8. Aquinas, *Compena. theologiae*, 2–2, qq. 163–165.
9. Aquinas, *Compendium theologiae*, 2, chs. 189–191; *Summa theologiae*, 2–2, qq. 162–163, and 165.
10. Aquinas, *Compendium theologiae*, 2, chs. 192–193; *Summa theologiae*, 2–2, q. 164.

CHAPTER THREE

St. Thomas's Faculty Psychology
of the Human Person

HAVING FINISHED examining divine providence, the natural place of human beings within the order of creation, and good and evil considered in general, since, beyond an adequate understanding of man's place in creation, an adequate understanding of St. Thomas's moral teaching presupposes an adequate knowledge of his faculty psychology of the human person, before considering the intrinsic and extrinsic principles of moral activity that St. Thomas identifies, need exists to examine what he says about his facultative psychology of the human person. Out of this facultative psychology of the human person, St. Thomas later develops a facultative moral psychology that constitutes the proximate first principle of all his other moral principles (such as, knowing, wanting, intending deliberating, consenting, choosing, and so on).

While many people who study St. Thomas are familiar with his teaching about intrinsic principles of moral activity, few of them tend to consider: 1) these principles as outgrowths of his faculty psychology of the human person (or powers of the soul); 2) that his faculty psychology of the human person generates a facultative moral psychology; and 3) that his facultative moral psychology gives birth to the intrinsic principles of moral activity and essentially relates to the external ones.

In short, a person's understanding of the moral teaching of St. Thomas essentially depends upon his or her understanding of his facultative psychology of the human person. His facultative moral psychology is the proximate principle that generates his moral principles. St. Thomas understands moral principles to grow out of a facultative moral psychology (faculties of the human soul naturally seeking facultative perfection and the perfection of the human soul and the entire person). More: Even a correct understanding of St. Thomas's teaching about the nature of philosophy and science essentially presupposes, and grows out, of his teaching about the faculty psychology of the human person.

1. The nature of the human soul considered in itself

Within the context of his consideration of the human soul, St. Thomas first studies the nature of the human soul considered in itself. After doing this, he talks about the soul in relation to the human body.[1]

St. Thomas starts his study of the nature of the human soul considered in itself with a consideration of the question whether the soul acts by virtue of its ability to act. While he develops his answer to this question through use of several objections and replies, his most direct and simple answer appears to me to be that in no composite being are acts identical with the faculty that generates them. Because God's act of existing and His ability to be are identical, God's action and ability are indistinguishable. Since all beings aside from God are composite (organizations composed of essential parts), the principle that causes something to exist cannot be identical with that thing's ability to act. If the soul were in act by its ability to act, it would be in act just by being able to act; and each faculty of the soul would always be active. For example, by the fact that hearing is a faculty (an ability) of the soul, a person possessed of the ability to hear would always actually be hearing (a situation which evidently contradicts common experience). Only in God do the ability to act and act essentially coincide.

Having settled the question about whether the soul's principle of action (its essence) is identical with its ability to act, St. Thomas next considers the question whether several powers (parts) exist in the soul (that is, to some extent, is the soul is a composite whole?). And, if it is a composite whole, what is its nature?

Regarding the nature of the human soul considered as a composite whole, like Aristotle before him, St. Thomas talks about the soul as the principle of life, growth, and development of an organized material body, a body *suitable* for it to exist in essential relation as that body's form. Among other things, important to note about what St. Thomas says regarding the human soul is that Jews and Catholics did not originate the idea of a soul as a principle of life and movement in a body. The ancient Greek physicists did, by reducing to the notion of "a soul" what the ancient Greek mythologists had considered to be "a god" intrinsic to a material body that accounted for movement in moving beings.

Early on in ancient Greek poetry and for the first philosophers (the ancient Greek physicists) the assumption existed that wherever motion exists life exists (life causes motion). Motion was considered a species of life, not vice versa. And wherever life exists, these early ancient Greeks assumed that a personal being, a god, must exist as its moving principle. This is why the first ancient Greek philosopher, the physicist Thales, could so easily say that water is the first material principle, *and* "all things are full of gods." Some god had to exist as a principle to explain how water could be the remote genus of all species of other things that exist in the universe. Some living principle had to exist to explain how water moves, and could be divided into species.[2]

The first point St. Thomas makes about the human soul (the principle of human intellectual operation) is that, considered in itself (that is, thought about as the *principle*, the human *soul*), it is a complete, immaterial, subsisting form. It does not need the human body to exist. He thinks that the intellect's ability to know all physical natures makes the soul's subsistent nature evident because the human intellect knows abstractly, in a dematerialized, not a materialized, way. The act of human knowing precludes material reception of forms, precludes having a material nature.

The reason for this is that things received in a material way (such as in a material organ) impede the ability impartially, indifferently, to understand things received after them. They preclude "absolute consideration" of a nature. Thomas gives the example of a sick man, whose tongue senses everything it tastes as bitter, being insensible to tasting anything as sweet; and that of the human eye receiving colors through a pupil colored like that of a glass vase that makes all liquid poured into it appear somewhat like the color of the vase.

Therefore, he maintains that if the intellect were material (for example, if it were the human brain), it could not know all bodies (for example, it could not know itself, sense itself as a whole). Consequently, Thomas concludes, because the human intellect can understand any and all things of a material nature (if something is material the human intellect can, to some extent, grasp its nature, organization), the human intellect executes its essential activity of knowing without co-operation from any bodily organ, apart from the body.

Since only a complete nature, complete substance, a subsisting being, can exercise such an independently essential act, can engage in "absolute consideration" of a nature, the human soul (which is the principle of the faculty called the "human intellect") must be a subsistent being.[3] Crucial to note about the nature of the human soul as a complete substance is that, in maintaining this claim, St. Thomas is not denying that the human soul considered as a principle separate from the human body is composite. Even though it is a complete substance, complete as the organizational whole that it is, it is still a composite of a finite form (a determinate potency: a limited ability to act) and an act of existing (*esse*) proportioned to it.

2. The nature of the human soul considered in relation to the human body

In considering how the human soul relates to the human body, St. Thomas maintains that, even though the human soul is a subsisting being in its nature and the principle of human knowledge, it is related to the human body as that body's form (chief intrinsic principle of organization). He defends this claim by arguing that nothing acts except in so far as it exists and is in act. A thing chiefly acts by the principle through which it acts. Because 1) a thing's form unifies its parts into an organizational whole, and 2) only organizational wholes are able to generate action in the created universe, the form is the chief intrinsic principle through which any created being or its faculties act. For example, physical health is a bodily form, a principle by and through which the body acts in a healthy way. And the act of existence (*esse*) is a principle, cause, of the soul, a principle by and through which the soul exists as living and causes health in the individual human person as a soul/body composite.

Thomas adds that the soul is more than a principle of the body. 1) It is the human body's first, or chief, principle, by and through which the body lives. 2) Because, through different operations in differing qualitative degrees, life is distributed throughout all the *parts* of the human body, the person must have some chief principle that unites these unequally related acts to one whole subject. The intellectual soul is that chief principle, the first principle of all these vital actions, of all our: nourishment, sensation, spatial movement—and knowing.

So, whether we choose to call this chief first principle by which we know by the contracted form "intellect," "soul," "human soul," or, more precisely, the "intellectual soul," it is the chief form (unifying cause of all the parts) of the body that causes a body to live. Following Aristotle's argument in his *De anima*, St. Thomas puts the burden of proof on any critic of his position to explain, in any other way, *how the act of knowing is the action of this individual man*. In short, absent a faculty psychology, how can anyone explain how *one* person does (causes) *many* acts?

Each human being is evidently aware that he or she is this numerically-one being, not, as David Hume thought, *some social multitude feeling itself to be one* that knows. Again following Aristotle, Thomas claims that we can attribute an action to a person in one of three ways. A thing moves, or acts: 1) as a whole self (for example, the way a human being who is also a physician heals); 2) as a part (for example, when a woman sees by and through an eye); or 3) through some accidental quality (for example, when a caucasian housing contractor builds, caucasian is accidental, incidental, to being a building contractor).

When we say that Socrates knows, we are predicating knowing essentially, *per se*, not accidentally, of Socrates because *we are attributing this act to him as one composite whole*: *this man* as the proximate cause of the knowing through his individual knowing faculty. In attributing the act of knowing to Socrates, we have two choices. 1) We can say that Socrates understands by virtue of his whole self, maintaining that man is an intellectual soul. Or 2) we can say that the ability (faculty) to know and act of knowing are a part of Socrates (that Socrates knows in and through these parts).

We cannot rationally hold alternative "1)" because *numerically-one and the same man* is conscious that, as numerically-one being, he exercises *many* living acts: knowing, sensing, eating, living, and so on. Since we cannot sense without a body, a body composed of sense organs must be an essential part of our individual human nature and *many acts of sense knowing* that we perform in and through faculties of soul somehow conjoined to this organic body. Consequently, rational coherence demands that we accept alternative "2)." *The faculty by which we know is an essential part of us, somehow essentially united as a first principle of life to the human body and its many acts.* As a result, we cannot hold alternative "3)," that a human being chiefly knows through an accidental quality not a faculty essentially flowing from its essence (some principle existing outside the human body). St. Thomas attributes a version of this alternative to Plato, who held that the intellect is united to the body as its motor.

Apart from Plato's teaching, St. Thomas thinks the nature of the human species proves the same point. The way a thing acts essentially reflects the way it exists. Knowing is a human being's proper operation, our specific difference, because by means of it we excel in kind, in virtual quantity, all other animals. For this reason, Thomas says Aristotle concludes man's highest good, happiness, must consist in knowing. The human species must derive its specific difference from the intellectual soul, the principle of the act of knowing. Since everything derives its species from its form, the intellectual soul must be the proper form of human nature.

According to Thomas, based upon the principle of virtual quantity (limited qualitative ability to possess existence, unity, and action), a hierarchy of forms (genera, species, and individuals) exists throughout the created universe. The more perfect, less deprived in being (*esse*), a form is, the less it is united to and depends upon matter to exist and perform its actions; and the more it excels matter in its natural faculties and acts. Principles of elementary bodies are less perfect, individually free or independent, in existence, form, and way of acting than are elementary bodies. Plant life is more perfect in form, more individually free or independent in existence, form, and way of acting than inanimate being. Sense life is more perfect in form, more individually free or independent in existence, form, and way of acting than vegetative life. The human soul is the highest, is the most qualitatively perfect in form, and most individually free or independent of forms. By the fact that the human soul has a natural faculty and act (the intellect, and intellectual "act") totally independent, free of dependence upon corporeal matter, in which corporeal matter in no way shares, St. Thomas holds that the human soul excels all other bodily forms.

Consequently, as St. Thomas sees it, because the intellectual soul is his essential form, no explanation other than the one Aristotle gave is capable of explaining how *this particular man understands*. The proper act of the human intellect makes clear that the intellectual soul is united to the human body as its form.

St. Thomas maintains that the soul is a proximate principle, cause, of life in the body that it generates to the body through a multitude of powers or faculties that vivify human organs. Considered as such, instead of seeing the human soul as a principle of life simply existing within some sort of a composite whole called a "body," St. Thomas thinks of the body as growing out of faculties of the human soul. Instead of understanding the soul to be some sort of life energy that the body or its parts generate, that the soul exists in the body as some sort of effect (epiphenomenon) the body produces, St. Thomas considers the body to exist in, and grow out of, the soul.

The human soul generates a multitude of faculties (like nutrition, growth, and reproduction; internal and external senses) and these faculties, in turn, generate bodily organs suitable to conduct life within and through them. Hence, just as a human faculty exists in relation to the human soul as a conductor, or distributor, of an act (the act of human life), so a bodily organ exists as distributor of this or that faculty of life. For example, the soul causes life within a sense faculty (limited conductor/distributor of life, like the faculty of hearing), and that sense faculty causes that facultative life to be distributed to a compositely whole body through a physical organ that we call an "ear."

Since an animal body is a complicated, composite whole having many vegetative and sense faculties, in answer to the question whether several powers exist within the soul, St. Thomas's reply is evident. From simple observation, he knows that many facultative abilities (like seeing and hearing, tasting and touching) belong to numerically-one, organically-whole being. And he knows that, for one being to possess many qualitatively different principles of action, one being must have different faculties (the faculties being the proximate principles of the actions being observed). Hence, he knows he has to conclude that, for one and the same agent simultaneously to have the ability to act in a multitude of qualitatively different ways, that agent has to have a multitude of qualitatively different principles, or faculties. Consequently, in answer to the question whether several powers exist within the soul, his answer is "Yes," as many as are needed for it to obtain its good in its highest degree.

Analogously, if someone were to ask St. Thomas whether a corporation has parts, his answer would be "Yes, because it needs divisions and departments so as to be able to act as an organizational whole." If, then, a person were to ask him how many divisions and departments a corporation needs, his reply would be, "As many as are required for it to be as good as it possibly can be (perfect) as this or that organization; as many as it needs to be completely whole, qualitatively perfect, as the kind of organization that it is."

Having admitted that the human soul exists as a life-communicating principle to an organic body through a multitude of faculties, St. Thomas does not appear to be saying something about the human soul and its relationship to the human body that is odd, difficult to understand, or radically different from the way in which many, if not most, human beings have, for millennia, understood the nature of the human person.

However, because, strictly speaking, all actions are essentially effects of relations and are invisible, difficult for any and every human being to understand is how to distinguish one action that anything performs from any other action it performs. For example, consider the acts of walking, conversing, seeing, or hearing. Surely, the person who is walking, conversing, seeing, or hearing, easily distinguishes one action from the other; but how? Where does the act of walking, conversing, seeing, or hearing exist?

For instance, where does the act of conversing exist? In two people? Between two people? In and between two people? If it exists between two people, how do we sense or know *the act of being between*? If *being between* is a relationship, how do we sense, or know relationships? Are not relationships invisible? Consider another example: the act of love. Surely, it exists, exists between and in people, and, to some extent, is invisible. Hence, how do we know, identify, it?

While acts like seeing, hearing, conversing, and walking might appear simpler to comprehend than love, such is not the case. Again, where does walking exist? In a person? Between a person and a surface? If no surface exists, can walking occur? If no relationship can be established between feet and a surface, can walking exist? As a necessary condition for walking to happen, would not a relationship first have to be established between feet and a surface?

Clearly, the answer appears to be "Yes." But walking has to involve more than simple contact between feet and the surface. Sitting and standing involve contact between feet and a surface, and neither one of those acts is the act of walking. Walking has to involve moving along, or across, a surface. But, again, we have the problem of what do "moving," "along," "across," and "surface" mean?

While my motive for asking many of the immediately-preceding questions might puzzle some readers, I ask them because St. Thomas's answer to the question of where acts exist is that they exist within *a genus*, or what today we would call an organization, or organizational whole. Strictly speaking, created acts exist within organizations, organizational wholes; and, for us to comprehend them, we have to relate them to the organizations in which they exist.

For example, the act of hearing, walking, or conversing is the effect of a coincidence of opposites: of being able to unite two opposites into an organizational whole. For instance, the act of hearing is the effect caused in the power to hear by an external stimulus (which St. Thomas calls a "formal object") that we call "sound." Hence, St. Thomas says that powers (faculties) are distinguished by their acts and acts by their formal objects. By this he means that acts are effects generated within organizations *through a relation that unites an ability and an external stimulus.*

Moreover, the external stimulus can be considered either as a first act that initiates a thing to move from the state of rest or a last act that it executes after having been moved out of a state of rest. For example, the thing heard and the agent doing the hearing are contrary opposites belonging to one and the same genus: the same organizationally whole act, of hearing. Some noise-making thing is the external stimulus, or formal object, that activates the power to hear. And we only know that hearing exists to the extent that some external noise moves the hearing faculty from being able to hear to actually hearing.

Consequently, St. Thomas maintains that powers are known by their acts; but, since, as knowable by human beings, acts are always composite, or organizational, wholes, we only know an act like hearing by referring it to the stimulus that activates it and with which it seeks to remain in contact. Hence, the fact that the faculty of hearing is stimulated by sound, by natural inclination, that faculty inclines to remain in union with the sound that is stimulating it (its formal object now considered as an end, not as an initial stimulus). Once activated to hear, the faculty of hearing naturally inclines to hear and to hear for as long and as best as it can.

Having explained how powers are distinguished by their acts and acts by the formal object, St. Thomas next examines whether an order exists among the powers of the soul, and his answer to this question is, "Yes." Again, while St. Thomas's reply is more complicated than I am presenting here, basically he answers that an organizational whole can only exist among unequally qualified parts, among parts that are more or less perfect, *because if they were all equally perfect, they would be identical; and the organization could not be a composite whole!*

A genus, or organizational whole, is composed of, generated by, unequally perfect, species, or parts. And, once again, the reason for this is that two beings that are exactly the same in perfection are identical, in no way different. To be different one being has to be more or less perfect than the other. Hence, *an order or organization composed of equally perfect parts could not be a composite organization because, by being equally perfect, its parts would be identical, exactly the same: numerically-one, not two.*

Consequently, St. Thomas states that a twofold order of qualitative perfection exists among the powers of the soul in terms of the lower, less qualitatively-perfect, powers being generated first, and preparing the way for the subsequent generation of the more qualitatively-perfect powers. For example, the vegetative powers of nutrition, growth, and reproduction that one finds universal to all living beings need to be generated in nature before the sense faculty, and the sense faculty needs to be generated before the intellectual faculty. And this is the case even though, from the standpoint of being qualitatively more perfect as an agent (being less dependent upon external assistance and aid to engage in one's natural act), being qualitatively the more immaterial, the act of intellection is a more perfect act than the act of nutrition.

According to St. Thomas, the qualitatively more powerful a

faculty is: 1) the less it depends upon external assistance to generate an action (the greater the liberty with which it causes); 2) the more extensive it is in its causing power; 3) the more deeply and firmly (ineradicably) it enters into the subject it causes; 4) and the more immaterial is its formal object (external stimulus).

For such reasons, St. Thomas compares the imperfection of insensible plant life to that of intellectual human life to being one in which a plant has its head in the ground and its feet in the air while a human being has his feet on the ground and his head in the air. St. Thomas understands the qualitatively more perfect powers to act as the final cause of the existence of qualitatively less perfect powers just as the building of a house is the final cause of all the preparatory work in which a builder engages before bringing a house to perfect completion in the final act of trimming it.

Next, St. Thomas asks whether all the powers of the soul exist in the soul as in a subject. By this he is asking whether all the powers of the soul grow out of the soul or depend on it like properties existing within a subject (like shape in a body). And his answer to this question is, "No," not all the powers of the soul exist in the soul as in a subject. Some powers of the soul exist in the soul simply as a soul, an immaterial principle (for example, the human intellect, will, and intellectual memory), while other powers of the soul exist as part of a soul/body composite (like the vegetative powers of nutrition, growth, and reproduction, and the internal and external sense powers). After considering the above question, St. Thomas wonders about a question I have already answered: whether the faculties of the soul flow out of, are generated by, the soul. Once again, his answer is, "Yes." Just as the many parts of the universe flow from God as from a proximate first principle, the many powers his soul flow from the soul. And, to answer a subsequent question, one power of the soul can come from another power of the soul inasmuch as (as I said above), the more perfect powers act as final causes for the generation of less perfect ones that operate like tools to fulfill necessary conditions for the generation of the more perfect ones.

The final question St. Thomas considers related to powers of the soul is whether all of these powers remain in the soul the way it exists independently of the body after death. His reply is that only understanding, will, and intellectual memory remain *in the soul separated from the body*; vegetative and sense powers do not. [4]

3. How the natural faculties of the human soul are united and divided, and the order that exists among them

According to St. Thomas, to explain how numerically-one human being can perform many acts, we have to maintain that the intellectual soul moves the individual, indirectly (not directly), through many natural powers. St. Thomas gives two chief reasons for the conclusion he holds.

1) Because power (or potency) and act divide being and every kind of being (every essence), a power and its act must belong to the same genus; the essence must belong to another. If an act is done within one genus, the power generating the act (its principle) must be in the same genus. For example, if the act of drawing mathematical conclusions is in the genus of quantity, the habit that generates this act must be in the same genus (must be a quantitative habit of mind). But, according to St. Thomas, in God alone, are act and essence in the same genus. In all created beings, act and power are in one genus and essence is in another. Because the soul's act is not identical with its essence, is not in the genus of its substance, the soul's many acts must be performed by many powers, not directly by the soul's essence.

2) By its essence the human soul is a form activated, caused to exist, by a principle other than its essence. This principle extrinsic to the soul is the soul's act of existing or *esse*. If the essence of the soul were the immediate principle of the soul's subsequent action, Thomas maintains that whatever has a soul would always be exercising its

secondary vital operations. In the case of a human being, for example, a person with the faculty of sight would always be seeing.

According to St. Thomas, simply as a form, the soul's act is not ordained to a further act. The human soul's chief, or first act, its act of existing, of being a soul, a living principle causing a body to be alive, is the ultimate term of prior generation. To be in potentiality to another act does not belong to the soul according to its essence as a form. Being in potentiality to another act belongs to the soul according to a different power, a principle other than the principle, power, through which it exists, lives as a soul. As the principle of generating second acts, the soul's essence has a principle that is its first act: existing, being alive. But the soul has another principle within its essence whereby it is the principle of other acts, second acts. What has a soul is always actual with respect to existing, living; but not always actual with respect to second acts, like sensing.[5]

4. The many powers, faculties, of the one intellectual soul

For three reasons St. Thomas claims that the soul must perform second acts through many powers, or faculties, in the soul.

1) Referring to Aristotle, Thomas says that the lowest genus of beings cannot acquire perfect goodness in one act. Through many acts, it can acquire imperfect goodness (that is, more mature development). Through many acts beings that belong to a higher order can acquire perfect goodness. Still higher beings can achieve perfect goodness through a few actions; and the highest perfection exists in those beings that can acquire perfect goodness doing nothing.[6]

For example, the sickest human being can only acquire imperfect health (some improvement in health) by means of many activities. More healthy is the person who can achieve perfect health by means of many, but fewer, activities. Even more healthy is the person who can achieve perfect health doing a few things. And healthiest of all is he who has perfect health without having to do anything.

2) From this example Thomas concludes that beings that exist below human beings in the order of created being can acquire a limited goodness. So, they have a few determinate activities and powers, faculties. *Because man can achieve happiness, he can achieve perfect human goodness.* According to his nature, man is the qualitatively lowest of beings of those to whom happiness is possible. Hence, the human soul must exercise many different, operations and powers to achieve human perfection. For angels, use of a smaller number of qualitatively powers, acts, suffices to achieve perfection. And, being perfect act, God has no power or action outside His own essence.

3) The human soul exists at the meeting point of spiritual and bodily creatures; therefore, the powers of both meet together in the intellectual soul.[7]

5. How powers of the intellectual soul are distinguished, divided, by their acts, objects, and opposites

Considered as such, St. Thomas maintains that we distinguish powers by their acts. Since acts and powers are contrary opposites, powers are distinguished by their opposites, beings that activate powers. Since a power is essentially related, ordered, to a determinate act, St. Thomas claims that human beings use acts to which powers are essentially directed as the means for knowing the nature of a power, and the way the power is divided, diversified.

Thomas says that all natural powers are active or passive. Hence, every act is of an active or passive power.

The object of a passive power (like color related to the power of sight) acts as the extrinsic, initiating principle, moving cause of a passive power. For example, the quality "color" brings the form "seeing" from potency to act.

The formal object of an active power is not the extrinsic starting point of the generation of a form. It is its intrinsic term, end: the form, aim, it chiefly aims to generate, bring to be. For example, considered as an active, not passive, power, the formal object, aim, of the faculty of seeing is "to see," the proper act of the power of sight.

St. Thomas maintains that an act receives it species, or form, from these two principles (one active, one passive): that is, from 1) the external principle that, like color, activates the faculty of sight as a passive faculty (brings it from being a passive power to being an active one) and generates its form or act (seeing); and 2) the intrinsic principle that the previously passive power, when externally activated, naturally inclines to generate. Hence, he concludes that the powers are of necessity distinguished by their acts, objects, and opposites.

Nevertheless, Thomas observes that possession of a specific form that is accidental to a being does not change its essential nature, species. For example, having a specific color is accidental to an animal as an animal. Difference of color does not change, cannot divide, its species. *Only a difference necessarily related to what it is, a difference in what properly belongs to its nature as an animal, a difference in the sensitive soul (which can be rational or non-rational, brute) can divide the genus animal into its species.*

For this reason "rational" and "irrational" are differences that divide the genus animal. Similarly, St. Thomas says, not just any object, act, diversifies the powers of the soul, but a difference in that to which the power, of its nature, is essentially related. So, he claims, by its nature, the sense faculty is subdivided into sensory powers that essentially react to the acts of specific physical qualities like color, sound, and so on. Since it is accidental to the quality *qua* color that it exist in a large or small musician, grammarian, man or stone, such differences cannot activate the sense of sight. Hence, sense faculties cannot be divided by differences not essentially related to their proper natural acts.[8]

6. That an order exists among the powers of the intellectual soul

Since the intellectual soul is numerically one, and the powers numerically many, and since a number of things that proceed from one have to proceed in a definite order, St. Thomas concludes that some (a threefold) order must exist among the powers of the soul. He says two of them correspond to the dependence of one power on another. He takes the third from the order of the formal objects.

Thomas maintains that we can consider the dependence of one power upon another in two ways: 1) according to the order of nature and 2) according to the order of generation and time. Considered in the first way, by nature, perfect, maturely-developed beings are prior to imperfect, immaturely-developed, beings. In the second way, the immaturely-developed, imperfect, being is first because a maturely-developed one comes to maturity after first being immaturely, imperfectly, developed.

In the first way, the intellectual powers are prior to the sensitive powers. For this reason, the intellectual powers direct, command, the sense powers; and the sense powers are naturally inclined to follow these directions, commands. Analogously, the sensitive powers are prior in this order to the nutritive powers.

In the second way, the relationship is opposite. In this case, the nutritive powers are naturally prior by way of generation to the sense powers, for which they prepare the body. The same is the case regarding the relationship of the sense powers to the intellectual powers.

In the third kind of order, some sense powers (for example, sight, hearing, and smelling) are ordered among themselves. According to St. Thomas, the reason for this is that, since it is common to all higher animals and does not require any external clash of elements to apprehend, the power of sight naturally comes first. The power of hearing, however, is prior to that of smell because the air makes a sound audible to the faculty of hearing while the faculty of smell requires elements in the air to unite to activate, produce sound. Hearing is prior to smell, however, because smell results from mingling of elements, of which the act of smell results.[9]

7. How the powers of the intellectual soul are in the soul as their subject

Because the subject of an active power is a principle of action, and an active power is a principle that can act, St. Thomas says that, necessarily, the intellectual soul is the sole subject of all the powers of which it is the sole principle. He notes, however, that the intellectual soul can perform some actions without assistance of a bodily organ and some that require such assistance. In the first case, the powers of these acts are in the soul alone as their subject. In other acts in which the soul needs assistance of a bodily organ (for example, seeing using an eye and hearing using an ear) the composite, not the soul alone, is the subject.[10]

8. How the powers of the intellectual soul originate from the soul as from a principle

According to St. Thomas, substantial and accidental forms agree in two ways: each is 1) an act and 2) a principle of act. He says they differ in three ways: 1) a substantial form makes a thing to exist absolutely, and its subject is something purely potential; 2) accidental form causes a thing to be in a relative way, to be such, or so, great, or in some particular condition; and its subject is an actual being; 3) since what is less of a principle exists for the sake of what is more of principle, a substantial form's subject, matter, exists for the completeness of substantial form, so the substantial form can be complete as a form; an accidental form exists for completeness of the subject.

For this reason, Thomas asserts, we first observe the existence of a subject (for example, an existing man) before we observe the actions the man performs. The reason is that, if we do not know that (and, to some extent, what) some physical subject is, we cannot attribute any other action to this subject. In the case of an accidental form, Thomas claims we first notice actuality *in* the subject (for example, a man's intrinsic accident of color or size) prior to knowing the subject to be a man.

Thomas adds that, inasmuch as a subject is in potentiality, it is receptive to an accidental form. Inasmuch as it is in act as a proper, intrinsic, *per se* accident (property), it produces an accidental form. With regard non-intrinsic accidents, the subject is receptive only. An extrinsic agent causes the accident in the subject.

From what he has said, the subject of the soul's powers is: 1) the soul alone, inasmuch as it has some potentiality in it (as such, it can be the subject of an accident); or 2) this subject is the composite of soul and body. Since the soul makes the composite actual by making it live, whether the subject is the soul alone or the composite of soul and body, St. Thomas concludes that all the powers of the soul originate from the essence of the soul, as from their principle. As he has already said, inasmuch as it is actual, the subject is the principle of its accidents, inasmuch as it is potential, and is a recipient.[11]

9. How powers of the intellectual soul can be principles of other powers or faculties

St. Thomas explains how the powers, faculties, of the intellectual soul can be principles of other powers by first recalling that we know powers by their actions. Since the action of one power causes that of another (for example, the action of the external sense faculty causing the action of the imagination), and since all causes are principles, Thomas concludes that one power of the soul is the principle of another.[12]

To this general argument he adds that, in effects that proceed from one cause according to a natural order, just as the first is the cause, principle of all the rest, so what is nearer to the first is, in a way, a prior principle, cause of those that are more remote. He has already shown that several kinds of order exist among the powers of the intellectual soul.[13] Consequently, he concludes that one power of the soul proceeds from the essence of the soul through another.

Since he compares the essence of the soul to the faculties as an efficient, or moving, and final, principle, he says that separately, by itself, or in union with the body, those powers of the soul that precede the others in the order of perfection and nature are the principles of the others after the manner of the end and moving principle. This is because the agent and the end are more perfect, while the receptive principle, as such, is less perfect.

Giving an example to clarify his argument, he says the senses exist for the sake of, to help, the human intellect, the human intellect does not exist to serve the senses. The senses are imperfect participants in the human intellect. According to their natural origin, the senses proceed from the intellect as the imperfect from the perfect.

Considered as receptive principles, the more perfect powers are principles with regard to what they generate. Consequently, inasmuch as it is the principle of the sensitive power, the sense faculty is considered as the subject, recipient, something material with regard to the intellect. On this account, the more imperfect powers precede the others in the order of generation, for the animal is generated before the man.[14]

10. The number and division of the sense faculties and their appetites and how properly to distinguish the five exterior senses

Like many human beings, and Aristotle before him, St. Thomas Aquinas divides the sense faculties into five exterior powers and several interior ones, some of which will not be familiar to many people. Nonetheless, in what follows, St. Thomas gives good reason for dividing the sense faculties the way he does.

In explaining why he distinguishes the sense powers how he

does, St. Thomas first presents two ways that some people prior to him have attempted to divide the sense faculties and shows why these are not adequate: 1) Some people who have done so attribute to the sense organs a preponderance of one of the classical material elements commonly accepted by the ancient Greek physicists (for example, water, air, fire, earth). By others it has been assigned to the medium, which is either in conjunction or extrinsic and is either water or air, or such like. 2) Others have ascribed it to the different nature of sensible qualities, according to which, supposedly, a quality belongs to a simple body or results from composition.

Thomas finds neither explanation viable because the powers do not, by nature, exist to help the organs; the organs exist to service the faculties. Human beings do not have different sense faculties because we have different sense organs. We have different sense organs because we have different sense faculties. The organs are naturally adapted to assist the faculties perform their proper operations; not vice versa. In the same way, he adds, the natural order of the universe provides different media within which the senses operate, according to the compatibility of the acts to the powers. Moreover, the human intellect (better, the individual person), not the sense organs or sense faculties, know.

St. Thomas states we find the answer to the question about how properly to number and distinguish the exterior senses in terms of what belongs to the senses properly and *per se*. Since the exterior sense is a passive power, is naturally activated by some exterior sensible being suitable, qualitatively proportionate in power, relatable, to it *per se*, the sense faculty grasps the exterior cause, principle, of such activation. Hence, he concludes that the diversity of exterior causes, exterior sensible principles, diversify the sense powers.

He maintains, further, that the exterior principles that activate human sense faculties can be material or "non-material." He makes this distinction for two reasons: 1) sensing is a mode of human knowing and knowing is essentially an immaterial act and 2) to account for the unusual nature of the faculty of sight.

Material activation occurs through the reception of the act of a physical quality (form) according to its material mode of being into receiving sense organ and faculty (as, for example, the quality heat is received from a physically hot thing into a sense organ that becomes physically hot as a result).

Non-material activation happens according to the act of physical quality being received, without corresponding qualitative alteration, into the sense faculty (for example, when a likeness of some visible being appears within the pupil of the eye, the form of color received into the pupil causes the pupil to become colored; still the pupil, as such, remains transparent and the faculty does not sense the pupil of the eye becoming colored).

St. Thomas thinks that, as knowing faculties, all the sense faculties require this kind of immaterial activation because he maintains that sensible beings activate sense faculties by and through radiating a likeness (sensible species) of their natures. Since every species of knowing consists in an immaterial act, even sense knowing requires an immaterial activation of a sense faculty.

This likeness, an effect produced by a bodily quality, not the bodily quality, activates the sense faculty through reception into the sense organ. For example, the bodily quality *heat* heats another physical thing by radiating heat, an act, effect, that (as an effect) is physically like (a sensible species of) its principle, cause. Hence, through this organic sensible effect of heat generated from the hot thing, the sense faculty senses the heat coming from the physical agent.

If material activation alone sufficed to account for sense knowing, Thomas says that all sense faculties would experience sense alteration in their respective sense organs when these organs underwent alteration.

But this does not always happen. In some senses, we find sense knowing (for example, seeing, a form of knowing) without experience of accompanying organic alteration. In all sense faculties, however, we find sense knowing (an immaterial act) and qualitative alteration (on the part of the quality that activates the sense faculty only, or likewise on the part of the organ).

Regarding sound, some kind of air movement, percussion, happens in what we sense. In the case of smell, some change happens to carry odor through the air. For example, movement of a flower or cooking food. In both these former cases, a medium (air) transports the effect that is produced by the percussion or cooking, sound to the ear and odor to the nose. No direct contact happens between the sense organ and what is being sensed. In the case of taste and touch, direct contact does happen. The tongue is in direct contact with what a person tastes, and the mouth must salivate for taste to happen, at least in a complete way. And when a hand touches something hot, the hand becomes hot.

Because seeing occurs: 1) without needing qualitative change in the organ of sight (the pupil of the eye remains a transparent medium, does not have to become blue, for a person to sense the color blue) or in its object (the visible object does not have to be changed, altered to be transported across a medium), and 2) seeing appears to occur instantaneously, simultaneously, with the presence of something visible to an agent, St. Thomas finds the sense of sight to be: 1) the most immaterial, perfect, and universal of all the senses; and 2) the most naturally desired from the standpoint of the service it provides to living a life under rational direction. Because, in its degree of immateriality and action it most resembles intellectual knowledge, and because of its ability to help us identify individual details of things, from the standpoint of what it contributes to human beings leading an intellectual life, St. Thomas claims that, by natural inclination, we prize the sense of sight more intensely than we do any other sense faculty.

After sight in degree of immateriality, perfection, and universality, Thomas says, come the faculties of hearing and smell, which require a change in what we sense, but not a qualitative change in the sense organ. To preclude the need for any direct physical alteration in their organs as a necessary condition for exercising their acts, unlike touch and taste, St. Thomas states the faculties of sight, hearing, and smell, on the other hand, exercise their proper acts through external media.

Touch and taste are the most material of all the sense faculties because they require qualitative change directly in the organ, direct contact and internal qualitative change, for sensing to happen. Moreover, St. Thomas maintains that, due to their crucial importance to the preservation and protection of human life, by nature, 1) human beings and all animals prize the sense of touch more than any other external sense faculty; and 2) *the sense of touch plays a crucial role in moral education from the earliest age through adulthood.*[15]

Through the sense faculties, St. Thomas maintains that we can apprehend three kinds of sensible beings. He calls these three kinds of sensibles: 1) "proper"; 2) "accidental," and 3) "common."

1) "Proper sensibles" are qualities that first and directly activate the sense faculties through their organs, bring these faculties from potency to act, like color does to sight.

2) "Accidental sensibles" are sensibles that, unlike proper and common sensibles, neither directly nor indirectly produce change in a sense faculty (sensibles to which, in a way, a sense faculty is indifferent). For example, whether a substance sensed is a tree or a human being is accidental, incidental to activation of the sense

faculty of sight. However, if it is too small to see or not light or dark enough, it will not activate the sense faculty.

3) "Common sensibles" exist in between proper and accidental sensibles. They are all related to quantity, an intrinsic, or "proper" accident of a substance (also called a "property"). The quantified, surface body is the proximate subject of the qualities that cause alteration, as surface is of color. For this reason, St. Thomas says the common sensibles do not activate the senses first and of their nature; they do so secondarily (for example, the surface through color).

Examples of common sensible are size, shape, and number. Size and number are kinds of quantity (continuous and discrete). Shape is a quality related to quantity because shape consists of fixing the bounds of, limits, of magnitude, or greatness. We sense movement (change) and rest when the size, location, or quality of a subject is affected in one or more ways. For example, when a tree grows, a person walks, or something becomes hot or cold. In a way, then, St. Thomas says to sense movement and rest is to sense *a one and a many*.[16]

11. How properly to distinguish the four interior senses

St. Thomas maintains that four interior sense faculties exist: 1) common, or differentiating, sense; 2) imagination; 3) estimative sense (called "particular," or "cogitative" reason in human beings); and 4) sense memory.

Because a thing's nature does not fail in providing a substance with the necessary powers to exercise its proper act in a maturely-developed way, St. Thomas maintains that human nature must provide man's sensitive soul with as many faculties and actions needed for a human being to live the life of a *perfect* animal (that is, an animal that has all the sense faculties possessed by the highest species of the genus animal). He adds that, because a faculty of the soul is the proximate principle of the soul's operation, if one sense power cannot generate the needed acts, diverse powers must exist to help generate them.

To accomplish the task of knowing and doing *many* things necessary for the life of this *one* highest form or animal life, St. Thomas says man possesses a "proper" and "common" sense faculty.

According to him, the proper sense judges of the proper sensible (the sensible form that necessarily activates a sense faculty) by distinguishing one proper sensible from another (for instance, by differentiating white from black, or green).

Since neither faculty can know both (neither the faculty of sight nor that of taste can differentiate white from sweet), another, common sense faculty must possess a differentiating sense judgment. To this faculty, as to a common term, or judge, all apprehensions of the exterior and interior senses must be referred.

Hence, it must have the ability to sense all the qualities that the other senses sense; as when someone senses that he sees. A person cannot do this by the proper sense. This sense only knows the sensible quality form that activates it, in which its act is completed. From this completed act, St. Thomas says, another, more universal act, in the common sense is one that perceives the act of the proper sense faculty.[17]

According to Thomas, in the highest form of animal life, an animal apprehends a thing at the actual moment of sensation and when the thing is absent. If the animal did not do this, since animal action presupposes, follows, sense knowledge, an animal would not move to seek something absent. Such behavior is the contrary to what we observe in higher forms of animal life. Such animals pursue things presently sensed by the exterior senses and also absent things. Therefore, through the sensitive soul, a higher form of animal life must receive the species of sensible things when a sense faculty is actually affected by a sensible being and retain and preserve said species when not so affected.

Thomas claims that, due to the organic nature of sense faculties, *diverse principles generate the acts of receiving and retaining*. The reason for this is that, while some things (like something moist) readily receive, they retain with difficulty; and the reverse is true with other things (for example, something dry). Since the sensitive power is the act of a bodily organ, it follows that the power which receives the species of sensible things must be distinct from the power which retains them.

Beyond this he adds that, if an animal were moved only by pleasant and unpleasant qualities that affect the sense organ and faculty, it would not pursue and avoid many things an animal needs to seek or to avoid (specific, sense-apprehensible goods and evils), on account of advantages and uses, that or disadvantages. As an example, he refers to how, by natural instinct, a sheep runs away when it sees a wolf. It does not do this because of the wolf's color or shape. It does so because wolves are natural enemies of sheep. As a second example, he refers to how a bird gathers together straws, *because they are useful* for building its nest, not because it finds straw pleasant to its sense faculty.

Animals need to perceive such forms related to utility that the exterior sense does not perceive. Consequently, some distinct principle must exist for the animal to perform such actions. The perception of exterior physical qualities comes by an action caused by these externally sensible qualities. This is not the case with the perception of immaterial qualities like danger and difficulty, sense good and sense evil.

Thomas claims that two sense faculties exist for *reception* of sensible forms, sensible qualities. He calls these the 1) "proper sense" and 2) "common sense." Another sense faculty exists for the retention and preservation of these forms. While most people today call this faculty the "memory," St. Thomas properly calls it the "imagination": a storehouse of forms received through the external and internal senses.

Furthermore, for the apprehension of forms like danger and difficulty, which external sense qualities cannot convey, St. Thomas says an "estimative" power (which he sometimes calls "particular," or "cogitative" reason) is appointed. He claims that the *sense memory exists to preserve these forms.* As a sign of the difference between imagination and sense memory, St. Thomas points to the fact that we find animals strongly stimulated to remember by something harmful or otherwise. He adds that knowing the past, the time that we sensed something, is an act of sense memory, not of imagination.

Regarding external sensible qualities received and preserved through the external sense faculties, St. Thomas asserts that no difference exists between man and other higher animals. A physical sense quality activates the sense faculties of other animals. *The way man and other animals receive and preserve these sense qualities,* however, *radically differs.*

Other animals perceive forms of sense good and evil only by some natural instinct. Man perceives them through relating ideas. Hence, the power that in other animals St. Thomas calls "estimative," in man he calls "cogitative." Because *the way this faculty works is by discovering some sort of relation between individual ideas and human self-preservation,* he also calls it "particular reason." For it relates ideas in an individual way just as the intellectual reason relates them universally. *According to St. Thomas, physicians during his time assigned an organ, the middle part of the head, to this faculty of cogitative reason.*

Regarding the memory, St. Thomas states that, beyond sense memory, like other animals, man possesses an intellectual memory that transcends *an animal's sudden recollection* of the past. Intellectual memory works, in a way, "syllogistically," as it were, seeking for a recollection of the past by the application of individual judgments.[18]

12. Why the intellectual soul must have an appetitive faculty

Just as fire is inclined to rise, *because every existing form is naturally inclined to generate an appetite*, St. Thomas maintains that the intellectual soul must have an appetite it naturally inclines to produce. According to him, two kinds of appetites exist: 1) solely natural and 2) more than natural.

Since more perfect forms, those of higher virtual quantity (qualitative greatness), exist in those beings more perfect in existence, and since beings more perfect in existence are more immaterial, more intellectual, in such beings an immaterial inclination exists that surpasses in kind the natural inclination of completely material forms. In a form that lacks knowledge, he says the chief aim of each thing is not cognitively social, receptive to taking externally existing forms immaterially into itself in a way that cognitive beings do. As a result, the natural inclination that such a form generates is a material, or natural, appetite.

But in those things that have knowledge, each form is determined to its own chief end by its natural form in such a way that it is receptive, in an immaterial way, to assimilating itself to other forms, species of other things. As an example, he refers to the sense faculty being naturally open to reception of the species of all sensible things. In a similar way, the intellectual faculty is open to assimilating itself to all intelligible beings. As a result, in a way, by sense and intellectual faculties, the human soul is all things. Hence, in a way, he adds, quoting Pseudo-Dionysius the Areopagite, intellectual beings approach to a likeness to God, "in Whom all things pre-exist."[19]

Because forms exist in those things that have knowledge in a higher manner (according to a higher virtual quantitative possession) and qualitatively above the way natural forms exist, an inclination must exist in intellectual forms that surpasses a solely the natural inclination, a solely natural appetite. The appetitive power of the intellectual soul is this kind of superior inclination. Through it a human being can desire what it knows, and not only that to which its natural form inclines it. So, the intellectual soul must have its own appetitive power toward something suitable, good, for itself.[20]

13. That the sensitive and intellectual appetites are distinct inclinations of distinct powers

Following Aristotle, St. Thomas distinguishes two appetites within the intellectual soul: a higher that naturally moves a lower one, two distinct appetites that assist the intellectual soul to carry out its natural activity of knowing: [21]

To explain more completely why and how he makes this distinction, he notes an essential difference between a passive and active power. He says that a passive power is one naturally activated, caused to move, by what it apprehends. What generates a passive power to act exists toward it somewhat like an unmoved mover. In relation to what stimulates it to move, the appetitive *power* or *faculty* is initially passive, is moved by what activates it, which exists toward it like an unmoved mover. Considered as such, following Aristotle, Thomas says that an appetite is an active power, a moving mover, a power that reacts, moves, when activated.[22]

According to St. Thomas, because the mover must be qualitatively proportionate (proportionate in intensive quantity of its power) to what it moves (capable of moving it), and what is active to what is passive, we have to differentiate passive and movable principles according to the distinction of their corresponding active and motive principles. In fact, Thomas says, the passive power itself has its nature *from its relation* to its active principle. The being of a passive power is a relational being, exists only in relation to what moves it. Since what is apprehended by the intellectual power (a passive power) and what is apprehended by sense power (also a passive power) are generically, qualitatively, different, the intellectual appetite must be distinct from the sensitive because powers, faculties, are principles of their respective appetites. Appetites and powers must belong to the same genus.[23]

14. The nature and division of the appetites of the intellectual soul

According to St. Thomas, the intellectual soul has two natural appetites: 1) sense and 2) will. The sense appetite has the sense knowing power as its proximate principle. The will, or volitional appetite, has the faculty of human intellect as its proximate principle.

St. Thomas claims that the sense appetite is a natural inclination, a natural, determinate movement that follows, results from, sense knowledge. He maintains that, since the existence of what a sense knower knows completes the operation of the sense knowing power, the subsequent inclination of the sense appetite is not identical with the act of sense knowing. Moving the sense knower toward the desirable object known through the sense power completes the sense appetite. Hence, St. Thomas likens the operation of the sense knowing faculty to rest and the operation of the appetitive power to movement. Since by sensual movement we understand the operation of the appetitive power, "sensuality" is the name we give to the sensitive appetite.[24]

15. Why the sense appetite is divided into two parts: concupiscible (propelling) and irascible (contending)

Following the lead of Church Father Gregory of Nyssa and St. John of Damascus, St. Thomas divides the sense appetite into two parts: 1) irascible and 2) concupiscible.[25]

Using the term "genus" in the philosophical sense of a natural genus or proximate principle or cause (the way he does in explaining the nature and unity of a science), St. Thomas says the sensitive appetite is one generic power. As a generic principle, it proximately generates two appetites, species, within the sense appetite: the irascible and concupiscible.

To make the reason for this division clear, St. Thomas observes that natural, corruptible things only need an inclination to: 1) acquire their proper good, what is suitable, something physically good; and 2) avoid what is harmful, and resist corruptive and contrary beings that hinder a physical thing from avoiding what is unsuitable, properly bad and harmful. For example, he says, fire has a natural inclination to rise from a lower, unsuitable position toward a higher, suitable one and to resist whatever destroys or hinders such action. Consequently, since the sense appetite is an inclination consequent upon sensitive apprehension, as a natural appetite, it is an inclination following a natural form.

In a human being, Thomas maintains, the sense appetite of the intellectual soul needs to be divided in two: 1) an appetite through which the intellectual soul inclines to seek what is suitable, according to the senses and intellect, and to flee from what is hurtful (St. Thomas calls this the "concupiscible" appetite); and 2) another appetite whereby a human being resists attacks that hinder getting what is suitable, humanly good, and harms a human being (St. Thomas calls this the "irascible" appetite). He immediately adds that, because its tendency is to overcome and rise above difficulties that can hurt a human being, the proper object of the irascible appetite is something difficult, dangerous.

Thomas argues that these two appetites do not constitute one principle because, against the natural inclination of the concupiscible appetite, following the impulse of the irascible appetite, sometimes the soul inclines a human being to flee from pleasant things so that a person might fight against dangers and difficulties. In addition, sometimes the human emotions that are seated in the irascible appetite (for example, anger) oppose emotions of the concupiscible appetite because, once activated, a concupiscible (pleasure-seeking/pain-avoiding) emotion decreases anger; and, in many cases, anger diminishes concupiscible emotion.

St. Thomas argues the same point by indicating that, in a way, the irascible appetite champions and defends the concupiscible (for example, when it rises up against what hinders acquiring good things that the concupiscible appetite desires, or against what causes harm, from which the concupiscible appetite flees). For this reason, he adds, all the emotions of the irascible appetite rise from those of the concupiscible appetite and ultimately terminate in them. As an example, he says that the anger that pain, sadness, generates terminates the anger *in the joy of revenge*; and he adds that, as Aristotle says, for this reason, fights among animals are about concupiscible things: like food and sex.[26]

16. Why and how the irascible and concupiscible appetites are inclined to obey the human intellect, or reason, and the human will

In two ways, St. Thomas says, the irascible and concupiscible appetites are inclined to *listen to reason*, obey the higher part of the intellectual soul: the intellect, or reason, and the will.

1) They obey intellectual reason in their own acts because *in human beings the faculty of particular reason replaces the estimative power that in irrational animals is the proximate principle that moves the sensitive appetite*. For example, as St. Thomas has already said, a sheep, judging the wolf as a natural enemy, is actually afraid. But, St. Thomas adds, *universal* reason naturally guides and moves particular reason.

By "universal" reason St. Thomas means the numerically-one intellect that is a faculty seated in the intellectual soul. He means the intellectual faculty of the intellectual soul. He does not mean a universal mind in a human being. He is predicating the term "universal" in a causal, not logical, or chiefly predicative, sense.

Hence, to clarify his point, he makes an analogy. He says that just as in syllogistic matters we draw particular conclusions from universal principles, premises, so in matters relating to the relation between higher and lower faculties and appetites, universal reason directs the sensitive appetite (for example, just like a CEO directs middle management). Because the sense appetite divides into concupiscible and irascible, *in obeying particular reason this whole appetite and its parts obey universal reason.*

Thomas adds that, because drawing particular conclusions from universal principles *is an act of reasoning of the faculty of the intellect,* and not the work of the intellectual faculty considered as a whole; because reasoning is the proximate cause of the concluding act, strictly speaking, the irascible and concupiscible appetites are proximately inclined to obey particular reason, not the higher intellectual faculty. Nonetheless, remotely, in obeying particular reason, they obey the higher intellectual faculty. He adds that anyone can experience operation in himself when, by applying general judgments to a specific situation, he may modify or intensify anger or fear.

2) Following the lead of Aristotle, St. Thomas claims that the sense appetites obey the will as to their execution. The will is the proximate principle, mover, of these appetites. *In brute animals movement follows immediately upon judgment made by the estimative faculty that something is dangerous.* For example, St. Thomas observers, because it has no superior appetite (that is, a will) to oppose it, fearing the wolf, the sheep, *immediately* flees. It does not take time to stop to compose a syllogism about whether or not to run.

On the contrary, a man, at times, awaits the command of his superior (that is, his more *universal*) appetite, the will, before fleeing danger. He does not naturally incline immediately to follow the dictates of his estimative sense. According to St. Thomas, the reason for this is that, wherever an order (that is, a relation of higher [more universal, less particular] to lower [less universal, more particular]) exists among a number of motive powers, the second (less universal) only moves by virtue of the first (more universal). In and of itself, that is, the lower appetite is insufficient, unable, to cause movement unless the higher appetite consents.[27]

Also following Aristotle, St. Thomas, observes two motive principles within the intellectual soul: 1) despotic and 2) political. Aristotle claims that the soul rules the body by a despotic principle, while the intellect rules the human will and sense appetites the appetite by a political and royal principle.

The reason Thomas gives for this distinction in naming is that, properly speaking, we call a power by which someone rules "despotic" when he rules like a master over slaves, people who, because they have nothing of their own, have no right or ability, in any way, to resist the orders of the one that commands them. But, properly speaking, we call a power by which someone rules "political" and "royal" when it rules like a just governor over free subjects, people who, while subject to the government of the ruler, have moral and political power, something of their own by reason of which they can resist the orders of the person who commands.

Analogously speaking, in agreement with Aristotle, Thomas says that, because the members of the body can in no way resist the sway of the soul, the soul rules the body by a despotic power. At the soul's command, hand, foot, and whatever bodily part will immediately move. But, because the sensitive appetite has some ability (a virtual quantum strength) by which it can resist reason's commands, the intellect, or reason, rules the irascible and concupiscible by a political power.[28] *For more than particular reason guided by universal reason naturally directs the sensitive appetite: the imagination and other sense powers also influence it.* For this reason, St. Thomas says we experience that the irascible and concupiscible appetites resist reason at times. For example, when we sense or imagine something pleasant that reason forbids, or unpleasant, which reason commands. And so, from the fact that the irascible and concupiscible appetites sometimes resist reason in something, we cannot conclude that they do not have a natural inclination to obey reason. They have such an inclination, but it exists within a hierarchy of relations among a multitude of faculties, powers, and inclinations that influence the way it operates.[29]

—Notes—

1. St. Thomas Aquinas, *Summa theologiae*, 1, q. 75, prol.

2. Id., q. 75, a. 1, reply; q. 76, a. 7. For a more detailed analysis of the mindset of the early Greek physicists, see Peter A. Redpath, *Wisdom's Odyssey from Philosophy to Transcendental Sophistry* (Amsterdam and Atlanta: Editions Rodopi, B.V., 1997), pp. 1–29.

3. Id., q. 75, a. 2.

4. Aquinas, *Summa theologiae*, 1, q. 76; see, also, St. Thomas's references to Aristotle, *De anima* (*On the Soul*), Bk. 2, ch. 2; *Physics*, Bk. 5, ch. 1; *Nicomachean Ethics*, Bk. 10, ch. 7. Cf. St. Thomas's teaching of the unity of the person to that of Hume's understanding of a person as a collection of feelings in his *A Treatise of Human Nature* and as presented in Peter A. Redpath, *Masquerade of the Dream Walkers: Prophetic Theology from the Cartesians to Hegel* (Amsterdam and Atlanta: Editions Rodopi, B.V., 1997), pp. 49–65.

5. Aquinas, *Summa theologiae*, 1, q. 77, a. 1, reply.

6. Id., a. 2, reply. See St. Thomas's reference to Aristotle, *On the Heavens* (*De caelo*), Bk. 2, ch. 12.

7. Aquinas, *Summa theologiae*, 1, q. 77, a. 2, reply.

8. Id., a. 3, reply.

9. Id., a. 4, reply.

10. Id., a. 5, reply.

11. Id., a. 6, reply.

12. Id., a. 7, *sed contra*.

13. Id., reply and a. 4.

14. Id., a. 7, reply.

15. Id., q. 78, a. 3, reply. Regarding relation of the sense of touch to moral education, see St. Thomas's discussion of the nature of the virtue of moral education through use of pleasure, pain, and the moral virtue of temperance in his *Commentary on the Nicomachean Ethics of Aristotle*, Bk. 2, Lects. 2–3 and Bk. 3, Lects. 19–20.

16. Aquinas, *Summa theologiae*, 1, q. 78, a. 3, reply.

17. Id., q. 78, a. 4, reply, and ad 2.

18. Id., q. 78, a. 4.

19. Id., q. 80, a. 1, reply; see Dionysius the Areopagite, *On the Divine Names*, Bk. 5.

20. Aquinas, *Summa theologiae*, 1, q. 80, a. 1, reply and ad 2 and ad 3.

21. Id., q. 80, a. 2, sed contra; see Aristotle, *De anima,* Bk 3, chs. 9 and 11.

22. Aquinas, *Summa theologiae*, 1, q. 80, a. 2, reply; see Aristotle, *De anima,* Bk. 3, ch. 10 and *Metaphysics*, Bk. 1, ch. 7, 1072a26.

23. Aquinas, *Summa theologiae*, 1, q. 80, a. 2, reply.

24. Id., q. 81, a. 1, reply.

25. Id., q. 81, a. 2, *sed contra*; see Gregory of Nyssa, *Nemesius*, and *On Human Nature* (*De natura hominis*) and St. John of Damascus, *On True Faith* (*De fide orthodoxa*), Bk. 2, ch. 12.

26. Aquinas, *Summa theologiae*, 1, q. 81, a. 2, reply; see Aristotle, *On the History of Animals*, Bk. 8. Regarding St. Thomas's use of the term "genus" as a proximate principle, see *Commentary on the Sentences of Peter the Lombard*, Bk. 1, d. 19, q. 5, a. 2, ad 1; *Commentary on the Metaphysics of Aristotle*, Bk. 10, Lect. 12, nn. 2142–2144; and *Summa theologiae*, 1, q. 66, a. 2, ad 2 and q. 88 a. 2, ad 4.

27. Aquinas, *Summa theologiae*, 1, q. 81, a. 3, reply; see Aristotle, *De anima*, Bk. 3, ch. 11.

28. St. Thomas Aquinas, *Commentary on the Sentences of Peter the Lombard*, Bk. 4, d. 49, q. 2, a. 3. I thank Eduardo Bernot for

suggesting addition of this reference at this point in the chapter.
29. Aquinas, *Summa theologiae*, 1, q. 81, a. 3, ad 2; see Aristotle, *Politics*, Bk. 1, ch. 2.

–CHAPTER FOUR–

Human Happiness and Other Intrinsic Principles of St. Thomas's Moral Psychology of Human Acts

HAVING CONSIDERED the faculty psychology that St. Thomas maintains acts as a proximate principle of the facultative *moral* psychology that generates intrinsic principles of moral activity, enabling means now exist to consider his teaching about the nature of moral activity considered in relation to that moral psychology. Since, as a Catholic theologian, St. Thomas treats of these issues within the context of man being created in God's image, anyone who wishes to understand St. Thomas's moral science needs to recall this context before proceeding further. Consequently, that is where the focus of this Chapter will start.

1. Creation and human happiness

Because human beings are created in God's image, necessarily we belong to a created order, exist as parts of a wider organizational whole: a real genus, or organization that resembles a real genus. Since every member of a genus has an end, is part of a wider, whole organization, and, as such, inclines, by perfecting itself as an organizational part, to cooperate with other parts of that organization toward perfecting the organization as a whole, need exists to consider more precisely what is the nature of an organizational whole (genus) and what kind of beings constitute essential parts of the genus called "creation."

According to St. Thomas, a real organization, genus, is a composite whole comprised of a finite number of parts divided by extremes of perfect and imperfect species with more or less imperfect species generally existing in between. What unites these species as parts of a whole is *unequal relation* of each part to numerically-one act that, as an organizational part, through relation to a most perfect part, it contributes to effecting.

For example, all the parts of a crew team possessing unequal rowing abilities are parts of an organizational whole precisely because all are unequally related to contributing unequally perfect acts of rowing to numerically-one aim: winning a rowing race under the direction of a chief crew member. In the case of the genus of creation, all the parts of species consist of multitudes of beings more or less perfectly resembling God as divine images, likenesses, for the chief aim of manifesting God's perfection under the chief direction of the most perfect of human beings: the second person of the Trinity, the God/man Jesus Christ.

Like all organizational parts, human beings move toward our end by exercising the nature we have as an organizational part. Since, by nature, human beings are free agents, every human being moves toward the numerically-one end of manifesting divine perfection through the exercise of free choice involving free consent of the human will. Like all organizational agents, we get our specific difference as an organizational part by more or less perfectly possessing and executing the organizational aim (in the example of the crew member, being more or less perfect in executing the act of rowing) according to the nature of the part we play within the organizational whole.

As organizational wholes, all organizations grow out of, are generated, caused, by the unequally cooperative, harmonious, activity of their parts in relation to numerically-one, chief aim, or final act. For example, the organizational activity of medicine has numerically-one chief aim: to heal, or improve the health of, some actually, or potentially, sick person. Without the existence of actually or potentially sick people, the human ability to heal them, and the chief aim to do so, no medical profession, no health organization, could possibly, much less actually, exist. Eliminate the chief aim, and necessarily, the essential relation that unites a multitude into parts of an organization disappears. An organizational whole exists within the harmonious relation that exists within the cooperative activity of its organizational parts. And a chief end of an organization is a necessary condition for the existence of that harmonious relation.[1]

Regarding the organizational whole called "creation," the chief end, aim, of manifesting divine perfection causes an essential, harmonious relation to exist among its parts that make it a created organization. The other ends, aims, that exist within this organization (like those that exist within any organizational whole in relation to its chief end or aim) are sought only as enabling means for satisfying this chief aim of a composite whole: perfect organizational good. *The ultimate end of any agent moved toward an end as part of an organizational whole is to achieve union with, satisfy, the chief aim of its organizational nature, not the good of one of an organization's parts.*

Such being the case, the chief aim of each and every human being according to our specific difference of being free, moral, organizational agents within the order of creation is to perfect ourselves in the free exercise of human choice: to become as morally virtuous, perfect, as possible.[2]

That being so, for four general reasons, St. Thomas claims that human happiness cannot consist in *having*: wealth, honor, fame, political influence, or any and every external good (all of which are simply enabling means for executing perfect human operation: moral virtue). Happiness, in short, consists chiefly in: 1) an internal way of existing, not in a way of having anything or everything; 2) total self-sufficiency (lacking in nothing really good); 3) complete internal and external well-being; 4) the inability to be harmed by bad luck; and 5) perfect satisfaction of human nature.

For many reasons St. Thomas says that happiness cannot consist in *having*: 1) any bodily good; 2) physical pleasure; 3) any good of the soul; and any 4) created good.

He claims that no bodily perfection can cause human happiness because: 1) being of more perfect qualitative greatness (higher intensive quantity greatness), the qualitative perfection of human happiness excels the qualitative perfection of every other species of animal good; 2) while other animals excel human beings in some bodily perfections, just as no act of a part of an organization can satisfy the whole organizational good, no bodily perfection can totally satisfy the human soul, human nature considered as a whole, the whole person; 3) human happiness consists in a composite whole being united to a good beyond itself: its formal object (perfect union with God); 4) *in a way, being united to a good beyond itself is true of every created nature, every organizational whole*; 5) no bodily or created good is the kind of Perfect Good and Perfect Truth that can constitute the absolute perfection human happiness demands.

Because human happiness consists in being totally perfect in human nature, human happiness must consist in: 1) an activity, because each thing is perfect inasmuch as it is actual, not potential; 2) an activity perfectly satisfying the person as a composite whole (intellect, will, and glorified body); 3) an activity of delight (enjoyment of the will/volitional satisfaction) in the knowledge of achieving perfect union with the whole of Truth: Perfect Enjoyment of the Beauty of Perfect Good and Truth; 4) a contemplative activity satisfying the whole person, not just the human soul—a perfection of the soul overflowing into the body consisting in perfect vision of God's essence.

Evident to St. Thomas and from what St. Thomas says is that: 1) such happiness requires divine assistance to attain; 2) once attained, it cannot be lost; 3) while all human beings desire human happiness as complete satisfaction of the human will and human nature, not all of us explicitly realize in what this complete satisfaction consists; and, as a result, some of us do not achieve it.[3]

To help remedy this weakness in human understanding about the nature of moral activity and how to improve use of it so as to become happy, the rest of this Chapter will start to consider the nature of moral activity according to its intrinsic principles.

2. The intrinsic principles of moral activity: the internal human faculties and the facultative moral psychology that human beings use proximately to generate, cause, moral acts

Because, strictly speaking, moral acts are distinctively human acts, freely-chosen acts that free decision-making proximately generates, causes, St. Thomas claims that, strictly speaking: 1) voluntary action is proper only to rational animals (animals capable of exercising, at least in part, abstract decision-making about humanly-doable deeds); 2) voluntary activity springs directly from the human will *under the advice of* the intellect *to move toward or away from a perceived good, an end*; and 3) several internal principles, psychological faculties, influence the voluntariness of moral activity.

Chiefly, voluntariness in moral activity refers to: 1) acts the will *indirectly* commands through its influence on the human intellect (of which it is the appetite), and 2) the will's natural inclination to pursue its natural end. St. Thomas adds that, with respect to what the will commands, voluntariness can be increased, decreased, or nullified when done under coercion, constraint, or duress due to: 1) acts of violence; 2) emotional influence, especially of fear and pleasure; and 3) ignorance, which can be of three species: antecedent (which makes an act morally involuntary); conjoined (which causes an act to be morally non-voluntary); and consequent (voluntary/directly willed).

While St. Thomas maintains that, *considered as a human faculty*, facultatively the human will chiefly aims at union with real good as its chief end, nonetheless, due to the limitations of its nature as dependent upon knowledge contained within a finite intellect to move it to act, necessarily, *the human will is only able to will the good in the individual situation* (the means to the end that, by nature, it wills) *as known, apprehended,* as it *appears* to the human intellect! As a result, sometimes, through no intent on its part, even though, by nature, *facultatively, by natural inclination, it wills union with a real good,* through no fault of its own, the human will secures apparent good *as its means* (just as sometimes, someone who chiefly wants to marry Cinderella in reality winds up marrying her ugly stepsister; or someone who wants to marry Prince Charming winds up betrothed to a frog).[4]

More specifically considered, St. Thomas states that three psychological acts chiefly involve moving the will toward its natural end (real human good): 1) willing (volition); 2) intention; 3) enjoyment/delight.

By "willing" St. Thomas means the naturally-inclined movement of the intellectual appetite under the direction of the human intellect toward real human goods that satisfy real human needs and away from evils that do not. According to St. Thomas, by its nature, with necessity of natural inclination, the human will voluntarily wills: 1) its proper object; 2) its natural end; and 3) everything suitable for all natural human powers, including the good of the will's own power, that of the whole of human nature, of human faculties and habits, and everything that befits fulfillment of natural needs. Nonetheless, because it can only will these through knowledge contained within a finite, fallible, intellect for which it is the appetite, *sometimes it does not wind up choosing any of these!*[5]

By "intention" St. Thomas means: 1) an act chiefly of the will, not the intellect, but involving the intellect; 2) an act directly and chiefly relating to the end, not the means, of human desire; 3) what the will directly intends a person to do, stretches out so strongly to what it seeks, that *it moves a person to plan and perform appropriate means of action to secure this end*; and 4) an act of will that employs reason to direct and order (prioritize) actions in a suitable way to realize an end. Evident from what he says about intention is that intention is not identical with wanting, or desiring.[6]

By "enjoyment/delight" St. Thomas chiefly refers to appetitive satisfaction of the human will, not the human emotions, in pursuit of a good that a person considers to be real, one that satisfies real human needs. Enjoyment/delight is a property of the will: appetitive satisfaction of the will resting in a state of calm possession of its end. Since brute animals have no will, they have no appetitive experience of such joy as part of their animal emotions. In a way, because appetitive satisfaction of the human will can overflow into other faculties, intellectual joy can spread throughout all human faculties including into the human emotions.[7]

As far as human faculties and other principles that are involved in moving the will, St. Thomas identifies: 1) the intellect (through intellectual knowledge concerned with presenting a suitable, proportionate, good for the will appetitively to pursue); 2) the sense appetites and internal and external sense faculties (by influencing how the human intellect apprehends [conceives, judges, and reasons about] the good); 3) will (which can move itself toward means to achieve the end); 4) other enabling principles and means external to the will; 5) mental acts like deliberation; 6) God (as a universal and special creator and chief good of the universe, creator of the human soul, and source of grace); and 7) the Devil(s) (who can move the will indirectly through influence on the sense appetites and the human imagination).[8]

Beyond the acts of voluntariness, intention, and enjoyment/delight by means of which the human will is moved toward an end, and other faculties and principles just mentioned, St. Thomas maintains that the will is involved in five other acts of moral psychology by which the will moves to acquire means to secure an end: 1) deliberation/counsel; 2) consent; 3) choice; 4) command; and 5) use.[9]

Deliberation/counsel is the first of five facultative acts of soul that move the will as means to fulfill intention to act for an end. After the will calls upon reason to prioritize action, by nature, human reason is constrained to consider enabling means to secure satisfaction of the will's pursuit of an end. To some extent, these means are always essentially contingent, doubtful/uncertain, many; and include temporal and locational circumstances and conditions (differing contexts) within which means might, or might not, be able to be secured, by this or that individual or group. Hence, before concluding a judgment, *through the use of cogitative reason* (the estimative sense) and its own consideration, intellectual reason questions the relation (intensive quantum, or qualitative, greatness) of potentially suitable means to each other *and to the qualitative powers and abilities of the person, or persons, involved in making a choice under the circumstances involved.*

What was said in the paragraph immediately above about deliberation, counsel, indicates that this activity: 1) can involve one person, or many people; 2) cannot go on endlessly (because the will intends counsel to be limited); 3) consists in appetitive movement toward or away from something existing within or beyond a person's power; and 4) consequently, *must involve use of cogitative reason (the estimative sense)* measuring the nature of the agent's natural ability against the choice to be undertaken within the individual circumstances in relationship to the nature of the act being contemplated. Considered as thus described, strictly speaking, deliberation, counsel, is not an activity in which brute members of the animal species can engage.[10]

According to St. Thomas, "consent" refers to a generic application of appetitive movement to execute an action existing within a person's power and consists in an act that *concludes* a reasoning process. As a result, *consent puts uncertainty to rest* about an action to be chosen or a plan of action to be executed.[11]

"Choice" involves an initial act of reasoning that consists in comparing real possibilities, imperfect goods, that *terminates in a concluding judgment* that this or that good is more likable than another, and, should be pursued or secured, and the other, or others, should be avoided.[12]

"Command" is chiefly an act of reason that presupposes an act of consent of the will to execute choice through use of human faculties naturally amenable, directly or indirectly, to taking direction from human reason. Such faculties include reason moving: 1) itself to conceive, judge, or reason; 2) the will toward or away from the specific end or means, and other faculties that it can influence to act or not to act; 3) human sense faculties and appetites; and 4) bodily movements that can be influenced by movement of the human of appetites. In the act of command, by nature, *the will uses the command of reason* to move and be moved toward *real* means that promote securing real human goods that fulfill real human needs and away from *apparent* means that do not.[13]

Finally, "use" consists in *executing enabling means to secure an end commanded to be secured*.[14]

3. The goodness and evil of moral activity considered in general, and in relation to the interior act of the will and exterior actions

Having finished a general discussion of moral, or human (freely/deliberatively-chosen), activity, St. Thomas considers the goodness and evil of moral activity: 1) in general; and in relation to 2) the interior act of the will, and 3) exterior actions.

Regarding goodness and evil of moral activity considered

in general, St. Thomas says that, because form is the intrinsic principle that generates action in things, discussion of good and evil in things should be done by taking into account the form being considered. In created, material, beings, form (or nature): 1) is always a principle of a composite, imperfect, whole in the act of self-maturation of every finite, organizational, whole: 2) always more or less perfectly possesses organizational unity of its parts; and 3) can be deprived of the complete organizational wholeness that constitute its organizational perfection (for example, a human person as a body-soul composite is a natural whole constituted of facultative and organic parts [like the faculty of hearing], which can be qualitatively weak, unhealthy, and fail); 4) to be good, to act, an organizational whole must be complete in its essential parts (have all its essential parts); 5), if missing any organizational parts needed to act with full, maximum of, perfection, to the extent that the form is somewhat deprived, it is weak, bad: not absolutely, unqualifiedly, good, not perfect as an organization; 6) as a composite whole, causes every finite action to be good to the extent that the action is missing no part needed to be the composite whole that it is. Since every acting form is a species (a more or less perfect *having* of a generic, organizational whole, unity), we have to judge the goodness of all finite forms, or organizations, in relation to their more or less perfect participation in the goodness of their respective organizational aim (their *bonum ex genera* [generic, or organizational, good]), not their *malum ex genera* (organizational defect) inasmuch as this good exists within each and every part of the organization (in other words, we have to consider the intensive quantum, or qualitative, *greatness of having* of the organizational whole that a part contains to the extent that it has been able to absorb into its nature, as much as possible, the chief organizational aim).[15]

Considered as specific moral acts that human beings perform

as some sort of organizational whole, St. Thomas claims that: 1) to be specifically good or bad, *moral acts must be animal acts* within the genus animal *done by a rational animal*; 2) *moral good and evil are specific differences* in rationally-caused, freely-chosen, acts; 3) the moral goodness or badness of an act *qua* human is derived from it being voluntary and intended by the will inasmuch as the act under consideration is, or is not, well-deliberated: prudent (really good or evil *for* the species of rational animals intended as really good or evil *by* rational animals); 4) considered specifically as human acts, moral acts have a twofold component as an end intended: internal and external activity.

Consequently, 1) the moral goodness or evil of an external act is derived from the moral goodness or evil of an internal act; and 2) the moral goodness or evil of an internal act is derived from the moral goodness or evil of an internal act's aim and the means essentially intended to be chosen to secure it; 3) if the chief aim of a moral choice is to select an individual action as a real means leading to fulfilling the chief aim of human life in the individual circumstance (is a prudent choice leading to the soul's union with God), the individual choice made is specifically good morally, a morally virtuous choice; 4) if, on the other hand, the chief aim is to make an imprudent choice leading away from union of the soul with God, it is specifically bad morally, a morally vicious choice.

Special note should be made that not all conscious acts we human beings perform are moral (that is, voluntary, freely deliberated and chosen) acts. Some are morally neutral acts. Strictly speaking, only deliberately-chosen acts essentially related to choosing means toward perfecting the human soul in its pursuit of union with God qualify as moral acts. Eliminate consideration of the nature of the human soul and its perfection, beautification, and conversation about moral activity becomes essentially unintelligible, worthless.

An Introduction to Ragamuffin Ethics

Precisely considered, specification of the formal object of a moral choice as morally good or evil for this or that person to execute within this or that individual circumstance essentially involves consideration of the magnitude of the of the deed being considered to be chosen as measured against the magnitude of the power of the agent considering executing the act here and now. Essentially involved in that pursuit of perfecting the human soul is taking into consideration the circumstances in which a choice is executed!

While *sometimes* they do not change the species of moral good or evil of a moral choice, St. Thomas maintains that *sometimes* the circumstances of a moral act increase or decrease the greatness or intensity of that good or evil. *Sometimes, what had been incidental circumstances* (like place and time considered in general) *enter into a moral act as a quality* (like a specific difference!) *causing an act to be morally good or evil or good or evil of a different species as prudent or imprudent for this or that person to make.* In such a situation, *what had been a circumstance now becomes an essential part of the chief aim that makes choice of means prudent or imprudent. What had been an incidental circumstance now become like a specific difference!*

As examples, St. Thomas refers to the following cases: 1) stealing food from a wealthy, instead of a starving, person; 2) lying about someone in general in school and lying about someone under oath in a court of law; 3) returning borrowed weapons to a friend when he is sane, not insane (an example that, knowingly or not knowingly, St. Thomas appears to have gotten indirectly from Book 1 of Plato's *Republic*).[16]

St. Thomas continues his consideration of good and evil in relationship to the human will by maintaining, once again, that interior acts of will (including alternative choices) are specified by formal objects: in this case, in relation to choice of the means, a good presented to the will through reason as morally right or wrong, prudent or imprudent. *Unless they enter into the formal object presented to the will, what we usually call "circumstances" do not specify moral acts as morally good or bad. However, since a prudent or imprudent intellect is part of the formal object of the goodness of an act of will, such moral goodness or evil of doable deeds depends upon the quality of the reasoning faculty involved in choosing the deed: including the quality of cogitative reason (the estimative sense)!*

Because, through divine will and eternal law, divine reason governing the created order has established that the human will take direction from human reason, St. Thomas adds that the goodness of an act of will also depends upon eternal law and God's will. And he states, further, that: 1) even a mistake in conscience binds; 2) every act against reason is always morally bad, unless performed through invincible ignorance or rational disorder (like insanity); 3) the moral goodness of an act of will depends upon the good intention of the moral agent; and 4) even though good intention might not generate a good choice, often it strengthens, increases, goodness in the will that lends to promotion of a good choice.[17]

Extending his consideration to moral good and evil in external acts, St. Thomas claims that: 1) the nature of moral good or evil in outward acts essentially depends upon the species of act in question (which includes circumstances under which the act is performed; for example, to give alms to the poor to show off, which is specifically bad morally); 2) the good or evil that exists within an external act is first present in intention in an interior act of the human intellect and will and is only present derivatively in external acts by reason of the will's plan to execute that intention; 3) the entire goodness of an external act essentially depends upon the intention being good and choice being of the right means (presence of the moral virtue of prudence as commanding *and* controlling it); and 4) the external deed and some moral good or bad related to an intended act.[18]

Regarding unintended consequences that result from a previously-performed, morally good or evil act, St. Thomas states that these add nothing to, and take nothing away from, the moral good or evil of the preceding action. He claims that moral acts performed in conformity with right reason (the moral virtue of prudence) and eternal law are morally right, and moral acts that proceed in a contrary fashion are morally wrong. Because we are the authors of (cause) our own moral choices, St. Thomas tells us that *we must be praised or blamed, rewarded or punished, for the acts we freely cause under our control.*

Finally, regarding whether our moral choices will merit reward or punishment by God, St. Thomas states that, through the quality of being directed toward others individually and as members of communities, human actions that intentionally help others are meritorious of reward before God, the governor and ruler of the community of the entire universe, or, as we might put it today: the CEO of all CEOs. And those that intentionally harm others merit punishment.[19]

—Notes—

1. St. Thomas Aquinas, *Commentary on the Metaphysics of Aristotle*, Bk. 1, nn. 18–35; Bk. 3, Lects. 1–12; *Commentary on the Nicomachean Ethics of Aristotle*, Bk. 2, Lect. 1, n. 246; Bk. 6, Lect. 3, and Bk. 10; *Posterior Analytics*, Bk. 1, Lects. 10–21; see, also, Peter A. Redpath, in "How We can use Common Sense Philosophy to Renew the West," in *Studia Gilsoniana* 3: (2014), pp. 455–484, and "The Essential Connection between Common Sense Philosophy and Leadership Excellence," in *Studia Gilsoniana* 3:(2014), pp. 605–617.
2. St. Thomas Aquinas, *Summa theologiae*, Prol., 1–2, q. 1; *Summa contra gentiles*, Bk. 3, chs. 28–40
3. Aquinas, *Summa theologiae*, 1–2, qq. 2–5.
4. Id., Prol. to q. 6, and qq. 6–9.

5. Id., q. 10.
6. Id., q. 12.
7. Id., q. 11.
8. Id., q. 9, and Prol. to q. 6
9. Id., qq. 14–17.
10. Id., q. 14, and 1, q. 78, a. 4, reply.
11. Id., 1–2, q. 15.
12. Id., q. 13.
13. Id., q. 14.
14. Id., q. 16.
15. Id., q. 18.
16. Plato, *Republic*, Bk. 1, 330C–E.
17. Aquinas, *Summa theologiae*, 1–2, q. 19.
18. Id., q. 20.
19. Id., q. 21.

–CHAPTER FIVE–
The Human Emotions (Passions)
Considered in General and in Some Detail

1. St. Thomas's definition of emotion/passion (*passio*), the nature of emotional reaction, and the division of sensory appetites

St. Thomas defines what, today, we generally call an "emotion" (but what he calls a "passion") as a psychosomatic change, reaction: 1) caused within the sense appetite of a human being *located within particular, or cogitative, reason* by the presence of an image, 2) which draws a faculty toward or pushes it away from union with or separation from a formal object (external stimulus), 3) apprehended as sensibly agreeable (good, fitting, proportionate) or sensibly disagreeable *as it is in itself* (that is, as co-natural or not co-natural [proportionate] in qualitative strength of power to the faculty it activates).

He maintains that, to some extent, emotional reaction always: 1) starts with some physical modification of an organ or an image; 2) involves bodily changes, including influence on the heart and blood flow; 3) contains a sense image and has a cognitive, conceptual component; and 4) seeks to terminate in rest in pleasurable union with, or separation from, its cause.[1]

On the basis of different formal objects (following the method of Plato used centuries before him in the *Republic* and later adopted by Aristotle), St. Thomas divides the sensory appetite into two emotional parts: 1) the higher passions (irascible appetite), whose formal object is some sense good or evil considered as helpful with which to unite or helpful to avoid; and 2) lower passions (concupiscible appetite), whose formal object is sense good or evil considered as pleasurable, but necessarily helpful or harmful to avoid or not avoid.[2]

2. How to distinguish passions that properly belong to the concupiscible appetite from those that properly belong to the irascible

Because acts generated by a different generic principle, or power, differ in species (for example, seeing and hearing generated by the sense faculty) and since the irascible and concupiscible appetites are different generic principles, or powers, into which the sensitive appetite divides, St. Thomas claims the passions that the concupiscible and irascible sense appetites generate are specifically different.

Moreover, because different faculties, or powers, have different formal objects, including aims, the passions of different powers necessarily have different formal objects, including aims. Thomas adds that a greater difference in the object is required to divide the species of the powers from each other than to divide species of their respective passions or actions. Consequently, the objects of passions and actions of different appetites that differ in species differ less greatly than do the objects of the appetites that the passions and actions divide.

In the physical order, St. Thomas maintains that diversity of genus arises from diversity in material potentiality and diversity of species arises from diversity in form of common matter (that is, difference in form of a proximate principle, genus). So, too, he says, in acts of the soul, those that belong to different powers, different generic principles (like different sense appetites) differ in genus and species.

The sense appetite is the genus. The passion, act, is the species. Consequently, acts and passions that relate to different *specific* objects (have different specific external stimuli) included under the one common object of a single generic power (in this case, a single appetite) differ as the species of that genus. That genus generates them as species of its appetite.

Hence, to determine which passions are in the irascible appetite and which are in the concupiscible, we have to consider the proper object of each generic appetite, the form (external stimulus) that essentially relates to and activates each appetite, which generates its aim. According to St. Thomas the formal object of the concupiscible appetite is some sensible human good or evil, *simply considered, thought about, as such, that causes a person pleasure or pain.*

Since, at times, a human being necessarily experiences difficulty, struggle, in getting some such good, or avoiding some such evil, insofar as such good or evil is more than our human nature can easily acquire or avoid, this good or evil, precisely considered as difficult in nature, is the formal object (external stimulus) of the irascible faculty.

Therefore, whatever passions react to good or evil absolutely, precisely considered as such, belong to the concupiscible appetite (for example, love, hatred, pleasure, pain, and so on); those passions that essentially react to some good or bad *as difficult*, but possible in the future for a human being to get or avoid, when considered as such, belong to the irascible faculty (for example, hope, fear, daring, and so on). Since the forms of good these two appetites chiefly pursue are not identical, the appetites and their respective passions cannot be identical.[3]

3. The eleven different passions and kinds of opposition and relation they involve

According to St. Thomas: 1) in total, eleven different passions exist (five in the irascible appetite: hope/despair; fear/daring; and anger; six in the concupiscible appetite: love/hatred; desire/aversion; and pleasure/pain); and 2) ten out of the eleven passions involve contrary opposites within the same appetite, while one passion (the irascible passion of anger) has an opposite (calm) generated by pleasing cessation of anger. *But calm is not a contrary opposite because*: 1) *it exists within the concupiscible, not the irascible, appetite*: a proximate genus other than the irascible appetite and 2) *contrary opposites exist within the same genus and impede the action, movement, of their contrary.*[4]

Helpful to recall at this point is St. Thomas's teaching that: 1) four kinds of opposition exist (privation and possession, contradiction, contrariety, and relation) and 2) contrary opposition involves terms, limits, or opposites *that exist within the same proximate genus* (that is, are generated by the same proximate principle and have the same formal object). For example, extremes of good and bad, perfect and imperfect armies, exist as extremes within the same generic kind of organization: military.

In contrast, privation and possession, and relation can exist within and between genera; but contradictory opposites cannot. For example, nothing can simultaneously exist and not exist, belong to a genus (organization) and not belong to genus; but, in many opposing ways, a human being can be good or bad as a species of animal, parent, lover, moral agent, military person, and so on.

Because anger and calm do not exist within the same proximate genus (anger being a species of passion contained within the irascible appetite and calm being a species of passion contained within the concupiscible appetite), while they are remotely related: 1) they have different formal objects (one being the useful good, the other being the pleasurable good) and 2) qualitatively different proximate principles (appetites). Hence, while they definitely are opposites, anger and calm cannot be contrary opposites.

Furthermore, St. Thomas maintains that, because its formal object is the *useful, not chiefly* (but secondarily) *the pleasurable, good*, in the case of the irascible appetite, two kinds of opposition can exist: for example, 1) between the terms (useful and not useful) and 2) between the relations (moving toward and away from, like the soldier attacking an enemy) to fulfill a qualitatively greater, more necessary, and healthy pleasure: a real need and a co-natural pleasure that accompanies it.

In the passions of the concupiscible appetite (for example, the passions of pleasure and pain), St. Thomas claims that only a contrariety of terms (not of relations) exists between the two opposites (one of which is perfect [pleasure] and attracts us; and the other of which is imperfect [pain] and repels us). By nature, in all animals, the natural inclination of the concupiscible appetite is to move toward pleasure and away from pain.

In contrast, in the case of the passions that exist within the irascible appetite, St. Thomas says that the situation is more complicated. Both species of opposition exist. For example, regarding the passions of hope and fear, simultaneously, these passions can have contrary terms (such as the safe and the dangerous) and have opposite relational movements toward the same object (like moving toward and moving away from the fear-generating subject). A hopeful person might, for instance, attack something painful or dangerous and, if the thing in question was a real danger to personal health or safety, get a pleasure of a qualitatively greater kind in doing so.

In the case of the concupiscible appetites, the relational movement is simple: we move toward what we love, desire, and pleases us and away from what we hate, do not like, and pains us. A chief reason for this difference between the way in which our emotional experiences occur within these different appetites relates to the fact that objects of the concupiscible appetite attract us in a simple and straightforward way (as pleasurable goods), while objects of the irascible appetite attract us chiefly as useful goods, but, secondarily, as pleasurable or painful goods.

Hence, in different ways, we can simultaneously move toward and away from the same object. For example, in the case of the passion of hope in the face of danger, in different ways, we can experience pleasure and pain and moving toward and away from the same object (for example, as a presently painful and difficult to overcome object [obstacle] that is useful to attack now as an enabling means for some future safety that we presently hope will be accompanied by a qualitatively greater kind of future pleasure).

Moreover, we can experience a concupiscible emotion without experiencing an irascible emotion, but we cannot experience an irascible emotion without experiencing a concupiscible emotion. All human passions start in the concupiscible appetite. For St. Thomas, the passion of love (which is located in the concupiscible appetite) is the first principle of all other passions, whether they be passions of the concupiscible or irascible appetite. As a principle of all human passion, love is present wherever a human passion, emotion, is present. And, because pleasure consists in knowing that a person has achieved secure possession of something loved, pleasure is always present when love is satisfied.

Considered as such, love is the chief human passion and the chief passion of the concupiscible appetite. Nonetheless, hope, not love, is the chief passion of the irascible appetite, the first principle of all the irascible passions, all of which contain love and hope as essential parts of their composite, constitutional makeup.

Regarding the respective formal objects of the concupiscible and the irascible appetite, both have an essential time component connected to them. The passions of the concupiscible appetite focus on the present, while the passions of the irascible appetite focus on the future.

In addition, the passions of the concupiscible appetite essentially relate to anything imaginable, while the passions of *the irascible appetite focus only on doable deeds*. The formal object of the concupiscible appetite is anything we presently can imagine to be likable/lovable or unlikable/unlovable, while the formal object of the irascible appetite is anything we can imagine to be future, possible, and difficult. Hence, while we can delight in imagining doing really impossible deeds, strictly speaking, considered as rational agents, we can never really hope to achieve them.[5]

4. Why and how opposition, contrariety, exists among the passions of the sense appetites

Following Aristotle, St. Thomas maintains that a passion is a kind of psychic movement, a movement in the soul.[6] Therefore, contrariety in movement, change, is the principal reason for the existence of emotional contrariety. Aristotle maintains a twofold contrariety exists in changes, and movements, according to: 1) movement toward or away from acquisition and loss of the same term, or form; 2) opposition of terms, changes, within a genus (thus whitening, movement of color from black to white, is contrary to blackening, movement of color from white to black).[7]

Thomas says a twofold contrariety exists in the passions of the soul: according to: 1) acquisition and loss of (moving toward or away from) *the same term* and 2) contrariety of terms (good and evil). He claims that both forms of contrariety exist in the irascible appetite, but the second form of contrariety alone, based on objects, exists in the concupiscible passions.

The reason Thomas gives for this distinction is that the formal object, and end-term, of the concupiscible appetite is sensible good or evil considered absolutely, or as such. Since nothing naturally seeks to avoid the good, since all things naturally desire, aim to get, it, the good, considered as such, cannot be a term, principle, limit from which change starts. It can only be only a term, principle, limit toward which change aims. It can only be an end principle, an aim, something chiefly sought after; not something chiefly avoided.

Similarly nothing naturally desires evil. By nature, all things naturally seek to avoid it. So, evil, a privation, resistance to good, considered as such, cannot have the nature of an end-term, principle, limit, or something chiefly sought after. It can only be a principle, term, limit away from which something moves. Accordingly, every concupiscible passion (like love, desire, pleasure) naturally tends toward the good and (like hatred, aversion, pain) naturally moves away from evil. Hence, St. Thomas concludes that, in the concupiscible passions, *no contrariety of approach exists toward and away from the same object.*

The object of the irascible faculty is sensible good or evil considered under the aspect of difficulty, not absolutely. Hence it tends to cause in us a fourfold opposition. 1) The difficult, possible, future good, considered as *good*, is of such a nature that it produces in us a tendency to generate the passions of pleasure and *hope* to get, not lose, it. 2) Considered as *difficult, possible, future*, it gives us pain, inclines us to turn, hope to get away, from it: *despair.*

Similarly 3) the difficult, possible, future evil, considered as *evil*, has the aspect of something to avoid, tends to generate the passion of *fear*. But 4) it also contains in it some good aspect that inclines us to move toward it, as something difficult, but *not impossible* to overcome. As such, *it contains an aspect of hope* of overcoming evil that tends to generate the passion of *daring*. Consequently, in the irascible passions, we find contrariety in respect of good and evil (for example, between hope and fear): according to movement toward and away from *regarding the same term*, object of desire (for example, between daring and fear).[8]

5. Moral good and evil as it relates to the passions

Inasmuch as the passions are subject to command of reason and will, St. Thomas maintains that moral good and evil exist within them. In maintaining this position, he is directly contradicting the teaching of some leading, ancient Stoic thinkers; and he knows this. Consequently, in the following way, he addresses this opposition between their teaching and his teaching related to the question whether the human passions are always evil for human beings to experience.

According to St. Thomas, the Stoics, including Cicero, considered the *individual* human intellect and *individual* human passions to be identical. Hence, because the human will exists within the human intellect, they considered the *individual* will and the *individual* passions to be identical. That is, strictly speaking, according to St. Thomas, the Stoics were not so much opposed to the passions, or human emotions, as they were opposed to the *individuality* of emotional experience.

Essentially, they considered reason and will to be *social Reason* and *Will, not individual* reason and will. They adopted what today we might call a "socialistic" understanding of reason and will: only one faculty of reason, one intellect, exists within the universe. While St. Thomas does not mention this fact, like the early Greek physicists, the ancient Greek and Roman Stoics were thoroughgoing materialists. They thought that only matter exists, that even reason and will are material. Moreover, they identified *Reason* and *Will* to be a numerically-one faculty that they considered to be the mind and will of Zeus, while the Roman Stoics identified this with the mind and will of Jupiter.

In this classical, socialistic understanding of Reason and Will, the ancient Stoics considered reason, will, and the appetites to be good. However, because they thought the individualistic understanding of reason and will (and the reduction of reason to individual reason and will to that of the *individual will, which they identified with human passions*), St. Thomas thinks they falsified the truth about the nature of reason, will, and real emotions and appetites.

They considered all individual acts of reason and will that contained any individual passions associated with them to be false and evil. Only Reason and Will (which are conflated in the being of

Zeus/Jupiter) are good, and *individual* reason and will are good only to the extent that 1) they do not exist within any human being; 2) are removed from individuals. Since individual emotional experience prevents the Reason/Will of Zeus/Jupiter from entirely entering into and controlling the behavior of individuals (human and otherwise, to include animals, plants, and inanimate beings), most, if not all, leading ancient Stoics opposed any semblance of passion for individual material things and individual emotions to exist within the physical universe.

In contrast to the prevailing, ancient Stoic attitude toward the human passions, St. Thomas maintains that Aristotle considered: 1) all passions moderated by right reason (prudential judgment) to be good; and 2) right reason to be a principle that, when existing within the human passions, constitutes a golden mean between excess and defect, regulating the passions by a proper love, desire, and pleasure so as to become moral virtues.

Because right reason is the root of all human (that is, moral) good, according to St. Thomas, the greater the number of human parts directed by prudential human reason, the greater will be human goodness. Consequently, the more the human passions are directed by right reason, the better they become. Morally considered, those passions that incline toward what is really good (toward fulfilling real human needs) for us as human beings (what is really safe and healthy for us to have because, according to our generic, specific, and individual nature we really need it) are really good, and those that incline toward what is really bad for us are really bad.[9]

6. How the human passions may increase or decrease an action's moral worth

According to St. Thomas, not every emotional action increases or decreases the moral goodness or evil of a human action. Disordered passions, those not rightly ordered, related, to a rightly directed reason and will that fulfills real human needs for life and safety, diminish an act's moral goodness, increase its moral evil. But if a rightly-ordered reason and will direct the passions, the human passions are part of the perfection of a human being. The perfection of moral goodness in human action chiefly consists in rational control of human passions and external actions. So, rational control of the human passions is part of moral perfection. It does not diminish it. And it is part of artistic and scientific perfection as well.

St. Thomas maintains that willing and doing the good is a greater perfection than only willing it. Moreover, complete human perfection requires that all the faculties subject to control of reason execute good actions. Hence, the human will and sense appetites should participate in doing the human good.

He adds that the human passions are related to rational decision-making in two ways: 1) antecedently and 2) by way of choice.

In the first way, if they are disordered, they interfere with right judgment, upon which a moral act's complete goodness essentially depends. By so doing, they diminish the moral goodness of a moral act. And even if rightly ordered, doing a charitable work from rational judgment alone is of greater moral worth than from doing it out of pity alone.

In the second way, consequently, human passions relate to reason in two ways: 1) by redundancy because, when the higher part of the soul is intensely moved to anything, the lower part also follows that movement (for example, the passion that results in consequence, in the sensitive appetite, is a sign, effect of the greater intensity of the will; so, it indicates greater moral goodness involved); 2) by way of choice (when, for example, someone chooses to be affected by a passion to work more promptly with the co-operation of the sensitive appetite). In this way, a passion increases an action's moral goodness.[10]

7. The passion of love, or liking, considered in general

According to St. Thomas, in human beings the generic act of love exists in three species: 1) volitional, 2) emotional, and 3) natural.

In natural subjects, he identifies love with an appetitive movement generated in two stages: 1) an external subject (formal object) imparting a form (external stimulus) to a receiving subject; and 2) movement of an appetite (a natural inclination consequent upon a form existing within a receiving subject) *toward union with its formal object* (external stimulus).

While *love has many species*, according to St. Thomas, it has *only one cause*: a suitable (proportionate) good. Moreover, love consists in a co-natural reality, compatibility, congeniality, between a lover and something loved. Within a human appetite, St. Thomas maintains that *love consists in a known and congenial good*, in a good in which a proportion, virtual quantum (qualitative) similarity, exists between the appetite and what it desires.

In other words, love consists in a virtual quantum proportion between the lover and the thing loved (a proportionate relation of qualitative equality in power in which the lover experiences what is loved as a congenial good, a good co-natural with, proportionate to its natural or facultative power [not too little, not too much, for its receptive power to experience proper, healthy, pleasure]). Considered as such, love is the experience of something as a beautiful, perfecting, good.

After considering the different species of love in general, St. Thomas next considers the different species of human love and the emotional effects that love has on human being.

St. Thomas divides human love into two species: love of 1) desire and 2) friendship (or of another for another). In addition, whether considered as love of friendship or love of desire, St. Thomas claims that, strictly speaking, love is always chiefly for a person (something evidently true since love is an act of a human person chiefly sought for the betterment of a human person—at least that of the lover).

Beyond the existence of two species of human love, St. Thomas states that human love has six effects: 1) union; 2) mutual indwelling; 3) transport; 4) jealousy; 5) being essentially helpful; and 6) being the first cause of everything a person appetitively does.

8. Why love is a passion in the intellectual and sense appetites

Following Aristotle in one respect, St. Thomas locates love in the sense and concupiscible appetite. He does this because he says good, the formal object of love, is also the formal object, chief end or aim, of all appetites. Hence, love formally differs according to the difference of appetites inasmuch as different appetites relate in analogous ways to a different form of the good.

St. Thomas often says that the terms "being," "good," "true," and "one" are convertible. By this he means that, strictly speaking, in different ways, they are signs of the same idea or really-existing being. A being is what is or has existence. A good is a being *related to*, existing toward (*ad esse*), an appetite. Something true is a being *related to*, existing toward, an intellect. Being one is being *related to* indivision, undivided being, a way being that resists division.

In short, good, true, and one contain in their natures, proper definitions, *relation, reference, to something else, an opposite*, with which they can establish a union. Since what is related, in some way, fits together with an opposite (like a hand in a glove, or foot in a shoe: both have opposing figures, shapes that can unite), Thomas understands the good and the true to be "fitting," "suitable," or "*proportionate*" being. Since being is identical with act, St. Thomas considers truth to be *suitable being* for an intellect, good is *suitable being* for an appetite, and unity is *suitable to being undivided*. Because it essentially activates it, the formal object, *the good* of a power (like a colored being for sight), is *suitable*, or *fitting*, *being* for a power: the good of the power, the act that can activate it. That is, it is a being *suitably, or fittingly, related* to (not too qualitatively weak or strong for; not too weak or strong in virtual quantity for) the power it activates.

Another way of saying the same thing is that the good, true, and one *are the attractive*. The good attracts an appetite; the true attracts an intellect, unity attracts, does not divide, a being.

St. Thomas maintains that appetites are relational movements toward an end that forms generate within their subjects, and that many appetites exist. For example, he calls a "natural appetite" an inclination toward what is "suitable" to non-sentient beings according to their nature (by reason of a knowledge that is in God [the author of their nature] and not in them). The tropism, or vegetative appetite, of a plant is an example. He understands a "sense appetite" to be *an inclination to what is suitable* to a sentient being arising from an agent's sense knowledge. In human beings, St. Thomas claims, the appetite has some share of freedom insofar as it is naturally inclined to listen to, obey, cogitative, or particular, reason (the estimative sense), which itself, in human beings, is inclined to obey the intellectual faculty of the human soul. Finally, the human will, the intellectual appetite, follows freely and directly from an intellectual apprehension in the human subject.

In each of these appetites, St. Thomas gives the name "love" to the principal, or chief, movement toward the end, or formal object, "loved" by an appetite. In the natural appetite the principle of this movement, "natural love," is the appetitive subject's co-natural suitability with the thing to which it tends. He gives the co-naturalness of a heavy body for an Earthly center by reason of its weight as an example.

Similar is the inclination of the sense appetite or will to some good: its *suitable union* with its *suitable being* is its "sense," "rational," or "intellectual," good. Hence, St. Thomas concludes, that, just as intellectual love is in the intellectual appetite (the will), sense love is in the concupiscible appetite because the formal object of this appetite is the good appetitively-desired absolutely as a sense good, and not under the formal difference of difficulty, which is the formal object of the irascible faculty.[11]

9. In what ways, as an intensive quantity (limited quality) of ability and satisfaction, love is the chief concupiscible passion

Because evil is a privation of, resistance to, good, that exists within the determinate potency, or power, of some being, good can exist without evil; but evil cannot exist without good. The relationship that exists between good and evil is unequal, not equal: one of privation and possession. By nature evil depends upon good for its existence; good does not depend upon evil for its existence. For this reason, even though good and evil can be objects of the concupiscible passions, good precedes evil in the order of emotional experience and desire. Prior to being able emotionally to experience an evil, we must first know, desire, its contrary good. Hence, St. Thomas says pursuit of a good is the reason for avoiding the opposite evil.

Good that activates an active power (like the faculty of sight or hearing) has the nature of an end, aim. For this reason, it is the first, highest, motivator, in any human being's plan of pursuit, order of intention (to see or hear); but it is last in the order of execution, or accomplishment (actually seeing or hearing). This being so, we can consider the concupiscible passions from the point of view of the order of intention or execution. In either case, we are considering them from the standpoint of *relation. The human appetites and passions, as well as all natural human faculties and habits, are essentially principles of human relation to everything in and around us* (hence, the common translation of the Latin word *"habitus"* to refer to "relation" in English).

In the order of execution, St. Thomas maintains that the first principle, or moving factor, belongs to what first moves a being that pursues an end. Because nothing naturally tends to a disproportionate end, one unsuitable for it, one to which it is totally unreceptive, unrelatable, or impossible for it to attain, whatever naturally tends to an end: 1) has, as a first principle, an aptitude, intensive quantitative receptivity, or proportion to that end; 2) is moved to that end; and 3) rests in the end, after having attained it as a proper good (and, in the case of an animal or human being, experiences *proper* pleasure).

For these reasons, Thomas concludes that love is an intensive quantity of ability, receptivity, or proportional capacity of the appetite *toward* the good and the intensive quantity of satisfaction that rests in the good. *Love, in short, is the first appetitive principle of all human relations*! He adds that desire is an in-between movement toward good; and pleasure, or joy, is rest in good (satisfaction of desire). Hence, in the order of execution, love precedes desire and desire precedes pleasure; but, in the order of intention, the reverse is true: the pleasure, enjoyment, intended causes desire and love. For *pleasure is* the enjoyment of the good (*love resting in a good*). In a way, then, just like the good, having enjoyment of the good, *love resting in the good, is the chief end of the concupiscible appetite.*[12]

10. How love is, and is not, a passion

According to St. Thomas, a natural agent produces a twofold effect on a passive (receiving) power. It gives it: 1) its form and, in a way, 2) the movement, as an active power, that results from the form. For example, what generates a physical body gives it a quantum of weight and the movement resulting from that weight. *Today, we might say that the generating principle gives the body mass or a quantum of gravitational influence.* Since weight is a principle of movement from one place to another place, St. Thomas says "natural love" is something co-natural to that body inasmuch as it has weight. In an analogous way, he maintains that, as something naturally suitable for, relatable to, the appetite, the appetible object gives the appetite: 1) movement toward the appetible object and 2) an adaptation to itself (satisfaction, rest, in that object). *If what St. Thomas says is right, the physical principle of gravity would be a principle of mass and real relation!*

Following Aristotle, St. Thomas claims that the movement of the concupiscible appetite is "circular" because, by introducing itself into the appetite's order of intention, the appetible object (the good), moves the appetite, while the appetite moves toward *possessing* the good. In this way, the movement ends where it started. Hence, St. Thomas calls "love" the first change effected in the appetite by the good: emotional recognition of the good's suitability for the appetite. From this recognition results a movement toward that same object (desire). Then, rest in the good: enjoyment. Since love consists in a change that the good effects in the concupiscible appetite, properly speaking, love is a passion. In an analogous sense, St. Thomas says love is in the will.[13]

In both cases, love is effected by *union* first recognized or achieved. From this start, the lover *stands in relation to* what he or she loves (exists as a term of a love relation as though it were himself or herself, or part of himself or herself).[14] Hence, strictly speaking, love is not the relation of union. *Love is a principle of union. Union is a result of love.* Strictly speaking, love does not denote the movement of the appetite in tending toward a good (desire). It denotes a movement by which the good changes the appetite by first causing the appetite passionately to know it as suitable for it, and, after pursuing it, to rest in the knowledge of possessing it.[15]

11. Human love's two chief divisions and why human love is always of a person

Again following Aristotle, St. Thomas holds that human love essentially involves wishing some person well. Because human love is always the act of a human agent, this is true even if the subject loved is some *thing, not some human being, loved. We always want some good for some person, even if that person is the one loving.* Whatever the nature of the good loved, Thomas says the movement of love always has a twofold tendency: 1) *toward the good* that *someone* wants for himself or herself, or to another person and 2) and *toward the person* for whom he or she wishes some good. For this reason, he says love has two chief divisions: 1) toward the good considered as such (love of concupiscence) and 2) related to a person (love of friendship toward the person to whom he or she wishes good).

He adds that the parts of these divisions are related as primary and secondary. Primary is what is loved with the love of friendship because this is loved first and foremost, absolutely, simply and for itself. But what is loved with the love of concupiscence is loved secondarily (because something else is first loved), not simply and absolutely for itself. It is loved relatively, secondarily, for some person, as a means to an end.[16]

12. Why the human good is the formal object and proper cause of human love

Considered as a passion of an initially passive power, love relates to its formal object as to the formal cause that initiates love's movement or act. Hence, whatever initiates love must be love's object. According to St. Thomas, the good (by which he means *being suitable* for a human) is love's formal object. As he has said, love implies some recognition of suitability of what is loved and the lover, an intensive quantitative proportion to it. Hence, it follows that the human good, *what is good for a human being, is the proper cause of human love.*[17]

Because love starts with some kind of knowledge of the good, someone might object that the beautiful, not the good, is love's formal cause. In reply, St. Thomas says the beautiful is the same as the good, that they differ only relationally. Since good is the chief aim, or end, of all desire, appetitively possessing the sense good calms sense desire. Beholding, intellectually knowing, the good (the beautiful being the good related to the will and intellect) calms the intellectual appetite: the will. For this reason: 1) the human intellect engages the most intellectual of the sense faculties, sight and hearing, to know physical beauty; and 2) we tend first and foremost to speak of beautiful sights and beautiful sounds, but less so of tastes and odors. Thomas says that beauty adds to goodness a special relation to a knowing faculty. Hence, "good" chiefly means what simply calms the appetite; and "beautiful" *is chiefly something that calms the will*, and secondarily other appetites, when intellectually apprehended.[18]

13. How knowledge is a cause of love

Agreeing with St. Augustine that no human being can love what he does not know, St. Thomas maintains that, as its formal object, good is, indirectly, not directly, the cause of love. Strictly speaking, the *good as known*, or the *known good, is the sense and intellectual appetite's formal object*. For this reason St. Thomas says Aristotle states that sense love starts in bodily sight. In an analogous way, St. Thomas claims contemplation of spiritual beauty or goodness is the principle of spiritual love. He adds that knowledge causes love for the same reason that good does: only a known good can be loved.[19]

Hence, just as sense knowing involves assimilation to the sensible species on the part of cogitative reason and/or cogitative reason and another sense faculty, so sense loving involves assimilation of the sense appetite to the sensibly known good, emotional apprehension of the *adaequatio*, "suitable *union*," between a known good and a sense faculty and the sense appetite. *The formal object of every faculty is always a suitable being for it*, some being essentially relatable to it, a facultative good. Knowing this union to exist within a knowing faculty causes a human being to love, and experience proper pleasure in what he or she knows through the appropriate appetite. Saying that knowledge of the good is a necessary condition for loving it does not mean that such knowledge must be perfect. St. Thomas holds that, while knowing something perfectly is required for perfection of knowledge, it is not required for the perfection of love.

Because knowledge belongs to the intellectual order, and because judging (dividing things that, in reality, are divided, and uniting things that, in reality, are united) is a knowing act, analysis and synthesis are chief judging acts of the intellect. Because, by nature, human beings cannot be totally satisfied considering a thing just as a whole, completeness, perfection, of human knowledge demands that we terminate knowledge in an act of judgment in which we know distinctly all that is in a thing (such as its parts, powers, and properties).

The appetite, however, relates to things, finds them suitable or unsuitable, the way they are as a whole. Completeness of love demands that a thing be loved according as it is known as a whole, not analyzed into all it all its parts. For this reason, Thomas says we love a thing more than we know it because we can love it completely without knowing it completely. He maintains that the truth of what he says is most evident in the sciences, which some people love through general knowledge they have of them. For example, because a man knows that rhetoric is a science that enables him to persuade others, he loves rhetoric. The same applies to human love of God.[20]

14. How likeness is a cause of love

While the known good is the chief cause of love, properly speaking, St. Thomas says likeness is also a cause of it. He explains why by observing that likeness (*oneness, unity, in quality*) between things is twofold: 1) actually having the same quality (for example, two things actually being blue) and 2) one thing actually being blue and another thing having determinate potential (potential by way of inclination, real proximate receptivity) for the color. For example, a fish living momentarily existing out of its natural habitat *is like* another fish existing in its natural habitat: or again, according as determinate potentiality bears a resemblance to its act; since, in a way, act is contained in the determinate potential. In this way, an all-star athlete not actively playing at present resembles one who is.

According to Thomas, the first kind of likeness causes love of friendship, or well-being. For the very fact that two women are alike, having, as it were, one form, makes them to be, in a manner, one in that form. Consequently, two women are one (undivided) in the species of humanity, and in womanhood. Hence, the appetitive inclinations of one tend toward, not away from, the other, as being one in species and sex. In this respect, one woman wishes the other good and wishes good to herself.

St. Thomas maintains that the second kind of likeness causes love of concupiscence or a friendship founded on utility or pleasure (not friendship in the chief sense) because whatever is in potentiality, as such, has the desire for its corresponding act; and, if it is a sentient and cognitive being, it takes pleasure in its realization.

In the love of concupiscence, properly speaking, in willing the good he desires, he says, a man chiefly loves himself. By natural inclination, one individual man loves himself more than another because he is *one* with himself substantially. He is *one* with another only in the likeness of some form. As a result, if this other's likeness to him that arises from relation to a common form hinders him from gaining a good that he loves, he can become hateful of another man; not for being like him (being a man), but for hampering him from getting the good. St. Thomas claims that this is why people in the same business profession sometimes quarrel among themselves, become jealous of each other: because they hinder one another's gain; and why proud people sometimes fight, become envious of each other—because they hinder each other from attaining some position they covet.[21]

15. How love causes every other passion

Because every psychic movement implies movement toward, or rest in, something, St. Thomas claims that every passion presupposes some kind of love. *All the other passions relate to love as a many to a one!* Every movement toward, or rest in, something arises from establishment of some prior *relationship, suitable union of opposites* (determinate potency and act). This suitable union of opposites is precisely in what love consists. *Love is the intensive quantum limit, measure, principle of appetitive union with a formal object! Considered as such, love determines the intensity of union that any and every passion can, does, have with its formal object! How intensely, completely, we love determines how intensely, completely we hate, desire, experience pleasure, pain, joy, sadness, hope, daring, fear, anger, and so on. No human passion other than love can cause every other passion because no other human passion can cause all the disparate human passions to become united as parts of a whole and cooperate as harmonious parts of a whole psychic unit. Hence, while, through its relation to love, some other passion might cause some particular love: it does so chiefly through the power of love in which it participates!*[22]

16. How union causes love

According to St. Thomas, because union of lover and something loved is twofold, union causes love in a twofold way: 1) actually (for example, when what is loved is present to a lover) and 2) potentially (for example, when what is loved is present in affection).

Because movement of the appetite follows apprehension, St. Thomas asserts we have to consider this union in relation to some preceding knowledge. Since love is twofold (of concupiscence and of friendship), each form arises from a kind of apprehension of unity of the thing loved with the lover. For example, when we love a thing by desiring it, we apprehend it as *one* with our well-being. Similarly, when we love someone with love of friendship, we will good to that person, just as we will good to ourselves. Hence, we view a friend as another self. For this reason, Thomas quotes Aristotle saying that a friend is called a person's "other self" and St. Augustine calling a friend "half of a person's soul."

Thomas claims that a final cause is the first of these unions referred to immediately above because love moves us to desire and seek the presence of the beloved, as of something suitable and united to us. Love causes the second union by formal cause because love is this union or bond. In this sense, he adds, Augustine calls love a vital principle uniting, or seeking to unite, a lover and a beloved. In describing love as "uniting" Thomas refers to the union of affection, without which no love exists and in saying that love seeks to unite, while Augustine refers to actual union.[23]

17. Six effects of love as a form of union considered in brief

Regarding love considered as a form of union, *being one*, St. Thomas maintains that union relates to love in three ways: as 1) a cause, 2) an effect, and 3) a relation of union existing between a lover and someone loved. Considered as an effect of love, St. Thomas maintains that love is the efficient and formal cause of union in reality and/or in affection in appetite and thought in both species of human love.

Considering mutual indwelling, St. Thomas states that love is constantly in the mind and appetites of lovers (in times of good and bad fortune).

This mutual indwelling (ecstasy), in turn: 1) is an effect of the desire on the part of lovers to transcend themselves and exist within the thoughts and appetites of a person loved and 2) constantly causes alteration in the inflation and deflation of the quality of a lover's intellect, reason, and appetites (making them more and less intense in perfection and operation, thereby affecting their virtual quantum [qualitative] greatness). Hence, sometimes love will cause a person to be appetitively relaxed and intellectually sharp; but, because it inclines to allow a lover to enjoy the good fortune and suffer the bad fortune of someone loved, it can also cause intellectual and appetitive fragmentation and weakness in these powers.

Because love makes a lover solicitous of the well-being and good fortune of someone loved, including oneself, jealousy and envy are also two of its effects. Hence, St. Thomas says that envy (dislike of a competitor in relationship to a commonly communicable and commonly desired good) consists in enjoyment of such a competitor's bad fortune and sadness over his good fortune; while, in contrast, jealousy can consist in 1) a love of desire caused by the love of some good, the loss of which a person considers possible and threatening due to the existence of some competition for a commonly communicable good; or 2) as a species of love of friendship, "jealousy on behalf of a friend" is solicitous of the well-being and good fortune of a friend and ready to take steps to protect that well-being and good fortune should they arise.

As far as love's effect of being essentially helpful, St. Thomas maintains that, strictly speaking, absolutely considered, love can never be harmful; but, incidentally, it can be by, for example, loving evil; or by the physiological and psychological changes it can cause as a result of four proximate effects it tends to produce: 1) pleasure; 2) a kind of appetitive and intellectual "melting" (by which a person is intellectually and appetitively disposed to be receptive to psychological influence from a lover); 3) languor (sadness caused by absence of someone loved); and 4) fervor (intense desire for possession of someone loved).

Finally, as far as being the first cause of everything a person appetitively does, the effect of love is evident: It is the chief principle, cause, of all our appetitive movements.

18. The passion of hatred, or disliking, considered in general

Regarding hatred, St. Thomas says its nature consists in a disharmony, qualitative disproportion, incongeniality, and repugnance existing between a sense appetite and sensed object which it apprehends as odious and harmful. Evident, once again, in relationship to hatred is how it is a passion caused by an awareness of a qualitative (virtual quantity) property of greatness of some object that is sensed as disproportionate in virtual quantity (qualitative) greatness of love (attraction) to the virtual quantity (qualitative) greatness of power of a sense faculty.

As far as hatred's cause is concerned, despite the fact that it might appear, at times, to have many causes, St. Thomas maintains *it has only one cause: love.* In addition, while, at times, hatred can appear stronger and to be more strongly experienced than love, according to St. Thomas, strictly speaking, because 1) love is the only cause of hatred, and 2) no effect can be stronger than its cause, hatred can never be stronger than love.

Consequently, St. Thomas explains the apparent and temporary appearance of hatred being stronger than love to be due to *initial experiences* of objects and *different experiences* of objects considered from different aspects. For example, when we first sense a highly noxious object that might really be good for us, it tends strongly to repel us, causing us to suspect maybe that hatred is stronger than love. And objects of different natures often have a similar effect when we consider them under different aspects (for example, as life-threatening or life preserving). Nonetheless, St. Thomas maintains that *hatred never overcomes love in relation to corresponding loves.*

Moreover, because hating either of these presupposes that a person must love them, St. Thomas asserts that, absolutely considered, a person can never hate himself or the truth. Although he says

Peter A. Redpath

that a person can hate: 1) a particular truth, wishing it not to be true; 2) the truth that prevents doing something (for example, pursuing a desired evil); 3) a truth a person wants kept secret; and 4) whole classes of things, multitudes of beings universally considered in relation to something that unites them both as abstract universals (for example, belonging to a different religion) and as operationally-causal universals (causes that generate universal effects considered as generating those effects [for example, the way in which the species of wolf naturally tend to appear to sheep]).

In contrast, St. Thomas contends that the passion of anger is different than hatred, that we always experience anger toward an individual. While, because the angry person always experiences anger in an individual way, what St. Thomas says is true, nonetheless, as contemporary experience shows, anger toward whole classes of people, identifying the individual with the class (like "the System"), and being angry with this or that person simply because he or she belongs to some class (like "the System," or some race or religion) appears possible because it actually happens. At the same time, if we consider a class (species) of individuals as numerically-one, St. Thomas is right. We can only be angry with it as *this* one religious class or *that* one race, for example.

19. How, in a way, evil causes hatred

Since a natural appetite is the result of apprehension (God's providence in the case of inanimate physical attraction), St. Thomas maintains that what applies to the inclination of the natural appetite, applies also to the animal appetite, which results from sense knowledge in the same subject. In the case of natural appetite, Thomas finds to be evident that, just as each thing is naturally receptive to (has a natural love for) what is *suitable* to it (the formal object of its natural love), so it has a natural resistance to, hatred for, what opposes and destroys it.

151

Hence, St. Thomas claims that in the animal, or intellectual, appetite, love is a kind of harmonious relation, *adequation*, between the appetite and what an appetite apprehends as suitable. Hatred, in turn, is a kind of disharmony, disequilibrium, between the appetite and what it apprehends as unsuitable for it. Just as whatever is suitable, as such, has some good proportionately related to it, so whatever is unsuitable, as such, has some evil related to it. Therefore, St. Thomas concludes, just as known good is love's object of love, so known evil is hatred's formal object.[24]

In making these claims St. Thomas adds that being, considered simply as being, or as such, does not repel because being is common to all things. But being, inasmuch as it is this determinate being, can be unfitting, or unsuitable, being for something. Hence, for that determinate thing it has an aspect of repugnance. In this way, one being is hateful to another, and is evil (though not in itself, but in relation to something else).[25]

20. The passion of concupiscence (*desire for* what is pleasurable) considered in general

Next in the order of experience within the concupiscible appetite after love and hatred is a psychological movement that resembles the passions of love and pleasure. The reason for this is that, by nature, on the sense level, we love something because we experience it as pleasant, while we hate it under the conceptual aspect of being painful. If the object that causes us pleasure is immediately present at hand, we immediately experience pleasure at, in some way, having it. If, on the other hand, some obstacle stands in the way of our being able presently to enjoy what we love, our natural inclination is to overcome that obstacle and secure union with what we love.

If the object confronting us is too powerful for us immediately to overcome, but we, nonetheless, still seek union with that object, we experience desire for that union: *the passion of concupiscence*. Hence, St. Thomas defines "concupiscence" as *the love of the pleasurable as absent*. And he maintains, further, that concupiscence properly belongs to the sense appetite involving the soul/body composite and differs from intellectual pursuit of pleasure, which, when secured, terminates in a qualitatively different kind of experience: joy, or intellectual delight.

Furthermore, St. Thomas maintains that: 1) by attracting the appetite toward itself, the good causes love; 2) by attracting the appetite toward itself as absent, the good causes desire, concupiscence; and 3) by satisfying the appetite as it rests in itself, the good causes pleasure or delight.

Additionally, St. Thomas states that some desires (found in brute animals) are naturally real in the sense that these animals are attracted toward them for the chief aim of satisfying real needs. In fact, following Aristotle, St. Thomas maintains that, aside from human beings, because they cannot distinguish between real and apparent goods, *all brute animals are naturally inclined to pursue all pleasurable goods as real*, even if not all pleasurable goods are really good for them. In contrast, only in human beings does the distinction between apparent and real goods exist within the genus animal. *And precisely for this reason, unlike other animals, human beings are moral agents in need of morally virtuous habits*!

Noting the powerful influence that pleasure and the pursuit of pleasure have within human beings, St. Thomas says that, in one way, human desire is finite: inasmuch as it is a natural desire for a formal object (real end) that really fulfills a human need (like healthy food does for the faculty of human nutrition). On the other hand, he states that, inasmuch as human beings can successively and repeatedly engage in different kinds of acts (like eating, drinking, sleeping), in principle, means to secure this real end are potentially infinite in principle if not in time and exercise. If we had the power, some of us would repeat such acts *ad infinitum* because, in principle, pursuit of real goods like health, wealth, fame, political power is potentially insatiable.

21. The passion of pleasure considered in general

St. Thomas defines the passion of pleasure as a psychosomatic movement within the concupiscible appetite having, in a final instant, achieved a perfection in harmony with a facultative nature. He says that *pleasure is unimpeded co-natural operation consisting in a state of rest involving a sense of being whole that occurs consequent upon the fulfillment of an appetitive movement*. He claims, moreover, that pleasure: 1) is an action, not a process; 2) need not involve time; and 3) differs from joy, which is intellectual, inasmuch as sensory pleasure involves bodily change, while intellectual pleasure is greater in species (qualitatively greater, greater in intensive quantity) than is physical pleasure.

Since every passion is a movement of the sense appetite as a result of sense knowledge, in agreement with Aristotle, St. Thomas maintains that pleasure is a passion, a psychic movement, "instantaneously and sensibly constituting a being as existing according to its nature."[26] St. Thomas gives a more complete explanation behind his conclusion by arguing that, just as some inanimate physical things, some animals achieve a natural way of existing suitable, naturally agreeable, to their natures.

While *movement toward* this natural state does not happen instantaneously, Thomas contends that attainment does. He claims that a difference exists between animals and inanimate physical things in that, when some animals reach this state they perceive it, while inanimate beings do not. From this perception of reaching a naturally agreeable state of existing, an animal's natural good, Thomas maintains that a psychic state arises in the sense appetite: pleasure.

Hence, St. Thomas says that, by calling pleasure "a movement of the soul," or "a psychic movement," he is designating pleasure's genus. In calling pleasure "a state of existing constituting a thing in agreement with its nature," he is assigning the cause of pleasure presence of "its co-natural good," the good suitable to its nature. By saying that this state happens is "all at once," he means this state is not a process. He means it is the terminus of a process that happens in an instant. He maintains he is agreeing with Plato that pleasure is not a "becoming." He is saying it is a "complete fact" of existing. Lastly, by saying that this constituting is achieved sensibly, he is excluding the states of suitable ways of existing of insensible beings that has no pleasure connected to it.[27]

As evidence of the qualitatively greater nature of intellectual joy to that of sensory pleasure, among other things, St. Thomas refers to the fact that: 1) people tend to reflect more repeatedly and intensely on intellectual acts than we do on acts of sensation; 2) we naturally incline to prize the sense faculty of sight (the qualitatively greatest of the human sense faculties) precisely because it is most like intellectual activity in its operation; but 3) we naturally incline to prize sanity over sight, would prefer to be sightless and sane instead of being sighted and insane, precisely because of the qualitatively more delightful emotional experience we get from having a healthy intellect than we do having even perfect vision.

Moreover, *if we consider absolutely* the three things essentially needed to experience pleasure: [1] the good of the thing with which a person is to be united (a sensory or intellectual good); 2) the part of a person to which a good is united (the intellectual soul or the sensory soul); and 3) the union to be achieved (intellectual or sensory)], in all three instances, St. Thomas maintains that, because it is more perfect, intimate, and lasting, intellectual union is qualitatively greater (of greater virtual quantum intensity) than is sensory union.

Furthermore, if we consider sensory pleasures relative to us *regarding the quality of their intensity*, St. Thomas states that, while, initially, sense objects are better known to us than are intellectual objects, this is not the case long-term; and sensory pleasures are intense chiefly because they essentially involve bodily modifications related to self-preservation and as medicinal remedies for physical defects and ailments. Their intensity is not chiefly due to their perfecting us as being human beings considered as a whole.

Comparing the sense faculty of sight to that of touch relative to sensory pleasure, St. Thomas claims that, unlike brute animals, human beings chiefly delight in the faculty of sight more than any other faculty for the contribution it makes to securing us knowledge, while we prize the sense faculty of touch more for bodily preservation. In contrast to human beings, he states that, because they lack an intellectual faculty, brute animals are not inclined to pursue their natural perfection in terms of perfecting the intellect to know truth about things (and, for example, know the difference between a real and an apparent good). They are inclined to pursue pleasure solely in terms of individual bodily, and species, preservation.

Consequently, agreeing with Aristotle, St. Thomas maintains that a dog does not chiefly delight in the sight (for example, the beauty) of a rabbit, and a lion does not chiefly delight in the sight, in the scent or sound of prey. *They chiefly delight in anticipating and actually eating them as a meal*! He states, moreover, that, because only a human being is a rational animal, only a human being can take pleasure in the objects of different sense faculties considered as such, only a human being can delight in speculatively knowing the nature of this or that object as the object of this or that sense faculty.

The highest sense faculty that brute animals possesses is the *estimative sense*, which, in them, is essentially ordered to: 1) take pleasure in objects of sense inasmuch as they relate to the sense of touch and 2) the passion of pleasure inasmuch as the estimative sense can use the irascible passions to use pleasure to safeguard individual, and species, animal life.

22. Why, strictly speaking, desire for pleasure, concupiscence, is a specific passion that exists only in the sense appetite

According to St. Thomas, pleasure is twofold: 1) intellectual and 2) physical. He says the first, which he generally calls "joy," appears to be a possession of the soul alone; while, because the sense appetite is seated in a bodily organ, the second appears to belong to the soul and body. Hence, he holds that sensible good is a good of the whole composite, while intellectual good appears to be chiefly of the intellect. Since concupiscence appears to be an appetite for physical pleasure, properly speaking, St. Thomas locates this inclination in the concupiscible faculty, which, he says takes its name from it (from concupiscence).[28]

Hence, not every good is the appetitive good of the concupiscible appetite. Just as *good is suitable being*, the good suitable for the sense faculty, which gives pleasure to the senses, is the formal object of the concupiscible faculty. For this reason, we distinguish the different sensible passions according differences of sense good.

Thomas explains, further, that the difference of this object can arise from the side of the nature of the object or from a difference in the active power that moves, or does not move, toward it. He claims that: 1) difference of object that arises from the nature of the active power's object causes a material difference in passions and 2) difference in active power relative to the nature of its chief aim or end causes a formal diversity of passions, in respect of which the passions differ formally.

He claims, further, that the nature of an active power's end, or good, differs according to whether this good is actually present or absent. For an active power a present good and absent good are different ends, different formal objects. And the nature of the end causes different effects in the active power. An actual good causes the faculty to find rest in it. An absent good causes the faculty to move toward it.

Hence, St. Thomas states, the formal object of sensible pleasure causes: 1) love in the concupiscible appetite inasmuch as it, so to speak, harmonizes and conforms the appetite to itself; 2) desire for pleasure, inasmuch as, when absent, it draws the faculty to itself; and 3) pleasure, inasmuch as, when present, it causes the faculty to find rest, calm, in itself. Accordingly, St. Thomas claims concupiscence differs "in species" from love and pleasure and sense desires for this or that pleasurable object differ "in number."[29]

23. Precisely why the desire for some pleasures can be boundless while others cannot

St. Thomas defines concupiscence as the appetite for pleasurable good. He contends that something can be pleasurable in two ways, because: 1) *it is suitable* to the nature of some animal or human being (for example, food, drink, and so on), and concupiscence of such pleasurable things is said to be natural; 2) some human being thinks that it is not naturally suitable for a human being; but, nonetheless, takes pleasure in it as something suitable. St. Thomas calls the first kind of concupiscence "natural" and the second kind "non-natural."[30]

Regarding the possible limitlessness of natural desire, St. Thomas says that, because nature tends toward what is determinate, fixed, limited, suitable to it, and naturally necessary for it (what satisfies a natural need), strictly speaking, natural concupiscence cannot be actually infinite. Hence, by nature, no man ever desires infinite meat or drink.

But, just as in nature, a potential, successive infinity can exist, so can natural concupiscence be successively infinite. For instance, after getting food, a man might later want more; and so of anything else that nature requires: because these bodily goods, when obtained, do not last forever, but fail.

Regarding non-natural concupiscence, because this results from an act of intellectual consideration, St. Thomas claims this can be infinite and desires of reason, wishes, can proceed to infinity. Hence, a person who desires riches might desire to be rich beyond measure.

St. Thomas adds that, in his *Politics*, Aristotle gives another reason, based upon the difference between desire of ends and means, to explain why one concupiscence can be finite, and another infinite. According to Aristotle, in a way, concupiscence of the end is always infinite because, while the end (for example, health) is desired for its own sake (health), greater health is more desired, and so on to infinity. On the other hand, concupiscence of the means cannot be infinite because concupiscence of the means consists in *suitable proportion* to the end (being a real, not fictional, means). As a result, Aristotle argues that those who place their end in riches considered as such have an infinite desire for wealth, but those who desire riches to fulfill the necessities of life want a finite measure of wealth sufficient for the necessities of life. Thomas adds that the same reasoning applies to concupiscence of any other thing.[31]

24. The moral and non-moral dimensions of pleasure

Since, according to St. Thomas, not all pleasures are morally good or evil considered as such, he maintains that pleasures are good when they come to rest in what agrees with right reason. If we take pleasure in doing good acts, the pleasure we take is morally good. If we take pleasure in performing evil acts, the pleasure we enjoy is morally evil. In agreement with Aristotle, *St. Thomas asserts that pleasure of a good will is the chief measure by means of which we judge all moral good! Principally, we judge moral rectitude in relation to whether or not the human will delights in taking pleasure in the activities and choices measured by the rule of right reason* (*prudence*): *a reasoning faculty intentionally conformed to fulfilling real over apparent needs and choosing greater over lesser goods*! Because, by nature, such pleasures are species-specifically and generically healthy and safe, St. Thomas calls such pleasures generically "natural" and "proper" pleasures.

In addition, St. Thomas considers some pleasures to be generically unnatural for all animals when they are contrary to the preservation of individual and species life. Hence, he finds some pleasures unnatural, and species-specifically and generically unhealthy and unsafe (not proper pleasures) from the standpoint of the innate animal inclination toward self-preservation. For example, for an animal to be inclined to be repelled by natural animal acts like pursuing and eating food, seeking shelter, and sleeping. Such behaviors are a sign of an animal being species-specifically appetitively unhealthy from the standpoint of the natural inclination of all animals to seek individual animal self-preservation. Analogously, St. Thomas considers such animal acts as failing to engage in reproduction and in subsequent nourishment, protection, and education of children to be unnatural from the standpoint of species self-preservation at least with respect to higher forms of domestic, animal life.

At the same time, St. Thomas maintains that some animal acts that are specifically natural can be non-natural for an individual. For example, something that is against the inclination of human nature regarding being rational for preserving the life of the body might be co-natural to some individual because of a corrupted, physically or psychologically unhealthy, nature. For instance, the inability to see is natural to a blind person, but unnatural to the species human.

25. The unique animal situation of human beings as moral agents and how this relates to the passion of pleasure

Because of the unique position that human beings occupy within the physical universe as free agents, St. Thomas indicates that human beings stand in a unique relationship regarding experience of the passion of pleasure within the concupiscible appetite. As has just been noted in the Section 21 above, St. Thomas considers pleasure to be an *unimpeded activity* that conforms to a natural inclination. Considered as such, pleasure is something good, a state of rest in a condition of emotional satisfaction. Considered as such as an extreme within a genus, pleasure would be a maximum good.

Within a genus the normal situation is for one contrary opposite extreme to be a perfection and the other contrary opposite extreme to be a privation. It is not for both contrary opposite extremes to be equally perfect or both to be deprived. For example, in the genus health, one contrary opposite is the living body in most perfect health, while the other is the living body in least perfect health. It is not for living bodies to be in equally good health

In the concupiscible appetite, for instance, pain is a privative negation (a resistance, impediment) to pleasure. Were two pleasures to exist as contrary extremes, neither would appear to be able to act as impediment to the other, and no hierarchy of species would appear to be able to exist within a human appetite as more or less perfect possessors of some generic good. Since contraries are two species existing within a genus that impede each other, and since two equal goods, pleasures (equally unimpeded activities) do not appear to be able to impede each other, a genus composed of two equal extremes of pleasure would appear to be no genus at all.

In the case of genus of moral activity alone, however, St. Thomas claims that such a condition is possible inasmuch as two pleasures (like cowardice and rashness) exist as extremes of vice mutually contrary to the virtue of prudence. Hence, while two virtues cannot be mutually contrary, cannot mutually impede each other, within the genus of moral activity, two vices can; and the one virtue of prudence can impede the two extremes of moral vice.

26. The causes of pleasure

According to St. Thomas, the existence of pleasure requires three conditions: 1) the pleasurable object; 2) union of an appetitive faculty with that object; and 3) knowledge of that union in the present, in memory, or in anticipation. Such being the case, St. Thomas asserts that the following can cause pleasure: 1) activity in so far as the activity unites with its object *and we appetitively know this union*; 2) change, or movement, because human nature is changeable and appetitively being united to a change and knowing about it can cause pleasure; 3) hopes and memories inasmuch as they are forms of union satisfy us almost as much as real union; 4) sorrow, inasmuch as it recalls a past good, or inasmuch as we recall it is not present; 5) other people's actions, if they are good considered in themselves; if they cause us to recognize a good in ourselves; or if the people happen to be friends or enemies (such as good things happening to friends and bad things happening to enemies); 6) to effect a good for a friend, in the hope of getting a good for oneself, or in knowing a person has the ability to do good, to do something good through possession of a good habit, or to motivate a person to do more good; 7) similarity inasmuch as it contains three things needed for pleasure mentioned at the start of this section above; and 8) wondering inasmuch as wondering contains real hope of achieving union with something pleasant.

27. The effects of pleasure

As effects of pleasure St. Thomas lists the following: 1) psychological enlargement of spirit involving intellectual expansion of knowledge and appetitive expansion of emotional receptivity including an inclination to surrender to the cause of pleasure; 2) sometimes a thirst for more; 3) sometimes (if the pleasure involved naturally inclines to accompany use of reason), an increase in the ability to use reason; or, if it does not naturally incline to accompany use of reason, the inability to reason; and 4) sometimes perfecting or impeding action toward an end (in the sense of being anything that is a compatible, suitable, good), or as an efficient cause that makes work more enjoyable.

28. Pain/Sorrow, its causes, effects, remedies, goodness and evil

St. Thomas claims that sorrow is chiefly an appetitive reaction in the human will that accompanies sensory displeasure caused by one's own misfortune, or that of another person. He identifies four species of sorrow: 1) pity: sorrow at another person's bad fortune; 2) envy: sadness at another person's good fortune; 3) anxiety (*angst*), a sadness consequent upon fear in the face of the inability to flee from an impending danger; and 4) torpor: a sadness that generates organic immobilization.

According to St. Thomas, sorrow has one chief cause: some impediment that, *because it is too strong* for the appetitive faculty to resist or overcome, frustrates desire for, or union with, some perceived good.

As effects of sorrow, St. Thomas lists the following: 1) physical immobility; 2) diminished ability to learn; 3) delighting in a variety of pleasures and actions; 4) emotional depression that, when intense, psychologically weighs a person down and swallows him up; 5) appetitive contraction, withdrawal, accompanied by physiological reactions like bodily contractions and muscular aches and pains; and 6) physical disease and muscular disharmony, especially to the heart and lungs.

As remedies for sorrow, St. Thomas identifies the following: 1) pleasurable activity in general, such as eating; 2) crying; 3) sympathy of friends; 4) contemplation of truth; 5) relaxation activities like sleep, bathing, taking a walk.

Regarding the goodness and evil of pain and sorrow, St. Thomas maintains that: 1) absolutely considered and in itself, because they disturb facultative health and prevent rest in a healthy facultative good, all pain and sorrow are evil; but 2) considered in relation to something else (for example, doing a morally vicious deed), experiencing pain and sorrow can be a morally virtuous and useful good. For example, experiencing the pain and sadness of shame for doing a vicious deed is morally healthy, is a sign of personal, moral goodness. Indeed, not to experience shame as a result of doing something morally vicious is a clear sign of an unhealthy, ugly soul: of unhealthy emotions and estimative sense faculty, reason, and will.

He states that two reasons could exist for this psychological condition: 1) a person does not have the sense experience of the vicious act as being unhealthy to do, or 2) has the sense experience, but does not estimate this experience to be something about which to be concerned. Since both of these reasons are signs of having unhealthy emotions and an unhealthy estimative sense, they are signs of aberration and pathology in moral psychology.

Regarding the moral utility of pain and sorrow, St. Thomas maintains that: 1) considered simply from the standpoint of being a concupiscible passion, because the concupiscible appetite only considers the present and does not consider utility, pain and sorrow have no utility; but 2) considered in relation to the irascible appetite (which inclines to avoid and expel painful and sorrowful evils), for three reasons, pain and sorrow can be useful. 1) Avoiding something can be right, healthy, because, in and of itself, something is unsafe, dangerous, to life and health. Or because, 2) while not unsafe, dangerous, threatening to life and health in and of itself, relating to something in one way or another can serve as the occasion for being exposed to such evils; and 3) because they add another good reason to avoid it, experiencing pain and sorrow about that which we ought to avoid is always useful.

Just as taking pleasure and joy in doing good deeds causes us to seek more intensely to do good deeds, experiencing pain and sadness in doing evil deeds inclines us more intensely to avoid them. While, by nature, all human beings incline to seek what is really good for us and to take pleasure in the good and to avoid pain and sorrow considered as facultatively unhealthy, evil considered as such is something we naturally, and should habitually, incline to avoid. According to St. Thomas, this is especially true regarding moral evils, which more than any bodily pain, prevent us from experiencing human happiness of the qualitatively highest degree and kind.[32]

29. Hope and despair

Just as love is the first principle of all the human passions, especially of the concupiscible passions, so hope is first principle of all the irascible passions. According to St. Thomas, hope's formal object is some future, possible, difficult, appetitively-achievable good. Hope, in short, does not, strictly speaking, involve what is temporally past, nor an easily or impossible-to-achieve good. For the subject of this formal object is the irascible, not the concupiscible, appetite: the sensory appetite chiefly concerns itself with pursuing real, achievable, and useful goods (goods really useful for preserving, promoting, and protecting individual and species life and health).

While it is chiefly seated in the sense appetite, hope has cognitive elements related to it including that of cogitative reason, the estimative sense. Even if this is not an intellectual awareness (but is based upon possession of animal instinct, implanted in them, as St. Thomas says, by the divine intellect), no surprise should exist, then, that some other animals that have some awareness of time should experience this passion. Regarding the causes of hope, St. Thomas states that these consist in anything that can cause a person to consider an action personally doable, such as: 1) experience; 2) inexperience, stupidity, foolishness; 3) age; 4) mental or physical condition (like intelligence, health, strength); 5) wealth; 6) beauty; 7) friends; 8) social status; 9) political influence; and 10) love.

Because, in one way or another, they lack experience and prudent judgment and are inclined to exaggerate their abilities (in short, have a weakly-developed estimative sense), as prime examples of hope, St. Thomas gives young people, drunkards, and fools.

As far as hope's contrary opposite (despair) is concerned, from what St. Thomas has already said, despair's nature, causes, and effects are fairly evident. As the contrary opposite of hope, despair is caused by the conviction that some future deed is undoable, impossible to achieve, either because of: 1) personal weakness, 2) the intervention of some overwhelmingly powerful and evil impediment, or 3) a combination of the two.

Despair's causes include many of the causes of hope listed above as well some of their opposites, and some that are related to effects that fear causes. Moreover, while hope's effects more closely resemble those of desire, pleasure, and joy, despair's effects closely resemble those of aversion, pain, and sorrow. Hence, no need exists for me to consider them further.[33]

30. Fear and the moral psychology of the daring person and how it differs from the moral psychology of the despondent individual

Among all the passions causing psychological depression, St. Thomas lists fear as second to sorrow. Since the first principle of all human passions is love, love is one of the causes of fear; but, since all the passions located in the irascible appetite are proximately caused by the passion of hope, hope is a proximate first principle of fear.

Such being the case, no surprise should exist in the fact that the formal object of fear somewhat resembles that of hope, but, since fear is emotionally somewhat opposite of hope, fear's formal object consists in some future, difficult, evil of a magnitude great enough to incline a person to move away from it as unlikable.

Like all human passions, St. Thomas considers fear to be essentially natural and, considered simply as a human passion, something good (not irrational) to experience. Indeed, like hope, because the passion of fear inclines a person to recognize and sense the existence of real evil, *fear is one of the chief passions that helps keep us in touch with reality*!

Our ability to recognize and properly *estimate* the passions of fear and hope as healthy passions to experience and real human goods lies precisely in the fact that they can only be healthy to the extent that human beings are convinced about the reality of good and evil as being facultatively-independent principles (not being considered to exist only in some psychological faculty). For if we are not convinced that good and evil are real, *if we are convinced that nothing can really help us and nothing can really hurt us*, then the passions of hope and fear, *and all the irascible emotions*, are irrational to experience as healthy.

If real good and evil do not exist, neither can real safety or danger, real health or disease, anything really useless or useful. As a result, the rational way for anyone accepting the truth of such an evidently false conviction about reality would be to evaluate real good and evil, all the irascible emotions, anything supposedly really useful or useless, healthy or unhealthy like some ancient Stoics did (and some contemporary political ideologues do): *as forms of a mental disorder*.

With logical consistency, anyone convinced that nothing psychologically independent of us can really be useful or helpful to us as human beings should conclude that the rational decision for us to make regarding such supposedly fictional beings would be to consider as forms of mental disorder all the passions and moral virtues that are naturally inclined to pursue goods under the aspect of being useful (all the irascible passions) as life- and health-promoting: like daring, courage, and justice. Rationally-considered we should judge all these to be delusions.

Going beyond his introductory remarks regarding fear's nature and formal object, St. Thomas identifies six species of fear: 1) laziness (which he calls "timidity in the face of labor"); 2) embarrassment (fear of reputational damage for what a person is presently doing); 3) shame (fear of reputational damage for what one has done in the past); 4) wonder/astonishment (fear caused by something unanticipatedly great, the suddenness of which overwhelms us with a sense of our own weakness); 5) stupor (fear caused by an unexpectedly strange experience that immobilizes the imagination by its unfamiliarity and, consequently, impedes a person's ability to judge precisely how intelligently to react to it); and 6) agony (a fear caused by an unforeseeable and unforeseen evil of such a magnitude that it presents itself as terrifyingly unavoidable).

Regarding fear's formal object, given the roots of fear in hope, evident is that this formal object includes the notions of being a present (not an absent), disagreeable, unavoidable, difficulty considered possible to escape in the future. Regarding the sense faculty that enables human beings to experience it and all the irascible passions, beyond that of imagination, is *the estimative sense*, especially because fear has two chief causes that are essentially causes of all the irascible passions, a sense of: 1) personal weakness and 2) strength of evil confronted that is of some possibly-overpowering magnitude.

As far as fear's causes are concerned, St. Thomas lists these as: 1) death and natural weakness; 2) great, unavoidable, pains; 3) an image of future, damaging things; 4) sometimes guilt; 5) sometimes fear itself; and 6) love of life.

Regarding these causes, as well as fear's nature, its causes, and effects, special note should be made that none of these is intelligible without taking into consideration St. Thomas's often-used principle of virtual quantity, or qualitative greatness. For without a comparison being made between the powers of the individual and the magnitude of the strength that those powers confront, no irascible passion can possibly be experienced, including fear.

Concerning the effects of fear, St. Thomas identifies these as chiefly two: 1) psychological and physical contraction and 2) an inclination consequent upon this psychological experience to deliberate about available options to flee. As far as the nature of psychological and physical contraction is concerned, St. Thomas describes this as: 1) an appetitive movement of withdrawal, 2) accompanied by an organic contraction of muscles resulting from withdrawal of heat from the extremities of the body toward the heart and accompanying cooling of the muscular extremity of the body; and 3) difficulty breathing and, sometimes, speaking, and, always, heart irregularities.

In contrast to fear exists daring (fear's contrary opposite), which St. Thomas says is moved by possible hope of future escape. As far as the moral psychology of the daring person, St. Thomas describes this as follows: 1) Hope attacks an evil of some magnitude in the future pursuit of some good. 2) Estimating the real possibility of a personal damage ensuing as a result of personal weakness due to the magnitude of the evil involved, fear inclines the hopeful person to shrink back. 3) In reaction to this momentary intervention of fear, daring causes a person to attack the fearful and disagreeable object.

In contrast to the daring person who is inclined to confront the evil to which fear is inclined to succumb, in opposition to the hopeful person, who, like the daring person, is inclined to attack a formidable evil, the despondent person gives up hope of avoiding evil and the pursuit of the good that accompanies that hope. Consequently, the psychological state of the despondent person is an essential consequence of the loss of hope necessarily connected to an irrational refusal, or rational acceptance of, a person's inability to do the daring.[34]

31. Anger and related considerations

St. Thomas defines anger as a psychosomatic, emotional inclination to attack a person for committing a suspected injustice in the form of undeserved contempt or disrespect against another person.

He maintains that anger: 1) is chiefly rooted in hope of revenge against another person; 2) strictly speaking, cannot be directed against an inanimate object; and 3) is, also, rooted in a natural, intensive quantum level of disposition (*habitus*) toward being just, prudent, temperate, and courageous that exists within all human beings; and 4) chiefly has one cause: the suspicion of being treated unjustly or disrespectfully.

Hence, even to this day, most people in the world: 1) appear to maintain that, no matter how badly educated a person might be, not knowing that acts like, murder, lying, stealing, are morally wrong is humanly impossible; and 2) appear to do so out of a sense of righteous indignation (justice related to the nature of the wrong involved).

In contrast to *many* people, just as he does not abstractly consider pleasure, or even hatred, to be essentially evil or irrational, so, abstractly-considered and in principle, St. Thomas does not claim that anger is essentially evil, or irrational. Indeed, in practice, like Socrates, Plato, and Aristotle before him, he maintains the passion of anger (the inclination to attack real acts of injustice) is a necessary condition for the existence and survival of human communities and political life. Nonetheless, in exercise, considered in relation to this or that circumstance, he asserts that anger often can be morally evil and irrational.

Beyond identifying the nature and cause of anger, St. Thomas maintains that three species of anger exist: 1) quick-temperedness (named from the way it starts); 2) incessant/bitter (named from the memory of unjust sadness it causes); and 3) vindictive/furious (named from the chief end sought: vengeance).

Peter A. Redpath

Concerning the moral psychology of the angry person, St. Thomas touches on this in his definition of anger as a condition in which an angry person emotionally reacts to a suspected act of disrespect, diminishment of personal dignity. Such being the case, Thomas notes three opposing ways of behaving toward another person that can increase or diminish the magnitude of anger caused: 1) knowledge or ignorance; 2) passion or lack of passion; 3) intention or lack of intention.

The moral psychology of the angry person is such that someone angry always inclines initially to identify the cause of anger to be *a moral slight*, a suspicion of being treated unjustly, *being intentionally diminished in relation to personal perfection*. Hence, knowing the different ways of slighting another person is useful for understanding how to increase or diminish anger.

According to St. Thomas, at least three ways exist in which intentionally to slight another person: out of 1) insolence, 2) contempt, or 3) spite. Because a person can slight another person out of ignorance, passion, or unintentionally, and because such ways of slighting someone are evidently at least somewhat involuntary, if a person slighted knows this condition of involuntariness was involved in the act of suspected disrespect, reasonable to expect is that this person's anger might not arise at all or, if it does, be less intense, of less duration. On the other hand, a person who is voluntarily treated unjustly out of contempt, spite, or insolence (all of which are forms of voluntary slighting) tends to magnify the intensity of angry response.

Finally, regarding the effects of anger, St. Thomas lists these as six in number: 1) joy of revenge (he says that the pain of anger terminates in the joy of revenge); 2) fervor in the heart/blood (fervor causing intensity of heat in the blood, which facilitates ease of muscular movement to attack a perceived evil); 3) other bodily changes that display signs of activities occurring in the heart, lungs, and facial expression (that is, changes in facial expression with respect to the eyes, reddening of the face, intensity of breathing, increased beating of the heart, and changes in speech pattern); 4) an increased or diminished capacity to reason; 5) when uncontrolled, most damaging to the use of reason; and, 6) when uncontrollable, causes us to become taciturn, morose.

Regarding remedies for anger, St. Thomas mentions that passage of time and inability to get revenge (especially over an extended period) help to decrease it. And it can be totally diminished by achieving what a person estimates to be just revenge.

Most interestingly, while what tends to eliminate one passion is it being extinguished by a contrary opposite passion, this is not the case with the passion of anger. In fact, once again, anger is the only passion that has no contrary opposite. Just why it has no contrary opposite appears to be related to the fact that human psychology necessarily involves ultimate termination of the human passions in the sense of pleasure and of the essential connection between anger and having a sense of justice (because only a person with a sense of justice is able to get angry).

In a sense, because of its roots in a sense of justice, anger is the most social of the human passions. And the other passions need to call upon it to stimulate acts of reasoning to go beyond existing acts of temperance and courage when these are not enough to effect peace, bring about calm within the human passions and the human community at large.

Hence, that one passion existing in the irascible appetite should have to return to the concupiscible appetite to find the pleasure that hope provides against despair, and daring against fear, suggests a unique quality of perfection that is contained within pleasure to teach human beings that the perfection of justice cannot lie within anger, that it can only be tempered by a pleasure identified by reason in perfect pleasure: calm (not concupiscence, but something more akin to temperance practiced toward another: friendship).

For this reason, most human beings are inclined to be more forgiving of the behavior of the angry person than we are of the hateful person. As St. Thomas notes, because an angry person acts out of a sense of justice, the angry person intentionally seeks limits to the damage done to another (has a sense of equity), while a hateful person does not (has no sense of equity, mercy). St. Thomas says that, while an angry person is inclined to experience sadness when acts committed out of anger tend to exceed the measure of justice, a person filled with hate would just as soon see another person not exist. Hence, moral acts committed out of hatred tend to be worse in kind than those committed out of anger. And, like acts of incontinence in general, most human beings tend more easily to forgive an angry person than we do a hateful one.

According to St. Thomas, the passion of anger is unique among all other irascible passions in this: *while it does have an opposite that terminates it*, it cannot have a *generic opposite* (a contrary opposite) according to approach and withdrawal (moving toward or away from), or opposition according to contrariety of good and evil. The reason Thomas gives for the peculiar nature of anger is that a presently-considered difficulty causes anger and confronts us with different possible ways of reacting; and because contraries are extreme differences, opposites, that belong to the same proximate genus, have the same generic principle, or common principle that generates them. While anger has an extreme difference that stops its movement, this opposite comes from a different, not the same, genus (proximate principle) as anger: from the concupiscible, not the irascible, appetite.

According to St. Thomas, when a person considers such an evil present (even if it not actually present), the sense appetite must engage or not engage. If the concupiscible appetite experiences dislike or sadness, the sense appetite must accept the situation or engage the irascible appetite to attack the perceived evil. If a person suspects the evil is undeserved, unjust, the irascible appetite will generate the passion of anger to attack it. In this situation, the irascible appetite cannot have a movement of withdrawal: because the evil already exists or has been done. The evil, difficulty, is not in the future. It is supposed to be already present or past.

Thus, no passion in the irascible appetite contrary to anger according to contrariety of approach and withdrawal is possible. No present withdrawal from the evil is possible. Given the perceived present or past nature of the evil, the appetite can only hope to the future to get revenge against an evil already done or presently happening. It cannot hope to avoid the present or past evil.

Similarly, no generic contrary of good and evil can exist because the generic opposite of *present* evil is *present* good. Present good does not have identically the same nature as possible future good secured by attacking difficulty. Once good is obtained, no movement toward the good or away from evil remains because rest in the good, satisfaction, has been achieved. This is the state of pleasure or joy, a concupiscible passion.

Hence, St. Thomas says that no psychic *movement*, no emotional movement of the soul, can be a contrary opposite (extreme, exact opposite in the same proximate genus) of the movement of anger. *Rest, not movement, terminates anger!* For this reason, St. Thomas has said that the pain of anger terminates in the *joy* of revenge. No contrary within its proximate genus (the iranscible appetite) can stop the movement of anger. Only the repose achieved in and through the concupiscible appetite (a different proximate genus of appetite) terminates anger. For this reason, quoting Aristotle, St. Thomas says "calm is anger's contrary" and he adds that this type of opposition is between possession and privation. Strictly speaking, it is not an opposition between contrary opposites (extreme differences that belong to the same, proximate genus).[35]

—Notes—

1. St. Thomas Aquinas, *Summa theologiae*, 1, q. 78, a. 4; q. 81; 1–2, q. 22.
2. Id. See Plato, *Republic*, Bk. 3, 386A–412B; and Aristotle, *De anima*, Bk. 3, ch. 11.
3. Aquinas, *Summa theologiae*, 1, q. 77, a. 3 and q. 81, a. 2; 1–2, q. 23; see Aristotle, *Physics*, Bk. 3, ch. 3 and Bk. 5, ch. 5.
4. Aquinas, *Summa theologiae*, 1–2, q. 23, a. 4, reply.
5. Id., q. 23; Aristotle, *Physics*, Bk. 3, ch. 3 and Bk. 5, ch. 5.
6. Id., 1, q. 81 and 1–2, q. 22; see Aristotle, *Physics*, Bk. 3, ch. 3 and Bk. 5, ch. 5.
7. Id.
8. Id.
9. Id., 1–2, q. 24.
10. Id., a. 3, reply and ad 1.
11. Id., q. 26, a. 1, *sed contra* and reply; see Aristotle, *Topics*, Bk. 2, ch. 7.
12. Aquinas, *Summa theologiae*, 1–2, q. 26, ad 2, reply.
13. Id., q. 26, a. 2, reply; see Aristotle. *Rhetoric*, Bk. 2, ch. 10.
14. Aquinas, *Summa theologiae*, 1–2, q. 26, ad 1.
15. Id., ad 2.
16. Id., a. 4, reply; see Aristotle, *Rhetoric*, Bk. 2, ch. 4.
17. Aquinas, *Summa theologiae*, 1–2, q. 27, a. 1, *sed contra* and reply; see St. Augustine, *de Trinitate*, Bk 8, ch. 3.
18. Aquinas, *Summa theologiae*, 1–2, q. 27, a. 1, ad 3.
19. Id., a. 4, *sed contra* and reply; see *de Trinitate*, Bk. 10, chs., 1 and 2; Aristotle *Nicomachean Ethics*, Bk. 9, chs. 5 and 12.
20. Aquinas, *Summa theologiae*, 1–2, q. 27 a. 2.

21. Id., a. 3, reply.
22. Id., a. 4, reply.
23. Id., q. 28, a. 1, reply; see Aristotle, *Nicomachean Ethics*, Bk. 9, ch. 4; St. Augustine, *Confessions*, Bk. 4, ch. 6 and St. Augustine, *de Trinitate*, Bk. 8, ch. 10.
24. Aquinas, *Summa theologiae*, 1–2, q. 29, a. 1, reply.
25. Id., a. 1, reply.
26. Id., q. 31, a. 1, reply; Aristotle, *Rhetoric*, Bk. 1, ch. 11.
27. Aquinas, *Summa theologiae*, 1–2, q. 31, a. 1, reply; see Plato, *Philebus*, 32A–34A, and Aristotle, *Nicomachean Ethics*, Bk. 7, ch. 12.
28. Aquinas, *Summa theologiae*, 1–2, q. 30, a. 1, reply.
29. Id., a. 2, reply.
30. Id., a. 3, reply.
31. Id., a. 4, reply; see Aristotle, *Politics*, Bk. 1, ch. 3.
32. Aquinas, *Summa theologiae*, qq. 31–39; see, also, 1–2, q. 6, a. 6, and Aristotle, *Nicomachean Ethics*, Bk. 3, ch. 1; *Rhetoric*, Bk. 2, ch. 3.
33. Aquinas, *Summa theologiae*, 1–2, q. 40.
34. Id., qq. 41–44.
35. Id., q. 46, a. 1 and a. 6, ad 1.

–CHAPTER SIX–
Habit, Virtue, and Law

1. St. Thomas's definition of "habit" ("*habitus*")

Having finished examining the nature of the human passions, St. Thomas next considers the definition of a habit. In so doing, he defines a habit: 1) generically as a quality (intensive quantity) of soul and 2) specifically as a quality of soul existing within a natural faculty that acts as a *principle* essentially relating the operation of a faculty of soul to its natural end.

Fully to appreciate the meaning of this definition, need exists to recall that a facultative end is a faculty's formal object (the act that stimulates a determinate power essentially to react to its stimulation and naturally incline to seek union with it; for example, sound acts as the formal object of the faculty of hearing and naturally inclines that faculty to seek to remain in union with it because, by natural inclination, the faculty of hearing seeks always to remain in act, actually to hear). Qualities that exist within faculties determine the limits of greatness of facultative operation (for example, how perfectly a person sees or hears). Seeing and hearing habits limit perfection of the act of sight and hearing, the qualitative strength of a person's ability to see and hear. Good vision and hearing habits strengthen the quality of the person's sight and hearing, while bad vision and hearing habits weaken it.

Complicating a person's ability to understand what St. Thomas is talking about regarding the nature of the habit is the fact that,

177

according to him, a habit can be a 1) natural quality of the faculty or 2) an acquired one. For example, the natural habits of health and beauty relate to the vegetative faculty of the soul's limited biological ability to generate specifically proper, limited greatness in acts of health (like reproduction, growth, and nutrition) and beauty (like species-specific proportionate size and figure).

In this sense, a habit (*habitus*), is simply *a having*: a relation existing between a subject that has and what is had by the subject. It is not an *acquired* having, or possession; not a limit of having related to quality of being and operation that is innately possessed (like the habit of eating slowly or quickly).[1]

2. St. Thomas's definition of "virtue" ("*virtus*")

Analogously to the way in which the term "habit" can refer to an innately-possessed limit of having (a limited ability to possess or have something) and an acquired limit of having, so, too, according to St. Thomas, a "virtue" can refer to and innately-fixed strength (limit of qualitative greatness or excellence in something: like existence, unity, or action; an intrinsic measure of strength of excellence, perfection) or an acquired one.

Considered as such, whether naturally possessed or acquired, strictly speaking, St. Thomas understands a virtue to be a good (its species) quality (its genus) of soul (a form [principle of operation, an intensive quantum limit of greatness in existence, unity, health, beauty, and action]) existing as part of a nature, which exists as part of a whole living being. So considered, the term "virtue" signifies a *perfection* of a natural or acquired power: an ultimate, maximum, qualitative limit of excellence in possession of good. When used in reference to the intellectual and appetitive faculties of the human soul, "virtue" is properly defined as an *operative* habit that perfects the activity of the faculty—makes its possessor good and perfects its possessor's action.[2]

178

Peter A. Redpath

3. The subject of moral and intellectual virtue

According to St. Thomas, the subject (receiver) of moral and intellectual virtue is a faculty of the human soul. Since a virtue perfects the power in which it exists, in its subject (that which receives it), because one virtue cannot exist in more than one power as in its subject, St. Thomas maintains that a virtue can be in one subject chiefly and in other subjects subordinately inasmuch as one power directs another power in use, uses another power as an instrument.

Hence, the human intellect and human appetites can be, and are, chief subjects of virtue, through their use of other faculties that are naturally inclined to take direction from them. So, virtues of the human intellect and appetites can exist subordinately, by participation, in other faculties after the fashion of existing as tools or instruments of these faculties.

In two ways, St. Thomas claims that a habit can be ordered, essentially related to, a good act: 1) in determinate ability (that is, in limited ability to receive or to generate a good act), or 2) as actually operating well, doing some good.

Further, St. Thomas maintains that some faculty is good *absolutely* (totally, completely, *simpliciter*) when it has determinate capability to act well and acts well (for example, the faculty of sight when seeing as perfectly as it humanly can according to the species-specific power [qualitative, or virtual quantum, greatness] of the faculty of sight).

Such being the case, according to St. Thomas, strictly speaking, we predicate the term "virtue" *simpliciter*, or *absolutely*, of qualities of the human soul like wisdom, science, art, prudence, and temperance because, without qualification, they make their possessor (the subject faculty and the subject that possesses the faculty) and his or her actions good. In the case of a human being, St. Thomas maintains that, of all the qualities of the human soul that make a person good, the moral virtue *par excellence* that makes anyone morally good, is possession of a good will.[3]

4. The intellectual and moral virtues considered in general and in relation to the "habit of understanding" and *synderesis*

Given what St. Thomas has already said about the nature of virtue, he reasonably concludes that intellectual virtue is a quality of the intellectual faculty that perfects the faculty in its natural and supernatural operations. As subject to taking directions from the human will, he maintains that the speculative intellect is moved by the infused virtue of faith to assent to what is of faith just as, in its natural operations, the practical intellect is subject to be moved by prudence, right reason.

In addition, he claims that four cardinal moral virtues exist in the intellectual and sensory faculties and appetites: 1) prudence (rightly-directed reason) exists *simpliciter* in the human intellect and justice in the will; and 2) under the direction of the human intellect, prudence also exists in particular, or, cogitative reason (the estimative sense), while courage exists in the irascible appetite, and temperance in the concupiscible appetite. Moreover, the moral virtues exist chiefly in the human intellect and will and by participation in the sense and appetitive faculties that are naturally inclined to take direction from reason.

Regarding the species of intellectual virtue, St. Thomas identifies three as existing within the speculative intellect: 1) wisdom, 2) science, and 3) understanding; and two as existing within the practical intellect: 1) prudence and 2) art.

Considered in general, he says that the three speculative intellectual virtues (including the special virtue of understanding; also, sometimes called, "the habit of understanding"): 1) perfect the intellect and its consideration of truth; and 2) have truth as their formal object.

Regarding how the intellectual virtues enhance the quality of intellectual operation, this is chiefly related to perfecting the human intellect's ability to consider truths and command well-done good deeds. According to St. Thomas, the human intellect is able to consider truth (which comes to the intellect in the form of a composite whole [the being of things first grasped by the human intellect in and through conjunction with the human senses]) in two ways: 1) *per se notum* (known through itself) and 2) *per aliud notum* (known through another).

As far as a *per se notum* truth is concerned, St. Thomas maintains that the human intellect is able to grasp this truth immediately simply by grasping the essential connection between the parts constituting a whole, or the terms constituting a judgment. He adds that: 1) "understanding" (the habit of principles) is the habit perfecting intellect in this way of considering truth; and 2) to some extent, while this habit exists in all people in an imperfect way, the virtue of understanding perfects this natural habit.

Regarding a *per aliud notum* truth, St. Thomas asserts that it, too, is about a composite whole (*an ultimate singular, some numerically-one being*), *but this whole is not immediately grasped in the essential relation of its parts*; and this ultimate singular can be said of some genus, or of all genera (like human happiness).

Concerning the speculative intellectual virtue of science, St. Thomas claims that it comes to an understanding of truth (the essential part/whole relations constituting a whole) through an inquiry of reason and finally achieves this understanding through a demonstrative syllogism. The truth achieved is thus the conclusion of a reasoning process: *its end*, or, *term*, while the start of the reasoning process occurs with a *per se notum* truth.

Absolutely considered (considered in relation to all science), St. Thomas says that the speculative intellectual virtue of wisdom (metaphysics): 1) is the most qualitatively perfect way of knowing in any single science and 2) considers the part/whole relationship principles (organizational principles) common, or universal, to all sciences. Considered as such, the science of metaphysics is of greater virtual (or *virtutis*) quantity/qualitative greatness than any other single science. Considered relatively, or relative to one science, wisdom consists in the habitual ability of a scientist to answer the most difficult questions within that science.

Regarding the practical intellectual virtue of art, St. Thomas states that art is: 1) right reason (perfectly reasoned judgment): 1) about making a product or executing the activities of human faculties; 2) an operative habit (one that generates action or a product); and 3), unlike speculative virtues, not chiefly concerned with pursuit of happiness *considered as a whole*.

Instead, the virtue of art chiefly concerns the good operation of some faculty: enabling some human faculty, or combination faculties, to do or make something well. Except incidentally, *art is not chiefly concerned with the perfect operation of the whole person in leading an excellently-lived life. It is chiefly concerned with the perfect operation of that facultative part of a person in which, through, natural and acquired ability, one person qualitatively excels another in production or performance.* For example, it chiefly concerns being a good singer, dancer, athlete, or homebuilder. Its chief concern is not with developing excellence of operation of all parts of a human being so as to lead an excellent human life.

Nonetheless, even in their professional aspect, *arts and sciences cannot totally ignore the presence of a moral culture that acts as a principle that enables arts and sciences to exist.* Arts and sciences do not exist in moral isolation. They are generated by a moral psychology that brings them into existence so as to help perfect the whole of human life in all of its parts. Hence, the existence of any and every art and science presupposes a level of personal and professional honesty as a necessary condition, prior principle, for preserving the existence of any and every art and science.

Consequently, operating badly, unprofessionally, dishonestly, within arts and sciences *considered as an artist* is not to work artistically well, or at all. It involves not being a good performer or producer within some practical or productive profession. For example, strictly speaking, a medical doctor who chiefly aims to make people sick, unhealthy, is not, cannot be, a scientist. And, strictly speaking, an athlete who cheats, breaks the rules of the game, is no professional athlete. Arts and sciences are virtues, essentially health- and safety-generating qualities of the human soul. The natural moral desire to promote health and safety is an essential principle that generates the existence of arts and sciences. This desire precedes the existence of arts and sciences. Without it existing, they cannot come into existence at all.

Because only a stable, morally-healthy culture is capable of generating the social conditions capable of causing and sustaining the peaceful social interaction upon which the short- and long-term existence of arts and sciences necessarily depends, while the chief good of this or that art or science mainly concerns the perfect exercise of this or that artistic habit (quality of soul), the existence of this or that art or science as a cultural phenomenon necessarily remotely presupposes the existence of a moral culture of justice within: 1) a true artist or scientist and 2) the wider culture in which the artist or scientist exists. Hence. *strictly speaking*, any so-called "artist" or "scientist" who practices his or her profession in such a way as to undermine the moral culture, destroy the rules of the game, that enables arts and sciences to exist at all, is no artist or scientist.

Just as art and science presuppose an individual and social, moral culture as a necessary condition for their existence and exercise, so, even though they do not chiefly aim at producing a work or making a product, like practical and productive arts and sciences, liberal arts and speculative science always involve work, some pragmatic form of reasoning.

Nevertheless, because: 1) the arts and sciences acquire their proper name from the highest, or chief act (their chief end or aim) that orders all the other acts that are being performed within the art or science under essential relationship of a generic habit, and 2) all liberal arts and speculative sciences aim chiefly at perfecting a person's intellectual faculty in the work of simply understanding truth, escaping from ignorance, we properly name such arts and science "liberal" and "speculative."

Considering, next, the practical intellectual virtue of prudence, St. Thomas tells us that prudence chiefly aims at: 1) good operation of a human faculty; 2) right use of what is well made or well done for living a happy human life considered as a whole; and 3) in conjunction with the faculty of particular reason (*the estimative sense*) in touch with reality, making a faculty right and its use right.

Just as perfection and right ordering of action in speculative activities (right reasoning speculatively) depends upon, presupposes, "the habit of principles" (the virtue of understanding), intellectually apprehending *per se nota* truths, St. Thomas maintains that right reasoning (perfection in right ordering) about practical matters depends upon possession of a somewhat-developed natural habit of moral virtue that rightly disposes an appetite toward ends known by moral virtues as *per aliud nota* practical truths (ultimate singulars known by practical experience at living). St. Thomas calls this natural habit "*synderesis.*"

As a habit of right reason, for the simple reason that reasoning essentially presupposes knowledge in the form of understanding immediately-evident principles, just as the speculative intellectual virtue of science presupposes the existence of the speculative habit of understanding, the practical moral virtue of prudence (right reason) presupposes the existence of the practical habit of *synderesis*.

According to St. Thomas, prudence: 1) perfects our other moral habits (like temperance, courage, and justice), and cannot exist without them, just as they cannot exist without it; 2) consists in the ability to make right individual judgments, choices; 3) chiefly aims to make these individual judgments, choices in relationship to living a good life for a human being considered as a whole; and 4) is chiefly concerned with the activities of deliberating, counseling, and commanding well.

Moreover, these acts of deliberating, counseling, and commanding well involve two acts of speculative reason (acts of inquiring well and judging well essentially involved in the single act of good counsel and one act of practical reason [commanding well]).[4]

5. The moral virtues considered in general and identified specifically

After having considered intellectual and moral virtues in general, St. Thomas starts to focus attention on the nature of the moral, ethical, virtues considered in general and specifically by first examining the meaning of the Latin term for morals: *"mos"* (referring to habit and custom; from which we derive our English terms that refer to morals and *mores* and the Greek terms *"ĕthos"* [which refers to habit] and *"ēthos"* [which refers to custom]).

Regarding the term "moral virtue," according to St. Thomas, *Aristotle defines it as a habit of choosing the mean determined by reason as the wise and prudent man will determine it*; and he considers moral virtues always to be: 1) chiefly appetitive virtues; and 2) related to other faculties that appetites can influence.

Considering how they operate, to some extent, St. Thomas says *the appetites that the moral virtues are naturally inclined to direct always tend somewhat, but not totally, to resist that direction.*

Consequently, following Aristotle, he says that reason rules them "politically," while it rules the body "despotically." Furthermore, he asserts that: 1) the moral virtues cannot be entirely unaccompanied by a passion or an analogue to a passion (for example, intellectual joy), *and especially the passion of pleasure/joy*; and 2) different moral virtues essentially perfect different appetites and passions (for example, the moral virtue of courage perfects the irascible appetite and its passions like hope and fear; temperance perfects the concupiscible appetite, and passions like love, desire, and pleasure; and the moral virtue of justice perfects the human will).[5]

According to St. Thomas, Aristotle lists ten moral virtues related to the human passions (omitting prudence and justice because these chiefly relate to the human intellect and the human will): 1) courage; 2) temperance; 3) liberality; 4) magnificence; 5) magnanimity, 6) love of honor; 7) gentleness; 8) friendliness/amiability; 9) truthfulness; and 10) playfulness/amusement.[6]

6. The nature and causes of virtue, and especially of moral virtue

Having discussed the nature of moral virtue is general and identified specific moral virtues, while focusing more on the nature of moral than intellectual virtues, next St. Thomas examines the nature of both these species of virtue.

To start his examination he states that, *specifically and individually, moral and intellectual virtues are natural, innate to human beings, inchoately present within our souls and bodies in an imperfectly-developed state, as immaturely-developed habits existing in seminal form in our souls and bodies*. In their early stages, these virtues (innate principles for generating action, intensive quantity principles of action) exist within our bodily and psychological constitution as natural dispositions, faculties, and principles that incline us to act individually well or poorly in relation to specific acts of virtue. Speaking in more contemporary terms, these natural virtues are limits of perfection of natural ability with which human beings are born that incline us toward further development of intellectual and/or moral virtue.

Chiefly, Aristotle and St. Thomas maintain that moral virtues are socializing human virtues, qualities of soul that facilitate human beings to be able to live together in this world. They are socializing qualities principally located in the human appetites and completed in us through repeated, habitual submission to the rule of right reason (prudential judgment) to which they are naturally inclined to submit, but not without some resistance.

Imperfect moral virtues are imperfectly developed inclinations existing in us either by birth or habituation toward a really good action, while perfect moral virtue is a good habit inclining us to a good deed (end) well done (prudentially achieved through choice of the right means).[7]

7. Properties of moral virtues

In relation to the acquisition of right moral habits by imperfect-ly-formed moral virtues, St. Thomas tells us that *moral virtue is the mean*; but, *in the exercise of moral virtue, prudence is the mean.* According to St. Thomas, all human beings are born with some innate inclination to act in a morally-virtuous fashion: to be more or less temperate, courageous, just, and prudent, for example. By nature, some people are more emotionally disposed to attack dangers, control their fear, and remain calm in the face of danger. Similarly, some people have an easier time controlling their pursuit of pleasures, being temperate. By inclining the appetitive part of the soul in which an innately-, immaturely-developed virtue already exists, increasingly, with greater intensity, to submit to the rule of right reason (prudential judgment), an acquired moral virtue is a habit that perfects, brings to mature development, this natural inclination already innately and seminally existing within a person.

Imperfectly-formed moral virtues like courage and temperance are connected by inclining the human appetites toward pursuing real human goods and by being perfected as virtues by prudence, which properly disposes these innately possessed moral virtues toward the right choice of the right means to fulfill their proper end as virtues, considered as such.

In genus and species, St. Thomas maintains that one moral virtue is qualitatively greater than another according to its closeness to resembling an act of intellectual reason, to the extent that a reason in touch with reality controls its behavior. On the basis of the fact that it is a virtue of reason, as we might expect, *generically* (as the form of all moral virtues) *and specifically* (as a moral virtue specifically concerned with excellent deliberation), St. Thomas considers prudence to be the greatest of all the natural moral virtues.

Because the moral virtue of justice exists within the human will, which is the appetite of the human intellect, by nature, justice more closely resembles reason in its perfection as a virtue than does courage or temperance. Consequently, St. Thomas considers the moral virtue of justice to be qualitatively better generically and specifically than the emotionally-seated virtues of courage and temperance.

Since, by nature, the moral virtue of courage (which proximately governs hope, fear, and anger) is more naturally-inclined to listen to reason than is the moral virtue that governs concupiscence, by nature, courage is closer to being rational in genus and species than is the moral virtue of temperance (and, hence, qualitatively better, more perfect, as a moral virtue in genus and species than is temperance).

However, considered in itself in relationship to everything to which it extends (all pleasurable things) *and the number of persons who can possess it*, St. Thomas maintains that: 1) temperance is greater in degree than any other virtue (more so than courage, for example, because courage extends only to dangerous things and fewer people possess it than possess temperance, while justice only extends to socially-interacting things); and 2) more people are inclined to possess the virtue of temperance and courage than are able to possess the virtue of justice (which, in its perfect form of political justice, takes a lifetime to acquire).

Regarding the moral or intellectual virtues, St. Thomas says that, whether one is superior to another in genus and species depends upon how we consider them. Absolutely considered (considered without qualification), St. Thomas maintains that wisdom is the greatest of all natural virtues, while charity is the greatest of all infused virtues (thereby making it the greatest of all human virtues considered as such).[8]

8. A brief consideration of the nature and division of theological virtues

Since this book chiefly concerns St. Thomas's moral teaching related to living a good life in this world, it will not focus on a study of his treatment of the theological virtues of faith, hope, and charity. Nevertheless, because St. Thomas considers these to be the greatest of all human virtues, they deserve some mention in this work.

Since these are infused virtues, St. Thomas maintains that they are acquired as a spiritual gift through grace of the Holy Spirit through the human will to the human intellect and faculties that participate in direction by the human intellect. Such being the case, they are not initially acquired by induction of speculative or practical principles of speculative or practical reason by means of the natural habits of the soul of "understanding of principles" or "*synderesis*." They are acquired by supernatural grace and strengthened by means of supernatural exercise.

Of these three virtues, St. Thomas tells us that: 1) Faith is seated in the intellect, concerns the beginnings of supernatural perfection, and its formal object consists in truths to be believed. 2) Hope is seated in the will, and its formal object is spiritual union with God to which it reaches out as attainable. And 3) charity, or friendship with God, is seated in the will and its formal object is perfect the union with God.

Regarding the relationship between the natural moral virtues and the infused virtues, St. Thomas maintains that, to some extent, all the natural virtues can exist without charity, but charity cannot exist without the natural moral virtues. He maintains, further, that all the moral virtues are infused together with charity, and with the loss of charity all the moral virtues infused with it disappear. In addition, in the afterlife, since all the other moral and infused virtues become unnecessary, only charity remains.[9]

9. Exterior principles of moral activity: God, the Devil, and law (especially natural law)

After discussing 119 questions in Part 1 and 89 questions in Part 1 of Part 2 of his *Summa theologiae* (related to "interior principles of moral activity"), in his prologue to question 90 (which starts what students of St. Thomas commonly call his "Treatise on Law" running from question 90 through 97), St. Thomas says he will now consider "exterior" principles of moral activity. In his preface, he calls: 1) the Devil the exterior principle of moral activity inclining us toward evil, and 2) God the exterior principle moving us toward good by instructing us through law and supporting us through grace.

In considering these exterior principles of moral activity, St. Thomas states he will first examine law generically and specifically and then study grace.[10]

Considering law (which St. Thomas maintains we derive etymologically from the Latin term *"ligere"* [meaning "to bind"]) in general, St. Thomas discusses: 1) its essence and 2) its effects.

Considering its essence, he starts to define "law" by identifying its form as a commanding (rule or measure) activity of reason related to prescribing and prohibiting by which a person is led toward or away from some good or evil. From this beginning, he next: 1) identifies law's chief aim (final cause) to be human happiness; 2) and says that law's chief concern in relation to its chief aim is the order of movement toward the common good.

After doing this, he identifies *law's efficient cause* as: 1) the entire multitude of the community or 2) their representatives; and, to match the end, *because order to an end of free agents must include force* (because, by natural inclination of the human appetites, to some extent, the human will and passions actually incline to resist taking direction from reason), he maintains that laws must be made publicly known, promulgated, and enforceable.

Having made these preliminary remarks concerning the nature of law in general, he defines "law" as a command of practical reason essentially related to the common good of the community issued and promulgated by someone who has care of (governs) a community.

Related to the nature of law, St. Thomas states that "good" law has chiefly two effects: 1) to lead those ruled by it to *their proper virtue* (that is, toward human happiness and the enabling means to secure human happiness: real human goods, goods that are real, not fictional; that secure and promote perfection of individual and species human life); and 2) to command and forbid, reward and punish, members of the community for the choices that they make.

After defining law, St. Thomas proceeds to identify five species of law: 1) eternal; 2) natural; 3) human; 4) divine; and 5) law of sin, lust, or sensuality.

Starting with eternal law, St. Thomas explains this to be the supreme ordinance, highest law of the created order by means of which, through divine reason, God governs the whole of creation for the good of creation considered as a whole (just as the CEO of a major corporation governs all the departments of an organization for the good of the organization as a whole, not chiefly for the good of one of its divisions or departments).

After considering several points related to the nature of eternal law, in question 94, St. Thomas turns his attention to the topic of natural law, which he treats in six articles that total in length approximately 20 to 25 pages of an average-sized, contemporary paperback book: 1) What is natural law? 2) What are its legal precepts? 3) Whether all acts of virtue are from natural law? 4) Whether natural law is *one* for all human beings? 5) Whether natural law is changeable? And 6) whether natural law can be abolished from the human heart?

Despite the minor amount of space and effort that St. Thomas devotes to the topic of natural law within the context of his entire treatment of moral activity considered in its entire scope, for centuries, scores of major students of St. Thomas have behaved as if, in addition to the falsely-so-called "moral principle" of double effect, the principle of natural law comprised more or less the whole of St. Thomas's moral teaching. Instead, as is evident to anyone who actually reads what St. Thomas has to say about moral activity, natural law plays much less of a (but still a crucial) role in the moral teaching of St. Thomas than that for which it is much of the time given credit.

And, when involving two effects following from a moral choice and one of them is evil, the actual moral principles involved are the moral virtues of prudence (when the evil effect impacts solely on the doer of the act) and, in cases where individual acts can foreseeably have some negative impact on the life of someone else, justice also comes into play. The chief reason for this is that the chief intention for performing a moral activity is to do good and avoid evil. Hence, if we foresee that an unavoidable moral choice is going to effect a moral evil as an unintended outcome, the morally prudent choice to make is to do as little attendant harm as possible to oneself and others. Today, people in business generally refer to this as "cutting your losses."

Peter A. Redpath

St. Thomas maintains that natural law is a principle of governance that issues from divine reason strictly related to members of the human species in the way that we are governed as free agents. St. Thomas does not introduce this principle into Western intellectual history. Its roots go back as far as the tragic ancient Greek play entitled *Antigone*, written by Sophocles; and it is extensively treated in the writings of Cicero (with which St. Thomas had some familiarity), for example, in *On Duties* (*De officiis*).

Aside from the fact that St. Thomas considers this principle of rule specifically different from the way in which God rules inanimate beings and creation considered as a whole, he introduces it to indicate a really-existing and special legal principle through which, in a radically different way than *by instinct*, God rules rational animals. Because we possess a faculty of reason and a deliberative power of free choice, He rules the distinctive animal species called "human" by a rule befitting rational natures: *law, not instinct*.

In addition, St. Thomas introduces natural law as a principle of rule existing in-between eternal law and human (civil) law to indicate the progressively more individualistic way in which God rules human beings as part of the created order. St. Thomas maintains that good law must be *proportionate, suitable*, in power to the nature of the community being ruled. As a principle, law must have a limit of power extensive enough to enable it to move and to stop the movement of a multitude over which it has command.

Eternal law is a generic law, somewhat like international law, ruling individual members of a multitude of qualitatively different communities (nations). *Such a law is not* specialized, particularized, enough to rule members of a more specialized and particularized community like a particular nation existing at a particular time and geographical location (like a city in the state of Texas, within the United States, within the year 2016). Analogously, eternal law, which

rules inanimate and animate beings, material as well as spiritual creatures (like angels), is not specialized, particularized, enough to be
able to move and restrain the behavior of individual species belonging to the animal genus.

Hence, God rules brute animals through a different principle of
rule (namely, instinct) than He rules inanimate beings and animate,
physical, human beings (namely, natural "law").

Nonetheless, even though this legal principle called "natural
law" is a special principle of rule directly designated to rule rational
animals, it rules rational animals *considered as members of a species*, not as members of a nation, city, natural human family, or hap-
piness-seeking individuals. Considered in this way, because it rules
us only as members of the genus *animal* and the species *human*, *St.
Thomas considers natural law to be an inadequate legal principle
through which human beings can secure happiness*!

The chief reason for this is that, as members of the animal
genus, natural law only commands us to satisfy those real needs that
we share: 1) generically with all creatures (for example, to remain in
existence as created being and to seek the preservation and continued
well-being of the created order); 2) in remote genus with plant life
(for example, to incline to remain in existence the way all living
beings are inclined to do: by staying alive, nourishing ourselves,
reproducing); 3) in proximate genus with all animals (for example,
to stay alive the way all animals tend to do: by avoiding dangers
that threaten animal life, pursuing forms of security that protect
animal life, like means to defend health and safety; and to stay alive
the way higher species of wild and domestic animals do: by forming
natural communities of more or less social stability [uniting for a
time through sexual reproduction in different ways (monogamous,
polygamous, and so on) between a male and a female, nursing and
educating their young for longer or shorter periods of time]); and 4)

in proximate species with all human beings (for example, the form of a natural family between a husband and wife; nourishing ourselves the way human beings, not brute animals, tend to eat; sexually reproducing the way healthy human beings, males and females, are naturally inclined to do so as to be able to maintain a healthy family, educate and protect children to adulthood; and form cities and wider political communities to help more perfectly live together as natural family members and members of wider cultural communities).

Evident from this discussion about the nature of natural law so far is that its precepts are not adequate to secure for human beings all the real human goods that human beings need to achieve even the goods we naturally incline to pursue and secure as members of the animal species (just staying alive and remaining healthy as a animals), much less to secure the kind of social goods we need to acquire to live the good human life for the whole of a human life: the moral and intellectual virtues.

For this reason, St. Thomas maintains that natural law needs to be supplemented by human (that is, civil) law and divine law (the Old Law of justice toward God and neighbor given by God to the Israelites and the New Law of love of God and neighbor given by God to the whole human community).

According to St. Thomas, all the precepts of the natural law are derived from this single, generic principle (known through the natural habit of *synderesis*) issued in the form of a command of practical reason: "Do good and avoid evil!" He maintains that we derive all other specific precepts of the natural law from this first command of practical reason *according to the threefold order of generic and specific inclination that exists within the nature every human being*: 1) generically with all living beings to preserve existence of the whole of creation and life; 2) more specifically with animals (for example, to procreate and raise children); and 3) most specifically with all human beings.

Moreover, derivation of all these other precepts does not happen overnight. It takes centuries, even millennia, without the aid of revelation (or even with it) for some human communities to recognize that activities like cannibalism, incest, rape, wife-beating, child-abuse, and slavery are morally vicious. While all these immediately preceding modes of behavior might be evident violations of natural law to some people, at some times and places, that they are morally vicious ways of behaving that natural law condemns is a specific precept derived, *per aliud notum,* from the generic precept "Do good and avoid evil!"

Consequently, in reply to the question about whether all acts of virtue follow from natural law, St. Thomas says that, in a way, they do; and, in a way, they do not. For a person with extensive experience possessed of the virtue of prudence, for example, that slavery is morally vicious, is a violation of natural law, is evident. To an intemperate, brutish individual, it is not, and never will be.

Hence, in reply to the question whether natural law is the same, *one,* for all human beings, again, St. Thomas says, in a way, "Yes," and in a way, "No." Generically considered, the first principle of natural law (Do good and avoid evil!") can never be eradicated from human nature. No human being who has possession and control of the ability to engage in practical reason can be unaware of it. It can never be changed, and can never be abolished from the human heart.

Regarding some other questions related to St. Thomas's teaching about civil law and the law of sin, lust, or sensuality, St. Thomas says several things, many of which I will not consider in this work for the simple reason that answers to them will become evident from topics that will be discussed in later chapters. However, I will consider three further points related to natural law with which I think all students of St. Thomas's moral teaching should be aware:

1) In answer to the question whether human positive law is derived from natural law, St. Thomas says that, *precisely because of the inadequacy of natural law* to supply the commands for the direction of human life that human beings need to understand in order to behave with perfect moral virtue in a multitude of different individual conditions and circumstances with which the general precepts of natural law are woefully inadequate to handle, civil law needs to supplement natural law.

2) In answer the question whether civil law should attempt to restrain all vices, in agreement with St. Aurelius Augustine, St. Thomas maintains that it should not. Civil law, he claims, chiefly relates to ordering, harmonizing, the behavior of a multitude of people of different levels of moral virtue so as to enable us to live in peace and cooperation for the perfection of a prudently-lived earthly life (which would include helping us to get to Heaven).

Moreover, he says that civil law is directed toward individual members of a community precisely as members of that community. To try to govern a community composed of a mixture of intemperate, incontinent, and virtuous people as if all were saints will not succeed. Laws should be enacted according to the moral condition of the majority of the community. Hence, prudent man that he was, St. Thomas concludes that attempting to require a level of moral excellence of citizens incapable of achieving it is likely to cause those citizens to become more vicious, not more virtuous. Consequently, the good ruler should chiefly focus on eliminating from a political community those vices that are most disruptive of civic peace and dangerous to the common good.

3) Finally, in answer to the question whether a human law should command all acts of moral virtue, St. Thomas responds that it cannot and should not. Doing so is not the job of civil law, is beyond

its capability. Instead, a ruler should focus attention on encouraging those acts of behavior among citizens that secure the common good, enable people to live at peace with one another.[11]

—Notes—

1. St. Thomas Aquinas, *Summa theologiae*, 1–2, qq. 49–54; *Commentary on the Metaphysics of Aristotle*, Bk. 5, Lect. 20, nn. 1058–1064.
2. Aquinas, *Summa theologiae*, 1–2, Prol., q. 55.
3. Id., q. 56.
4. Id., q. 57; and 1, q. 79, a. 12.
5. Id., Prol., q. 58 and qq. 58–60.
6. Id., q. 60.
7. Id., qq. 58–60.
8. Id., qq. 58–61 and 63–65.
9. Id., 1–2, qq. 62.
10. Id., Prol., q. 90.
11. Id., qq. 90–97; and 107; see, also Peter A. Redpath, "Classifying the Moral Teaching of St. Thomas," in *The Medieval Tradition of Natural Law*, ed. Harold J. Johnson (Kalamazoo, Mich.: Medieval Institute publications, Western Michigan University, 1987), pp. 137–138, and "Why Double Effect and Proportionality are not Moral Principles for St. Thomas," in *Vera Lex* (Winter, 2004), pp. 25–42.

CHAPTER SEVEN

The Nature of Moral Science and Its Relation to Happiness

SEVERAL TOPICS that Chapter 6 of this book considered, especially concerning the nature of habits, virtue, law (in particular the fact that natural law essentially needs to be supplemented by civil law so that human beings might have adequate moral guidance to satisfy real human needs within the individual circumstance) serve as a great segue into the start of St. Thomas's "Introduction" to his *Commentary on the Nicomachean Ethics of Aristotle* where he states that, since wisdom is the perfection of reason, by nature, the wise man's specific activity essentially involves ordering things.

1. St. Thomas's introduction to his *Commentary on the Nicomachean Ethics of Aristotle*: An essential responsibility of the wise man is to recognize and execute order

In his first "Lecture" in his *Commentary on the Nicomachean Ethics of Aristotle*, St. Thomas states that, because good habit perfects reason, and science in its most perfect species is wisdom, unequally perfect, *different habitual ways of considering unequally perfect modes of order* (ways of being organized/perfected) *is the chief cause of differentiation in the sciences*. In short, qualitatively different (higher/more powerful) habits of knowing different orders of perfection in being organized in terms of part/whole relations, causes differentiation in the sciences. The reason for this involves the fact that higher sciences know qualitatively higher, more universally powerful (qualitatively more powerful in virtual, or intensive, quantity) causes in qualitatively higher, more powerful, ways.

Consequently, in a fashion consistent with Aristotle, many students of Aristotle before St. Thomas, and scores of students of neo-Platonic philosophy before him, St. Thomas maintains that, qualitatively considered, the scientific habit of mind (the intellectual virtue) of metaphysics is, *qua* science, an intellectual quality that studies beings of utmost perfection in existence and difficulty for the human intellect to know, and does so in a way that, qualitatively, perfects the human intellect and its natural operations more than any other intellectual quality (intellectual virtue) is capable of doing.

According to St. Thomas, the more powerful a cause, the more deeply and widely it enters its effects. The act of existing (*esse*) is the most generic and powerful cause in the universe, entering into all natures more widely and deeply than any other cause. He maintains, further, that, *by nature*: 1) every other, secondary, or specific cause naturally inclines to preserve the order of creation more deeply than it does the existence of its species; 2) every individual seeks to preserve the existence of its species more than it does its individual existence; 3) every individual seeks to preserve and perfect its own existence as an essential part of these two higher orders of existence: the order of creation and its species; and 5) every individual part of the universe is social.

According to St. Thomas, in the finite order: 1) only the human intellect, human reason, knows the order of one thing to another and 2) a twofold order exists within things: of parts to parts, and of parts to a whole and the whole to an end through a highest part.

He claims that this second order constitutes one in which: 1) the action of the whole and of the parts are identical; 2) a combined, or cooperative action (what today, we would commonly call an "organizational" or "corporate" act) constitutes numerically-one act (like an entire army attacking an enemy or all the parts of a crew harmoniously rowing together). The first order (of parts to parts) resembles departmental actions that occur within contemporary corporations in which the actions of this or that department do not constitute that of the whole corporation.

St. Thomas claims that different sciences study different species of order. Hence, different divisions of moral science (or the science of ethics) study individual moral acts considered as different departmental divisions (species) of the organizational whole called "moral science," or "science of ethics." For example, 1) monastics studies the moral activity of individual human beings; 2) domestics studies the interaction of individuals considered as parts the more inclusive organizational whole of social groups; and 3) politics, or political science, studies the interaction of these smaller, individual and social organizations to that of the wider and more-inclusive organizational whole of a civic community. Considered as a whole to which all these smaller organizations exist as parts and to which they contribute is moral science, or the science of ethics.

Generically considered as a whole, St. Thomas claims that science has two widest divisions: 1) "theoretical" or "speculative" (today, the term "observational" tends to be synonymous in meaning with "theoretical" or "speculative"); and 2) practical, which, like Aristotle before him, St. Thomas often subdivides into productive activities (what, today, the terms "making," "producing," "manufacturing," "building," "constructing," closely, if not perfectly, convey); and practical activities (what, today, the terms "doing" and "performing" tend to signify).

Essentially, productive activities involve toolmaking for performance acts of use, while practical activities involve *acts of use* (*using* tools). For example, 1) the productive art of shipbuilding constructs a ship for the performance art of sailing; 2) the productive art of homebuilding constructs a house for the performance activity of living in it; 3) and the productive art of manufacturing basketball equipment constructs tools to use in the performance art of playing basketball.

According to Aristotle and St. Thomas, by nature, arts and sciences are hierarchically ordered according to an essential relationship in which the lower arts provide, and themselves serve as, tools for higher performance arts and sciences. For example, the productive art of shipbuilding essentially exists to make tools for people who possess the practical know-how, skill, performance art of sailing. Lower arts and sciences exist to help bring into existence and service higher and higher performance arts and sciences, the highest of which is metaphysics.

Regarding the order that the human intellect, reason, considers, St. Thomas states that this is fourfold, one in which it contemplates order and three in which it causes order. The one in which it contemplates order consists of already-existing parts and wholes (like the classical speculative sciences of metaphysics, mathematics, and physics). The three that it causes order in consist of the arts and/ or sciences of: 1) grammar and logic: ordering the parts and wholes of verbal expressions one to each other and principles of reasoning one to each other and to their conclusion; 2) ethics and performance activities (like cultural arts); and 3) planning/manufacturing/making external products.

2. The order, organizational whole, that moral philosophy/ science studies and the way it studies it

In moral philosophy/science, St. Thomas claims that the composite whole (part/whole relations) that constitutes the formal object of this habit of the soul is human (that is, voluntary) activity springing from the human will (that is, what the will executes) as commanded by reason (that is, as reason has ordered, prioritized it). The subject of ethics is voluntary human activity ordered through intellectual and volitional habits of the human soul to the perfection of human operation consisting in the moral virtue of human happiness.

Since St. Thomas maintains that, by nature, we human beings are social animals needing many things to achieve *perfect* operation, to live as *perfect* rational animals in the present life, by nature, we incline to live as parts of different groups that help us to live well (for example, as parts of: 1) a species; 2) a natural family that inclines, by nature, to give birth to us (by natural birth) as infants, nourish and educate us (including morally) after birth, and help us provide for life's necessities to adulthood; and 3) civic groups to help provide for us more than the necessities of life (*and provide more complete moral instruction through fear of punishment, especially of young males that parents often cannot control!*).

Since the natural family is only one of several social groups to which a human being belongs, St. Thomas maintains that ethics must study human activity as: 1) species-specific (monastic); 2) familial (domestic); and 3) civic, or political.

In Book 1 of his *Nicomachean Ethics*, Aristotle: 1) explains what he will do in other books of that work; and 2) states how practical sciences like ethics are diversified by a diversity of ends and means. St. Thomas comments on this explanation and statement of Aristotle by saying that consideration of order of ends and means is proper only to human reason. In practical matters, he says that two principles are essentially involved: 1) reason (considering order and choice), and will, which engages in execution of action; 2) and moral behavior as activity of the "appetitive intellect" (that is, the intellect commanding appetitive execution of actions). And *he maintains that moral education does not proceed like speculative education. It does not proceed by abstract syllogizing. Instead, it proceeds by concretely commanding, essentially involves choosing right means in relation to hierarchically-ordered ends. It is perfected chiefly through practice, not through lecture!*[1]

3. The essential connection between the moral science of politics and human happiness

Having discussed the nature, divisions, and general intrinsic principles of ethics (like reason, will, habit), St. Thomas starts to specify the subject (chief good intended by) of moral science as chiefly practical and related to ordering a finite number of ends and means. In so doing, St. Thomas states that the ends and means ethics studies must be finite because moral activity is moved: 1) by choice of something actual to satisfy a real end, put a desire to rest; and 2) in relation to actual desire (a desire that is reactive to an external stimulus, formal object, drawing a subject toward union with it). As desire for something really possible to get, it cannot be ordered to an infinite number of means to satisfy this desire because choice of the actual cannot be of the impossible; and trying to choose an infinite number of means to secure a real end is to attempt to do the impossible, an undoable deed.

This study has to belong to the supremely architectonic science of politics, moreover, because politics is the supremely architectonic performance science. In practical sciences, sciences of performance activity naturally rule over productive sciences because productive sciences exist solely for the aim of providing enabling means (tools) for performance sciences to exercise their proper activities: productive sciences essentially exist as tools to enable performance sciences to execute their proper activities as performance sciences.

Furthermore, the order of performance science is consequent upon the order of natural human needs and natural inclinations to live safe, healthy, lives. Therein, speculative, leisure, sciences that satisfy wants (like those in which we engage chiefly for purposes of relaxation, and not for intellectual perfection), not natural needs (like speculative study of the science of biology), are subordinated to sciences that, like biology, study subjects that fulfill chief natural needs.

More than any other performance science, following Aristotle, St. Thomas maintains that political science deals, first and foremost, with fulfilling human needs. Given their essential relationship to political science as tools for the exercise of its own proper act, *political science exists in a natural state of relational superiority* over these other sciences to which they are naturally inclined to submit. Consequently, political science naturally inclines to dictate to other practical and theoretical sciences specification of their exercise (use of their skill, like that of a smith) in relation to a specified activity (such as making swords) within individual circumstances of time and place (for example, during a specific war). And subordinated sciences have a natural inclination to take direction from political science regarding such activities.

Regarding speculative and practical sciences, according to its nature, St. Thomas maintains that political science can rightly dictate to some people, for example, to teach or learn geometry for military goals. However, by nature, since it lacks the natural qualification to do so, it cannot dictate to any science the formal object that specifies it, how properly to exercise its activity, and what conclusions it has to draw. *Specification of the nature of any and every science is derived from habits of the soul existing in relation to some sort of organizational whole acting as the formal object of the habit, stimulating it to exercise its proper activity*!

Properly considered, St. Thomas says political science uses the art of legislation to command and control the existence and exercise of other sciences. It can command for some sciences to exist, and others not to exist; for some to be exercised, and for some not to be exercised. One thing it cannot do is to determine the nature of the science, which includes: 1) the formal object, or subject, the science studies; 2) the essential method it uses to study this subject; and 3) and the chief aim for which, by nature, it studies this subject or formal object.

St. Thomas maintains such a study, which includes investigation of the nature of many societies for the good of many populations, is the generic subject of the ethical science of politics. Nonetheless, the subject that studies the ultimate end of the whole universe (theology) considered as such is qualitatively greater.[2]

4. Essential qualities needed by students and teachers of moral science, and the method of study proper to the science

After considering the chief good with which moral science, including political science, deals, St. Thomas analyzes what Aristotle says about the qualities that students and teachers of the science must have and the method of study proper to the science.

On the part of students and teachers of science, St. Thomas maintains that the method proper to manifesting truth in any and every science should be *suitable* (qualitatively proportionate) to the subject being studied. Different subjects require different methods to make their essential part/whole relations manifest, precisely known.

Ethics chiefly studies human (freely chosen) acts: 1) internal acts of virtue; and 2) external acts of virtue and enabling means for executing virtue. Included within the science of ethics as one of its specific parts, divisions, political science chiefly studies just acts and the external enabling means for executing just acts. And both sciences study circumstances and conditions under which ethical acts are performed.

Because the subject-matter of moral science is somewhat variable, contingent, St. Thomas maintains that the method of study it uses: 1) has to be somewhat variable, and 2) cannot generate the same quality of certainty as non-contingent matters. Because *moral science studies acts generated by the human will as moved by what appears to be good in contingent and variable circumstances*, the method involved must reason from what is true for the most part to singulars.

Regarding students and teachers of this science, Aristotle and St. Thomas claim that: 1) A man educated in one particular subject can judge well about what belongs to that subject. 2) A man educated in all subjects can judge well about them all. 3) That is, we judge well about what we know, subjects with which we are familiar.

Consequently, young people, incontinent people, emotionally-immature people, people lacking emotional self-control (like brutish, intemperate people), cannot achieve much advance in moral science, which is useful only for people who start off with the ability to control their appetites! Essentially, people lacking in emotional self-control lack the essential element of moral teachability (*docilitas*), are morally unteachable. Attempting to teach them the science of ethics, moral science, is largely, if not entirely, worthless.

In the case of young people, considering ethics as essentially involving training in political science, like brutish people, *their lack of practical experience at living* (their weakly-developed estimative sense, or particular reason) *in general prevents them from making the moral induction of moral first principles from which moral science starts*! In the area of moral science, the act of inducing moral principles essentially involves practical experience of living, a necessary condition for every act of induction in the area of practical activity and practical science.

Similarly, people who are slaves to their emotions: 1) dislike prudence; 2) incline to choose the pleasurable over the real good; 3) cannot induce, recognize, the chief good at which moral science aims, a first principle of moral science: ending enslavement to the emotion of concupiscence and appetitively bad will; and 4) cannot apprehend the enabling means to overcome this enslavement in the individual situation.

St. Thomas maintains that young people, the emotionally immature, and the habitually morally vicious are defective in the needed development of cogitative reason (the estimative sense) *to induce the first principles of moral science, including that of its chief aim*! To such people, moral science, the study of ethics, tends to be useless. Today, some such people would consider this science as Aristotle and St. Thomas conceive it to be "hate speech."

Nonetheless, St. Thomas claims that moral science is very useful to people who: 1) have a knowledge of moral matter, have a healthy estimative sense faculty, and other requisite human faculties capable of enabling them to induce moral first principles; 2) possess emotional self-control; and 3) can execute external acts under the command of right reason (the moral virtue of prudence).[3]

5. Start of part one of Aristotle's investigation of the supreme human good: Happiness

Having finished investigation into the qualities needed to teach and learn moral science, next, St. Thomas considers part one (Book 1, Ch. 9) of Aristotle's three-part investigation into the nature of the supreme human good: happiness (in which Aristotle concludes that, generically considered, happiness is an activity flowing from virtue). According to St. Thomas, starting in Book 1, Ch. 13, Aristotle specifies this definition by investigating happiness as a kind of operation according to *perfect* virtue; and, subsequent to that, in the concluding Book 10 of the *Nicomachean Ethics* Aristotle will return to this three-part investigation of happiness by considering just what sort of perfect operation and of precisely what nature happiness is.

As far as the first part of this study about the nature of happiness is concerned, St. Thomas starts this by talking about Aristotle's investigations into the nature of happiness made by others prior to and around his time: *the Many*, and some Platonists.

Regarding *the Many*, Aristotle maintains that they tend to: 1) think that happiness is something apparent, obvious: sensible pleasures, riches, honors, and like; 2) disagree about which one of these is happiness; and 3) consider happiness to be nothing fixed, something relative, what is most desired depending upon what good a person most lacks at some time.

As far as some Platonists are concerned, Aristotle maintains that they consider happiness to be a good separate from all sensible goods.

At this point, instead of continuing investigation into the nature of happiness, St. Thomas interrupts that examination to talk about Aristotle's method for studying the opinions of others. According to St. Thomas, in practical matters Aristotle uses investigation *quia* (reasoning from effect to cause), not investigation *proper quid* (reasoning from cause to effect), because in such matters effects are at first better understood by us. More specifically, Aristotle's habit in investigations of such practical matters is to start by noting *what the Many say as a generic understanding from which to induce practical first principles of right reason*!

Because some of these opinions are essentially irrational, such a method of induction, however, does not involve considering all the opinions that all people have about a specific subject such as happiness because doing so tends to be useless for a good philosopher. Still, because the nature of human faculties is to react to an external stimulus from formal objects about which, for the most part (unless, in some way, facultatively or organically impaired), *most of us cannot be totally wrong in judgment* (but must tend, by nature, to achieve at least a modicum of generic understanding of the truth) about the nature of the subject under consideration, Aristotle maintains that considering some opinions (like that held by custom by a majority of people) and those held by "the Learned" amounts to considering *likely* or *probable* opinions in which at least a generic grasp of the truth will often exist.

As an example of such reasoning from effect to cause (*quia*), Aristotle starts by taking as a principle *that something is universally so*: for example, fasting restrains concupiscence. Clearly, in Aristotle's mind, *one of the essential psychological foundations for the generation of this moral universal resides in an induction made by custom* (common experience) *by cogitative reason (the estimative sense) of the Many, the Learned, or both.*

For example, just as, in Book 1 of Plato's *Republic*, the youthful Socrates is able to induce practical principles of moral reasoning through his conversation with the elderly and morally-experienced and prudent man Cephalos (moral principles regarding the relation between old-age, youth, and human happiness), so Aristotle is convinced (perhaps by reading Book 1 of Plato's *Republic*!) that this is the chief method of induction used in practical matters especially related to ethics: inducing our first principles through our own practical experience or that of some others. However, in the matter under consideration at the moment, to know the precise reason why fasting restrains concupiscence, we need more than first principles of induction (more than principles of right reason, prudence, derived from practical experience of living). We need to study what effects those principles cause when applied to deliberative choice within individual circumstances and conditions!

Related to the question about the nature of human happiness, *Aristotle applies his inductive method by considering different opinions held by some men that he deems reasonable and probable*: that happiness is a good belonging to this life consisting in one of three types of life: 1) held by *the Many* and some eminent and upright people (such as some Epicureans), which identifies happiness with a life of pleasure; 2) held by some men of culture, refinement, and good practical reason (that happiness consists in a life of public service, such as the political life); and 3) held by people who tend to be lovers of the speculative life: that happiness consists in a life of contemplation.

About those who identify happiness with pleasure, following Aristotle, St. Thomas says that they have to: 1) identify happiness with intense pleasure of eating, drinking, and sex, with something that cannot possibly be human, something brutish, and 2) justify their choice, sometimes, by appeal to the unbridled pursuit of pleasure by "powerful" people.

Based upon the above threefold division of happiness proposed by *the Many* (the Uncultured and Unlearned) and *the Few* (the Cultured and the Learned), Aristotle makes the following threefold division of happiness based upon three kinds of real goods that exist: 1) honor; 2) utility; and 3) pleasure.

Considering each of these understandings of the nature of happiness in order, following Aristotle, St. Thomas maintains that happiness cannot consist in honor because: 1) happiness should exist preeminently in a person and be hard to remove; 2) honor exists more in the giver than in the receiver; and 3) people tend to seek honor to confirm from sound judges (people they consider virtuous [prudent]), the good opinion they have themselves (to confirm to them that they possess virtue for which they deserve honor; thereby indicating that, in actuality, they seek virtue more than honor).

Regarding a somewhat popularly-held opinion that happiness consists in virtue, Aristotle maintains that happiness cannot consist in virtue because people possess virtue even when they are asleep or lack the opportunity to exercise a virtue; but happiness consists in perfection of activity, not in its lack of exercise.

Moreover, happiness cannot consist in possession of useful goods because useful goods are instrumental, coercively-liked goods, like money (goods that we have to like incidentally as enabling means, necessary instruments for obtaining what we chiefly like).[4]

6. A sketch of happiness: Happiness provisionally defined generically

After considering the three above-cited understandings of happiness, St. Thomas cites Aristotle as maintaining that *a common agreement exists about happiness being the best of things, the ultimate end and best and self-sufficient good. Using this commonly-held agreement* (what the *Many* and the *Learned* say) about the nature of happiness *as an induction of* a generic definition from which to start further inquiry and specification, Aristotle *induces* the genus of happiness by examining this commonly-held agreement in relation to the chief aim of human nature considered as an organizational whole. In so doing, Aristotle is inducing the nature of happiness as a final cause, a chief first principle through which to identify the chief organizational activity of human beings pursued through the perfective exercise of human faculties: the chief action *of the whole nature* of man, the action that all human faculties naturally incline to generate.

With this chief aim in mind, St. Thomas says that *the final good of every composite whole or organization is its ultimate perfection* (that is, an organizational whole's qualitatively greatest act). The form, however, is an organizational whole's first perfection (the intrinsic first principle that generates an organizational whole's final perfection: perfect organizational operation). *The formal perfection of an organizational whole is perfectly harmonious operation*, the first principle of which is the organization's form, or nature (the qualified part/whole relations that generate harmonious organizational activity in relation to perfect execution of numerically-one act [for example, the skills possessed by the members of the crew team that are the proximate first principles that generate the more or less perfectly harmonious operation of the crew members]). Aristotle and St. Thomas induce the form of happiness from happiness considered as the final cause of the facultative operation of the whole of human nature.

Hence, St. Thomas says that happiness is man's proper operation. Just as each department within a corporation has a proper departmental operation, so, through the perfectly harmonious cooperation of its facultative parts and their respective virtues, each natural faculty and each virtuous habit within a natural faculty has a proper operation through which a human being *as an organizational whole* has a natural inclination to generate perfect human activity as a whole agent. Even incidental human acts, according to St. Thomas, have a proper operation.

The proper operation of living parts and living wholes is living operation. The proper living operation of a living whole is not that of any one part. It is the coordinated, harmonious action of all its parts through coordination of the topmost part that harmonizes (like an orchestra leader) all the parts to cooperate.

In human beings, St. Thomas maintains that our rational soul is our first, qualitatively highest, perfection. And this rational soul has two essential parts or divisions: one which he calls *rational by nature*, and another which he calls *rational by participation*.

On the basis of Aristotle's identification of happiness as consisting in a human being's highest (qualitatively greatest) activity, St. Thomas maintains a likelihood exists that this activity consists in an act that is rational by nature. In that case, happiness should consist in an activity of soul in accord with right reason (prudence).

Moreover, since happiness is the act of a superlatively good man, it would have to consist in acting well in a superlative way, according to reason: an act of highest virtue. As the product of a highest virtue, habit, St. Thomas claims that happiness requires: 1) continuity/perpetuity; and 2) continued repetition of good deeds throughout the whole of a person's life according to the best of our ability and virtue.

Having finished giving *a sketch* (general, good description) of happiness, St. Thomas says that Aristotle starts to move beyond this good description to a good definition by talking about the importance of learning from predecessors and engaging in repeated practice of moral virtue.

Consequently, Aristotle begins to talk about the fact that *the proper method of study in practical science is to examine the natures of things for their utility*; not to understand the natures exhaustively and speculatively. The proper method of study is to seek chiefly to identify the causes considered as such, *that this or that is the cause*, not to probe the cause's nature considered as such, but considered *as useful* for generating this or that activity!

Whether our chief aim is to examine the nature of things to understand the causes of those natures in depth and considered as such, or for their utility, all human reasoning, including philosophical/scientific reasoning, starts with a generic knowledge (induction) we have of the nature of something, of some organizational whole (*a one existing in a many*). All reasoning, right as well as wrong, starts with, presupposes, some organizational whole that we know: *with an induction of some chief relation that harmonizes, orders, some disparate multitude into being parts of a whole that we immediately, instantaneously, recognize*!

Despite popular and widespread contemporary misunderstandings of the nature of induction as a logical process of reasoning from a concrete particular to an abstract universal idea, strictly speaking, induction, in the form of: 1) initially recognizing the nature of something, or 2) philosophical/scientific induction, is no process at all; especially not a logical or non-logical one of reasoning from some concrete particular to an abstract, universal, idea. Properly understood, regarding initially recognizing the nature of something, or in the case of philosophical/scientific induction, *induction is an instantaneous act of understanding, immediately apprehending, in terms of the parts that*

214

harmonize to constitute, compose, it, the generic kind of organizational whole that a person is intellectually grasping.

For example, in the two cases referred to in the paragraph immediately above, induction is no logical process and it does not require numerous acts of "empirical experience" of sense data about which we logically reason to achieve. How complicated the act of induction needs to be essentially depends upon: 1) the intellectual excellence of individual human being who is doing the inducing, 2) the more or less complicated nature of the organizational whole which that person is attempting to understand; and 3) the extent and depth of familiarity with that organizational whole that person has.

Essentially, the act of induction involves instantaneously apprehending the chief principle of unity (a one) *that exists within a multitude* (a many) *that harmonizes, orders, that multitude into being parts of this or that kind of a whole!* Essentially, induction involves being able to grasp the chief principle that essentially causes: 1) organizational harmony, order; 2) some multitude to be unified as harmoniously-connected (ordered) so as to generate this or that kind of whole and the acts which that whole naturally inclines to cause (the organization's chief aim: cooperatively to accomplish numerically-one act).

For example, within moments of walking into a business organization, school, church, military or medical facility, charitable foundation, political party, or orchestral performance and sensing how it operates, an intelligent person with extensive experience working with one or more of these organizations just mentioned can immediately induce its nature, and determine whether its activities are healthy or unhealthy, strong or weak. For such a person, doing so requires no extensive process of empirical verification, logical reasoning, or mathematical testing for the simple reason that *the inductive skill resides within the high-quality of harmonious cooperation existing between the organization being experienced and the estimative sense faculty, cogitative reason, and virtuously-trained intellect of an expert.*

As Aristotle and St. Thomas well understood much better than did René Descartes, Sir Francis Bacon, and the overwhelming majority of contemporary self-professed "intellectuals," people, experts, induce different principles in different ways. For example, a medical doctor induces principles related to health and disease differently from the way in which a geometrician induces principles of a circle, square, or polygon; or a musician induces principles for musical composition, or a sculptor or painter induces principles for composing a statue or painting a mural.

Some professionals induce their principles simply by knowing the relation of terms in a premise, or observing the behavior of some composite whole (for example, a medical doctor diagnosing whether a person is sick induces the nature of a disease by recognizing external signs [medical symptoms] and immediately understands, induces, its cause). Or he or she might run a battery of tests to induce a plan for healing an illness (somewhat like a painter or sculptor might work on this or that material, or a pianist might work with this or that brand the piano, to induce its quality, suitability, for serving as a means for composing a statue, painting, musical arrangement). And, as Aristotle and St. Thomas have indicated, human beings can induce the existence of a being that has the nature of a moral agent (that such a person must possess a faculty of free choice) by simply observing a person being praised or blamed, rewarded or punished, for choices he or she has made.

Knowledge of principles and how they are derived is crucial to understanding how properly to reason to sound conclusions related to any subject of study. As Aristotle and St. Thomas recognized, the whole of science is virtually contained in, emerges out of, its

216

principles. Hence, St. Thomas says that one well-understood and completely thought-out principle answers many questions we seek to answer in a science.[5]

7. How Aristotle and St. Thomas confirm the soundness of Aristotle's generic definition of happiness

Keeping the above understanding of induction in mind will enable recognizing precisely why Aristotle makes the moves he now does related to confirming the generic definition of happiness he has just given. For if that definition is sound, and if, to some extent, human beings have a natural ability to know the nature of happiness as the formal object of human nature considered as a whole, the generic definition that Aristotle has given of happiness should agree with what other people incline to say about happiness: *with inductions* of *the Many* and *the Learned*.

Since investigations proceed from principles, and definition is a principle of reasoning, St. Thomas maintains that, thoroughly understanding principles, including definitions, at the start of the reasoning process is crucial for best hope of success in the end. Such being the case, beyond understanding definitions, *in practical matters, crucial to understand is the nature of the chief end*, or aim, pursued. The chief reason for this is, as Aristotle and St. Thomas say, because, in practical matters, the chief end, or aim (the ultimate singular, one final act we most desire to perform) generates all the other acts involved in a practical operation. They are caused, brought into existence, for only one reason: *as tools* to cause the last act, chief end, aim. The ultimate end, last, numerically-one act, is the first principle, and is essentially included in the generic definition given at the start of a scientific investigation.

To ensure a more careful scientific study, St. Thomas tells us that, as part of our reasoning process, we have to examine: 1) the premises and conclusions of our reasoning and 2) the observations made by others about principles being used. We have to make sure all our reasoning harmonizes with the truth, with, if they are right, the principles we are using (*because we achieve the good only in concurrence of all factors pertaining to the perfection of a composite whole*, chief among which is the principles from which we start our reasoning).

In this process, in agreement with Aristotle, St. Thomas maintains that even false opinions help. Evil, mistakes, arise in many ways through a defect in one part. Nonetheless, because we know evil, what is false only in reference to the good, the true, no evil, no mistake, exists that, in some way, does not reflect the good and the true.

Bearing the above fact in mind, to carry out his stated goal to examine the opinions of others in relation to his provisional definition of happiness, St. Thomas says Aristotle divides human goods into three species: 1) external (like riches, honors, friends); 2) internal psychological (like knowledge, virtue); and 3) internal bodily (like physical strength, beauty, and health).

After doing this Aristotle states that some philosophers make one of two chief claims about the nature of happiness. One group maintains that, in three different ways, happiness consists in virtue: 1) in any virtue, but especially moral virtue, which perfects the appetites that come under control of reason; 2) in the act of prudence, which perfects practical reason; or 3) in wisdom, which perfects speculative reason. Another group claims that happiness consists in any, or all of, these above-mentioned understandings, *plus pleasure*, that is: 1) virtue and pleasure almost in equal measure comprise happiness; 2) happiness lies *chiefly* in virtue and *secondarily* in pleasure; or 3) happiness lies in these two immediately-preceding conditions just mentioned *plus a full measure of external goods*.

In addition to these above-mentioned opinions of *the Learned*, Aristotle also considers some opinions held by *the Many* (the common people and some ancients), which include: 1) among *the Many,* that, to be happy, we need pleasures, riches; and 2) among *a minority of distinguished men*, that happiness consists in goods of the soul.

This survey having been completed, Aristotle claims the likelihood to be that: 1) none of these teachings was totally wrong or right; 2) some were right on some points; and 3), to some extent, all these teachings agree with his definition, but his definition is more complete.

Such being the case, Aristotle shows why he considers his definition to be better from the standpoint of reason and customary speech. 1) From the standpoint of reason, he claims that his definition is better because, by nature, *virtue inclines toward perfect operation as its end*; by nature, virtuous operation is more perfect than possession of virtue. And 2) from customary speech, in reference to a popular saying during his time related to the Olympic Games, *only those who compete, run the race, win the prize*. Of those who are good and best in virtuous living, only those who perform good deeds are illustrious and happy.

Beyond these instances of confirmation already given, Aristotle proves his claim by saying the following: 1) We attribute pleasure only to beings having perception, animals; activities of soul; and existing in union with what we love, find agreeable. And 2) by nature, virtue pleases all human beings because all people seek and delight in *perfec*t natural operation.

He adds that *the pleasures commonly pursued by human nature (proper pleasures, prudent pleasures) as real, not apparent, goods are naturally pleasant to people with an uncorrupted soul* (prudent, not incontinent, intemperate, brutish, people). The pleasures in which *the Many* delight: 1) are contrary to naturally higher (proper) pleasures and prudence; and 2) relate to apparent goods of the concupiscible appetite like pursuing and squandering money. In contrast, the pleasures loved by *men of virtue* essentially relate to: 1) naturally higher pleasures (joys) of the soul to fulfilling real needs of human nature regarding species and individual preservation and perfection: protecting the health and safety of individual human life and species existence; 2) possessing real, not apparent, good; and 3) doing naturally good acts.

The pleasures loved by vicious men, moreover, are: 1) acquired through habitual use of corrupt habits; 2) result from the habitual exercise of imprudent choice; and 3) are not delightful by healthy natural inclination. *Crucial to note about what Aristotle says regarding the unhealthy pursuit of unnatural pleasures of imprudent individuals is that all instances of such pursuit are external signs of the existence of an unhealthy estimative sense, unhealthy passions, and a bad will.*

In contrast to the many external and unhealthy pleasures that incontinent and intemperate people pursue as instances of happy activity, Aristotle maintains that the virtuous life needs no incidental or external pleasure to delight it. All it needs is the operation of its nature to give pleasure. *Proper pleasure necessarily belongs to virtue, pertains to its nature! A morally virtuous person naturally delights in doing virtuous deeds. And, strictly speaking, people who do not delight in doing morally virtuous deeds cannot be virtuous!*

The chief reason for this is: 1) that the act of a virtuous person *issues from a proper habit*, a habit directed by prudence that satisfies the natural desire of its faculty; 2) because of fitting arrangement of its parts, *noble, beautiful, of virtuous activity*; and 3) because virtuous activity is rightly ordered to (harmonizes with) its end, is good. Aristotle adds that *pleasure, beauty*, and *goodness* essentially belong to virtuous actions in a high degree (with a high degree of intensive quantity). *He maintains that proof of this is that the good man considers virtuous pleasures so much that he prizes them higher than any other pleasures.*

Since happiness consists in virtuous actions, Aristotle concludes that *happiness is the best, most perfect, and most beautiful of actions.* Moreover, properly understood, happiness is not a single act generated by a single part, or faculty, of a human being. *Properly understood, happiness is a single act caused by the whole of the human person considered as an organizational whole having all of its parts cooperate to generate a perfect activity through perfect possession of moral virtue.*

Such being the case, Aristotle proves his definition of happiness to be superior to definitions of happiness given by those who claim that happiness consists in possession of external goods by saying that, while happiness chiefly consists in virtuous activity, essential, *at times, to exercising virtue* is having the right instruments and the right circumstances (like good luck).[6]

8. The cause of happiness

Having started to consider the cause of happiness in general to consist in the exercise of perfect moral virtue, Aristotle starts to specify our understanding of this cause by stating that it must be: 1) *per se* and determinate or 2) incidental and by chance. If *per se* it must be: 1) divine or human and 2) caused by speculative learning, moral practice, or military exercise (like drill).

Regarding whether happiness is divinely caused, St. Thomas replies, because this is the most excellent of human goods, that it be divinely caused is eminently reasonable, and consistent with the fact that in the created universe higher beings and virtues give direction to lower beings and virtues. Nevertheless, such a consideration is proper to metaphysics, not to moral science.

Moreover, while God is its chief cause, human beings contribute to happiness in two ways: 1) Happiness is the reward and end of virtue, something most excellent, divine, blessed, and Godlike. And

2) if happiness is the end of human nature, it must be achievable by all human beings, cannot consist in communication with separate substances, and cannot be caused by chance.

Indeed, chance cannot cause human happiness because: 1) nature produces what is suitable, proportionate, for agents to achieve their ends; and 2) if chance were the cause of the most perfect of all human goods, the pursuit of all of the goods would collapse as essentially irrational.

According to St. Thomas, evident from the preceding inquiry is that: 1) happiness is an activity of the rational soul in accord with virtue influenced by some divine cause; 2) what happens according to reason does not happen by chance; 3) happiness springs proximately from a human cause and remotely from God as a first cause; 4) while other goods play a part in causing happiness, happiness does not chiefly consist in them; is enhanced by some of them, instrumentally helped by others; and is the chief end, aim, of political science.

Consequently, St. Thomas maintains that political science is especially concerned with framing laws and apportioning rewards and punishments to bring into being good citizens who are doers of good works. Moreover, strictly speaking, what also follows is that irrational animals and children cannot be happy because neither can share in the activity of perfect virtue, which demands being able to perform the best operation and continuous, good action.[7]

9. How Aristotle answers Solon's problem regarding whether, because of changes in fortune, strictly speaking, anyone can be called "happy" in this life

At this point, St. Thomas turns his attention to Aristotle's consideration of the famous question Solon had raised regarding whether anyone in this life (which is sometimes beset by quick and dramatic changes in fortune) can properly be called "happy": 1) when, at any time in life, the misfortune that beset King Priam could beset anyone; and 2) because happiness should be permanent, not easily changeable.

For several reasons, Aristotle rejects the claim that we can only judge a person happy after death because: 1) Since death is the worst of evils and happiness is the greatest good, such a conclusion appears unreasonable. 2) Happiness is a kind of activity. However, the dead appear to have no activity and suffer loss of consciousness. Consequently, the dead cannot be affected by goods and evils that happen related to them.

In reply to Solon's problem, Aristotle argues that, while external goods subject to fortune are essential to the performance and perfection of virtuous actions, virtuous actions are the chief and predominant factor in causing human happiness. *We properly call people virtuous and happy because they act virtuously, cause virtue, and do beautiful deeds*!

Because they are material and corporeal, Aristotle states that, by their nature, external and internal bodily goods are subject to change. In contrast, goods belonging to the human soul are changeable only indirectly. Moreover, moral virtues are longer-lasting than intellectual virtues, more fixed by frequent practice. And among virtues: 1) the most noble and beautiful appear to be more intense, to last longer because more intense are those virtues that are practiced more; and 2) moral virtue appears to last longer than intellectual virtue because it consists chiefly in appetitive acts essentially related to fulfilling real needs, which incline by nature not to be as easily destroyed by forgetfulness.

Indeed, Aristotle maintains that, if happiness consists in moral virtues that exist in the human appetites that protect and preserve human life on a daily basis by constantly fulfilling natural needs: 1) happiness can last a lifetime; 2) the happy man will act always, or almost always, according to virtue in everything he does; and 3) he will be eminently prudent in all matters; and be perfect in all the cardinal moral virtues.

In addition, good and bad fortune will not tend to affect the happy man because: 1) short runs of good and bad luck do not change life from happiness to misery and conversely; but 2) great and frequent runs of good luck make life happier, while bad luck will cause external annoyance and internal affliction (sorrow) that hinder execution of some external good works.

Still, Aristotle maintains that virtue makes good use even of bad luck, thereby enabling the good of virtue to shine forth gracefully in courageous and magnanimous endurance of great suffering, not because, as some Stoics falsely held, the virtuous man feels no sorrow. Unlike these Stoics, who considered external, bodily things not humanly good, Aristotle maintained that: 1) sadness affects the virtuous man appetitively and intellectually, but does not overwhelm his reason; 2) the virtuous man's prudential reason moderates the effect the sadness; and 3) similar to death, madness, and other similar disorders can cause cessation of virtue.

Nevertheless, if virtuous actions dominate in the life of the happy man, the happy man will not become unhappy due to misfortune or perform vicious acts because of it. The happy man will: 1) bear all changes of fortune, even misfortunes like those that beset Priam, becomingly, *beautifully*, like a truly good and wise man; and 2) act according to virtue under every condition according as the circumstances, conditions, and materials permit. Conversely, no matter what fortune brings, the vicious man can never be happy.

Consequently regarding Solon's question about who, properly, we can call "happy," Aristotle concludes that nothing stops us from analogously calling "happy" a man who acts prudently, in accord with perfect virtue and has sufficient external goods to act virtuously for a long time. Nonetheless, in the most perfect sense possible, a happy man will live the life just described and live prudently. According to Aristotle, this is the sense in which Solon was talking about happiness: happiness in its most perfect sense. And, since natural desire cannot be in vain, St. Thomas adds that perfect happiness is reserved for meta-perfect virtue in the afterlife.[8]

10. What causes happiness and virtue to be goods deserving of honor and praise

After he finishes answering Solon's question about what person we can properly call "happy," Aristotle starts to consider the question of precisely what causes happiness and moral virtues to be goods deserving of honor and praise by noting that: 1) honor signifies manifesting a person's excellence by word and deed, whereas praise consists only of manifesting a person's excellence through use of words; and 2) while honor and praise are given due to some excellence, two kinds of excellence exist: absolute (for which honor is due) and in relation to some end (for which praise is due).

Bearing these distinctions in mind, Aristotle maintains that, because happiness is of the genus of perfect and best things, happiness belongs to the genus of things to be honored. He adds that we praise human beings for having virtue of mind and power and strength of body; and, while we do so, we praise the person with virtuous habits because these habits are ordered to the work of virtue. But *something absolutely praiseworthy*, like happiness, is praiseworthy under all circumstances. Praise is given to things whose goodness is considered in relation to something within a genus; but best things are not ordered to anything better. They are to be honored because other (*praiseworthy*) things are ordered to them. Consequently, being the best of things, happiness is a good to be honored (something better than praise exists for the best), while virtue is a good to be praised.[9]

11. Aristotle returns to the discussion of the relation between happiness and virtue

Having finished his preliminary discussion of happiness in Book 1 of his *Nicomachean Ethics*, Aristotle ends the last chapters of this Book by returning to the discussion of virtue that he had started several chapters previously because, since happiness is an activity according to perfect virtue, we cannot fully comprehend happiness without fully comprehending, and relating happiness to, virtue. Moreover, because its chief aim is to produce good citizens, citizens who obey the law, political science needs to study virtue. And, to study virtue and happiness, political science needs to study the soul (*moral psychology*) because, in a person, the soul is the virtue-generating principle and moral virtue is the happiness-generating principle.

Just as the medical doctor must study the virtue of the body (health), Aristotle asserts that the statesman needs to study the virtue of the soul (wisdom and other virtues). And, just as the medical doctor must study many body-related subjects, so the politician must study many soul-related subjects. The soul must be studied relative to virtue and human actions because the soul is their proximate generator. *They grow out of the human soul as out of their proximate principle*!

Relative to the production of virtue, consideration of soul essentially involves examination of that part of the soul which is rational by nature (the human intellect) and that which is irrational by nature and rational by participation (the sensory part of the soul and its irascible and concupiscible appetite). Consequently, Aristotle ends Book 1 of the *Nicomachean Ethics*, by considering the human soul and its subdivisions.[10]

12. The sensory part of the soul and its subdivisions

According to Aristotle, the human soul is the life-generating principle of the human body, the principle that generates within the body vegetative faculties (like those present within plant life) that enable human beings to digest food, grow, and have the ability to reproduce. Considered strictly from the standpoint of a biological principle, he contends that ethics has no relation to the operation of these faculties. *The chief concern of ethics is with the sensory division of the irrational part of the soul, in which are located cogitative, or particular, reason (the estimative sense)* and the irascible and concupiscible appetites and their passions. Regarding this part of the human soul, moral science is chiefly concerned with that division of the soul that, by nature, is: 1) in the case of the incontinent man, somewhat inclined to listen to, and somewhat inclined to oppose, reason; and 2) in the case of someone in a state of doubt, with moral virtue inclined to listen to reason.

Moral reason is not related to the human passions as intellectual reason is related to an intellectual habit like logic or mathematics. St. Thomas maintains that moral reason works like: 1) a father giving advice to a son; a 2) friend offering advice to another; 3) the reproach of a seasoned veteran to a novice; and 4) the entreaties of novices to each other.

Furthermore, intellectual reason (to which the particular reason of the sensory part of the soul is essentially inclined to listen and from which it is naturally inclined to take direction) is not governed by the motions of the heavens and not directly subject to command of the passions. By nature, human beings are free agents. Finally, since praiseworthy habits and virtues exist in both divisions of the human soul, Aristotle contends that politicians need to study both parts of the human soul.[11]

—Notes—

1. St. Thomas Aquinas, *Commentary on the Nicomachean Ethics of Aristotle*, Lect. 1, nn. 1–18.

2. Id., Lect. 2, nn. 19–31.

3. Id., Lect. 3, nn. 32–42.

4. Id., Lects. 4–5, nn. 43–73; see Plato, *Republic*, Bk. 1, 328B–329A.

5. Id., Lects. 9–11, nn. 103–138.

6. Id., Lects. 12–13, nn. 139–164.

7. Id., Lect. 14, nn. 165–175.

8. Id., Lect. 15–16, nn. 177–202.

9. Id., Lect. 18, nn. 213–223.

10. Id., Lect. 19, nn. 224–230.

11. Id., Lect. 20, nn. 231–244.

Chapter Eight

Moral Virtue Considered in General

HAVING COMPLETED his introduction to the nature of moral science, including chiefly what it studies, and how it studies it, in Book 2 of his *Nicomachean Ethics*, before defining "virtue" and discussing the nature of intellectual, and speculative, virtues, Aristotle considers the nature of moral virtue in general and precisely how and why habit, not human nature, proximately causes all virtue.

1. The habits that cause virtue: How and why habit, not human nature, proximately causes virtue

In moral science, Aristotle and St. Thomas maintain that *we seek a definition of virtue chiefly to become good, not chiefly to know the truth. Since, in habit formation and habit perfection, actions control formation of right and wrong dispositions within our natural faculties*, we must know precisely what sort of actions these are. Moral virtue, they say: 1) aims chiefly at knowing changeable truth about contingent things and 2) consists in appetitive modification (qualitative modification in the appetite) caused by repeated impression of reason in an appetite by appetitive use of the appetite under direction of right reason.

Since such knowledge of changeable truth about contingent things is possessed by moral "science," St. Thomas maintains that it must be in accord, harmonize, with right reason and the virtue of prudence because: 1) all good actions *are in proportion to* (do not exceed the power of, and are proportionate [intensive quantum] likenesses of) the form that generates them; 2) existing form (a composite whole, organization) generates all good actions; and 3) because effects resemble causes, all human actions must harmonize with, be an image of, their form.

Since investigation must be conducted in harmony with the subject investigated, Aristotle and St. Thomas maintain that the method of investigation used within moral science must be somewhat provisional, *like that used in medicine: relative to the subjects studied and the remedies prescribed*. Given the fact that Aristotle was the son of one of the leading medical doctors in the West of his time (Philip of Macedon), that this method closely models that of a medical doctor should come as no surprise to most people. Evident from what he says is that, as a moral scientist, he knows that his method of procedure related to caring for the health of the human soul analogously resembles that of a medical doctor.

According to St. Thomas, in speculative science, we achieve our goal when we know the truth, what causes a determined effect. In practical (moral) science, in contrast, we achieve our goal when we know: 1) what determined cause causes a determined effect (this something) and 2) how to employ that cause to cause this effect. In moral science, once again, we seek a definition of virtue not chiefly to know the truth about things, but, by repeatedly doing good deeds, to become *psychologically-healthy* human beings.

Moral science chiefly studies prudent and imprudent actions: 1) individual causes of freely chosen activity; 2) done at the present time within individual circumstances; 3) after due deliberation.

Aristotle and St. Thomas maintain that all virtues and actions that cause virtues are destroyed by excess and defect in the exertion of effort in action, *by wrongly estimating* the qualitative (intensive quantum) greatness of effort to apply relative to a person's natural or acquired ability within this or that circumstance. To support this claim, they present evidence related to bodily activity: 1) In athletics, excessive exertion of activity and lack of exercise weaken bodily strength. 2) Eating too much or too little food and drink (especially of unhealthy food and drink relative to a person's bodily condition) impairs health. And 3) moderate exercise, eating, and drinking promote bodily health. *Analogously, the same is true of the soul*!

For Aristotle and St. Thomas, in moral matters, ethics, *we determine the golden mean, the right measure, of choice and action within the individual situation according right reason taking into consideration our limited capabilities* (not chiefly according to *dimensive*, but chiefly according to *intensive*, quantity: personal capabilities relative to actions being considered by prudential reason as part of particular reason within individual circumstances). When dealing with moral matters, two major questions we must repeatedly ask ourselves when considering performance of an action or making a choice are: 1) "Is this action something doable by any human being?" and 2) "Is it doable by me?"[1]

2. How pleasures and pains, joys and sorrows, act as signs indicating that moral virtue or vice is generating an action

Aristotle and St. Thomas claim that every moral virtue is concerned with human beings being rightly ordered in our pleasures and pains, joys and sorrows; with perfecting the lower (concupiscible) human passions of pleasure and joy, pain and sorrow. They maintain that, before any and every virtue (moral or otherwise, but especially moral) is completely possessed, lack of facultative harmony and strength of action (qualitative perfection of a habit: virtue) causes pain and drudgery in doing good deeds relative to that faculty being exercised. Once, however, we perfectly possess a good habit, virtue, within one of our human faculties that is naturally capable of being habituated, a pleasure and joy agreeing with the natural inclination accompanies doing good deeds through the exercise of that faculty. While pleasure is not the formal object of all virtues, *Aristotle and St.*

An Introduction to Ragamuffin Ethics

Thomas claim that pleasure accompanies all acts of virtue, is part of the essence of all virtue, including moral virtue!

They assert that the morally virtuous person experiences pleasure making right choices, while the morally vicious person experiences pleasure doing evil. Moreover, 1) every moral action engages the will and passions under the aspect of an end, aim: a good; and 2) when the will/passions come to rest at the end of an action, they experience pleasure or pain, joy or sorrow. Consequently, Aristotle asserts that *pleasure and sadness build and destroy all virtues.* All moral virtues essentially involve a person: 1) experiencing joy in performing rightly-ordered actions, 2) making prudent choices, and 3) experiencing sadness at making imprudent choice.

In support of his contention, Aristotle refers to Plato's advice regarding moral education that, from the earliest years, youth need to be accustomed to take pleasure in doing good, and to be grieved by doing evil, works

At times, moreover, St. Thomas maintains that moral virtue serves a medicinal use: to restore appetitive health. And this always involves experience of proper pleasure and, health-restoring pain. Indeed, he states that pleasure and pain/joy and sorrow accompany all our choices.

He maintains that three humanly-selectable objects exist: 1) perfective (agreeable to reason, good or virtuous) or debilitating; 2) helpful (also agreeable to reason) or harmful; and 3) pleasurable or painful. Regarding these he says that the virtuous man disposes himself rightly while the vicious man disposes himself wrongly.

Moreover, because pleasure exists in both the intellectual and sensitive powers, all animals are capable of experiencing it. Nonetheless, for two reasons, Aristotle and St. Thomas maintain that, *only the human intellect recognizes the virtuous and the useful*: 1) by definition, the virtuous act is an act performed in accord with reason,

232

and 2) the "useful" essentially implies order of one thing to another, and human reason (*including particular reason, the estimative sense of human beings, which participates in intellectual reason*), not the external senses, or the common sense unaided by particular reason, recognizes, and properly orders, one thing to another.

St. Thomas notes, further, that, as a facultative disposition, every habit has an inclination to concern its activity with doing things by which a faculty is brought to perfection in its action. Every faculty, moreover, naturally delights in exercise of a pleasure proper to it, one which keeps it healthy and strong: proper pleasure. In naturally pursuing perfection of the facultative health and operation, a virtue naturally inclines to delight in causing a faculty's proper pleasure. *We naturally regulate our activities in the individual circumstance through application of pleasure and pain under the direction of cogitative reason, the estimative sense, setting the mean*! Pleasure and pain are involved in building and destroying all acts of virtue.

Regarding pursuit of some pleasure as a real moral good, especially related to moral education, St. Thomas observes Aristotle's disagreement with ancient claim made by some Stoics that, by nature, experience of passion is evil. On the contrary, St. Thomas claims that the business of virtue is not to exclude all passion, including pleasure. It is only to exclude inordinate passions, inordinate pleasures. In fact, the business of moral science is precisely to determine the right kind, and limits, of pleasure or pain, joy or sorrow with respect to choosing this or that act in this or that circumstance.

Pleasure and pain accompany all our acts of sensing from our first childhood sensation. By nature, we delight in healthy exercise of our sense faculties, not in abusive exercise of them. Hence, the whole business of moral, and political, science concerns the moral psychology of right and wrong use of pleasures and pains within individual circumstances!

More than pleasure and pain accompany all our acts of virtue. According to Aristotle and St. Thomas, so too does difficulty. Because anyone can operate well related to easier activities, St. Thomas tells us that, like art, virtue always concerns the more difficult deed.

Because moral education always involves taking enjoyment in prudent application of pleasure to a specific activity within specific circumstances, from its initial beginning, moral education always essentially involves training the concupiscible appetite in acts of temperance. And, because moral education always involves prudently and with pleasure doing the more difficult deed, choosing the higher good over the lower and the real good over the apparent, in the individual circumstance, from its initial beginning, moral education, always involves prudent application of temperate activity to engage in courageous acts. In this way, the temperately-educated estimative sense faculty (particular reason) helps execute courageous acts to perfect the irascible appetite to perfect our behavior toward ourselves and toward other human beings: that is, to perfect our ability to act courageously (honorably) and justly.[2]

3. Comparison of moral virtue and art

After Aristotle has shown that actions cause habits and virtues, as he repeatedly does, as a pedagogical tool to help the learning process, he raises a sophistic objection to a claim that, in moral activity and art, action precedes habit development and habit perfection. According to this objection, what is true of art is true of moral activity. And, in art, the truth is that, just as producing a grammatical work requires that a person must first be a grammarian and producing a musical work demands that a person must first be a musician, so just as no person produces a work of art except a person who possesses the art, no one does a good moral deed without possessing moral virtue.

Aristotle answers this objection by saying that three conditions exist for acting in the morally right way: 1) knowing the right, 2) choosing the right as pleasing, and 3) choosing the right deed by habit.

Of the three conditions given immediately above, Aristotle says that, to persist in being able to act in a morally virtuous way, a morally virtuous person must repeatedly fulfill all three conditions, but that, for some artists, fulfilling all three conditions is not as crucial. For a person to be a good artist, for example, sometimes persistent practice, and even enjoying the application of one's art is unnecessary. Some artists can execute their art well for a long time with little or no practice or taking special delight in it. Crucial, however, to the artist is to be able to execute, and some artists can excel at what they do without always taking pleasure in their activity or habitually practicing.it.

He says, too, that speculative knowledge has little or no importance in a person becoming morally virtuous. Crucial to a person becoming morally virtuous is repeatedly to make the right choices in the way that virtuous people do. Consequently, he criticizes those who think they can become morally virtuous through speculative study. Today, that would be like a person thinking he or she could learn to become an excellent driver by studying a driver's manual, instead of by repeatedly getting behind the wheel of an automobile.[3]

4. Aristotle starts defining virtue generically

After having discussed virtue and the difference between virtue and art, St. Thomas says that Aristotle starts to define virtue generically by taking for granted that an animal soul has three principles of living action: 1) passions (emotions), powers (natural faculties), and habits. Such being the case, he states that virtue must be a species of one of these.

He maintains that passions are evidently not part of the vegetative power of the soul, and, because they involve no bodily changes (while passions essentially do), passions cannot be part of the intellect or will. Consequently, Aristotle locates the human passions in the sensitive appetite of the soul, which, as St. Thomas has already mentioned, Aristotle divides into the irascible and concupiscible appetites.

Next, Aristotle calls habits dispositions (principles of relations) determining a power in reference to something. He states that constant use of our faculties habituate them. Constant right use of our faculties habituates them well, while constant wrong use of them habituates them badly. Good habits, in turn, determine a faculty's actions to be well executed, while bad habits determine its actions to be badly executed.

He claims, further, that moral virtues are not passions because we are not called good or bad, praised, or blamed, just for having a passion. Passions are not interior choices, nor do they always involve exterior choice. Passions, emotions, are movements of the soul that often arise without choice.

Moreover, for two reasons, Aristotle maintains that virtues are not faculties or powers of the soul, because: 1) we are not praised or blamed for being able to have any motion; and 2) powers are generated in us by nature while virtues (at least in the case of acquired virtues) are generated in us by choice.[4]

5. Aristotle defines virtue specifically

After Aristotle defines virtue generically, he starts to define it specifically by noting a common quality of virtue: it makes its possessor and a possessor's work good. For example, he says that the virtue, power, excellence, of an eye or horse, make them excel at their proper act. Moreover, we judge, measure, the power, virtue, of the thing by: 1) the best thing that it can do, 2) its excellent performance, and 3) its perfect operation. That is, we judge, measure, a thing's power or virtue in terms of its *virtual quantity greatness*: in terms of its qualitative perfection, the intensive quantum maximum of greatness in acts it is capable of causing. Hence, Aristotle maintains that everything is good, operates well, according to its virtue (its intensive quantity greatness, perfection, of possession of form).

Under three headings Aristotle next investigates the specific difference of virtue in terms of a virtue's quality (strength of having, participating in, form) according to: 1) its proper operations; 2) its special character of good and evil; and 3) it being the mean in every action that makes the action good.

St. Thomas adds that virtue deals with three things, the 1) more, 2) less, and 3) the equal in continuous, contingent, and divisible matters according to dimensive and intensive quantity. In relation to these three things, he maintains that the equal holds a midpoint between more (excess, too much) and less (defect, too little) according to both *absolute quantity* between accidents and things and by *intensity* and in distinctness of a quality (that is, according to intensive quantity) in a subject. He adds that the mean according to absolute quantity is the equal taken from the things compared, from the quantity of the thing, while *the mean relative to us* is the mean proportioned, suitable, to our power (the mean according to us, like the size of a shoe relative to the size of the person's foot that it fits or does not fit), and is not the same for all. *Because he has a healthy estimative sense* and, as a result, *has a good sense of personal capabilities*, the virtuous, prudent, man, seeks and knows the mean relative to him.

Aristotle maintains that every practical science works in the following twofold way: 1) in planning, it aims at the mean and 2) in execution, it carries out its work according to the mean. Hence, 1) *people say that from a work well done nothing can be added or subtracted* and 2) the mean achieves and preserves a work's good.

Moral virtue, moreover, inclines us to work, as nature does, in one, determined, way just like art. And moral virtue is better than art because, while art makes us capable of doing a good work, *moral virtue causes us to do it.*

Furthermore, relative to actions and passions, Aristotle claims that the morally virtuous mean avoids excess and defect and indicates righteousness and a praiseworthy act.[5]

6. St. Thomas concludes Aristotle's definition of moral virtue

After specifying moral virtue in terms of making an agent and an agent's acts qualitatively good, St. Thomas starts his analysis of Aristotle's further specification of virtue's definition by citing a passage from the work *De divinis nominibus* by Pseudo-Dionysius the Areopagite referring to the fact that good results from a single and complete cause, a complete whole, but evil arises from any single defect. Hence, St. Thomas states that, *like health and beauty*, moral goodness arises when all the parts of a composite whole are well proportioned and of the healthy color (in short, when all of the parts of a moral act are beautiful inasmuch as *a beautiful quality in a moral agent is causing* moral activity). In short, goodness in action results from perfect harmonization (*beauty*) of all of the parts involved in the performance of the moral activity (including the virtuous qualities of the agent and the perfect suitability of the agent's choice to the circumstances in which it is freely exercised).

In attempting as completely as possible accurately to represent Aristotle's complete specification of moral virtue, St. Thomas makes the following four points: 1) The genus of moral virtue is an act of habit of soul. 2) The habit is specified by its act, which is determined by its object. 3) Moral virtue's formal object is *the mean relative to us*. And 4) the mean relative to us gets its goodness by being determined by prudence: right reason about the means to be chosen by this person, at this time, in these circumstances.

St. Thomas says moral virtue: 1) discovers the mean by reason and chooses it by will; 2) uses the prudent mean relative to choices involving actions and passions; 3) in its species and definition is a mean; and 4) as it acts or guides well in a determined genus is an extreme because the moral habit has the form of good by following, and being in harmony with, prudence.

In its specific nature as an intensive quantity, quality, or right proportion, *moral virtue is beautiful and a mean.* In the way it acts, it is an extreme between two evils of doing too much and too little; an extreme that, because it is beautiful, is a perfect measure to which nothing can be added and from which nothing can be subtracted.

In their specific nature, because they are essentially imprudent in relation to real human needs and fulfilling real human goods, St. Thomas maintains that some actions and passions, appetitive dispositions (like envy, shame, and bad will) can never be prudent/ beautiful, while actions like temperance, justice, and courage essentially connote moderation by prudence and a kind of intrinsic harmony and beauty.[6]

7. By applying Aristotle's definition of moral virtue in a special way to individual virtues, St. Thomas makes this definition more precise

After explaining Aristotle's generic and specific definition of moral virtue, following Aristotle's lead, St. Thomas maintains that, when considering actions, considering definitions abstractly, without applying them to singular causes, such definitions are not of much use within individual situations. *In practical science, the practical scientist considers definitions, which represent natures (organizational wholes) as proximate generators of individual actions, not as abstract universals. In practical science, natures generate individual actions and complete natures terminate their actions in the generation of individuals.*

Need exists at this point to recall, once again, that moral science aims, chiefly, not at speculative knowledge of the causes of action considered in general, but at practically controlling and directing individual actions. In such a situation, Aristotle and St. Thomas maintain that studying concrete particulars is more effective and accurate than abstract considerations of natures for the chief purpose of understanding how to command and control these actions because universal, causal natures are verified in particulars.

Focusing attention on the way in which moral virtues act as principles of action in the individual situation, St. Thomas distinguishes moral virtues in two ways: 1) in relation to prudential control of the passions by the four cardinal moral virtues and 2) in relation to potential execution of actions. And, he tells us that the reason for this distinction is due to the fact that passions have an inclination to resist control by reason, while actions like buying and selling do not. Regarding actions involving exchanging things (commutative exchanges), St. Thomas claims that equality of rectitude (fair price) is generally sufficient.

St. Thomas maintains that, in two ways, the passions involve a kind of inclination that can be contrary to prudential reason: 1) by drawing reason away from real goods and needs, and toward apparent goods and wants (as often happens in relationship to the irascible passions of hope and anger, and the concupiscible passions in general); and 2) by drawing the passions away from following prudential command as a result of passions of fear, hatred, and so on. In case one referred to immediately above, reason has to suppress and restrain the passions from distracting it, while, in case two, reason has to establish right order, the mean, by stabilizing (*calming*) the appetitive part of the soul about what conforms to reason.

On the basis of the two ways that emotional inclination can be contrary to reason, St. Thomas distinguishes the operations of the four cardinal moral virtues as follows: 1) Prudence determines the right mean in the individual circumstance. 2) Justice determines the right mean in exchanges. 3) Courage stabilizes, calms, the soul by making it constant in following prudence. And 4) temperance restrains concupiscence.

Next, St. Thomas distinguishes the cardinal moral virtues based upon their formal object considered as follows: 1) Prudence chiefly considers knowledge of commanding, not knowledge of all truth. 2) Justice chiefly concerns actions involving equality related to another person, not all acts of equality. 3) Temperance chiefly considers restraining the concupiscible appetite regarding desires and pleasures of touch and taste, and not restraining all pleasures. And 4) courage chiefly concerns stabilizing the soul, making it constant causing it to be calm in the fear of danger and death, not making it constant in all acts. Since St. Thomas maintains that all other moral virtues are reduced to these four, not as species of them, but as secondary virtues to primary ones (for example, virtues dealing with lesser pleasures or fears), analogously, the distinctions made immediately above apply to such virtues also.

Further, St. Thomas says that, since all human passions relate to bodily life, internal human acts, and external goods, moral virtue involves regulating passions related to each of these divisions. Nonetheless, St. Thomas states that, in his initial discussion of moral virtue, Aristotle does not discuss justice and prudence in detail. He restricts himself to discussion of temperance and courage, and of some other, secondary, virtues, in some detail. And, Aristotle starts to do this, first, by talking about virtues related to passions essentially connected to the preservation and protection of bodily life and, second, about virtues related to passions essentially connected to external goods.[7]

8. Aristotle's initial discussion of the moral virtues of courage and temperance, liberality and magnificence

Concerning Aristotle's treatment of the moral virtue of courage, St. Thomas says that Aristotle talks about it in relation to dangers destructive of life as a means concerned with fear and daring related to danger of death existing between the extremes of rashness and cowardice.

Regarding temperance, St. Thomas states that Aristotle considers temperance as it relates to being an enabling means for preserving life in the individual via food and drink and in the human species via sex. He adds that, properly speaking, temperance is not a mean related to all pleasures and pains. It is a mean related to all pleasures and pains of touch, and chiefly to pleasures essentially related to food and sex. He says that Aristotle calls a person who over-indulges in such pleasures "intemperate," while he labels as "insensitive," a person who avoids participating in such pleasures entirely or as much as possible.

After briefly discussing these two virtues, St. Thomas says that Aristotle engages in a similarly brief examination of virtues related to external goods like riches and honors. Regarding virtues regulating riches, Aristotle talks about liberality (moderation concerning wealth-related goods) and magnificence (moderation concerning disbursement of great wealth related to major cultural undertakings).

Aristotle calls "liberality" a mean between the extravagance of a spendthrift and the stinginess of a miser in giving and receiving money. And he calls "magnificent" people who avoid being extravagant (squanderers) and stingy (cheap) in great matters.[8]

9. Aristotle's initial discussion of some other moral virtues related to external matters regarding riches and honors

Extending his treatment of moral virtues related to external *actions that prepare human beings to be able to socialize with other people, get along with them, and eventually practice the virtues of justice and friendship toward them as members of the political community*, Aristotle starts to talk about moral virtues related to the external goods of riches and honors by saying that, just as in relation to riches magnificent people avoid being squanderers and cheap, magnanimous people avoid being presumptuous and fainthearted regarding great honors due them.

And just as liberality is the mean of virtue in small matters and actions related to riches that avoids being extravagant and stingy, the person who is morally virtuous regarding small honors is neither ambitious nor lacking in ambition.

Regarding anger, Aristotle says that the person who avoids extremes is even-tempered and mild, not quick-tempered or apathetic.

Regarding virtues related to external speech, Aristotle says that one is truthfulness, while the other is amiability: simply being pleasant and truthful in the way we talk to, and about, other people.

Considered as a mean, the virtue of truthfulness embodied in the behavior of a truthful person avoids the extremes of the: 1) boasting of the boaster; 2) bragging of the braggart; and 3) dissembling of the dissembler as either a harmless pretender or duplicitous person.

And the virtue of amiability embodied in the behavior of the amiable person achieves the mean of being: 1) witty, amusing, in word and deed related to leisure activities while avoiding the extremes of the buffoon and the boor; and 2) legitimately friendly and affable related to serious matters like work and politics while avoiding the obsequiousness of the sycophant and flatterer who act as counterfeit friends for their own benefit and the contentious person who is inclined not to be able to get along with anyone.

Finally, Aristotle talks about some praiseworthy passions related to external actions in which the mean is: 1) moderation related to extremes of being bashful and shameless in personal relations and that of 2) righteous indignation of the reasonable person who is grieved by the prosperity of the wicked and avoids the extremes of the envious person who grieves over everyone else who prospers and the devilish person who rejoices over the success of the wicked.[9]

An Introduction to Ragamuffin Ethics

10. Opposition among virtues and vices

Having completed his examination of virtues related to external goods concerned with riches and honors, St. Thomas next examines Aristotle's consideration of opposition among virtues and vices.

To begin this study, St. Thomas maintains that Aristotle does three things. He shows that: 1) a twofold opposition exists between vices to each other and of both vices to a mean; 2) the opposition of vices to each other is greater, stronger, than their opposition to the mean; and 3) one of the extremes is more strongly opposed than the other to the virtuous mean.

In saying that virtue opposes both extremes, St. Thomas maintains that Aristotle is indicating that, to some extent, the mean partakes of both extremes. Moreover, precisely as it partakes of one extreme, it is contrary to the other. For this reason, he says that a motion exists against the mean as against a contrary. And, as Aristotle observes, to persons of both extremes, the virtuous person appears extreme in the contrary direction (for example, to a coward, the brave man appears rash).

For two reasons, St. Thomas maintains Aristotle shows that vices are more greatly opposed to each other than to the mean: 1) because opposition is a kind of distance, the more distant two things are from each other, the more opposed they are; and 2) because complete dissimilarity exists among two vices, but moderate similarity exists between the mean and its vice.

For two reasons, St. Thomas claims Aristotle says one extreme is more opposed to virtue than the other: 1) Sometimes the more opposed is the excessive or the defective (for example, cowardice is more opposed to courage than is rashness; and self-indulgence, not insensibility, is more opposed to temperance). 2) These extremes relate to virtues essentially involving individual passion, not to virtues related to interpersonal actions and relations. Such virtues

244

preserve the good of reason against extremes of passion especially against concupiscence; and they chiefly aim at restraining, resisting, acting with excess. In this respect, excess resembles virtue (strength); and the weaker extreme is like fear, which tends to withdraw.

Finally, regarding the opposition among virtues and vices, St. Thomas states that the chief aim of virtue is to restrain those vices toward which we have a stronger inclination. He asserts that those vices that are somewhat innate to us are more opposed to virtue than are vices not so strongly innate to us. Most innate in us, he says, is the inclination in us inordinately to pursue, not flee, from pleasures. Hence, the moral vices of self-indulgence, intemperance, tend to be stronger than any other moral vices.[10]

11. Aristotle's teaching about how to become morally virtuous

Before considering Aristotle's teaching about how to become morally virtuous, St. Thomas reviews some things Aristotle says about moral virtue, namely that it is a mean: 1) relative to us (a virtual quantum mean, virtual quantity); 2) between two vices: one of excess, the other of defect; and 3) that aims at choosing a mean in passions and actions.

Because finding the mean is difficult, while deviating from the mean is easy, Aristotle states that becoming virtuous is difficult. To help alleviate this difficulty somewhat, he: 1) shows us how we can discover the mean in general and 2) gives us three points of advice that we can use to assist in determining the mean in the individual situation.

Regarding how to discover the mean in general, Aristotle tells us to: 1) strive to avoid the extreme more opposed to virtue, the greater vice; 2) know the vices to which we are more inclined, recognizing that we are vehemently inclined toward actions that give us the greatest pleasure and actions toward which we tend naturally to be inclined; 3) draw ourselves to the opposite vice, extreme (like straightening a sapling); and 4) keep ourselves on guard regarding pleasures.

Lastly, regarding Aristotle's final three points of advice about determining the mean in the individual situation, he says: 1) Recognize that determining the mean in the individual situation is difficult. 2) Do not deviate much from the mean, if we deviate at all. And 3) recognize, as St. Thomas more precisely than Aristotle articulates the point, that judgment about how much deviation is permissible (*moral verification*) *needs to look to cogitative reason and prudence, which terminate their judgment in cogitative reason, or the estimative sense* of human beings![11]

—Notes—

1. St. Thomas Aquinas, *Commentary on the Nicomachean Ethics of Aristotle*, Bk. 2, Lects. 1–2, nn. 245–264.
2. Id., Lect. 3, nn. 265–279.
3. Id., Lect. 4, nn. 280–288.
4. Id., Lect. 5, nn. 289–305.
5. Id., Lect. 6, nn. 306–318.
6. Id., Lect. 7, nn. 319–332.
7. Id., Lect. 8, nn. 333–344.
8. Id., Lect. 9, nn. 345–357.
9. Id.
10. Id., Lect. 10, nn. 358–368.
11. Id., Lect. 11, nn. 369–381.

–Chapter Nine–

Voluntariness, Choice, and Willing as Intrinsic Principles of Moral Activity

AFTER FINISHING his consideration in Book 2 of his *Nicomachean Ethics* of moral virtue in its essence as a habit and mean related to passions and actions, pleasure as a sign of moral virtue, and how to become morally virtuous, Aristotle starts to talk about intrinsic principles of moral activity other than habits and related matters: chiefly regarding: 1) voluntariness and involuntariness as related to moral virtue, 2) choice, and 3) willing. Within the context of my current study, I will repeat some things St. Thomas has said about these topics in his *Summa theologiae*.

1. Voluntary and involuntary activity considered in general and in relation to praise, blame, reward, punishment, and moral virtue and vice

St. Thomas starts his examination of Aristotle's Book 3 of his *Nicomachean Ethics* by doing three things: 1) noting that, because moral virtue works by means of choice, Aristotle defines it as a habit of right choice; 2) stating that Aristotle discusses choice together with voluntary activity and willing; and 3) claiming that the voluntary is common to choice, willing, and anything freely done; choice concerns means related to an end; and willing concerns the end.

Shortly after making these observations, St. Thomas states that Aristotle's prior discussion of moral virtue indicates that, in matters of actions and passions that concern ethics: 1) praise is due anyone acting virtuously; 2) blame is due anyone acting viciously; 3) no praise is due virtuous acts involuntarily done; and 4) no blame, but pardon, befits vicious acts involuntarily done.

He adds that, sometimes, Aristotle says more than pardon, pity, is due and total exoneration of blame for a wrong choice. According to St. Thomas, the difference between pardon and pity consists in this: pardon results from a judgment of reason that involves lessening, or totally canceling, punishment and blame, while pity results from a passion (sadness).

He states that acts of moral virtue and vice especially merit, and are diversified by, praise and blame, which, in turn, are diversified by the voluntary and the involuntary. Hence, *he maintains that people who want to study moral virtue and vice need to study voluntary and involuntary acts. And, they need to do so first, externally, from their effects: from the praise and blame, reward, and punishment that their actions and choices publicly receive!*

Regarding the nature of first principles of understanding as first principles of right reason, the immediately-preceding statements St. Thomas makes are crucial to understand. They indicate that Aristotle's method of investigation throughout his *Nicomachean Ethics* repeatedly starts with negative reasoning, the way of remotion (*remotio*), *demonstratio quia* (from effect to cause), to: 1) establish the existence and nature of his subject (moral activity) and all its principles and 2) achieve the proper starting point for practical reason—*a sound* per aliud notum *induction of a moral first principle derived from practical experience at living!*

The readily-observable fact that, within all social communities, we human beings incline publicly to praise and blame, reward and punish, human beings for choices we make indicates to Aristotle and St. Thomas the sound moral induction of a moral first principle: that we human beings possess internal faculties, powers, that enable us to exercise free choice (faculties of voluntariness, willing, and choice). The effect (praise and blame, reward and punishment) acts as an external sign that *human beings universally incline to take for granted, consider as an evident inductive truth, the existence of internal human faculties of voluntariness (first principles) that generate free human activity and make us responsible moral agents.* Consequently, Aristotle maintains that legislators, especially, should find study of voluntary and involuntary acts (that is, proximate principles of moral activity) especially useful for determining honors and rewards for the law-abiding and punishment for lawbreakers.[1]

2. Involuntary and voluntary acts

According to St. Thomas, because its causes are fewer and easier to understand, using his standard pedagogical method of reasoning from the better known to the less well known, as a good teacher, because it is easier to comprehend, Aristotle studies involuntary activity first (its causes being ignorance or violence and easy to understand) and voluntary activity second (its causes being knowledge, many, and more difficult to understand).

Then, St. Thomas maintains, Aristotle achieves his explanation of the nature of involuntary activity in three stages. He: 1) divides the involuntary into two species (by violence and ignorance); 2) examines the first division; and 3) after so doing, proceeds to examine the second division.

Since voluntariness is caused by cognition via sense or reason of *an apparent* good, and because the appetites of passion and will cause cognition of an apparent good, St. Thomas maintains that involuntariness can be caused by: 1) exclusion of the appetite (will or passion), violence, or 2) cognition (sense or intellectual reason) due to ignorance.

Next, he divides the involuntariness that violence causes (morally-forced actions) into two species: 1) physical force (which he calls violent *simpliciter*) and 2) actions executed out of fear (which he calls violent *secundum quid*).

An Introduction to Ragamuffin Ethics

According to St. Thomas, Aristotle: 1) considers violence to neutralize, destroy, appetitive participation in a choice and action; 2) maintains that violence must always be caused by an exterior principle because the essence of a violent act is that an interior appetite resist it; 3) claims that not every action caused by an exterior principle is violent to a faculty; and 4) holds that a violent activity results from an exterior principle acting *contrary to the natural direction in which the appetitive faculty is inclined to move* (that is, contrary to the natural end that it naturally inclines to pursue).

Regarding involuntary acts done out of fear, in his *Summa theologiae* that we considered, St. Thomas referred to these as acts of "mixed-voluntariness." In his *Nicomachean Ethics*, Aristotle refers them in the same way. Like St. Thomas, regarding the case of sailors who throw merchandise overboard to save the ship at risk, Aristotle states that (absolutely considered, considered in general), such an act is more voluntary than involuntary. At the time, when it was committed in the individual circumstance it was voluntary. The reason for this is that the nature of a choice is fully achieved, completed, made whole in the individual act. Before that, it does not completely exist.

In moral activity, the numerically-one, individual act of executing free choice in the individual situation functions as a chief, causal principle (aim) of universal relation to the many acts of intention, deliberation, consent, and prudence or imprudence that precede it. What Aristotle calls "the ultimate particular" (this individually-chosen act), is the numerically-*one* act that these *many* preceding acts cooperated to cause: the last act, the end (like the many different kinds of acts a builder executes are universally caused by the numerically-one house that he finally completes with his last act of nailing in a last piece of trim; or winning the race is the numerically-one act that universally causes, and finally terminates, the whole act of a rowing crew).

Such a composite act is the act of a whole, the corporate, practical universal that generates moral activity (just as it does other kinds of practical activity [like architecture, engineering]) being called "scientific."

According to St. Thomas, among the many voluntary acts that merit praise, blame, reward, punishment, and pardon, Aristotle includes acts of mixed-voluntariness (freely-chosen acts mixed with fear) because he maintains that some people are praised, honored, for suffering evil they do not deserve (including sadness, grief) for the sake of preserving a greater good, including virtue. Indeed, some actions done out of fear are done precisely because the evils feared tend to be beyond human endurance (like lying to avoid being burned alive). And some actions people take they take to avoid doing evils of such a great magnitude that no magnitude of force should be able to compel our doing them.

In contrast to people who make an effort to avoid involuntarily choosing an evil, Aristotle observes that people who suffer evil to preserve no greater good tend to be criticized because their disordered, psychologically unhealthy, desire prefers lesser to greater goods that are destroyed by greater evils.

Regarding precisely what acts merit praise and blame, reward, punishment, and pardon, Aristotle maintains that, at times, in the concrete situation, judging what should be chosen to avoid an evil, to be endured so as not to be deprived of a greater good, is difficult. In such a situation, this is chiefly a judgment call of reason. Prudent judgment must be the referee.

Even more difficult than judging what should be chosen to avoid as evil and to be endured so as not to be deprived of a greater good, he says, is to remain passionately steadfast in a decision involving mixed-voluntariness. Doing so takes courage because, at times, the choice to avoid evil involves suffering disgraceful, sometimes blameworthy, indignity. The choice to endure such a situation merits praise.

An Introduction to Ragamuffin Ethics

In sum, about such acts, St. Thomas claims that Aristotle says chiefly three things: 1) Absolutely considered, violent acts are acts to which a person contributes nothing as an intrinsic appetitive principle. Their cause is totally extrinsic. At most, they serve as an incidental, instrumental cause violently wielded by an extrinsic agent. 2) By reason of some circumstances at some time, violently-influenced acts are somewhat voluntary because, in these circumstances, the human appetites somewhat consent to choose them. 3) Determining the act we should choose in such a circumstance is difficult because, among other reasons, singular acts present us with many differences in options. Judgment about them cannot involve an exact rule. *It has to be left* (*like the leaden, flexible, rule of a mason*) *to the judgment of the prudent man.*

While Aristotle and St. Thomas do not say so precisely in this part of their work, the reason for using such a flexible rule is clear: *because such a situation essentially involves using a rule capable of measuring the proportion of intensive quantity possession of the power* (qualitative greatness of power) *existing relationally between the nature of the agent and the nature of the act being considered in the individual situation. People who deny the existence of natures in things cannot make prudent choices according to any fixed habit or rule because they have no rationally-determinable rule to measure, determine, free, responsible, agency within an individual situation. They have no healthy principle of estimative sense* by means of which impartially to measure, judge, the magnitude of power (ability to act) the individual person possesses at an individual moment in time within an individual situation relative to the magnitude of danger and difficulty he or she faces relative to the magnitude of power possessed by the nature of the thing he or she confronts. As a result, *nothing exists within the choice and action of the agent that can possibly be recognized by such people lacking in principles of moral induction to judge as really honorable, praiseworthy, or blameworthy!*

Peter A. Redpath

For five reasons, St. Thomas maintains Aristotle rejects the claim made by some philosophers that, because reason is man's specific difference, only acts performed in agreement with the determination of reason are voluntary. When, because of some pleasure, act of greed, or external good, a person acts contrary to reason, these philosophers falsely maintain that he acts involuntarily. They falsely maintain, further, that, simply by being external, pleasurable, external goods like riches violently compel a person to act against his reason.

St. Thomas summarizes Aristotle's five reasons as follows: 1) If, precisely as they are pleasurable and apparently good, objects of choice cause violence, no human action would be voluntary; all human choice would be violent. 2) Everyone who performs acts as a result of violence acts involuntarily, with sadness. But people who act to acquire something good do so with pleasure, not sadness, and not involuntarily or by violence. 3) For people to attempt to excuse moral blame for yielding to pleasure of external goods is ridiculous. It denies the power of individual moral freedom. Only what possesses the nature of a universal and perfect good compels human nature to desire it. Choice is always of the apparent, imperfect, good. 4) For a person to call himself the cause of his virtuous acts, but not the cause of his vicious acts because they induce desire, is ridiculous. Virtuous and vicious acts are contraries, and contraries are caused by the same principle (in this case, appetitive reason). Such a claim makes a person free only to cause good. Finally, 5) although the principle inclining the human will to pursue or avoid a perceived good is external, the principle to consent and choose is internal; and the final decision is the proximate, internal, determining cause.

Regarding involuntary acts resulting from ignorance, as St. Thomas does in his *Summa theologiae*, in his *Nicomachean Ethics*, Aristotle distinguishes three kinds of moral ignorance: 1) voluntary,

2) involuntary and 3) non-voluntary. And he notes that, in different ways, all three acts get the names by being related to the human will.

Aristotle and St. Thomas refer to: 1) involuntary acts of ignorance as acts of ignorance the will opposes as unknown; 2) non-voluntary acts of ignorance as acts of ignorance as unknown, but not necessarily unwilled (disagreeable to the will); and 3) voluntary act of ignorance as will-caused of known ignorance (willful ignorance).

Remarking about involuntary acts of ignorance, Aristotle claims that, emotionally, such acts tend to sadden a person, a person tends to take no pleasure in doing them, finds them painful; and, after the fact, a person repents choosing them, and would be inclined to change them if they could be changed.

Regarding acts of ignorance considered in general, he says that they essentially differ from acting *out of* ignorance (acts that ignorance partly causes, generates); and acting *in* ignorance (an act in which ignorance is conjoined to the act), such as tends to be the case with someone whose acton is generated by anger or by the vice of intemperance. Such a person acts unknowingly in some respect about the personal damage the action does or might cause. This ignorance happens simultaneously with the act, is conjoined to it, but does not cause it. Such a person acts *with* ignorance, not *out of*, or *because of*, ignorance.

Similarly, Aristotle and St. Thomas maintain that *every vicious person acts partly in ignorance of the real good he should do and the evil he should avoid at this moment in this situation.* By repeatedly acting in ignorance of the real good to be done, the intemperate/ angry person increasingly becomes like the voluntarily-wicked person, increasingly: 1) becomes unjust toward others, wicked; 2) acts voluntarily; and, while Aristotle and St. Thomas do not expressly say so at this point in the discussion, 3) loses touch with reality.

In addition to voluntary, involuntary, and non-voluntary

ignorance, Aristotle adds *negligent ignorance* as a kind of voluntary ignorance: a privative kind of ignorance of what a person ought to know in the individual circumstance, such as the sort of ignorance a person claiming to be a professional in some enterprise would claim to have. Hence, this is a sort of ignorance people do not tend to expect from "professionals": ignorance of what is suitable for professionals, what they should know, under the circumstances.

In two ways, Aristotle claims a person can be ignorant of what is suitable, proportionate, under the circumstances: 1) out of voluntary ignorance related to a particular choice (whether to fornicate now), or to a general choice (whether to fornicate ever); and 2) out of involuntary ignorance of singular circumstances under which an act is executed.

Regarding the circumstances of an act, while, strictly speaking, these are eight in number (who, does what, about what [to whom or what], with what, where, why, when, and how), the way Aristotle lists them in Book 3 of his *Nicomachean Ethics* can give the mistaken impression that only six are involved: 1) who is acting (the chief agent); 2) what is the agent doing (the genus of the act); 3) concerning what or whom/this (the object in relation to which the agent acts and the time and/or place in which the agent acts); 4) with the help of what; 5) for what end; and 6) in what way. Aristotle claims that only an insane person could be totally ignorant of all these circumstances.

According to St. Thomas, Aristotle defines the cause he calls "voluntary" by "removal" of the causes of an act being involuntary: 1) violence, physical or psychological compulsion and 2) ignorance. Since physical and psychological compulsion and ignorance cause involuntary acts, a voluntary act appears to be what an agent causes (considered as such, such an act excludes violence) in such a way that the agent knows the individual circumstances that concur with the act (considered as such, this excludes ignorance).

In addition, St. Thomas claims that, for five reasons, Aristotle rejects the assertion that not everything an agent originates through knowledge of circumstances is voluntary because sometimes the passions, not the will, chiefly cause human act. 1) St. Thomas says Aristotle's first and chief reason for rejecting this assertion is that an action is voluntary because the agent causes it according to the agent's natural inclination to act. It is not because the will is its proximate cause. The passions can be the chief cause, especially when they have the natural inclination to take direction from, to listen to, reason, but refuse to do so. If this were not true, Aristotle maintains that young children and non-rational animals could not perform voluntary acts ("voluntary acts" being here analogously predicated by Aristotle of non-rational animals). 2) If evil actions done as a result of anger and intemperance are voluntary, so should be good actions caused by passion. But, Aristotle says that, since the human will is the chief cause of morally good and evil acts, emotionally-influenced human actions cannot come to be in act without consent of the will. And, at times, reason incites passion to seek a good we should seek and evils we should avoid. Acts executed under such emotional influence are voluntary. 3) Aristotle repeats that sadness, pain, accompanies actions we do involuntarily under the imposition of violence, while the emotion of pleasure accompanies actions we do voluntarily. 4) Whether successful or unsuccessful, we tend to condemn voluntary moral mistakes, but not involuntary acts. And 5) since the human passions are naturally inclined to obey reason, actions that proceed from them are voluntary.[2]

3. Choice, voluntary activity, the passions, wishing, and opinion

After examining voluntary and involuntary acts, Aristotle examines the nature of choice. Among other reasons, he says he does so because: 1) choice appears especially proper to moral virtue, which is of chief concern for ethics; 2) while the habit of moral virtue generates a choice and outward action, we chiefly judge virtue and vice by inner choice; and 3) good reason exists to use inner choice as the measure of moral virtue and vice because, sometimes out of fear, a vicious person performs a virtuous act.

In several ways, Aristotle proves that choice is a species of the genus of voluntary activity. Like all genera, he says voluntariness is universally predicated of choice. While every choice is voluntary, in the following way, he proves that not every voluntary act is a choice. Children and irrational animals do, and suffer, things voluntarily because both lack the ability to deliberate, neither uses choice as part of voluntary action. Whatever we cause through a cognitive appetite, principle, within us, without resistance and with receptivity, he maintains, we do voluntarily, even if without deliberation.

Beyond the preceding comments, on the basis of the fact that, to be identical, no difference or opposition can exist between two things, Aristotle claims that choice cannot be identical with: 1) sensual desire or any passion of the concupiscible or irascible appetite; 2) any act involving reasoning such as deliberation or wishing; or 3) opinion.

Because all such acts contain principles of human cognition, Aristotle states that some people have been inclined to reduce choice to one or more, or a combination, of them. Nonetheless, Aristotle refutes the claim that choice consists in any human passion because: 1) some brute animals experience irascible and concupiscible passions like pleasure and pain, anger and fear; 2) *choice, which requires deliberation (involves abstract consideration absent emotional involvement) exists in no brute animals*; 3) while sensual desire, not rightly-reasoned choice, proximately causes acts of the incontinent man, the continent man acts from right choice and contrary to sensual desire; 4) sensual desires are contrary to choice in incontinent and continent people (the continent person chooses according to reason what the incontinent person chooses according to concupiscence and contrary to reason; sensual desire opposes choice in the continent person, while it agrees with choice in the incontinent person); 5) that choice and anger are not identical is easier to prove because anger tends to shut down deliberation and inclines to generate sudden actions (the angry person does not incline to wait for perfect direction by reason); and 6) concupiscence acts less suddenly and more closely resembles choice.

Next, Aristotle maintains that choice cannot be identical with wishing because, while both are acts of the will: 1) choice essentially involves a voluntary act ordered to a means, while wishing relates to any and all good, and to an end and a means; 2) choice is essentially related to generating action, doing something actual, which precludes the impossible, while wishing can be directed toward the impossible; 3) wishing can be concerned with an action someone else causes, while choosing only relates to what a person thinks he or she can do; and 4) all the above differences chiefly refer to the fact that choice is directed toward acts *within our power* to cause.

After showing that choice is not any appetitive activity, not an act of the irascible appetite, the concupiscible appetite, or of the human will (such as wishing), next, Aristotle shows that choice is not opinion considered in general or in particular.

First, he maintains that choice cannot be opinion considered in general because: 1) Opinion can be about everything, impossible things, things lying within our power, and external things; while choice only concerns actions within our power. 2) What is divided by different contraries cannot be the same. Opinion is chiefly an act of the knowing faculty divided by contraries of true and false, while choice is chiefly an act of the appetitive faculty divided by contraries of good and bad.

To this first argument, Aristotle adds five reasons why opinion and choice cannot be identical:

1) We are judged morally good and bad according to our actions, not according to our opinions.

2) Good will, not natural or acquired ability, having a good intellect, or right opinion, chiefly causes a person to use well natural or acquired ability. Hence, Aristotle says that a habit is a quality by which a person acts well when he wishes.

3) Good will causes a person to act well according to every capability, every habit obedient to reason.

4) We call a person "good," "morally good," and "absolutely good" simply for having a good will; while, from the fact that he has a good intellect, we call a person "relatively good." Chiefly, the will causes choice, while the intellect causes opinion. Choice chiefly concerns actions, not things, while opinion chiefly concerns things, not actions; and knowledge, opinion, about our actions is not sought chiefly for truth. It is sought chiefly for the purpose of action, to do good or evil. *The good of choice consists in rightness of the appetitive faculty ordering and action toward an end!*

When Aristotle maintains that we praise choice because it chooses what it ought, he means we praise choice because it rightly chooses (chooses in the right way) what it ought: the real good, the real means. We praise opinion for being true about something, while we praise choice for rightly directing action. The perfection of opinion is truth, right judgment, while the perfection of choice is right direction of action. Because things that have different perfections are different, opinion and choice a different. Choice is accompanied by certainty because we choose especially what we know to be good, what we know we like more, while opinion is accompanied by uncertainty because we have opinions regarding things about which we admit our knowledge might be false. If opinion and choice were identical, people who make the best choices and people who have true opinions about the best choices would be identical; but, the contrary is true:

sometimes, because they have a bad will, people who have a right opinion about a better choice of action, knowingly, willingly, choose the worse action.

5) Since it is not an irascible or concupiscible passion, wishing, or opinion, Aristotle defines choice in terms of its genus as voluntary (not every voluntary act being deliberately intended) and in its specific difference as deliberately intended (because counsel, an act of reason, precedes choice).[3]

4. Counsel, its order and method, and how it compares and contrasts with choice

After determining the difference between choice and opinion, Aristotle next considers counsel, which, in nature, precedes choice. According to St. Thomas, he starts his study by determining counsel's formal object, by asking whether we should take counsel about matters about which *the Many* (including fools and the insane) or *the Prudent* and *the Wise* take counsel (deliberate).

Next, by considering the matters about which *we do not take counsel*, reasoning negatively (from effect to cause) by means of a *demonstratio quia*, Aristotle maintains that we *do not* take counsel about: 1) eternal things (things that do not change); 2) unimportant matters; 3) necessary things: things that can be in only one way; 4) chance events; 5) things that cannot be affected by our forethought or action; and 6) everything.

After doing this, Aristotle says that four species of cause can generate things: 1) nature, 2) necessity, 3) fortune (luck), and 4) the human intellect. He claims that the first three are irrelevant to counsel. And, while the human intellect is different in all human beings in degree of power and ability (intensive quantum greatness, quality of power and ability), each person takes counsel about practical matters, deeds *doable* by him.

Regarding how counsel occurs related to human arts, he asserts that, where the method of proceeding in an art tends to be universally known and fixed (like in grammar), counsel rarely happens. The chief reason for this is because we only deliberate about *doubtful* matters, matters about which some doubts can exist.

In doubtful matters he maintains we deliberate about *our abilities* and other issues that can affect performance, getting job done. In other words, even though Aristotle and St. Thomas do not make explicit note of this fact at this point in their discussion, deliberation, counsel, *always essentially involves work of the estimative sense*! Hence, people who are unaware of, or deny the reality of, human nature and an estimative sense faculty (particular, or cogitative, reason), cannot possibly comprehend the nature of counsel, deliberation!

Continuing with Aristotle's, examination, he asserts that we deliberate more about some doubtful matters than about others: matters more crucial to us, which can limit our abilities to act. For example: 1) the medical doctor deliberates more about a patient's health and strength; 2) the businessman deliberates more about supply and demand, needs and wants, time available to get a job done; 3) a sailor deliberates more about weather than about some other matters; and 4) an athletic coach deliberates about other matters specific to the abilities of athletes. Crucial to note is that all deliberation relates, in some way, to intensive quantum greatness (quality of faculties, powers) and knowing abilities essentially involving the estimative sense relative to individual circumstances of action.

Moreover, Aristotle observes that we tend to deliberate more about artistic activities and practical and productive sciences (how to put something together) and less about speculative/observational sciences (how something is put together).

Then, he states that matters about which we take counsel involve essentially three qualities relative to the subjects about which we deliberate: 1) the time, frequency, of occurrence (how often they tend to occur); 2) the greater or less extent of their unsettled nature (to what extent a more or less fixed rule exists about how to handle them); and 3) how crucial they are to the individuals taking counsel.

Having finished discussing the nature of the subjects about which we take counsel, Aristotle next considers the method, order, of taking counsel. Likely, today, many of us would refer to this method as "the steps," "priorities," or "plan" involved in taking counsel.

Taking his lead from Aristotle, St. Thomas starts his commentary on Aristotle's discussion about this topic by: 1) defining counsel as "a practical deliberation about things to be done"; and 2) saying that, just as in speculative science, where we assume principles from which we seek, reason to, conclusions, so *in practical science we assume ends and seek, reason to, means*! That is, we reason negatively from effect to cause via a *demonstratio quia*.

To clarify his claim St. Thomas refers to four examples that Aristotle gives of people who take counsel, *and what they do not do*: 1) The medical doctor *does not* deliberate about whether to heal a patient. 2) The orator *does not* deliberate about whether he should persuade people. 3) A statesman *does not* deliberate about whether to achieve peace. And 4) nobody who engages in practical action deliberates about whether to pursue an end. In practical matters, the end is a first principle.

Taking for granted that a numerically-one, *last act* (a singular extreme, or ultimate singular), final act of completion, is a first principle of practical investigation, St. Thomas notes three points about the order and method (steps) to be taken related to acts involving deliberation. People who deliberate tend to ask the following questions in the following order: 1) How, by what motion, action, can we attain the end? 2) What means must we use to execute this motion, action? 3) When we can attain an end using several actions and instruments, by which of these can we, in a better way, more easily achieve the goal?

If only one means (action and/or instrument) exists to achieve the end, the prudent counselor concludes that need exists to persevere and use care related to this action, means, and/or instrument. If this means should not be readily at hand, this person concludes that need exists to investigate how to get it *so as to be able to use* it to achieve the desired end.

Just as in geometry, St. Thomas maintains practical investigations proceed analytically (by breaking wholes down into their essential parts and reducing conclusions to first principles). Consequently, counsel is a kind of inquiry, process of discovery, that seeks to get to the first principles of operation because the last in analysis is the first in productive activity.

As a prime example of the analytical reason related to counsel, St. Thomas talks about *the moral psychology of prudent business leaders, about how business professionals tend to think and how hope of success tends to guide their reasoning from start to finish.* He states that, in the point of deliberation where they have to execute *a first action*: 1) If they find the desired end impossible to achieve (for example, due to lack of money), they immediately give up. 2) If they find the action doable, they immediately start it. 3) If, after starting, they discover they need the help of others, they count the number of friends they have with the qualifications to help. 4) If, in addition to friends, they find they need tools, they ask how can they can get these tools, who/where is the supplier? 5) If they discover they can acquire these tools, they ask, "Do we know how to use them?" 6) If they do not know how to use the tools, they ask, "Can we get help from others who do?" 7) If so, they inquire, "Where are these people, and how can they get their help?"

To put what St. Thomas says in more contemporary business language, good, prudent, counsel proceeds by asking these questions in this order: 1) Is this action something we need to do? 2) Do we need to do it now? 3) Are be able to do it by ourselves? 4) If not, do we know a friend, or some professional we can trust, who can do it for us? 5) If we are able to do it ourselves, can we do so easily, without outside help and/or resources? 6) If we need outside resources, what friends with right qualifications, or professionals we can trust, can we find to supply these resources? 7) What are the best resources available? 8) Do these resources include people and tools? 9) If so, where can we get these? 10) If we can find them, will they be readily/easily available to us? 11) If so, how quickly can we get them? 12) Once we get them, will we need special training to use them? 13) If so, do we have the internal resources/money available to secure the training? 14) If not, can we, should we, try to secure financing to do so?

After having determined in precise detail the kind of analytical questions that a prudent counselor intends to ask, St. Thomas indicates three generic considerations that Aristotle determines to be the universal, intensive quantum, or qualitative, limits of all real counsel: 1) Every individual takes counsel about actions *doable by him or her* toward an end. 2) A limit exists in the number of means counsel can consider; it cannot be of the infinite. And 3) inquiry about means must be limited to means essential to the activity at hand.

After having considered the three, generic, qualitative limits that Aristotle maintains exist related to every real act of counsel, to make even more evident the precise nature of counsel, he next makes a final comparison between counsel and choice. Counsel, he says, inquiries about possible means to choose, while choice ends that inquiry /deliberation, and, if several means exist, starts the process of prioritizing among them. By example, he says that the ancient Greeks considered kings to be *guides* to the people whose vote determined their choice.

Aristotle concludes his comparison of choice and counsel by defining choice in a general way, without giving a detailed explanation. He says choice is: 1) a desire arising by means of counsel for things in our power; 2) a deliberating desire inasmuch as, through counsel, a man arrives at a judgment regarding the things that had been discovered by means of counsel.[4]

5. The formal object of willing: Real, or apparent, good?

Having finished discussing the nature of counsel, Aristotle turns his attention to the question of whether the formal object of the will is real, or apparent, good.

In answer to that question, St. Thomas says that the human will is a faculty, and regarding any faculty, we name the facultative act from the faculty *in relation to* that toward which it chiefly, and of itself, tends: that is, the chief end, stimulus, formal object, that activates it.

Regarding willing he says that disagreement exists about whether the act's formal object is a real or apparent good. Those who regard real good as the formal object of willing sometimes falsely claim that a person who will's real good as a formal object does not will when choosing badly and acquiring real evil.

In reply to that false claim, St. Thomas says Aristotle refutes it by stating that, in fact, sometimes what the will wills is not a real good. Moreover, knowingly or not to them, their false claim maintains that no generic object, external stimulus, is identical for the faculty of will that exists in all human beings. He maintains that, knowingly or not to them, this false claim is analogous to asserting that no generic object, external stimulus, is identical for the faculty of sight in all human beings: that apparent, not real, color is the formal, natural object of sight.

Hence, if this claim were true, just as the faculty of sight would have nothing visible as its formal object, so the faculty of will would have nothing naturally lovable as its formal object. Because every natural faculty has some determinate, definite, formal object, external stimulus, evidently this claim is false.

St. Thomas maintains that Aristotle resolves this disagreement by saying that, for the really good (prudent) man, the real good and the apparent good (what pleases) are identical. For the vicious man, these are not identical because the vicious man considers all good to be apparent, considers pleasure to be the only good.

Right *estimation* of real good is a right estimation of qualitative perfection existing within facultatively-independent, existing organizational wholes, a perfection that does not depend upon the vicious man's sense of pleasure. His experience of pleasure does not make the internal relations that perfect real wholes, that cooperate within the parts of a whole to harmonize in such a way as to generate a perfect whole, what they are. The pleasant harmony that a spectator experiences of the crew team that makes it a perfectly-harmonized, organizational whole (a winning team) is a real good existing within the real relations of the real parts of the members of the crew team. It does not depend for its existence on its being experienced as good by either the prudent or the imprudent man, or some other spectator.

Nonetheless, because the estimative faculty of the prudent man exists in a healthy condition, inclines to be in touch with reality, while the estimative faculty of the vicious, imprudent, man naturally inclines not to be in touch with reality, just as a person whose sense of taste is physically ill, or whose sense of sight is color-blind, is no sound judge of the way in which what exists should appear to a sense faculty of taste of sight, so the estimative sense of an imprudent man is no sound judge of healthy and unhealthy, really good and really bad, pleasures.

According to Aristotle, right estimation of real good is a right estimation of qualitative goodness relative to the agent. Such estimation is a unique quality, virtue, of the prudent human being. Just as the person with healthy organs is the measure of healthy body temperature, so the prudent man is the measure of real good (*of right, proportionate, relation* between his facultative power of choice and the end to be achieved relative to the means to be chosen by him in the individual situation). Hence, the prudent man rightly judges about individual means that lead to really good ends in the individual circumstance. And the imprudent man does not. According to Aristotle, while vicious, imprudent, people follow a badly-educated, unhealthy estimative sense (particular reason) and concupiscible appetite in attempting rightly to relate real means to real ends in the individual situation, morally virtuous, prudent, people do the contrary opposite.[5]

6. Why behaving morally virtuously and viciously must be within our power

Having discussed voluntary activity, choice, counsel, as principles of human acts, Aristotle next discusses virtue and vice as principles of moral activity. According to St. Thomas, Aristotle starts to do so by demonstrating that moral virtue must be within our power because: 1) The formal object of virtue consists in real means to a real end; and real means are possibilities, not impossibilities. 2) Virtue and vice, the power to act/not act, to act well/or badly, belong to the same faculty: the voluntary. 3) Affirmation/negation, receptivity/ resistance, belong to the same genus. If the operation is within us, so is the habit which is its principle.

Next, Aristotle refutes the claim made by some that no person is voluntarily (willingly) evil or involuntarily (unwillingly) good because, by nature, the will tends toward the good. All human beings naturally seek the good and avoid evil. No one seriously doubts that a man is the cause of his actions just a father is a principle of children. If counsel, choice, willing are principles of our actions, Aristotle maintains we are principles of our good and bad actions. Because the principles of good and bad actions are in our power, the actions are in our power.

He states that the way private individuals behave in their everyday lives supports his argument. For example, fathers tend to punish children and servants who misbehave and reward those who behave. Lawmakers legislate punishments of different severity and greatness, and different honors, to encourage virtue and restrain vice within different kinds of political orders. Because encouragement before doing an act is useless regarding impossible acts, no one tends to encourage a person to do things not in his or her power (like not to be hot during the summer) and to do actions that are not voluntary.

Special note should be taken that Aristotle's arguments about restraint and encouragement just given relate to acts that we recognize to be within our power, our abilities, acts that are essentially related to a faculty psychology and the faculty of estimative sense (cogitative, or particular, reason).

Further, related to acts within our power, Aristotle maintains that, while ignorance causes an act to be involuntary, in some way not within our power, it does not do so when the ignorance is willed to excuse moral responsibility. Also not excused is ignorance of right behavior due to negligence in right education: a vice that leads to loss of ability to reason well (like the contemporary plague of drug addiction).

Having refuted the false claim that no human being is ever voluntarily evil, St. Thomas starts to refute this assertion by addressing a false claim that not everyone is naturally able to be diligent about acquiring good habits of soul. According to this false argument, by nature, some people have a negligent disposition that prevents them from developing virtuous habits; by nature, some people take pleasure in pursuing and doing evil.

In reply to this argument, St. Thomas states that a human being can be of a natural disposition in two ways: 1) physically—influenced by qualities of body chemistry, physical environment, and passions; and 2) psychologically—a state chiefly determined by the human intellect and will.

Regarding body chemistry, physical environment, St. Thomas maintains that these can exercise no more persuasive power over the human intellect than do the human passions and external sense faculties, which incline by nature to take direction from human reason.

Regarding influence of habits of the soul (intellect and will) on voluntariness, he states that blameworthy bodily and psychological defects are voluntary. Among other reasons, we know this because we are censured on account of them by ourselves, our conscience, our emotional sense of shame and embarrassment, and by other people. Moreover, moral habits are voluntary with respect to formation and are not easily voluntary after formation.

In addition, evil habits differ as evil actions do, in two ways: 1) They withdraw us from doing good. In this case, we cause our own evil lives because we are not diligent in doing good deeds. We live carelessly and make little to no attempt to do good works. 2) Evil actions incline us to do evil to ourselves through incontinence and intemperance and to others inasmuch as, by our own viciousness, we behave unjustly toward others.

St. Thomas continues that habit formation is natural to human beings. Through it we perfect and strengthen, or weaken, our facultative operations. Evident is that our good or bad acts cause good or bad facultative habits.

St. Thomas makes the same point about habit formation by relating act to a habit as its proximate cause, and saying that, if we will some cause from which we know a particular effect results, we will the effect; at least indirectly because we will that it exists more than we do choosing to refrain from this action. While the effect is not voluntarily willed in and of itself, it is willed as necessarily related to, conjoined with, this action. To will to do unjust, intemperate actions, but not to will to become unjust and intemperate, is irrational according to practical and speculative reason.

He continues that, once formed, evil habits are not easily reversible by acts of will. As an example, he refers to a once-healthy person who, through bad dietary and exercise habits becomes sickly. The principle (facultative habit) by which we become just or incontinent lies within our power. Once executed, that principle cannot quickly and easily repair subsequent damage. Consequently, we tend to reproach people for their vices, not for their birth defects.

Regarding the claim that we have no knowing faculty that knows the good, St. Thomas says Aristotle starts to refute this assertion by maintaining as a fundamental principle that, just as natural desire, or inclination, follows the form naturally generating it, so *animal desire follows perceived form*. To be desired by any animal a subject must be perceived as good. As a result, some people might claim that human beings have no power over the way things appear to us because our imagination can cause them to appear to us other than they are.

In reply, St. Thomas says that, in two ways a thing can appear good to someone. In the first way of appearing good, the judgment about good follows no particular natural inclination. It follows speculative consideration of reason judging about actions, some of which might be good or bad. In the second way of appearing good, a subject may do so in two ways: 1) absolutely (in all respects) in itself is a good in conformity with the nature of the end, a natural need; and 2) not absolutely (in some, not all, respects) we judge according to present psychological reaction to an individual situation.

The appetitive faculty inclines toward an object in two ways: 1) under emotional influence (corresponding to scenario "2" immediately above), which is an inclination according to how something psychologically appears to us in the present situation (for example, to throw goods overboard because the ship is sinking); and 2) by habit, by which we judge a thing really good or bad in light of practical experience (corresponding to scenario "1" above). The claim that human beings have no power over the way things appear to us because our imagination can cause them to appear other than they are is the sort of imaginative reaction that occurs in scenario "2" listed in the paragraph immediately above, not in scenario "1."

In reply, a sophist might claim that: 1) some people are born with the ability to see the real good and take delight in what is really good for us, while others are not; 2) this ability is not teachable; 3) nor is the self-control over the imagination that supposedly can be taught.

In answer to this sophistic argument, in agreement with Aristotle, St. Thomas replies: 1) To some extent, all human beings are born with some natural ability to apprehend the real good and take delight and what is really good for us. 2) *For both virtuous and vicious people, no matter how some individual person perceives it, just like hunger and breathing, perception of the facultative good, end, is innate to the human faculty*! He adds that, if, because we cause the habits by which we incline to move toward our innate end, a natural need, virtues are voluntary so, too, are vices.[6]

7. Courage (Fortitude) and vices that oppose it

Having finished his treatise considering the nature of virtue in general, Aristotle next considers particular virtues, starting with the virtue of the irascible appetite: courage, or fortitude. Before considering virtues related to external goods in Book 4 of the *Nicomachean Ethics*, in Book 3 Aristotle examines two moral virtues essentially related to protecting and preserving human life: temperance and courage (fortitude).

According to St. Thomas, starting with courage, Aristotle defines it considered in general as: 1) a firmness of soul by which the soul remains unmoved by fear of dangers; and 2) a kind of mean between fear and rashness. Strictly speaking, the formal object of courage according to Aristotle and St. Thomas is one (not all) species of fear: *fear of death*, a kind of fear that they maintain is good, not bad, to experience. Indeed, St. Thomas maintains that some species of fear are naturally good to experience, naturally bad not to experience, so as to help us lead a morally good life. As examples, he says that: 1) a person who does not fear evils like loss of respectability/honor is disgraceful/shameless; 2) reasonable fear of poverty, physical illness, and other such avoidable evils (like and personal physical injury to himself or his family) is good, not bad, to experience.

Aristotle maintains, further, that the person who remains *calm* in the face of the most terrifying dangers is unqualifiedly brave. The courageous person does not lose the ability to reason well, *remains calm,* when confronted by terrifying dangers while fighting for a noble cause.

According to him, courage consists in *prudential hope* in a specific kind of death: honorable death for a good cause in battle. This is virtue as the maximum in the faculty of courage.

Regarding courage's formal object, St. Thomas maintains that, generically considered, it is identical with that of fear, but, in some way, is qualitatively greater, greater in intensive quantity.

Describing the psychology of the courageous man, St. Thomas maintains that this person: 1) experiences fear the way a *prudent man* does (prudentially), especially regarding matters concerning evils in the individual circumstance; 2) endures the evils he needs to endure and flees through fear the evils he ought to fear in the right way, at the right time, and in right relation to all the other circumstances involved in the individual situation.

St. Thomas claims that the chief reason that this is the moral psychology of the courageous man is because every moral virtue accords with prudence: right reason about things to be done.

He adds that the proximate, proper, end of every habit is to impress a likeness of that habit on its act. In this way, habits, customs, act like second natures. *While St. Thomas maintains that the remote end of every naturally-operating agent is a perfect good: the good of*

Peter A. Redpath

the created universe, he states that its proximate end is to imprint a kind of likeness of itself on another! Hence, he asserts that the good that the brave man intends is not the habit of courage (which already exists in him), but the likeness of this habit in act.

After considering acts of cowards (the nature of which, as contrary opposites of courage, should be evident and, consequently, a topic we need not examine in this chapter), in five ways, St. Thomas next contrasts real courage with counterfeit courage in relation to three ways an act of courage can fall short of real courage, by: 1) not operating with knowledge; 2) being caused by passion not choice; and 3) being motivated by imprudent choice.

His first three ways of contrasting real and counterfeit courage refer to cases of civic courage in which ordinary citizens undergo dangers chiefly to secure honors from, or avoid punishment by, the State. Since performing an act that attacks danger chiefly for the aim of securing honor is chiefly motivated by the passion of shame, fear of public disgrace, and since the virtue of courage essentially involves doing the right thing precisely because it is right and doing so with an emotional sense of pleasure, not fear, why this first way of behaving is properly identified as counterfeit courage is evident.

Closely resembling this first case is the second scenario in which citizens face dangers for the chief aim of fear of avoiding legal penalties; and the third scenario in which, through use of fear of punishment, political leaders compel/coerce citizens to fight.

Case four involves the courage of soldiers in a particular case in which, because none of us tends to fear doing what we know how to do well, and because, in war, many ways exist to be unarmed, well-trained, but not necessarily courageous, soldiers fight like the armed against the unarmed, until they face a formidable and unfamiliar danger. When this occurs the difference between counterfeit and real courage becomes glaringly evident.

Finally, similar to the case four, but comparing the courage of the citizen to that of the soldier, St. Thomas describes well-trained soldiers who lack real courage easily fighting while they do not apprehend real danger (one that does not exceed their skill; for example an enemy of a small number). From the start of their military careers, soldiers with counterfeit courage expose themselves to dangers because they *estimate* themselves to be more powerful, better-trained and armed than the enemies they face. When, however, they encounter an enemy they *estimate* to be more powerful than they are, they cut and run, fearing death more than dishonor and shame. In contrast, in the same situation, a person who possesses a citizen's counterfeit courage fears disgrace, dishonor, more than death, and consequently refuses to cut and run.

Besides the kinds of wrongly-motivated acts just considered, St. Thomas next examines counterfeit courage motivated by anger. About this, he says that, while an angry man is inclined to attack danger and tends to resemble a courageous person, strength (qualitative, virtual quantum, greatness) of soul, the real good, not anger, chiefly motivates people who are brave. The counterfeit courage of an angry man resembles that of enraged animals. Still, St. Thomas maintains that, because it is motivated by justice, the courage of angry men most closely resembles real courage.

After counterfeit courage motivated by anger, St. Thomas considers bravery motivated by *high hopes*. Since people with little experience and high hopes (like young people, drunkards, and fools) have a weak estimative sense faculty, and, consequently incline, at times, to *over-estimate* their abilities, in attacking dangers, they often appear to resemble courageous people.

In contrast to the emotionally-generated, counterfeit courage of such individuals, St. Thomas maintains that a really brave man (a person with a healthy estimative sense faculty) inclines to react: 1) by habit, not spontaneous passion, especially in situations of extreme danger and unexpected terror in which no passion is so vehement to preclude use of reason; and 2) *with calm*, without need to deliberate.

Finally, the last species of counterfeit courage that St. Thomas examines is that of *inexperienced overconfidence*, the sort of psychological condition found, once again, in people possessed of an unhealthy estimative sense faculty (in people who underestimate the magnitude of the dangers they face relative their personal facultative strengths). St. Thomas maintains that such people are more lacking in courage than people with high hopes because people with high hopes rightly estimate the dangers, but overestimate their abilities. Consequently, people with high hopes tend to fight longer than do people who underestimate the dangers. As a result, people with inexperienced overconfidence tend immediately to flee once they rightly estimate the real magnitude of the danger they face.

Having completed their examination of the difference between counterfeit and real courage, Aristotle and St. Thomas next consider properties of courage related to pleasure and pain.

In so doing, St. Thomas starts by stating that, while courage relates to fear and daring, it does so differently; and that praise of this virtue consists more in praise of the courageous person being undisturbed by terrifying events than in performing a courageous act.

While this second statement that St. Thomas makes might appear strange, he makes it because he claims that standing up to a stronger person is more difficult than facing a person of equal or weaker strength. *The passion of daring, and, with it, the moral virtue of courage, starts in the irascible appetite located within the estimative sense*, with a person's *estimation* that the person he attacks is not too powerful to defeat.

After making this observation, St. Thomas discusses a special relationship between courage and pain; starting this discussion with the observation that fear and pain share a common generic object: evil (pain's generic object being an evil affecting a person in present time and fear's generic evil being one of possible effect in future time). While the brave man stands fast against future dangers, St. Thomas maintains that he continues steadfastly in the midst of these dangers.

Regarding praise of a courageous person, St. Thomas asserts this essentially relates to his stout-heartedly enduring (that is, enduring with qualitative greatness, intensity, even pleasure) painful, harmful, immediately-threatening, dangers. And he observes that we praise virtue considered in general essentially for the same reason: a person endures distressing events; and enduring pain and harm is more difficult than abstaining from pleasure. Consequently, he maintains that courage is more praiseworthy than is temperance.

Related to a special relationship that exists between courage and pleasure, St. Thomas reports that Aristotle talks about this as follows. Since courage exists in enduring distressing events, a brave man appears to take some (a greater) pleasure in attaining the end of attacking danger than does the non-courageous person. While this pleasure appears to be weakly felt at the time a person initially experiences a present grief, like boxers and soldiers, who endure much drudgery and pain to achieve a greater pleasure, the brave man suffers wounds and faces death to attain the pleasure and good of virtue and to avoid the disgrace and pain of the act of cowardice.

At the same time, this fact in no way supports the mistake of some Stoics, which claims that the virtuous man feels no pain. On the contrary, according to St. Thomas, in the following way, Aristotle proves that *very intense* (qualitatively great) pain befalls the virtuous man. He claims that, according to Stoic teaching, virtue (totally unemotional reason) is the only human good. Aristotle disagrees. He maintains that: 1) human beings are naturally inclined to be saddened by the loss of any good; and 2) two circumstances can increase sadness at the loss of any such good: the greatness of the good lost and the injustice involved in the loss. For example, loss of life of the virtuous man is a cause of great sadness. Such an event causes a virtuous man distress. St. Thomas adds that hope of future life makes this death desirable; and the brave man willingly suffers loss of many lesser goods as a result of death to achieve the one greater good of living virtuously.

Next, Aristotle modifies a claim that, previously, he had made about virtuous operations being pleasurable. Regarding courage, he now says this is true only about the end, not about the means. And he adds that nothing prevents men who are less brave (like mercenaries) from being good soldiers.

Finally, he finishes his discussion of courage with a general definition of it as a moral virtue concerned with fear and daring consisting in a mean according to right reason because of the good.[7]

8. Temperance and intemperance

After considering courage, which concerns terrifying evils destructive of human life, Aristotle examines temperance, which concerns pleasurable goods like food, drink, and sex that preserve and protect human life specifically and individually.

According to St. Thomas, Aristotle claims that both courage and temperance agree in being: 1) seated in the sensitive part of the soul that inclines to listen to reason (that is, in particular, or cogitative, reason, the estimative sense); and 2) sense appetites.

As St. Thomas reports, temperance is located in the concupiscible appetite and concerns pleasures of food, drink, and sex. He adds that *natural animal fear of death is a chief reason temperance exists in the sensitive appetite.* Moreover, courage and temperance belong to this part of the soul more than simply because they are passions: because the formal object of all human passion is sense goods and evils as they are perceived good by animals for animals.

At this point, Aristotle starts to define temperance generically as a mean concerning contrary opposites: pleasures and pains (sorrows). Immediately, to locate temperance's specific difference, he follows this generic definition by distinguishing two kinds of pleasure: 1) purely of the soul completed by interior apprehension within the soul alone and 2) of the soul completed in some bodily affection of a sense faculty.

As a chief example of psychological pleasure purely of the soul, Aristotle: 1) refers to love (the principle, cause, of pleasure); and 2) says that *pleasure arises from knowledge that we have, possess, what we love.* Moreover, no external sense, only the interior power of the soul, apprehends: 1) having, possessing, and 2) love.

Aristotle adds that temperance concerns bodily pleasures, not psychological joys, like honor and learning, which are the concern of other virtues. He maintains that the joy that accompanies honor and learning has no bodily cause.

Nor, he says, is temperance concerned with: 1) other psychological joys, like storytelling, contingent events, and unnecessary deeds; 2) external goods like money and friends; nor, essentially, with pleasures of sight, hearing, and smell (indeed, he notes that vices related to these are not called "intemperate"). Moreover, *he maintains that pleasures related to these three external sense faculties belong only* incidentally *to other animals!*

Strictly speaking, he asserts that *the formal object of temperance is intense pleasures of touch (chiefly) and of taste (secondarily), the sense faculty of touch being essentially related to the natural animal inclination to preserve existence of the animal genus and species and individual animal life. He contends that other animals take delight in the sense of sight, hearing, and smell only indirectly, by reference to taste and touch. He supports this contention by saying that dogs do not chiefly delight in the scent of rabbits. They chiefly delight in eating them. And lions chiefly delight in the sounds and sight of other animals as signs that a meal is near!*

Peter A. Redpath

Brute animals have sense faculties and appetites solely to assist and instruct them in individual, bodily and species self-preservation. Human beings, on the other hand, have sense faculties and appetites for individual and species bodily self-preservation *and, additionally, to lead us to a knowledge of the existence, and commands, of reason.*

Having discussed the external sense faculties to which temperance does not chiefly apply, Aristotle next discusses the two sense faculties to which it directly applies: touch and taste.

Before considering that discussion, most helpful is to recall a previous analysis in which St. Thomas had noted: 1) how knowledge of having and not having what we love (pleasure) and do not love (pain) is a first principle of all other passions; 2) that, by nature, we naturally love having human life; 3) that *this natural love of having human life causes our facultative loves as natural likenesses of itself*; 4) that the sense of touch generates all of the sense faculties, and is naturally loved by all animals for being life-preserving; and 5) how no exterior sense (including touch and taste) generates knowledge of having and loving.

These points having been duly noted, before considering the relationship of touch and taste to temperance and intemperance, need exists to note what Aristotle has to tell us regarding taste, namely: 1) that taste is not the chief interest of intemperate people; 2) intemperate people care little about perfectly distinguishing distinct tastes and flavors, have little or no use for taste; 3) intemperate people's chief interest related to taste is in gluttonously gorging themselves ("pigging out," as the popular contemporary phrase well describes their emotional state); 4) the chief interest of intemperance resides in touch, the pleasure of which taste sometimes enhances, increases, intensifies; 5) the formal object of intemperance is the sense of touch inasmuch as touch relates to eating, drinking, and sex: the chief activities related to preservation of individual and species life. To support this claim Aristotle gives the example of Philoxenus Erichius, an ancient Greek who, reportedly, wanted to possess a throat as long as that of a crane so that the delightful experience he had of food resting in his gullet would endure for a much longer time.

Because all animals share the sense of touch, and because having a healthy sense of touch is crucial to the experience of sense reality related to the preservation of individual and species life, according to Aristotle, intemperance naturally inclines to appear to human beings to be *the most beastly*, and least-properly human, of all moral vices. Hence, he asserts that such vices possess the most disgusting shamefulness and make human beings most *small-souled*, and *most like beasts*! Through their performance, he says, notorious evil and blameworthy acts result.

In reply to the objection that, aside from beastly pleasure, some properly human delight, good, should pertain to touch, Aristotle says that pleasures of touch that are naturally appropriate and delightful for human beings are those that we use according to right reason (prudentially, like an athletic massage); and pleasures of touch that are: 1) ordered to the health of the body considered as a whole and 2) not ordered to some parts of the body to delight the sense of touch of that bodily part to the detriment of the health of the body as a whole and the preservation of individual and species bodily life.

To explain the nature of intemperance more precisely, Aristotle distinguishes among several modes of human choice: generic, specific, and individual related to generic and specific nature. He says that all human beings naturally desire to satisfy natural needs for goods like food and drink, needs that all animals must satisfy to stay alive and remain healthy. He adds that natural need is not identical with individual preference for this or that kind, taste, or the amount of food and or drink.

In the case of generic and specific desires, he maintains that most human beings do not make mistakes related to eating or drinking what we really need to stay healthy. Instead, most of us make mistakes related to eating or drinking too much or too little of what we really need to remain healthy.

Natural animal desire related to the preservation and promotion of animal life and health is only that the natural need be supplied. Related to intemperance, his chief point is that intemperance unnaturally subordinates the natural need of the preservation and protection of individual life and species survival to satisfaction of the sense of touch of one or a couple of bodily organs. It resembles the psychological disorder of sacrificing healthy sight for pleasing touch of the organ of sight. *He says "belly-mad" people, gluttons, are very brutish because they fill their bellies with no sense of limits*!

In short, like all vices, intemperance does not conform to the prudent measure in the individual circumstance. According to Aristotle and St. Thomas, the prudent measure is the right measure as determined by the circumstances that bring the act of choice to its individual completion. As a result of their intemperance, the moral psychology of intemperate people inclines them to take pleasure in: 1) things they should not eat and drink to preserve and promote their health; 2) eating in the wrong way, at the wrong time, in the wrong place, with the wrong people, and so on. Hence, Aristotle concludes about the moral psychology of intemperate people in general that it tends to be to enjoy objects highly unsuitable, blameworthy, unhealthy, that they ought, by nature, not to enjoy; and, even when they enjoy real goods, they do so to excess.

Regarding pain and sadness, Aristotle says that: 1) temperate and intemperate people are physiologically and psychologically, differently disposed; 2) temperate people are chiefly praised for the way they endure sorrows and pains (nobly, honorably), not chiefly for enduring them; 3) the coward, and not the intemperate man, is blamed for refusing to undergo pains; 4) the intemperate man is blamed for the way he undergoes sorrow and pain: *like an infant*; 5) unlike the coward, the intemperate man's grief is not generated by real harm or serious discomfort, but simply by not having the pleasure he wants when he wants it; 6) the temperate man is praised for not complaining over the absence of pleasures and comforts.

Contrasting courage and temperance, Aristotle maintains that courage chiefly concerns pains and sorrows that follow from the presence of some really harmful thing that causes death and bad health, while temperance chiefly concerns pleasures that follow from the presence of pleasurable goods. According to Aristotle, pleasure is essentially a cause of sadness for the intemperate man because he chiefly wants all pleasurable goods, not just some of them. He wants the whole genus of pleasure in the most intense degree. As a result, his desire is insatiable. Sensual desire, not prudence, drives his passion to choose pleasurable goods. Hence, when he does not get what he covets, he desires pleasurable things more than anything decent, useful, honorable, and really good for a human being.

While St. Thomas says that, as a cause of sadness, pleasure might appear incongruous to some people, still pleasure distresses the intemperate man like a pilotless ship distresses people who do not know how to sail.

Aristotle adds that the vice of insensibility (being incapable of experiencing pleasure, or experiencing it less than we should for our health and well-being) is a rare human disposition and contrary to brute animal and human nature. Moreover, because other animals differentiate food chiefly by virtue of the pleasure it gives, the natural disposition to be capable of experiencing pleasure, not the natural disposition to be incapable of so doing, appears to be common to all animals. As a result, a person who takes pleasure in nothing appears to other human beings to be abnormal, less than human.

Next, Aristotle details how the temperate man behaves toward pleasures, saying that he: 1) follows the golden mean (prudence) regarding pleasure, sorrow, and desire; 2) does not delight in shameful evils that delight the intemperate man; 3) is saddened by these; 4) tends not to rejoice in things in which he should not rejoice: real evils, and to rejoice in what he should: real good; 5) is not excessive in any circumstance, sad beyond measure; if at all, is saddened by absence of healthy, pleasurable goods; 6) does not long for absent pleasures, or longs for them in the right measure, when he should, in accord with prudence.

Accordingly, Aristotle asserts that the temperate man: 1) desires all pleasures useful to bodily health and well-being; 2) all such pleasures prudently; 3) all other unnecessary pleasures (wants) under three conditions: that they do not hinder human health and well-being (like excess, or naturally unhealthy, food and drink); are not contrary to sexual decency (like fornication) or imprudently excessive; and do not exceed a person's ability to possess (for example, pursuing impossible delights, and going financially broken the process).

In contrast to the temperate man, Aristotle maintains the intemperate man, the man wrongly-disposed to pleasure, pursues pleasures: 1) harmful to his health and well-being, 2) to a degree in kind contrary to what is honorable (goods of a higher quality and greater need) that exceed his means.

To complete his discussion of the moral vice of intemperance, Aristotle compares it to the vices of cowards and children. To make this comparison, he talks about how each moral vice involves a different kind of voluntariness.

By nature, he maintains that intemperance is more voluntary than cowardice (which is motivated by fear of danger). We delight in what we do voluntarily and are saddened by what we do involuntarily. The intemperate man moves toward the pleasure he wants, while the coward flees pain he fears. Pain is contrary to emotional appetite and will. Something involuntary, naturally repugnant, causes the coward to flee, while something voluntary, naturally repugnant, attracts the intemperate man. Because something naturally contrary and harmful causes pain, pain immobilizes and corrupts the nature of its possessor. Consequently, pain tends to impede intellectual work.

As a result, regarding voluntary acts, St. Thomas says: 1) choosing good merits praise; 2) choosing evil merits blame (as does choosing the evil more easily avoidable); 3) consequently, the vice of intemperance is more disgraceful than that of cowardice.

Since the contrary virtue can enable us to avoid every contrary vice, becoming habituated to good action in matters of temperance is easy because: 1) many opportunities exist almost every day in human life to practice temperance in eating, drinking, and sexual matters; and 2) such actions tend to involve no danger, no great risk, unlike acts of courage in war.

St. Thomas adds that the pain that causes fear is involuntary, in some way external. Moreover, abstractly considered, the human inclination to experience fear appears to be voluntarily caused, while, in the individual situation, it tends to be involuntarily caused. In the case of intemperance, he maintains that pursuit of intense pleasure in the abstract tends to be involuntary for intemperate people, while it tends to be the norm for them in the individual situation.

St. Thomas explains that, as the inclination of the habits of the soul approaches toward particular goods they desire, their vehemence (intensity) tends to increase. In the case of an intemperate soul, this natural inclination inclines to cause the intemperance to become more intense and voluntary, while, in the case of cowardly soul, this natural inclination inclines to make the cowardice less voluntary.

After talking about the voluntary and involuntary activity related to cowardice and intemperance, Aristotle considers how the vice of intemperance resembles the infantile vices of children because: 1) children especially live under the influence of sensual desire; 2) need exists to restrain, chasten, chastise, children less they fail to develop prudent habits; and 3) as it increases within the soul of an intemperate person, desire for pleasure becomes increasingly insatiable, like childishness, foolishness.

Consequently, the less intemperate we are, the more efficient becomes our ability to reason, and reason well, like adults should. Hence, restraining intemperance is crucial for all human beings in order to: 1) behave like adults, not like children; and 2) become prudent and remain in touch with reality.[8]

—Notes—

1. St. Thomas Aquinas, *Commentary on the Nicomachean Ethics of Aristotle*, Bk. 3, Lect. 1, nn. 382–391.
2. Id., Lects. 2–4, nn. 392–431.
3. Id., Lects. 5–6, nn. 432–457.
4. Id., Lects. 7–9, nn. 458–487.
5. Id., Lect. 10, nn. 488–495.
6. Id., Lects. 11–13, nn. 496–527.
7. Id., Lects. 14–18, nn. 528–594.
8. Id., Lects. 19–20, nn. 595–648.

–CHAPTER TEN–
Liberality, Magnificence, and Magnaminity

ST. THOMAS STARTS his analysis of Book 4 of Aristotle's *Nicomachean Ethics* by remarking that, having finished studying courage and temperance (*moral virtues that chiefly concern means for preserving and protecting human life*), Aristotle next starts to examine virtues, means, related to lesser goods (enabling, instrumental, coercively-needed, means) for the exercise of the cardinal moral virtues. He considers these means (such as, the rewards of riches and honors) to be *coercive and constraining* because, if we want to exercise a cardinal moral virtue, to some extent, we must use them. They essentially limit our ability to choose, secure, what we chiefly want. Considered as such, these are not the chief objects of our desire; but, without using them, we cannot secure and exercise those chief goods we want more than the means to them.

1. Liberality as an external good for preserving and protecting individual and species human life

As the external good he starts to examine, because of a likeness between liberality (generosity) and the crucial, concupiscible, moral virtue of temperance, Aristotle selects liberality as the chief external good with which to begin his examination of moral virtues related to possession and use of riches.

St. Thomas remarks that, just as temperance moderates the desires related to having tactile pleasures, which enables us to control them well, liberality moderates the desire related to *getting* and *having*, wealth: a tool for obtaining another tool (tactile pleasure).

He says that liberality chiefly involves being able to *handle* well possession of wealth, to be able to receive and distribute wealth well. He claims that liberality's *proximate matter is love of, getting, wealth*, and its remote matter *is* wealth (although, more precisely, its remote matter appears to be not wealth, but *having* wealth).

Further, he maintains that extravagance (spending like a glutton, *drunken sailor*), and miserliness (being stingy, tight, a hoarder, cheap) are vices related to liberality.

By "wealth" Aristotle loosely understands anything we can measure in terms of exchangeability. Comparing the spendthrift to the intemperate man, Aristotle considers the term "spendthrift" to signify wasteful, extravagant people, squanderers, prodigal people, and the like. He maintains that wealth is a tool, and liberality consists in *prudent use of wealth*. While he considers the chief act of this virtue to consist in making disbursements of wealth, he asserts that possessing this virtue tends to enhance a person's ability to act courageously and temperately.

Next, Aristotle distinguishes liberality from *saving*, which he considers to be a kind of preservation, habitual retention of wealth: a taking, or acceptance, of wealth that produces retention of it.

From what he has said, Aristotle concludes that a liberal person tends more to distribute wealth to the right people than to take it from the right sources and refuse it from the wrong sources. He adds that, more characteristic of the liberal person is to spend well and to avoid spending badly, to give well instead of receiving well. *He claims, moreover, that a useful, not honorable, friendship (the sort that inclines to exist within business relations) inclines especially to love the liberal person.*[1]

2. The act of liberality

Regarding the chief qualities of liberal giving, Aristotle says *the first* is that the giving *fulfill all the properties of prudence*, while the second is *to experience pleasure in giving, or at least no sadness*; *or, if with some sadness*, with less than that which other people suffer. In addition to the just-cited emotion of sadness when giving, Aristotle stresses that a quality of giving the liberal man avoids is that of imprudent giving by excess and defect.

To the chief acts of liberality that Aristotle mentions, he adds: 1) receiving prudently, 2) saving and investing well, and 3) restraining from wrong giving. To these acts he adds four properties of liberality he observes among people who give with liberality. 1) He says they give eagerly, generously, and prudently. 2) They give proportionately to their means: not too much nor too little according to the wealth they possess. 3) Perhaps remembering what Cephalos tells Socrates in Book 1 of Plato's *Republic*, among liberal givers who have inherited wealth, Aristotle says these are inclined to be spendthrifts, while those who have inherited wealth tend to protect it like good parents protect their children. And 4) the liberal man is not easily made rich. Because becoming rich is not the inclination of his character, not because of imprudent giving, the liberal man does not tend to become rich.[2]

3. The illiberal vices of the spendthrift and the miser

Because opposites are mutually revealing, St. Thomas says that, to make the nature of the virtue of liberality more evident, Aristotle next contrasts the imprudent habits of the spendthrift and the miser to those the person possessed of the virtue of liberality.

Regarding whether being a miser or a spendthrift is the worse, St. Thomas says that, for three reasons, being a miser is a more serious fault: 1) Like fools, spendthrifts quickly exhaust their wealth. As a result, ensuing poverty or age tend to cure this vice. 2) The vice of the spendthrift closely resembles the virtue of the liberal man, and the spendthrift can be more easily educated to prudent spending than can the miser. The spendthrift's vice arises more from ignorance than from vicious appetite. 3) The spendthrift helps many people, while the miser hurts everyone, even himself, and has the disposition of a thief.

Regarding the person who is a mixture of a spendthrift and the miser, St. Thomas claims that imprudent givers tend to be imprudent takers: loan-sharks. They incline to give out of love of giving, and they incline not to care how they acquire the wealth they give. As a result, they tend to enrich bad people, impoverish good people, and become intemperate themselves.

Related to the vice of miserliness, Aristotle and St. Thomas observe that the many bodily defects, weaknesses, and disabilities that beset human life incline some people to seek to possess external things to compensate for their personal weaknesses, poverty. Because riches help to protect us from danger, some misers tend to be takers of wealth, not givers. Generosity and miserliness involve opposing actions of giving and receiving. They add that, since many species of giving and receiving exist, so many kinds of stinginess (of taking too much and giving too little) exist.

They claim that, as contrary opposites, both these vices simultaneously do not dominate in the same person. Simultaneously, some people have one vice, while other people have the other. Aristotle identifies the following people as having the moral psychology of deficient givers, being cheap, those who: 1) spend little; 2) hoard everything; 3) are tightfisted, give nothing and take nothing; and 4) those people live by the motto "neither a borrower nor a lender be."[3]

4. The moral psychology of misers and why miserliness is difficult to cure

Next, Aristotle explains the moral psychology of misers, or tightfisted, people.

First, he states that some among them reason that, if they give what they have, someday they might need to have it, and have to shame themselves by begging to get it. They tend to: 1) think that, by its nature, taking anything from someone else is shameful; and 2) shy away from taking something because this might someday obligate them to give something in return.

Next, he maintains that others among them tend to be thieves, unjust takers, people who often get themselves involved in especially shameful professions (such as being a pimp, grave robber, gambler, drug dealer, plunderer, loan shark, extortionist, or someone involved in bribery). Often disgraceful names are used to refer to such people; and, in all such cases, they involve people who want to enrich themselves by impoverishing others.

For two chief reasons Aristotle maintains that being cheap is a greater vice than being a spendthrift: 1) It is more difficult to cure; and 2) men tend to commit worse vices, more shameful acts, because of it than they do because of being a spendthrift.[4]

5. The moral virtue of magnificence: Being a doer of great deeds, giver of great gifts

After discussing Aristotle's treatment of the virtue of liberality, St. Thomas next talks about the way he considers another virtue concerned with wealth (magnificence) by first contrasting it with liberality.

St. Thomas maintains that, while liberality concerns giving and taking regarding all money matters, magnificence concerns only giving and taking regarding *great expenditures related to great events*. Considered as such*, evident is that the virtue of magnificence essentially involves use of the estimative sense and understanding the nature of intensive quantity, qualitative greatness.*

Regarding the terms "magnificent," "great," St. Thomas remarks that: 1) they are predicated analogously; 2) the expenditures must be judged great relative to the thing for which they are being made and the person making the expenditures.

By defect, he claims that the vice opposed by defect to the

virtue of magnificence is being *classless*, while the opposing vice by excess is being *tacky*, *gaudy*. Supporting the claim just made that the virtue of magnificence can only be understood in relation to the notion of virtual quantity, St. Thomas maintains that this virtue is taken according to "right reason," "prudence," *not according to* "absolute," that is, *dimensive*, quantity.

According to Aristotle and St. Thomas, qualities of the magnificent giver and magnificent giving include: 1) making great disbursements in a prudent way; 2) expending the right amounts for a great good; 3) spending great sums cheerfully, promptly, and readily; 4) planning how to achieve the best, most splendid, work (not planning how to spend as little as possible for doing an adequate job); 5) being magnificently generous; and 6) while incurring great expense, getting the maximum of quality and beauty for the expense incurred (*getting the most bang for the buck*).[5]

6. The objects of magnificence

St. Thomas starts his discussion about Aristotle's treatment of the objects of magnificence by stating *that the magnificent person preserves proportion* between money expenditures and what is received. In other words, as the virtuous mean, prudent expenditures are: 1) well-proportioned; 2) rightly related; 3) suitable; 4) beautiful/ harmonious; 5) measured in terms of virtual quantity, qualitative, greatness; and 6) hit the virtual quantum mean between excess and defect relative to the event undertaken. And, in performing magnificent acts, by participating in, possessing, the virtue of prudential judgment, the magnificent person becomes the virtuous mean, measure, of magnificent expenditures.

According to St. Thomas, *all virtue consists in*: 1) *a unity, a proportion, between opposites belonging to the same genus*; 2) a privative negation of extremes between the opposites; and 3) a measure of the mean between the opposites in terms of use of virtual quantity. He says that the prudent man behaves as the proportionate equal, one, limit (resembling a leaden rule used by a mason), qualitative balance scale (measure), between too much and too little power, exertion of effort, in act within individual circumstances, relative to him.

Recall that, because choice concerns what is actual, it is always of the possible, not the impossible. *Choice presupposes voluntariness and is naturally ordered toward real, not fictional, means*, which means that it is essentially ordered toward exercise under the direction of the virtue of prudence (right reason and right appetite): virtuous, prudent, perfect, harmonious union (right proportion and reason) *between the capabilities of the agent and those of what the agent chiefly seeks to effect*. Considered as such, virtuous, prudent, choice is beautiful.

In executing a particular act, this beauty includes properly qualifying the action and consideration of all the right circumstances that are essential parts of a single act of self-adjustment to the individual circumstances. Moral virtue, thus, operates analogously to an internal modulator, gyroscope, enabling opposites to be properly related to surrounding influence so as to be able to unite and generate a perfect fit between the agent and what is being done within the individual circumstances so as to generate a perfect action. Considered as such, moral virtue has the property of being a moral universal, a command and control universal, the universal principle generating perfect moral activity. It acts as a self-adjusting balance-of-power scale properly ordered to relations between an agent's personal abilities and a choice to be effected so as to enable opposites to be perfectly united, harmonized, to comprise a perfect fit.

As a particular moral virtue, magnificence involves: 1) executing honorable acts; psychologically more beautifying, more spiritually perfecting acts of qualitatively, higher intensive quantity of greater goodness; and 2) performing these acts most perfectly/beautifully.

Aristotle maintains that the objects of such expenditures are: 1) chiefly divine, religious, undertakings, public welfare projects; and 2) secondarily related to private persons regarding events that happen once, or rarely, not often and permanently, and relate to pursuit of the common good.

In giving, the magnificent person makes expenses commensurate with the merit of the work. Because the person choosing and what is chosen are extreme differences, the chooser and what is chosen belong to the same genus as extreme terms (opposites) of a relation of virtuous activity.

Unlike the magnificent person, the person not magnificent, vicious by the extreme of excess (the classless person) spends lavishly, imprudently, on fools; while, the person not magnificent, vicious by the extreme of defect (the tacky or gaudy person) is extreme by defect in at least five ways: 1) falling short in expenditure; 2) paying late; 3) dwelling on spending as little as possible; 4) spending gloomily/painfully; and 5) when done, thinking he spent too much![6]

7. The moral virtue of magnanimity and the moral psychology of the magnanimous person

According to St. Thomas, as its name suggests, the virtue of magnanimity is a beautifying and perfecting quality: 1) concerned with executing great deeds, and receiving honors; 2) performed by people who think themselves able to do great deeds and receive great honors; and 3) the act of a prudent, not a foolish, person, who knows well his powers and abilities and acts accordingly.

While, considered in a wide sense, a temperate person is a person of moderation in small deeds, like a beautiful person, the magnanimous person displays: 1) some greatness of size, 2) being well-built, and 3) having spiritual heft.

According to St. Thomas, the vice by excess of magnanimity is thinking too much of oneself: 1) having an inflated ego, 2) being conceited, 3) being pompous; while the vice by defect of magnanimity is thinking too little of oneself: 1) pusillanimity, 2) being small-souled, and 3) lacking in initiative/the desire to undertake and execute great deeds.

The chief object of concern that is part of the moral psychology of the magnanimous person is to do the greatest of all externally great deeds, to effect the greatest of all public works and achieve the greatest of all public honors related to public service.

When it accompanies other virtues, Aristotle and St. Thomas maintain that magnanimity is a special virtue; for example, striving for great deeds in courageous action.

Because prudence generates magnanimity, Aristotle concludes that: 1) no evil person can be magnanimous; 2) magnanimity is a special virtue perfecting, beautifying, other virtues; and 3) magnanimity is difficult to achieve because it presupposes having great virtue.

Following Aristotle, St. Thomas says that the magnanimously courageous person: 1) does not expose himself the dangers for trifling matters, 2) is not a lover of danger considered as such; 3) does not undergo danger for trifling and insignificant reasons; 4) braves great dangers for great goods such as religion, public welfare, and justice; and 5) braves such dangers ardently, preferring death to dishonor.

St. Thomas identifies the following as five properties of moral psychology of the magnanimous person: 1) being proficient in doing good for others while being hesitant to accept favors from others; 2) if he accepts benefits from others, he is anxious to return greater ones; 3) he cheerfully confers benefits on others, but reluctantly receives benefits from others; 4) he cheerfully listens to talk about the benefits he has bestowed on others, but does not take pleasure in listening to talk about benefits bestowed on him; and 5) he does not incline to show himself in need of anything, but promptly inclines to minister to the needs of others.

Peter A. Redpath

Other traits of the magnanimous man include displaying honor, dignity, and equality appropriate to other people of dignity and wealth, while not displaying superiority to ordinary men. Because the virtuous man accurately knows (has a healthy estimative sense of) his self-worth among superiors, he has no need to show off among them or inferiors.

As magnanimous traits especially related to the human intellect, St. Thomas identifies: 1) being open, transparent, truthful about who are his friends and enemies (for the simple reason that he has no reason to fear either); 2) caring more about truth than the opinion of others; 3) being transparent in speech and action; and 4) not tending to lie, but liking to joke, in the presence of some people.

Related to the human appetites (will, and passions), St. Thomas identifies the following as psychological traits of a magnanimous person: 1) enjoying the company of a few, honorable, pleasant, friends; 2) eschewing flatterers and being popular; 3) not trying to please everyone; 4) not being a gossip; 5) being quick to express admiration of others; 6) busying himself with internal goods, not having many external ones; 7) because he is too busy being concerned about God and the common good, he rarely speaks about other people and himself; 8) not tending to hold a grudge; 9) not being chiefly interested in having many external and useful goods; 10) because he is self-sufficient, preferring honorable to wealth-generating goods; 11) in bodily movement he walks deliberately, slowly; 12) speaking in measured speech and solemn voice; and 13) because he does not tend to hold possessing external goods of value, he is not contentious about possessing them.[7]

8. Vices opposed to magnanimity: Being conceited and small-souled

According to Aristotle, the vice by defect to magnanimity is being small-souled, while the vice by excess is being conceited (*both of which, once again, are defects involving particular reason [the estimative sense*]). By underestimating his abilities, Aristotle maintains that, by not trying to work to get them, the small-souled man: 1) deprives himself of greater goods that he deserves; 2) becomes satisfied with lesser goods, and becomes lazy; and 3) shrinks away from performing virtuous acts, great deeds, and studying speculative science.

Unlike the small-souled man who is stupid and ignorant of his ability, Aristotle maintains that the conceited person attempts great, honorable, deeds totally beyond his ability, thereby publicly embarrassing himself. Because he thinks too much of himself, the small-souled, conceited person externally practices the vice of external glorification and displays external signs of pomposity in dress, walking, actions, and speech.

Of the two vices, Aristotle claims that the vice of being small-souled is more opposed to the virtue of magnanimity than is the vice of conceit because the natural inclination of virtue is to restrain our inclination to evil. Human nature more strongly inclines us to do good, virtuous deeds that it restrains us from avoiding evil. Consequently, omitting the practice of virtuous deeds is worse than failing, through conceit, to attempt them. It makes us less virtuous because we become virtuous by attempting difficult deeds.[8]

9. The virtue concerned with desiring small, ordinary honors

Aristotle maintains that analogous to liberality in relation to magnificence is the virtue concerned with rightly desiring small honors. While he claims that this virtue has no proper name, it conforms to prudence, and involves a striving to be honored rightly under all circumstances in the right way regarding the right deeds.

Regarding vices related to this virtue, he says that these concern wanting the wrong honors and/or wanting the right honors in the wrong way.[9]

10. The moral virtue and vices related to inhibiting and provoking anger

Having considered virtues and vices dealing with external goods of riches and honors, St. Thomas says Aristotle next considers virtues and vices dealing with external goods that restrain and provoke anger.

Regarding these virtues and vices, St. Thomas identifies mildness, *being calmly inclined,* as the mean or virtue, between these two extremes. While Aristotle says that this mean has no name, its extreme by the defect is sheepishness, while its extreme by excess is called "irasciblibility, " or "being hot-tempered." Of the two vices, Aristotle maintains that sheepishness is worse.

The calmly-inclined man that is the mean to which Aristotle refers closely resembles what today we would call someone who is "even-tempered" or "cool-tempered," the person who gets prudently angry at the right acts, in the right way, under the right circumstances.

For three reasons, Aristotle refutes a Stoic claim that all anger is blameworthy because he maintains that: 1) at times, getting angry conforms with prudence, a species of wisdom; 2) at times, anger helps justice to punish actions that should be punished by stirring up, disturbing, reason to help *engage* its judgment in right choice and action; and 3) only a sheepish man tolerates being treated like a doormat.

Concerning the vice of hot-temperedness in general, St. Thomas says that hot-tempered people possess the imprudent trait of inclining to excess of anger in all circumstances. *Simultaneously,* because of their naturally self-destructive nature, these circumstantial excesses cannot co-exist within one person. Were they to be able to do so, hot-tempered people would live a life of perpetually-intense anger, which no human being could long endure.

More precisely, he identifies three species of hot-temperedness and the moral psychology distinctive to each: 1) being too angry with the wrong people about the wrong issues (a kind of hot-temperedness that St. Thomas says is, sometimes, the result of body chemistry, family inheritance, or both that tends not to last long, to dissipate quickly; and inclines, therefore, long term to be good for the heart and good for health); 2) broodish (sullen/melancholy) anger that tends to last long, be unhealthy for angry people, making them difficult to live with and inclining punishment to be the only remedy for this anti-social kind of anger; and 3) morose anger, being angry at the wrong things in the wrong way, for too long a time (the length of time the anger exists being caused by the fixed resolve of the angry person in the length of time involved for the anger to be satisfied by just revenge).

Aristotle maintains that excessive anger, especially of the morose kind, which tends to hide the anger from public view, is more opposed to even-temperedness than is sheepishness because: by nature, being social animals, unless injured, *human beings incline toward being calm*, while excessively angry people incline toward being anti-social.

Finally, Aristotle concludes that: 1) precisely determining with certainty at what actions, in what way, we should be angry is not easy; 2) we should not greatly blame the person who departs from the mean too much or too little in great or small matters; 3) at times, we praise people for doing both; 4) determining precisely how much deviation from the mean is praiseworthy is difficult; and 5) evident is that the prudent mean is praiseworthy, while excess and defect are blameworthy: less so, if they are slight; more so, if they are great; and most so, if they are most great.[10]

11. The essential connection between possessing the friendship-like virtue of good personal relations (amiability) and being able to exercise moral virtue toward others

As Aristotle moves closer to his discussion of the nature of justice in Book 5 of the *Nicomachean Ethics*, in the last chapters of Book 4, he starts to discuss external human actions that chiefly impact upon social life: acts of sociability, personal relations (like generally behaving in a pleasant way toward others, being inclined to tell the truth, laughing in public at oneself, and experiencing shame) as necessary conditions for being able to act justly.

According to St. Thomas, Aristotle does this related to matters that are: 1) serious (more work-and politically-connected) and 2) humorous (more leisure-connected) personal relations; and he first starts his study of personal relations with those of the serious nature by studying the social virtue of amiability (being pleasant) and its vice by excess of obsequiousness and by defect of being a contrarian, or being habitually socially disagreeable.

Considering the social vice by defect of being socially disagreeable, first, St. Thomas says that, in the area of human communication and conversation in which human beings naturally incline to associate as companions: 1) some human beings go to excess in the use of words and deeds by straining, at all costs, to please, not to offend, others (praising everything others do so as to make others like them; never contradicting anyone out of fear of causing pain/ sadness and offense); 2) while other people tend to be contrarians (socially-disagreeable people who incline to contradict and criticize everything other people say or do, emphasizing anything that will tend to make life miserable for others).

In contrast to these moral flaws in social personal relations, Aristotle maintains that the virtuous mean rightly accepts and praises what others rightly say and do and rightly rejects and blames whatever they wrongly say and do.

From its likeness to friendship, St. Thomas says Aristotle names this virtuous mean "amiability." According to St. Thomas, Aristotle does this because, in external act, this habit closely resembles friend-

An Introduction to Ragamuffin Ethics

ship. The person disposed by this habit behaves toward others in a way that fosters agreeable association. In a way, he claims, this virtue resembles honorable friendship (loving those with whom we live), a friendship moderated by prudence.

St. Thomas asserts that this virtue differs from friendship because it does not manifest the sense passion of love and the will's act of affection that accompanies friendship. The amiable person treats everyone (strangers and acquaintances alike) as a result of a habit of being amiable, pleasant, and not being a sycophant, obsequious, quarrelsome, contentious. Considered as such, the amiable person resembles liberal givers who donate chiefly because they are free spenders, not chiefly because they love a person. Moreover, this virtue does not extend to all acts. It concerns simply being able to live together and get along with other people.

From his observation of the way in which amiable people incline to communicate with each other, Aristotle enumerates five properties of the moral psychology of amiability. He says the amiable person: 1) communicates *fittingly*, *proportionately*, with others; 2) chiefly aims at living together without offense and with pleasure; 3) sometimes refuses to give pleasure to another and chooses to give another pain (this can happen in two ways: when a person speaks disrespectfully to him; or when a person he lives with does something disgraceful, which the amiable person will incline to correct); 4) respects social distinctions and talks accordingly; and 5) chiefly strives to give pleasure, avoid offending; but will offend, at times, if he suspects that future living together requires doing so.[11]

12. The amiable, social virtue of veracity

Because Aristotle says that examining individual virtues as we do research into this study of moral science is useful to this science, he adds that, by so doing, we come to understand that *all virtues are medicinal states related to particular habits*! Consideration of verac-

300

ity, truth-telling in words and deeds further extends moral science in external acts, contributing to making us more or less sociable. Regarding truth-telling, Aristotle identifies its vice by excess as boasting, and its vice by defect as dissembling.

About the boaster, Aristotle contends that the boaster pretends to have praiseworthy qualities (powers/abilities, a level of intensive quantum, or qualitative, greatness) that he does not have at all, or does not have as greatly as he claims to have.

Regarding the dissembler/liar, Aristotle maintains that he claims to be less powerful, knowledgeable, than he is. And, he adds, that the virtuous mean of being rightly self-admirable consists in being genuine, real, truthful, transparent, in word and deed (appearance and reality).

Moreover, these habits can relate to a means to an end or just to an end (taking pleasure in being what you are).

Because words are signs of what is, and we use science chiefly to represent things as they are, Aristotle maintains that liars are vicious, evil, because their actions cause disorder within human relations and communication, thereby helping to destroy language and social life.

St. Thomas, in turn, says that someone who speaks the truth constitutes the mean in human communication because the truth signifies a thing as it is, consists in a proportionate equality (*adaequatio*) between the human intellect and the thing known. Further, he maintains that the truthful person about whom Aristotle speaks is the person: 1) habitually inclined to tell the truth in everyday conversation, not the person coerced to tell the truth under oath; who 2) loves telling the truth considered as such; 3) aims to live affably with others through love of truth; 4) hates a lie; 5) considers lying essentially shameful; and 6) inclines toward understatement, not overstatement and excess.[12]

13. The moral psychology underlying boasting and dissembling, the objects about which people boast and dissemble, and why; and when, if ever, these acts are evil

Considering the boaster, Aristotle states that, sometimes, this person boasts for: 1) the pleasure he gets out of so doing, and not for any evil aim; 2) honor and/or glory; or 3) some good honor and glory often help secure. While Aristotle maintains that boasting for the first aim is not evil, he claims that doing so for the second or third end just cited is evil.

About the objects about which people tend to boast and why, Aristotle maintains that: 1) people who tend to boast for enjoyment purposes tend to do so chiefly for that reason (for example, to make people laugh); while 2) those who tend to boast to gain honor and/ fame do so chiefly for personal gain (like physicians, diviners, and Sophists, who pretend to be professionals with some sort of esoteric knowledge so as to take the advantage of the ignorance of the general public).

Dissemblers, on the other hand, sometimes: 1) incline to do so for a good purpose, like Socrates did, to avoid becoming hubristic, 2) as a way of boasting, appearing greater than one is, as Aristotle maintained Spartans did regarding dress; and 3) neither to affirm nor deny a great deed, and, in so doing, to please, and get along with, other people.

Regarding which vice, that of the boaster or dissemblers, is worse, Aristotle maintains, because it inclines to be more opposed to the mean: being truthful, that of the boaster is worse.[13]

14. Amusement, laughter

Considering next behavior related to non-serious, relaxing, activities, St. Thomas starts by saying that: 1) at times, human beings need such activities as useful means to rest from bodily and mental work; and 2) they involve listening and talking, chief activities of human socialization, about pleasant things and pleasant ways of acting.

Aristotle says we call people with this virtue of amusement "witty." Today, we might call such persons "humorous," "funny," "comical," or "comedians."

The extreme by excess, he calls a "buffoon" (someone who aims, at all costs, to get a laugh, who tends to make fun of everyone) and in the extreme instance, a "mocker" (someone who chiefly aims at publicly making fun of someone to shame that person), while he calls the extreme by defect a "boor" (a conversationally useless person, someone who hates humor, jesting).

Aristotle claims that the witty person: 1) tells jokes that are tactful, decent, like those of the liberal soul, not gross, like those of a slavish soul; 2) jests in a cultured, not obscene, way that intends to please, not offend; and 3), at times, reproaches for amusement for the chief aim to correct someone.

Aristotle concludes his discussion of amusement and laughter by saying that species of communication exist in words and works with different chief aims: 1) veracity (truthfulness in words and deeds) and 2) emotional expression in work-related activities (serious matters to which the virtue of amiability applies) and leisure-related activities (non-serious matters to which the virtue of amusement, laughter, applies).[14]

15. Shame

Having finished discussing qualitative (intensive quantum) means regarding the ability to act well (engage in virtuous activity), next, St. Thomas says, Aristotle examines the qualitative mean that can, at times, assist some people to become virtuous and prevent others from becoming vicious: the passion of shame.

St. Thomas contends that passions are movements of the sensory appetite that affect bodily organs. Hence, they employ heat and cold and blood flow to influence bodily actions. Passions essentially involve organic change! Hence, we judge their existence by observing bodily changes as signs of their presence.

Because virtuous people do not experience shame (because *qua* virtuous they do no wrong), virtuous people do not experience such bodily changes. Like Aristotle, St. Thomas maintains that shame is a passion, not a virtue; and that it consists in fear of disgrace or fear generated by a condition of psychological confusion. Like some frightened people as an external sign of their emotional condition, he says that ashamed people tend to blush, while terrified people incline to turn pale.

The chief reason St. Thomas gives for this difference between the physiological condition of the terrified person in contrast to that of the ashamed individual is that bodily energy inclines to rush to the bodily location where the soul judges the life and health of the body to be in greatest present danger. In the case of the experience of the intense fear of death that produces terror, the life principle inclines to rush toward life's chief organic principle: the heart, drawing heat from the extremities to protect the heart against external attack. Because shame causes a person to experience loss of an external good (honor) or psychological confusion due to the sudden presence of a threatening evil that causes a person to sense personal weakness, the soul rushes bodily energy toward the body's surface to facilitate attack against an incoming evil.[15]

—Notes—

1. St. Thomas Aquinas, *Commentary on the Nicomachean Ethics of Aristotle*, Bk. 4, Lect. 1, nn. 649–665. Regarding Cephalos' discussion with Socrates about wealth, see Plato, *Republic*, Bk. 1, 330B–331B.

2. St. Thomas Aquinas, *Commentary on the Nicomachean Ethics of Aristotle*, Lect. 2, nn. 666–677.
3. Id., Lects. 3–4, nn. 678–696.
4. Id., Lect. 5, nn. 697–706.
5. Id., Lect. 6, nn. 707–718.
6. Id., Lect. 7, nn. 719–734.
7. Id., Lects. 8–10, nn. 735–783.
8. Id., Lect. 11, nn. 784–791.
9. Id., Lect. 12, nn. 792–799.
10. Id., Lect. 13, nn. 800–815.
11. Id., Lect. 14, nn. 816–830.
12. Id., Lect. 15, nn. 831–839.
13. Id., nn. 841–849.
14. Id., Lect. 16, nn. 850–866.
15. Id., Lect. 17, nn. 867–884.

CHAPTER ELEVEN

Justice

AFTER FINISHING his study of the definition of moral virtue chiefly as an appetitive mean between excess and defect regarding internal and external relations and actions of the individual person, in Book 5 of the *Nicomachean Ethics* Aristotle considers justice chiefly as a mean between excess and defect in social relations between people. To start to do so, St. Thomas maintains that Aristotle talks about three differences between justice and previously-examined virtues.

Previously, Aristotle had chiefly considered how internal faculties and habits internally and externally influence (qualify) choice and actions. He had considered external actions chiefly as effects caused by internal principles like the intellectual faculty, will, particular reason (the estimative sense), the passions, habits, and virtues.

Now, St. Thomas maintains that Aristotle will chiefly consider the virtue of justice (starting with commutative justice) *in relation to external action*, and secondarily in relation to how internal principles (like faculties and habits) help or hinder the performance of just acts.

Previously, Aristotle had considered the mean of virtue taken chiefly from right reason and prudence. Now, he will start discussion of the mean of commutative justice taken from a midpoint, an equal in actions between individual people (a mean of social interaction), not directly from the mean of right reason and prudence. In fact, toward the end of Book 4 of his *Nicomachean Ethics*, he had already started to prepare for application of this mean by making reference to the psychological effect of shame that conscience is capable of generating, and which necessarily depends upon the existence of social relationships.

1. Justice considered chiefly as a mean between excess and defect in social relations between people

As just noted above, Aristotle maintains that justice is not the mean between two extreme habits of action related to personal vices. It is the mean between two extremes (excess and defect) of action between people.

After explaining the difference in approach to what Aristotle has done and what he will do, St. Thomas says that Aristotle distinguishes between particular (personal, ordinary, individual) justice, which exists between individuals and legal justice (defined through legislation enacted by a political organization).

Next, St. Thomas says Aristotle starts to examine particular justice by defining justice in general in relation to three effects that common agreement appears to claim the habit of justice causes: 1) an inclination to do just works, 2) just action, and 3) a desire to do just acts.

Then, making the appropriate changes, Aristotle defines injustice as a habit by which men are disposed to perform unjust deeds and by which they will and do unjust acts. By so doing, St. Thomas says Aristotle intentionally focuses attention on the human will (which is the prime mover of external human actions): the chief subject, generator, and cause, of justice and injustice.

According to St. Thomas, a chief aim of the will as a moral principle is to will and to perform just deeds and not to will and to perform unjust acts. To support his claim, he makes reference to Aristotle's observation that, while contraries exist in faculties and sciences (for example, the colors black and white in the faculty of sight and more or less perfect knowledge in science), *contraries do not exist in habits considered as firmly-fixed dispositions*!

An Introduction to Ragamuffin Ethics

For example, considering health as a firmly-fixed habit of a living body, health, not disease, proceeds from this habit, or virtue. Only those acts that agree with, essentially relate to, are not contrary to, health proceed from the fixed habit, inclination, of health (from health as a bodily virtue or excellence).

Analogously considered, while science as a knowledge (but not a firmly-fixed habit) studies health and disease, *as a firmly-fixed habit of right judgment, science chiefly relates to, inclines to generate, cause, knowing one contrary: the truth, and not judging falsely*. Since contrary habits belong to contrary generating principles (forms, qualities, like healthy and unhealthy), one inclination to act, and one act, belongs to one fixed habit (for example, a sickly habit inclines to, and actually, generates illness, while a healthy habit generates health). Hence, we incline to know healthy and unhealthy qualities from the habitual condition of the body that causes health and disease. For example, being in shape, muscular, inclines to cause health; while being out of shape, flabby, inclines to cause disease.

Again, analogously considered, science as a firmly-fixed habit possessed by a professional scientist is firmly fixed on generating knowledge of the truth, not on judging falsely. The habit of science is no more professionally disposed as a virtue to judge falsely than is the habit of the professional musician to generate noise.

As another example, in contrast to the unfixed habit of the incontinent man, the habit of the temperate man, the moral virtue of temperance, is firmly fixed on generating temperate acts. As a result, while *shame* can, in some instances, be used as an effective propaedeutic in the moral education of the continent and the incontinent man, it *is totally useless in relation to the moral education of the temperate and intemperate man.*

In the case of the intemperate man, it has no influence because he has no moral conscience; while, in the case of the temperate man, were shame to influence his moral choice, that very fact would indicate that so-called "temperate" man was devoid of the virtue of temperance. No virtuous person, a person in whom virtue is a firmly-fixed habit, is moved to perform an act of virtue out of fear of shame. Love of doing a good deed, not fear of shame, motivates virtuous people to perform virtuous acts.

Note should be taken that, in beginning in his analysis of justice, as we will show throughout Book 5 of the *Nicomachean Ethics*, Aristotle heavily concentrates on negative reasoning, remotion, to help define justice from knowledge of injustice, and from use of *demonstratio quia* reasoning (reasoning from effect to cause), from observed actions as external signs of the facultative habits that cause them.

Keeping this note in mind, easily observable is the negative way in which Aristotle approaches preliminary definitions of justice and injustice by explaining that we predicate these terms analogously, just as we do the terms "habit" and "virtue." For example, he says we talk about the unjust person in three ways, as: 1) a lawbreaker; 2) unfair by excess: greedy (wanting too many good things); and 3) unfair by defect, wanting too few evils.

From these ways of talking about injustice, Aristotle concludes that we speak of the just person in two ways, as: 1) law-abiding and 2) fair (the equal being the mean opposing the two extreme ways of being unfair). Further, he concludes that, because law is a habit, and acts of habits make known their formal objects toward which acts of habits incline, we call "just" what is lawful and fair, and "unjust" what is unlawful and unfair.

St. Thomas adds that a greedy person wants too many goods that all men want, especially pertaining to good and bad luck (goods we need, but can lose). In addition, these goods are not always beneficial, expedient, and proportionate to what is really good for this man, what the greedy man really needs in the individual situation. In pursuing goods and avoiding evils in this imprudent way, St. Thomas maintains that a person develops vices of greed and injustice. And Aristotle observes that the unjust person is not always called "unjust" because he chooses too much good. Sometimes, he is called "unjust" because he chooses too few evils, burdens.

Finally, Aristotle explains how the lawbreaker is unjust according to the norm of law, that *what is illegal* is a kind of inequality because the lawless man is *not equal to the measure of law* as determined by this or that political order, not because the man is necessarily unjust. In fact, the political order, not the person who breaks one of its laws, might be the chief generator of injustice.[1]

2. Legal justice

After having considered justice most generally in relation to legal and particular justice, Aristotle says that legal justice concerns legal enactments as *relatively, somewhat, just acts*. He maintains that laws chiefly aim at encouraging *a citizen's virtue*, behavior that promotes, is *useful* to, fostering civic virtue, being a good citizen of this or that type of political regime. They seek to encourage behavior that promotes the one chief activity (means to happiness) of main concern to the specific kind of regime in question. Since Aristotle maintains that just polities can involve the rule of the best persons, one person, the many, or the few, for the benefit of all, the best (virtuous), the many (poor), the few (rich), or the one (the ruler), what a political order commands as just might not conform to what is really just.

Once again, predicating the term "just" analogously, Aristotle calls "just" those laws that chiefly cause, promote, and preserve happiness and the things that make for happiness in a civic community. Civic laws command civic virtues and forbid civic vices. Good civic laws do so under the direction of civic prudence.

Because justice commands the work of all the virtues, St. Thomas maintains that it is called perfect *secundum quid*, not *simpliciter*, nor absolutely. Legal justice, in turn, is perfect by commanding every virtue the law prescribes and forbidding every vice it prohibits. He adds that legal justice is the most perfect species of virtue because it alone practices virtue toward another; and because perfect virtue is a *communications activity*, and communications necessarily involve the existence of other people. As the sole social virtue, justice makes all virtue complete.

Since the job of the ruler is to arrange things ordered toward the common good, ruling/legislation are essentially communications arts. Just as legal justice is a general virtue, so illegal acts are general vices. And just as the most vicious person practices vice toward himself and others, so the most virtuous person practices virtue toward himself and others. In a way, virtue and justice are identical because justice is all virtue practiced toward another. In a way, temperance approaches justice because temperance aims at quieting shameful desires; and we incline to experience the passion of shame as a result of awareness of a vicious action we have performed becoming publicly communicated.[2]

3. Particular, or individual, justice

Having completed his analysis of legal justice, Aristotle starts his examination of individual justice (justice between individuals) by showing, in three ways, the difference between legal justice and individual justice.

First, he says that a man considered legally just or unjust can be individually just or unjust, and the two need not be identical. For example, while, individually considered, a person who breaks a traffic law might not be doing anything morally unjust from the standpoint of particular, or individual, justice, from the standpoint of legal justice, he would be. Second, *because the ordering of an act to an end changes whether the nature of an act is virtuous or vicious,* the man who commits adultery to satisfy lust is chiefly concupiscent (violates individual justice). Third, the man who commits adultery to rob a woman is chiefly a thief (violates individual and legal justice).

Just as nothing is contained in a genus that is not contained in the species, so Aristotle and St. Thomas maintain that whatever is legally unjust is reduced to an individual vice. Hence, 1) the legally cowardly soldier is reduced to the individual vice of cowardice; 2) whatever is legally unjust is reduced to the individual vice of injustice; 3) the person who commits illegal assault is reduced to the vice of anger; and 4) the legally-judged thief is the individually unjust thief.

Aristotle maintains that we determine the mean of legal and particular justice in terms of an equal. Whether legal or particular, the unjust, illegal, act is unequal. He adds that, while every excessive act is unequal, not every unequal act is excessive; for example, strictly speaking, having too few burdens is defective, not excessive. Similarly, the inequality of individual (particular) injustice is not identical with the inequality of illegal injustice. For example, the inequality of individual injustice exists as part of a whole in relation to illegal injustice.

Next, Aristotle says that, as he has already noted, inasmuch as legal justice involves using every species of virtuous act toward our neighbor, it conforms to the nature of complete virtue. Making the appropriate changes, analogously, he claims that the same is true of injustices that violate just civil law: they conform to complete vice.

He adds that, considered in general, civil law commands us to live according to every virtue and forbids us to live according to any vice. Nonetheless, some laws do not *directly* relate to any virtue. For example, laws related to commutative justice involving exchanges of external goods indirectly, not directly, relate to the quality of the soul of a person engaged in a commutative exchange.

Nonetheless, Aristotle states that, in its relation to justice, positive law tends to educate the soul in virtue by giving instructions to citizens about right and wrong behavior in relation to the civic good. Beyond this kind of legislative instruction in virtue, Aristotle maintains that another kind of moral instruction about how to become individually virtuous exists: political science; but, that is a topic he says he will discuss in his work on *Politics*.

Regarding the relation between individual and legal justice, St. Thomas observes that, in the Book 3 of his *Politics*, Aristotle states that to be a good man and to be a good citizen are not necessarily identical in every State. Indeed, some States are not worthy of honor, do not allow a person to be a good person while simultaneously being a good citizen. In the best polity, however, these coincide.[3]

4. Distributive and commutative justice as forms of particular justice

Leaving aside the study of legal justice, Aristotle and St. Thomas next examine distributive and commutative justice as forms of particular justice. Regarding distributive justice, St. Thomas says that this virtue consists in distributing (*dividing up*) some common goods and evils (like money, work, expenses, and so on) among people who are members of the same social community.

In contrast to distributive justice, St. Thomas states that commutative justice consists in voluntary or involuntary *transactions and exchanges*. Then, he divides commutative justice into two species: 1) voluntary on the part of both parties (involving, for example, activities such as buying/selling, bartering, mortgaging, lending, depositing, and renting); and 2) involuntary on the part of one party (such as, theft, adultery, beating, poisoning, kidnapping, defamation of character, different forms of personal abuse, and slave enticement [apparently similar to the contemporary business practice of trying to hire talented workers away from business competitors]).

St. Thomas adds that, since injustice can happen in both voluntary and involuntary transactions, the species of injustice is twofold, doubles, when it involves involuntary exchanges because, in voluntary exchanges, if a person is unwittingly treated unjustly, return of the loss contributes just recompense. But in involuntary exchanges, the victim loses some external possession and suffers personal injury, is dishonored, psychologically damaged, through an act of violence to his or her person, or soul!

Since involuntary acts can be done out of violence and ignorance, Aristotle divides such acts into 1) openly (plainly, out in the open) involuntary and 2) secretly (hidden, surreptitiously) involuntary.

Having made these initial observations about the natures of commutative and distributive justice, Aristotle next starts to talk about how and why we need to understand the equal as a mean in relation to commutative and distributive justice.

Starting with distributive justice, regarding this species of justice, he says that *a mean should be taken according to a relationship of proportions, a proportionate equality*, by which he means a *qualitative equality* based upon a need to counterbalance any inequalities in contributions and merit.

To explain more precisely what he means by "proportionate equality," Aristotle repeats something he had already said: that the unjust man wants an inequality of good and evil, and that the unjust thing consists in the inequality (*unjust relation*) the unjust man wants.

To understand precisely what Aristotle means by "proportionate equality," necessity exists, once again, to return to the teaching of Aristotle and St. Thomas about the nature of virtual, or intensive, quantity. Aristotle considers the just to be a mean (midpoint) relation between relations of *having* too much and too little: a virtual quantum mean in a generic relation of excess and defect, a privative negation, opposite, *of having* between too much and too little. In the case of the proportionate, generic relation of the just act to specific extremes of injustice, Aristotle says that the just act consists in equality among at least four objects: two *persons* and two *havings*—two things (goods and evils).

In distributive justice, he claims that just as the things (goods and evils) to be divided are related, so is the *having* of the persons. Otherwise, the persons will not *have* shares proportionate to their contributions and merit.

However, he says that different political regimes (for example democracies, aristocracies, plutocracies) understand "merit" differently, that is, *they measure what a person deserves "to have" according to a different standard of quality (having), or intensive quantum* (qualitative) *greatness*!

After showing that the mean of distributive justice consists in a mean (a proportionality), he now shows precisely what is the mean of what proportionality, and in what way this precise mean is understood.

To do this he starts to explain the nature of proportionality by saying that what is distributively just is a proportion because *we find proportion not only in counting, arithmetic. We find it wherever we find number*. According to Aristotle, need exists to recall that two kinds of quantity exist: discrete (divided into the two species continuous and discrete) and virtual (a qualitative quantity that St. Thomas calls "spiritual greatness," and corresponds to the kind of quantity possessed by a body that has weight: *spiritual heft, greatness of soul*).

Regarding Aristotle's teaching about proportionality in geometrical equality, St. Thomas explains that we find proportionality in geometry in terms of the geometrical equality expressed in the phrase "this is to this is that is that." Put in terms of merit regarding labor, for example, the proportion involved is the relation of one intensive quantity (work) to another (pay).

Use of proportion as a measure is possible because proportion is a property of quantity (both virtual and discrete quantity), and quantity has the nature of a measure according to numerical unity.

From numerical unity (a mode of unity being precisely what equality is) the concept of unity (and with it all its essential properties) can be transferred to every kind of quantity: *including intensive*, like that existing between geometrical shapes. Merit pay is an intensive quantum (qualitative) equal related to qualitatively unequal relations of contribution and recompense: equal pay for equal quality of work and unequal pay for unequal quality of work! Aristotle says that mathematicians (geometricians) call this "geometrical equality" when comparing different geometrical figures of the same kind (for example, squares) of different sizes.

According to Aristotle and St. Thomas, properly applied, distributive justice does not consider different (disproportionate) relations among persons as persons (for example, whether one of the person is the son or daughter of someone with political clout with an employer who is paying workers to do the same kind of work of equal quality). Today, we would say that, properly applied, distributive justice does not "show favoritism." It applies to persons *as more than persons*: *as qualitative contributors*! Properly applied, an employer/employee relation uses a standard of merit pay. For equal quality of work it rewards equal quantity of money (measured in terms of *greater or less* numerical dollars). For equal quality of work it does not pay one person *more* than another because he or she is politically-connected, of a specific sex, religion, race, or color. It pays one person *more* than another *for better quality* work.

According to Aristotle and St. Thomas, *one vice exists against distributive justice*: *favoritism*, failure to consider the inequality of a person's qualitative contribution to a work.[4]

5. The mean of commutative justice and how to find it

In commutative justice, Aristotle and St. Thomas maintain that the mean is chiefly the arithmetical, not the proportional, geometrical, equal. Commutative justice chiefly considers transactions, exchanges that occur between individuals. It only considers the nature of an injury (personal damage), when one occurs. In matters of commutative justice, the judge attempts only to make good the laws, restore what was taken away (for example, in terms of money; and when psychological damage [dishonor, loss of respect] results in addition to loss of money, restoration of honor, respect [payment for psychological damage]). No concern exists about whether one of the individuals involved in a transaction or exchange is a morally virtuous or vicious person, or of this or that sex, race, religion, or color. In a commutative exchange, if a morally good man injures a morally bad one, the morally good man is held to be at fault.

The exchanges involved are measured chiefly in terms of the natures of the things exchanged, not chiefly in terms of the natures of the parties engaged in the exchange. For example, in the case of a commutative exchange involving physical injury (like a murder), a just judge will attempt to compensate the parties injured (including the political community), through a commensurate sentence (one that fits the crime), like life imprisonment or death.

From what he has said about commutative justice thus far, Aristotle deduces the following conclusion about the nature of the just act as a kind of equal in commutative transactions: the equal is a mean between "a gain" (getting more of the good) and "a loss" (getting more of an evil) as these terms are commonly understood (having more gain and less loss).

However, Aristotle notes that, at times, use of the terms "gain" and "loss" in cases of commutative justice does not appear suitable. Not all instances of commutative transactions, exchanges, are as simple as buying and selling goods at a fixed price. While commutative justice chiefly focuses upon the transaction involved, often it has to take into consideration the nature of the parties involved. For example, in the case of buying and selling in which a contract is involved, the contract might not be between individuals of equal social status. One might be an adult and another an adolescent. In a case involving personal injury, the person injured might be damaged physically and psychologically; or might be of a social status within a political order in which, beyond personal injury, the political order is seriously damaged by the personal injury. Assassination of a sitting president of a nation is a case in point.

Because of the difficulty involved precisely in determining the mean in commutative and distributive relations, people often go to court, to a judge, a mediator, intermediary, mean, between disagreeing parties. Hence, Aristotle states that *the judge who determines the mean should be a living embodiment of justice.*

In the case of commutative exchanges, Aristotle maintains that people go to see a judge when they are in doubt about the mean of gain and loss.

To indicate how a judge determines a mean in commutative justice, Aristotle uses an example taken from continuous quantity: a straight line. He says that, to establish equality between the parties, the judge imagines a line divided into longer and shorter parts. He takes a quantity from a longer part and gives it to the shorter to equalize them. He gives some other examples, too, but these are not necessary to consider because his point is clear.

Finally, Aristotle says that the terms "gain" and "loss" used to refer to commutative interactions were first derived from business transactions.

St. Thomas thinks that, from what Aristotle has said thus far, the equal in exchanges involving commutative justice is evident. It involves having an equal amount before and after the transaction even in involuntary interactions.[5]

6. The false opinion of some Pythagoreans about the mean: That it is reciprocation, an eye for an eye and a tooth for tooth

In several ways, Aristotle criticizes the retributive teaching about the just mean attributed to some Pythagoreans. He critiques their reduction of the whole of justice to retributive justice because he maintains that their understanding of the mean as an eye for an eye and a tooth for a tooth does not: 1) make intelligible the mean related to distributive justice, and 2) it does not cover all acts of commutative justice even though this is what these Pythagoreans had intended to cover. Aristotle maintains that even the famous legislator Rhadamanthus had held this false understanding of the just mean.

While, in exchange of things, commutative justice ordinarily considers equal rank, as already indicated, in personal injury cases, it does not, cannot. Aristotle maintains that injury to a ruler of a commonwealth is injury to the commonwealth. Moreover, commutative justice involving involuntary interactions can increase or mitigate punishment.

In commutative justice, voluntary offenders tend to be punished more severely than involuntary ones, or not at all (unless, for example, the involuntary offender is voluntarily ignorant because, in such a case, the offender acts with intention and contempt).

To some extent, equality of proportionality measures commutative exchanges because, while equality of the thing is always involved in such exchanges, sometimes inequality of persons is involved (as, for example, in the example given above of exchanges between adults and adolescents related to business contracts).

Aristotle claims that proportional equality is sometimes required in commutative exchanges because doing acts of kindness, returning favors, enables citizens to live as friends, on friendly terms. By nature, he thinks that all citizens desire to follow the golden rule. When following this rule, we do not seek proportionate injury for injuring another or being injured by another. We do not even tend to seek proportionate good when doing good for another because returning favors is an act of gratitude, and doing acts of gratitude is natural to human beings and increases acts of gratitude to be done, thereby promoting concord within a political society.

Nevertheless, without just retribution, Aristotle claims that a kind of servile mentality (what, today, some people call an "entitlement mindset") tends to develop within a political order. Moreover, without the presence of equality of proportion (qualitative equality) and arithmetical equality, Aristotle and St. Thomas maintain that business exchanges would be destroyed, something most important to remember for understanding the nature of money and the role it plays in maintaining and promoting strong political regimes.[6]

7. Money

While Aristotle's and St. Thomas's teachings about economics are often ridiculed today, actually what they had to say about this issue is quite profound.

According to them, a type of proportionality in commutative exchanges is an essential part of business activity that qualitatively makes intelligible the nature of money and economic exchange. A chief reason for this is because, to preserve justice in terms of proportionate equality within commutative economic interactions, the natural qualitative inequality of products produced by different professions and professionals for satisfying natural human needs, real human goods: 1) must be publicly recognized and 2) equated according to a uniform measure of equality. *The greater qualitative contribution that some professions make economically to a political order must be publicly recognized and justly compensated. If this does not happen, Aristotle and St. Thomas maintain that economic exchanges within a particular political order and between political regimes will stop*!

If a uniform measure of proportionate equality between and among professions of unequal quality (between those more and less necessary for promoting and preserving human life, health, and safety) is preserved within a political society, they say all things capable of being economically exchanged can, thereby, be compared to an equal unit measure so as to make known which is more or less great in relation to market demand and fulfilling real human needs.

They maintain that money, currency, was invented as a measure of market demand to establish fair pricing in relationship to fulfilling real needs! The invention of money, therefore, becomes a measure of paying: 1) too much, 2) proportionately equal (fair price), or 3) too little, chiefly relative to a real need.

To make intelligible the nature of money as a measure of fair price and market demand, they give the following example related to the exchange of one house for X number of sandals or X amount of food. While, generally considered, St. Thomas says one house is of qualitatively greater good *for the preservation and promotion of human life* than one sandal, over a long period of time, one house is qualitatively (has the intensive quantum greatness: a greatness of power relative to preserving and promoting human life) equal to so many sandals. And, over a short period of time, one house has a qualitative good for the promotion and preservation of X number of people.

In short, some goods have a qualitative greatness relative to the preservation and promotion of real human needs (the greatest of which is the preservation and promotion of human life) expressible in arithmetically-quantifiable terms through a physical sign numerically-expressed: by money!

The farmer, builder, and shoemaker produce qualitatively-unequal useful goods, goods unequally useful for executing performance activity and keeping people alive, safe, and healthy. If human beings do not recognize the hierarchical inequality of business, and other, professions for the unequal contribution they make toward the preservation and promotion of human life and safety, perfecting the quality of human life, Aristotle and St. Thomas maintain that human beings will refuse to exchange goods and products, will refuse to engage in economic activity. Hence, some means for equating qualitatively unequal goods and activities, hierarchically-ordered professions, must be discovered or invented.

Money enables the real wealth (quality of talent of qualitatively unequal, but talented, people) and the generically unequal goods they produce (like those of the farmer, builder, cobbler, baker, and cosmetologist) to become members of the same genus of economic goods (enabling-means, goods productive of real, life-enhancing good) to be measured by a generically-common standard of use value. Wealth is chiefly measured in terms of personal talent and that of how many talented people a talented person can get to work for him for free.

According to St. Thomas, only one standard truly measures all goods, including economic ones: demand, human needs. All human goods have one chief measure—natural need to stay alive and preserve health. Hence, St. Thomas says we do not measure economic good according to a metaphysical standard of greatness. If we did, a mouse would be of greater good than a pearl! We measure economic good, price, according to a human being's relationship to needing something for some human use to fulfill some real human want or need in the present that some talented person can satisfy.

As further proof that human need is a chief measure of economic price, St. Thomas says that if human beings had no real needs, no human exchanges would happen. Nor would they happen if we did not have like needs. We would not exchange something for which we have real need for something for which we have no need. He maintains that the etymology of the word "money" in Greek is from the Greek word for law (*"nomos"*). And he maintains that the etymology relates to the fact that: 1) demand measures all economic exchanges; 2) money arose as a conventional agreement among men because of the need, natural demand, to exchange necessary goods; 3) money is a physical sign of an agreement (an IOU) that, upon demand and by law, what a person needs will be given to him in exchange for money. St. Thomas calls this *exchange-power of money a virtue* of money, part of its intensive quantum, or qualitative, greatness.

Because money can become useless if not backed up by the force of law, St. Thomas adds that, while human demand, need, is the measure of all good according to nature, money is the measure of all economic good according to human convention by law.

Further, money enables us to have a measure by law within and between States, a measure of the quality of labor of a State, and of the productivity of a State's workers: of the reciprocal proportionality of economic worth of labor and the hierarchy of professions within and between States. Hence, in a way, money is the measure of the social health of a State.

By the law of supply and demand, and convention, money directly equates exchange with goods and labor and indirectly equates exchange with human needs. According to St. Thomas, money's *virtue*, nature, consists in uniting qualitatively unequal (hierarchically-ordered) goods and labor within the same genus through an arithmetically-quantifiable measure.

Put simply, money replaces the balance scale to enable weighing proportionate equality (intensive quantity greatness/qualitative greatness) of goods and labors exchanged Money is chiefly a sign, measure, of comparative quality analogously expressed in terms of a numerical greatness. Considered as such, money enables us to dispense with carrying a universal balance scale.

St. Thomas explains the great good that money provides to social human life by saying that, when human beings are so related that one, or both, does not need another, no mutual exchange happens. Exchange happens when a farmer needing wine has a neighbor who is a vintner who needs grain so that a poundage of grain is exchanged for X number of bottles of wine. Because money is not chiefly a weight or arithmetic number, but can analogously measure both, he says that money fosters exchange activity and human socialization. Moreover, *when money loses its exchange power, its virtue*, St. Thomas maintains that *human communication stops*.

He adds that money has the additional power, virtue, of serving as a tool for future exchanges of many goods because not every need is immediate and involves exchange of wine and grain. Thus, money's virtue includes the ability to serve as a kind of *insurance policy* that, in the future, in exchange for money, someone will get what he needs or wants.

Because, like other goods, the demand for currency can fluctuate up and down, because it can lose its *virtue*, purchase power, St. Thomas states that legal protections need to be put in place to enable money to retain its exchange utility more so than other things do.

Since the hierarchy of human needs, arts, and sciences, differ so greatly in quality, St. Thomas maintains that no measure to equate them can exist according to reality and the nature of things. The best we can do is to compare the quality of contributions made by the arts and sciences to human needs at this or that time, and in this or that circumstance, by convention, established by law.[7]

8. Just action as a mean, or equal

From what he has said thus far about justice, Aristotle concludes that justice is an equal, a mean, between doing what is unjust (doing too much good) and suffering what is unjust (receiving too much evil). Justice is a mean between having more, or less, than is due.

As a mean in *having, possessing*, it is a qualitative, virtual quantum, measure: an equality of doing and having, and receiving and having. In the most precise sense, however, Aristotle claims that justice is not a mean in the same way as other moral virtues are a mean: between two vices. It is chiefly an operational mean between doing what is unjust and suffering what is unjust.

Justice, that is, is a mean between doing an unjust act and tolerating (suffering) and unjust act, which, in some cases, is no vice and can be a virtue. It is a mean in external social relation, not in individual, internal appetitive extremes.

Because virtue is a habit by which, through deliberate choice, a man acts virtuously, Aristotle maintains that justice can be a virtue in two ways, in: 1) exchanges—in personal relation regarding one man's treatment of his neighbor and 2) distribution—in relation to a judge's treatment of the relation between two other men.

In relation to distributive goods like rules and honors, Aristotle asserts that the just man and just judge do the just deed by making an equal distribution according to proportion. They do not act so as to have for themselves or one or another of the litigants more than is proportionately due the parties involved.

Contrary to justice, injustice is a habit that, by deliberate choice, does what is unjust. Injustice operates by the vice of excess and defect to secure for oneself more or less of benefit or damage than is proportionately due

Aristotle maintains that injustice produces a twofold evil effect: 1) a defect of benefit and an excess of harm to the person who deserves benefit, not harm, from a social interaction; and an excess of benefit to the person who does not deserve it and a deficiency of harm to a person who merits it in the same social interaction; and 2) qualitative damage related to the human soul of the unjust party.

From his preceding remarks about the nature of justice as a mean related to social interaction, Aristotle derives three conclusions: 1) to do an unjust act is a vice pertaining to injustice; 2) to suffer injustice is no vice, is to have a vice done to oneself; and 3) injustice is not a mean between two vices. It is an extreme of excess

and defect committed by one party in a social interaction, communication, against another.[8]

9. The unjust man and political justice

Having finished treating justice and injustice in a general way,
Aristotle next starts to talk about unjust deeds related to the unjust agent by
noting that not every doer of an unjust act is an unjust person; sometimes
unjust acts are committed as a result of passion and/or ignorance, not
committed by deliberate choice. St. Thomas says Aristotle proceeds in
this way so that, by means of so doing, he may achieve a more complete
understanding of the nature of justice considered as such, and, eventually,
acquire a more complete understanding of its nature in a qualified sense
in terms of political justice.

According to Aristotle, political justice consists in a community
of life (an organizational whole) ordered to a self-sufficiency of things
pertaining to human living (having all the enabling means needed
for living a self-sufficient communal life). He maintains that a State
should be such a community in which everything sufficient for the
real needs of human life exist within it.

According to him, political justice exists in free (self-deter-
mined, self-ruling) people (those in which the measure of rule is
proportionately equal in qualitative greatness to the virtue, power,
of the self being ruled). Hence, it cannot exist in slaves, in persons
possessed of an anarchic soul, someone incapable of self-determination and self-rule, like intemperate people. He maintains that free
men exercise over slaves (in the sense of persons morally incapable of self-determination, self-rule) justice of dominion, self-control.
And political justice can only exist among equals, people equal in
the ability to exercise self-rule (moral adults), not among beings one
of whom is subject to the other by natural or political (moral) order.

Further, he maintains that political justice is of two species: 1)
distributive—proportionate equality; and 2) commutative—numeri-

cal equality. Political justice exists in free and equal people because, being enacted by law (reason), it is found in those for whom law is enacted: people who are receptive, and able, to take direction by reason and in whom injustice can exist (people who can resist taking rational direction). That political justice extends to those capable of being unjust is evident to Aristotle because legal punishment is a judgment about what is unjust. The law exists for human beings between whom just and unjust actions can exist.

Because not every virtuous or vicious action is an act generated by virtue or vice (virtuous or vicious people), Aristotle concludes that, in governing a community, law or the prudent man should rule, not those who act out of whim or passion, not anarchists, nor the imprudent.

St. Thomas says that the reason for this is that a *princeps* (ruler) who ignores the communal equal and rules according to passion, whim, rules unjustly. Because the ruler should rule for the benefit of the ruled, the reward given to rulers should be honor and glory, not wealth. Tyrants rule to acquire wealth.

St. Thomas calls justice of a master over a slave or a child (over someone psychologically incapable of self-rule) "paternal justice": justice of dominion. In a State, this is benevolent despotism. He maintains that, while both differ from it, paternal justice and benevolent despotism share some likeness to political justice.

Even though, previously, Aristotle had identified political and legal justice, had conflated them, at this point, for the sake of greater precision, he divides political justice into two species: 1) legal and 2) natural. In political regimes, he maintains that political justice has the same force and power: to induce doing good and restrain from doing evil. So, too, does the inclination to act justly.

Natural, justice, however, differs from justice by decree/ legal enactments inasmuch as legal enactments presuppose it as an evident first principle. By natural inclination our specific human nature inclines us, by reason, to distinguish the honorable from the dishonorable, the qualitatively lower from the qualitatively higher good. Aristotle maintains that jurists call "natural" (*ius naturalis*) man's generic nature as an animal to marry, have and educate children, and so on, in contrast to "the right of peoples" (*ius gentium*): man's natural inclination as a rational animal (free agent). They consider ways of behaving according to international law and agreements part of *ius gentium*. By "natural right," Aristotle understands man's nature considered as composite whole: a synthesis of *ius naturalis* (man's generic nature) and *ius gentium* (man's specific nature).

Aristotle continues that, in three ways, some types of behaving are called "legal justice": 1) habitual ways of interacting between people that become written down; 2) by starting out as a particular decree; and 3) as judicial decisions/legal enactments.

Citing Cicero, St. Thomas claims that legal/positive justice always originates from natural justice, but not as an evident conclusion from a principle. If it did, it would be applied always and everywhere. Instead, it arises through judicial decrees in two ways: 1) mixed with error, and 2) without being mixed with error.

He gives as examples of positive justice arising from natural justice the conclusions that: 1) thieves should be punished (arising from natural justice as an end to be pursued) by paying a particular fine (arising from legal justice as a means, unmixed with error, to satisfy the end); and 2) benefactors should be honored (arising from natural justice as an end to be pursued) by acts of worship (arising from legal justice as a means, mixed with error, to satisfy the end).

St. Thomas notes further, that, in ancient Greece, a man who claimed to be a follower of Socrates, Aristippos, had denied the universal nature of natural justice and had maintained that legal enactments are the origin of justice.

At this point in his analysis, Aristotle starts to prove the uni-

versal nature of natural justice by: 1) claiming that, in nature, heavenly bodies are unchangeable while earthly/human bodies change
internally and externally; and 2) saying that, while all just acts in the
world are, to some extent, changeable, some are naturally just, while
others are just by judicial decision.

He observes that just as a natural act in this world happens in
the same way in a greater number of cases, and fails in a few, so acts
that are just by nature (for example, that a deposit made to a person
should be returned) must be observed in the majority of cases, but
can fail in a few.

While human nature as a principle of action in us is unchangeable,
due to the changeable nature of individual circumstances and
conditions, habits, actions, and movements that this unchangeable
principle generates are changeable. So, too, while, in its nature, as
a principle of organizational action, justice is unchangeable (for
example, the prescription, "Thou shalt not steal!"), actions that justice
generates in the individual circumstances are changeable.

Moreover, the legally just act is: 1) always changeable, just by
arrangement, advantage, and convention for some human utility; and
2) a conventional measure, like money and scales: more diverse in
some human interactions (like in a wholesale business) and uniform
and others (like in a retail business).

While only one form of government (the just) is everywhere
best according to nature, civil law/state administration cannot be universal and uniform. *All laws are framed as needed for the chief end
for which a State is arranged*: 1) *safety*, 2) *personal perfection*, or 3)
personal freedom.

*Each legal enactment is related to individual human choices as
a causal/operational (relational) universal*: as an enabling means for
performing a doable deed to satisfy a natural need.

While the acts that justice effects are many, the cause is one, an end that justice commands: for example, that a deposit must be returned. Just how this end is to be satisfied is determined by legal enactments that differ from State to State.

Finally, while, before being executed, strictly speaking, the just and unjust action do not exist, Aristotle maintains that, in principle, they do.[9]

10. Actions that make a person just or unjust

Having considered the nature of justice and what just and unjust actions are, Aristotle next considers how: 1) what is just and unjust to do can exist without a just or unjust action; 2) a just and unjust action can exist without a just or unjust agent; and 3) a person acts justly or unjustly when acting voluntarily.

According to Aristotle, what is just considered in itself exists when the just act is considered as an organizational whole having all the parts essentially needed as a proximate principle to generate a just act. Considered in itself, what is just exists in the intellect and will of a voluntary agent who intends to execute a just act, in the praiseworthy intention of that agent.

Considered as a just action, what is just is specified by the arrangement of parts essentially needed to make the act completely whole as a just act, including voluntariness on the part of an agent to execute a just action, in the individual circumstance.

To act voluntarily, a person must: 1) be acting through his own power; 2) know precisely what he is doing; 3) and know precisely by what means and for what chief end he is doing it. For example, he must know that he is hitting someone (like a strong or weak friend/enemy or father/stranger) by means of his own power, alone, or with assisted power, within this or that individual circumstance, for a chief aim (for example, self-defense).

Since all the circumstances of an act (who is doing what, about what [to what, with what], where, why, when, and how) influence the voluntariness of an act, and since only a voluntary act can be a moral, or ethical act (a freely-chosen act), *St. Thomas maintains that these circumstances necessarily enter into the specification of an individual act as voluntary, non-voluntary, or involuntary and the determination of the nature of the individual choice and act as morally virtuous or vicious*!

Accurately to judge the nature of the whole human act, we have to know the chief aim, the enabling means, and the personal abilities of the agent, all of which comprise part of the circumstances of the act. The circumstances of the act constitute essential parts that enable the completely virtuous or vicious act to be generated in the individual circumstance: constitute all the generating principles needed to execute a morally virtuous or vicious act.

A moral act is an act authored (voluntarily caused) by someone who is a causal principle of his action (an act that an agent has the power to cause), that is in control of the agent as being executed in the way the agent intends it to be executed. *Completely voluntary actions are actions to which we consent and command that we author and control up until the total completion in this or that time or place* (only upon their successful completion can we more or less accurately determine their precise nature as voluntary, involuntary, or non-voluntary). *Considered as such, such acts essentially depend upon participation of particular reason, the estimative sense, in their execution: in their command and control*![10]

11. Whether a person can voluntarily suffer injustice and a just person easily execute unjust acts

After considering how a person can voluntarily perform just and unjust acts, in three ways Aristotle starts to answer the question whether a person can voluntarily suffer injustice: 1) Evident, he says, is that some people unwillingly, involuntarily, suffer injustice (for example, blows, flogging, robbery). 2) He asks whether a man who involuntarily suffers blows, flogging, or robbery essentially, or incidentally, is a victim of injustice. And, 3) he asks whether, if a person can voluntarily suffer injustice, such suffering can, in some way, still be involuntary.

Next, Aristotle attempts to answer the immediately preceding questions by defining injustice generically as essentially voluntarily inflicting injury.

After doing this, he gives the example of an incontinent person voluntarily inflicting injury upon himself and, in so doing, apparently voluntarily doing injustice to himself.

Then, he poses the question whether, if an incontinent person can permit another person (for example, a prostitute) to injure (for instance, beat or rob) him, could the incontinent person voluntarily suffer injustice? As another example, Aristotle talks about whether a person does injustice to himself by tolerating such injustice for a greater political good.

Aristotle resolves the question whether a person can voluntarily suffer injustice by stating that, without qualification, the definition he had given of doing injustice as voluntarily inflicting injury was incorrect. *Strictly speaking, doing injustice is voluntarily inflicting an injury on another person against his will.*

Absolutely speaking, *with a complete will*, Aristotle maintains that no one willingly suffers injustice because, strictly speaking, *doing injustice is to inflict harm upon someone else against his will. With a complete will*, he maintains that no one, not even the incontinent man (although, at least in part, he is willingly hurting himself), *completely wills* to hurt himself, or will, in any way, to suffer injustice.

As a result of concupiscence, then, in a moment not totally driven by intense, overpowering, passion, one in which the incontinent person does not think what he wants to do is really good, the incontinent person is attracted to seek a lesser, or apparent, not real, good (a real evil), nonetheless, once overpowered by intense passion, he subordinates whatever he possesses of prudent judgment and good will to command of his disordered sensitive appetite and chooses the apparent over the real, or lower over the higher, good.

Consequently, Aristotle's conclusion is that, absolutely speaking, because the principle of action is in the agent, doing injustice is voluntary; and, *because the principle (proximate cause) of suffering injustice is the unjust doer of injustice*, suffering injustice is chiefly involuntary.

Having resolved one question about injustice, Aristotle considers another: In distributions, who does injustice: the giver, the taker, or both?

He resolves this question by saying that, if the conclusion he just drew about suffering injustice is true, a problem appears to arise because, at times, people knowingly, willing, give more good to others than they do to themselves. Moreover, virtuous people are inclined to accept less good than they give.

In proposing his solution to this question, Aristotle notes a twofold difficulty about this situation. Sometimes, while the giver gives a greater external good away, he receives a qualitatively greater internal good in return (for example glory, a moral/honorable good, a good of greater quality/intensive quantity for a person than, for example, receiving money).

For three reasons, therefore, Aristotle maintains that a person who accepts too little or too much good from another does not always commit an injustice: 1) Only a person who voluntarily wills to commit an injustice can do an injustice. 2) A person can act as a chief, or instrumental, principle of an act; be the recipient of an injustice, an instrument of injustice, and not be its cause. And 3) in distributions, the giver is analogous to a judge in exchanges. In distributions, if the giver knowingly shows favoritism to one party over another, the giver acts unjustly. On the other hand, if the receiver receives such a distribution in ignorance, he does not act unjustly.

After resolving this question, St. Thomas presents Aristotle as refuting some false opinions about doing injustice, starting with the false notion that being habitually unjust is easy. According to St. Thomas, Aristotle starts to undermine this notion by maintaining that, while the opportunity to do unjust acts is sometimes great and immediate, doing unjust acts immediately and with pleasure is not easily and immediately in our powers.

Precise knowledge of the just and unjust action in the individual situation is not easy to possess, requires prudence, *a special kind of estimative and adaptive knowing and ability to adjust to a situation* that, in the prudent man, enables universal principles to be used as right regulatory guides (measures) in individual circumstances. In short, doing injustice with the skill analogous to that of a craftsman would require a healthy estimative sense of the qualitative greatness that only a prudent man possesses, which the habitually unjust person does not possess.

Second, Aristotle refutes the false claim (represented, for example, by Plato, in his famous fable of the "Ring of Gyges") that the just man can do injustice as easily as anyone else because he has a greater knowledge of how to do unjust acts. Strictly speaking, Aristotle maintains: 1) this claim is false, 2) that, by disposition of justice, the just man is the person least capable of doing injustice. Virtue inclines its possessor easily to use goods well, not badly, to have its possessor's acts naturally reflect the nature of its proximate principle. Hence, just people incline easily to execute just acts, and to perform unjust acts with great difficulty, against their habitual inclination; and unjust people easily incline to execute vicious acts.[11]

12. Equity

Having considered justice in general, under the following three topics, Aristotle next considers equity, a general directive of justice: 1) its formal object; 2) its subject; and 3) the kind of habit it is.

To start his inquiry, he: 1) distinguishes the equitable act/person from the just act/person; 2) says that the equitable act/person is better (or more just) than the just person considered as such; 3) claims that, sometimes, the behavior of the equitably just person departs from that of the legally just person; and 4) says that people tend to praise the equitable person as "manly" and "perfect."

After shortly wondering about how the equitable person can possibly be better than the just person and more praiseworthy, and not be better if not more praised, he solves this problem by saying that the equitable act is one species of just act better than another species of just act. Equity is a habit of justice different from the habit of legal justice. Because natural justice is the proximate principle that generates legal justice/positive law, the equitable act is a species of natural justice, and natural justice is a species of justice higher in quality, intensive quantum greatness, than the species of justice existing within legal justice/positive law.

Since natural law governs individuals and actions considered as species individuals and species acts, but positive law governs implementation of natural law within individual circumstances, Aristotle and St. Thomas maintain that prudence dictates a person should correct mistakes in the application of positive law when they happen in particular circumstances (for example, like outdated safety laws).

Because legislation cannot possibly cover all the different ways in which the naturally just act can possibly be applied in all different times and places, application of natural justice to positive law invariably generates defective precepts. Nonetheless, because this is the only way in which legislators can legislate, they include such defective precepts as part of legislation with the understanding that, in the individual circumstances, through use of equity, just legislators will correct such mistakes if they can.

The mistake in positive law arises from the nature of individual human actions, which always exist within different circumstances. Hence, Aristotle and St. Thomas maintain that the nature of the equitable is clear: it is a natural law corrective and directive of positive law where positive law is defective in a particular case. They maintain that positive law can never be applied with absolute rigidity in individual cases. *It must be applied proportionately to the situation like with the leaden rule of the mason! That is, to be a real equity a law must be applied under the direction of a healthy estimative sense faculty: prudentially!*

Hence, an equitable judge should: 1) not be a zealot; 2) not add more punishment than is needed to be medicinal; 3) possess a healthy estimative sense, when directed by the moral virtue of prudence.[12]

13. Whether a person can be unjust to himself

Aristotle ends Book 5 of the *Nicomachean Ethics* by examining whether a person can be unjust to himself.

For two reasons, Aristotle claims that, strictly speaking, the answer is, "No": 1) Law commands acts that are, appear to be, considered of themselves, just according to some virtue. Law forbids acts that are, appear to be, considered of themselves unjust according to some virtue. Consequently, law does not command a person to commit suicide because, considered in its nature, suicide appears to be forbidden as naturally unjust. 2) A person who injures another person contrary to law voluntarily does injustice. A person who takes his own life in anger willingly injures himself contrary to law.

While a person can voluntarily, willingly, kill himself, according to Aristotle, strictly speaking, he cannot "murder" (unjustly kill) himself because, by definition, no person with complete will, voluntariness, can suffer an injustice. By definition, *an injustice is an act involuntarily received as by an instrument*. Consequently, at times, States impose possible punishment related to suicide (for example, dishonoring the body of the man who commits suicide by dragging it in public or leaving it unburied) as a public expression of injustice committed by the perpetrator of suicide against the State and to discourage its practice.

In terms of particular, or individual, justice, for three reasons Aristotle says no one can commit an injustice against himself: 1) According to particular justice, a man who does injustice receives more than his due good, and the person who suffers injustice receives less than his due good. If a person could do injustice to himself, *simultaneously* a person could give to and take from himself contrary opposites of more and less good (like health and disease) in the same part of himself. 2) Doing injustice to oneself must be done voluntarily, with deliberate choice, *prior to* suffering injustice. The man who voluntarily injures himself must, then, with deliberate choice, simultaneously, involuntarily, against his choice, suffer from the effects of this unjust act before it has been executed. 3) If a person voluntarily could do injustice to himself, suffering injustice would not be a violent (involuntary) act.

Aristotle maintains that the problem of whether or not a person can act unjustly toward himself is completely solved by recognizing that, by definition, unjust acts *are involuntary acts on the part of the receiver* (who, as a receiver, exists as an instrument of, not a chief principle of, an act of injustice) and voluntary on the part of the doer.

Next, Aristotle asserts that doing injustice is morally evil, that doers of injustice receive more good and less evil than is their due, and that, while suffering injustice need not be morally evil on the part of the receiver, those who suffer injustice receive less good than is their due.

Finally, because it is more shameful, doing injustice is morally worse than suffering injustice. Even though, incidentally, suffering injustice can result in more injustice down the road, in no way, strictly speaking, can the person who suffers injustice be considered, called, morally "evil."[13]

—Notes—

1. St. Thomas Aquinas, *Commentary on the Nicomachean Ethics of Aristotle*, Bk. 5, Lect. 1, nn. 885–899.
2. Id., Lect. 2, nn. 900–912.
3. Id., Lect. 3, nn. 913–926.
4. Id., Lects. 4–5, nn. 927–946.
5. Id., Lects. 6–7, nn. 947–964.
6. Id., Lect. 8, nn. 965–977.
7. Id., Lect. 9, nn. 978–991.
8. Id., Lect. 10, nn. 992–999.
9. Id., Lects. 11–12, nn. 1000–1034.
10. Id., Lect. 13, nn. 1035–1049.
11. Id., Lects. 14–15, nn. 1050–1077; see, also, Plato, *Republic*, Bk. 2, 358E–360E.
12. Id., Lect. 16, nn. 1078–1090.
13. Id., Lect. 17, nn. 1091–1107.

–Chapter Twelve–
Intellectual Virtues

ACCORDING TO ST THOMAS, after finishing his study of the definition of moral virtue, Aristotle devotes Book 6 of the *Nicomachean Ethics* to a consideration of the definition of intellectual virtue by first noting that, whenever science is at work, the intellectual virtue of right reason is at work. Since right reason is at work in both speculative and practical science, we might expect Aristotle to talk about right reason in both these species. Instead, at this point in the *Nicomachean Ethics*, Aristotle ignores speculative science as a species of right reason and only considers practical reason and its subdivisions.

1. Right reason and practical science

Before discussing the species of practical right reason, St. Thomas notes how, *wherever it is found, right reason determines a mean between excess and defect: a state of perfection*! While Aristotle and St. Thomas do not precisely say so at this point, in speculative science, that mean would be truth (*adaequatio*), *a relation of equality of proportion* expressed in an intellectual judgment regarding the human intellect and what is. To explain more precisely the nature of right reason in practical science, St. Thomas claims that, in all moral virtues considered thus far and all art, a man with right reason keeps his eye on a mark, and object.

St. Thomas says this mark, object, virtue's formal object, is analogous to a rule for a craftsman: 1) what is becoming/fitting; 2) what we must not add to or fall short of; 3) *the proportionate equal*;

339

4) the mean of virtue; 5) *a proportionate equal relating contrary opposites within the same genus.*

Because right reason is crucial to understand so as to comprehend the natures of virtue and science, St. Thomas adds to, specifies, Aristotle's claim that further inquiry about the nature of right reason is needed. He starts doing this by noting that right reason is something, and, the universal principle, measure, used in all human occupations involving practical science (like strategy, medicine, and so on) and also in speculative science. In all science, neither too much nor too little should be done nor passed over. What determines, measures, is what holds the middle and accords with right reason.

But, St. Thomas adds, the man who considers this common measure, rule, alone, because of its generality (the many ways it can be applied), will not know how rationally to use it in the individual situation. For example, knowing the right measure in science is right reason, if, in an individual situation, a person asked a medical doctor precisely what prescription should be given to this person at this time to restore health, based upon the rule of right reason, the physician could not answer that question with precision. *The right prescription is a right plan of action.* So, too, is good law in civil matters.

As an example, St. Thomas gives the following analogy. Just as the right plan of prudence (order of choice) is the right guide (measure, prescription) in moral matters, so the right plan of art (order of choice) is the right guide in art.

Extending this analogy to speculative matters, following St. Thomas, we can rightly assert that the right plan of speculative science is the right guide in speculative science (that is, the right order of judgment, reasoning).

At this point, St. Thomas adds that, again, such examples taken from human habits are insufficient to know precisely how to operate in the individual situation. Put in contemporary military terms, while they give the right strategy, they do not give the right tactics. Such examples are too generic. To make up for such deficiencies, we need a precise, specific definition of the limits of right reason, a precise, specific, determination of the norm of right reason.

To start to give such a specific, precise definition, determination, St. Thomas says that Aristotle begins a study of the intellectual virtues that regulate, order, human reason; but, *because we cannot know the virtues without first knowing the soul,* he prefaces this study with a discussion of the soul's nature.

St. Thomas, then, tells us that Aristotle resumes study of the human soul by recalling its specific divisions into: 1) rational absolutely considered (*simpliciter*), whose formal objects are necessary beings, whose principles are unchangeable and invariable, that exist and act in one fixed way; and 2) rational relationally considered (*secundum quid*) by participating in reason perfected by moral virtue, whose formal objects are contingent beings, whose principles are somewhat contingent, variable.

St. Thomas justifies this division by saying that different parts (faculties) of the soul should correspond (be proportionate) to different formal objects (proportionately in intensive quantity, qualitative, receptivity and capacity) that essentially stimulate them to act. The qualitative, intensive quantum, receptivity and capacity of the faculty must be qualitatively proportionate in qualitative power of receptivity to the intensive quantum activity of the agent that activates it.

Knowledge, he says, exists in parts of the soul according as they have some greatness of likeness (a proportion of likeness) to the thing known. According to its peculiar nature, each faculty of the soul is qualitatively proportioned, proportioned in receptive capacity, natural ability, to know formal objects that stimulate it to act. Aristotle calls "scientific" that part of the rational soul whose formal object, external stimulus, is necessary beings: beings that exist and act in only one way. He calls "estimative" that part of the rational soul whose formal object is contingent beings. He maintains that estimating, deliberating, refer to the same formal object, what is changeable, contingent. Because no one deliberates about what acts, exists, in only one way, he says that deliberation is an inquiry not yet concluded, like argumentation.

St. Thomas, however, *doubts this division* that Aristotle makes is suitable, saying that Aristotle divides the intellect into: 1) the acting (the power of operating on all things) and 2) the potential (the power of becoming all things). So, by their very nature, they have the same formal object: *the true.* Hence, they must belong to the same genus. The true about necessary matters and the true about contingent matters belong to the same genus. If, by the same power, we apprehend extremes of the same genus, if for example the faculty of sight, which is less noble in power than the intellectual power, can see incorruptible beings (like the material bodies existing in the everlasting heavens) and contingent Earthly bodies, so can the intellectual power know necessary and contingent truths.

St. Thomas solves this apparent contradiction by saying that we can understand contingent beings in two ways: abstractly and concretely. Abstractly, we understand contingent natures according to fixed part/whole relations in terms of their organizational parts being capable of generating their generic acts. Concretely considered, we understand contingent natures according to the way they operate, exist, in the contingent situation.

Abstractly considered is the way speculative sciences like physics and the division of physics like astronomy study necessary and contingent beings: as abstractly considered movers/agents.

Concretely considered is the way practical sciences like prudence and art proceed. Prudence and art consider things as they concretely exist, composite wholes as generating, causing, specific acts in individual circumstances. They do this through use of particular reason, the *estimative sense*, which, initially, individually *collates*, mnemonically *specifies* into a quasi-nominalistic, sensory, experiential universal, some multitude into a temporal, generic relation: for example, that whenever, in the past, some person has been sick with this disease, when given this medication, this person's health has been improved, or totally restored. Thus understood, contingent beings and *operational universals* can be formal objects of speculative intellect.[1]

2. Intellectual virtues as they relate to different parts of the soul

After dividing the parts of the soul, St. Thomas tells us that Aristotle examines the intellectual virtues by which each part is perfected by first proposing a generic definition of virtue as "what renders good a thing's work."

After giving this generic definition, Aristotle says he needs to consider the most excellent habit (the best virtue) of each part because this most excellent habit, virtue, perfects the proper operation of each part. When it guarantees that an action is performed in the best way (with highest virtual quantity, highest quality) perfection, this habit would be best (of maximum intensity of greatness in quality!).

To determine the proper operation of each part, Aristotle considers the end, good, of each part. Regarding the intellectual part, Aristotle says two activities are proper to human beings: 1) knowing the truth and 2) self-mastered action; and three principles in the soul have mastery over these two activities: the human intellect and the intellectual and sense appetites. Since neither the senses nor the sense appetite are psychological principles of truth, considered as such, in and of themselves, the senses and the sense appetite play no essential role in generating self-mastered (emotionally self-controlled) moral action.

An Introduction to Ragamuffin Ethics

Because they lack an intrinsic principle of voluntary activity (the power rationally, abstractly, to deliberate), while brute animals have senses, these animals do not have within them principles that enable them proximately to generate moral interaction. St. Thomas maintains that the intellect and sense appetitive faculty can achieve a kind of unity and harmony (peace) inasmuch as what the intellect declares good, the appetitive faculty pursues, and what it declares to be bad the appetitive faculty avoids. This peace, harmony, is not found in other animals.

St. Thomas maintains that the appetitive faculty and intellect can harmonize because they have proportionate, complementary, analogous, relatable powers. The intellect has two chief actions in judging: 1) affirmation, by which it assents to (accepts, is receptive to) what is true; and 2) negation, by which it dissents from (rejects, resists) what is false. Analogously, proportionately, these two acts correspond to two acts of the appetitive faculty: 1) to be receptive to, tend, adhere, to the good; and 2) flee, withdraw from, resist, dissent from, the bad.

He maintains that, in well-ordered moral choice and activity, these actions of the intellect and appetite harmonize, cooperate. St. Thomas calls *choice* "the appetitive faculty deliberating" because choice essentially involves what has been rationally pre-considered, deliberated about. He asserts that choice is the concurrence of reason and appetite, an act of the intellect commanding, prescribing action. For choice to be completely good, he maintains that what reason commands must be true and what the appetitive faculty pursues must be good or what it avoids must be evil.

St. Thomas claims, further, that, in speculative knowing, absolutely considered, the abstractly considered true is good and the false is bad. The good of the practical intellect, however, is not abstract conformity, abstract harmonization of the intellect with what

344

is. It is concrete conformity of the truths of the intellect with the right appetite (a prudentially-, rightly-guided appetite), an act of the intellect conforming to right desire. Choice is essentially a composite act of the: 1) *intellect commanding* and 2) *appetite consenting*.

St. Thomas asserts that man as a free agent is a proximate principle of moral choice. If truth of the practical intellect is determined by conformity with right appetite, and right appetite is determined by the fact that the appetite agrees with right reason (prudence) conforming with, fulfilling, real human needs, man's end is determined by nature, not by social contract or choice. *Rectitude of the appetitive faculty to fulfilling real human needs, as determined by human nature, is the specific, precise prescription, measure of truth, for practical reason*!

Moral virtue is a habit of free choice. As a voluntary activity, free choice is directed toward *real*, not fictional, *means* that actually fulfill natural needs. The truth of practical reason (the means that actually satisfy real human needs, the means really healthy to choose) is the precise, specific, rule, measure, of rectitude for the appetitive faculty. Hence, the appetitive faculty is called "right" inasmuch as it pursues the means that reason considers true, suitable, fitting/proportionate, healthy, in the individual situation.

Like the speculative intellect, the practical intellect *starts* its reasoning from a universal consideration of a generic subject, but it terminates, concludes, its reasoning in an individual, doable deed judged to be such in conjunction with particular reason (the estimative sense)! *The doable deed is the subject, genus, of practical science! Satisfaction of the doable deed terminates practical science just as a true conclusion terminates speculative reason.*

According to St. Thomas, both universal and particular reason have a relation to action. *Because it determines whether or not a deed is doable for this or that individual within the context of this or that situation, particular reason, the estimative sense, specifies the action that universal reason generically considers.* In both its speculative and practical divisions, the human intellect is a principle of action: of 1) speculatively judging what is and 2) practically choosing what can be a real means to a real end. Choice is the appetitive faculty, under the direction of reason, commanding, organizing, action after rational deliberation. Considered as such, it is an efficient cause, proximate principle, of action. Choice is the appetitive faculty ordered to a means, commanded by reason as suitable for this or that end in this or that situation. In the act of choice: 1) reason proposes an end and subsequently starts to deliberate about suitable means to achieve this end; 2) after reason terminates deliberation, the appetite consents or does not consent to the end or means.

The effect of choice in action (good or evil action) cannot exist without comparing the deliberating intellect to some inclination existing within the appetitive faculty. Consequently, prior to choice being effected, the human intellect and the estimative sense must cooperate in comparing choice as a cause and the appetitive faculty being commanded to cooperate in effecting the cause.

While the human intellect is a principle of action, St. Thomas maintains that, considered in and of itself, the speculative intellect moves nothing else because the speculative intellect prescribes and commands nothing about pursuit and flight. The intellect as a principle of practical action is an intellect *intent on* achieving, satisfying, an end *by harmonizing operation*, generating an individual action or thing as an end. Aristotle gives an example of the productive arts of a builder constructing a house for use as a shelter. This is a concrete, individual product, not an abstract one, for a concrete, individual end. In moral activity, in the individual situation, the choices *that prudence arranges* (harmonizes) are acts of the appetitive faculty as a means to an end of perfect operation.[2]

3. Enumeration of the intellectual virtues and how every science can be taught

After finishing his study of the nature of human choice, Aristotle starts to examine particular intellectual virtues by first specifically defining intellectual virtues of wisdom, science, understanding, prudence, and art as habits by which the soul expresses the truth by affirming and denying.

Starting with the virtue of science, Aristotle says it is a habit perfecting the intellect regarding necessary things. He maintains that knowing with certainty is proper to science because, properly speaking, science is the best form of human knowledge. The best form of human knowledge knows with certainty. Only the necessary, what can be in only one way, removes doubt. Without qualification, the subject of science is what is unchangeable, necessary.

Nonetheless, St. Thomas claims that even the science of the producible and perishable (like physics) can exist, but its principles for determining truth cannot be based upon contingent particulars subject to generation and corruption. All science must be based upon universal, necessary, perpetually existing, or eternal, principles.

Explaining science by its cause, Aristotle says that every noble thing can be learned by someone with the ability. All teaching, science, must arise from some prior knowledge. We cannot arrive at knowledge of some yet-unknown thing except by some known thing.

Moreover, by means of things known a twofold teaching and way of learning exists, by: 1) *induction* by which we understand some principle and some universal experience of singulars; 2) *syllogism*, which proceeds from universal principles known by induction. Induction is a principle of the syllogism.

Not every syllogism, however, generates scientific knowledge and causes speculative science. Only demonstrative syllogisms generate speculative science. Hence, speculative science is a habit caused by demonstration.

To have science, first principles of knowledge must exist, be known by a scientist, be assented to, and understood better, with higher qualitative greatness, than the conclusion because the cause must be more powerful (of greater intensive quantity, qualitative intensity) than the effect. That which causes science must be more, better, known than science.

Aristotle maintains that, to perfect knowledge about different species of contingent things, the intellect must use: 1) prudence regarding the act to be done (performance activity) and 2) art regarding the thing to be made (productive activity). A habit that, through reason, causes action (prudence) is not specifically identical with a habit that, through reason, produces things (art) because the habits of art and prudence have different formal objects, different subjects of formal interest.[3]

4. The nature of prudence

After considering in general the specific difference between the nature of prudence and art, next Aristotle starts to examine the nature of prudence by saying he will do so by studying the behavior of people we tend to call "prudent." He asserts we commonly call a person "prudent" in two ways, essentially related to two different kinds of contingent matters. 1) Generally, we call person who gives good advice about proper (proportionate) and useful goods in some particular matter "prudent in particular," or "relatively prudent" (*secundum quid*). And 2) we call a person "prudent absolutely" (*simpliciter*), unqualifiedly, who gives good advice about proper and useful goods for the whole life of man.

A quality common to people who possess either or both forms of prudence is that they assume the end pursued is good because, to make deductions, correct inferences about things (means) useful for an evil end is as contrary to prudence as it is for a dentist or medical doctor to assume that disease is the chief aim of dentistry or medicine.

To start defining prudence through negative reasoning (from effect to cause), Aristotle observes that no one deliberates about things that are unchangeable or beyond our power. That is, from the outset, in starting to define prudence negatively, Aristotle takes for granted that this method of definition must involve use of cogitative reason (particular reason), or the *estimative sense.*

From this intellectual first principle involving use of estimative reason, Aristotle concludes that, strictly speaking, because the principles of prudence are somewhat variable, flexible, not totally rigid, strictly speaking, prudence cannot be "science" (speculative science) because *demonstration causes speculative science*; and the subject whose principles prudence considers are not amenable to strict demonstration. Prudence is about giving good advice regarding organizing plans of action (strategies and tactics) related to changeable matters worthy of deliberation: concrete actions to take in variable situations.

Furthermore, Aristotle maintains that prudence and art cannot be identical because they are different intellectual acts having generically different formal objects, qualitatively different kinds of doable deeds. Prudence studies the genus of action, chiefly aims at terminating choice in a well-done deed, while art studies the genus of making, and chiefly aims at terminating choice in a well-made product, producing some organized whole (like a house or a bridge).

Aristotle and St. Thomas maintain that knowledge of contingent beings cannot possess truth's certainty in affirming truth and rejecting falsehood, and cannot perfect the intellect as speculative knowing can. However, it can perfect the intellect as commanding, controlling, prescribing the useful, doable deed, and directing human acts to satisfy ends. As Aristotle says, art is a habit concerned with making something through reason. Hence, every productive habit directed by reason is art.

St. Thomas maintains that art's subject-matter includes two parts: 1) the product made or activity done and 2) the act of the craftsman, artistic performer, that the art directs. He adds that a threefold operation exists in art, to: 1) consider how to make or do something; 2) work on the external material or subject to be organized; and 3) make something or perform some action. Art is also concerned with preparatory work: qualifying the material and observing how art may make or do something.

In productive arts, St. Thomas maintains that two things especially need to be considered on the part of the work undertaken: 1) whether products can or cannot be made; whether or not the subject of interest to produce is a contingent and improvable being; and 2) whether the principle of artistic creativity exists in the artist alone as an intrinsic principle, or whether it also exists in the thing made as an extrinsic, instrumental, principle.

St. Thomas states that mathematics and metaphysics consider necessary causes existing in their subjects of study. Physics, in turn, studies causes of motion intrinsic to its subject, mobile bodies. Further, art gives directions for making; prudence gives directions for action.

He says that prudence is a habit concerned with: 1) action; 2) things good (healthy) and bad (unhealthy) for human beings; and 3) causing human actions that perfect human beings in our ability to satisfy real human needs. For example, because general contracting is a productive art, the chief aim, end, last act at which the art of general contracting aims is completing construction of a building, an edifice external to the builder. In contrast, the chief aim and last act at which prudence aims is excellent, perfect, action, operation: action internal to the agent, not transient action terminating in a product made. This is because prudence is a performance excellence.

Other species of performance excellence also exist: performance arts. For example, fine arts like music and dance, poetry. Such forms of practical excellence chiefly aim at perfecting different faculties of the human person; they do not chiefly aim at perfecting human life considered as a whole: perfecting human nature and the whole of a human life lived under the direction of a perfected human nature. Professionals concerned with this specialized way of knowing are people who can estimate well about what is good for themselves and other human beings from the standpoint of living a qualitatively perfect human life, perfect as an organizational whole. Often, historically, people have identified political philosophers/scientists as engaged in this sort of profession.

St. Thomas says that prudence derives its name from the Greek word *"phronēsis"* ("reasoning") while temperance derives its name from the Greek word *"sophrosyne"* ("preserving reasoning"). Precisely by monitoring pleasures and pains of touch, temperance preserves a right *estimation* of good acts to be done and bad acts to be avoided. While pleasure and pain have less of an impact upon right reason related to speculative judgments, they tend to have a major impact upon right reason related to specifically, precisely, *estimating* what needs to be done and avoided in practical matters in the individual situation. St. Thomas maintains that this major impact occurs because, in practical actions, what is best in the genus is the last act, *the numerically-one act* for which all the other acts are planned, harmonized, used as tools, done: the final act that all the other acts exist cooperatively to generate, for which they do everything they do.

For a person experiencing intense pleasure and pain, judgment of what is really best is often distorted. *As a result, the judgment of the intemperate man does not see clearly the doable end* (a first principle of prudence), becomes unable to desire this as his real end. *He takes his eye off the ball, as we might say today. He loses the appetitive strength to maintain focus under the pressure of emotional conflict involving pleasure and pain.* Today, we would say that such a person inclines to *choke under pressure*!

As a result, *because his moral psychology is essentially unhealthy*, to choose and do everything as a means for satisfying his real end, satisfy his real needs, no longer appears necessary to the intemperate man. Like every moral vice/bad habit, *the imprudent judgment of the intemperate man distorts the health of particular reason, the ability of the estimative sense rightly to apprehend real ends, real needs, and the prudentially-grasped enabling means to secure them.* In distorting right estimation of the right end, the vice of intemperance distorts right desire; and in distorting right estimation of the right means to satisfy real needs, it distorts right reason's ability to recognize the real means to do so in the individual situation.

From what he has said thus far about prudence, Aristotle concludes it is necessarily a habit of action directed by right reason toward the real good of man, the really good doable human deed.

While not essentially part of their chief aim according to their professional activity, nonetheless, to some extent, St. Thomas claims that every productive and performance art essentially depends upon prudence to be able to maintain a professional moral culture that sustains the health of the productive or performance activity generated by the art. As St. Thomas says, these arts do not depend upon prudence so that they can fulfill their nature considered as such, but they do depend upon prudence rightly to regulate the proper use of these arts within different circumstances and situations. They depend upon prudence to preserve their principles, the natural abilities of the respective arts, including the strength of appetitive ability and physical health needed to focus on pursuit of the chief aim of the art and appetitively to support right reasoning about the right means to satisfy the aim within the individual situation.

For example, while a general contractor might, in virtue of his art, have the ability to construct a good building here and now, some vice of intemperance (like drug addiction) might cause him to become lazy or physically ill to such an extent that he is no longer able or willing to do so. Analogously, the same scenario applies to athletes, movie stars, investment bankers, and all other professional artists.

While a moral virtue, like justice, might intervene and cause such a person to start to use his or her art out of a sense of duty (for example, to help a friend in need), after an art is acquired, to be consistently maintained as securely possessed, the artist will still need to exercise the moral virtue of prudence to regulate right use of the art.

Moreover, after prudence is acquired, additional moral virtue is needed to regulate right use of a professional activity because prudence is essentially joined to directing moral virtues that preserve individual human beings, species life, and real human goods. While prudence helps us rationally to focus, fix on, the right means to achieve a right end (the right reasoning to do so), the cardinal moral virtues of justice, courage, and temperance keep us appetitively focused on the right ends to pursue (the right desires that satisfy real needs).

For the principles of prudence to be preserved, rectitude of the appetitive faculty's conceiving of real ends and fulfilling real needs (right desire) must be preserved. The other moral virtues preserve the right desire in the appetites for the right ends, while prudence preserves the ability to focus the faculties of universal reason and estimative sense on the right reasoning involved to secure the right means to satisfy those ends within the individual situation.

Consequently, St. Thomas says prudence is not an art consisting in knowing the truth of reason. It is a moral virtue commanding rectitude of appetite like that possessed by moral virtue. Even though prudence is chiefly an intellectual virtue, by participation (*secundum quid*), *it is an intellectual virtue existing in the estimative, conjectural, part of the soul just as in a subject.* Unlike art, it is not connected to an act of reason alone. Prudence is a cooperative act of right reason (including right estimation) and right appetite (right desire).

St. Thomas concludes his treatment of prudence by saying that cessation of right desire, not lack of use, causes prudence to be lost, forgotten. So long as right desire exists, is engaged with things, ends, belonging to prudence (that is, with desire to fulfill real human needs), to some extent, the ability to act prudently exists.[4]

5. The intellectual virtue of understanding

After examining the intellectual habits of right reason through which the intellect is perfected, St. Thomas says Aristotle next considers intellectual first principles that right reason presupposes in all its species: 1) understanding, from which demonstrative reason, science, is generated; and 2) wisdom, from which all other principles of right reason are, to some extent, derived.

Aristotle says that science is a judgment about universals and necessary and unchanging beings. He maintains that particular and contingent beings, which fall within the apprehension of the senses, do not attain scientific certainty. Because science (which is found in demonstrative reason that proceeds from principles to conclusions) reasons from cause to effect (*proper quid*), he states that some principles of science necessarily involve demonstrable conclusions. Hence, the principle of demonstrative science necessarily is not a prudence, art, or science, not even the science of metaphysics.

According to Aristotle, strictly speaking, first principles of demonstrative science: 1) must be indemonstrable causes; 2) cannot proceed to infinity; 3) cannot be contingent; and 4) are what we know best. Because the subjects they consider are contingent beings, in some, not all, beings (not what we know best), strictly speaking, art and prudence cannot provide principles of demonstrative science. And metaphysics cannot provide these principles because the metaphysician starts reasoning from indemonstrable principles of speculative reasoning to arrive at first principles of being (first principles of existence and organizational operation).

Since, whether they consider necessary or contingent subjects, nothing false can be a first principle of an intellectual science; and since prudence, art, science, and wisdom are species of virtues of right reason, *the intellectual virtue of understanding grasps the first principles of all other intellectual virtues.* By the habit, or virtue, of understanding, St. Thomas says he does not mean the human intellect considered as a faculty. He means a particular habit of the intellectual faculty by which a man, in *virtue of the light of the intellect engaged in acting* naturally and immediately (*that is, by means of induction!*) understands principles (like every whole is greater than a part) from a knowledge of the terms.[5]

6. The intellectual virtue of wisdom

Having considered the virtue understanding, Aristotle next considers wisdom in a qualified sense (relatively) and in an unqualified sense (absolutely). In so doing, he states that, in a qualified sense, wisdom is the highest excellence of any particular art or science, the maximum of perfection in an art or science. Among architectonically-arranged arts, wisdom is that one art whose principles direct and command lower arts, like tools servicing a higher art. For example, arts of performance, doing, or use govern arts of production just as sailing governs the art of shipbuilding. But, in an unqualified sense, wisdom, the science of metaphysics, studies principles of being most noble in themselves.

Considered as such, the science of wisdom is not a highest art or science within some genus of art and science. Because it knows first principles of all being (organizations), not just of all demonstration, the science of wisdom is the perfection of all sciences, is the most certain of sciences, of all modes of knowing. It judges about principles of demonstrable science in order to explain them, make them more intelligible. It does not do so to prove them. It does so to declare their truth and defend them against those who attempt to deny them.

Of all the intellectual virtues, St. Thomas says Aristotle considers wisdom to be the highest, and he shows why it must be the chief intellectual virtue and science. Considered as such, wisdom can be no ordinary science. Aristotle considered it to be a science of the most honorable things, a science of divine things: of beings of highest quality, intensive quantity, greatness of being, and highest good/perfection. Within its nature, in some way, as the chief of all sciences, it contains all the principles of the other sciences.

Just as the senses located in the human head direct all the movements of the other bodily parts, St. Thomas says that, because, to some extent, all the sciences take their principles from it, wisdom directs all the other sciences, is the command and control science of all science. Following Aristotle, St. Thomas claims that philosophers who maintain that political science (which governs the multitude) or prudence (which governs a single person) is the highest science are wrong. No science *of use* can be the highest science, best of sciences.

The best science has as its subject the best of all subjects, goods, beings: the most perfect of all natures (the being of greatest quality, intensive quantity, of goodness; the most perfect of beings existence). Since human beings are not the best of all beings, Aristotle maintains that political science cannot be the highest science.

Some things that exist are contingent, variable (have composite natures comprised of parts chiefly existing in proportion, relation, to each other). Such beings exist in unequal proportion, relation, intensity, quality, perfection, to qualities and conditions said of them. Such qualities and conditions are predicated unequally of the subjects to which they refer according to unequal relation, analogously of the subjects that possess them. Other beings are predicated according to equal relation of their subjects, univocally, like white of colors and straight of figures. According to Aristotle, divine beings (like the Intelligences that move the planets) *in which wisdom resides as a nature* are always the same, unchanging. The wisdom that resides in such beings is always the same, predicated univocally of them. And wisdom that is the science of all first principles includes study of such beings.

But prudence, which exists in finite things, human beings, is predicated relationally, analogously, participatively, according to the unequal power of receiving of the subject of which is said. For example, a person of different levels of prudence, and human beings and other animals.

If any and every science were wisdom, since many sciences exist, many wisdoms would exist, and political science would be wisdom. But, metaphysics studies unchanging principles and all beings without qualification. In contrast, politics studies somewhat variable principles of human communities. Hence, it cannot be wisdom considered in an unqualified sense.

Even though man is the most excellent of animals, St. Thomas maintains that God, angels, separate substances, are more excellent than principles of less excellent beings. Analogous to the intellectual virtues of science and understanding, wisdom is science and understanding of the most honorable beings, the highest principles. While prudence considers human goods, wisdom considers goods better than human.[6]

7. Prudence as the chief virtue in human relations

According to Aristotle and St. Thomas, deliberating well is the work of prudence, not the work wisdom. The prudent man without qualification is a good counselor, advisor, someone who can *estimate* among different alternatives what is best to do. Because prudence is a principle of action, prudence considers both universals (in which action does not occur) and singulars, principles of action. Since action chiefly has to do with singulars, concerning action, knowledge of singular principles of action is more crucial than knowledge of universal principles. Nonetheless, since prudence is right reason concerning the doable deed, the prudent man needs knowledge of universals and of singulars.

While wisdom is the chief intellectual virtue considered in an unqualified sense, Aristotle and St. Thomas assert that prudence is the chief intellectual virtue related to human affairs. While wisdom does not consist of knowledge of human affairs, *as a kind of architectonic command and control principle, prudence exists in practical reason as a form of universal knowledge rightly regulating individual choices through particular reason toward successful fulfillment in achieving their chief end pursued.*

In the matter of human affairs, Aristotle and St. Thomas distinguish between individual and civic prudence similar to the way in which Aristotle distinguishes legal justice from individual justice. Considered as prudential as such, they define both forms of prudence as right plans, ordering of action of things to be done, in relation to what is good or bad for respectively one person or a civic multitude. St. Thomas gives the analogy of civic prudence being related to individual prudence just as legal justice is related to individual justice. Located between civic prudence and individual prudence, they talk about household (domestic) prudence as a mean.

They maintain that civic prudence is divided into two parts. One deals with this or that civic group or part of the State, while the second concerns the State considered as a whole. They divide this into two parts: 1) architectonic, or legislative, prudence, which concerns determining the civic duties of citizens; and 2) administrative prudence, legislative enactment (concerning what kinds of deeds are doable).

To help make intelligible this twofold division of civic prudence, St. Thomas compares laws to doable deeds as universals to particulars. Similarly, legislative, or architectonic, prudence frames laws, and executive, or administrative, prudence puts into effect, and attempts to conserve, what the law prescribes as doable. Considered in this administrative capacity, executive prudence is simply an application of universal reason to some particular, doable deed.

Strictly speaking, St. Thomas maintains that a legal decree is a "decree" only in relation to a doable deed, a singular precept. A decree concerns a singular extreme, limit, in a civic relationship between a ruler and those ruled about which the decree as a decree is deliberative and operative. A decree that commands doing the impossible is no legal decree at all. Simply put, a decree is simply a prescriptive statement, command to "Do this, not that!"

St. Thomas says that the individual legal decree is called a "singular extreme" because our knowledge *starts* from it, *proceeds* to the universal reason generating the decree, and terminates by way of assent or dissent to the individual act commanded. He adds that it is also called a "singular extreme" because it applies a universally (abstractly) stated law to a singular, concrete doable deed (does not command the impossible).

Since only those who execute enacted laws are active in civic affairs, analogously, Aristotle compares them to manual workers who execute architectural plans, thereby comparing legislators to architects.

While both legislative and executive civic prudence are acts of prudence, Aristotle maintains that personal prudence is especially prudence, prudence absolutely. St. Thomas says that Aristotle refers to the other types of prudence (household/domestic and civic [legislative and executive]) as prudence by participation [*secundum quid*]).

Considering the nature of prudence in more detail, St. Thomas maintains that prudence is divided into two parts: 1) consultative and

2) judicial. Moreover, he says that not only in reason, but also in the appetites, does prudence exist universally and in particular. He adds that all the species of prudence he has mentioned up to this point are species of prudence to the extent that they do not exist in reason alone, but, to some extent, also exist in the appetites.

If these aforementioned activities exist only in reason, then, since they are not being actualized in the individual circumstance, but exist like objects of speculation, St. Thomas says that the proper name for them is "practical science," "domestic ethics," or "politics" (apparently because they exist more like subjects of syllogistic demonstration than they do like subjects of practical action).

Whatever the case, St. Thomas maintains that, since a whole is of a greater priority than a part, the city than a household, and a household than one human being, civic prudence must be of greater import than domestic prudence, domestic prudence must be of greater import than personal prudence; and legislative prudence is of greater import among the parts of civic prudence and absolutely of greatest import among acts a person must perform.

In reply to objection that only a man who cultivates things having to do with himself appears prudent, while those who devote themselves to concerns of the multitude appear lacking in prudence, Aristotle gives the example of a soldier in a play of Euripides, who asked how he could be prudent when he neglects care of himself. Aristotle replies that the good of the part cannot be attained without the good of the whole. In human affairs, individual good cannot be perfectly attained without domestic and civic prudence. Simultaneously, without personal prudence, civic and domestic prudence are insufficient. Even with them in place, how to dispose personal affairs is not evident.

St. Thomas clarifies Aristotle's argument by saying that prudence is concerned with universals and particulars. Evidence of this special nature of prudence is that, while young people can excel in speculative sciences like geometry and arithmetic, they do not appear able to become prudent. The particulars, *individual principles*, *singular extremes*, that prudence must know demand sense experience.

Comparing prudence to understanding, St. Thomas says that both science and prudence are receptive of, in contact with, have some agreement with, understanding as a habit of principles. Understanding concerns indemonstrable principles, extremes, for which no proof exists. *Doable deeds are first principles, singular extremes, of prudence evidently known to the estimative sense, particular reason, of the prudent man for which no proof exists*!

Such principles, singular extremes, doable deeds, the nature of prudence as a moral virtue cannot be proved by reason, but are immediately known by themselves by the prudent man! St. Thomas maintains that *prudence* is concerned with, *chiefly focuses its attention on, the singular doable deed*: a singular doable deed that must be taken as a principle of things to be done. He adds that no scientific knowledge exists for the singular doable deed because no scientific knowledge exists for singular terms (extremes of a relation; in this case of the estimative sense, particular reason, of the prudent man to a doable deed).

This singular extreme, the doable deed, is not apprehensible by any external sense faculty as a proper sensible. St. Thomas maintains it is apprehended by the inner sense faculty through which we perceive the sensibly imaginable, like a triangle. Then he states that *prudence perfects particular reason to judge singular relations, know doable deeds*!

He notes that even brute animals endowed with the natural *estimative power* are called "prudent." The internal sense that has the ability to distinguish among proper sensibles like colors, flavors, and so on (the common sense) is incapable of judging the singular relations involved in apprehending the natural strengths and weaknesses present in performing doable deeds. Transcending the virtual quantum power of the common sense, *as a property of the estimative sense, particular reason, prudence agrees with understanding in that both consider extreme terms of a relation* (starting points, principles). Prudence differs from understanding in that understanding does not incline toward inquiry, while prudence inclines to a deliberation, which is a kind of inquiry (for example, Is this doable? Is it doable by me? Is it doable by me now?).[7]

8. Virtues connected to, and closely resembling, prudence: *Eubulia* and *eustochia*

To make more precise the nature of prudence, Aristotle next examines virtues connected to, closely resembling, prudence: 1) *eubulia* (excellence in deliberating) and 2) *eustochia* (lucky guessing). Once, again, inquiring like a good teacher who instills confidence in his students by being able to indicate to them real differences between beings that closely resemble each other, Aristotle studies *eubulia* and *eustochia* negatively by showing how they are not identical, and how they are not science nor prudence.

Because *eubulia* is a kind of deliberation connected to inquiry, Aristotle maintains that *eubulia* cannot be science because people with science are certain, do not deliberate, inquire, about what they know.

For two reasons, he maintains that *eubulia* cannot be *eustochia*: 1) because lucky guessing is instantaneous, exists without rational inquiry. He says *eustochia* exists in deliberation in some men who have rich imagination, sensitive external senses, and exceptionally-quick and accurate, natural judging ability rightly *to size up* situation; and it also exists in people with wide experience. In contrast, *eubulia*, excellence in deliberating, takes time to develop, involves slow deliberation over a long time. Its nature recalls to St. Thomas the proverb that prudential matters should be quickly executed, but deliberated slowly beforehand. 2) if *eubulia* and *eustochia* were identical, Aristotle says they would have no differences.

But, being quick of mind is a species of *eustochia*, lucky guessing (right opinion immediately jumping to a conclusion) about the means to an end. Such ways of behaving are not marks of deliberation. *Eubulia* is a kind of deliberation, while *eustochia* is a kind of opinion, and opinion is a fixed judgment involving no deliberation. Moreover, *eubulia* is a kind of right deliberation, not a kind of science; and *eustochia* (opinion) consists in a declaration of what one imagines, not what one has proven, to be true.

Further to develop his argument, Aristotle maintains that we predicate the term "rectitude" in four senses: 1) properly of good things (like of a good person, Socrates) and figuratively of bad things (like of a good burglar); 2) of ends; 3) of means; and 4) of manner.

Then, he maintains that the rectitude of *eubulia* is about good things that contain a good end, of the right means; in the right way toward the proper end, manner, and time; about a rightly qualified or unqualified end.

From Aristotle's analysis St. Thomas concludes that *eubulia* has four properties of rectitude in practical matters: 1) right deliberation 2) about an absolutely good end, 3) by suitable means, and 4) at the right time.[8]

9. The virtue of *synēsis* is distinguished from common sense, opinion, *gnome*, and the virtue of science and *eustochia*

After showing how *eubulia* involves rightness of investigation, inquiry, Aristotle starts to distinguish *synēsis* from common sense, science, opinion, and *eustochia* by noting that, while all human beings have some science (in the sense of knowledge, and opinion), not all have common sense. If *synēsis* (knowledge) and opinion were identical, all human beings would have common sense. *Synēsis* is no particular science (for example, medicine, physics, metaphysics); it concerns matters about which we can doubt and deliberate, about which prudence doubts and deliberates.

To make the idea of *synēsis* more precise, Aristotle compares it to speculative matters involving investigation and judgment. While *eubulia* deliberates, investigates, well, *synēsis* judges well about matters already well deliberated and investigated. Unlike speculative reason, which concludes in judging, St. Thomas says that practical reason investigates (like *eubulia*), judges in an un-prescriptive way (like *synēsis*), and commands (like prudence).

Unlike *synēsis*, which is descriptive, prudence is prescriptive. *Synēsis* is right judgment about what happens in the majority of cases (the doable deed); it resembles judgment in matters of legal justice. *Synēsis* also resembles *gnome*, which is right judgment about the equitable.

Prudence combines, synthesizes, right investigation with right judgment found in legal justice and equity (merciful adjustment) and then adds commanding well to this synthesis.

Like prudence, *synēsis* and *gnome* consider individual extremes, limits, starting points. And, like science, deliberation presupposes understanding. Understanding, in turn: 1) occurs in both speculative and practical knowledge and 2) considers first principles, singular extremes, *from which all reasoning starts*!

According to St. Thomas, two kinds of understanding exist: 1) speculative and 2) practical. Speculative (the habit of understanding) considers unchangeable first principles of demonstration. These include the first things we know, which (because our knowledge of them cannot be removed from us) are immutable. Practical (the habit of *synderesis*) considers the singular and contingent, what is to be done: means for an end.

Because we take our understanding of universals from singulars,

St. Thomas says, *evident is that singulars have the nature of principles*! For example, we conclude that this herb has the universal, medicinal power to cure from the fact that this herb cures this man. He claims that, because we know singular first principles through the senses, we need to have experience of these singulars (which St. Thomas calls "principles" and "singular extremes") by both the exterior and interior sense. Immediately, *St. Thomas adds that prudence belongs to sensory power of judging called "particular reason."* In addition, he maintains that, *inasmuch as its object is sensible and singular, we call particular reason* (the estimative sense) *"understanding!"*

St. Thomas asserts, further, that, since the habits of *eubulia* (inquiring well), *synēsis* (judging, estimating well from a majority of cases), *gnome* (right judgment about the equitable), and prudence (commanding well) consider singulars, in some way, they must be in contact with the sensitive faculties that operate by means of bodily organs. Moreover, these principles appear to be "natural," *not in the sense that they are entirely from nature*, but in the sense that some human beings are inclined to them by natural physical disposition so as to be perfected in them with little experience.

In addition, he notes that such a disposition does not happen with speculative intellectual habits like geometry and metaphysics, which, in some way, by considering singulars, must also consider physical natures. St. Thomas says that no one is born wise, a geometrician, or a metaphysician. While some men are naturally more apt to develop these habits, this speculative disposition is more intellectually remote than the proximate, practical disposition for *synēsis, gnome,* and sense understanding.

He maintains that an indication of the sensory aptitude for these habits is that they tend to happen in old age after intense bodily changes have ceased. Common sense/understanding appear to come to man as if nature cause them. From what he has said, St.

Thomas infers that, like speculative understanding, *particular reason* (*understanding of practical matters*) *concerns principles, but does so as a kind of aim, or end*!

St. Thomas reminds us that, in speculative matters, demonstration proceeds from principles considered by the habit, or virtue, of understanding, and that no demonstration of speculative reason exists for these principles. In practical matters, however, while demonstration also proceeds from first principles (practical ones), which practical reason cannot demonstrate, in a way, demonstration by speculative reason exists for them. For example, the speculatively observable success or failure of a person to be able to execute an action based upon this or that practical principle: successfully doing a deed.

In practical argumentation (which essentially involves reason commanding action, prudence or imprudence), the major premise is the prescriptive statement, or command: "Do good and avoid evil!" The minor premise is a singular— for example: "This is good." And the conclusion is the command, prescriptive statement: "Do" (or "Do not do") "this!"

From the preceding claims he has made about the nature of practical principles and the way they are rationally applied, St. Thomas concludes that the perfection of particular reason (understanding of singulars), which essentially deals with practical principles (means to ends), follows from age and experience. *Special note should be made that this perfection of particular reason* (*the estimative sense*) *through the virtue of prudence is the chief concern of moral, or ethical, education*!

Hence, in practical matters, especially those of moral concern, we must pay special attention to the opinions and decisions of experienced, especially prudent, old men. While such opinions and decisions do not lead to demonstrations, in practical matters, St.

Thomas maintains they lead to something more crucial: right moral induction, apprehending principles of practical understanding.

Just as in universal principles of speculative understanding, absolute judgment about singular principles of practical understanding (*singular extremes*) belongs to understanding (in the case of practical judgment, to sense understanding: particular reason, the estimative sense). Prudence, *synēsis*, *gnome*, and *eubulia* chiefly belong to particular reason (which concludes from one of these to the other), a part of the soul different from that of intellectual reason, but which participates in intellectual reason, which intellectual reason, and with it, the human will, ultimately commands and controls.

In conclusion, St. Thomas maintains that wisdom (the chief virtue in speculative matters) and prudence (the chief virtue in practical matters) exist in different parts of the soul.[9]

10. Answering some possible objections about the utility of wisdom and prudence for human life

Immediately following this conclusion, St. Thomas notes that some people might raise possible objections about the utility of wisdom and prudence for human life. For example, since wisdom considers first principles of being (what makes something an organizational whole), and, strictly speaking, does not consider first principles of operation generated by an organizational whole, it appears useless to making human beings happy.

And, in relation to prudence, someone might object that, while prudence considers actions by which we might become happy, it appears unnecessary because, by an inner habit of inclination, not knowledge (the concern of prudence), a person performs noble and honorable (that is, useful) deeds toward himself and just deeds toward others. While, in some cases, from a knowledge of his art, an artist acts well as an artist, such intellectual influence is incidental to the art. The habit of the art, repetition of action, not knowledge, generates the good of the art. Hence, virtuous habits, routines of action, not prudence, induce a man to do the good.

Aristotle and St. Thomas respond to such claims by saying that, because prudence would not be useful when men are already good, such replies appear to be unreasonable. To become virtuous, we need prudence; and to start to become prudent, we need instruction by prudent men.

They reject another reply that questions the superiority of wisdom over prudence. This response maintains that, while wisdom appears superior to prudence in excellence because it considers universal principles of being, while prudence considers singular principles of singular operations, political science (a species of prudence) gives orders about what sciences should be possessed in a State, what sciences someone should learn, and the length of education. Since, to give orders is the function of a judge and a superior, prudence appears to have authority over wisdom. That the less perfect should exercise authority over the more perfect appears unreasonable.

Next, they resolve general doubts about the usefulness of prudence and wisdom by saying that, even if prudence and wisdom do not give to a human being the qualities of soul that generate well-made products or that enable a person to become a better performer in one act of human life or another (like being a better singer or dancer), they produce a far greater quality of good. *They contribute to human happiness by causing every artist to be psychologically healthy as a whole human being*!

Regarding the objections about prudence contributing nothing to happiness, they say, further, that both prudence and moral virtue perfect the work of virtue. In a work of virtue, we need two things: 1) right desire for the end that moral virtues like temperance, courage, and justice provide and 2) right reason about the means to secure these ends that the preceding virtues pursue, and which prudence

Peter A. Redpath

provides (*which includes taking delight in the right means, which the other moral virtues cannot provide!*).

In a morally virtuous operation, a concurrence of prudence and these other moral virtues exist. Prudence cannot exist without the moral virtues of temperance, courage, and justice; and the moral virtues of temperance, courage, and justice cannot exist as complete or perfect virtues, without prudence. Without prudence the moral virtues of temperance, courage, and justice are not complete as moral virtue; and without temperance, courage, and justice, neither is prudence complete as a moral virtue.

For total moral virtue to exist two operative principles must exist: 1) right desire and 2) right reason. Not everyone who does temperate, courageous, or just acts (even habitually) is morally virtuous (for example, when we do just acts under the force of law, out of ignorance, or chiefly for personal gain). To be morally virtuous, a person must *know* and *love, take delight, pleasure*, in doing the temperate, courageous, or just deed.

For this to occur, the means designed by nature, means naturally proportionate to right reason and right desire (prudential choice), real, not fictional, means (means that actually lead us to, and enable us to secure, the end), *must be known, loved, and chosen considered as such!*

Aristotle and St. Thomas maintain that an operative power *resembling* prudence exists in particular reason, the estimative sense: shrewdness, craftiness, cleverness—and the ability to execute well acts ordered to an end, *whether morally good or evil!* They claim, moreover, that prudence is a species of shrewdness, craftiness, or cleverness ordered to the morally good.

Because shrewdness, craftiness, or cleverness is sometimes identified with prudence, and prudence is sometimes conflated with wisdom, some people mistakenly conclude that prudence and wisdom are not needed for happiness. Nonetheless, they claim that the habit of prudence is never united to this *estimative* power related to choosing means to an end without right desire, moral virtue.

Just as universal first principles of reasoning exist for speculative science, so, in practical science, the supreme good, happiness, exists as a universal first principle (a singular extreme, singular ultimate) of practical reason. To the morally virtuous man, through *synderesis*, the supreme good as a final end, and the temperate good as a proximate end (an enabling means we need to pursue in the individual circumstance) are evidently known as causal principles of each and every right choice (universal principles) just as evident first principles of speculative reason are immediately apprehended by a person who knows the meaning of "part" and "whole."

Because prudence and moral virtue exist within this person's estimative sense power, and because the virtue of prudence simultaneously exists (but in different ways) *as a command and control principle within the universal (intellectual) and particular (or sense) reason of the prudent man, within the individual circumstance, this morally virtuous man apprehends with precision universal and singular first principles of moral choice (the universal and singular extremes). What is really good considered as an end and a real means in the individual circumstance appears really good to the estimative sense of the prudent man!*

St. Thomas maintains that moral vice perverts the judgment of reason and causes deception in the conception of practical principles, doable deeds, on the level of universal and particular reason. Since we cannot reason well when we are mistaken about principles, the moral psychology of imprudent, vicious, people prevents them from being able habitually to reason well in practical matters. Their unhealthy moral psychology prevents them from being able habitually and precisely to conceive the human good, the good doable deed, or the means to it within the individual circumstance.

Consequently, I think that Aristotle and St. Thomas would conclude that, strictly speaking, modern science (mathematical physics) is a form of mathematically-regulated, constrained, and controlled shrewdness, craftiness, or cleverness, which, by having intentionally divorced itself from wisdom and prudence, lacks the moral and metaphysical culture needed for it to be science in a professional, or real, sense. Considered as such, it has become a serious threat to the survival of Western civilization and global peace!

After considering in some detail that prudence cannot exist as a complete virtue without the other cardinal moral virtues, Aristotle and St. Thomas show how the cardinal moral virtues of temperance, courage, and justice cannot exist completely as virtues without prudence.

To start their argument, they first distinguish between natural and moral virtue, stating that moral virtue as a perfectly possessed habit presupposes the existence of some level of natural moral virtue by which some men appear to be naturally disposed to some extent to be temperate, courageous, and just.

Next, they consider these natural moral dispositions and three ways that they exist in relation to practical reason, the human will, and sense appetite.

In relation to practical reason, they maintain that first principles like "Do no evil!" are naturally implanted by human nature within human reason.

In relation to the human will, they claim that the will is naturally moved by the good apprehended by the human intellect (the good *as it appears good to the human intellect*) as its proper object.

In relation to the sense appetite, in turn, they assert that some men are naturally inclined to react with too much, too little, or with moderation, to different passions like anger, pleasure, and so on.

And, finally, they say that the natural inclinations of human reason and the human will are common to all human beings.

Nonetheless, St. Thomas asserts that, without addition of another principle through which they exist more perfectly (reason), even children and brute animals (like the often-called "noble"/"brave" lion) display morally virtuous inclinations. And, he adds that, unless guided by right reason, a man with a strong inclination toward moral virtue can do much harm to his body, external things, and other people. In its proper sense, moral virtue is natural virtue rightly guided by right reason.

Just as in the reasoning part of the sensory soul (particular reason, or the estimative sense) two principles of operation exist: [1) natural shrewdness and 2) prudence], so, in the appetitive part of the soul pertaining to moral virtue, two principles exist: [1) natural virtue and 2) moral virtue]; and without prudence, moral virtue cannot exist in the soul.

St. Thomas maintains that Aristotle confirms St. Thomas's claims about the need for two kinds of moral principles (natural moral virtue and prudence) by criticizing Socrates for saying that moral virtues are kinds, species, of knowledge, in a sense of intellectual prudence. St. Thomas contends that Aristotle thought Socrates was right to maintain that moral virtue cannot exist without prudence, but Socrates neglected too much the role that appetite, right desire, prudence, plays in particular reason, or the estimative sense.

To correct this mistake on the part of Socrates, St. Thomas thinks Aristotle maintained that moral virtue must accord with reason, but reason must accord with right desire (satisfy real needs). Moreover, the reason possessed by the man of natural moral virtue (the naturally-inclined morally virtuous person, the person naturally inclined to be temperate, courageous, and just) need not be directed by prudence in its imperfect state of moral virtue. To be perfect moral virtue, moral virtue must accord with right reason (prudence), but prudence need not accompany, direct all (imperfect) moral virtue.

Next, Aristotle and St. Thomas refute philosophers who claimed that one virtue can exist without another by saying that: 1) even though one person is naturally inclined, with practice, to possess all virtue, acquiring a virtue to which one is not strongly inclined by nature is difficult; 2) in a way a person naturally inclined to some virtue knows this inclination to be the case, has right reason about it (as Socrates maintained); 3) strictly speaking, no virtue can exist without prudence, nor prudence without other virtues.

When prudence (a single virtue) exists, Aristotle and St. Thomas maintain that, simultaneously, all the moral virtues will exist. Without prudence, St. Thomas claims that no virtue will exist formally, but only materially.

Moreover, St. Thomas asserts that different species of prudence do not exist for different species of virtue (for example, one prudence for temperance another prudence for courage, and a third for justice). The same principle of prudence (rule by right reason and right desire) applies to, commands and controls, all species of moral virtue. In addition, while, through a lack of enabling means, a prudent person inclined to generosity might be too poor to exercise the virtue of generosity, if those means are acquired, the complete moral virtue of generosity will exist in that person.

From his previous discussions about prudence, evident to St. Thomas is that, even if prudence were not operative in the soul, we would need it because it perfects particular reason, or the estimative sense of human beings. Prudence is operative right choice, moral virtue in a complete sense. Moral virtue rightly disposes us to the end, real good, the good that really fulfills human needs. And prudence rightly directs us toward the real means to secure the real end toward which moral virtue rightly disposes us.

Finally, Aristotle and St. Thomas end discussion of the moral virtue of prudence by solving some doubts previously raised about the wisdom and prudence as to whether prudence rules over wisdom or wisdom over prudence. In reply, they say that, while the art of medicine commands what a person should do to become healthy, this art has no power over the health-generating power of the soul. It gives orders to people about how to secure health, but it can give no orders to the health-generating faculty of the soul commanding it to heal the body. So, they maintain that, while individual prudence and (in its civic, social form, something superior to individual prudence and civic prudence) political science give orders about things to do to obtain wisdom, since wisdom, by nature, has a qualitative greatness naturally superior to prudence and political science, these do not, cannot, give orders to wisdom about how to judge about divine matters.

Indeed, according to Aristotle, to claim that, because it gives directions about everything people do in a State, prudence rules over wisdom is like claiming it rules over the gods.[10]

—Notes—

1. St. Thomas Aquinas, *Commentary on the Nicomachean Ethics of Aristotle*, Bk. 6, Lect. 1, nn. 1109–1123.
2. Id., Lect. 2, nn. 1124–1141.
3. Id., Lect. 3, nn. 1142–1160.
4. Id., Lect. 4, nn. 1161–1174.
5. Id., Lect. 5, nn. 1175–1183.
6. Id., Lect. 6, nn. 1184–1194.
7. Id., Lect. 7, nn. 1195–1216.
8. Id., Lect. 8, nn. 1217–1234.
9. Id., Lect. 9, nn. 1235–1256.
10. Id., Lects. 10–11, nn. 1124–1291; see, Aristotle, *Nicomachean Ethics*, Bk. 6, ch. 13, 1145a10.

CHAPTER THIRTEEN

The Moral Psychology that Causes Moral, Cultural, and Civilizational Decline: From Incontinence to Brutishness

AFTER HAVING FINISHED defining and considering intellectual and moral virtues in Book 6 of his *Nicomachean Ethics*, in Book 7 Aristotle starts to talk about incontinence, an imperfect moral state close to moral virtue. St. Thomas says he does this to ensure that he has not overlooked any issue related to moral activity that needs to be considered. His procedure now is to study progressively worse stages of moral decline related to moral vice from: 1) incontinence, to 2) intemperance, to 3) brutishness. Since intemperance and brutishness are kinds of moral vice, unhealthy, psychological qualities, Aristotle starts his study with a definition of moral vice.

1. The progression of moral vice from incontinence to intemperance through disease of particular reason, or the estimative sense, and the human will

To determine a right definition of moral vice, St. Thomas says Aristotle begins by noting that a good moral act is a synthesis of right reason and right desire. He states that a disordered relationship between these two faculties can cause an act to be morally vicious. If a disorder in this relation is partial, so that reason still remains right, incontinence results; if the disorder is total, the result will be the vice of intemperance, or worse: brutishness.

St. Thomas says that the incontinent person is not vicious because, while the appetitive faculty of the incontinent man is disordered, the desire for reason to remain right (in touch with reality) remains in the incontinent man. In the vicious person *the disordered appetitive faculty dominates reason so much that reason follows the end pursued by the disordered appetite as a first principle, an ultimate end.* Consequently, an evil person performs evil acts with complete voluntariness, by choice.

Eventually, because the natural inclination of a human being to take direction from right reason (a healthy estimative sense and good will) is destroyed, the result of such viciousness is brutishness. Just as, St. Thomas says, physical illness results from an improper proportion of metabolic agents (poor digestion), generating toxic chemicals (humors) in the body that create disordered body temperature, bad eating habits destroy physical health, so a disordered appetite that disorders the harmonious psychological relation between reason and appetite causes a human being to degenerate from being morally healthy to the level of a brute. A rightly-ordered appetite, right desire, preserves the natural, healthy, psychological harmony (the healthy, proportionate, good) between the faculties toward which, by nature, all human beings are inclined.

In one way, St. Thomas adds, psychological disharmony of this kind can happen without totally destroying a person's ability to order choice like a psychologically healthy human being. A partial psychological appetitive disorder, even of the extreme kind like incontinence, will not so corrupt human choice that it will resemble that of a brute. However, St. Thomas claims, wrong reason, wrong desire, can become so extreme through intemperance that the result is analogous to a man's body becoming changed into that of a lion or a pig.

Contrary to these morally disordered states, St. Thomas lists: 1) for brutishness: heroic, or divine, virtue; 2) for incontinence: continence; and 3) vice: virtue. Then, he lists three ways of becoming brutish, through disorder caused by: 1) bad laws; 2) psychological, or physical, illness; and 3) habitually becoming more vicious.

After giving this general introduction to the devolution of human beings from moral virtue to moral vice, Aristotle starts to talk about incontinence by first discussing continence, perseverance, and being morally resolute in the face of pleasure and pain. He commends continence when concerned with pleasure, and perseverance when concerned with pain, as laudable; but he claims that neither is a virtue. Then, he concludes his introduction to the study of continence and incontinence by noting its essential limitations, saying that he will proceed in his usual way regarding ethical matters: by stating what appears probable.

Following this procedure, he maintains that, in moral matters, we cannot explain everything. The best we can do is start by stating what appears probable and, when difficulties arise, resolve the questions we can. He asserts that doing this will help us to identify the most probable, most likely, truth.

Using this method he makes the six following probable statements: 1) Continence, perseverance, are good, while incontinence and irresoluteness are bad. 2) The continent man appears prudent; the incontinent man appears imprudent. 3) The continent man knows particular acts are evil and avoids them for this reason; the incontinent man does the contrary opposite. 4) The temperate man appears continent and persevering. 5) Some people say the prudent man cannot be incontinent, is godlike. 6) Sometimes, people who get angry, who pursue honor, gain, are called "incontinent."

According to St. Thomas, the proper way to consider, study, a subject involves six steps—proceeding in the following order: 1) in general (generally); then 2) specifically (its proper nature); 3) the act its proper nature generates (the way it specifically acts); 4) by comparing it to beings the same as it; then 5) comparing it to things that differ from it; and, finally, 6) considering it in relation to its external surroundings. St. Thomas mentions this procedure to explain why

Aristotle does not address six doubts about six probable statements he has just made about continence and incontinence in the order in which he has presented them. Instead, Aristotle's first doubt addresses his probable statement three (the continent man knows particular acts are evil and avoids them because of reason; the incontinent man does the contrary opposite) instead of his first probable claim: continence and perseverance are good; incontinence and irresolutenessare bad.

In addressing this third probable statement, St. Thomas realizes that Aristotle is directly criticizing Socrates' well-known claims that: 1) to know the good is to do the good (right judgment made as a result of knowledge precludes a person from being incontinent) and 2) vice is a kind of ignorance. And St. Thomas maintains Aristotle answers Socrates as follows: 1) Evident is that some people do what they know is wrong; and 2) if incontinent people only commit vicious acts when under appetitive influence, studying this influence is helpful because without it the incontinent man is continent.

In the following way, Aristotle next rejects the argument given by some to salvage the teaching of Socrates, which claims the incontinent man acts under the influence of opinion, not knowledge. When acting, the incontinent man has either a weak or strong opinion. If the opinion is strong, then the act the incontinent man does is just as morally blameworthy as the act people perform when they knowingly do what is morally wrong. And if his opinion is weak, the action of the incontinent person appears not to be blameworthy, not to be a vice.

As far as the claim that a prudent man can be incontinent, Aristotle considers, and, for two reasons, rejects, the opinion to explain the truth of this claim proposed by some of Socrates' followers: Even though prudence (right reason) directs him toward moral virtue, because prudence is the strongest of opinions, the prudent man can be incontinent *if he has a strong opinion contending against evil desires.* 1) If this opinion were true, it would allow a prudent man simultaneously to be prudent and incontinent. This appears impossible because it would declare performance of the basest actions to be prudent (to be a moral virtue). 2) The prudent man correctly, rightly, judges the individual act in the individual situation (*knows the right principle of means, is guided by synderesis and synēsis to induction of the right means*), but, also, has all the other moral virtues (knows the right principles about the right ends). In short, the prudent man is totally virtuous.

Next, Aristotle presents several arguments against his probable claim that the temperate man appears continent and persevering by saying: 1) A man is called "continent" because his reason does not succumb to vehement, evil desires. If this is true, a temperate man will not be continent, nor the continent man temperate because *the virtuous man is temperate, has no vehement, evil desires*; but the continent man does. 2) Since, if the temperate man has no vehement, evil, desires, he cannot be continent because the continent man has such desires and conquers them; and, if he were continent and had evil desires, and the continent man had good, not evil, desires, the following absurd consequent would result: some kinds of continence would be undesirable and incontinent. 3) If the evils the incontinent man resists are not vehement, resisting them requires no virtue.

Turning to objections against his probable claim that the continent man appears prudent, while the incontinent man appears imprudent, Aristotle presents the following argument: A continent man lives by reason, but a man who lives by reason is irresolute because he is open to be persuaded by every opinion, not reject any (to be tolerant) of all opinions. But, since an opinion can be false, and since what is false is evil, some kind of continence is evil, cannot be prudent.

At this point, Aristotle rejects the above-given, sophistic argument and strengthens his probable claim that the incontinent man is imprudent by saying that, if to abandon every opinion is sometimes good, and, at times, prudence joined to incontinence is good, virtue will be a synthesis of two vices (incontinence and imprudence), which is impossible.

After doing this, he strengthens his claim that continence and perseverance are good and incontinence and irresoluteness are bad by saying that the person who performs evil actions after reasoning (because he is persuaded they are good and pursues, chooses, evil pleasures as if they were good; that is, makes the choice out of bad reasoning, not out of incontinence) is better than a person who chooses evil acts as a result of incontinence and not because of bad reasoning. Aristotle maintains that *the person who has to be persuaded to misbehave* appears to be more ethically corrigible than does the incontinent man who needs no persuasion to make a vicious choice. Because of a weak will and weak emotional disposition, *the incontinent man does not incline to listen to reason and cannot be helped by any good advice.*

Finally, regarding his probable claim that, sometimes, people who get angry and pursue honor and personal gain are called "incontinent," Aristotle says he thinks he has solved why this is so in some of the cases he has already considered. Some of these angry people who are called "incontinent" are mistakenly given this name, their anger being due to something other than incontinence; but, to some people, he maintains, the name aptly applies, not absolutely, but with some qualification.

St. Thomas considers Aristotle's final resolution of doubt about his six probable claims regarding continence and incontinence by returning to Socrates' contention (which appeared to be that incontinence cannot exist) by saying that, to answer Socrates, Aristotle must first resolve the question whether continence and incontinence exist. And, to do that, Aristotle says he must consider the kinds of pleasure about which a man can be incontinent and continent and whether continence relates to some or all pleasures.

Since the continent person and the persevering person are not totally identical, St. Thomas considers whether they differ specifically regarding some common matter (that is, whether they are species of a common genus), or whether they differ only in the way they deal with some subject of consideration.

To answer these questions, St. Thomas notes that Aristotle distinguishes between continence in an unqualified sense and continence in a qualified sense. Then, he says a person can be continent and incontinent only regarding some limited subject and also in relation to the way he conducts himself toward that limited subject.

He notes that the incontinent man pursues a pleasurable object when it is present, but not in the same way (and with the same kind of moral psychology) as the intemperate man, who *reasons it is wrong to choose but chooses it anyway*. In contrast, the incontinent man chooses what is unhealthy, what he reasons to be wrong, because he is appetitively weak, because, appetitively, he is too weak to do otherwise, cannot help himself.

Aristotle claims that his argument is right whether the cognition that generates incontinence is knowledge or opinion. For some people are as tenaciously led by force of opinion as they are by knowledge.

Habitually, he continues, we human beings know in two ways: 1) by having a habit and not presently using it and 2) by having a habit and presently using it. If we fail to take into consideration these two different ways of knowing (and only think about knowing in the second way), for a person to act contrary to what he presently knows is difficult to understand: *but for him to act contrary to what he habitually knows, but does not consider*, think about at the moment, is easy to understand. *Practical reason uses two modes of judging*: 1) universal reason and 2) particular reason. No problem exists understanding how person can habitually know in both ways, but in the individual circumstance only consider the universal way of judging and not the particular.

Moreover, a universal can be considered in two ways: 1) abstractly, in abstraction from the way it exists in any particular; and 2), concretely, as it exists in some particular. For example, some person may know, abstractly, that all healthy food is good for a human being to eat, and, concretely, that this food is healthy and that he is a human being. So, while a man might know habitually and actually know the abstractly-considered universal, he might not know it habitually, or actually, as it exists in some particular in the present. When considered according to these three different modes of knowing (actual and habitual, universal and particular; abstract and concrete), what appeared impossible and unreasonable to Socrates appears possible and reasonable.

For an incontinent man to have one kind of knowledge (the abstract) and not another (the concrete) appears reasonable. Beyond the above, distinctive, modes of knowing, St. Thomas adds that we can understand differently the acts of knowing by way of habit and act.

For, example, sometimes a habit is highly, or not highly, responsive to direction by reason; sometimes it goes into act immediately, slowly, or not at all. This happens especially when we act under emotional influences like anger and sexual desire.

St. Thomas says that, at times, such passions generate so much heat that they can cause people to behave crazily. Hence, he maintains that incontinent men resemble people asleep, drunkards, and, at times, maniacs: that is, *people who have practical science impeded regarding particulars all of whom have an impaired (unhealthy) estimative sense!*

According to St. Thomas, to someone who uses the following appeal as a means to refute Aristotle's claim that the incontinent man has an active appetitive habit restrained by reason: "The 'supposedly' incontinent man's use of scientific terminology indicates that he is too profoundly intelligent to be incontinent," Aristotle replies with two examples:: 1) Even drunkards and crazed people can mouth demonstrations and cite abstruse material in poetic verse, soothing sounds. 2) Even children who start to learn can put together words that sound profound, but they do not understand. To understand what we hear, in a way, what we hear must become "co-naturally" part of us. *It must become perfectly impressed in the estimative sense and intellectual soul*!

For this to happen, much time must pass so that, by much meditation and deliberation, what is intellectually received in the rational intellect becomes intensely possessed and confirmed in the particular intellect. This is true even of the incontinent man who can mouth the right words, but does not actually hold to be true what he says—pretends what he says is what he thinks.[1]

2. The moral psychology of the incontinent man

If we want to understand how the incontinent man can, contrary to his knowledge, say one thing (know the right thing) and do another (the wrong thing), St Thomas says we have to understand the two stages of judging involved in the natural process of practical reasoning. Judgments that constitute an act of practical reason may be universal (known abstractly by intellectual reason) or particular (known concretely by particular reason, the estimative sense). For example, by practical universal reason a person might know, "Every dishonorable act must be avoided"; and, by practical particular reason, the estimative sense, a person might know, "This act is dishonorable."

Since these two acts unite to form one nature of a practical reasoning activity, practical science, at least three conclusions necessarily follow: 1) If the conclusion reasoning aims at is speculative, not practical, we draw the conclusion and command no act to follow upon it. 2) If the conclusion reasoning aims at is to generate action (is, strictly speaking, an act of practical science), the conclusion we draw immediately moves us to act. And 3) if the judgment of universal (abstract) reason is that "we must taste" every sweet thing, and the judgment of the estimative sense, particular reason, is that "this is sweet," following this flawed reasoning as if it were one of right reasoning and prudential judgment, *even a temperate man will immediately taste this thing.*

Analogously, the incontinent man rightly reasons abstractly in the same way about avoiding doing something shameful. *But,* because, in the concrete situation his unhealthy practical reason tells him, "Every pleasure is to be 'pursued,'" at this point, on the level of sense desire, due to appetitive weakness, even though on the level of practical reason, he knows the conclusion he draws that he must taste this sweet thing is wrong, abstractly reasoning *univocally,* the way the extremely incontinent man actually tends to reason in such a situation, *because he identifies pleasure and good,* the incontinent man will taste this thing.

While the moral psychology of the incontinent man is flawed, unhealthy, St. Thomas claims that it is not so morally flawed, unhealthy, as that of the intemperate man. *Before acting,* by dispassionate universal reason, the incontinent man knows that not every pleasure is morally good and to be pursued, that some pleasures are morally evil and should be avoided; that physical pleasure and good are not identical. But, in the individual circumstance, *overwhelmed by intense emotion, his dispassionate, abstract, reason becomes blinded to the genuine concept of the universal good to be pursued; he cannot see it.* His appetite blinds him to it.

So, for example, when, under the influence of the principles of *synēsis* and *synderesis*, his universal practical reason abstractly proposes this command, "Do not eat anything sweet after 8:00 PM!", his concupiscible appetite proposes that he change that practical negative prescription into a positive universal prescription: "Every sweet thing must be eaten at all times." From this universal prescription, with logical consistency, he then judges, "This is sweet." And concludes, "Eat this."

In so doing, his estimative sense (what most people call "common sense") *loses touch with the principles of synēsis and synderesis, proper induction, and reality*; and he becomes unable to distinguish fact from fiction, real good from apparent good. In contrast, at least initially, and for quite some time (*until the intemperate man's psychological constitution, the passions and will, eventually, reduce all good to physical pleasure!*), *the intemperate man knows the evil he does is evil, is against right reason, and this is precisely why he deliberately chooses it*!

St. Thomas maintains that the process of practical reason happening in the way he has described in the case of the incontinent man is evident from the fact that, in the incontinent man, concupiscence so overwhelms reason that the incontinent man freely inclines to replace what reason declares with a universal judgment with what the concupiscible appetite declares to be the universal. In the incontinent man, universal practical reason and the estimative sense are so weak, unhealthy, and the appetite so strong, that reason cannot prohibit this change. St. Thomas adds that concupiscence, not reason, causes this opposition, disharmony, inasmuch as concupiscence opposes universal reason; reason never itself opposes the judgment of right reason.

In contrast to human beings, because brute animals possess no intellectual reason, universal reason, St. Thomas says they cannot make a universal judgment that concupiscence can oppose.

Imagination and memory of particulars moves them. They make no distinction between apparent and real goods and evils. *To them all goods and evils are real.*

As a prescription to cure the ignorance of the incontinent man, St. Thomas proposes the following. Since the incontinent man's ignorance about the particular act involves incorrectly identifying what is (the real nature to be considered) with what is not (a fictional nature), recovery of knowledge of reality is the same as the treatment used for alcoholics and people asleep. Physical change has to happen to put the incontinent man back in touch with reality. Since passions like anger and concupiscence cause bodily changes that disrupt our ability *calmly* to sense the real, physiological changes that *calm* these passions need to be prescribed. St. Thomas maintains that determining such prescriptions relates to skills of natural philosophers (medical professionals who analyze bodily movements). Hence, their professional advice needs to be consulted at such a point.[2]

3. Based upon distinction between universal and particular reason (the estimative sense), how Aristotle is able to refute the argument of Socrates

Based upon what he has said about universal and particular reason, St. Thomas claims Aristotle is able to refute the argument of Socrates in this way: 1) Particular judgment is made according to sensible knowledge directive of actions concerned with particulars. 2) A person under the influence of intense passion either does not have this particular judgment as a habit, or has a restrained habit that causes him to be blinded to the particular like an alcoholic who repeats profound intellectual sayings but cannot appetitively restrain from taking a drink. True is that the man under intense passion does not know the universal that is known by dispassionate, abstract, science. 3) Since, in truth, the universal known by abstract science is not the proximate cause, generator, of practical actions, passion is not present in the apprehension of abstractly-considered universals; but it is present in the apprehension (weakened particular reason, weakened estimative sense) of the man choosing under intense passion, Socrates' conclusion appears to follow: in a way, the incontinent man does not knowingly do evil.[3]

4. The generic matter (subject) of continence and temperance

Having shown that, in a way, human beings can knowingly perform evil acts, Aristotle next considers two questions, whether: 1) anyone can be incontinent absolutely, without qualification; and 2) if someone can be totally incontinent, regarding what matter? In short, Aristotle is asking what is the formal object of the incontinent man? What precisely stimulates his appetite? Aristotle's reply to this question is that *the formal object of the incontinent man's appetite is intense pleasure and pain of taste and touch essentially related to food, drink, and sex.*

To explain why this is so, Aristotle observes that, among those subjects that cause us pleasure, some (the matter, formal object, of continence and temperance!) are: 1) necessary for the preservation of individual and species human life, 2) not necessary for the preservation of individual and species human life, but are desired for another reason. Among other unnecessary things, he mentions some goods desirable in themselves, like honor, riches, and the like. He says that people who pursue these goods to excess, in a disordered way, are not called "incontinent" *absolutely*. They are called incontinent *by way of likeness*, analogously, relative to these goods.

He confirms his claim through an analogous example in which we tend to call "soft" people who cannot undergo hunger and thirst, any discomfort, not people who cannot, like most of us, undergo something like poverty. Consequently, Aristotle locates the intemperate and incontinent man within the same genus; but he considers them to be specifically different. The intemperate man deliberately chooses excess, while the incontinent man does so because a passion overpowers his reason.

Because the intemperate man knowingly does wrong, chooses evil, he does wrong, evil, under the influence of an evil will, not under the influence of overpowering emotion. Aristotle says the vice of such a person is worse than that of the incontinent man because, he asks, "What would such a person do if he were to experience youth's intense desires, or the serious discomforts that poverty causes?"

In the following way, Aristotle shows that, in the case of unnecessary goods, no absolute incontinence can exist. He says three kinds of pleasure exist: 1) some to which we incline by nature; 2) some to which we incline against natural inclination; and 3) enabling means that exist between both extremes (for example, honor, victory, money, and so on). Of people who go to excess, beyond the measure of right reason about naturally good things (like honors, care of children and parents), their behavior is not totally blameworthy.

Considered in itself, each is naturally desirable, praiseworthy. They become blameworthy only when pursued beyond the measure of right reason, prudence. No complete incontinence exists in these pleasures. Considered in themselves, they are naturally desirable, good. They are bad only when pursued imprudently. Hence, Aristotle concludes that only partial incontinence relates to such pleasures; absolute incontinence relates to necessary bodily pleasures of life, sex, food, drink, and the like; and pleasures of touch.[4]

5. Natural and unnatural pleasure and the appetitive disposition and moral psychology of incontinent and brutish men

Having considered the difference between calling a person "continent" and "incontinent," absolutely, totally, and partially, Aristotle next examines another way of talking about continence and incontinence: as 1) brutish and 2) human. Depending upon whether or not his passions, pleasures, are inclined to be directed by prudence,

Aristotle says, in different senses, we call, name, a person "continent" or "incontinent."

To explain what he means, Aristotle starts by dividing pleasures into two species: 1) in agreement with natural human inclination, 2) not in agreement with natural human inclination.

Then, he states that some pleasures are naturally delightful to different species of animals: for example, 1) plants to herbivores, and 2): animals to carnivores. Moreover, by bodily disposition, some people naturally prefer hot or cold food.

Before explaining the nature of what he refers to as "unnatural" pleasures, he says that some pleasures are naturally delightful because of privation, sickness, sadness, mental imbalance, habitual disorder, or vicious nature. As examples of such unnatural pleasures, Aristotle gives cannibalism, compulsively pulling the hair out of one's head, eating dirt, homosexuality, and torturing others.

Next, he reduces the causes of such unnatural pleasures to a tendency: 1) of bodily temperament possessed from birth; or 2) generated through childhood habituation.

Having identified the preceding unnatural, and brutish, pleasures, he says that these unnatural pleasures: 1) dispose some people to incontinence in a qualified, partial sense; and 2) do not totally dispose to incontinence absolutely, in all respects. So, he maintains, that no one will accuse anyone who, from birth or bad education, has such a flawed nature with being incontinent absolutely and unqualifiedly.

St. Thomas adds that, while such men have some universal judgment in them, being weighed down by bad physical disposition and malignant nature or education, they resemble brute animals who use no universal judgment, use only imagination and memory of particulars. Hence, just as we do not call brute animals "continent" and "incontinent," *since even the strongest rational arguments against*

their appetitive proclivities will appear weak to them, since little rea-
son exists in them, we should call them "continent" and "incontinent," in a qualified, not an absolute, sense.

The nature of incontinent acts, moreover (their natural basis
residing in badly-disposed body chemistry, other physiological
conditions, emotional dispositions, and/or poor moral training),
inclines Aristotle to state that, strictly speaking, absolute incontinence
does not apply to them.

As far as brutish habits are concerned, Aristotle maintains that
absolute brutishness exceeds ordinary viciousness. He asserts that
brutishness is no ordinary human vice. Instead, it is a malignant,
close-to-incorrigible, pathological habit. He claims that some people
are brutish by nature, others by mental or physical illness, and still
others by habit. Some people within these groups oppose all virtues;
while others oppose some of them (for example, foolishness opposing
prudence; timidity opposing courage; and intemperance opposing
temperance). And, finishing his discussion of brutishness, he claims
that barbarians and native peoples especially incline toward this
moral defect.[5]

6. Comparison of different kinds of incontinence to different kinds of pleasure and the moral psychology of the angry man

Having shown how incontinence is related in different ways
to different pleasures, next, Aristotle compares different species of
incontinence to each other. In so doing, he says that absolute, total,
complete, incontinence concerns matters of touch. Hence, a matter
like anger concerns only partial incontinence. Following Aristotle,
St. Thomas adds that incontinence related to anger is less disgraceful
than incontinence related to pleasures of touch, incontinence considered strictly speaking, or considered absolutely. Then, he makes four
points to support this claim: 1) To some extent, anger listens to reason
because reason tells the angry man to get revenge. 2) Anger inclines

the angry man to listen poorly, imperfectly, to reason because anger causes him not to be careful to listen attentively about the amount and mode of punishment to inflect. 3) The angry man acts like a servant who hastens to do something before hearing all the directions given by a master, like a dog who barks at the first sound of someone knocking. And 4), under the influence of bodily passion, the man in a state of incontinent anger starts to administer punishment before hearing reason's complete injunction.

St. Thomas reports Aristotle's analysis of the moral psychology of the angry man in this way. As soon as reason or sense declares something to sense to be delightful, sensual desire moves without reasoning to enjoy it. A man who suffers injury, contempt, however, sometimes knows about this immediately from a report of reason or imagines an injury or slight has happened even though one has not. Apparently, before reason has time to decide the proper punishment, the man stirs himself by anger, decides to attack, and inflicts improper punishment.

St. Thomas explains the reason for the incontinent, angry man's behavior as follows. A pleasing object has the nature of being desirable in itself, is like a principle of action toward an end, like a logical premise is in reference to a conclusion. Ordinarily, to a psychologically healthy person, damage to be inflicted on another does not appear as an end. It appears as an enabling means, instrument. To the incontinent man, however, it appears as an end.

By nature, an irascible emotion like anger inclines to follow reason. By nature, a concupiscible desire does not incline to listen to reason, unless an irascible passion can incline it to do so. Unless directed by an irascible passion, its natural inclination is immediately to follow its own decision.

As a result of the way the sexual appetite inclines to operate in human beings, *St. Thomas says something shameful happens in human affairs when the incontinent man does not listen to reason.* In the case of immediate pursuit of sensual desire, pleasure, St. Thomas maintains that the incontinent man is more shameful than the incontinent man acting out of anger because, to some degree, the angry man can listen to reason, while essentially, without restraint from an irascible emotion, the incontinent man is incapable of so doing.

St. Thomas, then, presents three more arguments from Aristotle to show that the incontinent man's behavior is more shameful than that of the angry man.

1) If a man acts imprudently regarding ways of behaving toward which human beings are naturally inclined (like matters of food and drink, not *fancy* food and drink), people are inclined to pardon him because, since anger is more natural and difficult to resist than superfluous and unnecessary pleasures that the intemperate man seeks, we are more inclined to pardon the angry, incontinent man than the intemperate one.

The tendency toward anger results from an individual's emotional nature, habits, and bodily dispositions. Even though, by nature, for the most part, human beings are naturally inclined to be peaceful, by nature, some people are more prone to anger than are others. A disposition to anger can even be biologically inherited. So, a man naturally disposed to anger behaves less shamefully than does an intemperate and absolutely incontinent man.

2) Deceitful men are more unjust than are truthful men. The angry man is truthful, wants the person being punished to know precisely why he is being punished; and anger does not arise secretly. It arises impulsively. Like the goddess Venus, who binds reason by sensual desire, incontinence binds the judgment of reason in practical matters, tends to work deceitfully, secretively, and is more unjust and shameful than is the incontinence of anger.

3) No one voluntarily injuring another acts with sadness. The man

who acts immediately with anger acts with some sadness, as a result of having been injured. We appear to do with sadness any involuntarily acts we do. The angry man acts somewhat involuntarily, under provocation. If the more unjust act is the one about which we incline to be more angry, and the incontinence of sensual desire inclines to make us more angry, because it is done with pleasure, not sadness, with complete voluntariness, not some involuntariness, then, by being more unjust, the absolutely incontinent act of sensual desire is more shameful than the partially incontinent act of the incontinent, angry man.

St. Thomas summarizes Aristotle's conclusion about incontinence by saying that, in an unqualified sense, continence and incontinence concern sensual pleasures related to the senses of touch and taste. Such incontinence is more shameful than the qualified incontinence related to anger.

Comparing human incontinence to brutishness, he says temperance and intemperance concern sensual desires natural to human beings. Absolutely considered, we do not call brute animals "temperate" or "intemperate." We do call some animals more "unclean," "stupid," "voracious," and "rapacious," than others. In contrast to these, by a kind of likeness to human beings, we call some animals "temperate" and "prudent." Insane people, who have lost the use of reason, resemble wild animals, brutes. But, strictly speaking, temperance and intemperance do not exist in brutes and brutish men.

Considering the animal condition of brutes and the brutish condition of brutish men, St. Thomas says that brutes are less evil and more frightening than brutish men. While brutish animals might tend to cause more physical damage to us, the brutishness of a vicious man is more to be dreaded and morally blameworthy.[6]

7. A more detailed comparison of the moral psychology of continence and incontinence to that of temperance and intemperance

After discussing in detail the nature, and moral psychology, of continence and incontinence, Aristotle compares these in detail to temperance and intemperance. He does so first by noting that they share the same formal object and subject of chief interest: intense physical pleasure and pain related to the sense faculties of touch and taste. Both the temperate and the continent man are related to intense pleasures of touch and taste. Both are strong-souled, persevering, and able to resist temptations.

In contrast, the incontinent man is weak-souled, soft concerning the same matters. The intense physical pleasures with which temperance and continence deal essentially relate to necessary, real, not apparent, goods: goods essentially connected to self- and species-preservation. While such physical goods are necessary up to a point of quantitative, virtual and discrete, greatness, beyond that point, they cause damage to the possessor and to preservation of individual and species life and health.

Because the concupiscible appetite is not directly inclined to listen to reason, it tends to cling to its object as an end considered in itself, not as an enabling means, or useful good. As a result, *in immediately pursuing pleasure and avoiding pain, it inclines not to experience shame or guilt. It tends to experience these through the influence of the irascible passions and particular reason, or estimative sense!* Hence, the intemperate man, who intentionally plans to ignore reason, tends not to experience shame or embarrassment, sorrow, guilt, or remorse about the base pleasures he seeks or has sought. The frigidly-intemperate man, who is insensitive to pleasure by an emotional defect of being unable to experience pleasure, deviates as much as, if not more so, from the means pursued by the temperate man than does the intemperate man who is a slave to pleasure.

The moral psychology of the incontinent man differs from that of the intemperate man chiefly because incontinent man is inclined to take direction from prudentially-guided reason; but, appetitively, is too weak, irresolute, to do so. Recognizing this personality defect, like any morally healthy man or woman, the incontinent man experiences shame and embarrassment, guilt and remorse, sorrow; *and has a conscience*. Unlike the intemperate man, the incontinent man is no sociopath.

The intemperate man tends to be dispassionately wicked in the pursuit of pleasure or in the cold-blooded infliction of intense pain and wickedness, and tends to be pathologically evil. In contrast, the incontinent man tends to be emotionally weak and delicate. The intemperate man cold-bloodedly tends to seek shameful and intense pleasures and to inflict shameful and intense pains, dispassionately delights, by deliberate choice, in behaving imprudently, wickedly. About such a person Aristotle asks, "What might such a person do if he were passionate?"

Aristotle maintains that, with some struggle, perseverance, now and then, the continent person can restrain and contain intense emotion. But the continent man must struggle, persevere, someone to do so. He claims that the continent man is not identical with the persevering man because, while he still struggles somewhat to make the virtuous choice regarding pleasures and pains, the continent man has mastered the pleasures and pains with which he tends to struggle. The persevering man has not yet achieved marginal victory over the pleasures and pains with which he tends to struggle, is still on the way to so doing, but manages to stand his ground.

Still, the continent man is not totally victorious, temperate. The incontinent man, is, once again, soft-, not strong-souled, small-, not great-souled, weak in intensive quantity strength of soul. While the incontinent man still struggles greatly against intense pleasures and pains, he is better than the man no longer able to persevere: the sad-sack, wretch, who can no longer endure pain and work, hardship and difficulties. While the intemperate man might be thought to be more inclined to pursue amusement as a form of pleasure, this is more the inclination of the incontinent man, the class clown, who seeks emotional outlets to distance him from self-awareness of his pain of failure, his sense of guilt and shame.

According to Aristotle, two species of incontinence exist: 1) impetuous, or impulsive, which cannot wait for reason to deliberate (found in angry and depressed men); and 2) emotional softness, which, appetitively can wait for reason, but, when it does so, is unable to take good advice.[7]

8. A special note about how the concupiscible and irascible passions relate to pleasurable and useful goods and the importance this has for understanding the nature of moral education

Special note should be taken of how Aristotle considers the concupiscible and irascible passions to relate to pleasurable and useful goods. He considers the concupiscible emotions directly to react to pleasurable, not useful, goods. The formal object of the concupiscible appetite is a pleasurable, not a really useful and healthy good. In contrast, the irascible emotions directly relate to instrumental and useful goods, goods that tend to improve human life and make it safe, help perfect productive and performance activities of human beings. The concupiscible appetite no more recognizes and reacts to this kind of good than the faculty of sight recognizes and reacts to sound.

Recognizing this radical distinction between these sense appetites and their formal objects helped Aristotle realize that ethical, or moral, education is chiefly concerned with emotional and appetitive education *proximately achieved through the particular reason, or estimative sense.* As he, and even more so, St. Thomas, came to realize, by nature, under the direction of the virtue of prudence, the estimative sense inclines to use the emotion of pleasure to teach the irascible appetite to delight in restraining and encouraging, moderating, training, and educating, the concupiscible appetite to take direction from particular reason to execute commands of universal reason. As they realized, *education in continence and temperance is the chief appetitive tool of moral education* to help individuals who tend to have some level of natural temperance, courage, and justice to take increasing pleasure in being prudentially guided in performing habitual acts (moral virtues) that involve hope, fear, daring to overcome dangers and difficulties in individual situations related to protecting and, as much as possible, perfecting individual and species human life.

9. Some additional reasons why the intemperate man is morally worse than the incontinent man

Chiefly because the intemperate man voluntarily, deliberately, refuses to listen to right reason, prudence, Aristotle considers him to be morally worse than the incontinent man and, in fact, educationally-incorrigible, unteachable, in the area of morals. While both the incontinent and intemperate man tend to choose bodily pleasures as their chief end and cannot clearly see, recognize, real human, transcendental goods like courage, temperance, justice, and prudence, the incontinent man readily repents and experiences sorrow after submitting to intense pleasures and unhealthy activities that he is convinced are personally unhealthy, dangerous. In contrast, the intemperate man delights in his imprudent lifestyle. For this reason, *incontinence is more curable and intemperance tends to be educationally incorrigible.*

St. Thomas says that incontinence resembles a short, intense illness, while intemperance resembles a long, incurable one. Their differences are so extreme that, in relation to moral activity, in at least one respect, St. Thomas maintained they belong to different genera. The reason for this is that intemperance is a fixed vice, while incontinence is a disposition toward viciousness. To a vicious man, a vice does not appear to be a vice; it deceives a vicious person into thinking that what he desires, the choices he makes, are really good.

This self-deception is not present in the incontinent man. Hence, the incontinent man is still in his right mind, still possesses a somewhat healthy estimative sense faculty (what people often call "common sense"), still knows that the apparent good that attracts him is really personally unhealthy, unsafe, evil.

Since hidden evil is morally worse than overt evil, the intemperate man is worse than the incontinent man. The intemperate man can, and does, reflect in advance, and can act in a self-controlled way, but takes pleasure in disobeying right reason, being imprudent. Hence, just as continence is almost a virtue, incontinence is a quasi-vice, while intemperance is full-fledged vice.

The incontinent man, who sins out of soft bodily constitution and emotional dispositions, is more to be pitied, helped, than blamed, does something vicious, but not in the way the vicious person does. Because he knows that pursuing bodily pleasures against the command of right reason, prudence, is really harmful, when he does so, he repents.

In contrast, because of his wicked habit, while the intemperate man can, and does, reflect in advance, and can act in a self-controlled way, because he is convinced that the brutish pleasures he pursues constitute good in itself, happiness, he takes delight in disobeying right reason. The incontinent person, on the other hand, is habitually unconvinced that what he chooses is right.

In the sphere of moral activity, Aristotle and St. Thomas claim that vice destroys, while virtue preserves, knowledge of the end: the chief principle of moral action for the sake of which we engage in free acts. In practical activity, the end, the last act to be done, replaces, is analogous to, first principles of speculative reasoning in speculative science. Just like the habit of understanding in speculative knowledge, St. Thomas says that such principles of practical knowledge cannot be taught. They are induced by nature and practice. By the habit of virtue naturally known, or learned by custom, we acquire *right estimation* of the ends to be pursued.

While the incontinent man momentarily exceeds the limits of right reason, through repentance, he returns to the limit of prudential judgment in determining the end. Because reasoning presupposes, cannot teach, the principles it assumes, people who, like the intemperate man, make mistakes about principles cannot be corrected by appeal to reason, or in any way easily. Not being amenable to being penitent, feeling sorrow, shame, embarrassment, they cannot be educated, are totally lacking in moral teachability, until the bad habit is destroyed. Hence, a temperate man is the right measure regarding the means, the end, related to matters involving intense bodily pleasures and pains.[8]

10. Continence: Its precise species, how the moral psychology of the continent man differs from that of the obstinate man, and more precisely from that of the incontinent, temperate, and intemperate man

According to St. Thomas, Aristotle starts to settle the question about the precise species that is continence by saying that the continent man abides by every right principle of choice; and, hence, to right reason and virtue by following the mean of right reason. Considering a question whether any of the following is continent or incontinent, Aristotle starts to narrow down with precision the specific difference that makes a continent act continent—whether a man is continent or incontinent who abides by: 1) any principle or choice whatsoever, whether it is good or bad; 2) no principle or choice; 3) the right principle of choice; or 4) the wrong principle.

In answer to this question, Aristotle replies that a man who responds to any principle whatsoever is, strictly speaking, not continent, is continent incidentally, because we name a person properly from what he chiefly aims to choose. The continent person must chiefly aim to choose the good, not just any principle whatsoever. The proper object of any appetitive faculty is the good it essentially desires. What is outside that direct desire of intention is desired incidentally. A man who adheres to true reason is essentially, totally, absolutely, continent; while he who adheres to false reason thinking it is true is continent incidentally, partially; and he who adheres to false reason knowing it is false is incontinent absolutely, in all respects.

Next, Aristotle observes that obstinate, strongly-opinionated people resemble incontinent people. He explains the difference by first considering two ways that exist to change a person's opinion on the part of reason: 1) with a better reason, or 2) a passion swaying rational judgment, especially in practical matters. He maintains that the continent man's opinion tends to be swayed by reason, not passion, by rational judgment, especially in practical matters; while the obstinate man's opinion tends to be swayed by passion, especially by irrational pleasures. Being intellectually undisciplined, unreceptive to being taught by anyone, obstinate people tend to be unable to entertain anyone else's opinion. They tend to love when they win arguments, hate when they are proved wrong, and more resemble the incontinent, not the continent, man.

Next, Aristotle notes that, sometimes, abandoning a principle, especially a weaker one, is good and worthy of praise. He adds that not everyone who pursues pleasure is evil, incontinent, and intemperate. Only someone who pursues shameful pleasures is.

Moreover, Aristotle shows how, by pursuing a mean, continence relates to virtue. He says that, sometimes, someone enjoys physical pleasures not for a vicious end, but out of disgust, less than he should, and resembles the insensible, intemperate, man. Such a man's behavior is not in accord with right reason, which sees pleasures as a human good. The continent man constitutes a mean between the excesses of the insensible, intemperate man (by defect), and the incontinent, impetuous, and weak-souled man (by excess). Since excess and defect do not adhere to the measure of right reason, Aristotle concludes that, because continence is a like a virtue and must adhere to right reason to be a virtue, it must be a mean between two bad habits of excess (sensuality) and defect (insensibility).

He, also, notes that, often, people do not recognize continence and intemperance as a mean between extremes because the defective extreme of insensibility rarely happens. He says that extremes are opposed to continence in two ways: 1) from the side of reason, excess of reason, abstinence is to continence like prodigality is to generosity: an unstable weakness in the application of right reason; and 2) from the side of desire: restraining too much (the defect of insensibility, having no desire for pleasure) and restraining too little (the excess of sensuality, evil desires being excessively attractive).

While the temperate man is not battered about by the incontinent man's evil desires, like the temperate man, the continent man is not seduced by evil desires. And, while the temperate man is not delighted contrary to reason, sometimes the continent man is, but, like the temperate man, is not seduced by these.

Finally, Aristotle compares and contrasts incontinence and intemperance by saying that both agree in pursuing intense bodily pleasures, but they differ in that the temperate man thinks this is good to do while the incontinent man does not, knows it is bad.[9]

11. The psychological difference between the prudent and incontinent man: why prudence cannot co-exist with incontinence

After comparing and contrasting incontinence and intemperance, and the moral psychology of the incontinent man to that of the intemperate one in detail, Aristotle employs two arguments to demonstrate that prudence cannot co-exist with incontinence.

The first argument maintains that prudence accompanies all moral virtue, causes moral virtue to be morally virtuous. The prudent man is morally good, virtuous. Because the passions of the incontinent man are morally seducing, the incontinent man has no moral virtue, is essentially morally imprudent. The second argument claims that prudence essentially involves knowledge and judging, practicing and commanding; while the incontinent man does not totally fail in knowledge, he fails in practice.

Next, Aristotle gives the reason why, sometimes, incontinent people appear prudent: they are only apparently prudent. Shrewd, clever, people have a reputation for being prudent, even though, strictly speaking, they are not. Especially shrewd, incontinent people greatly resemble prudent people.

Nonetheless, according to Aristotle and St. Thomas, the prudent and incontinent man differ in the following ways:

1) Both appear to reason correctly, but only the prudent man can execute. *The incontinent man reasons speculatively and poorly, not practically and well, has a deficient estimative sense faculty.*

2) And even regarding speculative knowing, actually, the incontinent man does not habitually speculate well. He does not habitually know, speculate thoroughly, completely, about the individual circumstances of an act. Lacking in a sound estimative sense (common sense), he resembles a dreamer, a drunkard, someone in whom the habit of reason in touch with reality has been suspended.

3) In a general way, he knows the circumstances of an act, and he chooses somewhat willingly, voluntarily. He is not a morally bad person, because not every voluntary act is an act of choice, deliberate act.

4) When passion does not overwhelm him, his choice is good, equitable, he means well; but when the passion of pleasure or pain overwhelms him, his choice crumbles, and he wills evil.

5) The moral psychology of the prudent and incontinent man also differs in relation to deliberate choice. The prudent man's choice is deliberate, uncorrupted. The incontinent man's choice is voluntary, but corrupted in the deliberating process.

6) Consequently, the incontinent man is partly bad, not absolutely evil and unjust; is not an evil-doing schemer, con-man, is not deliberately evil.

7) One species of incontinent man is impulsive and impetuous, inclined toward anger, highly sensitive emotionally, sad, melancholic; cannot deliberate at all or listen to good counsel.

8) Another species of incontinent man is a weak deliberator, fearful, prone to laziness, timid in the face of labor, a dreamer, lacking in resolve, and lacking in the ability to take good counsel.

12. Aristotle concludes his comparison and contrast of moral psychology of the continent man to that of incontinent, intemperate, and prudent man

Having completely compared and contrasted continence and incontinence, Aristotle concludes that the specific difference they share relative to intense pleasures of taste and touch is chiefly in the human will, not in the human emotions. The continent man is strong-willed, while the incontinent man is weak-willed. The continent man voluntarily chooses rightly, while the incontinent man voluntarily chooses wrongly.

Aristotle compares the incontinent man to a city that plans intelligently, arranges everything logically necessary, has good laws but is unable to follow any of its laws. He says the incontinent man is incapable of using the right reason he possesses.

In contrast, the intemperate man, using perverse reason, resembles a city observing bad laws that does not deserve good laws. The continent man follows a mean of right reason *greater in intensity* (intensive quantum greatness) than the majority of men, but less than that of the prudent man.

The majority of men do not have the habit of right reason because they do not master sensual pleasures. Related to moral activity, right reason is a habit of mastery over the concupiscible appetite, sensual pleasures. The incontinent man abides by right reason less than the majority of human beings because he cannot overcome the sensual desires that most men can.

Of the two kinds of incontinence, St. Thomas says that the impetuous kind dominated by anger is easier to cure because it is naturally inclined to listen to reason, while the sensual kind dominated by concupiscence is not naturally inclined directly to listen to reason.[10]

13. Why moral and political science need to study pleasure and pain

After explaining why prudence and incontinence cannot co-exist, Aristotle and St. Thomas start to examine why moral/political scientists need to study pleasure and pain. In considering this issue St. Thomas says that the reason they need to do so is because political science is the topmost division of moral science. He adds that the whole of any science is reducible to its chief science because *this science contains its first principles*. Just as the end of the master art measures, commands, and controls all the activities of the lower arts, so pleasure, *the chief end of political science*, is the chief principle, subject matter, of moral science!

In a way, Aristotle and St. Thomas maintain that pleasure and human happiness are identical. This is because, in any art, the principle, end, rule, chief subject of consideration, is that to which all other actions are referred as making them intelligible and desirable. *In ethics, political science, habits and actions are measured good or bad relative to the qualitative, or intensive quantum, greatness of the pleasure desired!*

Note that, the end of the master art is the good of maximum intensive quantum (*qualitative*) greatness, the highest, most perfect, beautiful, good: the good of greatest qualitative satisfaction. As such, *it must maximally please. To be morally virtuous, the virtuous man must be pleased by doing good, intrinsically-pleasing, beautiful, deeds!*

In contrast, the vicious man is pleased by doing *evil*, *ugly*, deeds. Because the duty, job, of the moral philosopher is to investigate virtue and vice, principles attracted to *the beautiful in act, beautiful qualities of acts (their harmonization relative to their end) that recognize what pleases when perceived, the job of the moral philosopher is to investigate pleasure and pain, beauty and ugliness, in human activity*. Hence, St. Thomas notes that *the Many* among the Greeks and *the Learned* connect happiness *"beatus"* (derived from the verb "to rejoice exceedingly") with pleasure.[11]

14. Aristotle's refutation of six arguments supporting four sophistic opinions held by some ancient Greek philosophers claiming to prove that pleasure is not good and the highest good

Following the pedagogical device he often uses to strengthen in the minds of his students about the truth of a claim he has made, at this point, Aristotle presents four sophistic arguments found in the works of some ancient Greek philosophers objecting to his claim that pleasure and human happiness are, in some way, identical: that 1) no connection exists between pleasure and good; 2) if the pleasurable thing is good, pleasure and good are not identical; 3) while some pleasures are good, most are evil; and 4) even if all pleasures are good, none can be the highest good.

Next, he follows the above-listed assertions with six arguments in their defense, the first of which is taken from a definition of pleasure as an experience, process (movement) of the senses toward a natural end.

When something co-natural to us is produced in us, according to Aristotle, we delight in it. No such process, however, belongs to the genus of ends (for example, being built). It belongs to the genus of means (for example, becoming built). The good has the nature of an end. Consequently, a pleasure is good.

Aristotle's second argument is that no one is praised as virtuous for avoiding good. The temperate man is praised for avoiding pleasure. Since the temperate man is virtuous, pleasure is not a good.

His third argument maintains that the prudent man seeks freedom from pain (an imperfect kind of pleasure). So, he seeks freedom from pleasure. Since pain is not good, neither is pleasure.

Aristotle's fourth argument states that no good impedes prudence. Pleasure and more intense pleasures, like sex, however, impede prudence to the point of not simultaneously being able to exercise acts of pleasure and understanding. In short, pleasure and prudence cannot co-exist. Therefore, pleasure cannot be good.

His fifth argument is that every human good is the product of some art. Pleasure, however, is the product of no art. Consequently, pleasure is no good.

Finally, Aristotle's sixth argument in favor of the four opinions that pleasure and good cannot be identical is that what is pursued by the childish, the animal, in man, is shameful, not good. The childish and the animal in man pursue pleasure. Consequently, pleasure is no good.

In sum, even if all pleasures are good, no pleasure is the highest good because the end is the best, and pleasure is a process, a means to an end, not the highest good.

Having stated the six arguments favoring the philosophers' false assertions about the relation of pleasure and good, Aristotle and St. Thomas prepare to refute these arguments by saying that the arguments advanced do not really prove that pleasure is not good, is not the very best thing. To advance closer to presenting their refutations, Aristotle and St. Thomas distinguish two ways of being good: 1) absolutely and 2) relative to some individual.

By nature, and according to habits, they say all things are ordered to good absolutely and relative to some individual. Because movements, generations, proceed from particular natures and habits, in some way, they must be related to the natures and habits that generate them: to some good absolutely and some good for a particular individual.

On the supposition that pleasures are movements, processes, four kinds of pleasure exist: 1) some absolutely good, as pleasures taken in virtuous works; 2) others, absolutely bad, although, by reason of some necessity (for example, medicine) desirable to a particular individual—a sick man; 3) still others, not chosen by anyone consistently over a long period, but chosen consistently for a short time (for example, taking food rarely to prevent death); and 4) counterfeit, disordered, pleasures, taken as a remedy for a sickly disposition in which a person delights (like twisting, turning, in bed; taking better food, engaged in to relieve pain).

Next, Aristotle and St. Thomas make a second distinction about two ways of being good: 1) as an activity (for example, contemplation), and 2) as a habit (for example, science).

Further, they make a *crucial*, third distinction between: 1) formation-developing habits and perfectly-developed habits: virtues.

This last distinction is crucial to understand because a formative habit, a habit in the process of being developed, appears to be an imperfect good precisely because it is not yet maturely developed, *is in the process of formation, being generated*, coming to initial completion, perfection. In contrast, activity appears to be perfect good because it is an additional perfection consequent upon being a complete organizational whole. *Consequently, Aristotle maintains that genuine, perfect, pleasure exists in the good that consists in an activity caused by knowledge of being a perfect whole*!

Those actions, movements, that produce a formative habit within a nature or faculty (natural formative habits) are only incidentally, secondarily, good. They are virtue-formation habits, habits that form other habits, like doing the hard work to develop skill, virtue, science. As any professional athlete, entertainer, educator, or businessman knows, the pleasurable activity that derives from virtue-formation habits (doing the hard work needed to acquire a skill), in and of itself, is not qualitatively as pleasurable as the pleasure experienced by exercising the perfected skill. If it were, the subsequent pleasure experienced in the exercise of a virtue or skill would add nothing qualitatively different, different in intensity, from that experienced in exercise of a habit-, or virtue-formation habit.

Again, as any person who has ever developed a skill well understands, skill-formation habits are imperfectly pleasurable and are essentially accompanied by pain. In contrast, skill-formed, virtue-formed, habits are much more intensely delightful and need be accompanied by no pain. *A person on the top of his or her game does not struggle, experience pain, resistance to perfect exercise of activity; makes a difficult job look easy, and experiences it as such, and delightfully so.*

With pain a novice covets the pleasure derived from performing acts of virtuous habits: a pleasure of higher quality, intensive quantity greatness than those experienced as a novice. *A pleasurable activity accompanied by a desire for the pleasure of higher quality* that accompanies that of the exercise of a perfectly-formed habit *does not belong to a perfect habit.* It proceeds from a natural, or dispositional, principle accompanied by pain, an imperfectly-formed habit. Not without pain do we desire a natural perfection we do not yet have, of pleasure unaccompanied by pain, and further desire due to their imperfection.

Not all pleasures are of this perfect quality, but some are. Evident from pleasures that accompany contemplation is that such pleasures do exist. *Satisfaction of a natural bodily need does not generate such pleasures. Perfection, satisfaction, of reason, intellectual delight, causes them*! Pleasures connected with habit-formation and virtue-formation habits are pleasures in an imperfect manner and sense. They are not pleasures in the perfect, maximum, qualitative sense: pleasures that proceed from knowing yourself to be a perfect, beautiful, organizational whole.

Pleasures that help, assist, natures and habits maturely to develop into complete, perfect, wholes are qualitatively-incomplete pleasures. If such pleasures were completely, maximally, enjoyable, they would be so under any condition. But a gorged nature (present in a man who has over-eaten, for example) and a temperate nature do not experience the same kind, quality, of pleasure.

Nature, habit, properly-controlled by right reason, prudence, delights, enjoys, life-, and health-promoting and protecting pleasures, states, and conditions for human nature specifically and individually. Consequently, St. Thomas notes that people with healthy diet enjoy pungent and bitter-tasting foods that act as dietary supplements and digestive aids, while gluttons do not. As more perfectly enjoyable things, goods, are compared, he says, so are the pleasures they cause: goods that can be enjoyed with greater quality, more intensive quantity.

Having established the principles needed to refute the false teachings of some philosophers related to good and pleasure, Aristotle starts to do so by saying that no need exists to consider pleasure as a process (a coming to be) because the state of being is qualitatively more perfect than a state of becoming. Because they conceived of pleasure as a state of coming to be, and recognized that the pleasure of happiness, the pleasure that accompanies experience of the qualitatively highest good, must consist in a qualitatively better pleasure, some philosophers mistakenly concluded that they had to exclude pleasure from being a highest good or having any connection with it.

As Aristotle has convincingly shown, however, not all pleasures are processes; not all pleasures are accompanied by some process. *Habit-formation pleasures, process pleasures, are pleasures of means, of becoming a whole, perfect. But, not all pleasures are pleasures of means. Some pleasures are pleasures of ends, of complete perfection, of being whole!* Such pleasures come from virtuous use, not from virtue formation. They do not arise as pleasures that come from forming habits. They arise from the exercise of already-formed, good habits, as essential properties accompanying their exercise.

The first argument, which defines pleasure as an "experienced" process is wrong precisely because it defines pleasure in terms of imperfect pleasure. Properly understood, defined, pleasure is the co-natural activity of an already-formed habit/virtue. Instead of an "experienced" process, better, more precise, would be to call such pleasure "unimpeded."

Hence, most properly understood and defined, St. Thomas calls pleasure an unimpeded habit that is a natural harmonizing with the nature of its possessor. A better, more precise definition, because an impediment to operation causes difficulty in operation, impedes, prevents, experience of pleasure.

Since some philosophers mistakenly identified good chiefly with generation (coming to be), not with what it principally is (a completed, generated, being; a developed whole), they mistakenly concluded, like so many modern and contemporary intellectuals tend to do, that, precisely speaking, and most properly understood, pleasure is a kind of process. Operation, activity, originates from a completed nature, is not a process. Movement is a process. In the most proper sense, pleasure accompanies, is co-natural with, action.

Aristotle disposes of the false claim that, even if a pleasurable thing is good, pleasure and good are not identical by saying that the reason some philosophers held this was because they recognized that, at times, some pleasurable goods involve, lead to, evil. If this were the case, however, Aristotle maintains we would have to say that some healthful activities are evil because they cost money.

Regarding the claim that the prudent man seeks freedom from pleasure, considers pleasure evil, St. Thomas replies that the co-natural pleasure of every habit facilitates, does not impede, its proper operation. Pleasures alien to co-natural pleasures impede virtuous, perfect, operation of a habit. Hence, pleasures that accompany investigating and learning cause us to delight in learning, to learn more, not less, with greater intensity, facility.

Regarding the false claim that pleasure is the product of no art, like Aristotle, St. Thomas argues that, properly speaking, pleasure accompanies activity, not process. Art does not have the power directly to cause activity, has the power directly to cause the principle, faculty, from which activity arises. Consequently, art is the remote, not proximate, cause of pleasure: the cause of the means that cause pleasure, like the arts of cooking and performing.

St. Thomas maintains that the fact that the temperate man (referred to in the second argument Aristotle refutes) is praised for avoiding pleasure, that the prudent man seeks a life free from pain and pleasure (referred to in the third argument he refutes), and that children and dumb animal seek pleasure do not prove that pleasure and good are not identical because pleasures can be considered absolutely, and unqualifiedly and relatively and qualifiedly. Some pleasures are good absolutely, by nature for all human beings everywhere and at all times. Other pleasures are good for particular individuals, depending upon the individual bodily constitution and condition, their psychological condition and external circumstances. Physical pleasures of this or that person accompanied by pleasure or pain are not good absolutely considered. From their excess, we become intemperate. Hence, a temperate man avoids them. Other pleasures, those proper to a temperate man, he seeks and delights in![12]

15. That one pleasure (happiness) is the highest good, and why

According to Aristotle, as he immediately starts to prove,

properly speaking, not only is pleasure a human good, one pleasure (human happiness) is the highest human good.

As a first step in developing his complete proof, St. Thomas reports Aristotle maintains that everyone admits the truth of the following two claims: 1) Pain is bad and should be avoided; and is of two kinds: evil absolutely, unqualifiedly, in every way and relatively, qualifiedly, in a way. 2) Evil relatively is a hindrance, impediment to good, and hinders a soul from doing good.

Just as evil and good are, or resemble, contrary opposites so are/do pleasure and pain. Pleasure opposes pain as good opposes evil.

Aristotle maintains that Speucippus was wrong to claim that pain is opposed to pleasure as greater to less evil, as one extreme evil to another (both pleasure and pain supposedly being evil). According to Aristotle, the teaching of Speucippus maintains that pleasure considered as such, in its own nature, is evil: something no one can plausibly hold.

While, according to Aristotle, the Platonists maintained that pleasure is not a good, is an obstacle to good, something imperfect, Aristotle says they never went so far as to hold pleasure to be evil absolutely considered in itself. (In saying this, although, in a way, praising Plato and the Platonists, Aristotle appears to misrepresent Plato, who, while he did consider pleasures that turn the soul toward the material universe to be evil, appears to me to have held just the opposite regarding pleasures that turn the soul toward invisible realities, to separated Forms. Such pleasures of the soul he considered to be good.)

Whatever the case regarding the Platonists, Aristotle maintains that happiness is both: 1) an unimpeded activity and 2) an activity that causes pleasure. Because happiness is *perfect activity*, and no perfect activity contains an imperfection or impediment, by nature, everyone actually, understandably, essentially connects pleasure and happiness, actually thinks that the happy life is pleasurable and delightful. *Happiness is an unimpeded activity that causes pleasure.*

Because happiness is unimpeded activity, it requires all the enabling means for exercising unimpeded activity: 1) bodily goods (like general good health, lack of injuries) and 2) external goods (called "goods of fortune," or "goods of luck").

Aristotle and St. Thomas maintain that, strictly speaking, people who, like the Stoics, claim that, even when tossed about and overcome by great misfortune, the virtuous man is happy, talk nonsense. Indeed, so closely do human beings incline to identify happiness and pleasure, because happiness demands good fortune to be pleasant, Aristotle says that some philosophers considered happiness and good fortune to be identical.

Still, Aristotle disagrees that happiness and good fortune are identical. Because too much wealth, good fortune, often hinder us from doing acts of virtue, often makes us lazy, and happiness consists in performing acts of virtue, strictly speaking, we should not call superabundance of wealth "good luck," "good fortune," because the *measure* of real good fortune is established by comparison to real happiness.

Because the opinion of *the Many*, that pleasure is the highest good, cannot be totally wrong, St. Thomas states some indication exists that Aristotle is right in his claim. Nature does not fail in most cases. What we find in most people appears to arise from nature, which inclines to generate nothing false and evil.

In reply to a possible criticism that what all men admit about happiness is that it consists in pleasure, and a highest pleasure, is wrong, Aristotle claims that different people disagree about the nature of this pleasure. According to natural (species-specific) desire, all human beings want the same highest pleasure: happiness. According to individual judgment, they differ as to the nature of this pleasure.

By nature, inasmuch as all men desire to know and excel at

knowing the truth, by nature, St. Thomas claims all human beings identify the same pleasure as the highest: contemplation of rational truth. The reason for this is that all people have in us a divinely-implanted inclination derived from God and/or our substantial form to know truth.

Nonetheless, because bodily pleasures are the ones most commonly experienced, easy to know, and needed to be satisfied to live, survive, many people, even philosophers, do not recognize this. Because *the Many* do not tend to experience contemplative pleasures, have reduced the term "pleasure" to their narrow understanding of it as a process, not an act of perfect satisfaction, they do not recognize that the pleasure which consists in happiness is contemplative in nature.

Finally, if, strictly speaking, pleasure and pleasurable activity are not good absolutely, if the life of the virtuous man, and his activities, are not essentially pleasurable (which is false because, in producing good, virtue necessarily produces pleasure), the happy life might not be pleasant, and living in pain might not be evil and something to be avoided.[13]

16. Pleasure and pain as related to continence and incontinence

After having considered pleasure and pain in general and the essential relation of pleasure to human happiness, Aristotle next talks about pleasure and pain in relation to continence and incontinence.

He starts to do so by saying some people claim that some bodily pleasures are especially worthy of choice, while others (intemperate ones) are not. According to Aristotle, bodily pleasures are good: 1) inasmuch as they drive away opposing pains; and 2) not absolutely, but in some respect, because every bodily pleasure is caused by some bodily movement, activity, or habit.

If, in a habit, a superabundance of the better (too much good) cannot exist, neither can an excess of pleasure. According to Aristotle and St. Thomas, such is the case regarding bodily pleasures, but not regarding contemplative ones. Everyone desires bodily pleasures up to a physical maximum, beyond which we suffer personal damage. But, the more we contemplate the truth, the better we become intellectually and personally, the qualitatively greater, greater in intensive quantity, becomes the personal pleasure we experience.

According to St. Thomas, we even blame some people for not experiencing bodily pleasures. As the foregoing arguments show, up to a point, bodily pleasure is good. We do not call someone "evil" because he wants these bodily pleasures. We call someone "evil" because he wants them to exccess, to a point that they damage him, harm his life and health.

While we rightly avoid some good, Aristotle and St. Thomas maintain that we rightly avoid all pain! Absolutely considered, no pain is good. By nature, all human beings flee from pain as evil. Even a man of virtue, St. Thomas says, flees absolutely all pain.

Pain, then, cannot be the contrary opposite of excess of physical pleasure. If it were, we would only flee excessive physical pain, and not all pain. Pain would be something, in some cases, to be tolerated, not totally shunned. Some people, however (the incontinent), are pained by even a minuscule absence, privation of pleasure. Moreover, excess of physical pleasure is bad because it causes pain, from which, by nature, all human beings are inclined to flee.

According to Aristotle and St. Thomas, more discussion is needed to explain why, even though, as is the case to all human beings, by nature, to *the Many*, bodily pleasures are known to be qualitatively inferior to intellectual ones, nonetheless, *the Many* incline to pursue physical pleasures as qualitatively greater than intellectual ones. After all, intellectual pleasures are good absolutely, while bodily pleasures are only good to some extent.

In an attempt to explain this paradoxical phenomenon more

completely, Aristotle says that, one reason that physical pleasure is often desired more than intellectual pleasure is because, by its intensity, it drives out pain. Hence, to protect ourselves from pain, some human beings seek an abundance of intense bodily pleasures.

Because intellectual pleasure is perfect pleasure, strictly speaking, no intellectual pain opposes intellectual pleasure absolutely, can be absolutely opposed to it. Pain is a privation of pleasure, just as evil is a privation of good. Hence, drink appears more intensely pleasurable to thirsty people and solid food to hungry ones. Because two kinds of bodily pleasures exist (naturally, properly, desirable and excessive), to some people, bodily pleasure considered as such appears to be evil.

Considered as naturally evil, unhealthy, harmful to life, safety, and health, some bodily pleasures are considered as naturally harmful, evil, to brute animals, but as desirable to brutish men. Other bodily pleasures are naturally good as medicinal remedies for physical ailments. Such pleasures belong to someone in natural need (like food and drink to a hungry and thirsty man). Moreover, while *to be already* perfect is better than to be *becoming* perfect, medicinal pleasures are needed by those who are being perfected, but not by those who are already perfect.

Such pleasures are not good absolutely, but incidentally good, *useful goods*, for a time. Since, strictly speaking, what makes pleasures good is that they are medicinal (life- and health-enhancing), physical pleasures *qua* physical (material) are not good or bad. Their essential goodness for *human beings* comes chiefly from their being life-and health maintaining and improving, and only accidentally, incidentally, from their being physical. Since physical pleasures are not good simply as physical, but good as life-and health-enhancing, medicinal, some people incline falsely to conclude they are not good at all.

Because they exceed the proper *measure* of right reason, some vehement bodily pleasures are not medicinal, are physically or psychologically life- and/or health-threatening. Considered as such, they are organically, facultatively, naturally, and morally, harmful/ evil for those they so threaten.

Because, by nature, we human beings seek the intense pleasure of a qualitatively different kind of joy than bodily pleasures can cause, and because some of us lack the proper habituation to delight in the kinds of intellectual pleasures that generate such joy, some people unwittingly attempt to satisfy their desire for such pleasures of a higher intellectual quality by using artificial stimulants like recreational drink, drugs, or dangerous lifestyles of one sort or another.

Since these people do not have the spiritual resources to secure these other forms of intense delight, St. Thomas says that to enjoy such pleasures is not so bad so long as they do not physically or morally hurt themselves or others through reprehensible acts like committing adultery, eating poisonous foods, and so on.

In addition, he says that, by nature, we need recreational pleasures as a remedy for painful work. As physical scientists will confirm, he states, natural movements involved in physical labor cause stress, especially to those highly sensitive to enduring pain of any kind; and, in and of itself, hard work tires the human body. Even constant seeing and hearing can cause physical strain and fatigue to these organs. Hence, animals need to sleep to rest, relax, from the everyday living of an animal life. Because, by nature, we delight in sight, hearing, and knowing, sometimes we do not recognize the physical damage we cause ourselves by over exerting our organic and inorganic faculties.

Because of their bodily chemistry related to growth, St. Thomas maintains that young men especially seek pleasure, and resemble alcoholics in bodily disturbances.

Emotionally depressed people, also, have a constant medicinal need for pleasure because their depression toxifies their body. This need is often intense. Hence, depressed people often become intemperate/brutish.

Because, as acts of the intellectual soul, intellectual pleasures directly cause none of these negative side-effects, they serve as a natural and proper, not incidental, medicinal, remedy for such pain/harm.

Incidental remedies, pleasures, please inasmuch as they can cure, and return a person to a healthy condition. But, when such medicinal remedies are sought outside their medicinal need, they incline to cause harm. Natural remedies of intellectual and moral virtues do not cause such harm.

St. Thomas observes that human nature is not simple, unchanging. It is composite, constantly attracted by different things, constantly physically deteriorating. As a result, if we do one action pleasurable to one of our parts, this pleasure often causes pain to another. Indeed, due to our composite nature, the pleasures of contemplation that are naturally desirable to our intellectual faculty transcend the natural power of the human imagination, especially so for some human beings. Hence, contemplation is not even always enjoyable to some of us all the time.

Nonetheless, St. Thomas says, if man were only intellect, like God, he would always take pleasure in contemplation, even a state of immobility. He adds that, because the activity of the human intellect is *unimpeded by the imperfection of motion*, the pleasure the human intellect produces without a motion, at rest, is qualitatively greater, of higher intensive quantity greatness, than that of the imperfect pleasure generated through the sense appetite in process. Even now, in this life, the human intellect experiences such pleasure.

But, because, by nature, we human beings are physical and constantly change, even though they are imperfect and we often know them to be imperfect, we tend to delight in pleasures involved with change.[14]

—Notes—

1. St. Thomas Aquinas, *Commentary on the Nicomachean Ethics of Aristotle*, Bk. 6, Lect. 1, nn. 1292–1309; regarding the ancient Greek teaching about humors, see http://www.greekmedicine. net/b_p/Four_Humors.html.
2. Id., Lects. 2–3, nn. 1310–1338.
3. Id., Lect. 3, nn. 1339–1353.
4. Id., Lect. 4, nn. 1354–1367.
5. Id., Lect. 5, nn. 1368–1384.
6. Id., Lect. 6, nn. 1385–1403.
7. Id., Lect. 7, nn. 1404–1421.
8. Id., Lect. 8, nn. 1422–1434.
9. Id., Lect. 9, nn. 1435–1454.
10. Id., Lect. 10, nn. 1455–1468.
11. Id., Lect. 11, nn. 1469–1482.
12. Id., Lect. 12, nn. 1483–1497.
13. Id., Lect. 13, nn. 1498–1515. Regarding Plato's teaching about pleasure as it relates to the soul turning toward the body and the World of Forms, see his *Phaedo*, 82C–85B.
14. Aquinas, *Commentary on the Nicomachean Ethics of Aristotle*, Bk. 6, Lect. 14, nn. 1516–1537.

CHAPTER FOURTEEN

The Moral Psychology that Causes Moral, Cultural, and Civilizational Greatness: Friendship

After Discussing continence and incontinence in Book 7 of the *Nicomachean Ethics*, St. Thomas reports that Aristotle starts Book 8 of the same work by presenting six arguments defending the claim that moral philosophy/science must study friendship.

1. Six reasons why moral philosophy/science must study friendship

According to St. Thomas: 1) since moral philosophy studies virtue and, reductively, friendship is a kind of justice or accompanies justice as an effect of virtue, moral philosophy necessarily studies friendship; 2) moral philosophy considers all things needed for human living. Friends are so necessary an external good for human life that no sane human being would choose to live without them (in support of this last claim he gives examples of how, naturally, socially, psychologically, even wealthy people, rulers, and other powerful people need friends to help acquire, preserve, and protect external goods. The poor, young, and people in their prime of life also need friends as a refuge and restraint against doing vicious deeds and to help them to do good acts); 3) the moral philosopher/scientist needs to study what is naturally good. By nature higher forms of animal life feel friendship for other members of the same species, especially those closest to them in kind: for example, parents for their children and adult birds for their young. People of the same race, who have common customs, ancestry, and social life, tend to experience friendship toward one another. And, by nature, human beings incline to experience a natural friendship for other human beings, even for strangers; 4) moral philosophy appears ordered toward the good of the State. Friendship appears to be especially necessary for the preservation of States. Hence, because discord threatens the security of a State, to preserve harmony and concord, rulers incline to prefer friendship and equity even to justice; 5) when perfect friendship exists, no need exists for justice; but if human beings are just, they still need friends. If we are not perfect friends, perfect justice helps us preserve/strengthen friendship. Hence, for a political scientist, studying friendship is more crucial than studying justice; 6) finally, Aristotle argues that friendship is more than a necessary good as a means for strengthening the State and inter-personal relations: a good honorable and lovable considered in itself.

In reply to a hypothetical objection that friends like people who like them because likes like likes, but they do not like people who are competitors, Aristotle says, absolutely considered, friendship is rooted in a natural love that people have for other people. Incidentally, some people dislike some other people because they consider these people to be obstacles to their possession of a good. For example, people in the same business sometimes dislike each other because a business competitor deprives a business owner of an economic good: a customer.

In ancient Greece, Aristotle claims some intellectuals like Euripides, Heraclitus, and Empedocles had attempted to give cosmological arguments to explain why friendship exists; but he rejects considering such explanations in favor of principles derived from human nature and choice. He, also, rejects an error made by some philosophers who claimed that, because friendships are compared to more or less, only once species of friendship exists. He does so because he knows that specific difference derives from *unequal*, not *equal*, having of generic being. Differences of more or less, however, are specific differences of a common genus.[1]

2. Good as friendship's formal object, or external stimulus, and friendship as properly and improperly defined

Having finished his introduction regarding the need for moral philosophy to study friendship, next, St. Thomas says, Aristotle investigates the nature and definition of friendship and its essential relationship to its formal object. To simplify this investigation, he considers the formal object of love from which love and friendship get their name. Then, he notes that not everything is love's, or friendship's, formal object.

Considered as such, evil is not loved, is unlovable. Only the good considered: 1) absolutely (the intrinsically perfect/pleasing whole, the perfect good), the pleasurable good considered as an end, or 2) relatively, relationally as the essential enabling means (the enabling good, the useful/pleasurable as enabling means) are essentially lovable objects of love and friendship.

Absolutely considered, as they exist in themselves, Aristotle maintains that the good and pleasurable are identical. Conceptually considered, as they exist relative to this or that person, Aristotle holds that the good and pleasurable need not be identical. Conceptually considered, we may distinguish the good and pleasurable as: 1) the intrinsically perfect and desirable (good) and 2) the intrinsically perfect and *desirable as possessed by this or that person in relation to this or that appetite in which it rests as pleasurable.*

Next, to expose a falsehood so as to incline a student more readily to accept a truth, Aristotle poses a problem related to love's formal object. He asks, when loving, do we love the absolute good or (because, sometimes, these are not identical) the good relative to us? For example, while to philosophize is good absolutely considered, it is not good for a pauper. And, while something sweet is pleasant absolutely considered, it is not so to someone with a sour taste in his mouth.

Aristotle argues that, facultatively considered, by nature, every faculty tends toward, takes delight in, loves what is *proportionate* to itself according to its intensive quantum strength (a facultative mean), proper facultative (healthy) pleasure. Absolutely considered, from the standpoint of the faculty considered as a species faculty, we pursue the facultative good within the species limits proper to the species as a species mean between excess and defect. For example, a specific limit of food or drink exists for all human beings beyond which drinking or eating is not good (healthy) for any individual member of the species.

Relatively considered, *proportionate* to the individual facultative power of this or that brute animal or human being, we pursue the limit of good as a mean relative to us (for example, that limited exercise of the faculty of sight that, under these conditions and circumstances, here and now, in which we are we are able to engage in the act of seeing without causing damage to our individual faculty).

Again, as a pedagogical tool to incline a student more readily to accept a truth, Aristotle argues against the conclusion he just drew by stating that *every man loves what appears good to him, not what is really good for him*. Hence, to say that what is lovable by us is good for us is false.

To this criticism, Aristotle replies in a twofold way: 1) when we love we love what we love as something really good for us, even if it is not really so; 2) three possible objects of human love exist: the good considered absolutely (the perfective good) as naturally and facultatively perfective; the good considered as an enabling means to become naturally and facultatively perfected (the useful good); and the good considered as imperfectly pleasant (the pleasing good), loved as facultatively pleasing, but not necessarily as the perfecting natural end of facultative operation and health. In all three cases, we love something that, to some extent, is really good for us, although not necessarily perfectly so.

For Aristotle, absolutely considered, the good *qua* good is the intrinsically-perfect whole desirable and pleasing considered in itself as the formal object that stimulates a faculty to act. It is a perfect whole operating as a proximate principle of act, just as, absolutely considered, the one is a principle of measure and generates measure, limit. *So, properly understood, strictly speaking, the good generates pleasure, is chiefly a pleasure-generating principle, a principle that attracts some other being to it as a final, perfecting, cause.*

Considering friendship relative to human love's three possible objects of desire, Aristotle first notes that friendship does not, cannot, consist in loving inanimate things and human beings in the same way. Because inanimate things cannot return love, strictly speaking, human beings cannot will good to inanimate things in the same way they love other human beings with benevolence.

Even if we love wine to last, he says, we do so chiefly for self-love, not for friendship with the wine. He adds that, when we love another human being chiefly for the good of that person without any desire for return of good, we love out of benevolence, not out of friendship. Strictly speaking, friendship is a kind of exchange of love of mutual benefit between equals generated by a sense of commutative justice. And, to be complete, the concept, definition, of friendship must add that it is: 1) a mutually-recognized, mutually-desired, benevolence and love; and 2) a mutually-desired benevolent good recognized as such by both parties for a perfective, useful, or pleasurable good.[2]

3. Aristotle's division, and discussion of, the three species of friendship: perfective, useful, and pleasurable *and how these relate to having the right moral psychology* for a lasting friendship

Having properly defined friendship and divided it into

three species (perfective, useful, and pleasurable) on the basis of qualitatively unequal ways of having friendship (qualitatively completely possessing the definition of friendship), next St. Thomas reports that Aristotle notes perfect friendship is chiefly/ primarily friendship of mutual good will. Imperfect friendships, on the other hand, consist in friendships of enabling means, in utility and imperfect pleasure. In these forms of friendship, Aristotle says a person does not act chiefly out of love of another, to give love. Instead, a person chiefly acts to receive a good from another. He adds that such friendships are easily dissolved, and are based upon something incidental to a person's nature as a person, and to his or her natural and facultative perfection.

Such imperfect friendships, he adds, tend to belong to the following groups: the young, old, sick, needy, rich, poor, fellow-travelers, the incontinent, and *business professionals*, all of whom tend quickly to change their personal relationships as life's situations change.

Perfect friendship, on the other hand, tends to perfect because it exists between virtuous people, people perfectly good (prudent), people who wish good to others to perfect them and to be perfected by them. Consequently, it contains all the elements needed for friendship. It is useful, really pleasant, and of real mutual benefit; but Aristotle states, such friendship is *rare*, and takes a long time to develop.

Following his normal method of defining the subject considered as a whole before comparing and contrasting its parts, having defined friendship as a whole, Aristotle next compares imperfect friendships (showing first how they are alike and contrasting them by showing how they differ). To start doing this, he examines both in relation to the chief reason, aim, for loving found in perfect friendship.

He has already noted that perfect friendships tend to last chiefly because: 1) their chief reason for loving is reciprocal good will, benevolence; and 2) they are based upon possessing specifically like habits. If either one of these two elements is missing, he claims that friendships tend not to last. Since, at least to some extent, friendships based chiefly upon utility and imperfect pleasure have these two elements, such friendships tend to last for a while.

Because friendships depend upon reciprocation, and pleasures widely differ, friendships based upon pleasure (like sex-based friendships) have a difficult time enduring for any length of time. Also, if their chief aim for being friends differs, Aristotle claims that people have a difficult time remaining friends (for example, people who return a useful good for a pleasure [like money for sex], or a pleasure for a useful good [like sex for money]). Aristotle notes that only virtuous people have the enabling psychological qualities (*the right moral psychology*) to form perfect friendships, and they can only do so with each other.

For the sake of pleasure, he notes that any of the three species of friendship (the virtuous [the perfective], pleasant, and the useful) contain principles that can enable human beings, if they are not totally evil, to be friends.

However, evil men have a kind of moral psychology that enables them only to form friendships to use people for personal pleasure/ gain; they do not have the psychological constitution to enable them to reciprocate virtuous good for virtuous good. As a result, at best, they are able imperfectly to form the semblance of real friendship.

To be perfect friends, Aristotle maintains, friends must have the right moral psychology that enables them to be perfectly *friend-worthy*, just (*which means having qualities of soul* such as being honest, trustworthy, and prudent). As a result, virtuous friends incline not to believe moral evil of a friend. When a party involved in a virtuously-rooted friendship discovers that the person he or she thought to be really virtuous is not so, Aristotle says such friendships can quickly dissolve.

In other kinds of friendship, imperfect ones, especially those based upon a moral psychology of pleasure, believing a friend to act unjustly, be morally evil, is less of a, or no, problem, *Professional dishonesty in business friendships, however, tends to be a problem.*[3]

4. Aristotle's consideration of the nature of perfect friendship in general and the moral psychology that it necessarily demands

After having compared and contrasted imperfect acts of friendship, St. Thomas says Aristotle next examines the nature of perfect friendship considered in general. To do so, he first makes a distinction between two ways in which we properly name natures: according to 1) power and 2) act.

For example, at times, we call people "virtuous" because they: 1) most properly possess the habit of virtue or 2) perform an act of virtue. Analogously, he says, most properly, we call people "friends" who: 1) *actually* live together harmoniously, pleasantly, and enjoy delight in doing good for each other; but 2), in a way, we call people "friends" who have a psychological disposition to act in this way.

Because maintaining regular, mutual, activity tends to be necessary to cause friendships to last, Aristotle explains how three classes of people have a hard time being lasting friends: 1) those geographically separated from each other for a long time (because, since causes precede their effects in nature, and friendship is an act of a habit, prolonged absence of friends tends, first, to cause *forgetfulness* of friendship; then *weakness*, and, finally, *disappearance*, of it); 2) since inclination toward being pleasant/sociable is a necessary condition for becoming friendly, people lacking these dispositions do not tend to form friendships (for example, gloomy, morose, mean-spirited; people not pleasant to be around; people wracked by pain;

the elderly, and the shy); and 3) benevolent people who do not, or cannot, live together.

Living together, bestowing favors on each other, *rejoicing in the same activities and things*, getting the best out of each other, appear to be essential acts of perfect friendship. Friendship is chiefly a habit of good will, not an emotion. Love that exists in the sensitive appetite (love as a passion/emotion) is not sound, and tends not to last; is not love in the properly-human sense. In sum, Aristotle maintains that enduring friendship chiefly involves three acts: 1) living together; 2) repeatedly doing favors for each other; and 3) sharing the same pleasures; repose of appetites in the identical kind of good.[4]

5. Aristotle's consideration of the moral psychology of perfect friendship in relation to its chief subject: the friend-worthy person

Having considered the nature of friendship in general and different species of friendship, Aristotle next continues to examine imperfect friendship in relation to perfect friendship, chiefly regarding the qualities that make a person friend-worthy, having the kind of *moral psychology* capable of generating friendship and entering into friendships. He says that such qualities chiefly consist in sociability, liking people, being able to: 1) be agreeable (pleasant); 2) get along with others; and 3) enter into conversation.

Chiefly, Aristotle considers friendship to be an activity of pleasing communication between people. Hence, people who delight in talking readily, tend to agree with others, find pleasure in the company of other people (like young people do), and quickly make friends. Because they do not tend to live with *and take pleasure in* the company of many people, old people, morose, quarrelsome, critical people, can be benevolent, but (because they have the wrong moral psychology) have a difficult time making and maintaining friendships. Their problem of entering into friendships is complicated by the fact that, by its nature, friendship does not lend itself to one person having many friends, especially among virtuous people, who tend always to be few in number.

The superabundant, excessive, love that perfect friendship demands is designed by nature for one, not many, people: a best friend. As an example, Aristotle gives the attempt of one man excessively to love many women.

In perfect friendship friends possess a moral psychology that enables them to be exceedingly pleasing to each other. Because being displeasing to others is possible in so many ways, perfect friendship is hard to form and sustain. To be perfect friends we have to form habitual association, and doing so with many people is difficult.

For two reasons, in imperfect friendships, one person can have many friends: because we can have many 1) pleasing and 2) useful friends. Often, forming such friendships takes little time and effort. But, even in the case of imperfect friendships, forming them can be difficult when the chief aim of the friendship differs among the parties (when, for example, one person wants utility and another pleasure). Youthful friendships tend to be an exception in imperfect friendships because, even in the case where they involve utility, the moral psychology of youthful friendships tends to be chiefly concerned about wanting pleasure.

In pleasurable friendships the moral psychology that tends to dominate is one in which friends incline to love each other more generously than they do in useful relationships, which tends to be the moral psychology more common in business activities. Hence, friendship based upon pleasure more perfectly resembles perfect friendship than does friendship based upon utility.

Because they are rich and tend to have no need of many useful people, rich people tend to possess a moral psychology inclined to form friendships based upon pleasure. And, in general, Aristotle maintains that we human beings tend to have a psychological makeup that enables us to bear unpleasant behavior in others for only a short, not a long, time. He adds that we could not even stand the good life if it did not please.

Next, Aristotle asserts that people in positions of power tend to form friendships based upon pleasure and utility, not upon virtue. For utility, they especially like people who are shrewd and funny, not qualities generally found in one person.

In reply to a possible objection that, because virtuous people are also pleasant and useful, the powerful can be friends of the virtuous, Aristotle replies that *virtuous people do not incline to be friends with powerful people as powerful, but for their virtue; and powerful people do not incline to be friends with virtuous people as virtuous, but to use them, and only insofar as they defer to the powerful as more powerful*. The virtuous person, however, is not inclined to defer to the powerful person as more virtuous or powerful, and the powerful man is not inclined to defer to the virtuous person, except as useful. Moreover, usually men who excel in power and riches do not excel in moral virtue, but reluctantly recognize the morally virtuous as their qualitative betters.

Finally, Aristotle notes that, in all three species of friendship, friendships are based upon proportionate equality and ability to love and be loved in relation to a chief end. Only perfect friendship is properly named. The other forms of friendship are said analogously as they more or less resemble the perfect.[5]

6. The nature and moral psychology of friendships between unequals, and the crucial role the estimative sense plays in being able to form them

After discussing three species of friendship based upon equal relations between friends, Aristotle next talks about friendships essentially involving unequal relation between the friends. Chiefly, he is thinking about family and civic friendships, friendships rooted in qualitative inequality in friend-worthiness.

In this form of friendship, he maintains that a qualitative difference exists between the friends that causes them to have difficulty engaging in commutative exchanges in goods. They tend not to be able to give and return goods of equal quality and kind.

Since the normal psychological disposition of friendship is to be disposed to do favors of equal proportion to each other, this form of friendship is unique because it involves friends who cannot equally reciprocate favors of the same kind. As examples of such friendships, he gives that of: 1) parents to children and children to parents; 2) a superior to and inferior; and 3) a husband to a wife and a wife to husband.

Different reasons for loving, abilities to love, cause different kinds of friendship and are at play in these species of friendship. Aristotle maintains that these friendships are preserved by each party contributing what is suitable, fitting, proportionate, and proper to the relationship according to unequal status and ability. The equality involved in these relationships more closely resembles that of contributive/distributive justice than that of commutative justice.

While equality is the goal of justice, Aristotle claims it is the starting point of friendship. Friendship starts with knowing the kind of equality that the relationship demands. This is crucial to know because, he says, friendship cannot exist between people widely differing as equals related to a common aim.

Such being the case, while neither Aristotle nor St. Thomas explicitly says so, this means that, at least in part, essentially, *the starting point of friendship lies within the estimative sense, the particular, or cogitative, reason!* This is chiefly because: 1) *entering into a friendship that a person seeks to have last presupposes from the start that those seeking to become friends have the right moral psycholo-*

gy: possess self-knowledge, understand their abilities, strengths and weaknesses, and that of the other partner, to contribute long-term to exchanging in the specific kind, or kinds, of goods that the relationship requires; and 2) *the estimative faculty is the chief psychological principle of individual self-knowledge, sense estimation of personal abilities, strengths and weaknesses, of oneself and that of others.*

Aristotle maintains that great differences in inequality tend to cause friendships (like that between the gods and human beings, kings and peasants, the best and wisest and evil people and fools) to be impossible to form and not to last. And exact determination of the greatness in inequality that will prevent friendship formation or destroy friendship is impossible to determine. *The best we can say is that inequalities too great make friendships psychologically impossible to form and last. Such being the case, a well-educated estimative sense faculty, cogitative reason, is crucial, essential, to any hope of forming strong and long-lasting friendships.*

From the prior discussion, someone might object, it appears to follow that human beings cannot wish the greatest of goods for some friends because then they could no longer be friends. Aristotle answers this objection by saying that, when we wish others good, we: 1) do so to them as human beings, not as a god; and 2) we wish good to ourselves most of all, including not to lose a friend.[6]

7. The nature and moral psychology of loving and being loved as related to friendship

Having finished examining the moral psychology of friendship between unequals, Aristotle next considers: 1) how the moral psychology of loving and being loved relate to friendship; and 2) in three ways shows how loving, not being loved, is more of the nature of friendship.

He starts doing so, first, by noting that *the Many* appear to want to be loved, not to love, because they associate being loved with being of greater, qualitatively better, honorable, or more honorable, good.

For this reason, *the Many* tend to take pleasure in flattery and love people fawning over them. According to Aristotle, however, the flatterer tends to be of a psychologically-low moral status, character, pretends to be a friend by loving more than wanting to be loved more. Because of an inordinate love of honor, men wish to be loved, instead of to love. Yet, according to Aristotle, people who seek to be honored do so chiefly for being good, because honor is a sign of goodness. Hence, they desire honor only incidentally; and do so from people they consider good so as to verify to themselves their intrinsic goodness, virtue.

Some such flatterers chiefly seek honor from: 1) the powerful (hoping to obtain something from those who honor them) and 2) the just (to confirm the flatterer's self-opinion). They do so because, considered in and of itself, having friends appears to them, and appears to be, a sign of honor because it is a sign of some internal personal good, virtue. Nonetheless, according to Aristotle, since the essential is more excellent than the incidental, loving and honoring are more excellent than being loved and being honored.

In several ways, Aristotle next shows how the psychological excellence of friendship consists in loving and being loved. He starts to do so by stating that friendship is a psychological habit. A habit terminates in operation, not in being acted upon. As an example, Aristotle gives good mothers who take more pleasure in loving their children than being loved by them.

He adds that friendship is maintained by loving according to: 1) excellence and ability and 2) proportionality. And he maintains that friendship is as lasting as the greatness of the proportion love is able to achieve between the friends. Hence, friends tend to be praised for loving, not for being loved, *and for doing so proportionate to their ability*.

The likeness that preserves friendship, he adds, is found maximally in virtuous people, whose psychological disposition is to want to love more than to be loved so as to get the best out of their friends. Consequently, the friendship of evil men is the least stable and enduring because intrinsically it is hateful, self-serving. Evil men have a psychological disposition that inclines to find nothing really good, pleasant, that mutually satisfies them. As a result, they can remain friends only for a short time; and chiefly to use other people for personal advantage.

Aristotle observes, further, that friendships of pleasure and utility tend to last longer than those of the wicked so long as the pleasure and utility last. And friendships between people of opposite social and economic conditions appear to be chiefly those of utility, based upon mutual need. Such utility can also exist in friendships rooted in pleasure, but Aristotle maintains they do not tend to exist among virtuous people because no disparity of condition tends to exist among them. Further, sometimes disparity of an opposite condition can cause ridicule to a person who thinks more of himself than he deserves.[7]

8. The nature and moral psychology of friendships that exist within civic associations

Having considered friendship among unequals, next Aristotle considers friendships in relation to different human associations, saying that *every association is a kind of communications relation*, and that friendship, justice, tend to hold together such associations. According to him, we diversify friendships chiefly based upon the psychological diversity of aims for associating, and communicating, with each other. Indeed, were no communication to exist, no friendship could exist; which indicates that, from the start, whatever friendships we can form essentially depend upon the quality of communication that exists between friends.

Aristotle continues that acts of injustice and justice increase in moral magnitude as they involve closer, associates, friends (for example, to steal from another friend tends to be morally worse than to steal from a stranger). By nature, he says that all human associations are enabling means for, aim at, acquiring something useful, needed, for living.

For utility's sake, we human beings appear psychologically to incline to associate and remain together for common interest. Private associations do so for private utility and gain, and even those based upon pleasure seek some utility. By nature, private associations aim, beyond themselves, to generate a moral culture of civic association to benefit us all during life, to generate a State and to order it for long-term right living.[8]

9. Distinction of political societies and households based upon the number of people who rule and the moral psychology they employ to rule

Having shown that, by nature, all forms of friendship psychologically aim at generating civic friendship, next Aristotle starts to discuss different species of friendship in relation to different species of political society.

As is well known, Aristotle divides political societies chiefly on the basis of the number of people who rule (one, the few, or the many) and the moral psychology involved in way they rule (justly or unjustly). Just rule by one person he calls "kingship"; unjust rule by one person, "tyranny." Just rule by a few people, "aristocracy"; unjust rule by a few people, "oligarchy" or "plutocracy." Just rule by many people, a "timocracy"; and unjust rule by many people a "democracy."

Aristotle observes that, while the first form of unjust rule (the tyranny) suffers from the defect of intending the good of only one person (the ruler), the last two forms of unjust rule resemble each other by suffering from the defect of intending the good of one political class: the rich or the poor. The oligarchy, or plutocracy, chiefly intends the good of the wealthy, while the democracy intends only the good of the poor.

Next, Aristotle shows how the moral psychology of different political orders resembles the moral psychology of different family/household relations. Benevolent paternalism of fathers over this sons, he claims, resembles kingship, while malevolent paternalism resembles a master/slave relation, similar to that of the way Persian fathers treat this sons: like slaves. And while he considers this relation between a father and his children unfitting, he maintains that to use slaves for household profit is all right, appears to be right.

Lest we incline to glory in our own contemporary moral superiority in considering Aristotle's claim that to use slaves for household profit is all right, we should recall that Aristotle understood the terms "slave" and "slavery" to apply to much wider groups of people than we do today. For example, in his time, he would consider anybody who worked for another for a wage, a person we would call, today, an "employee," to be a slave. Moreover, because the ancient Greeks lacked machines to perform the manual and servile work that machines do for us today, Aristotle maintained that formation of a household essentially required employment of slaves.

Given his more finely-nuanced understanding of the terms "slave" and "slavery," we should not be surprised, then, to find that his attitude toward the household relation between a husband and wife is far less chauvinistic than many people today might expect from an ancient Greek. For example, instead of maintaining that a husband has complete dominion over his wife, Aristotle considers the husband/wife relation of household rule to be essentially aristocratic, not that of a benevolent or malevolent ruler over a natural or political inferior. Each, he says, has dominion over what pertains to each, to what each can do with his or her excellence, virtue.

Hence, he states that husbands should not arrange everything and leave the wife in charge of nothing. *And wives who are heiresses should not arrange everything and leave their husbands in charge of nothing*, rule based on their inherited riches and power. Instead of ruling like despots, each should rule according to his or her excellence, competence.

While he makes no mention of relation of sisters to rule within a household, he states that rule of a household by brothers who are close in age resembles a timocracy (rule by people who chiefly aim at acquiring honor).

Regarding democratic rule within a household or a political society, he states that such rule resembles companions staying at an Inn. No one is responsible for anything, including paying the bills. If anyone has authority, the authority is weak.[9]

10. The nature and moral psychology of friendships existing within political societies

After distinguishing the different kinds of political and household associations, St. Thomas says, Aristotle next shows how the moral psychology involved in organizations of political societies resembles that involved in friendships. This is so, he maintains, because every real political order is a species of justice involving a kind of friendship.

To start showing how these two species of organizations analogously resemble each other in moral psychology, Aristotle says that kingly rule is analogous to benevolent paternalism: friendship between unequals. While the benefaction of a king is quantitatively greater than that of a father because it extends to a greater number of people, benefaction of a father to one person, a son, for example, is greater because the father is the cause of a son's three greatest goods: 1) life, 2) upbringing, and 3) education. All such unequal friendships have a common principle: excellence of one person over another.

Friendship between a husband and wife, on the other hand, resembles a friendship between equals: aristocrats possessing different excellences. And democracy is analogous to fraternal friendship.

Since little justice (and, consequently, little friendship) exist within them, Aristotle maintains that the following friendships correspond to corrupt forms of government.

The least friendship exists in a tyranny, where the moral psychology of a tyrant inclines him to treats citizens like tools and slaves. Since no human being can have a real friendship with a tool, Aristotle reasons that no master *qua* master can have a real friendship with a slave (but he can have a real friendship with a slave as another human being). And no tyrant can have a real friendship with those he rules.

In contrast to the tyranny in which friendship exists least extensively, Aristotle asserts that friendship exists most extensively in a democracy, a form of rule that attempts, by unjustly rewarding them, to make untalented people equal to talented ones.

And, in contrast to the tyranny and democracy, the extent of friendship within an oligarchy tends to be somewhere in the middle.[10]

11. Division of friendships into species based upon their psychological awareness of sharing other kinds of things in common

Having distinguished personal, domestic, and civic friendship as forms of common participation toward an end, Aristotle next divides friendship on the basis of sharing something in common into that between and among blood relatives, non-blood relatives, close associates through common upbringing, close friends, inhabitants of the same village, city, State, or nation, and fellow travelers. Before so doing, however, *Aristotle notes that the friendship existing between parents, a husband and wife, is the natural foundation of all subsequent friendship because, by nature, parents are naturally inclined to have a moral psychology that involves loving their children as part of themselves. As a result, the friendships between a parent and child is closest to that of natural self-love, from which all friendship naturally derive!*

For three reasons Aristotle and St. Thomas say that, by nature, parents are psychologically inclined to love their children more than their children love them: 1) the more a person knows the causes of love, the more intensely he loves; 2) parents know their children as part of themselves, know the causes of the children's generation; 3) children only know their parents first and foremost as authors of their existence.

Moreover, the relationship of blood relatives one to another always involves the relation of a procreator to offspring to which all offspring have an unequal relation of dependency. Such a relation is like that of a whole to a separable part. While such parts are separated from their natural whole, they retain a natural closeness for it because the whole includes them, but they do not include it.

As procreators, parents naturally know and love their children for a longer length of time (from birth) than children know and love their parents. Hence, by nature, mothers naturally incline to love their children more than do fathers because mothers know better than do "fathers" those who actually fathered the children. In addition, in regard to time, mothers conceive affection of love for their children longer and more intimately than do fathers—from conception.

As begotten by the same parents, brothers: 1) are inclined to love each other as being generated from the same principle; 2) have more of a natural closeness to each other than they do to other human beings other than their natural parents; 3) are reared/educated together generally within the same household, at least in their early years; and 4) tend to live close together like friends from birth.

Other blood relatives: 1) share common ancestors, giving them natural domestic proximity; and 2) are more or less closely related as members, parts, of the same family in relation to blood ties, temporal proximity, and common ancestors.

An Introduction to Ragamuffin Ethics

Because parents are, by nature, the greatest of benefactors to their children, children have a natural psychological inclination to experience friendship toward parents as to a superior good. Hence, in proportion as they live together in common, children and parents tend to share more of pleasure and utility toward and with each other than they share with other friends.

Among family relations, Aristotle and St. Thomas maintain that, for reasons already given, the friendship between and among brothers is like friends living together, but naturally stronger. Analogously, the same is true friendships among other blood relatives.

Regarding the special and unique familial friendship between a man and a wife, like recourse to a higher natural principle, Aristotle and St. Thomas say that, while human beings are political animals, we are more conjugal than political because the conjugal relation between a man and a woman is, by nature, not generated by convention, nor social contract, and is the natural first principle of all other human associations.

Because this conjugal union is generic, part of animal nature, the natural inclination to preserve it is qualitatively stronger than the inclination to preserve any civic association, including States. Hence, Aristotle and St. Thomas would likely consider contemporary "same-sex marriage" and political orders that support such intemperate unions to be examples of human associations that, when push comes to shove, by natural inclination, most human beings would have a strong, natural, inclination to reject as socially dangerous for humans.

Furthermore, they say that, while union between a male and a female among other animals exists exclusively for species preservation (generation of offspring), among human beings, conjugal friendship between a man and a woman proximately generates a natural, psychological need to provide for: 1) the self-sufficiency of their resulting natural family, and 2) long-term preservation of the

440

strongest, natural, familial relationship that exists—that between a husband and wife. This natural, strongest of all, domestic friendship (that between a man and a woman) serves as the natural, proximate principle of all subsequent social and civic associations through which only men can get out of women goods that other women cannot get out of them and vice versa.

In so doing, the natural family generated by the conjugal relationship between and a man and a woman generates all higher forms of social life out of which, by nature, all civic society, including modern States, arise. Beyond this, Aristotle and St. Thomas maintain that the conjugal friendship between a man and woman creates an essential means for generating and maintaining the transgenerational civic good (*the natural connection with commonly-known ancestors*) *that strengthens political societies long-term.*

Regarding this conjugal friendship between a man and a woman, Aristotle adds that it can be chiefly based upon pleasure, utility, or virtue. Based upon everything he has said previously within his *Nicomachean Ethics*, he would consider conjugal friendship based upon virtue to be the strongest of conjugal bonds.

Regarding children, Aristotle says, they appear to strengthen, not weaken, conjugal union. As a sign of the truth of this claim he refers to: 1) a phenomenon that was apparently common within his time, that sterile couples tend to separate more often than do married couples; and 2) his conviction that couples whose conjugal union essentially includes the well-being of children born of that union tends to last longer than a conjugal union which does not.[11]

12. The nature and moral psychology of quarrels and complaints that tend to arise within friendships between equals and advice about how to resolve them

After finishing his discussion of different kinds of friendship and their psychological foundations, Aristotle next discusses complaints (quarrels) that incline to arise within all the different species of friendship, especially quarrels based upon merit and equality and inequality.

While Aristotle recognizes that quarrels can exist within any of the three species of friendship, he maintains they happen most in friendships based upon utility, not those based upon virtue or pleasure. *He reasons that the chief cause for this occurrence is that utilitarian friendships chiefly tend to arrive from business dealings; and they do so because the nature of such dealings essentially involves using the participants within such activities for personal advantage, for some sort of personal benefit on both sides of the relationship. In general, people involved in business dealings are naturally inclined to want to get more out of such dealings than they give.*

Consequently, beneficiaries within such dealings incline to complain about not getting as much as they should have gotten, especially when they have contributed so much. Simultaneously, the benefactors in such relationships tend to say they have no more to give, that they have given too much already. Aristotle notes that such quarrels do not tend to happen within the context of virtuous friendships because, in such friendships, people incline to give more than they get. Indeed, they incline to enter into such relationships precisely to give a greater good than they get.

Regarding reasons for quarrels arising within utilitarian friendships, he says this can happen between equals and unequals, and in private and legal matters. Since friendship is essentially rooted in justice, and justice is of two species (personal and legal), friendships can be of two kinds (personal and legal, or professional).

He also notes that quarrels rarely happen in friendships based chiefly upon pleasure because, if friends in this relationship enjoy each other's company, each has what he or she wants. If he or she does not, not to stay in the other's company is usually possible, often easily so. He notes that complaints in utilitarian friendships are especially prone to arise as a result of confusing these two kinds, orders, of friendship: personal and professional.

For example, in a business deal, one person wants justice according to law while another expects it according to personal relation. Also, while some legal, professional, contracts are explicitly spelled out in writing, some are based upon a handshake, or a combination of the two. Within such business dealings, even if not explicitly spelled out, a "moral utility" often tends to exist in which, while not formally expressed in writing, people who freely give a good, do a favor, are psychologically inclined to expect to get something, often a favor, in return.

Because to confer a benefit without receiving one is noble, and the utilitarian man wants to appear noble, even if he is not, publicly he will sometimes pretend not to want to profit from doing a good deed beyond the call of duty, from performing a benevolent act within the context of the business deal. Nonetheless, generally, he will incline to expect a favor down the road, if not immediately, for a presently-executed benevolent act.

To show how to avoid quarrels in utilitarian relations, Aristotle advises people, first, to avoid becoming involved in utilitarian exchanges without first establishing a fixed agreement on the terms of such exchanges. When freely receiving a benefit from another, he says the recipient should, from the start, consider: 1) the person who is giving the benefit; 2) whether the gift is being freely given or has strings attached to it; and 3) under what conditions he is receiving the benefit (whether he is able or not to make a return [for example, to a loan shark]) before deciding whether or not to receive the benefit. *In short, a person considering entering into such a relationship should have a well-educated estimative sense awareness about the relationship into which he or she might become involved, and should recognize from the start that utilitarian friendships are not chiefly based upon benevolent exchange of virtue.*

Hence, in a suspected utilitarian relation, a benefactor within such a relation should make return worthy of the gifts received because he should not: 1) make someone a friend against his will; and 2) be willing to receive for free what a person is not willing to give for free.

In attempting to determine suitable repayments within the context of utilitarian relationships, Aristotle notes that a difficulty often arises about *how to measure* the repayment in terms of the benefit conferred on the action of the giver. To resolve this problem, because the benefit received could only have been as much as the receiver actually received, Aristotle recommends that, generally, the repayment in utilitarian relations be measured by the beneficiary, not the benefactor, according to the actual benefit received (which the beneficiary should generally know better than the benefactor).

Within the context of virtuous friendships, however, Aristotle says that repayment should be measured according to the intention of the giver because, in such friendships, the will of the giver has the likeness of a measure.[12]

13. Quarrels and complaints that tend to arise within friendships between unequals and advice about psychological, and other, means to resolve them

Generally considered, Aristotle maintains that quarrels in friendships tend to arise when one party *thinks* he or she should have gotten more than he or she did. In virtue-based friendships, the more virtuous tends to think he or she should have received more, while, in utility-based friendships, the more useful person thinks that he or she should have received more, just as in business relations the bigger investor expects the larger returns. In both cases, Aristotle says both parties, in general, appear to reason rightly: that something *more* is the *right measure*. To the beneficiary, this is the greater monetary gain. To the benefactor, this is the greater honor.

In such an unequally-based, utilitarian relation, Aristotle claims that honor is suitable compensation to a benefactor for the benefactor's act of virtue (generosity), while, simultaneously, monetary gain provides suitable assistance against need for the beneficiary.

Observance and recognition of proportionate excellence, Aristotle says, creates proportionate equality among friends; and it preserves friendships within political societies. Psychologically, friends tend to ask, expect, of friends what is possible, proportionate to their ability, not what is mathematically equal, or impossible. And not often possible is for the same person to get riches and honors. Since not all benefits to God and parents, for example, can be repaid, St. Thomas says, the just, virtuous, act is *to repay what we can and not to try to do the impossible.*[13]

14. Proportionate properties of friendship, and how a psychologically-healthy (prudently-regulated) estimative sense can serve as a remedy for disturbances arising related to friendship

Having finished his discussion of friendship's nature and kinds within Book 8, Aristotle starts Book 9 of his *Nicomachean Ethics* with consideration of the general topic he will discuss throughout this Book: proportionate properties of friendship.

He initiates doing so by observing that fair return tends to preserve friendship. And, immediately after so doing, he explains how, to preserve friendship in relations involving distributive justice (friendship between social unequals like that of a father or employer and a son and an employee), *use of proportionate equality tends to dominate.*

Before going into detail about the nature of such proportionate equality, first Aristotle explains how disagreements about fair distribution tend not to happen in exchanges related to commutative justice in which money, a commonly-accepted, numerically-equal, standard is used. In *qualitatively* different exchanges (like that involving emotional affection and business services), in contrast, he observes that lack of the right, proportionate, measure tends to disturb friendship.

He notes that we human beings *tend to judge* repayment and friendship in two stages: 1) internally as an act of love and 2) externally in terms of giving gifts and performing services. And we tend to complain about doing too little or too much in both.

Sometimes, the complaints arise because people involved within the relationship do not get what, psychologically, they expect, or as much as they expect, out of the relationship. For example, a lover wants pleasure while a beloved wants utility. In such a case, neither provides or is provided with what he or she wants, and the friendship ends.

As remedies against disturbances in friendships involving *qualitatively unequal* exchanges, Aristotle recommends that, because *negligence* on this person's part is the chief cause of complaint in *qualitatively unequal* friendships, fair repayment should be measured by the person who first receives the benefit. Since *right estimation of the proportionate benefit* to return cannot accurately be measured without first determining the benefit received, as Aristotle and St. Thomas note, within this context, a *well-educated particular reason, or estimative sense, is crucial for being able to remedy against such disturbances and friendship*. As they say, payment ought to be made based upon virtue. Within such a situation, they claim that, to avoid excess and defect in repayment, the measure of proper repayment becomes the prudent man, *the person possessed of the habit of right estimation*.

The amount of the payment is properly determined by considering the benefit bestowed by the benefactor and the benefit received by the beneficiary. This, however, is often impossible precisely to determine. As an example of just such a case of impossibility precisely to determine fair benefit received, because payment for learning wisdom can never be commensurate with the good received, Aristotle refers to the case of Protagoras, who asked for repayment of his services to students in ancient Greece *that they be the measure* what they paid him according to the educational benefit that *they estimated* they had received from him.

In useful friendships, he says the right measure should be determined in terms of the help received. In pleasurable friendships, he suggests that the right measure should be equality of pleasure given and received. From a legal standpoint, regarding voluntary, personal exchanges, he notes that legislators tend to use the principle of what was later called *caveat emptor* (*let the buyer beware*) in cases where no redress is possible, the burden of responsibility falls upon the buyer, the recipient of a possible benefit to be the party chiefly aware.[14]

15. Some doubts about duties related to friendship

Having given advice about how to preserve friendship through the proper moral psychology related to proportionate repayment, Aristotle immediately raises some doubts about what he has said regarding repayment between unequals. For example, someone might ask, to which superiors should and inferior chiefly listen? Another person might wonder whether a friend has a moral duty to help a friend before helping a virtuous person. A third person might wonder whether someone should first repay a benefactor before giving a gift to a friend.

Aristotle replies that, in the abstract, no easy way exists to resolve these problems. As a general rule, however, in the case of repaying a benefactor, he recommends that, if a person cannot simultaneously do both, except in extreme emergencies (for example, a situation such as kidnapping), the honorable choice is to repay the benefactor first, just as if one were repaying a loan.

Nevertheless, in some cases, Aristotle says a benefactor should not be repaid (for example, if the benefactor has become morally depraved or, as in the case that Socrates presents to Cephalos in Book 1 of Plato's *Republic*, a person had received weapons from a previously sane benefactor who subsequently, after going insane, asks for their return).

Regarding what person should be honored more, Aristotle recommends that this be done according to that person's merit.[15]

16. The crucial relation of self-love and good will to having the needed moral psychology to generate acts of friendship; and how the moral psychology of the good man differs from that of the evil man

After giving the above advice about how to preserve friendship through having the proper psychological attitude toward the nature of proportionate repayment, Aristotle immediately considers some minor doubts about the dissolution of friendship which are not crucial for consideration within the context of this work. Hence, I will skip them here, except for one sage observation that Aristotle makes about fraudulent friends: that *people who counterfeit being friends are worse than people counterfeit money!*[16]

That tidbit of wisdom being noted, this study of Aristotle's and St. Thomas's moral teaching continues at the point where Aristotle traces the proximate origin of friendly acts within the individual to the psychological act of self-love, personal good will. According to Aristotle, and St. Thomas concurs, the chief reason a person acts benevolently toward others is because he inclines to act benevolently toward himself—because he possesses a good will. A will in touch with reality, the good will possessed by the prudent man, is friendship's chief proximate cause within any and every human being.

Since benevolent acts are effects of benevolent wills, effects of friendship, Aristotle divides such benevolent acts into three species: 1) voluntarily doing good toward another with no expectation of any reciprocal good; 2) a friend willing another friend's existence and continued life for his friend's sake, not for his own benefit/gain (just as good mothers naturally incline to will the existence and life of their children); and 3) friendly acts that promote close contacts, shared emotions (such as loves/pleasures and dislikes/pains), and shared ways of thinking.

Because people tend to think that people having the essential quality of at least one of these species of friendship have the essential quality of friendship, we tend to define friendship in relation to these qualities. As far as he is concerned, Aristotle says all these qualities belong essentially to the virtuous, or prudent, man and to other people inasmuch as they think they are virtuous, or prudent.

He, then, immediately explains how he thinks these virtuous qualities exist in the non-virtuous person by saying virtue/good appears, by natural desire/inclination, to be the standard of human excellence for all people. In fact, insofar as he considers himself virtuous, every human being naturally inclines to do good toward himself because virtue and the good man appear to be the natural, proper, measure of right human action.

Aristotle maintains that, *in any order (genus) of reality, the perfect species is the maximum, measure,* because all other things within a genus are judged more or less perfect to the extent that they approach toward, or recede from, this maximum. Since virtue is our proper perfection as human beings, the virtuous, prudent, man is the maximum of perfection in the human species. Consequently the virtuous, prudent, man should be taken as the measure in moral activities.

The morally virtuous man, however, suitably (proportionately) has/possesses what is proper to: 1) beneficence (doing good); 2) good will; and 3) peace/concord. Hence, he wishes for himself that his friends acquire real and apparent human goods because, for him, these are identical. Moreover, because the mark of a good man is to work for the achievement of real good, he generates these goods for himself and his friends.

Because virtue makes its possessor and possessor's works good, the morally virtuous person especially wants virtue for himself and his friends; and, especially, for the most perfect part of the human person, the intellectual faculty. Hence, a morally virtuous person always strives to do what is reasonable and wishes for himself and his friends to be prudent. He always wishes for himself and his friends *perfection of the absolutely good soul and life and conservation of the part of the soul in which wisdom resides: once again, the human intellect.*

Most especially, the morally virtuous man wishes himself *to exist* so that his identity can be preserved, to exist like God, says St. Thomas, who remains eternally in His existence. Because we are most like God (incorruptible/unchangeable) in our intellect, St. Thomas maintains that the morally virtuous man: 1) thinks of his existence chiefly in terms of his intellect; 2) especially wishes himself to exist and live; and 3) especially wishes to live in accord with prudence.

In contrast, Aristotle and St. Thomas maintain that *the morally vicious person, who wants chiefly to live for the imperfect pleasures of the body, does not really want to exist and to live, is not essentially pro-life.* Put in contemporary terms, *the moral culture of the vicious man is the culture of death.*

Most fittingly, therefore, St. Thomas asserts that the morally virtuous man: 1) possesses in himself the qualities of soul proper *psychologically* to cause peace, concord, and harmony; and 2) wants most of all, with pleasure, to return to his soul and meditate alone.

With pleasure, the virtuous man meditates about, delights in, fond memories of the sweetness of his past triumphs, hopes, and anticipations of future success in moral conflicts; and his present true and useful knowledge. He is at peace with his passions and keenly experiences all sorrows and joys as an integrated unit with psychological integrity with the whole of his being. Because the virtuous man rightly identifies real and apparent good, he knows/feels these with the whole of his being. He does not know and love one with the intellectual part of the soul while, simultaneously, knowing and loving its contrary opposite with the sensitive part of the soul, like the members of the crew team simultaneously rowing in opposite directions.

In the virtuous man, these two parts harmoniously cooperate, are not at war with each other. The sensitive part of the soul is so much subject to reason's promptings that it readily obeys them, or does so, with weak resistance. Hence, the virtuous man: 1) delights in always acting according to reason; 2) does not have regrets; and 3) is at peace with himself.

At this point, Aristotle talks about how a friend should be psychologically disposed to act toward friends: as he acts/feels toward himself, as another self. Then, he immediately contrasts this to the way evil men are psychologically disposed to treat each other.

Because they cannot understand friendship the way virtuous men do, do not have the psychological make-up to be able to do so, Aristotle maintains that evil men can never find total self-satisfaction. The chief reason for this is that, because the more virtuous we are, the more we know ourselves to be virtuous. Because we like ourselves, we become pleased with ourselves. Because most of the people who are evil know they are evil, they can never find total self-gratification, can never be totally pleased, and at peace, with themselves. As a result, as they become increasingly more evil, St. Thomas maintains they become increasingly inclined to loathe themselves and others.

Aristotle maintains, further, that *wicked men do not have the psychological qualities suitable for performing acts of friendship*: good will, beneficence, and peace and concord. Because, simultaneously, they want, and delight in, opposing pleasures agreeing with the sensitive and intellectual parts of the soul, they are constantly at war with themselves, cannot get along with themselves, or with others. They have incontinent, intemperate, souls and reap the fruit of such souls.

Lacking in good will, St. Thomas says that the most wicked among them eventually wind up committing the most gruesome crimes (for which other people tend to hate them, and for which they tend to hate themselves). As a result, they tend to find life burdensome and, at times, eventually commit suicide. *Lacking the ability to do good to themselves or to others, they can have no real friends and cannot converse with others, with themselves, and cannot meditate, contemplate.*

When morally evil men turn their souls outward to communicate with others in words and works, St. Thomas maintains they try to forget themselves in such external activities. Because their memories of past deeds and hopes for future ones leave them intellectually and appetitively (*psychologically*) empty, they tend to remember their past evil deeds and moral failures.

As a result, they anticipate engaging in the same sorts of evil actions in the future. Experiencing nothing in themselves worth loving and to hope for, they tend to hate themselves and become increasingly unable to love others in a psychologically healthy way. In an attempt to find internal peace through repeated acts of intemperance, incontinence, that increasingly divide the appetitive parts of the soul, they become increasingly unable to experience pleasure and pain, joy and sorrow, as an integrated whole.

One part of the soul draws an evil man in one direction, while simultaneously, another part of the soul draws them in the opposite direction; both parts being dissatisfied and distressed in the process, rent with conflicting appetitive drives and dissatisfactions. Never being able to achieve intellectual or appetitive satisfaction, evil men tend to become filled with remorse, regrets; and, because they lack the qualities of soul that make a person friend-worthy, they become increasingly unable to make real friends.

If living without self-love and real friends is among the greatest of human evils, Aristotle and St. Thomas recommend that we should strongly avoid becoming morally vicious and make every effort to become morally virtuous.[17]

17. How the moral psychology of good will relates to friendship

After discussing the three acts, or works, of friendship in general, Aristotle starts individual discussion of them in relationship to good will, which, he says: 1) is an interior liking for a person; 2) is not the habit of friendship, but a proximate principle of that habit; and 3) resembles friendship because all friends must have good will.

Since we can experience good will toward strangers and the act of good will involving strangers need not be reciprocal, Aristotle says that good will cannot be identical with friendship. In contrast to perfect friendship, good will resembles a lazy friendship. Because good will is a proximate principle of friendship, it is a necessary, but not sufficient, condition for friendship.

Good will, also, is not love because, strictly speaking, love considered as an emotion extends the soul with a kind of violence toward an existing object while, in contrast, good will is a single movement of the will, not of any emotion, toward an object. Moreover, inasmuch as it requires vehement impulse that increases with familiarity, emotional love demands familiarity to develop. Good will, in contrast, can arise in an instant. For example, spectators at a sporting event can experience it when witnessing an act of courage in an athletic competition.

Aristotle maintains that good will appears to exist in the souls of people who have some moral virtue and sense of equity and who are able to recognize some good, excellence/beauty worthy of praise in another. And, it does not develop into friendship in a soul that has no room for it.[18]

18. How the moral psychology of concord relates to friendship

Discussing concord after good will, Aristotle maintains that concord appears to be an effect of friendship, but not, as some people think, an identity of opinion because people who do not know each other can have identical opinion without sharing concord. Moreover, concord does not consist in common agreement about speculative topics, preferences, or likes; nor does it consist in unity of appetite about means and ends related to things to be done.

To help more precisely to understand the nature of concord, Aristotle presents as a prime example of concord citizens who agree among themselves about working together to effect a project of mutual interest. Based upon the behavior of such citizens, Aristotle concludes that concord chiefly concerns practical matters of two kinds: 1) of some major import to some group of people; 2) related to things that can be shared, possessed, by a multitude.

Consequently, Aristotle concludes that, if realized as such, something no one can possibly share cannot be a concern of concord. Moreover, concord does not consist in the fact that the parties involved wish good for themselves. It consists in people (a meeting/ unity of wills/minds) that they are all getting what they want out of a project of mutual interest to them. Concord and political friendship, in short, appear to be identical.

Moreover, such concord is found among virtuous people because only among such people do the minds and wills, appetites, remain one. Only the wills of virtuous people can remain fixed and unchangeable in the identical good.

Consequently, concord cannot be found among vicious men because, except through some principle of force, they cannot tend to agree.[19]

19. How the moral psychology of beneficence relates to friendship

After his brief discussion of concord, Aristotle starts a lengthier examination of beneficence with the paradoxical claim that benefactors appear to love those they benefit more than those they benefit love them. This situation appears contrary to reason because the beneficiaries are in debt to their benefactors, and have a moral duty to love them. The moral psychology of the relationship between benefactors and beneficiaries appears to be that of lenders to borrowers. Benefactors, in contrast, are not in debt to their beneficiaries, and, as beneficiaries, have no moral duty to love them.

Appearances to the contrary, Aristotle asserts that this situation is actually not contrary to reason. Even though borrowers are in debt to lenders, often borrowers do not tend to feel indebted to lenders. To be free of a debt, and any sense of moral obligation to repay it, once they have money in fist, borrowers often wish their lenders did not exist. While beneficiaries are not identical to borrowers and benefactors are not identical to lenders, nonetheless, the psychology of the beneficiary often closely resembles, if it is not identical with, that of a borrower. For example, beneficiaries tend not to be solicitous about returning thanks to benefactors any more than borrowers are solicitous about paying off debts if they can get away without doing so. Often both borrowers and beneficiaries prefer to be excused from paying debts. Often, like debtors, beneficiaries love their benefactors very little, and tend to be ingrates.

While this analysis tends to portray human nature in a bad light, Aristotle says, nonetheless, it does appear to be quite human, accurate. Most of us tend to forget benefits received and those who have given them to us soon after they have been received. Most often we want to get more than we give.

When considered from the perspective of the benefits received, this situation appears to be irrational. When considered from the perspective of the benefactor, a man of good will, however, the situation is quite rational because the moral psychology of the benefactor is not identical to that of a lender (who wishes a beneficiary to live for the lender's benefit: financial profit).

Benefactors, however, love their beneficiaries like, by nature, good mothers are inclined to love their children and poets are inclined to love their poetry: with a real love and affection, even when their recipients are not now useful to them and never promised to be useful to them in the future. For, without beneficiaries, benefactors realize that they could not be benefactors, could not do the honorable deed that only the existence of a beneficiary enables a benefactor to do and to be honored for. While a money lender is suitably repaid by a return on investment with a suitable profit, a benefactor receives a much greater good in the form of suitable honor, something, in kind, of much greater worth than monetary profit

In a way, Aristotle concludes, benefactors consider those they help to be somewhat their creations. And he adds to his argument that the chief reasons for such loves is that: 1) by nature, all human beings incline to cherish and choose existence over non-existence and 2) to the extent that something exists, it is good and lovable.

He says that human existence consists in living and acting. No life exists without being a living act of some individually living being. By nature, all human beings desire to perform living, human acts. Because the producer actually producing, in some way, exists in the effect produced, the action of the mover, cause, is in the moved, the caused. Hence, because, by nature, craftsmen, parents, and benefactors love their own existence, they incline to love the existence of their own productions. This is especially so when the product is, in actuality, what the cause is in potentiality.

Since man's first act of existing through the soul causes his second, final act (the effect generated by a faculty of soul), man's products consist of the soul existing in its acts (effects), causing a likeness of itself within them. The benefactor's good, what satisfies him completely, consists in the act of bestowing good, whether or not it is appreciated. Without the existence of the recipient, he knows he could not be a benefactor, could not improve the quality of his soul the way he does. As a result, the benefactor loves the beneficiary as the term, end, in which his good is achieved and rests.

Because nothing virtuous exists in the recipient of a good from another, the recipient finds nothing noble in the benefactor. If the recipient sees any good in receiving a good, it is as a useful good (fulfilling a need), not as a noble good, making the benefactor less worthy of love than the beneficiary.

Aristotle reinforces his argument by claiming that all activity occurs in the past (memory), the present (knowledge), or the future (hope); and pleasure relates to knowledge of all three such activities: the 1) present that we know; 2) past that we remember; and 3) future for which we hope. For the benefactor, so long as his beneficiary exists, so, too, does the pleasure of the honorableness of his activity. For the beneficiary, the utility he receives passes quickly as a memory of the past. Even the memory of past honorable deeds is pleasant, while that of useful goods is either not pleasant (for example, because they have been lost) or, if pleasant, qualitatively less pleasant than that of honorable ones.

On the contrary, expected future useful goods tend to be more pleasing than expecting more honorable ones. The reason for this is that only a known, not an unknown, good gives pleasure. Except for the person who has it, no one knows an honorable good. Hence, if they are in the past or present (but not if they are in the future), these honorable goods are known to the beneficiary. Even when past goods have vanished, useful goods are known in the past and future. Because help from useful goods in the future pleases as a remedy against future needs, a man tends to be more delighted with hope of useful goods than with memory and hope of honorable ones; but he takes more pleasure in the memory of having honorable goods.

Hence, a benefactor inclines to remember an honorable good, while the beneficiary inclines to remember a useful one. For this reason, the beneficiary is more pleasing and lovable to the benefactor than vice versa.[20]

20. Some doubts and answers about the moral psychology of self-love

After talking about the preservation and dissolution of friendship and its effects, Aristotle raises some doubts about self-love, especially about whether: 1) a person should love himself or another more and 2) self-love is blameworthy, shameful.

Aristotle resolves these problems by arguing that someone can be a self-lover in two senses: 1) blameworthy, selfish, evil, and vicious; or 2) praiseworthy, selfless, good, and virtuous.

St. Thomas maintains that the benevolent relation that a human being has to himself individually, specifically, and generically is the natural source of all benevolent acts toward others because *it essentially consists in a psychological synthesis of right reason and right desire, the perfection of human nature toward which all human beings are naturally inclined.* He adds that this act of self-benevolence generates in an individual a kind of *psychological integrity, wholeness, virtuous unity* that establishes a proper relation of prudent activity on a personal level that enables a person to practice acts of virtuous friendship toward other people. These, in turn, help to promote concord in civil society, the human species, the animal genus, and the whole of creation.

Aristotle and St. Thomas agree that people who cannot rightly love themselves lack the qualities of good will needed to love others. They maintain that the sort of self-loving that is evil is the kind of self-loving that exists within those who chiefly love the irrational part of the soul, one generated by an evil, individual will, the intemperate/incontinent loving common to incontinent, intemperate, and imprudent men.

Contrary to the vicious self-love of evil men, Aristotle claims that the virtuous man's self-love: 1) is the noblest/most praiseworthy; 2) does not incline to assign to himself an excess of physical goods;

and 3) inclines to seek the noblest kinds of goods, those of the intellectual part of the soul. *Having a healthy moral psychology operating as a proximate moral principle for all he does, a person of this kind always bestows good things on the intellectual part of the soul.* By so doing, he induces all the parts of the soul to follow right reason, act prudently, and delight in so doing.

As Aristotle and St. Thomas well understood, the more interior a principle is to a whole subject in *virtual quantity of power* (qualitative greatness) the more widely and deeply it influences the behavior of all the parts of that whole. The soul as the life-principle of the whole person (the soul/body composite) is a prime example. By influencing the most internal principles within a whole, the more a first principle influences all its secondary principles. Hence, Aristotle says that the person who wishes to be the most perfect in good works must love himself in a high degree. To prove this claim Aristotle proposes three arguments.

1) The person who loves the most interior, dominant, strongest principle of intensive quantity, highest quality, greatest good in him (the intellectual faculty and its perfection) especially loves himself by loving the highest and noblest of human goods. An analogous example of this situation exists in the political society in which its most authoritative, chiefly directing, leading part (the ruler; today this would also apply to a corporate CEO) appears to be chiefly identical with the political society as a whole. The maximum in the generic whole called the "political society," or the "State," is its highest part: the ruler. Hence, what rulers of States do the whole State is said to do. So, what a human being does in his or her most influential directing, commanding, noblest, principle (in a human being's chief command and control principle) especially appears to be a human act. The self-controlled, continent, prudent, man, not the incontinent and imprudent man, is, therefore, the true self-lover, truly loves human beings.

2) Our rightly reasoned, prudent actions, those generated by our most interior and perfect influential principle of choice, appear to be human, voluntary, and free acts in their highest qualitative, intensive quantum, greatness. What we do under the influence of passions like concupiscence and anger, we do not do as a perfect, harmonious fully-integrated whole, in a completely human, voluntary, and free, way.

Instead, we do them in a partly-rightly-desired, voluntarily-conflicted, weak-willed, way, under the influence of external impulse, against our right reason, right desire, and better judgment. In a special way, we are especially human in what we do in conformity with our intellect/reason. We are especially, most intensely, in our chief principle, our intellectual soul because this is the highest, perfective part in the human species. Because the intellectual soul is the first principle, a proximate generator of all other human faculties, because all the other faculties naturally grow out of it like out of a root, it is our most interior and causally-influential principle of our human life and action.

3) Because he loves what chiefly preserves a person as an organizationally-integrated whole, the virtuous person loves the highest part of the intellectual soul, perfectly perceives and obeys it, and is the highest of human self-lovers. He is the highest human self-lover because he loves chiefly according to right reason, right desire, and right pleasure; and chiefly seeks what is really good, and a qualitatively higher good. He is the contrary opposite of the shameful self-lover who seeks useful and apparently-pleasing goods, lesser goods over real and higher ones. Such a virtuous man is worthy of highest praise, not blame. This person is helpful to himself and others, eager to do exceptionally good acts, "great-souled," and a model citizen. If all were like him, Aristotle and St. Thomas agree, a political society would be perfect!

After finishing his three arguments in defense of his claim

that the person who wishes to be the most perfect in good works must love himself in a high degree, Aristotle maintains that the best of social situations results from such a person being a self-lover because, in so doing, he helps himself and others. In contrast, the worst of situations results from a vicious, imprudent, intemperate man being a self-lover because he is a fool who inclines to choose fictional over real goods.

Far beyond other human beings, the prudent man will perform great acts of sacrifice for the sake of other citizens, friends, and his country, even at the sacrifice of his own life, disdaining all external and lower goods in favor of internal, honorable, higher, ones. He will incline to choose to delight for a short time in brilliant, intense, works of virtue over a long life of mediocre acts of virtue.

He will prefer to delight in the illustrious life of one year to an ordinary life of many years; a single, notable, good deed to many insignificant ones. While those who die for virtue might live few years, by dying for a friend, in this one act they do a greater good, a good of greater intensive quantity, of higher quality, than the many acts done by lesser human beings. They choose a great good for themselves, and, in so doing, demonstrate that they love themselves, and others, very much.

By loving honorable goods more than external ones, giving money away to friends, they acquire a good of higher intensive quantity and more intense quality. In so doing, they manifest a higher moral quality of soul (magnanimity) in themselves and their actions, and concretely demonstrate that they love themselves more by giving themselves a greater good. Analogously, the same is true, for the good of friends, to disdain the honors, positions, that most people, *the Many*, cherish. In each case, the virtuous man always does what is really better for himself and others by assigning to himself more, and a higher-quality of, virtue: the beautiful good, the good that perfects, beautifies the soul.[21]

21. Resolving a doubt about a happy man needing friends

After solving the doubts about self-love, in two ways, Aristotle resolves another doubt about whether a happy man needs friends.

First, he answers an objection (that, because they are self-sufficient, have all good things, happy human beings need no friends) by saying that an essential part of human self-sufficiency consists in having access to all required enabling means to exercise virtuous activity. Having friends, the greatest of external goods and enabling means for exercising virtuous activity, is evidently a necessary condition, an essential part of, exercising virtuous activity. A virtuous person needs friends that, in times of plenty and need, health and sickness, joy and sadness, he can benefit to get the best out of themselves; and they can benefit him to get the best out of himself.

Aristotle adds that, to live a solitary life is unnatural for human beings. Nonetheless, he asserts that the happy person does not need the kinds of friends that *the Many* consider friends, people to be enjoyed and used for personal advantage.

In a minor way, the virtuous person needs friends in a pleasant way for relaxation, laughter; but the happy life is pleasant considered as such. The happy man does not need virtuous friends as a superfluous addition to the happy life. *Having virtuous friends is an essential part of living the happy life.* The happy life essentially consists in virtuous living (in habitually doing good deeds), which cannot happen without virtuous friends; and is most pleasing considered in itself.

Moreover, human beings take pleasure only in what we know. Since, because of an inclination to be biased toward ourselves, repeatedly to have a better-educated, improved, estimative sense of our current moral condition, studying the behavior of virtuous friends and virtuous friends of theirs is of great assistance.

Beyond the reasons already given, people who live a solitary life, tend to live a hard, burdensome, unpleasant life, one often interrupted by the need to provide for natural necessities. Remaining continuously active by oneself is difficult. Living with another virtuous person tends to make the life of a virtuous person continuously pleasant. Hence, when lived together with another virtuous person, a person who can provide constant companionship in virtue, the virtuous man should be able to live a continuously pleasing life.[22]

22. Some other reasons that a happy man needs friends

Having finished resolving the doubt why a happy man needs friends, Aristotle proceeds to give some other reasons for the happy man needing them.

First, he says that, for a happy man, virtuous friends comprise the greatest of external goods, essential enabling means of being happy because, to the good man, every living creature's, every virtuous man's existence, life, is naturally lovable. While, in other animals, life is defined in general as the capacity for sensation, in human beings it is defined in general by: 1) the capacity for perfection relative to what we share in common with other animals, *or* 2) the capacity for thought relative to what we have proper to other human beings.

Operation is the proper perfection of every determinate potency. Act, not potency, is the chief, highest human perfection; is existence and life in the fullest, most complete, perfect, sense. For an animal, life in a complete sense is sensory life. For a human being, it is perfect intellectual life.

From the fact that life is something determinate, definite, undivided, one, it is good and is numbered among what is pleasant considered in itself. Because it can be *many* things, but becomes *one* by means of act, Aristotle identifies potency without any act as a pluralization, chaos, as deprived potency, indeterminate, evil. So, just as the perfection achieved by act constitutes the nature of unity, goodness, and beauty, a substance is evil, ugly, divided in its nature to the extent that it is indeterminate, an un-unified plurality.

Since the virtuous, prudent, man is the measure, limit, of perfection in the human species, and life is naturally pleasant to all human beings, *life is maximally pleasant to the prudent man.* On the contrary, the vicious life of the imprudent man, *as vicious*, lacks proper unity (integrity), is indeterminate, without proper nature and definition, just as a bad athlete, *as bad*, does not properly, perfectly, fulfill the definition of an athlete.

What exists in its essentially-related principles and parts makes a composite whole, determinate, one, complete, and good. If these parts are not properly related (like the crew of a rowing team), the whole will not exist in the parts, or at all, because the principles will not be parts. In the case of an organization like a crew team, the parts will row indeterminately, not harmoniously. Just as a sick body is indeterminate and ill, so is a vicious, ugly, soul.

Aristotle maintains that: 1) perception of being alive is desirable and pleasant to the virtuous person; and 2), by nature, perceiving and understanding our facultative acts causes us pleasure. The more perfect, completely-intellectual, highly-perceptive, is this awareness, the more pleasant is the awareness it generates. The perception, understanding, of their own goodness, being good, living well, causes the way they live their lives to be maximally pleasing to virtuous, prudent, people.

The virtuous man feels toward his friend as he does toward himself: a friend's existence, life, and acts of virtue delight him almost as much as his own. Aristotle claims that constant communication in such a way of life is appropriate to human beings, not to cattle (as is the life of the vicious).[23]

23. How many friends a virtuous man should have and why

According to Aristotle and St. Thomas, from the preceding analysis, the answer to the question about how many friends and virtuous man should have is evident: a few, who can live close together. They claim this answer is evident because only the virtuous person can excel at being a real friend in the most proper sense. Because virtuous people tend to be few in number, and can only be real friends to other virtuous people, no human being can be a real friend to many people. For this reason, virtuous friendship can never be identical with political friendship. By their nature, political friendships can involve many people.

Also evident to Aristotle and St. Thomas from the preceding discussions is that human beings need friends in prosperity (to share in the prosperity) and in adversity (to help lessen sadness). Consequently, friends should promptly invite friends to share in personal prosperity and hesitate to have them participate in adversity. If needed in a situation of adversity, a friend should ask of a friend only to do what is doable.[24]

24. The nature of friends living together

Having finished discussing the need for, and number of, friends, Aristotle ends Book 9 of the *Nicomachean Ethics* with a discussion of the nature of friends living together.

To start, he remarks that friends living together is based upon a likeness to sensory love in which lovers most of all desire *to see* the people they love. Among other reasons, Aristotle maintains that we prefer the sense of sight to other external sense faculties because the motion of love especially starts by seeing, and is preserved by seeing, because *love is stimulated especially by beauty perceived by sight.* Friends' pleasure in living together is analogous to seeing in this way: seeing a beautiful sight! Just as lovers delight most in seeing each other, so friends delight in living together in all circumstances.

Further, according to Aristotle, friendship is a species of communicating/sharing ourselves with each other. Hence, as a man behaves toward himself, he tends to behave toward a friend.

When a person finds his own existence and life desirable and delightful, he inclines to take delight in knowledge of his friend's existence and life. This sort of knowledge is especially present in living together, through which, by reason of their mutual activity, friends see each other, communicate with each other, closely and continuously. Hence, friends incline to live together.

Moreover, friends most wish to share with friends the activity for which they chiefly live and exist, the activity they most enjoy and around which they incline to order all they do. For example, some friends most enjoy drinking, gambling, sporting events, hunting, studying, together. Each species of friend most wants to remain, be at rest, with his or her friends in *that one* activity he or she loves best among all others in life pursuits. In so doing, we mutually engage in acts that we greatly enjoy, that give us great pleasure, that we think constitute the whole of life (what life is all about) for us. Partaking (being a part of, sharing in) these activities gives friends a sense of living together as parts of a whole, being one, united, not separate, belonging to the same organization, community.

From the preceding analysis in Book 9, Aristotle concludes two things: 1) the friendship of the vicious man is evil, finds pleasure most of all in doing evil deeds with another vicious man and, always, by imitating each other, progressively goes from bad to worse; and 2) in contrast to that of vicious men, the friendship of virtuous men is good, always increases in pleasure and goodness by exemplary community life, and progressively becomes better and more delightful as they work together, love each other, and constantly give each other good example.[25]

—Notes—

1. St. Thomas Aquinas, *Commentary on the Nicomachean Ethics of Aristotle*, Bk. 8, Lect. 1, nn. 1538–1550.

2. Id., Lect. 2, nn. 1551–1561.

3. Id., Lects. 3–4, nn. 1562–1595.

4. Id., Lect. 5, nn. 1596–1606.

5. Id., Lect. 6, nn. 1607–1623.

6. Id., Lect. 7, nn. 1624–1638.

7. Id., Lect. 8, nn. 1639–1656.

8. Id., Lect. 9, nn. 1657–1671.

9. Id., Lect. 10, nn. 1672–1687. For Aristotle's teaching about slavery, see his *Politics*, Bk. 1, chs. 4–7,

10. Id., Lect. 11, nn. 1688–1701.

11. Id., Lect. 12, nn. 1702–1725.

12. Id., Lect. 13, nn. 1726–1743.

13. Id., Lect. 14, nn. 1744–1756.

14. Id., Bk. 9, Lect. 1, nn. 1757–1772.

15. Id., Lect. 2, nn. 1773–1784; see Plato, *Republic*, Bk. 1, 331C–331E.

16. Id., Lect. 3, nn. 1788.

17. Id., Lect. 4, nn. 1797–1819.

18. Id., Lect. 5, nn. 1820–1829.

19. Id., Lect. 6, nn. 1830–1839.

20. Id., Lect. 7, nn. 1840–1854.

21. Id., Lects. 8–9, nn. 1855–1882.

22. Id., Lect. 10, nn. 1885–1899.

23. Id., Lect. 11, nn. 1900–1912.

24. Id., Lects. 12–13, nn. 1913–1943.

25. Id., Lect. 14, nn. 1944–1952.

–CHAPTER FIFTEEN–

Pleasure and Happiness

HAVING FINISHED considering friendship in Book 9 of the *Nicoma-chean Ethics*, in Book 10, in three ways, Aristotle examines the end (chief aim) of moral virtue that perfects man considered in himself. He does so chiefly in relation to the common good of the whole State, but also in relation to divine things. He starts doing so by reconsidering "pleasure," which he had incompletely studied in Book 7 in relation to continence and incontinence.

1. Three reasons St. Thomas gives for reconsidering the relationship between pleasure and happiness

For three reasons, St. Thomas says Aristotle reconsiders the relationship between pleasure and happiness.

One is because pleasure appears to be especially adapted to human nature, and most so to human education in general and moral education in particular. Hence, 1) parents especially use pleasure and pain to educate and teach their children; and 2) people who want to encourage children to be well behaved and discourage them from being badly behaved will also use these as teaching aids. Since moral science/philosophy studies human behavior, part of its job essentially involves studying pleasure and pain.

Two is because, as human beings, we are naturally inclined to love and enjoy what is really good, and hate and abhor what is really bad, for us. *Because moral virtue consists chiefly in regulation and education of the concupiscible appetite in which is located the emotions of love/hate and pleasure/pain (emotions*

468

that generate all other appetitive movements, including those of the irascible appetite and the human will), pleasure and pain extend to all phases of human life and exert great influence upon us to become virtuous and live happily.

Unless our pleasures and pains are properly and rightly disposed and subordinated, ordered and related, harmonized, *prioritized*, this cannot happen. We human beings often choose unhealthy, harmful, pleasures and avoid healthy, helpful, pains. A person who wants to become morally virtuous and happy should not choose pleasure and reject pain considered as such or commit evil deeds and avoid virtuous actions to get pleasure and avoid pain. Just as moral science needs to study moral virtue and happiness, it needs to study pleasure and pain.

Reason three is because much uncertainty and many different opinions exist about these passions and how they relate to human happiness. For example, for different reasons, some highly intelligent people say pleasure is a kind of good, while others claim it is something very bad.

Aristotle states that some of those who say that pleasure is something very bad do so because they are convinced this is true. Others claim that, while it is not incarnate evil, to withdraw us from pleasure toward which most of us are slavishly inclined, they judge it better for human living to call pleasure unqualifiedly "evil." Like people who tend to be somewhat puritanical, or those that ascribe to Plato's advice to us that, periodically, we need to tell a "noble lie" for self-benefit or the benefit of others, such intellectuals think that misleading incontinent men to have aversion to all pleasure is a better teaching tool than telling them the truth.

Aristotle and St. Thomas disagree. Because "actions speak louder than words," they do not consider saying what we do not hold to be true to be prudent. *If we do the very action we say is evil, we en-*

courage by example more than we restrain by words and arguments. They maintain that all of us incline to choose the object of human actions as it appears good to us. *When a person's arguments are manifestly contrary to his actions, people tend to ignore his arguments and the truth they express is destroyed.*

Sound arguments convince to the extent that they accord with behavior, and are understood by their audience. Most people, however, are inclined to identify good with what appears good to us in the individual situation. Often, we cannot distinguish by judgment real from apparent good. Arguments do not incline to move and persuade the Masses and the Many, who cannot comprehend them, especially when they see a person arguing against pleasure while simultaneously pursuing it. They encourage to follow them those who understand them.[1]

2. Aristotle continues his discussion of pleasure by considering Eudoxus' teaching about it

Because Eudoxus was well-known in ancient Greece for being a wise and good man, Aristotle continues his discussion of pleasure by considering Eudoxus' teaching about it. Before immediately doing so, however, Aristotle prefaces what he is going to say by observing that all animals pursue pleasure because pleasure is a naturally and facultatively good mode, way, of being.

What all animals choose appears to be a proper animal good, one to which an animal is facultatively inclined to move by natural desire. Because it attracts every appetite to itself (serves as a principle of animal appetitive motion), pleasure has a great influence in animal life. The fact that pleasure is not only "a good," but moves all animals to it as a formal object, indicates that pleasure is a most excellent good. Because evident is that all animals naturally seek to find what is naturally good for us as animals, pleasure as an object sought by all animals is good by nature for all animals, including human beings.

Aristotle maintains that, because Eudoxus was a virtuous man, his virtue gave his arguments special persuasive force with *the Many* and *the Virtuous* (that is, *the Learned*). He adds that, because all animals by nature are inclined to avoid pain, considering Eudoxus' argument from the standpoint of pain is equally compelling.

Considering Eudoxus's teachings first from the standpoint of pleasure, Aristotle presents two arguments from Eudoxus to demonstrate that pleasure is the greatest animal good.

Eudoxus' first argument is that evident is that pleasure added to any good makes that good more desirable. Hence, additional pleasure to a just or temperate action makes it more pleasurable, better. A man who takes pleasure in the work of justice, temperance, science/philosophy is better in these activities, more just and temperate, more of a scientist/philosopher, considered as such, than is a man who takes no, or little, such pleasure in these activities.

Regarding this argument that pleasure enhances goodness in all human action, Aristotle says that Eudoxus sought to conclude from this that pleasure is the greatest of human goods. Aristotle disagreed. He claimed that, while the argument proves that pleasure is a human good, it does not prove that it is greater than any other human good, or the greatest human good. One reason for this is that when we join any good to another good a greater good results. To this reason Aristotle adds several others that he takes from Plato.

According to Aristotle, against Eudoxus, Plato had argued that, because, when accompanied by prudence, pleasure becomes a greater good, pleasure cannot be the highest human good. Because what is the highest, most intense, good does not become more perfect through the addition of something else, Plato maintained that pleasure cannot be the absolute, universal, or most perfect good. According to St. Thomas, Aristotle claimed that Plato did not consider pleasure to be a good considered in itself, or absolutely. He said Plato considered the highest good, good absolutely considered, to be the form/essence of good just as man absolutely considered, absolute man, is the essence of man.

Further, Aristotle asserted Plato to hold that this essence of goodness is perfect goodness, that nothing can be added to, or taken away, from it. While other things can *appear* good by sharing/participating in it, whatever additional goodness exists in reality beyond the perfect good is an apparent, not a real, good (an imperfection, imperfect likeness) derived by participation in the highest good, from the essence of goodness. Hence, in no way, can this addition of a deprivation of goodness (pleasure) make the highest good better, more perfect, or the less good really good.

Because it removes perfection in being good from being in this world as an essential part of this world and of human life, essentially associated with human life as improving it *in this life*, St. Thomas maintains Aristotle rejected Plato's argument. In Plato's teaching, no human action, mode of behavior, will be absolutely, perfectly, maximally good because, if we accept Plato's teaching, we will be able to find nothing associated with real human life that can be really improved, made really more perfect, when a good is added to a good.

As understood by Aristotle, Plato removes perfection from good in this life. Good and perfection are only identical in the World of Forms. Hence, in this life, Plato's teaching makes impossible for any perfection to be added to goodness. Perfect good exists in another world. In this world, all that exists is a semblance of perfect good.

But, Aristotle tells us the good that moral philosophy/science seeks is a good of just such a nature: a perfect good in this life, one that makes this life to be more perfect, absolutely good, by being added to it in this life. People commonly hold that pleasure is a human good to which addition, perfection, beautification, can be made here and now in this life; not a divine good to which nothing, no perfection, can be added in this life.

Beyond Plato, Aristotle said some Platonists countered Eudoxus by replying to his first argument (pleasure added to any good makes it better) by denying that what all animals/humans naturally desire is real good.

Aristotle rejected this counter-argument of the Platonists as "nonsense," evidently false, because, to some extent, natural judgment cannot be totally wrong. The natural judgment of our natures, faculties, at least generally, has to be right. True, Aristotle says, is that, since the concupiscible appetite tends only to what *appears* good, what we all desire through our concupiscible appetite is *seeming*, not real, good. Nonetheless, Aristotle maintained that what the concupiscible appetite of each individual person desires is the good as it *seems to every* individual human to be a *real* good. So, collectively considered as a numerical universal, the pleasure we all desire in this way is good, the good universally considered by each one of us as a *real* good.

The person who, like Plato and some Platonists, rejects as false what everyone accepts as true needs to defend the reason for so doing. Otherwise, his claims are of no more intellectual weight than the ones he rejects. The burden of proof is on him.

If, by nature, only brute animals and evil men desired pleasure as good, suitable, proper, the claim of some people that we human beings do not, by nature, desire real good might be defensible. Because the *external senses* only judge good in its sensory particularity, in the present, *as it appears*, not as it really is in its nature, real good escapes the notice of the *external* senses, and of the internal sense faculties of common sense, imagination, and concupiscible appetite!

But, as St. Thomas notes, since, beyond animal instinct or a brute animal estimative sense, some animals (human beings) possess a particular, or cogitative, reason that is naturally inclined to take direction from an intellectual reason, this argument is rationally indefensible.

Such animals evidently pursue pleasure as a real good, a suitable, natural, proper good. Such animals, human beings, can understand the natures of things here and now, concretely considered as such; unlike brute animals, can explicitly recognize that they consider all goods as real goods. Thanks to the possession of particular reason and intellectual reason, by nature, to some extent (unlike brute animals), all human beings have the ability to distinguish between real and apparent goods and greater and lesser goods. Even in wicked men some desire for real good might still be probable because even in them some natural inclination to real good still remains and tends by nature to be desired as a real human good.

Just as virtue improves, strengthens, and perfects, more intensely unifies and harmonizes, a natural composite whole (a real nature), moral virtue improves, strengthens, and more intensely unifies a human composite with a qualitatively greater, more intense, and unbreakable strength of organizational unity and action.

Moreover, vice, on the contrary, is a corruption, fragmentation, pluralization, and imperfecting of a natural, concrete, composite wholeness, unity/harmony (integrity), and organizational strength and action. *Qua* vicious, evil men become fragmented, divided, from each other as organizational natures, parts, and civic beings—doers of good deeds. Vice, *not pleasure*, divides. By nature, pleasure inclines to unite. According to Aristotle and St. Thomas, the contrary pleasures they pursue, *not pleasure properly understood and considered as such*, fragments evil men and causes them to lose touch with reality.[2]

3. Four arguments Aristotle gives against some people St. Thomas calls "the Platonists" related to pleasure not being a good

Next, Aristotle presents four arguments against some people St.

Thomas calls "the Platonists" designed to show that they are wrong to claim pleasure is not a way of being good, a mode of goodness.

The first argument claims that good appears to be a species of the genus quality because when asked what the quality of something is we tend to reply "good." Nonetheless, because pleasure is not a quality, it is not a good.

Aristotle's reply to this claim is that, even if pleasure is not a species of quality, it is still good. We predicate good of all genera; it is not a genus or species. *It is a principle that both genera and species presuppose in order to exist.*

The second argument claims that good is a determinate unity, causes a multitude to have unity, be limited, one (become an organization, or composite whole). From the fact that it admits of degrees, pleasure is indeterminate, not one, unlimited, a cause of fragmentation, decomposition, disorganization, chaos. For this reason, pleasure appears not to belong to the genus of good.

Aristotle refutes this second argument by maintaining, first, that any genus, or thing, admits of degrees, or specification, in two ways: 1) abstractly and 2) concretely. What exists as a part of an organizational whole has an organizational unity and simplicity. *Considered abstractly in itself,* a part, form, unity, admits of no degrees of more or less. Because the subject in which it exists has, possesses, this part, form, unity with greater or less intensity and perfection, strength (more or less strongly), what it has, possesses, can be said, predicated, to be *more* or *less.* For example, while, abstractly considered in its nature, light admits of no more or less in its being and intelligibility, as it exists in something according to the capacity of the receiver to have/possess it, the subject in which it exists is said to have more or less light.

Moreover, Aristotle argues that a form can admit of degrees even according to its own nature *when its nature expresses a relation of proportion of a many to a one as to a principle*: that is, when its nature considered as such expresses more or less harmony/proportion. As examples, he gives health and beauty, different species of harmonious unity.

Evident, then, to Aristotle is the reason why unity *abstractly considered*, unity as a principle of determinacy and limitation that causes an organization to be an organization (*not unity as a principle of harmonization of an organization as a principle of action*), cannot admit of degrees. The former generates an organization, causes it to exist. The latter harmonizes the actions of its parts once the organization exists!

If the Platonists hold that, because it admits of degrees in the concrete, pleasure is indeterminate, lacks unity, definiteness, is essentially chaotic, Aristotle reasons that they will have to maintain the same claim about justice and other virtues, and about just and virtuous actions and people. Either virtues will not be ways of being good, or the argument of the Platonists is false.

On the other hand, if they maintain that, like a harmony, pleasure admits of degrees, that would appear to be distinguishing different kinds of pleasure: 1) perfect/pure, uncomposed/unmixed, unimpeded and 2) imperfect, composed, mixed pleasure, like a musical harmony or the beautiful blending of tastes and colors.

Aristotle maintains that, just like the unimpeded action of an army acting as an organizational unit is totally agreeable, simultaneously whole, to all its parts, pure pleasure of an unimpeded, intellectual faculty (one that is instantaneous) admits of no degrees. Mixed pleasures that harmonize sensibles of different kinds, on the other hand, produce pleasures more or less agreeable to: 1) one faculty, 2) different faculties, and 3) human beings considered as a whole.

Nonetheless, Aristotle says, nothing prevents mixed pleasures that result from harmonization (like health) from being determinate.

They might become more perfect in definiteness, determinacy, even though they might not be totally so; or totally one inasmuch as they come close to it as toward a proper end. Analogously, nothing prevents us from calling them "definite," "determinate," like we call the harmonious integration of bodily chemistry "health."

We tend to call "sickly" a body that in no way approximates such harmony. Even then, unless dead, health remains in a human being to some degree. Analogously, the same is true of imperfect pleasure!

Aristotle's third argument against the Platonists is against two of their claims: 1) The good considered in itself is total perfection. Good and perfection are identical. 2) Because motion is act as deprived act, motion, processes of generation, are imperfect, essentially evil. Hence, no motion or process of generation belongs to the genus of good. Pleasure is a motion, a process of generation, or belongs to the process of generation. Consequently, pleasure is no good.

Aristotle starts his refutation of the argument by maintaining that, because every motion appears to be swift or slow, involves speed/time, the Platonists appear to be wrong. *Abstractly considered* in their nature, swiftness, slowness, and time are not essential to motion. Swiftness and slowness (speed) are predicated of a moving body relative to something else; and time is a qualitative fragmentation of the whole existence of a motion into an orderly, successive, kind of positioning and limiting of its existing acts (ordinal numbering) in place in terms of before/after in relation to motion of the heavens. While pleasure can happen in an instant, time cannot.

Aristotle continues his refutation by stating we call "fast," or "swift," a body that moves a *long* distance in a *short* time and "slow" a body that moves a *short* distance in a *long* time. Considered as such, in their natures, just as what they are, swiftness and slowness are not attributed to pleasure. While a man can come to be, reach the point of being pleased or angry quickly or slowly, strictly speaking, he cannot be in the state of anger or pleasure quickly or slowly. While we say a person can be quick-tempered (quick *to become* angry), while we can call "anger" hot/intense or cold/mild, of short or long duration, long or short lasting in time, strictly speaking, *we do not call it as it exists now, but only as it comes to be and subsides*, "*slow*" *or* "*fast*."

Strictly speaking, *pleasure is an act of being, not a process of coming to be*. It exists in the present moment*, in a doing now*, not in *an approach to a doing, almost a doing,* now. Because generation (motion) presupposes (exists in the genus of) relation, and relation presupposes the existence of terms, of limits, boundaries (a starting point and an end point extremes existing within the genus), pleasure is not some indeterminate process of generation. Generation is no indeterminate process. *Generation, motion, exists within a genus, proceeds from a definite relation as from a proximate first principle*! *The indeterminate, chance, generates nothing*!

Since the terms of its relation regarding what is the subject that is coming to be and what this subject is going to be, *its potency as a subject* (an organization, or composite whole) is determinate, *so is its external stimulus or formal object*. Motion, change, does not just happen by chance. It happens within a genus *after a relation has been established/fixed* between a determinate potency (for example, the faculty of sight) and a formal object/external stimulus (for example, a colored body)!

Whatever moves, changes, in any way, gets its initial impulse to move, change, from a determinate agent: one with an act *proportionate in intensive quantum greatness to the faculty or habit it activates, proportionate to this faculty's or habit's qualitative, receptive capacity* (its intensive quantum greatness *to receive an act proportionate to its power*: to receive an act that has been able to establish an organizational [generic] relation: unity, with it). For example, *too intense a colored body cannot establish with too weak a power of sight the generic relation needed to move the faculty to act through harmonization of its parts! Generation necessarily presupposes the ability to establish a real relation between a determinate power and determinate stimulus.*

In saying that pain is a defect, privation, of what exists according to nature, Aristotle claims some Platonists considered pain to be a diminishing principle in something as opposed to pleasure, which is an opposite replenishing principle.

Aristotle rejects this argument because he says: 1) Pleasure is a cogitative activity of the soul. Strictly speaking, if the body is replenished, the *body* should be the proximate subject experiencing pleasure. But, strictly speaking, the whole human being, not the body or soul, feels pleasure; and a human being does so through the emotional appetite of the soul just as the whole man, not the organ or faculty of sight, sees. And 2) pleasure is no process of becoming replenished because *pleasure is no process of becoming at all*. It is a state of *being* within an organizational whole, a genus, that has become unified into a perfect, composite whole (like the harmonization of unity of specific parts within the crew of a rowing team or business organization).

Aristotle attributes this mistaken understanding of pleasure chiefly to the pleasures/pains we experience relative to being hungry and eating and being thirsty and drinking. But, he says, not every pleasure involves replenishing deficiency. For example, intellectual pleasures of learning and exercising intellectual and moral virtue involve no replenishing of deficiency. Even the simple acts of enjoyment related to sight, hearing, smell, and so on, need no process of generation involving opposites of replenishment and privation. The same is true of many delightful hopes/memories involving no prior defects. Pleasure can exist without pain, and is no correlative opposite of pain.

An Introduction to Ragamuffin Ethics

From these preceding arguments Aristotle claims "the Platonists" drew another argument based upon pleasure's supposed vileness. They referred to pleasures like drunkenness and adultery to conclude that pleasures are not modes of good, contributing factors to being good.

As one counter-argument against this teaching, Aristotle said, *absolutely considered*, shameful pleasures are not pleasant. Because some intemperate people sometimes delight in doing vicious actions, the conclusion that all pleasure is morally evil is false. The right conclusion to draw is that, sometimes, some pleasures are not good for some people.

While considered in relation to a faculty it activates as a proper, or formal, object, all pleasures (proper pleasures) are delightful and good as such, relative to the intensive quantity strength of a faculty, the amount or intensity of the facultatively proper good, pleasure can be bad, painful, damaging, too weak or strong (for example, hard-to-digest food for a person with a weak digestive power). Just as foods that are healthy for healthy people and appear so to them, such foods can appear, and be, unhealthy for a sickly person. The concretely-considered *pleasure* for human beings considered as really good for us in the individual situation is what is pleasant to the estimative sense, cogitative reason, of a prudent person.

As a second counter-argument against those who claim pleasure is not a real good, Aristotle argues that abstractly, unqualifiedly, absolutely considered, pleasures are a real, desirable, good. Concretely, qualifiedly, relatively considered, however, they are not desirable/good for all people at all times.

Aristotle maintains, further, that the difference between a real and an apparent friend (flatterer) proves that different kinds of pleasure (honorable/shameful) exist, that not all pleasures are shameful. No healthy human being would choose to retain a childish

480

mind and appetites all his life so that he could enjoy the pleasures of a child or to choose delighting in the shameful pleasures of youth into adulthood, even if he never had to suffer pain from psychologically maturing. *This is how unhealthy, intemperate, people behave. They refuse intellectually and appetitively to grow up.* (Hence, in our time, like infants, they call critiques of their behavior like Aristotle just made "hate speech"!)

Aristotle and St. Thomas claim that some objects (like knowledge, memory, virtue, sight) would be desirable even if no pleasure accompanied them; but, without being good, nothing is desirable. Hence, abstractly-considered, pleasure and good are not desirable as concretely real goods considered as such for all people. But concretely-considered, some pleasures, virtuous ones, are desirable considered in themselves (just as, abstractly-considered by a mathematician, triangles have no color or texture while as they concretely exist in reality they always do).[3]

4. Aristotle starts properly to define pleasure

After arguing against the opinions of "the Platonists," according to St. Thomas, Aristotle starts properly to define pleasure by first saying that the act of seeing exists all at once whole at any instant. It requires nothing in a subsequent instant to perfect its form. The same is true of pleasure. Pleasure is a whole act completely existing in its first instant of being. No space/time in which the act exists makes its form, nature, more complete.

While every process of generation is perfected *after* a lapse of time, after some time is past, this is not true of pleasure, which is completely whole as an act in an instant. Every motion has a length of existence that comprises its time. The points that start and end the existence of motion are acts, instants, principles that start and end, number and order, the length of the motion's existence. Every motion is also a means to an end, a relational act from a start act to a final act;

An Introduction to Ragamuffin Ethics

has a first act from which it relationally starts and a last act it intends, moves toward.

For example, St. Thomas says, the act of building naturally intends, through completion of its final act, to finish in the last act what it first intends: a completely built, *finished*, house. The builder builds the house by means of, through, a multitude of ordered (an ordered multitude being a number) of imperfect, incomplete acts (motions). Since all these incomplete acts are ordered toward (essentially and successively related to) one final act (the finished house), these incomplete acts are processes, parts, of the whole act, one generic act, of building a house.

As a harmonious unity, these ordered acts get their species and proper name from their last act, which completes the house. This one whole act of building takes a length of time to finish, exists for a length of time, and consists in a harmonization of, ordering, sequencing, of a limited multitude of part acts, which are ordered acts that constitute a *number* (not a disordered or infinite multitude) of acts constituting parts of a whole. The *form of the whole operation* is one harmonious act with one chief end. The form of the parts that compose the whole operation comprise another operation with two ends: the chief end of the whole and the subordinate ends of the parts.

St. Thomas elaborates Aristotle's point through an example of temple building to explain the whole action involved in such construction, *which occurs over one whole length of time*. He says one part of that time involves fitting stones for a wall. Another, for sculpting, fluting columns. A third, the whole construction. *And all three operations are specifically different as determined by their respective chief ends*!

The terms (start/finish) of relation we call a "motion" specify it. In the case of locomotion, these terms are positions or places. A runner, for example, travels along a line existing relative, relationally,

482

to place (a starting line and finish line). Hence, in specifying motions, we do so as species of *a relation*, by referring to a beginning term and end term, a beginning/end boundary, or limit, indivisibles, *ones*: a start one and an end one of the same genus.

The whole of a local motion (movement from one place to another one place) is a movement from one boundary of a place-relation to another. According to the difference of boundaries that limit the relation and the subject that is being bounded by these limits, the movement (*generic relation*) involved *specifically changes*. Because *the terms of a motion* (which is a relation of a determinate potency to determinate act) *specify it*, building is a specifically different movement from walking; and one whole motion can be composed of many part motions with differing start and end points. At no moment in the process is any part of the motion the whole relation.

In the case of the form of pleasure, on the contrary, as an act of the whole person, pleasure is complete at any moment of its existence.

St. Thomas argues, further, that, except as existing in time and place, motion cannot exist. Pleasure, however, can exist in an instant, can take no time (process of before and after). Real time (not mathematically-measured time) is an imperfect way of *having existence* involving a succession of part acts, imperfect acts, existing between two whole acts (whole instants) of being; it is a way of having existence in the form of a becoming between two limits, instants, of being (for example, the first moments of being alive and being dead, two instants that *take no time*).

Following Aristotle, St. Thomas adds that the experience of pleasure is one instantaneously apprehended, that of a whole. Hence, he concludes that, strictly speaking, philosophers are wrong when they talk about pleasure as a motion or process of generation. Pleasure is no generation. It is a whole act, immediately complete. Since, properly speaking, we can predicate motion and generation only of some things (we cannot predicate them, for example, of undivided things that are instantaneously whole; we can only say them properly of divided things successively whole), strictly speaking, we cannot predicate them of pleasure.

To reinforce this last point, Aristotle makes some analogies. He says that, strictly speaking, we cannot speak of seeing as a movement to a process of generation successively attained. Seeing is a whole act complete in an instant. So, too, is a *point*, and a *real unity*, indivisibility. Neither is a process or motion.

Having demonstrated that, strictly speaking, pleasure cannot be a motion or process, Aristotle starts properly to define its nature, properties. He does so by observing that the activity of each sense faculty is the act of the faculty as externally stimulated by its formal object. Hence, perfect sense activity demands perfect condition of the facultative end of its formal object. A sense faculty operates at its maximum of intensive quantity, or qualitative greatness, when the power's qualitative greatness of receptivity is proportionate to, suitable for, perfectly matches, the qualitative greatness of its formal object (when one is not qualitatively too strong or weak for the other as terms of a generic relation of giving and receiving).

Next, St. Thomas says that, while, strictly speaking, the complete composite (the human person), not the soul, acts, whether strictly or loosely speaking, obvious is that perfection in facultative act, *perfect act*, proceeds from the union of the best-conditioned faculty and the best-conditioned formal object.

Then, he states that pleasure is the perfection of activity, acting perfectly with maximum of intensive quantum (qualitative) greatness. Considered in itself, the most perfect act is also the most pleasant. Whenever any activity exists within a percipient, to some extent, considered in itself, so, too, does a pleasant activity. In a most perfect percipient, considered *qua* perfect, a most pleasant activity exists.

He adds that pleasure co-exists with every sense faculty *and every contemplative intellect in a state of certainty*. The highest, most perfect, pleasure is that belonging to perfectly well-conditioned sense and intellectual faculties in relationship to the best of formal objects that stimulate them. *Hence, pleasure is the perfection of cognitive activity in its most perfect and beautiful state*!

The pleasure that exists in a perfectly-conditioned cognitive faculty united to a perfectly-existing formal object is qualitatively different in intensity from that which exists between an imperfectly-conditioned cognitive faculty and an imperfectly-existing formal object.

St. Thomas adds that a healthy body and the medical art cause restoration of health from which pleasure ensues. Pleasure perfects activity by way of a perfect formal principle. A suitable formal object perfects activity as a stable, unchanging, external stimulus. Every sense activity is exceedingly beautiful, pleasant, when it is at its maximum of intensive quantum, or qualitative, facultative strength and greatness, when it is a faculty stimulated by an analogously perfect formal object.

A pleasure is experienced as maximally beautiful, passionate, then, when the sense faculty is at its intensive quantum, or qualitative, maximum of receptivity and the formal object, the external stimulus, is perfectly proportioned to it, remaining unchanged in its maximum of qualitative intensity as it activates the sense faculty in question. So long as the sense faculty and the external stimulus remain unchanged, so does the pleasure, and its intensity.

Pleasure perfects the activity of the sense or intellectual faculty of the soul by maximizing its spiritual greatness, the perfection of the faculty, as a formal cause of its respective operations. According to St. Thomas, formal perfection is twofold: 1) intrinsic, constituting a thing's nature; and 2) added to an already existing whole. He maintains that pleasure does not perfect the soul in the first way, as a life-generating principle. It perfects soul in the second way, in the operations that it causes as a life-generating principle.

It resembles a blossoming, beautification, of operation attendant upon perfect possession of goodness. Today, a good analogy would be that of the running of a well-oiled machine, the maximum in qualitative greatness of operation. Aristotle and St. Thomas consider pleasure to be the reward of repose of the appetite and knowledge of its perfect operation.

They recognize that pleasure cannot last permanently in us human beings because the activity pleasure exercises on our bodily organs and the faculties that operate through them tire and exhaust these organs and faculties. Even intellectual activity causes bodily movements in the internal and external sense organs like sight, hearing, imagination, and estimative sense that exhaust these faculties and organs in even a strong and healthy person. New, strange, cognitive objects tend instantaneously, especially, to delight at first; but their novelty, unfamiliarity, causes the cognitive powers to work more intensely to grasp their natures, thereby tiring them.

Intense cognitive activity is pleasant considered in itself. It causes an intellectual pleasure, joy, *rush*, that immediately generates an intense desire to know more. All human beings naturally desire pleasure because: 1) we all naturally desire to live, and to live life to its fullest; 2) in its ultimate perfection, life consists in a way of acting/living. We are most active, devote ourselves most to, doing activities we most love. Since virtuous pleasure brings human activity to its final beautification of perfection, virtuous pleasure perfects life to a maximum of intensive quantity/qualitative greatness.[4]

5. The difference of pleasures and pains according to species

Having explained pleasure's nature and properties, St. Thomas says Aristotle next considers how pleasures differ in kind. He proceeds to do this first by distinguishing pleasures according to the activities they perfect, intensify in qualitative greatness. He maintains that specifically different perfections, qualitative limits of greatness, accompany specifically different operations of the soul. He adds that *essential principles of a species generate essential perfections and imperfections as limits of intensive quantum greatness of operation and receptivity and resistance to external acts*!

Following Aristotle, St. Thomas claims that proper, healthy, pleasure adds an intensive quantum, qualitative, limit of greatness of receptivity within a faculty to performance of the faculty's proper operation. And proper, healthy, pain, sadness, adds an analogous resistance to receiving any activity that impedes a faculty's proper operation.

Every facultative activity is facilitated, intensified, by its own proper pleasure. For example, seeing within specific limits of the faculty, organ of sight, is *specifically healthy*, pleasant, for every human being. Proper objects proportionately received into a faculty generate a natural, proper, pleasure: *a beautifying quality to the faculty*.

Analogously, St. Thomas says, just as perfect vision is naturally pleasing, beautiful to its possessor, so, too, is fruitfulness for a tree, fitting colors to a painting, shape to a statue, solidity and roominess to a home. So, too, do intensifying qualities, virtual quantities, virtues, of intellectual greatness facilitate, beautify, delight, performance of intellectual operations just as intensifying qualities, virtuous operation, of the sense faculties bring along with perfect sense operation their own proper pleasures to these faculties.

Pleasure and pain are species-specific intensifying principles, principles of intensive quantity receptivity to proper acts within brute animals and human beings, that accompany right desire! Proper pleasure facilitates, *beautifies*, specifies and limits, activities that perfect facultative operation. It *measures* their rightness or wrongness. *This is the end at which right desire chiefly aims*!

According to St. Thomas, every act of co-natural good of a knowing faculty that exists in the knowing faculty as a proper pleasure appears pleasing to it. Analogously, the same is true of co-natural evil. Co-natural pain, sadness, resists alien pleasures, joys, pains, sadness, which destroy the health of facultative acts.

Hence, *proper pleasures are natural virtues*! *Improper pleasures are natural vices*! Proper pleasures: 1) strengthen the activities of the faculties from which they proceed; 2) prolong these activities; and 3) beautify them so that they attain their natural end more perfectly and rest in it with maximum intensity of delight.

Improper pleasures and pains, on the other hand: 1) destroy proper pleasures and pains; 2) weaken the activities of the faculties from which they proceed; 3) diminish the length of these facultative activities; and 4) cause an ugliness in them that prevents them from attaining their natural end, beauty, and more perfectly resting in it with a maximum intensity of delight.[5]

6. The moral goodness and evil of pleasures and pains, joys and sorrows

After showing that pleasures and pains differ in species according to different activities, Aristotle and St. Thomas next show that pleasures and pains differ in moral good/evil according to different activities.

St. Thomas starts to demonstrate their case by claiming that *proper pleasure is virtuous pleasure, analogous to right desire, but better as a moral measure*. He adds that improper pleasure is vicious pleasure, analogous to wrong desire.

He proves these claims by first considering the nature of desires, and then stating that desires by which we want: 1) good and honorable (life and health-promoting) objects are praiseworthy, honorable, good (for example, to act justly, courageously); and 2) bad and shameful objects are blameworthy, shameful, evil (for example, to act unjustly, cowardly, to steal, fornicate).

Next, St. Thomas maintains that *the pleasures* by which we enjoy virtuous activities are closer, more proper, of more intensive qualitative and intensive quantum goodness, and more beautiful in spiritual greatness than are *the desires* by which we want to acquire and exercise these virtuous activities.

He says that desires are separated from activities by time and precede activities in time and execution. They differ in kind, qualitatively, from acts performed with pleasure; and are, by nature, acts of an imperfect whole, or organization. Desires, moreover, precede the existence of the whole act.

Pleasures, on the other hand, *are acts of the perfect whole, accompany it, facilitate its existence and the performance of its activities*. For example, wanting, desiring, to make the right or wrong choice is qualitatively different in kind of moral strength or weakness to doing these activities. And wanting, desiring, to make the right or wrong choice is also qualitatively less praiseworthy or blameworthy than choosing or doing so.

Along with right reason and right desire, St. Thomas asserts that *proper pleasures and pains are part of the essential intrinsic measuring principles of complete moral virtue*. They are necessary conditions for exercise of prudential judgment in the individual situation, *even more so than right desire*! The reason for this is that pleasures and pains are intrinsically connected to cognitive activities of sense and intellect because both: 1) are caused by the same faculty operating as an organizational whole a complete nature; 2) happen simultaneously in the present time and conditions and circumstances as the activity chosen.

Indeed, pleasure is so closely connected to cognitive activity that some people consider pleasure and knowledge to be identical. (Jean-Jacques Rousseau is a modern example.) But, while we can experience pleasure and pain only as an act of the intellect and will, the senses and the passions, the intellect and will, senses and passions, are not identical faculties. Pleasure and pain exist in the appetites, are appetitive principles of the will and passions. While the intellect and will, the senses and passions, can never totally be separated, they are not identical powers. Moreover, pleasures and pains differ qualitatively, according to the qualitative greatness, purity, or beauty, of soul that generates them.

Just as the act of sight is of higher purity, higher spiritual quality, greatness, and beauty, of greater intensive, or virtual quantity, or quality, is more highly intellectual, more immaterial in greatness than that of the sense of touch (because it is the most immaterial of the external senses, is the purest of all external sensory knowing powers, because knowing is an immaterial act), so virtuous pleasures and pains are of a higher spiritual greatness and beauty, or quality of soul, than are vicious pleasures and pains.

Just as the faculty of sight is of a higher qualitative greatness considered in itself, its formal object, and medium through which its formal object comes in contact with the faculty: color, so the pleasures of the intellect are purer, qualitatively more perfect in kind and intensity of immaterial, or spiritual, greatness. Since pleasure accompanies every natural and facultative activity, each species of animal appears to have its own species of pleasure just as it has its own specific activity, and just as it has its limits of due size.

Specific forms of animal life generate a proper specific pleasure within their natures and faculties. The truth of this claim is evident to observation by sense induction. It needs no proof. That in which a horse, dog, man naturally incline to take pleasure are specifically different. As the ancient Greek physicist Heraclitus once said, "The ass prefers grass to gold." Hence, animals alike in species have natural, specific, pleasures in which they incline to delight in kind and limits.

Peter A. Redpath

According to Aristotle and St. Thomas, the chief pleasure found in the human species is located in the prudent man! This pleasure synthesizes right reason and proper (species-specific) pleasure. The species-specific (proper) pleasures of other animals originate from species-specific inclinations generated in them by their specific forms as from a proximate principle. They know their proper pleasures through their species-specific instinct, not through rational deliberation and particular reason.

But, in the human species, St. Thomas maintains that *universal reason and particular reason* (*the estimative sense,* or instinct, found in brute animals) are the proximate principles through which we human beings come to know with precision our proper pleasures. Since the activities and pleasures of human reason are not determined specifically and individually by instinct, but by the natural inclination proper to humans (free decision, deliberate choice), what delights/places some men and saddens others in the individual situation is not identical.

All brute animals and human beings delight, take pleasure, in what we love. What we love essentially depends upon what we know. Knowing precedes, is a necessary condition for, loving. We love, delight, well or badly depending upon what we know.

In human beings delighting, loving, well in the individual situation especially depends upon having a healthy estimative sense faculty that can tell the sick man he is sick when what he tastes as sour is really something that he should taste as sweet or that what he experiences as cold to touch is really hot considered in itself. *Because he has such a healthy estimative sense faculty, the pleasures of the prudent man are the measure of proper human pleasure*! In all cases related to human appetites (the passions and will) and especially to loves, desires, and pleasures, what appears good to the prudent man, tends to be so. In the case of health, the judgment of the prudent man matches the sense pleasure of the healthy man and the natures of things. Hence, *prudence is the measure by which we should judge all moral affairs*, including whether a human being is morally good or not. No surprise, then, is that the delights of *the Many* and those of *the Prudent Man* (*the One*) tend to be contrary opposites.[6]

7. Happiness: the one, chief pleasure of the prudent man and the proper pleasure of human nature considered as an integrated whole

According to St. Thomas, after having discussed the nature and species of pleasure and pain, joy and sorrow, Aristotle says he will next consider the highest human pleasure: happiness. He says he especially needs to do so because, by nature, all human beings consider pleasure to be human happiness, to be the last end and first principle and mover of all human desires, what we most love, because all love rests in joy. To direct human activities unerringly to a last act, a chief end, we need to know what is that last act, that chief end: that first, greatest, and most intense, passionate, natural love.

To identify human happiness with utmost precision, St. Thomas maintains that Aristotle returns to his prior definition of happiness as chiefly an activity, not a habit. He does so because he says *happiness consists in perfect exercise of vital activity*, and not just an exercise of any kind of vital, living, activity (like sleep, or acts of the vegetative soul, like digestion). Also, if happiness were a habit, someone asleep for most, or all, of life could be called happy. Virtuous habits exist even in the extremely unfortunate and habitually good people living miserably. Aristotle, St. Thomas, and common human opinion disagree that, strictly speaking, such people are happy.

After having precisely located the genus of happiness as an activity, Aristotle proceeds to identify its specific difference as a virtuous activity. Then, he makes this definition more precise by saying happiness is a virtuous activity: 1) desirable in itself; 2) self-sufficient and in need of nothing further; and 3) lacking in nothing, unable to be desired as a means for anything else. Happiness is desirable *per se* as accompanied by intellectual joy, *not by childish amusement or delights of the animal part of the soul*. As such, *it is a great-souled, not a small-souled, activity properly generated by the intellectual part of the soul*!

Having shown that happiness is an activity in accord with virtue, according to St. Thomas, next Aristotle shows how happiness is: 1) an activity in accord with the highest human virtue; 2) is the best of all human goods, the chief goal of all human goods (all of them being inclined, like tools, to generate it); 3) the best activity of the best part of a person; 4) the active human life directed by the highest virtue proper to the highest faculty, and accompanied by the highest joy; 5) an activity flowing from the highest habit of the highest human faculty; and 6) *a contemplative, speculative, activity of wisdom, science, and understanding of truth*.

Aristotle and St. Thomas start to prove all these immediately-preceding claims by comparing the human intellect to human faculties of less spiritual, immaterial, qualitative greatness in kind and strength: the irascible and concupiscible appetites. While these appetites can, to some extent, resist taking direction from intellectual reason, Aristotle maintains that the intellectual soul rules over these appetites through a quasi-political rule, while it rules over the body just as over a slave, by despotic power.

He, then, gives some indication of the intellectual soul's superiority in immaterial/spiritual greatness by, in two ways, comparing its power/activity to that of divine beings: 1) by a special power whereby it knows divine beings; and 2) by a special inclination, appetite, it has to love divinities.

He adds that happiness is an activity of this best principle in us in accord with the virtue proper to it because the perfect activity required for happiness can come only from a power perfected by a habit that is the power's proper virtue making its activity good and most delightful. Such a power must be a contemplative one; and happiness must be a contemplative act because contemplative activity belongs to the intellect according to its highest, proper, virtue, and proper pleasure: wisdom, which includes science and understanding![7]

8. Why Aristotle maintains that human happiness consists in the virtue of contemplation of the highest truth

For three reasons, according to St. Thomas, Aristotle says the highest, qualitatively greatest (or greatest in intensive, or virtual, quantity), most perfect human activity is contemplation of the highest truth: 1) On the part of the faculty, this is the single, most immaterial, spiritually great, simple and un-composed act in which a human being can engage. Considered as such, it most resembles the divine act of self-knowing. 2) On the part of the things known, it is the most immaterial, spiritual, and divine. 3) Because of the immateriality of the human intellect and of the thing known, this act is the most continuous, uninterrupted, unimpeded, and lasting of all human acts. As such, it is the most intensely pleasant, satisfying, and long-lasting. While all human activities fatigue the body and cannot continue uninterruptedly, contemplative acts fatigue the body less than do other acts.

St. Thomas maintains, further, that the philosophical contemplation of wisdom is the most delightful of all virtuous activities because it is the most: 1) pure (that is immaterial, spiritually intense, qualitatively great); and 2) permanent from the standpoint of the faculty involved and the thing known, something eternal. He says that lasting enjoyment cannot be produced by the animal part of the soul or contingent beings, by an act like a dog eating a rabbit.

He adds that interruptions rarely happen in philosophical, metaphysical contemplation. Contemplation of truth is twofold: 1)

Peter A. Redpath

investigative pursuit and 2) reflective activity, resting in, loving, repose. Since the reflective is the term, end, of philosophical, metaphysical, contemplation, St. Thomas says it is the better of the two. Hence, people who already know the truth and have their reason perfected by its intellectual virtue (its intensive quantum, immaterial, greatness) through apprehension of forms of things spend their life more delightfully. He adds that the self-sufficiency (*autarchia*) that constitutes part of happiness exists most of all human activities in contemplation because to engage in contemplation we do not need leisure goods. We need only necessary goods required for social life by all virtuous men.

When the necessities of life are sufficiently provided for the prudent man, however, the prudent man still needs other virtuous people as helpers. The contemplative man does not. The contemplative can contemplate truth even alone. Contemplation of truth is almost entirely internal. And the more a person can contemplate truth when living alone, the more perfect is his wisdom because this man knows much and needs little help or instruction. While, for the most part, in intellectual and practical activities, two intelligent heads are better than one, in the act of wisdom, because those who seek to help cannot tend to have the intensely abstractive knowing ability needed to grasp the principles involved in doing philosophical metaphysics, the wise man tends to be on his own, be his own best helper.

Happiness in this sense is so self-sufficient that no good can be added to or subtracted from it. Contemplation is its own reward, except incidentally. Hence, chiefly, most of all, happiness consists in contemplation of truth considered as such.

So considered, Aristotle says that happiness closely resembles amusement because, like happiness, amusement involves rest in an end, leisure, and perfect enjoyment of an object. Chiefly, we busy ourselves with work and engaging in business to relax and have leisure to rest, delight, in what we most love. This situation resembles soldiers who make war to enjoy peace.

While, previously, Aristotle had said that rest is essentially ordered to subsequent activity (we rest now so we can work better later), at this point in the *Nicomachean Ethics* (because he is understanding perfect leisure as perfect rest in the perfect, or last, act [end] toward which all other instances of leisure and act are ordered as enabling means), he is considering leisure in its highest qualitative intensity as a special property accompanying happiness essentially order to know subsequent activity.

In this sense, leisure is not found in the activities of the practical virtues. Indeed, people of a practical bent, inclination, do not tend to understand leisure's nature in this sense. This is especially true of politicians, whose chief concerns are political acts (like war and peace) related to the common good; and even religious leaders, whose priestly duties chiefly involve concerns with religious ceremonies.

Acts of war, he continues, cannot be essentially ordered simply to more acts of killing. If they were, war would be essentially murderous and would turn friends into enemies so we could kill each other endlessly. Hence, even political life is ordered toward the contemplative life of the political body established by preservation of peace for pursuit of science in contemplation of truth. Because they concern preservation of the common good, Aristotle considers political, especially military, life a preeminent act of moral virtue.

Nonetheless, because we apply ourselves to contemplative activity for its own sake, for no further end, Aristotle and St. Thomas maintain that the contemplative activity of the human intellect toward which the contemplative virtues are ordered essentially differs from the contemplative activity toward which practical virtues are ordered in intensity of focus. Hence, the activities generated by the moral virtues, even that of prudence, cannot generate the *contemplative virtue of happiness*.

Contemplative activity produces a proper pleasure (happiness in its most perfect sense!) *proceeding from itself, augmenting it.* Hence, it provides for human activity the *beautifying, perfecting,* adornments associated with a happy life. Happiness, thus, consists in the proper pleasure involved in contemplative life of the intellect; and, since for complete happiness as a human life, no essential part should be missing, long life is necessary.

Moreover, *the kind of leisure needed for contemplation of speculative truth* transcends in kind the leisure through which our reason directs sensory activities: engaging solely in intellectual activities proper to superior substances that are solely intellect. Consequently, a human being living a contemplative life lives like something divine, unmixed with the bodily.

Just as the intellect considered in its purity differs from a composite of soul and body, so the activity of the contemplative intellect differs from the activity consequent upon moral virtue which is properly concerned with human affairs. Just as the intellect compared to man is something divine, so the contemplative life of the intellect is compared to the life of moral virtue as divine to human.

Rejecting the opinion of those who think otherwise, Aristotle recommends that, as far as possible, we must strive to attain immortality and live according to reason (the best of all the principles in man, who is really divine and immortal). While small in dimensive quantity as simple and immaterial, in intensive quantity, human reason surpasses everything human in power and goodness.

By its activities, which resemble those of divine beings, it excels all other human powers. Similarly, regarding the excellence of its nature, it excels all the parts of the body in goodness. If the intellect is the better part of man, in a way, it appears to be the whole of man.

Since all other parts of a human being are, in a way, tools of the intellect, which is our chief part (our command and control center), and since living a life chiefly under its highest part is natural and proper to all composite beings, Aristotle maintains that people like Simonides give foolish advice when they say human beings should not engage in contemplation of truth and metaphysical speculation. In fact, because it is the most immaterially, spiritually, great, the contemplative life is the most delightful and maximum in intensive quantum greatness of all human activities.

Considering us according to our composite human nature, contemplating the divine *is not* our properly human and most pleasing act. But considered from the standpoint of the chief command-and-control principle in us as human beings, the principle of maximum qualitative, or intensive quantum, greatness, the immaterial intellect (a principle most perfectly existing in totally immaterial beings, but imperfectly and by participation existing in us), this dimensively small part is greater in intensive quantity, qualitative, greatness than all other human parts. Hence, the person who gives himself to contemplating truths is the happiest a person can be in this life.[8]

9. The secondary kind of happiness that the activity of moral virtue causes

After showing how happiness consists chiefly in the intellectual virtue of contemplation, next Aristotle and St. Thomas show: 1) the nature of a secondary kind of happiness generated by the moral virtues directed by prudence; and 2) that the person who lives a life of moral virtue directed by prudence is happy with a secondary kind of qualitative greatness.

Just as wisdom perfects and contains within itself the other speculative habits of the human soul, so Aristotle and St. Thomas consider prudence to contain within itself and perfect all the soul's moral virtues. In four ways, according to St. Thomas, Aristotle proves that the contemplative life is happier than the practical life.

First, he maintains that, because they chiefly concern human affairs, the way human beings treat each other, *the inter-personal relations with which prudence and the other moral virtues are concerned essentially deal with human social interaction and relations, getting along with each other in communal life.*

He says that some matters of concern to the moral virtues deal chiefly with the human appetites (the human will and emotions), while others concern the body and external goods. Considered chiefly as an intellectual virtue perfecting the human will's relation to perfecting contemplation, prudence is connected to other moral virtues by a kind of affinity, but chiefly concerns the end of perfecting the intellect considered as such. Considered chiefly as an intellectual virtue perfecting the *estimative sense* (particular, or cogitative, reason) and the human passions, the ends of these moral virtues are not of the intellect as speculative. They are of the principles and starting points of prudence in relation to the practical intellect: to deliberation about means to practical ends. Considered in this way, prudence does not aim chiefly at helping to perfect contemplation of divine things. It aims chiefly at perfecting inter-personal relations.

In this practical sense of being chiefly concerned about practical affairs dealing with human relations, St. Thomas says, the other moral virtues and prudence unite in the estimative sense to create one nature through which to direct the human emotions as a synthesis of right reason and right desire/proper pleasure! Because the human emotions belong to the body and the soul, prudence and moral virtue direct the whole body/soul composite toward right social living.

Evident is that the other moral virtues and prudence concern the psychosomatic composite. In this respect, life lived under the direction of these moral virtues as command and control principles of prudence is most perfectly human inasmuch as the human composite is a composite of body and soul. Human life lived chiefly under the direction of these two principles is called "human" and "active." Nonetheless, contemplative life and happiness is of a qualitatively higher nature, is divine and more excellent in immaterial, spiritual, intensive quantum, greatness.

Aristotle starts his second argument to demonstrate that the contemplative life is qualitatively happier than that of the practical life by noting that the life and happiness generated by contemplative moral virtue has little need for external goods and personal relations. But the life of the statesman is chiefly concerned with human happiness as practical, and with contemplation only inasmuch as this concerns sciences necessary for the perfection of the political order. While both the contemplative and the practical man of action need life's necessities filled, the man whose chief concern is happiness in this life through perfecting inter-personal relations through daily exchanges with other people needs many external goods and the help of many other people.

Moreover, Aristotle maintains that, without visible external acts, man's will remains hidden, many unjust people can pretend they act justly. To show, for example, that we are brave we need to perform some externally courageous act. Consequently, a brave man should perform some such act. And to show temperance, a temperate man must have the opportunity to be tempted and to enjoy pleasure in an externally manifest way. If no occasion for observing *virtue and vice* in external behavior happens, is legally permitted, St. Thomas says that no occasion for judging, praising/ rewarding or blaming/punishing human beings for choosing an action is possible; *and with this disappears the chief enabling means of moral education: healthy pride and shame or embarrassment, arising from private and public conscience.*

While choice is more crucial proximately to perform a moral (that is, free) activity, choice and public, external, display of moral (freely chosen) acts are required for the acquisition and exercise of perfect moral virtue. For such public display, we human beings need many things of a greater, nobler, kind, *including actually doing great good deeds*!

Not so, St. Thomas says, in the case of the contemplative happiness of the contemplative man, who wants and needs few external goods and for whom many external goods become a hindrance. Evident, then, is that happiness of the contemplative man is more perfect than that of the practically-active man.

Aristotle's third argument for the qualitative superiority of the contemplative virtue of happiness over that of the practical moral virtue of happiness is based upon the claim that, because perfect happiness is divine, considered as such, it contains no active moral virtues dealing with human relations and external goods. Hence, it must be contemplative.

Aristotle's fourth reason in support of the same claim cited in the above paragraph is that, while, to some extent, brute animals, in a way, perform acts resembling moral virtue, they do so absent any contemplation of wisdom. Because gods have only intellectual life, the life of the gods is supremely happy. Analogously, the same is true of us. The more spiritually great, beautiful, we become in the contemplative part of the soul, the happier we become.[9]

10. Human happiness and external goods

After having shown the twofold nature of perfect happiness in superior/contemplative, and inferior/practical, modes, St. Thomas says Aristotle next discusses how the happy man is disposed toward other beings. According to St. Thomas, Aristotle starts to do this by maintaining human nature is not self-sufficient for the act of contemplation such as a god performs because, at a minimum, to contemplate we need food and a somewhat healthy body. Periodically, then, our intellects must become diverted from contemplating. While we do not need many external goods in order to engage in the act of contemplation, we need some—especially to execute virtuous external acts like justice.

In the case of the practical moral virtues, private citizens of moderate means are often able to perform more noble deeds in number than rulers because too many external relationships frustrate our ability to move and move effectively. Because *the Many* tend to ignore intellectual goods, they have a difficult time understanding how the best of human goods for us considered in themselves (in intensive quantum greatness, qualitative greatness and beauty) do not demand a person to be materially rich or powerful.

This difficulty is complicated by the fact that, because the chief aim of practical activity is conduct, in practical matters we test truth chiefly through deeds, not through argument. *We chiefly measure truth in practical activity by prudent conduct, not by arguments. In practical matters, conduct tells us more about whether a person knows what he is talking about than does syllogistic argument.*

Next, Aristotle tells his readers that, because they claimed that external things were evil, not needed for happiness (*yet, nonetheless, we have to pursue them for happiness!*), the argument of the ancient Stoics does not persuade Aristotle.

St. Thomas adds that, since the happy man is most well disposed toward God and things God loves/honors, we are right to conclude that God: 1) delights in this person and that part of him which is the most perfect part of a human being; and 2) loves and honors his intellect, and is most pleased with the philosopher, who is happy in the maximum way. Hence, evident is that, as St. Thomas says, Aristotle places happiness in the contemplation of wisdom, not in a series of actions commanded by the practical intellect.[10]

11. Why, according to Aristotle and St. Thomas, we need moral virtue plus prudent legislation to become happy: the moral psychology of the happy man as opposed to that of the incontinent and intemperate man

After determining that, in both its contemplative and practical manifestations, happiness is pleasure, according to St. Thomas, Aristotle considers the end of human life in terms of the pleasure associated with civic life by first asking whether his prior discussion of happiness of the active life of the practical man in relation to virtues of friendship and pleasure has been enough, or whether he needs to add something. Immediately, he settles the question by arguing that: 1) for human beings to become morally good and happy, we must become morally virtuous, habituated to morally virtuous living; and 2) to gain the habituation adequate to this end, we need direction by good civil law.

To achieve the end of moral science, he says, we do not need speculative knowledge about things. We need practical knowledge about how to do good deeds! Moreover, since we become virtuous, doers of good deeds in accord with virtue, we cannot do good deeds intermittently, now and then. We must habitually practice doing good deeds the way good people do them.

As is evident from experience, *persuasive words*, *rhetoric*, do not suffice to make us habitual doers of good deeds. Such words can challenge and move, encourage, us to do good deeds. Indeed, because they are well disposed to take good advice, when they are verbally incited to do good works, people who truly love doing what is good can become apprentices in moral acts of doing honorable deeds.

But, because they have no sense of honor, no fear of dishonor, no sense of embarrassment, shame, no conscience, extremely incontinent and, especially, intemperate men cannot be dissuaded from evil by embarrassment and shame. Only physical punishment, physical pain, can dissuade them from making vicious choices.

An Introduction to Ragamuffin Ethics

Attempting to use rational persuasion on such rationally anarchic individuals tends to be a waste of breath and time. Because they reduce the whole of good to physical pleasure and the whole of evil to physical pain, they incline to fear and dread pain, not rational arguments. Their natural inclination is to listen to arguments promising hope of pleasure and warning of fear of pain, not to unemotional, rationally-composed, argumentation.

By habitual bad choice, the moral psychology of the extremely incontinent, and especially, intemperate man is out of touch with reality and the natures of things. Such people naturally incline to identify good with physical pleasure, evil with physical pain; and right reason with what pleases them and hatred and fear of what causes them physical pain. Lacking a realist ability to sense real good and evil through a morally well-educated estimative sense (particular, or cogitative, reason), they cannot understand nor experience honor, embarrassment, and shame. Not understanding honor, embarrassment, and shame, they cannot be attracted by honor and repelled and punished by embarrassment and shame.

Living their lives chiefly under the direction of their concupiscible appetite's pursuit of physical pleasure and avoidance of physical pain, having reduced the whole of right reason to concupiscible delight, they incline to oppose as forms of hate and violence (what today is popularly called "hate speech") whatever opposes their unbridled pursuit of physical pleasure (such as rational claims that moral virtues exist that they incline to ignore).

To such people, anyone who attempts to persuade him or her out of such a life appears to be *full of hate*, essentially irrational, incarnate evil (today commonly called "a bigot" "intolerant"). Since to change a person's way of choosing, we have to change his or her way of thinking, and we cannot change such an irrational person's way of thinking by rational argument, the only alternative mode of

504

persuasion to use with such a person appears to be fear of physical punishment. Since they incline to reduce reason to an emotional state, they incline to estimate that anyone who opposes their thinking about pleasure must be a "hater," someone using *fear* (to which they reduce opposing reason) to change their minds.

Aristotle and St. Thomas consider such brutish persons to be moved chiefly by love of physical pleasure and hatred of physical pain, to be people who cannot comprehend honor and honorable goods and deeds, much less delight in them. Consequently, they maintain that such people lack the educational virtue of moral, or ethical, teachability (*docilitas*). Volitionally and emotionally, they lack the psychology of moral teachability, the moral psychology essentially needed to accept the sort of reasoning that inclines to generate moral virtue, and, especially prudence.

They maintain that, for anyone to change by rational argument anyone who holds conclusions by long, strongly, and passionately-held convictions is close to, if not totally, impossible. *To do so, you have to change their first principles, or their way of reasoning from them: both of which are held by long and strong bad habits, which is not easy to do.*

Regarding attainment of virtue, Aristotle says three chief philosophical teachings existed around his time, that: 1) we become virtuous by nature, natural disposition, plus influence of heavenly bodies; 2) we become virtuous by practice; and 3) we become virtuous through teaching.

To some extent, Aristotle claims that each teaching is true. He says that, by nature, all human beings have some natural disposition toward virtue, but he holds that this natural disposition to be courageous, temperate, and just is imperfectly possessed at birth. He maintains that its perfection requires command-and-control by the virtue of prudence, which is also imperfectly possessed at birth. If all these virtues were located in a disembodied intellect, perfect as an intellect, virtue would be knowledge and no habituation of the human will, estimative sense, and the emotions would be needed for human beings to be perfectly virtuous morally.

But St. Thomas maintains that such habituation in virtue is needed because these faculties are not born perfectly well-disposed to recognize and follow right reason and right desire/proper pleasure. Evident is that what pertains to human nature by birth in composing parts of a psychosomatic whole causes all our natural powers. To some extent, these powers come to us from: 1) external physical causes, like our environment and heredity, which influence our body chemistry and our bodily dispositions, including, emotional dispositions (like anger and fear, or emotional calm); and 2) God, who alone governs our intellect, inclining it toward all good, and the Devil, who inclines our lower appetites toward morally evil.

Because rational discourse and argumentation are not effective with everyone, and because, just as, like poor soil, an evil soul must be well-tilled abundantly to nourish seeds of virtue, initially, the man who identifies reason with, reduces reason to, concupiscible passion, inclines to identify prudent advice coming from particular reason (the estimative sense), and constraints imposed by the irascible appetite in the form of moral virtue *as an act of violence*! Such a person lacks the emotional maturity and disposition to be able to recognize, much less listen to, right reason and good counsel. *While good counsel can be effective in the soul of a listener prepared by many good customs and laws, St. Thomas maintains that, when the concupiscible appetite becomes firmly rooted by habituation in a person's soul, a person's higher reason and estimative sense (particular reason) lose touch with reality as from a first principle and become anarchic*!

As a result, a person becomes a slave to love of pleasure and finds listening to sound reason emotionally painful, intolerable, unbearable: an act of moral intolerance, violence, being violently imposed upon him. Generally speaking, Aristotle and St. Thomas maintain that nothing short of fear of criminal punishment and force of law can compel such a despotically-inclined nature to do good deeds. Evident is that, for intellectual persuasion to be effective as a moral, educational, tool, right emotional habituation through good family training, custom, and civil law must precede it so that youth come to love and delight in doing honorable deeds and to hate and abhor doing shameful ones.

Unless, from the earliest age, we are first emotionally educated under the direction of prudent legislators framing excellent laws that can command the concupiscible appetite to love and delight in doing really good deeds, Aristotle and St. Thomas maintain that, for anyone to be guided from youth to perfect moral virtue according to good customs becomes difficult.

Most of us, they claim, especially young males, who are prone to pursue pleasures and avoid pains, naturally find unattractive living a temperate and hard life that refrains from pleasures and does not abandon real good in favor of apparent good. Consequently, to educate young people to become good human beings and peace-loving citizens, good, childhood, moral education demands the existence of good lawmakers and good laws to accustom, even force, youth to become habituated in doing good deeds and loving/delighting in them. Through such good laws and the good moral education they incline to foster, moral virtue might be perfected through habitually doing really good deeds and, later on in life, be enjoyed as such after the fashion of a second nature. Indeed, Aristotle and St. Thomas maintain that such good laws are needed by young people and adults so that we become accustomed to do good deeds throughout the whole of our lives.

While legislation chiefly exists to help morally educate human beings to become just, and political friends, to contribute to the health and preservation of civil society, Aristotle laments that legislators tend universally to neglect its study. Prior to him, in fact, he says the science of legislation (political science putting prudence into customs), had been largely neglected. As a result, prior to engaging in his study of political science in a separate work, Aristotle ends his *Nicomachean Ethics* by saying he needs to show how to put into practice what some others have, prior to him, put into books about legislation and laws, but have not succeeded in putting into execution as such.[11]

—Notes—

1. St. Thomas Aquinas, *Commentary on the Nicomachean Ethics of Aristotle*, Bk. 10, Lect. 1, nn. 1953–1963.
2. Id., Lect. 2, nn. 1964–1979.
3. Id., Lects. 3–4, nn. 1980–2004.
4. Id., Lects. 5–6, nn. 2005–2038.
5. Id., Lect. 7, nn. 2039–2049.
6. Id., Lect. 8, nn. 2050–2064.
7. Id., Lect. 9, nn. 2065–2079.
8. Id., Lects. 10–11, nn. 2080–2110.
9. Id., Lect. 12, nn. 2111–2125.
10. Id., Lect. 13, nn. 2126–2136.
11. Id., Lects. 14–16, nn. 2137–2180.

Once Again, Mission Accomplished

In my "Author's Introduction" to Volume 2 of my *A Not-So Elementary Christian Metaphysics*, I claimed that, in that work, I had considered myself to be acting as a midwife for mentors of mine to formulate, in a completed nature, a radically-new and much-improved understanding of St. Thomas's teaching about philosophy/science, that some colleagues of mine and I had started to call "Born-Again Thomism" or "Ragamuffin Thomism," grounded in metaphysical principles that: 1) transcend centuries of misinterpretation of many of St. Thomas's key metaphysical doctrines and metaphysical principles the West had inherited from René Descartes and his Enlightenment intellectual descendants; 2) provide a much-improved understanding of St. Thomas's teaching about the real nature of philosophy/science than the major ones offered over the recent centuries; and 3) reunite philosophy, science, and wisdom into a coherent whole.

Analogous to that claim, in this work, I had considered myself, once again, to be acting as a midwife for mentors of mine and, in an increased way, *a reporter* of the teachings of others, to formulate, in a completed nature, a radically-new and much-improved understanding of St. Thomas's teaching about moral science, ethics, that some colleagues of mine and I have started to call "Ragamuffin Ethics." In this work, I had considered myself to be working like an archeologist: 1) finally to help teachers of mine unearth ethical principles of St. Thomas that transcend centuries of misinterpretations of his moral teachings since his death in 1274; 2) to provide a much-improved understanding of the real nature of St. Thomas's moral doctrines than the major ones offered over the recent centuries; and 3) show precisely how speculative and practical science belong to philosophy/science as a coherent whole.

As I said in my "Introduction" to this book, "My chief aim in writing this work is to present to my readers what, as far as I know, is a more lucid and complete *report* of the moral teaching of St. Thomas Aquinas than has been written by anyone in English within modern times, in language that most fairly-intelligent adults should be able to understand." Such an aim is: 1) not small, modest, and 2) not meant to be. It is meant to fill a glaring contemporary need within the modern West and the world as a whole.

Also, within my "Introduction," I said, "Except for the case of modeling moral virtue in personal behavior, the best apologetical moral tool bar none for the defense of universal moral principles that have guided people for centuries within the West and throughout the world are those contained within the moral teaching of Aristotle and St. Thomas as St. Thomas presents them in his writings: as habits of the human soul essentially ordered toward prudent living." Having completed my study of St. Thomas's moral teachings, I stand by the truth of these immediately preceding claims.

In addition, as further evidence of the truth of the apologetical power of St. Thomas's moral psychology for defense of classical Western moral teachings against charlatans who repeatedly misrepresent them, I include within this book a "Concluding Postscript," Thomistic critique, of perhaps today's most celebrated, and self-described moral psychologist: *Jonathan Haidt*, which a colleague of mine, Max Weismann, had been kind enough recently to publish and send out as a "Special Edition" publication to members of the Center for the Study of The Great Ideas.

Whether or not the claims I have made in concluding this book are true or false remains for intellectual history to affirm or deny. Hence, in closing, once again, I welcome those who challenge my above claims, or subsequent ones I make about Haidt's book, *The Righteous Mind*, to show me where and how what I have said has been incorrect.

The Moral Bankruptcy of Jonathan Haidt's *The Righteous Mind*

Special Edition

A Critique of Jonathan Haidt's *The Righteous Mind* as a Chief Cause of the Contemporary "Coddling of the American Mind": Written in Memory and Honor of Mortimer J. Adler

Peter A. Redpath

Senior Fellow, Center for the Study of The Great Ideas

Rector, Adler-Aquinas Institute

Close to 75 years ago, reflecting upon his career as a Ph. D. graduate in psychology from Columbia University, Mortimer J. Adler reported:

> I cannot help recalling my own career as a student of psychology. The textbooks through which I made acquaintance with this subject confessed, in their opening chapters, that psychologists had not been able to reach genuine agreement about the subject matter of their science. They quite belligerently proclaimed the complete independence from philosophy of psychology as a science; and at the same time they summarized the diverse "schools of thought"—each differing from the others, not because of contrary discoveries, but because of the 'point of view' which motivated its method of research and determined the restricted fields of phenomena it was willing to explore. Even to a sophomore, it was apparent that the

psychologists had shut the front door on philosophy only to indulge in some surreptitious "philosophizing" of their own. I taught experimental psychology for six years and tried my hand at various types of research in pursuance of a doctoral degree; but in all those years of teaching, throughout all my experimental efforts, and at the moment I received the degree—supposedly a competent worker in the field—I could not tell my students, my colleagues, or myself, what psychology was about, what its fundamental principles were, or what was the theoretical significance of all the data and findings that thousands of young men like myself had been collecting and sorting ever since the Ph. D. industry and the research foundations had encouraged such labors.[1]

Having had the above-described experience with the pseudo-science of modern psychology, and having spent most of his professional academic career leading the fight in American higher education against, and exposing as intellectual frauds and sophists, the many falsely-so-called "social scientists" that inhabited American colleges and universities while he was alive, were he still with us today, I suspect that Adler would be shocked and bewildered to find the magazine *First Things* (founded by Adler's and my friend Fr. Richard John Neuhaus, r.i.p.) seeing fit to publish an interview with Jonathan Haidt by Brother Dominic Bouck, O.P., in which Haidt's work appears to be celebrated as some sort of elixir against, instead of a chief promoter of, the PC culture that some academics (supposedly not including Haidt) have, wittingly or unwittingly, tended to encourage on American college and university campuses over the past several decades.[2] Interviewing Haidt to try to discover how to solve the problem of the contemporary coddling of the minds of contemporary

American college and university students is analogous to what my friend Curtis L. Hancock often refers to as asking an incendiary for help trying to extinguish a forest fire.

Were he alive today, I suspect Adler would have replied as forcefully as possible against such a positive portrayal of Haidt as someone who knows the chief causes and solutions to present problems facing American higher education. Since he is not alive, and since someone needs to expose Haidt for the charlatan and snake-oil salesman that he is, I have written this article in his place and have submitted it to Mortimer's partner-in-philosophical crime Max Weismann for publication to the members of the Center for the Study of The Great Ideas, which Mortimer co-founded with Max, the place where I consider it most fitting to be published.

1. General analysis of *The Righteous Mind*

Jonathan Haidt's *The Righteous Mind* is *chiefly* a cleverly-composed, fictional, historical narrative in the tradition of Jean-Jacques Rousseau's *Émile or On Education*, Gotthold Ephraim Lessing's "Education of the Human Race," and Immanuel Kant's "Conjectures on the Beginning of Human History" (what Kant calls "a pleasure trip" made "on the wings of the imagination").[3] In this fictional narrative Haidt purports to demonstrate that his "beloved topic of inquiry," his misguided version of "moral psychology—is the key to understanding politics, religion, and our (by which Haidt means "the Enlightenment West's") spectacular rise to planetary dominance" (p. 315). In saying this, Haidt is claiming to show that, in the history of the evolution of human consciousness, in Greek antiquity his "hero" Glaucon was supposedly "the guy who got it right," that "people care a great deal more about appearance and reputation than about reality" (p. 74). As for Plato, Haidt says, "the assumed psychology is just plain wrong" (Id.). Supposedly Glaucon showed us "the overriding importance of reputation and the other external restraints for creating moral order" (p. 315) and the Enlightenment intellectual David Hume supposedly "helped us to escape from rationalism and into intuitionism" (Id.).

From the start of his text, Haidt's argument essentially rests upon a series of unsupported, dogmatic assertions, false and exaggerated claims, partial truths, inadequate distinctions, overall sophistry, and sloppy scholarship.

He makes the first such unsupported, dogmatic assertion and false claim on p. 4 of his text when he maintains, "Some [moral] actions are wrong even though they do not hurt anyone."

As Socrates and Plato realized centuries ago, being wrong about anything (morally or otherwise) always causes damage to the person who is wrong. In the case of moral activity, which involves a cooperative activity of intellect, will, and emotions, making wrong choices damages the intellect, will, and/or emotions, some relation between or among them (such as prudent judgment), and the person who makes a moral choice (just as being wrong about the answer to the mathematical problem damages a person's mathematical ability).

Haidt follows up this mistake by making a false disjunction and distinction on p. 5 that assumes most people think "morality" must come from "nature or nurture." By coming "from nature" he means that moral knowledge is innate (coming pre-loaded, perhaps from God implanting it in us) or that it is contained in "evolved moral emotions" (like he thinks Charles Darwin claimed).

This distinction is false because it is a false disjunction. It assumes that a person must maintain that moral knowledge *cannot come partly from nature and partly from nurture*, which thinkers like Plato, Aristotle, Marcus Tullius Cicero, St. Aurelius Augustine, and St. Thomas Aquinas who have largely dominated the Western moral tradition from the start of philosophy with the ancient Greeks (and of whom Haidt displays little to no knowledge) up through the twentieth century held.

For example, Plato maintained that a world of Forms exists independently of the human knower that human beings once knew through immediate intuition. In this life we recall these Forms through sensible forms that the human soul apprehends in the human body like in a cave. Aristotle and St Thomas Aquinas held that innate powers, faculties, exist in the human soul and that these powers are specifically activated by correlative external stimuli, like color, sound, and real dangers, existing in physical things.

Based upon this false disjunction, Haidt immediately makes a false distinction about the nature of "empiricism" and "rationalism," terms initially coined to describe movements in "modern philosophy" that Haidt misunderstands and seeks broadly to use to classify all moralists as nativists or nurturists. As coined around the time of Immanuel Kant, "empiricism" and "rationalism" are forms of "subjective idealism." Subjective idealism is a kind of "solipsism," a teaching claiming the human beings can know nothing other than themselves or their psychological states. John Locke, David Hume, and Kant are often presented by modern "philosophers" as classic examples of empiricism and rationalism. All three claim that the only thing human beings can know is our own psychological states, effects made upon our sense organ of imagination. Like Locke, Hume is well known to call these states of imagination "perceptions," which Hume divides into strong, lively, sense "impressions" and weak, dull, recollections of sense impressions: "ideas."[4]

Just as he grossly and anachronistically misunderstands Plato after the fashion of a modern rationalist, Haidt grossly misunderstands Hume as an "empiricist" in the fashion that Haidt conceives of empiricism. Haidt thinks *"Empirical* means 'from observation or experience'" (p. 5; this, however, is not the empiricism of David Hume, something that Haidt does not know).

On p. 324 Haidt falsely claims, "*Empiricism* has two different meanings": 1), which he says psychologists typically use and with which he disagrees: a "belief, in contrast to nativism, that the mind is more or less a 'blank slate' at birth, and that nearly all of its content is learned from experience"; 2) the meaning used by "philosophers of science to refer to the devotion to empirical methods—methods of observing, measuring, and manipulating the world in order to derive reliable conclusions about it." Regarding the empirical method, Haidt says, "As a scientist, I fully endorse empiricism as a method." Haidt, then, thinks of the method of fictional history, the evolutionary sociobiology in which he engages in his book, as a "science."

Today, "empiricism" has more than two meanings. If by "experience" Haidt means sense knowledge, or any knowledge, of some mind-independent being, the "empiricism" he describes above is not the empiricism of David Hume. Like Bishop George Berkeley, who preceded him and whom Hume lavishly praises, Hume thinks that the only experience human beings have is of our own mental states. Like Kant, who came after him, Hume maintains that we know nothing about the natures of things outside of our mental states. In fact, Hume thinks human beings are simply a train of disconnected perceptions that "feel" as if they are related. According to him, no natures, no substances, exist. For the nominalist Hume, an existing thing is simply a name for a collection of feelings that feel themselves to be related. In short, feelings have people. People do not have feelings.

Starting with these misinterpretations of Plato and Hume, and of himself as a "scientist" (apparently because he employs the "empirical method"), Haidt derives what he calls (p. 318) his "first principle of moral psychology: "*Intuitions come first, strategic reasoning second*" around which he developed his "social intuitionist model" that he used to "challenge the 'rationalist delusion'" of thinkers like Plato, Kohlberg, and Kant.

While Haidt is right to challenge the rationalist delusions of Lawrence Kohlberg and Kant, his use of Glaucon to challenge Plato is largely a straw-man argument based upon Haidt's gross ignorance of Plato's teaching and of the role that Plato's brother Glaucon plays in Book 2 of Plato's *Republic*. On pp. 72 through 74 of his text, Haidt presents a superficial and majorly incomplete summary of the problem that Glaucon and his brother Adeimantos give to Socrates. Among his many errors, Haidt totally ignores what Adeimantos says in Book 2; he gives a partial, and grossly distorted, report of the story of the Ring of Gyges, and he portrays Glaucon as disagreeing with Socrates (when, in fact, he is agreeing with him, arguing as a kind of devil's advocate on behalf of the "popular" understanding of justice, the understanding of "the many" that Thrasmyachos had defended in Book 1, which is that justice is "following the law of the established government" or "might makes right").

Immediately below is a summary of what Glaucon and Adeimantos actually request of Socrates in Book 2 of Plato's *Republic*.

2. Summary of Book 2 of Plato's *Republic*

A. Introduction

After Socrates finishes his criticism of Thrasymachos' understanding of justice and injustice in Book 1, Book 2 starts with Plato's brother Glaucon joining in a discussion with Socrates asking Socrates whether Socrates *really* wants to persuade his listeners that, in every way, being just is better than being unjust, or whether he only wants *to appear* to have persuaded them. In short, is Socrates *really serious* when he says that, in every way, being just is more profitable than being unjust, and if not, the question readers would have to ask is why he would only want to appear to have persuaded them? (That is, is Socrates attempting to mislead them about his true understanding of justice so as to appear just and, thereby, be able to take advantage of those who accepted his appearance as reality?)

Glaucon tells Socrates that, if Socrates really wants to persuade them, he is not doing what he wants. To help Socrates in his work, Glaucon asks him where, within three categories of good, Socrates would place justice: 1) enjoyable class, good we like for its own sake, like joy but not for any consequences; 2) noblest class, the good we like for its own sake and for the sake of its consequences, like exercise; 3) laborious class, good we take no delight in for itself but which we like as a means for another good that we do like to have for itself, like medicine?

B. Initial discussion between Socrates and Glaucon (acting as devil's advocate for Thrasymachos' understanding of justice as praising injustice over justice)

While Socrates places justice in the second category, taking up Thrasymachos' argument as a devil's advocate, Glaucon argues that Socrates has not done justice to Thrasymachos' argument, which Glaucon thinks has more merit to it than Socrates gave to it. He maintains that, while Socrates might place justice in the second class of noblest goods, most people, *the many*, would agree with Thrasymachos and place it in the third class of laborious goods because men dislike justice as such and only choose it to avoid having to suffer injustice.

Glaucon says that, while he disagrees with this popular opinion about justice, this view has been drummed into his ears by Thrasymachos and many others, and he has never heard it adequately refuted. He has never heard anyone commend justice for its own sake, arguing that justice considered as such is unqualifiedly better than injustice, commending justice for its own sake. Glaucon thinks that he will most likely hear this from Socrates.

To assist Socrates in this effort, even though he agrees with

Socrates and not Thrasymachos, Glaucon states he will do everything in his power to praise the unjust life. He will show Socrates how he wants Socrates to speak when Socrates attacks injustice and praises justice.

Since Socrates finds this proposal agreeable, Glaucon starts his work by explaining the nature and origin of justice according to popular opinion.

According to Glaucon, in the popular view (*the one that Haidt praises*), justice is a laborious good, a necessary evil, an emotional compromise or social contract, lying between two emotional extremes of human desire: 1) *a greatest human good*, to be able to hurt other people with impunity and 2) *a greatest human evil*, to be hurt by other people and to be unable to get revenge.

A human being's greatest delight is to hurt other people with impunity (*this is happiness*). Simultaneously, a human being's greatest dislike is to be hurt by others and to be unable to get revenge (*this is misery*).

Of these two opposing desires, the dislike for being hurt by others coupled with the inability to get revenge (the dislike of misery) is stronger than the emotional attraction to hurt other people with impunity (the desire to be happy). Justice is an emotional mean between these two contrary extremes, an emotional compromise, or social contract, made in a moment of weakness by a person who has come to the realization that he or she is not powerful enough to hurt other people with impunity or to be able to get revenge for personal harms suffered from others.

The origin of justice, then, is a state of consciousness, mental awareness, of personal weakness. A person who never experiences this state has no sense of justice. Considered in itself justice is not desirable, is evil. Considered in relation to a greater evil, it is respected as a necessary, honorable compromise made between two people who have come to a mutual realization of mutual weakness. But "the many" say that if a man were powerful enough, were a *real* man, he would never enter into such an agreement.

To enable his listeners to perceive most clearly that those who practice justice do so involuntarily because they are not powerful enough to do perfect injustice, *Glaucon tells The Story of the Ring of Gyges*, about unbridled desire and power, to show that, if given the opportunity to do so with impunity, both the just and unjust man would behave the same: Unjustly.

C. The Story of the Ring of Gyges

This story is about Gyges the Lydian, a shepherd to the king of Lydia. One day while Gyges was tending his sheep, an earthquake occurred, and a chasm opened the earth. Gyges entered the chasm and saw a large, hollow, brazen horse, with windows in its sides. Inside a window he saw the body of a dead man, appearing bigger than human, wearing only a golden ring on its hand. Gyges went in and took the ring. Then, one day at a monthly meeting of shepherds to report to the king, Gyges discovered that the ring had the magic power of invisibility. When he turned the top of the ring downward, he turned invisible. And when he turned it to its original position, he became visible again. Discovering this power, Gyges managed to get himself appointed a messenger to the king. Eventually he seduced the king's wife, with her help killed the king, and took over the kingdom.

The moral of the story is that if two such rings existed and one were given to a reputedly just person and the other to an unjust person, given the ability to do wrong with absolute impunity, both would act identically and would do wrong. Moreover, if a person had the opportunity to have this ring and do wrong with impunity, in the popular mind, the person who did not use the ring to his advantage would be privately considered a miserable fool. Simultaneously, in public, "the many" would praise the actions of the just man, the one in private they think to be a fool, out of fear of each other that, lacking this power themselves, they might suffer injustice from another.

Glaucon continues that the only way properly to judge, *or measure*, the profitability of these two lives is to compare them in their most perfect states, in the lives of the perfectly just and perfectly unjust; strip the unjust person of any appearance of injustice and the just person of any appearance of any justice.

The supremely unjust person must have the appearance of being supremely just. He must have access to the instruments for seeming just while being unjust; be a politician; possess all the gifts of seeming; have the gift of public speaking and be able to persuade so as to be able to do injustice in the right way and, if caught, be able to talk his way out of punishment (*possess the science of moral psychology according to Jonathan Haidt*); be rich and in a position to help friends and hurt enemies; be able to behave as he must toward men and sacrifice magnificently to the gods so that he might reasonably expect that the gods will care for him more than they will for the just man (361b–361c).

In contrast, Glaucon says the supremely just man must be completely just while appearing supremely unjust. He must be unable to call upon anyone else for help; stripped of all power but justice; subjected to every form of persecution during his life, chained, set out on a rack, have his eyes burned out, and suffer a miserable death by crucifixion (362a).

Glaucon states that these are the kinds of things that that those who wish to praise the life of the unjust over the life of the just will say, that both the gods and men provide a better life for the unjust than for the just.

D. Discussion between Socrates and Adeimantos about the way popular opinion praises justice over injustice

At this point, Plato's other brother, Adeimantos, interrupted the conversation because he thought that Glaucon had only told half the story *about the way popular opinion talks about justice and injustice*; had only considered how "the many" talk *when they commend injustice*.

Adeimantos thinks they should also consider what "the many" say *when they praise justice*. He thinks that doing so will make more precise Glaucon's argument. So, he immediately describes how fathers and poets, priests, and others commend justice when they do so.

Starting with the fathers he says that, when they recommend that their sons be just, like those who dispraise justice, they treat justice as a laborious good, good only for the "seeming," not for its "being." They tell their sons that they should be just because, by being just, *they will get a good reputation among human beings and the gods*; having the reputation for justice in this life, they will be able to marry into rich and powerful families and become politically influential. Even the gods will hear about them. When they die, the gods will roll out the welcome mat for them; prepare a sacred banquet for them; allow them to spend their lives in partying and eternal drunkenness; and will bury deep in the mud those with a reputation for impiety and injustice, and will make them gather water in a sieve.

Worse is what poets, priests, and others say about these issues. While they all commend moderation as beautiful and good, they say that justice and moderation are difficult and painful; injustice and intemperance are easy. For the most part, unjust actions are more profitable than just ones; rich, powerful, evil men are called "happy"; honored in private and public, while they admit that they are better people, they disrespect and despise anyone weak and poor.

According to Adeimantos, most shocking is what they say about the gods and virtue. They say the gods have fated misfortunes and a miserable life for many good men and good fortune and happiness to many evil men; priests and prophets come begging at the homes of the rich telling them that the gods have allotted them special powers through sacred rites and chants whereby they can fix with pleasures and feasts any wrongs done by them or their ancestors. They call in poets as expert witnesses about the ease of vice and difficulty of virtue and the seduction of the gods. They say that if anyone would like to hurt an enemy, for a small fee, using special charms and spells, they can persuade the gods to do their bidding; and they cite such authorities to convince private citizens and politicians that, for a modest donation, by means of specific rites, they have the power to free men from damage caused by their vice in this life; and special rites, for a higher price, they can fix and absolve any punishment due in the next.

Since the power of *seeming* (*Haidt's moral psychology*) appears to overcome the power of *truth*, Adeimantos asks Socrates, when clever young people hear all these ways of talking about justice and injustice by people (*like Haidt*) who supposedly praise justice over injustice, what sort of affect he thinks this will have on their minds when they think about how they should live their lives?

What is the benefit of being just if doing so is unpleasant and reaps no real reward? *Would not the better, more profitable, way to live a life be to develop an art* (*like Jonathan Haidt's moral psychology*) to *enable a person to be evil while simultaneously seeming good*? Should not the calculating young man build defenses around himself (*like Jonathan Haidt's moral psychology*) to *seem* good and virtuous, while simultaneously developing the art of *being* bad?

Adeimantos tells Socrates if someone were to say that being bad without being discovered is difficult, this person might simply reply that nothing great in life is easy; if a person wants to be happy, this is the necessary way to do so.

To keep an evil life hidden from public view, a smart person will have to learn the art of sophistry (*Jonathan Haidt's moral psychology*) from professional mouth pieces (*ancient sophists/*

contemporary social scientists in the tradition of David Hume) who teach this art of public speaking before public assemblies and law courts; join clubs, organizations; develop friends in political positions to conspire against enemies and exert influence where needed.

If someone were to caution against evil doing because of punishment from the gods, this person can simply say that if no gods exist, or if they do but care nothing about human beings, what should we care what they think? If gods do exist, the only things we know about them are what the poets have told us in their stories and genealogies.

The poets say the gods can be bribed not to punish us for wrongdoing in this life or in the next. We have to believe the poets in everything they say about the gods, or in nothing. Such being so, why should we be just? If we are unjust, we can bribe the gods not to punish us. Why be just when doing so is unpleasant, difficult, unrewarding, only results in living a miserable life, and we can bribe the gods anyway if we do wrong? Instead, why not simply be unjust, bribe the gods if we have to, and gain all the rewards?

Given such an understanding of justice and injustice and their respective benefits and damages, Adeimantos asks Socrates why would any reasonable person choose being just over being supremely unjust? He tells Socrates that *the mass of public opinion* (*which Jonathan Haidt recommends we use as a higher measure than the opinion of experts in virtue*: people with experience being just) and the highest authorities (*Haidt's moral psychologists and contemporary social scientists*) declare that we will make out better in this life and the next in our relationships with other human beings and the gods if we are able to *appear* good but *be* evil.

Adeimantos asks Socrates what could possibly persuade any man of power to choose justice over injustice? He says that any man of bodily or psychological strength, wealth, or family influence would simply laugh at such a proposal. Such a person can find many excuses to be unjust and is not angry with people who advocate being just. He is simply convinced that no human being is ever voluntarily just, except a person who is born with a divine hatred for injustice or has learned through experience some reason to avoid it. He thinks, otherwise, old age, cowardice, or some other weakness, the inability to do it, causes people to avoid injustice. The person who has the first opportunity to be unjust, as much as possible, seizes it.

Adeimantos says that, most surprising about this situation is something he and his brother had previously told Socrates. In the whole history of ancient Greece, from the time of the primeval heroes to their day, no one who has professed to praise justice over injustice has ever done so on the basis of the nature of justice that makes it essentially good for its possessor. Not in poetry or private conversation has anyone ever shown what is the power of justice, what quality it possesses hidden from gods and men, that always benefits the soul of its possessor, to make it the greatest good; and what is the power of injustice that causes it always to damage those who practice it, to make it the greatest evil. To a man (*in the tradition that Jonathan Haidt recommends we should emulate*) they have all commended justice and criticized injustice on the basis of reputation, honors, and rewards that come from them.

Adeimantos maintains that Thrasymachos and those who share his view (*like Haidt*) would say such things and add others, too. While, like his brother, he has played the role of a devil's advocate, Adeimantos says he longs to hear Socrates advocate the opposite view. He begs Socrates to show them precisely what, by their respective natures, justice and injustice do to the souls of their possessors to make justice always good and injustice always bad.

He wants Socrates to omit from his argument any reference to reputation and external rewards, otherwise they will think that he

agrees with Thrasymachos (and Haidt) and is only advocating that
people seem good and be evil, but undetected.

More than simply showing that justice is stronger than injustice, Adeimantos wants Socrates to show them what justice and injustice do as essential properties of their action that, *whether visible or invisible to gods and men*, makes justice good and injustice bad.

Haidt incorrectly assumes that, unlike Haidt, who (pp. 120 and 121) claims to understand how "the moral mind actually works" (using observation "informed by empathy" [which is supposedly the approach taken by Haidt's hero and that greatest of Western moralists, David Hume]), Plato conflates reasoning with logic and thinks that reasoning precedes observation. As the preceding entreaties by Glaucon and Adeimantos make clear, Haidt does not know what he is talking about. As is evident from the discussion Socrates has with Jonathan Haidt's hero, Thrasymachos (which is summarized immediately below), *Socrates is not celebrating rationalist reason,* abstract logic, and theoretical reason in the classical sense. *He is celebrating prudential knowledge, practical wisdom.*

3. Summary of Book 1 of Plato's *Republic*

A. Introduction (327A–328B)

Socrates opens Book 1 of Plato's *Republic* by describing an encounter that Socrates and Plato's brother Glaucon had had with a friend of Socrates named Polemarchos and Plato's other brother, Adeimantos, after returning from observing a religious festival in the Piraeus (the harbor area of Athens) and paying their respects to the goddess Bendis, in whose honor the festival was being held.

As they were attempting to leave the festival, Polemarchos, Adeimantos, and some other friends caught up with them persuaded Socrates and Glaucon to go with them to the home of Polemarchos' elderly father and friend of Socrates, Cephalos.

B. Discussion between Socrates and Cephalos (328B–331D)

After getting to Cephalos' house, Socrates and the aging Cephalos first discuss the question of old age because, at this time, Socrates is young and, *since he has no sense experience with old age*, he wonders whether old age is a difficult time of life or not. Since Cephalos is old and has experience at living, Socrates suspects that Cephalos might provide him some *knowledge* (*what Haidt calls an "intuition"*) about old age *that he can use as a principle of experiential knowledge for reasoning* about the nature of difficulty and its relation to old age.

Cephalos replies that a man's *character*, not age, is the chief determinant of whether or not any time of life (youth or old age) will be difficult; for the reasonable man (that is, the man of moral character, practical reason, prudence) old age is no more or less difficult than youth. For an unreasonable man (that is, the man who lacks emotional self-control, practical reason, prudence), rich or poor, every time of life will be miserable. Having a good character (that is, possessing prudential and practical, not logical and speculative, reason) is more important than wealth or poverty for being happy.

After discussing how Cephalos acquired his wealth, in reply to Socrates's question "What is the greatest good that comes from having great wealth?", Cephalos says that, while some people might find this hard to believe, the greatest good that he finds from having great wealth is that it enables him always to tell the whole truth and give back whatever he has received from everyone, man or god. He explains that this gives a man a special peace of mind and hope, especially in old age, as the thought of death starts to enter more into a man's consciousness and things that might not have concerned him before start to work on his mind.

For example, he wonders about the afterlife and whether the stories people tell about the lives of the just and the unjust and rewards and punishments in the afterlife are true. Such thoughts can even cause nightmares to a man who has wronged people in this life.

Agreeing with the poet Pindar, Cephalos considers hope to be a great human good. He thinks wealth helps him to be hopeful about death.

Considering Cephalos' reply to be excellent, Socrates follows it up with another question in which, in response to his question about the greatest good that comes from having great wealth, Socrates interprets Cephalos, in part, to have just given him a definition of justice. Socrates asks Cephalos whether justice is simply to tell the whole truth and to give back what a person has received, or whether it is something else. If so, would not behaving this way sometimes be unjust? For example, if a friend, when sane, gave a friend weapons to hold, and then demanded their return while insane, telling the whole truth and returning the weapons would be unjust, not just.

Cephalos agrees with Socrates, but then his son Polemarchos interrupts the conversation to come to his father's defense. He says that, if we are to believe the poet Simonides, justice is what his father said it was ("to tell the whole truth and to give back what we have received").

Cephalos turns over his part of the conversation to his "heir," explaining that he must see to the sacrifices. Polemarchos agrees, and Socrates and Polemarchos enter into a discussion in which Polemarchos fails to persuade Socrates that justice, which is a virtue, can ever cause harm.

C. Discussion between Socrates and Thrasymachos (336B–354B)

At this point in the dialogue, Socrates says a member of the audience that the other listeners had previously restrained from interrupting, Thrasymachos, broke into the discussion in a rage, leaping on the two interlocutors "like a wild beast" ready to tear them apart and scaring them to death. According to Socrates, the sight was so terrifying that, had he not seen Thrasymachos first and been able to turn his eyes away from him, he would have been struck dumb.

After Thrasymachos accuses Socrates and Polemarchos of pandering to each other like a pair of fools, he demands that Socrates stop refuting arguments and give a *precise* definition of justice.

After a short exchange in which Socrates and Thrasymachos agree to give precise definitions of justice, Thrasymachos gives a first definition, saying that justice is "the advantage of the stronger" (339A). He thinks that this was a terrific definition and wants Socrates to applaud it.

Socrates replies that he will applaud it once he understands what Thrasymachos means. He then asks Thrasymachos whether he is saying that if a champion athlete like Pulydamas is stronger than the rest of us and a diet of beef is to his advantage, then we should all eat beef.

Thrasymachos damns Socrates for this reply, saying that Socrates understood what he said in just the way to ruin a great answer. Thrasymachos was not talking about the physical advantage of the physically stronger. He was talking about the political advantage of the politically stronger.

Because Thrasymachos did not *precisely* say this was his meaning, Socrates responds that Socrates did not ruin the answer. Thrasymachos simply had not been *exact* in his answer. Socrates now wants Thrasymachos to tell him *precisely* and *exactly* the definition of justice.

Thrasymachos offers the example of governments in which the rulers always establish the laws to their own advantage, laws that take advantage of the ruled for the benefit of the ruler, and then pronounce them just. He says that justice is following the rules of the established government, doing what rulers tell them to do.

Peter A. Redpath

Socrates immediately asks Thrasymachos whether rulers are infallible or whether rulers can makes mistakes. Thrasymachos admits that rulers can sometimes makes mistakes.

Socrates tells Thrasymachos that when rulers make mistakes about their own advantage they command their subjects to do things that the rulers *think* are to their advantage but *really are not*, thereby demanding that their subjects do what is to the ruler's disadvantage. Since the subjects must simultaneously *do what is to the ruler's* advantage and *do what the ruler commands*, when what the ruler commands is not to the ruler's advantage, the subject must simultaneously act in opposite ways, do contrary opposites, something humanly impossible: what is to the advantage and disadvantage of the ruler.

When Socrates asks Thrasymachos to clarify what he had said, Thrasymachos replies that the subjects had to do what the ruler "said," not what the ruler "believed to be" to his advantage, even if it was not to his advantage. He accuses Socrates of quibbling for the purpose of discrediting his argument.

Thrasymachos then reverses the claim that he had made shortly before about rulers being fallible and asks why Socrates would think Thrasymachos would say that rulers could possibly make mistakes when, in the *precise* and *exact* meaning of the term, "rulers" are infallible, never make mistakes. He claims *people* can make mistakes. Since a ruler is a human being, while, when making a *personal* decision about a *private* matter, a ruler might make a mistake, in the *exact* sense of the term, a "ruler" in the professional capacity as ruler never makes a mistake.

Thrasymachos gives examples of a physician and an arithmetician to support his definition. He says that, *strictly speaking*, neither makes a mistake in relation to professional activity. While knowledge fails in individual situations, art does not. *Precisely and exactly speaking*, no artist, craftsman or ruler ever makes a mistake.

531

Having told Socrates *precisely* and *exactly* what he meant by a "ruler," Socrates asks Thrasymachos to consider the definitions of a "physician" and a "pilot" in the *exact* sense of the terms: whether, in the precise sense of the term, a physician is a moneymaker or a healer of the sick; a *true* pilot is a "sailor" or a "ruler over sailors."

Thrasymachos admits that, precisely speaking, physicians are healers of the sick, not money makers, and pilots are rulers over sailors, not simply sailors. He also admits that, true of all arts is that they seek no other advantage than to be as perfect as they can be, the perfection of each lies in the advantage of its subject.

Thrasymachos then questions Socrates about what Socrates means in raising these questions.

Socrates replies by asking Thrasymachos whether bodies exist in a perfect, or deprived, condition. Thrasymachos agrees that the art of medicine was invented *precisely* because bodies, subjects, exist in a deprived, not perfect, condition.

Socrates follows the above question with the question whether the medical art is ill? Is any and every art a deprived subject like eyes are of sight or ears of hearing so that they need a higher art to investigate and provide what is advantageous to them, and so on *ad infinitum*? Or is it not the case that every art (medicine, sailing, horsemanship, and so on) relates to, is defined in reference to, providing an advantage to a specific kind of body or subject? Is it not the case that the art is complete as an art and fulfills its nature when providing for the advantage of something else over which it rules? In the *exact* sense of the terms, is not a "physician" a healer of the sick, not a moneymaker, and a "pilot" a ruler over sailors, not simply a sailor? Is it not true that no "ruler" rules for personal advantage, always ruling for the advantage of subjects?

At this point (343Aff.), Thrasymachos sarcastically asks Socrates whether Socrates has a nurse at home to wipe his nose because it is running. He says he asks because Socrates is not able to understand the difference between shepherds and sheep. Shepherds and oxherds only fatten their sheep to kill them and make a profit for themselves and their masters.

Thrasymachos adds that the just man will always get less and be less happy than the unjust man, get the worse in any contract, in all private and public affairs, he will pay more taxes, and will incur more anger from his friends and relations when he serves in and leaves public office because he does not steal from the treasury and does not favor them.

He declares that people are not just because they fear doing unjust deeds, but because they fear suffering injustice. Just men as Socrates understands them conceive of injustice on a small scale and consider injustice shameful because they are not strong enough to commit injustice on a grand scale, as an art (344A ff.)

Jonathan Haidt's hero, Thrasymachos, maintains that when he talks about justice as the advantage of the stronger, *he is conceiving of justice as the art of complete injustice, the art of absolute despotism through which rulers are able to subjugate whole nations and peoples. He is not talking about petty thievery and small–time criminal acts to which weak people, "the many," refer with shameful epithets and names as being "unjust."*

He claims that when a person is able to practice injustice on a great scale as a master artisan, other people do not refer to him with shameful names. They refer to him with honorific titles.

Hence, *true justice, justice in the exact sense of the term, is supreme injustice*: the advantage of the ruler and the disadvantage of the ruled.

After drenching Socrates with this flood of oratory and attempting to leave, under pressure from the other listeners to stay, *Socrates tells Thrasymachos what they are trying to define is no small thing. It is the whole conduct of human life, how each one of us might live as profitably as possible.* In Jonathan Haidt's term, they are talking about "moral psychology."

Socrates then accuses Thrasymachos of not caring at all whether, in ignorance of what he claims to know, the rest of them live better or worse lives.

Socrates claims he is not convinced that, *even if never observed,* injustice is more profitable than justice, or that the unjust man lives a more profitable life than the just. He wants Thrasymachos to convince him, stand by what he has said, or, if he changes what he has said, to do it openly, not in secret. While Thrasymachos wants Socrates to be *precise* and *exact* in his replies, and while Thrasymachos had previously agreed that the physician in the *exact* sense of the term was a healer, not a moneymaker, regarding the shepherd, Thrasymachos finds no need to be *exact.*

Just as the art of medicine, the art of shepherding takes care of its *precise*, not an incidental, subject. *Precisely speaking*, Socrates says the subject of the art of shepherding is the welfare of sheep just as *precisely speaking* the subject of medicine is the health of patients; money making is no more the art of the shepherd than it is the art of the physician; the subject of the art of the political ruler is the advantage of the ruled, their improvement, not that of the ruler; each art (like medicine, piloting) offers its own specific benefit depending upon the subject that it improves; unless Thrasymachos wants to reduce all arts to one (*like, in the tradition of René Descartes, Jonathan Haidt, David Hume, and Jean-Jacques Rousseau want to do*), the medical art provides health; the pilot's art a safe voyage; and the moneymaking art money.

Socrates then asks Thrasymachos whether Thrasymachos would call the art of money making "medical" if someone's health improves during the practice of making money? Or the medical art the "moneymaking" art if someone gets wealthy while practicing the art of medicine?

After Thrasymachos admits he would not, Socrates says the reason Thrasymachos would not is because each art has a specific subject that it improves. If some benefit comes to all the arts when each art practices its art, this common benefit must be the result of some art other than the specific arts in question. For this reason, Socrates maintains no artist, no ruler, chooses to practice an art, rule, without some form of pay, such as money, honor, or a penalty (such as that of the "best men," who only rule because they fear the rule of a worse person), because doing so involves taking on some other subject's difficulties. In no way, then, will he concede to Thrasymachos that justice is the advantage of the stronger.

So, Socrates returns to Thrasymachos' claim that perfect injustice is true justice and that justice as Socrates conceives it is not and asks Thrasymachos whether he calls injustice a vice, and justice as Socrates conceives it a virtue.

Haidt's hero Thrasymachos says he holds just the reverse, that injustice is a virtue, profitable; *a kind of wisdom, prudence*; and, while not a vice, Socratic justice is "naïve simplemindedness," unprofitable; *a kind of foolishness, imprudence. Put in Haidt's modern business parlance, Thrasymachos is saying that, so long as you can protect your brand, your reputation, and hide your injustice from public opinion, circling the wagons and being unjust is better, wiser, than being just and suffering damage to your reputation*!

To sum up Thrasymachos' view, Socrates asks Thrasymachos whether he considers unjust people *prudent and good*. Thrasymachos replies that he does, so long as they understand "unjust" people to mean "supremely unjust people," tyrants, if they are not caught, not petty thieves.

Socrates says that Thrasymachos' response surprises him. While

An Introduction to Ragamuffin Ethics

his reply puts his argument on a firmer footing, more difficult to refute, Socrates had expected him to hold the opposite. Then he immediately attacks Thrasymachos' understanding of injustice and justice.

He asks Thrasymachos whether:

1) a just man would seek not to equal (act specifically the same as) another just man, and would he ignore the limits of action used as a measure by another just man;

[To which Thrasymachos says he would seek to act equally to the just man; otherwise Socrates' just man would not be the pleasant simpleton he is.]

2) the just man would claim and think himself to exceed (be morally unequal, superior to) an unjust man;

[Thrasymachos says he would claim and think it, but would not be able to do it.]

3) the unjust man claims to exceed (be morally unequal, superior to) the just man;

[To which Thrasymachos replies, of course he does, since he claims to excel everyone.]

After inferring that the unjust man will not seek to match the unjust man and unjust action and will seek to get as much of everything he can, Socrates puts his argument another way. He says that the unjust man will seek to behave unequally to his like and unlike, but the just man will only seek to behave unequally to his unlike. According to Thrasymachos [*and Haidt*], the unjust man is wise and good, while the just man is foolish and bad. Each is like what he seeks to do.

[Thrasymachos agrees.]

Socrates then makes an analogy from the arts of music and medicine. He asks Thrasymachos whether the musical men and physicians exist and have opposites.

[Thrasymachos agrees they exist and have opposites.]

Then Socrates asks which is wise: the musical or unmusical man, the physician or non-physician?

[Thrasymachos says that the musical man and the physician are wise and the unmusical man and non-physician are not.]

Socrates takes Thrasymachos to mean that the musical man and physician are wise in their actions, and the unmusical man and non-physician are not.

[Thrasymachos agrees.]

This being so, Socrates asks about the behavior of musical and unmusical men, and physicians and non-physicians. In each case of opposites, Socrates wants to know whether a musical person would seek to exceed, or precisely match, another musical person in measuring the limits of tension in tightening strings of a musical instrument; a physician would seek to exceed, or precisely match, another physician in measuring the limits of a medical activity, such as how much a patient should eat, drink, or exercise?

[Thrasymachos says that both would seek to match, not exceed, the respective members of their professions, or as Socrates calls them "their likes" not "their unlikes," in what they are and in their actions. They are what they are like.]

Then Socrates asks Thrasymachos whether in every form of knowledge, *a person who knows would choose to do or say more than another person who knows. Would not such a person seek to do or say precisely as much as a person who knows, an expert, would do or say?*

According to Thrasymachos, are not such people like what they resemble? Are not people that know "knowledgeable people," people they are like?

When Thrasymachos agrees that, in such cases, this might be necessary, Socrates asks him whether an ignorant person would not seek precisely to match his like or unlike (that is, the knower or the ignorant person). If so, would he be like another ignorant person, would that be what he is like?

After Thrasymachos reluctantly agrees, Socrates draws the following conclusions: the man who knows is better, wiser, than the one who does not; the wise is good; the wise and good will not seek to exceed the good and wise, but only their opposites, the ignorant and bad; the foolish and bad, being foolish and bad, will seek to exceed everyone, will seek to conform their actions to no standard, of the good or the bad. because they had agreed that people are what they resemble (that is, analogously are what they essentially share in common with someone else), and they have agreed that the just man is like (that is, is a species of) the wise and good and the unjust man is like (that is, is a species of) the foolish and bad. Socrates has, thereby, demonstrated to Thrasymachos and their audience that that *the just man is wise and good and the unjust man is foolish and bad*

At this point, Socrates reports that he had to drag these conclusions out of Thrasymachos with a lot of effort and sweat, because they were in the middle of summer. He makes special note that Thrasymachos was doing something he had never seen him do before: *blushing* (thereby suggesting that Thrasymachos was *embarrassed and ashamed* because Socrates had publicly damaged his reputation and shown him to be weak!)

Socrates claims, further, that he has shown, and Thrasymachos has been forced to agree, that justice is wise and good and injustice is foolish and bad and that, having established these two principles, Socrates is now in a position easily to refute the claim that the injustice is strong and that the lives of the unjust are more profitable than the lives of the just.

Socrates proceeds to do this (still dragging Thrasymachos along) by maintaining that, because injustice is foolish and bad, it cannot be strong; reinforcing this simple argument by relating it to Thrasymachos' claim that supremely unjust people, tyrants, are strong; and criticizing this claim by asking Thrasymachos whether, when they oppress whole nations, tyrants do so in combination with, or completely without, justice.

Thrasymachos says that, if, as Socrates says, justice is wisdom, they would have to combine their actions with justice. If justice is what he said it is, they would not. He cannot maintain that claim for long, however, because he has to admit that Socrates is right when Socrates immediately asks whether any group of human beings (city, army, gang of robbers, and so on) that set out for some common, unjust purpose could not achieve that aim if they acted unjustly toward each other. Thrasymachos admits that the injustice would hinder their operation.

Socrates explains that the reason tyrants must use justice among their partners when behaving tyrannically toward others is because, wherever it exists (in an individual or a group) injustice brings factions, hatreds, disagreements internal conflict in one person and between different parts of the soul, making a man an enemy to himself; enemies among two or more people; and, if the gods are just, as Thrasymachos appears reluctantly to agree, it will make him an enemy of the gods (352A–352B).

Socrates maintains that Thrasymachos is wrong to say that injustice would hinder collective operation. Wherever it is present *it totally destroys* that in which it exists because *the power of collective action comes from justice*, not injustice. Absolutely unjust people are incapable of doing anything together. Perfectly unjust people can accomplish nothing together. The power of unjust people comes from the fact that such people are not completely unjust, that while, as a group, they treat someone else unjustly, they do not behave unjustly toward each other as they do so.

Having established that *injustice is foolishness* and *a universal principle of hatred and faction*, Socrates finds himself finally to be in a position to start to refute Thrasymachos' claim that the life of the unjust is happier than the life of the just. He says that this question is no minor issue. It involves how we should live.

He starts to refute the claim by making an analogy by means of several questions, asking Thrasymachos whether a horse and ears have a work (by which he means some one, whole act, or end, that all their parts cooperatively, or organizationally, incline to produce, such as being a horse in the case of a horse or hearing in the case of ears), some one act, that these things cooperatively, as parts, do best, or better than anything else.

Thrasymachos agrees they have a work. And, when asked, he also agrees that a pruning-knife also has a work in the sense that it is more useful for cutting a vine twig than is a regular cutting knife or a chisel.

Socrates then asks whether things that have a work also have a virtue (by which Socrates means some proper or precise act that initiates their work, the acts of seeing and hearing; for example, color for the eyes and sound for the ears). Without such virtues, necessary conditions of work, he says the eyes and ears could not do their work well, and Thrasymachos agrees.

Like the eyes and ears, Socrates next argues that the soul has a work, something like ruling, planning, caring, and living. He asks whether these acts are properly works of soul, and Thrasymachos agrees that they are.

This being the case, Socrates asks Thrasymachos whether the soul also has a virtue, something (that is, a quality) without which it can do none of its work well, and Thrasymachos agrees the soul has a work.

Such being the case, with Thrasymachos agreeing to everything else he says to the end of Book 1, Socrates says that they have already agreed that justice enables a soul to do its work well and injustice causes a soul to do its work badly. This means that justice enables a human being to live well, not badly. If just people live well and unjust people live badly, then just people are happy and unjust people (*no matter how much they try to hide their injustice and protect their reputations and brand, as Haidt would encourage them to do*) are miserable; since to be miserable is not profitable, and to be happy is to be profitable, Socrates concludes that Thrasymachos is wrong to claim that injustice is more profitable than justice and that the unjust live more profitable lives than the just.

4. Mortimer J. Adler's correct analysis of the Story of the Ring of Gyges

As then general editor of the board of editors of the *Encyclopaedia Britannica*, Mortimer J. Adler, sagely observed in a Christ Church sermon "On the Golden Rule," on August, 1991 in Aspen, Colorado, moral philosophy's first principle—its categorical imperative—*is not* the moral psychology principle of Jonathan Haidt: "*Intuitions come first, strategic reasoning second.*" It is, as Socrates, Plato, and Aristotle well understood: "You ought to seek everything that is really good for you and nothing else. Only when you know what is really good (e.g., truth is really good for human beings to know) can you draw any conclusions, such as seek the truth."

Given knowledge of this truth, Adler tells us we can face the most difficult problem in moral philosophy: the age-old problem that of the apparent opposition between altruism and selfishness that Glaucon raises in the Story of the Ring of Gyges.

To do this, Adler maintains that we must first recognize that real human goods exist, goods universal to human nature. "Only then," he states, "can we understand the difference between what is really good for all human beings and what is only apparently good to some individuals but not to others." Only then do we become able to discover what we ought to seek for ourselves and for others as individuals

Recognition of the difference between the existence of a universal human nature and real human goods allows us to derive the second precept of natural moral law derived from the first: Do no harm. Do not injure other people by depriving them of what is really good for them.

To make his argument clear, Adler considers what are traditionally called the four cardinal moral virtues: fortitude or courage, temperance, justice, and prudence. He says that, "of these, temperance and courage are entirely self-regarding virtues; and justice is entirely other-regarding."

He adds that, if a person can be temperate and courageous without simultaneously being just, he or she can seek the good and, simultaneously, hurt others: be unjust toward others.

And if that were the case, Adler concludes that the "golden rule" could not be a moral principle. A person would not have to do unto others what he or she would have them do unto him or her. Like Thrasymachos, we would want other people to be just to us because that helps us attain what is really good for us. But, if we could get away with it, we would be able to seek what is really good for us without being just toward other people. This, Adler says, is the problem raised by The Story of the Ring of Gyges: "If, with the ring of Gyges, you can be unjust to others and get away with it, why not do so? What's in it for you to be just to others, if you can seek your own good without being just toward them?"

If, on the other hand, seeking your own good without simultaneously being just to others is, as Plato maintained, impossible, then, assuming that we want others to do what is really good for us, we must act toward others as we would have them act toward us.

While Adler answers this question in terms of Aristotle (someone that Jonathan Haidt totally ignores, as if Aristotle contributed nothing to the debate about moral behavior in Western culture), the solution lies in the discussion that Plato had with Thrasymachos and Aristotle apparently inherited from Plato and Socrates.

As Plato recognized, these moral virtues are not existentially separate virtues. A person cannot have one without having all of them. We cannot have any one of the three without having the other two. Only a temperate person (one able to forego pleasure for a really higher good) can be courageous. And only courageous people can be temperate. Justice, in turn, is the habit of treating other people temperately and courageously. As Plato demonstrated to Thrasymachos, however, none of these ways of behaving is possible without being practically wise, without having the habit of practical knowledge called "prudence," which requires individuals often to seek counsel from individuals more knowledgeable than themselves (people with greater experience at living), to secure real individual goods.

As Adler says, "Prudence consists in choosing the right means for the right reason, the right end." Thus, even if he can do damage control by circling the wagons and protect his reputation, "there is no prudent thief or murderer, for his reason for being crafty is wrong." According to Adler, because the means he chooses for getting away with it is not a choice for the right reason: real human good, something that fulfills the real need of human nature, we should call such a person (*like Jonathan Haidt*) "clever," not "prudent."

By the natural inclination of human nature, only one right end exists for all human beings: habitually perfecting our human faculties so that we habitually incline to make choices under the direction of a prudent reasoning faculty, will, and emotions; choosing-faculties that are in touch, not out of touch, with what is and is not a real human good for us in the individual situation, or what Adler calls "a whole life enriched by the possession of everything that is really good for human beings."

If, as Plato and Adler maintain, prudence causes every moral habit to be a virtue, this is because prudence inclines all the faculties of human choice (intellect, will, and emotions) to be disposed to choose means for the same reason: because they are really enabling means for choosing a real human good over an illusory one and a greater human good over a lesser one in the individual situation.

In such a case, we cannot be temperate or courageous without simultaneously being just. As Adler notes, this is simply another way of saying that we cannot really act for our individual happiness without simultaneously acting for the happiness of others.

"Hence, there is no conflict between selfishness and altruism. The other-regarding aspect of virtue (altruism) is inseparable from the self-regarding aspects of virtue (selfishness)."

5. A more detailed analysis of the sophistry of Jonathan Haidt's
The Righteous Mind

While Jonathan Haidt cautions his readers (p. 316) to "Beware of anyone who insists," apparently like Mortimer Adler, "that there is one true morality for all people, times, and places—particularly if that morality is founded upon a single foundation," the person to beware of is not the person like Adler, but the person like Jonathan Haidt, who, by his own admission, in the tradition of his hero David Hume, celebrates fame, reputation, more than truth, more than being right.

While Haidt celebrates Hume as a paragon of moral excellence, Hume was so professionally shallow that, in his autobiography, he confessed that love of literary fame had been his ruling passion.[5] Hume's morally unprofessional behavior is confirmed by an event that historians of philosophy often note about him: when the first two books of his *Treatise of Human Nature* were not as highly acclaimed as he wanted, *Hume wrote a laudatory review of the previous works, hoping thereby to influence literary opinion on his behalf and prevent his third book from falling upon similarly deaf ears.*[6]

While being a professional does not demand that a person be a moral saint, it does demand a minimum level of professional honesty. Even Thramsymachos' *bands of unjust brothers* have to treat each other with minimum standards of professional honor among thieves, a standard that the unprofessional scoundrel (Haidt's *moral hero*) Hume was unable to achieve.

Hence, while Jonathan Haidt might want to claim that his moral psychology is radically different from that of Thrasymachos, that claim is belied, among many other things, by Haidt's choice of David Hume as a hero, Haidt's caricature of Glaucon, and his approval of the Rousseauean utopian socialist, Émile Durkheim's fascist claim (one with which Adolf Hitler, Benito Mussolini, Chairman Mao, and Joseph Stalin would heartily agree): "What is moral is everything that is a source of solidarity; everything that forces man to . . . regulate his actions by something other than . . . his own egoism." (Haidt, p. 270)

The utopian socialist nature of Haidt's moral psychology posing as science helps explain the extensive number of absurdities that Haidt would have his readers accept, such as that "anyone who tells you that all societies, in all eras, should be using one particular matrix, resting on one particular configuration of moral foundations, is a fundamentalist of one sort or another" (p. 316).

This claim is false, absurd. Every moral foundation rests upon an understanding of human nature, must accept that human beings are free agents, that we have intrinsic powers and abilities of intellect, will, and emotions that enable us freely to author, cause, our own acts that enable us to be rightly praised and blamed, rewarded and

545

punished as morally responsible agents—something that Haidt's moral hero David Hume categorically denies: existence of causality and individual powers and abilities.

A person cannot be wrong about human nature and right about the nature of morality. Human nature is the foundation, the one particular matrix, of all moral agreements and disagreements, of all moral principles for everyone, always, and everywhere.

Hume denies the reality of human nature, human faculties of knowing and willing, and of causality. In so doing, he undermines essential principles of all moral intelligibility and responsibility. Yet Haidt has the shameless gall to maintain (p. 116), "Hume got it right. When he died in 1776, he and other sentimentalists had laid a superb foundation for moral science."

Similarly false and outrageous are Haidt's claims that (p. 271), "The best known systems of normative ethics are the one-receptor systems I described in chapter 6: utilitarianism (which tells us to maximize overall welfare) and deontology (which in its Kantian form tells us to make the rights and autonomy of others paramount") and that (p. 315) his beloved topic of moral psychology "is the key to understanding politics, religion, and our spectacular rise to planetary dominance." Apparently, Haidt never heard of the natural law moral teaching of Aristotle, Cicero, St. Thomas Aquinas, and Jesuit natural law moralists like Francisco Suárez.

"Fundamentalism," in the sense of religious, or Haidt's secular, fundamentalism, is a species of skepticism and sophistry. Like skeptics, fundamentalists like Haidt and his hero Hume distrust reason. Like sophists, fundamentalists like Haidt and Hume deny the existence of natures, secondary causes, in things. They think that *feelings* are the measure of all things. People who are convinced that they possess reliable knowing faculties of sense and intellect are not fundamentalists. Those like Haidt and Hume, who distrust reason in touch with reality and sense knowledge of the real, substituting "gut feeling" for sense knowledge of the real are fundamentalists.

To give their rationally incoherent thinking the aura of science, because scientific talk is expressed in terms of "universals," generalizations, "All" statements (like "All hydrogen is combustible"), social science fundamentalists like Haidt and Hume maintain that words do not originate as natural signs, initially generated by individuals, of some mind-independent being, the nature of a thing.

Instead, words are social conventions, inventions of social agreement between people devoid of any and all vocabulary (even body language) to call some common feeling or thought by a common name. Because, like Hume, Haidt is a nominalist, he marvels at the supposed discovery by the expert on "chimpanzee cognition" Michael Tomasello that words express shared feelings, shared personal understandings. As Haidt says (p. 207), "Tomasello notes that a word is not a relationship between a sound and an object. It is an agreement *among people* who share a joint representation of things in their world, and who share a set of conventions for communicating with each other about those things."

Like all sophists who, going back to Protagoras in ancient Greece, maintain that words do not originate as individual signs of the natures of things, who claim that universal conceptualization is an effect of shared naming, Haidt and Tomasello cannot explain how human beings who have no knowledge of what individuals are can enter into a social contract to share with others names of things that, even by body language, they do not know or share. How does a person, even by grunts, name things a person does not know? Having no knowledge about what we want to communicate, how do we even use body language to grunt out these contracts?

Similarly absurd is for Haidt to have written a book connecting together over more than 300 pages of arguments that he appears to think are scientific, are the product of rational intelligence. Apparently, like Hume and Rousseau, by scientific intelligence Haidt means a name for a plurality of Enlightened, socially-evolved feelings. This would explain his numerous references to Charles Darwin and to the absurd claims that the brain and parts of the brain, like neurons, can be smart or dumb (p. 90).

The brain, neurons, no more think or decide than the human eye sees. No physical organ can apprehend its own activity. The eye cannot see it sees. To do so the eye would have to have itself presented physically to itself. For a similar reason the brain cannot know itself knowing. Human beings see, know, and know that we see and know. If we do not know we see and know, we do not see or know.

Haidt claims (Id.):

> We should see each individual as being limited, like a neuron. A neuron is really good at one thing: summing up the stimulation coming from the dentdrites to "decide" whether to fire a pulse along its axon. A neuron by itself isn't very smart. But if you put neurons together in the right way you get a brain; you get an emergent system that is much smarter and more flexible than a single neuron.

The chief problem in what Haidt says immediately above is that, no matter how many dumb neurons you have banging off one another forever, they will still be a bunch of dumb neurons banging off one another. Putting disconnected multitudes together requires that they share a common end or aim. Modern science was largely founded upon the denial of the reality of ends or aims in things. And even if aims, ends, do exist in things, because knowing is a living act, knowledge of such aims has to come from the principle that causes life in the organ, not from the organ considered in itself (once, again, because no organ can know its own act).

Peter A. Redpath

Moreover, if sense and intellectual knowing are acts of physical organs, they are subject to the laws of chemistry and physics. In such a situation, human beings are not free agents. Laws of chemistry and physics, not the free choice of the human will, determine moral activity. If that is so, moral activity cannot exist, and Haidt's moral psychology cannot, does not, exist.

If, by "reason," a person means logic, Haidt is right to caution readers about any *individual's* ability to reason. (He is a case in point.) A major problem that Haidt has, however, is that he conflates reason with sophistic logic. As a result, he thinks (pp. 88 to 90) we apprehend truth through sense feelings (sense intuition), that "anyone who values truth should stop worshipping reason," and that reasoning "evolved not to help us find the truth but to help us engage in arguments, persuasion, and manipulation in the context of discussions with other people," (p. 89 [*which appears, by his own admission, to be the chief reason Haidt wrote his book!*]).

Haidt's location of truth in sense feeling would help explain why he thinks he is a "scientist." Apparently, again, this is because he applies the method of empirical testing and sense observation. Even though no one can empirically verify that all truth lies in empirical verification, Haidt appears to think such a claim is evidently true.

Unhappily, however, application of empirical testing and sense observation is no essential sign of possessing truth or being a scientist. Verification is an act of the human intellect working in conjunction with the human senses. Considered in and of itself, empirical verification is an oxymoron. (For example, no chemist can empirically verify that "all hydrogen is combustible" because this would entail blowing up all the hydrogen in the universe.)

Neither the senses nor reason apprehend truth separate from cooperation with each other. Just as a person, not the sense of sight or hearing, sees or hears, so the person, not the intellect, or the sense

549

of sight or hearing, apprehends truth. If that is the truth, then Haidt's whole book is an exercise in sophistry, a behavioral contradiction, designed more (like his hero David Hume) to enhance his professional reputation than to get at the truth.

At the end of this article is a diagram of Jonathan Haidt's "Intuitionist's Model."[7] As anyone the least familiar with Plato, or anyone who has read Socrates's discussion with Thrasymachos, can recognize, Haidt's "intuitionist's model" is, with some incidental changes, largely a description of the Socratic method that Plato employs throughout his dialogues.

According to Plato, all reasoning is an act of recollection of a knowledge that human beings had acquired *through direct intuition* of the Forms (natures of things) in a previous life. For Plato, because we cannot reason about what we in no way know to be, human reason has only one possible object: what a person knows to be. Because in the present life matter obscures our direct observation of physical things, Plato maintained that we human beings cannot trust the external senses to give us precise knowledge. Hence, to get precise knowledge, we must, with the help of human reason, constantly test our present sense observations and other knowledge on the basis of what we know better than what we are now observing (by testing our intuitions recollected from our knowledge we had in a prior life against examples from sense, or intellectual, reality that we presently apprehend).

The chief difference between Haidt's model and that of Plato and Socrates is that Haidt thinks Humean-like feelings and popular reputation, not knowledge of being right and of making the right choice and respecting professional judgment made by experts in knowing and choosing (people with wisdom and prudence), should be the chief measures of science and human choice.

The Socratic method (*elenchos*) is essentially based upon

publicly shaming fools like Haidt out of their foolishness. It essentially respects expert opinion over the opinion of people who lack professional experience and knowledge of a subject. For this reason, in the *Crito*, when encouraged by Crito to leave prison because of the damage to their popular reputation that his friends might suffer, Socrates tells Crito they should not care about popular opinion, even if negative popular opinion can cause what Crito thinks is trouble. They should care about the opinion of the few, experts in virtue, who will know that things were done as they should have been done (*Crito*, 44B–D).

Plato agrees with Haidt that intuitions come first. He simply disagrees that intuitions are first apprehended in this life and are blind to intellectual content. Like his student Aristotle and St. Thomas Aquinas, Plato thinks that human beings have a natural ability to know what is happening in the human emotions. For this reason Plato claims that the human emotions have a sense knowledge of real goods and evils that cause pleasure and pain, hope, fear, and anger. According to St. Thomas Aquinas, the human emotions are contained within the sense faculty of cogitative, or particular, reason, which some other forms of animal life also share. Thomas attributes animal "instinct" to this faculty and explains that emotions like fear, daring, and anger react emotionally by sensing danger and difficulty that escape the notice of external sense faculties like sight and hearing. Hence, St. Thomas states that, by instinct, the sheep runs away from the wolf because the sheep has a natural knowledge that wolves are dangerous to sheep, and not because it does not like the color of the wolf.[8]

As Mortimer J. Adler observed in famous 1940 article presented in New York City at a conference on science, philosophy, and religion, entitled "God and the Professors," like the health and disease of the body, cultural health consists in organizational health, the harmonious functioning of its parts, and cultures die from lack of harmonious functioning of these same parts. He added that "science, philosophy, and religion are certainly major parts of European culture; their distinction from one another as quite separate parts is certainly the most characteristic cultural achievement of modern times. But if they have not been properly distinguished, they cannot be properly related; and unless they are properly related, properly ordered to one another, cultural disorder, such as that of modern times, inevitably results."[9]

In short, Adler was maintaining that, if, like David Hume and Jonathan Haidt, we do not properly understand the natures of things, especially of culturally-related organizations like religion, science, philosophy, we cannot properly relate and unite them as complementary parts of a coherent cultural whole, or healthy cultural organization. This, however, is precisely the problem we have with solving the decline of Western higher education and culture, and the coddling of the American college and university students in our time. We do not properly understand the natures of things, and especially of the natures of philosophy, science, and religion; the way common sense essentially relates to all these, and how, through this relation, the natural human desire to have common sense regulate all aspects of human life uses the natures of things, arts, philosophy, science, and religion to generate cultures and civilizations as parts of organizational wholes.

During the early part of the twentieth century, this lack of common sense was so bad that it prompted Adler to write his scathing 1940 *Harper's Magazine* article "This Prewar Generation" in which, among other things, he accused post-World War I American young people of having a mindset largely similar to that of Hitler's youth. "Our college students today, like Thrasymachus of old," Adler said, "regard justice as the will of the stronger; but unlike the ancient sophist they cannot make the point as clearly as or defend it as well."[10]

Immediately Adler went on to add that, while American

students might not have read *Mein Kampf* and might not have been inoculated with nihilism's revolutionary spirit, they have become the same sort of realists, "believing only in the same sort of success—money, *fame*, and power." While their understanding of "success" was not identical with that of the Hitler youth, while, by "success," they understood personal advancement (*individual* power, money, fame; not mystical identification of the individual with success of Germany, working for the Fatherland), post-World War I and pre-World War II American youth did not think that democracy was intrinsically superior to fascism. Hence, Adler claimed that American youth would continue to work for democracy only so long as democracy continued to work for them: only so long as it continued to serve their sense of pragmatic liberalism.[11]

Adler did not think that post-World War I American culture alone had initially generated this post-World War I mindset. He maintained that centuries of Western cultural change chiefly related to the replacement of classical philosophical realism by the bastardized substitute of "scientism" had prepared the minds of American youth to become sophists. He argued that this situation was "the last fruition of modern man's exclusive trust in science and his gradual disavowal of whatever lies beyond the field of science as irrational prejudice, an opinion emotionally held."[12]

While Adler considered "the doctrine of scientism" to be "the dominant dogma of American philosophy," during the early part of the twentieth century, he maintained that this last fruition of modern thought had received its finishing touches in university philosophy courses, reaching "its culmination in American pragmatism and all its sequelae—the numerous varieties of positivism." Adler added that all these varieties agreed about one and the same reductionistic point: "Only science gives us valid knowledge of reality."

Such being the case, Adler maintained that, at its best, philosophy "can be nothing more than a kind of commentary on the find-ings of science; and at its worst, when it refuses to acknowledge the exclusive right of scientific method to marshal evidence and draw conclusions therefrom, philosophy is either mere opinion or nonsen-sical verbiage."[13]

In philosophy courses, Adler continued, "the student really learns how to argue like a sophist against all 'values' as subjective and relative." Instead of being the last bulwark against the scientism that every other part of the curriculum, *especially social science*, professes or insinuates, he said, "philosophy courses reinforce the *negativism* of this doctrine by inspiring disrespect for any philosophy which claims to be independent knowledge."

To finish their job, Adler asserted that Philosophy departments used semanticism to implement the ancient sophistries they had revived.

> The student learns to suspect all words, especially abstract words. Statements which cannot be scientifically verified are meaningless. The abstract words which enter into moral judgments—such words as 'justice' and 'right' or even 'liberty' and 'happiness'—have only rhetorical meaning. Denuded of all deceptive verbiage, such judgments can be reduced to statements of what I like or what displeases me. There is no 'should' or 'ought.'[14]

While Adler rightly understood the sophistic nature of most twentieth-century American Philosophy Departments, most twentieth-century U.S. college and university Philosophy Departments were not examples of "the degenerative tendency of modern philosophy." They were, and still are, prime examples of the modern lack of philosophy, of the degenerative cultural effects of the neo-sophistry of "social scientists" like David Hume and Jean-Jacques Rousseau fulfilling its nature in modern culture under the rubrics of "philosophy" and moral psychology. While Jonathan Haidt deserves praise for the fact that, in principle, he rejects moral relativism and is seeking a way to transcend it, the principles he has chosen will never allow him to do so. As the great French historian of philosophy Étienne Gilson was fond of saying, "We think the way we can, not the way we wish." And as that great master of common sense, Gilbert Keith Chesterton once observed:

> Since the modern world began in the sixteenth century, nobody's system of philosophy has really corresponded to everybody's sense of reality: to what if left to themselves common men would call common sense. Each started with a paradox: a peculiar point of view demanding the sacrifice of what they would call a sane point of view. That is one thing common to Hobbes and Hegel, to Kant and Bergson, to Berkeley and William James. A man had to believe something that no normal man would believe if it were suddenly propounded to his simplicity; as that law is above right (*that neurons make decisions*), or right is outside reason, or things are only as we think them, or everything is relative to a reality that is not there. The modern philosopher claims, like a sort of a confidence man, that if once we will grant him this, the rest will be easy; he will straighten out the world if once he is allowed to give this one twist to the mind.[15]

Unhappily, Jonathan Haidt's science of moral psychology is one more instance of the tradition of modern snake oil peddled by modern academic confidence men under the rubric of "science."

Unlike classical philosophers like Plato, Aristotle, Cicero, and the medieval theologian St. Thomas Aquinas, throughout his entire book, Haidt never engages in a consideration of the human will or human freedom and choice. He never identifies or defines "good," "human good," or "human emotions." He repeatedly mischaracterizes the nature of human reason and fails to distinguish theoretical from logical and logical from practical and productive reason.

Beyond these failings, he falsely credits to modern social science the spectacular rise to planetary dominance of the West (p. 315) that, historically, were largely due to the vast college and university system and moral culture developed over centuries by religious groups (such as the Jesuits, who, within 250 years of their founding had established around 600 colleges and universities in Europe). He totally ignores the vast influence that the Oxford Plato scholar John Ruskin (not David Hume) had on Cecil Rhodes and other British aristocrats on the development of the British Commonwealth of Nations whose missionary zeal to spread the influence of Western culture, more than anything else, appears to explain the 20th century's "spectacular rise to global dominance."

To conclude, Jonathan Haidt has next to no familiarity with the Western intellectual tradition, especially its philosophical tradition in the study of ethics. As Mortimer Adler realized decades ago, Aristotle was the only thinker within the West or anywhere else who ever produced anything closely approaching a maturely-developed philosophically/scientifically-based moral psychology. Plato comes second to Aristotle, and he does not come close to Aristotle in his moral psychology. *Jonathan Haidt is no Plato or Aristotle.* Like David Hume, he is, at best, a clever sophist masquerading as a great discoverer, an expert in the "science of moral psychology," and the moral psychology of executive leadership. Even as a sophist, he is second rate, is no David Hume.

About classroom teachers in general, Adler once sagely observed that our proper role in relation to students is that of reading instructors, people who, by training our students to read books written by great discoverers, provide them with the enabling means to enter into first-hand conversation with great discoverers, the first and best of teachers (like Plato and Aristotle); and, thereby, become more highly educated. As Adler well understood, the decades-long coddling and closing of the American mind has chiefly been caused by classroom teachers like Jonathan Haidt who, hungering for professional glory, like David Hume and the sophists of ancient Greece, have presented themselves before generation after generation of uneducated audiences as original and great discoverers.

About a charlatan like Haidt, Adler once wrote, he or she "should not masquerade as one who knows and can teach by virtue of his original discoveries, if he is only one who has learned through being taught. The primary sources of his knowledge should be the primary sources of learning for his students, and such a teacher functions honestly only if he does not aggrandize himself by coming between the great books and their young readers."[16] Such masquerading is, and has been for decades, a chief cause of the coddling and closing of the contemporary American mind.

Unlike the classroom teacher Adler has just described, Haidt has not learned through being taught. His *The Righteous Mind* displays no evidence of his having learned any chief philosophical or scientific principles of moral psychology. He displays no competence to convey a high-school, much less an undergraduate or graduate, university level of understanding of the teachings of Socrates, Plato, Aristotle, Hume, Charles Darwin; or of social psychology or business ethics.

Haidt's claims that he is an expert in moral psychology and that his moral psychology is "moral science" are intellectually misguided or morally and intellectually dishonest. Hopefully, this article will help readers to understand: 1) why Haidt's moral psychology is no moral philosophy or science at all; 2) why they should avoid believing Haidt's caricature-of-Glaucon "got it right," while his caricature-of-

Plato "got it wrong"; 3) why Haidt is no authority from whom anyone should seek sound advice about how to end the current "coddling of the American mind"; and 4) that Haidt and his beloved David Hume are not better guides to living a happy life, running a successful business, and un-coddling the American mind than is the wisdom of Socrates, his student Plato, or Mortimer J. Adler.

Jonathan Haidt's "Intuitionist's Model"

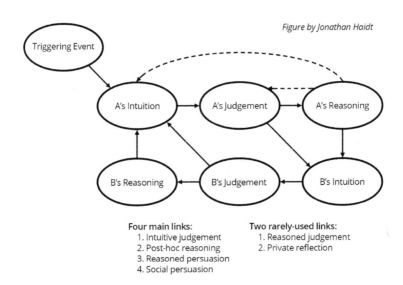

Figure by Jonathan Haidt

Four main links:
1. Intuitive judgement
2. Post-hoc reasoning
3. Reasoned persuasion
4. Social persuasion

Two rarely-used links:
1. Reasoned judgement
2. Private reflection

—Notes—

1. Mortimer J. Adler, "Introduction," in Robert Edward Brennan, *Thomistic Psychology* (New York: Macmillan Publishing Company, 1941), pp. viii–ix.
2. Dominic Bouck, O.P., "Revenge of the Coddled: An Interview with Jonathan Haidt, in First Things," https://www.firstthings. com/blogs/firstthoughts/2015/11/the-revenge-of-the-coddled-an-interview-with-jonathan-haidt, 18 November 2015.

3. Jonathan Haidt, *The Righteous Mind: Why Good People are Divided by Politics and Religion* (New York, Pantheon Books, 2013); Immanuel Kant, "Conjectures on the Beginning of Human History," in Hans Reiss (ed.) and H. B. Nisbet (trans), *Kant: Political Writings* (Cambridge, England: Cambridge University Press, 1992), pp. 221–222. For a detailed account of the Enlightenment principles that essentially generate Haidt's sophistic mindset, see Peter A. Redpath, *Masquerade of the Dream Walkers: Prophetic Theology from the Cartesians to Hegel* (Amsterdam and Atlanta: Editions Rodopi, B.V., 1998).

4. For a detailed understanding of the epistemological teachings of Locke, Hume, and Kant, see Redpath, *Masquerade of the Dream Walkers: Prophetic Theology from the Cartesians to Hegel*, pp. 33–184.

5. David Hume, *My Own Life*, 18 April 1776, http://www.bartleby.com/209/785.html.

6. Charles W. Hendel, "Editor's Introduction," in David Hume, *An Inquiry Concerning the Principles of Morals*, ed. Charles W. Hendel (Indianapolis, Ind. and New York: The Bobbs-Merrill Company, Inc., 1957), pp. viii–ix.

7. I thank Peter DeMarco, founder and president of the Priority Thinking Institute for providing me with this diagram of Jonathan Haidt's "Intuitionist's Model."

8. St. Thomas Aquinas, *Summa theologiae*, 1, q. 78, a. 4.

9. Mortimer J. Adler, "God and the Professors," in *Philosophy is Everybody's Business*, ed. Max Weismann, 9:3 (Winter 2003), pp. 7–24. I thank my friend Max Weismann (r.i.p.), former director of the Center for the Study of The Great Ideas, for providing me with a copy of this article.

10. Mortimer J. Adler, "This Prewar Generation," in Mortimer J. Adler, *Reforming Education: The Opening of the American Mind*, ed. Geraldine van Doren (New York: Macmillan Publishing Company and London, England: Collier Macmillan Publishers, 1988), pp. 7–9.

11. Id.

12. Id., 9.
13. Id., 9–11.
14. Id., 12.
15. Gilbert Keith Chesterton, *St. Thomas Aquinas*: *The Dumb Ox*, in George Marlin, Richard P. Rabatin, and John L. Swan (gen. eds.), *The Collected Works of G.K. Chesterton*, 3 vols. (San Francisco: Ignatius Press, 1986), vol. 2, p. 514. My addition in italics.
16. Mortimer J. Adler, *How to Read a Book* (London: Jarrolds Publishers, Ltd., 1949), p. 35.

CENTER FOR THE STUDY OF THE GREAT IDEAS
Founded in 1990 by Mortimer J. Adler & Max Weismann

A NOT-FOR-PROFIT EDUCATIONAL CORPORATION

21 W. GOETHE STREET - 8G
CHICAGO, IL 60610
E-MAIL: mailto:thegreatideas@rcn.com
HOMEPAGE: http://www.TheGreatIdeas.org

Questions for Study and Discussion

Author's Introduction

1. What is the chief reason the author gives for having written this book?

2. When he was a youth, what was a chief thing that had annoyed the author about the way St. Thomas's ethics had been taught?

3. According to the author, how should St. Thomas's ethics chiefly be taught?

4. According to the author, what is harmful and helpful about the casuistic-apologetic method of teaching Thomistic ethics?

5. According to him, what is "the best apologetical moral tool bar none for the defense of universal moral principles that have guided people for centuries within the West and throughout the world"?

6. Does the author of this work claim to have written this work chiefly as an ethicist? If not, why not? And in what capacity does he claim chiefly to have written it?

7. According to the author, how does this work complement a chief aim that he has had for writing two other works published previously to this one?

8. According to him, how are metaphysics and ethics "more than subjects of study in which some people in the past and present have had, or have, an interest"?

9. According to the author, how does the approach to metaphysics

and ethics taken by Aristotle and St. Thomas help to make intelligible and solve a "leadership deficit" present in the West today?

10. What is a chief claim upon which, for decades, the author's research into Western intellectual history has been based? Do you agree with this claim? If not, why not? If so, why?

11. According to the author, why does the reality of ethics and the existence of philosophy for the ancient Greeks depend upon the reality of a power psychology"?

12. According to the author, what did Socrates do to increase the ancient Greek understanding of philosophic/scientific thought?

13. According to him, what precise roles did Plato and Aristotle play in advancing ancient Greek philosophic/scientific, metaphysical and ethical, understanding beyond what Socrates had accomplished?

14. According to the author, what major intellectual fraud did seventeenth-century Western intellectuals perpetrate and what subsequent problems did this fraud cause?

15. In the trilogy of works that this author has recently written, why does he think he has not been doing anything especially novel? What does he think he has been chiefly doing?

16. What major teachings of St. Thomas does the author think Mortimer J. Adler, Jacques Maritain, and Étienne Gilson overlooked that caused them to be unable to understand St. Thomas's teaching about philosophy "considered as a whole and in detail"?

17. According to the author, what contributions to improving our understanding of the teachings of St. Thomas about philosophy and science did Armand A. Maurer, Charles Bonaventure Crowley, and Fran O'Rourke make beyond those contributions of Adler, Maritain, and Gilson?

18. According to the author, what chiefly caused Gilson to be unable to understand St. Thomas's teaching about the nature of genera and species?

19. According to him, what has been the devastating impact that the general ignorance contemporary Thomists have had about the actual teachings of St. Thomas on the contemporary Catholic Church and Western civilization considered as a whole?

20. What does he think will be the special impact of this general ignorance of the teachings of St. Thomas upon the Church's *new evangelization* movement and revival of Catholic education? Why?

21. Precisely what steps does the author think the Church must take for its new evangelization movement and revival of Catholic education to succeed?

22. Precisely what major obstacle does the author think exists within the Church that started around the time of Vatican II that his recent trilogy of books can help remove?

23. For what audience does the author say he *has not* chiefly written this book, and why?

24. For what audience(s) does the author say he *has* chiefly written this book, and why?

25. For what reasons does the author say he finally decided to subtitle Volume 2 of his *A Not-So-Elementary Christian Metaphysics* "An Introduction to Ragamuffin Thomism," and of this current work in ethics "An Introduction to Ragamuffin Ethics"?

26. What does the author mean by the terms "Born-Again Thomism," "Ragamuffin Thomism," and "Ragamuffin Ethics"?

27. Why does the author say he decided to entitle this book: *The Moral Psychology of St. Thomas*: *An Introduction to Ragamuffin Ethics*?

An Introduction to Ragamuffin Ethics

Chapter 1: The Wise Man's Job, God's Goodness, and the Goodness of the Created Order

1. According to the author, why does no way possibly exist to render an accurate report of the nature of St. Thomas's teaching about ethics without considering his understanding of human nature and the created universe?

2. According to a chief aim of this book, why does this book need to start to fulfill its nature by considering what St. Thomas says about human nature as part of the order of creation?

The office of the wise man within the created order

1. According to St. Thomas, why is the office of the wise man to know the order existing within things in both speculative and practical ways: to recognize and establish order in things?

2. Why is St. Thomas essentially correct when he says that arts and sciences are architectonically ordered or arranged?

3. Precisely how do performance arts and sciences essentially differ from productive arts and sciences?

4. What name does St. Thomas give to wholes generated by uniting qualitatively different and unequally perfect parts into a harmonious unit? What name might we commonly use today to signify such a unit?

5. According to him, what is the origin of all species?

6. According to St. Thomas, what does no specialized art or science ever study?

7. According to him, what must a person who is totally, or absolutely, wise (a metaphysician) study and know?

The twofold job of every science and every wise man

1. According to St. Thomas, what two duties does the nature of every science essentially involve?

2. In effecting its work, what does St. Thomas say the job of science essentially involves knowing?

3. What chief reason does St. Thomas give for every science essentially involving these two acts of knowing?

4. According to him, what three duties does a metaphysician's or theologian's job essentially involve?

5. As the person most perfectly possessed of science, what does St. Thomas claim is the special responsibility of the metaphysician, and why?

The fourfold way that order relates to human reason

1. According to St. Thomas, what is the fourfold way in which order relates to human reason?

2. For him, how does this fourfold order essentially relate to the existence of different arts and sciences?

3. According to St. Thomas, what do the organizationally-arranged (composite) wholes that reason studies comprise?

4. What does St. Thomas mean by the formal object of a science?

How differentiation of the arts and sciences naturally occurs on the basis of an essential relation existing between habits of the human soul and qualitatively more or less perfect organizations that the human soul needs to consider to satisfy its natural and supernatural life-perfecting need of being perfect as a human soul

1. According to St. Thomas, through the different orders and com-

posite wholes that reason considers through its habits, what effect is generated within the human soul?

2. For him, how does differentiation of the sciences arise?

The meaning of "perfect" and "good"

1. What does St. Thomas mean by "perfect"?

2. What does he mean by "good"?

3. How does St. Thomas distinguish the meanings of the terms "perfect" and "good" from that of the term "being" (*ens*)?

How the ideas of being (*ens* and *esse*) and good (*bonum*) intellectually and causally relate

1. According to him, how do the ideas of being (*ens* and *esse*) and good (*bonum*) intellectually and causally relate?

2. For St. Thomas, why is everything that exists, in some way, good and perfect?

The idea of "good" and its relation to efficient, formal, and final causes

1. According to St. Thomas, in what way does the idea of good in some way contain the ideas of final, efficient, and formal causes?

2. According to him, how do the ideas of unity, good, and beauty have the same foundation?

3. For St. Thomas, how do the ideas of unity, good, and beauty differ?

God's perfection in goodness and how it relates to that of creatures as a cause of diversity and distinction in them

1. What is crucial to understand about St. Thomas's teaching as a whole regarding God being the first efficient cause of everything?

2. According to him, what threefold perfection exists in God?

3. For him, why do diversity and distinction exist in things?

How, as an imperfect likeness of God, form causes generic and specific order, hierarchy of genera and species within the universe

1. According to St. Thomas, how does form cause generic and specific order, and a hierarchy of genera and species, within the universe?

2. According to him, how does form cause a kind of perfection, beauty, and goodness within a composite whole?

How inequality in qualitative perfection in having (possessing) is the origin of all plurality, diversity, difference, and order within all genera and species of things

1. According to St. Thomas, how is inequality in qualitative perfection in having, or possessing, the origin of all plurality, diversity, difference, and order within all genera and species of things?

2. According to him, why does form play a greater role than matter in the origin of all diversity and difference within material things?

A more precise consideration of how God causes diversity and differentiation in creation

1. According to St. Thomas, how do form and matter differ in the way in which they cause diversification within things?

2. According to him, how does division into species occur within a genus?

Chapter 2

1. Why does no real possibility exist adequately to comprehend St. Thomas's teaching about the nature of moral activity and moral science without an adequate understanding of his teachings about human nature and good and evil?

2. Why does no possibility exist for understanding St. Thomas's

teachings about the nature of moral activity and moral science apart from an adequate understanding of what he says about creation and the human situation within the *order* of creation?

3. According to St. Thomas, from where do we take the rule, or measurement, of government and for all things directed to an end, or good?

How the divine providence of an absolutely perfect being rules over the order of created beings

1. According to him, how does God rule over everything in the created order?

2. In contemporary terms, what is a helpful analogy to use to describe the way St. Thomas thinks that God rules over creation?

How good and evil exist in things

1. According to St. Thomas, how is the way good and evil exist in things related to his understanding of perfection?

2. What role does St. Thomas's principle of virtual quantity play in understanding his teaching about how good and evil exist in things?

3. How does St. Thomas understand the nature of evil?

4. How does St. Thomas' understanding of the nature of evil preclude the existence of a totally, or supreme evil, essence, nature, or substance?

5. According to St. Thomas, why can no human being desire evil considered as such?

6. According to him, what is the only way in which human beings can desire an evil?

Adam and Eve in the state of perfect harmony of original justice, and the subsequent state of human nature that resulted from the infection of human nature by the sin of disobedience

1. According to St. Thomas, to what does "the state of original justice" refer?

2. According to him, precisely what was the condition of Adam and Eve as they existed in the state of original justice?

3. According to St. Thomas, why was the "Tree of Knowledge" called a "tree of knowledge?

4. According to him, what effects resulted from Adam's and Eve's loss of the state of original justice?

5. According to him, why was eating from the tree of knowledge prohibited?

Eve's seduction by the Devil and Eve's coaxing of Adam as these relate to the irascible and concupiscible appetites

1. According to St. Thomas, what two steps did Satan take to seduce Eve to be inclined to listen to him?

2. According to him, what four sins did Eve commit by listening to Satan?

3. Unlike Eve, what does St. Thomas maintain caused Adam to disobey God's command?

The effect on human nature of the loss of state of original justice

1. What does St. Thomas say happened to human nature as soon as the human will rejected free submission to divine direction?

2. According to him, in what way is the loss of state of original justice a sin of human nature?

Chapter 3

1. Why does an adequate understanding of St. Thomas's moral teaching essentially depend upon an adequate understanding of his psychology of the human person?

2. Why does an adequate understanding of St. Thomas's moral teaching essentially depend upon an adequate understanding of his moral psychology?

The nature of the human soul considered in itself

1. How does St. Thomas start his study of the nature of the human soul considered in itself?

2. What does St. Thomas understand by a "soul"?

3. What is the origin of the Western understanding of a soul?

4. Precisely how does St. Thomas develop his answer to the question about whether the human soul acts by virtue of its ability to act?

5. How does St. Thomas answer the question whether several powers (parts) exist in the soul?

6. How does he answer the question whether, if the soul is a composite whole, what is its nature?

The nature of the human soul considered in relation to the human body

1. According to St. Thomas, how does the human soul relate to the human body?

2. According to him, how is the human soul more than a principle of the body?

3. What chief problem does St. Thomas think a person who denies the reality of the human soul confront? How does this problem confront, for example, David Hume?

4. How does St. Thomas use the principle of virtual quantity to help explain the way the human soul relates to the human body?

5. How does St. Thomas explain how the human soul causes acts of life, growth, and nutrition within the human body?

6. How does St. Thomas explain how one and the same agent simultaneously has the ability to act in a multitude of qualitatively different ways?

7. According to St. Thomas, where do acts of any created being exist?

8. What is a formal object, and what are two different ways in which we can consider it?

9. How does St. Thomas explain how an organizational whole acts?

10. According to St. Thomas, what twofold order of qualitative perfection exists among the powers of the soul in terms of the lower powers being generated first, and preparing the way for the subsequent generation of the more qualitatively-perfect powers?

11. How does St. Thomas answer the question whether all the powers of the soul exist in the soul as in a subject?

12. How does he answer the question whether, after death, all of these powers remain in the soul the way it exists independently of the body?

How the natural faculties of the human soul are united and divided, and the order that exists among them

1. What two chief reasons does St. Thomas give for the conclusion he holds about how numerically-one human being can perform many acts?

2. According to St. Thomas, how does being in potentiality to another act other than simply existing belong to the soul according to its essence as a form?

The many powers, faculties, of the one intellectual soul

1. What three reasons does St. Thomas give to defend his claim that, to perform many second acts, a soul must act through many powers, or faculties, within the soul?

2. Comment, as to their cogency, on the reasons Thomas gives to defend his claim that, to perform many second acts, a soul must act through many powers, or faculties, within the soul.

How powers of the intellectual soul are distinguished, divided, by their acts, objects, and opposites

1. According to St. Thomas, how and why are powers of the intellectual soul distinguished, divided, by their acts, objects, and opposites?

2. According to him, how do formal objects act differently on the powers, faculties, they activate?

3. According to him, from what does an act receive its species? Explain.

4. According to St. Thomas, what sort of difference divides a genus and diversifies the powers of the soul?

That an order exists among the powers of the intellectual soul

1. Why does St. Thomas maintain that a threefold order must exist among the powers of the human soul?

2. According to St. Thomas, in what two ways can we consider the order of dependence of one power on another?

How the powers of the intellectual soul are in the soul as their subject

1. According to St. Thomas, how are the powers of the intellectual soul in the soul as their subject?

2. According to St. Thomas, how are the powers of the intellectual soul *not* in the soul as their subject?

How the powers of the intellectual soul originate from the soul as from a principle

1. In what two ways does St. Thomas say that substantial and accidental forms agree?

2. In what three ways does he say that substantial and accidental forms differ?

3. Why does St. Thomas conclude that, whether the subject be the soul alone or the composite of soul and body, all the powers of the soul originate from the essence of the soul, as from their principle?

How powers of the intellectual soul can be principles of other powers or faculties

1. According to St. Thomas, how can the powers of the soul be principles of other powers or faculties?

2. According to him, how can one power or faculty of the soul be a principle prior to another?

3. According to him, how does one power proceed from another according to different orders of perfection?

The number and division of the sense faculties and their appetites and how properly to distinguish the five exterior senses

1. According to St. Thomas, in what two ways did some people prior to him unsuccessfully attempt to divide the sense faculties?

2. According to him, where do we find the answer to the question about how properly to number and distinguish the exterior senses, and what conclusion about the diversification of the exterior sense faculties does he draw from this answer?

3. Why does St. Thomas think that the principles that diversify the exterior sense faculties must be material and immaterial?

4. How does St. Thomas hierarchically distinguish the five exterior sense faculties based upon the immateriality of their operations?

5. In what way does St. Thomas think the senses of sight, hearing, and touch play crucial roles in human activity?

6. According to St. Thomas, what are the three kinds of "sensibles," and how does he precisely distinguish one from another?

How properly to distinguish the four interior senses

1. Why does St. Thomas maintain that human nature must provide man's sensitive soul with as many faculties and actions needed for a human being to live the life of a *perfect* animal?

2. According to St. Thomas, what are the four interior sense faculties?

3. Precisely how does he distinguish one interior sense faculty from another?

Why the intellectual soul must have an appetitive faculty

1. Why does St. Thomas think that the intellectual soul must have an appetitive faculty?

2. According to him, what two sorts of appetites exist?

That the sensitive and intellectual appetites are distinct inclinations of distinct powers

1. According to St. Thomas, why does the intellectual soul need two appetites?

2. According to him, how do we distinguish passive and movable principles from each other, and why do we need to do so in relation to the human soul?

3. According to St. Thomas, why must appetites and powers belong to the same genus?

4. According to him, to what genus do they belong?

The nature and division of the appetite of the intellectual soul

1. According to St. Thomas, what are the two different appetites of the intellectual soul?

2. According to St. Thomas, how do these appetites differ one from another?

Why the sense appetite is divided into two parts: concupiscible (propelling) and irascible (contending)

1. According to St. Thomas, why is the sense appetite divided into two parts?

2. According to him, what are these two parts and how are they respectively inclined to operate?

Why and how the irascible and concupiscible appetites are inclined to obey the human intellect, or reason, and the human will

1. In what two ways does St. Thomas think that the irascible and concupiscible appetites are inclined to obey the human intellect, or reason, and the human will?

2. What does St. Thomas mean by "universal" and "particular" reason?

3. What does he not mean by "universal" reason?

4. In order to understand how individual human beings act within individual circumstances, why is understanding the nature and difference between universal and particular reason crucial?

5. Why does St. Thomas say that two motive principles exist within the human soul?

6. What are these two principles, how do they differ from each other, and why is knowing this difference crucial for understanding moral science?

7. Beyond universal and particular reason, and the will, according to St. Thomas, what else guides the sense appetite; and why is this additional influence over the sense appetite crucial to know?

Chapter 4

1. Why must anyone who wishes to understand St. Thomas's teaching about moral science recall that St. Thomas considers human beings to be created in God's image?

Creation and human happiness

1. According to St. Thomas what constitutes a real genus, and how does the created order constitute, or resemble, a real genus?

2. For what four general reasons does St. Thomas claim that human happiness cannot consist in *having*: wealth, honor, fame, political influence, or any and every external good?

3. From the fact that moral acts are distinctively human acts, freely-chosen acts that free decision-making proximately generates, what three claims does St. Thomas make?

The intrinsic principles of moral activity: the internal human faculties and the facultative moral psychology that human beings use proximately to generate, cause, moral acts

1. According to St. Thomas, what three psychological acts chiefly involve moving the will toward its natural end (real human good)?

2. Explain what St. Thomas means by willing (volition), intention, and enjoyment/delight.

3. According to St. Thomas, aside from willing, intention, and en-joyment/delight, what other intrinsic and extrinsic principles move the human will?

4. Explain what St. Thomas means by deliberation/counsel, con-sent, choice, command, and use; and explain how each of these in-fluences St. Thomas's moral psychology.

The goodness and evil of moral activity considered in general, and in relation to the interior act of the will and exterior actions

1. What does St. Thomas say about the goodness and evil of moral activity considered in general?

2. What four things does St. Thomas say about specific moral acts that human beings perform being of some sort of organizational whole?

3. According to St. Thomas, how do we derive the moral goodness or evil of an external act?

4. According to him, how do we derive the moral goodness or evil of an internal act?

5. If the chief aim of a moral choice is to select an individual action as a real means leading to fulfilling the chief aim of human life in the individual circumstance (is a prudent choice leading to the soul's union with God), what does St. Thomas maintain is the specific na-ture of such a choice?

6. If the chief aim is to make an imprudent choice leading away from union of the soul with God, what does St. Thomas consider to be the specific nature of such a choice?

7. Are all conscious acts we human beings perform moral acts? Why, or why not?

8. What happens to conversation about moral activity if we eliminate from it consideration of the nature of the human soul and its perfection and beautification? Why?

9. Precisely considered, what does specification of the formal object of a moral choice as morally good or evil for this or that person to execute within this or that individual circumstance essentially involve?

10. According to St. Thomas, while *sometimes* they do not change the species of moral good or evil of a moral choice, *sometimes* what do the circumstances of a moral act increase or decrease?

11. According to St. Thomas, how do the circumstances of a moral act *sometimes* become like a specific difference of a moral act?

12. Why does St. Thomas say that the goodness of an act of will also depends upon eternal law and God's will?

13. What does St. Thomas say about whether mistakes in conscience bind or do not bind; acts against reason being morally good or bad; and the moral goodness or evil of an act of will in relation to the intention of a moral agent?

14. What does St. Thomas say about unintended consequences that result from a previously-performed, morally good or evil act?

15. What does he maintain regarding whether our moral choices will merit reward or punishment by God?

Chapter 5

St. Thomas's definition of emotion/passion (*passio*), the nature of emotional reaction, and the division of sensory appetites

1. How does St. Thomas define what, today, we commonly call an "emotion," and he calls a "passion"?

2. To some extent, what four characteristics does St. Thomas consider an emotional reaction always to display?

3. Into what two emotional parts does St. Thomas divide the sensory appetite, and on what basis does he make this division?

How to distinguish passions that properly belong to the concupiscible appetite from those that properly belong to the irascible

1. According to St. Thomas, why are the passions that the concupiscible and irascible appetites generate specifically different?

2. According to him, why do the passions of different powers necessarily have different formal objects, including aims?

3. How does St. Thomas account for diversity of genus and species arising within the physical order?

4. According to him, how do acts of the soul differ in genus and species?

5. Regarding the sense appetite and a passion, which does St. Thomas say is the genus, and which is the species? Why?

6. According to St. Thomas, how do acts and passions that relate to different *specific* objects come under one common object of a single generic power?

7. According to him, how do we determine which passions are in the irascible appetite and which are in the concupiscible?

8. According to him, how does the formal object of the concupiscible appetite differ from the formal object of the irascible appetite?

The eleven different passions and kinds of opposition and relation they involve

1. According to St. Thomas, how many passions or emotions exist; how many exist within the concupiscible appetite, and how many exist within the irascible appetite?

2. Name the passions that exist within the concupiscible appetite.

3. Name the passions that exist within the irascible appetite.

4. How many of these passions involve contrary opposites within the same appetite?

5. Which passion has no contrary opposite within the same appetite?

6. Does the passion that has no contrary opposite within the same appetite have a contrary opposite? If not, does it have an opposite, where does this opposite exist, and why is it not a contrary opposite?

7. Why can privation and possession, and relation exist within and between genera; but contradictory opposites cannot?

8. Why can anger and calm be opposites, but not contrary opposites?

9. According to St. Thomas, why can two kinds of opposition exist within the irascible appetite but only one within the concupiscible appetite?

10. What are the two kinds of opposition that St. Thomas says can exist within the irascible appetite?

11. What is the one kind of opposition that he says exists within the concupiscible appetite?

12. According to St. Thomas, why is love the chief human passion?

13. According to him, why is the passion of love present wherever any human passion is present?

14. According to him, why is pleasure always present when love is satisfied?

15. Why do the passions of the concupiscible and irascible appetites both have time components connected to them, and how do these time components differ in relation to these different appetites?

Why and how opposition, contrariety, exists among the passions of the sense appetites

1. According to St. Thomas, what is the principal reason for the existence of emotional contrariety?

2. According to him, why is the opposition that exists within the passions of the irascible appetite more complicated than the opposition that exists within the passions of the concupsicible appetite?

Moral good and evil as it relates to the passions

1. To what extent does St. Thomas maintain that moral good and evil exist within the passions?

2. How does St. Thomas address the opposition between the teaching of ancient Stoic thinkers and his teaching related to the question whether the human passions are always evil for human beings to experience?

3. How does St. Thomas understand the prevailing teaching of the ancient Stoic thinkers, including Marcus Tullius Cicero, regarding the passions of the soul and their moral worth?

4. According to St. Thomas, how does Aristotle's teaching about the passions differ from the prevailing teaching of the ancient Stoics?

How the human passions may increase or decrease an action's moral worth

1. According to St. Thomas, why does not every emotional action increase or decrease the moral goodness or evil of a human action?

2. Relative to the passions and external actions, in what does St. Thomas think perfection of moral goodness in human action chiefly consist?

3. What does St. Thomas think complete human perfection in moral action requires?

The passion of love, or liking, considered in general

1. According to St. Thomas, into what three species is the generic act of love divided?

2. In natural subjects, with what does St. Thomas identify love, and in what way does he consider natural love to be generated?

3. Considered in general, in what does St. Thomas think love consists; and what does he maintain is its only cause?

4. Within a human appetite, in what does he think love consists?

5. Expressed in terms of virtual quantity, as St. Thomas defines it, in what does love consist?

6. Into what two species does St. Thomas divide human love; and, strictly speaking, why does he think love always chiefly consists in love for a person?

7. According to St. Thomas, what are the six effects of love?

Why love is a passion in the intellectual and sense appetites

1. According to St. Thomas, in what way is what is good naturally related to an appetite as what an appetite loves?

2. What does St. Thomas mean when he claims that "being," "unity," "truth," and "good" are convertible terms?

3. What does St. Thomas mean when he says that a formal object is "suitable," "fitting," or "proportionate" to a faculty?

4. What does St. Thomas mean by the term "appetite"? Name some appetites that St. Thomas identifies and explain how they operate.

5. According to St. Thomas, in what way do some human appetites have a "share of freedom"?

6. In relation to an appetite, to what does St. Thomas give the name "love"?

582

In what ways, as an intensive quantity (limited quality) of ability and satisfaction, love is the chief concupiscible passion

1. Why does St. Thomas claim that pursuit of a good is the reason for avoiding the opposite evil?

2. In what way does what activates a natural power have the nature of a good as an end?

3. In what way does some good exist as the first, highest, motivator, in any human being's plan of pursuit?

4. From what two different points of view can we consider the concupiscible passions? In either case, how are we considering them?

5. For what reasons does St. Thomas conclude that love is an intensive quantity of ability, receptivity, or proportional capacity, of the appetite *toward* the good and the intensive quantity of satisfaction that rests in the good?

6. Why does he consider love to be the first appetitive principle of all human relations?

7. According to him, how does love differ from desire and pleasure, or joy?

How love is, and is not, a passion

1. According to St. Thomas, what twofold effect does a natural agent have on a receiving power?

2. In what way, for St. Thomas, is "natural love" something naturally suitable for, and relatable to, a natural appetite?

3. According to St. Thomas, what two effects does an appetitible object generate in an appetite?

4. If St. Thomas is right regarding the way he speaks about natural appetites in the way they operate, why would gravity be a relation?

5. Why does St. Thomas claim that movement of the concupiscible appetite is circular?

6. Why does St. Thomas call "love" the first change effected in the appetite by the good, and what does he mean by this claim?

7. In what way does St. Thomas claim that love is a passion, in what way does he claim that love is an act of will?

8. In what ways does St. Thomas think love is a principle of union?

9. According to St. Thomas, strictly speaking, what does "love" denote, and what does it not denote?

Human love's two chief divisions and why human love is always of a person

1. According to St. Thomas, no matter what the nature of the good loved, why does the movement of love always have a twofold tendency?

2. Why does he say that love has two chief divisions, and why does he say that the parts of these divisions are related as primary and secondary?

Why the human good is the formal object and proper cause of human love

1. According to St. Thomas, why is the human good the formal object and proper cause of human love?

2. How does St. Thomas reply to someone who might say that, because love starts with some kind of knowledge of the good, the beautiful, not the good, is love's formal cause?

3. According to St. Thomas, how do the ideas of the "beautiful" and the "good" somewhat differ?

How knowledge is a cause of love

1. According to St. Thomas, how is knowledge a cause of love?

2. According to him, how does sense loving involve assimilation of the sense appetite?

3. According to St. Thomas, does saying that knowledge of the good is a necessary condition for loving it mean that such knowledge must be perfect? If not, why not?

4. According to him, how does completeness, perfection, of love differ from completeness, or perfection, of knowledge?

5. Why does St. Thomas say that we can love a thing more than we know it and that we can love a thing completely without knowing it completely?

How likeness is a cause of love

1. According to St. Thomas, in what way is likeness between two things twofold?

2. According to him, how does this twofold way of being alike cause different kinds of loving?

3. What are these kinds of loving and how do they specifically differ?

How love causes every other passion

1. According to St. Thomas, how is love the principle of every other passion?

2. According to him, how does love determine the intensity of union that any and every passion can, or does, have with its formal object?

3. Why does St. Thomas maintain that love precisely consists in a suitable union of opposites?

4. Why does he maintain that the intensity of love determines how intensely, completely, we hate, desire, experience pleasure, pain, joy, sadness, hope, daring, fear, anger, and so on?

How union causes love

1. According to St. Thomas, how does union cause love?

2. According to him, why does union cause love in a twofold way? What is this twofold way that union causes love?

3. Why does St. Thomas assert that we have to consider the union that causes love in relation to some preceding knowledge?

4. According to St. Thomas, why is a final cause the cause of love of concupiscence?

5. According to him, why is a formal cause the cause of love of friendship?

Six effects of love as a form of union considered in brief

1. Regarding love considered as a form of union, in what three ways does St. Thomas claim that union relates to love?

2. In relation to union as an effect of love, what does St. Thomas say are the six effects of union? Explain the nature of each.

The passion of hatred, or disliking, considered in general

1. How does St. Thomas define the passion of hatred?

2. How is some awareness of virtual quantity related to experiencing the passion of hatred?

3. Despite appearances that might exist to the contrary, why does St. Thomas maintain that hatred has only one cause? What is that cause?

4. While, at times, hatred can appear stronger and to be more strongly experienced than love, why does St. Thomas maintain that, strictly speaking, hatred can never be stronger than love?

5. How does St. Thomas explain the apparent and temporary appearance of hatred being stronger than love?

6. According to St. Thomas, absolutely considered, why can a person never hate himself or the truth?

7. According to him, in what way can a person hate the truth and himself?

8. According to St. Thomas, how does the passion of anger differ from that of hatred regarding the ability to hate individuals?

How, in a way, evil causes hatred

1. In a way, according to St. Thomas, how is evil able to cause hatred?

2. According to him, how is hatred the result of a perceived disequilibrium within an appetite and what it apprehends?

3. According to him, why can being, considered simply as being, never have the ability to repel, cause hatred?

4. According to St. Thomas, when does being, considered as determinate being, have the ability to repel, cause hatred?

The passion of concupiscence (*desire for* what is pleasurable) considered in general

1. How does St. Thomas describe the psychological experience of concupiscence in relation to the experience of emotions of love and pleasure?

2. How does St. Thomas define "concupiscence," and how does this definition differ from the way in which he defines "love"?

3. Why does St. Thomas maintain that concupiscence properly belongs to the sense appetite involving the soul/body composite and that it differs from intellectual pursuit of pleasure?

4. According to St. Thomas, what are the different ways in which what is good causes love, concupiscence, and joy?

5. According to him, in what sense are some animal desires "real" and others "apparent"?

6. According to him, why do only human beings have the ability to distinguish between real and apparent pleasures?

7. From the fact that, among all species of animals only human beings are able to distinguish between real and apparent pleasures, what conclusion does St. Thomas draw regarding a special need human beings have that other animals do not have?

8. In what way does St. Thomas say that human desire for pleasure is infinite?

9. In what way does he say that human desire for pleasure is finite?

The passion of pleasure considered in general

1. How does St. Thomas define pleasure?

2. Strictly speaking, why does St. Thomas claim that pleasure: 1) is an action, not a process; 2) need not involve time; and 3) differs from joy? How does he defend his claim against those who would object to it as being false?

3. In calling pleasure "a movement of the soul," or "a psychic movement," what does St. Thomas claim he is doing?

4. In calling pleasure "a state of existing constituting a thing in agreement with its nature," what does he maintain he is doing?

5. By saying that the state of pleasure happens "all at once," what does St. Thomas mean?

6. As evidence of the qualitatively greater nature of intellectual joy to that of sensory pleasure, among other things, what does St. Thomas refer?

7. To what does St. Thomas chiefly ascribe the qualitative intensity of bodily pleasures?

8. To what does he chiefly ascribe the qualitative intensity of intellectual joy or delight?

9. When comparing and contrasting the natural pleasure that the act of seeing generates to the natural pleasure that the sense of touch generates, what does St. Thomas note regarding their qualitative differences relative to human beings and to brute animals?

10. For what chief reason do Aristotle and St. Thomas think that a dog delights in the sight of a rabbit and a lion in the sight or sound of prey?

11. Why does St. Thomas think that, of all animals, only human beings have the natural ability to enjoy the acts of their sense faculties considered as such?

Why, strictly speaking, desire for pleasure, concupiscence, is a specific passion that exists only in the sense appetite

1. According to St. Thomas, why does the psychological state that he calls "joy" or "delight" appear to be a possession of the soul alone; while concupiscence appears to belong to the soul and body?

2. From his observation that delight appears to be a possession of the soul alone while concupiscence appears to belong to both the soul and the body, what does St. Thomas conclude?

3. According to St. Thomas, how does the formal object of the concupiscible appetite differ from the formal object of the intellectual appetite (the will)?

4. According to him, how does the formal object of the concupiscible appetite differ from the formal object of the irascible appetite? Why?

5. According to him, what three effects does the formal object of sensible pleasure cause within a human being, and why?

Precisely why the desire for some pleasures can be boundless while others cannot

1. According to St. Thomas, in what two different ways can something be pleasurable?

2. According to him, what is the difference between natural and non-natural concupiscence?

3. Why does St. Thomas say that natural concupiscence cannot be infinite, but, in a way, non-natural concupiscence can be infinite?

The moral and non-moral dimensions of pleasure

1. Why does St. Thomas maintain that not all pleasures are morally good or evil considered as such?

2. According to him, when are pleasures morally good, and when are they morally evil?

3. According to him, what is the chief principle by which we measure all moral good?

4. Why does St. Thomas consider some pleasures to be generically natural and unnatural for all animals? Precisely what makes such pleasures generically natural and unnatural for them?

5. What does St. Thomas mean when he maintains that some animal acts that are specifically natural can be non-natural for an individual?

Peter A. Redpath

The unique animal situation of human beings as moral agents and how this relates to the passion of pleasure

1. Why does St. Thomas maintain that among all other animal species, human beings stand in a unique relationship regarding experience of the passion of pleasure within the concupiscible appetite?

2. Why does he consider the genus of moral activity in which only the human animal participates to be unique among genera to which an animal species belongs?

The eight causes of pleasure

1. According to St. Thomas, what three conditions does the existence of pleasure necessarily require?

2. According to him, what are the eight causes of pleasure, and why?

The effects of pleasure

1. According to St. Thomas, what are the four effects of pleasure?

Pain/Sorrow, its causes, effects, remedies, goodness and evil

1. According to St. Thomas, chiefly what is sorrow (or sadness) and what are its four species?

2. What does he say is sorrow's one chief cause?

3. According to him, what are sorrow's six effects?

4. What five remedies does St. Thomas identify for sorrow?

5. Absolutely considered, and considered in relation to something else, what two things does St. Thomas maintain about pain and sorrow?

6. According to St. Thomas, of what is the inability to experience shame as a result of doing something morally vicious a clear sign?

7. What two possible reasons does St. Thomas offer for the psycho-

logical inability to experience shame as a result of doing something morally vicious?

8. What does St. Thomas say regarding the moral utility of pain and sorrow considered simply as concupiscible passions?

9. For what three reasons does St. Thomas say that pain and sorrow can be morally useful in relation to the irascible passions?

10. According to St. Thomas, more than any bodily pain, what is especially bad about moral evils?

Hope and despair

1. According to St. Thomas, in relation to the irascible passions, how is hope analogous to love in relation to the concupiscible passions?

2. According to St. Thomas, what is the nature of hope and what is its formal object?

3. Even though hope is seated in the sensory appetite, in what way does it have cognitive elements, including that of cogitative reason?

4. What are the ten causes of hope that St. Thomas identifies?

5. Why does St. Thomas present drunkards, young people, and fools as prime examples of hope?

6. According to St. Thomas, what are despair's nature, causes, effects, and contrary opposites?

7. What do despair's effects closely resemble? Why?

Fear and the moral psychology of the daring person and how it differs from the moral psychology of the despondent individual

1. Why does St. Thomas list fear as second to sorrow among all the passions causing psychological depression?

2. Why should no surprise exist in the fact that the formal object of fear somewhat resembles that of hope?

3. Does St. Thomas consider the passion of fear to be something in some way naturally good to experience? If so, why? If not, why not?

4. If real good and evil do not exist, what implications follow with logical consistency regarding the passions of hope and fear?

5. According to St. Thomas, what are the species of fear? According to him, what causes these species of fear?

6. According to him, what is fear's formal object, what does the formal object include?

7. Beyond the internal sense faculty of imagination, what internal sense faculty is most necessary in order to experience fear, and why?

8. According to St. Thomas, what are the six causes of fear?

9. Why is the principle of virtual quantity especially necessary for us to understand the nature of fear?

10. According to St. Thomas, what are the two chief effects of fear?

11. How does St. Thomas describe the nature of the physiological and psychological contraction that accompanies the experience of fear?

12. How does St. Thomas describe the moral psychology of the daring person?

13. How does he describe the moral psychology of the despondent person?

Anger and related considerations

1. How does St. Thomas define anger?

2. What four things does St. Thomas say about the roots of anger, the object with which it is chiefly directed, and what chiefly causes this passion?

3. According to St. Thomas, is anger essentially morally evil and irrational? If so, why? If not, why not?

4. According to him, what are the three species of anger and how do they differ one from another?

5. How does St. Thomas describe the moral psychology of the angry person?

6. According to St. Thomas, what three opposing ways of behaving toward another person can increase or diminish the magnitude of a person's anger?

7. According to St. Thomas, what are the three ways of slighting a person? Of these different ways of slighting someone, which tend to magnify, and which tend to diminish, a person's anger, and why?

8. According to him, what are the six effects of anger?

9. What does St. Thomas mention as remedies for anger?

10. Why is anger the only passion that has no contrary opposite?

11. Does anger have an opposite passion that terminates it? If so, what passion is it, and why does it terminate anger?

12. In what sense is anger the most social of all the passions?

13. Why does St. Thomas think that most people are more forgiving of an angry person than of a hateful one?

14. According to St. Thomas, why is the passion of anger unique among all other irascible passions?

Chapter 6

St. Thomas's definition of "habit" ("*habitus*")

1. Generically and specifically, how does St. Thomas define a "habit"?

2. What are some things that complicate understanding St. Thomas's teaching about the nature of a habit?

St. Thomas's definition of "virtue" ("*virtus*")

1. Generically and specifically, how does St. Thomas define a "virtue"?

2. What are some things that complicate understanding St. Thomas's teaching about the nature of a virtue?

The subject of moral and intellectual virtue

1. According to St. Thomas, what is the subject of moral and intellectual virtue?

2. According to him, how can one moral or intellectual virtue simultaneously exist in many subjects?

3. In what two ways does St. Thomas claim that a habit can be ordered, essentially related to, a good act?

4. According to St. Thomas, how can a human faculty be good *absolutely*?

5. According to him, strictly speaking, what enables us to predicate the term "virtue" *absolutely* of qualities of the human soul like wisdom, science, art, prudence, and temperance?

The intellectual and moral virtues considered in general and in relation to the "habit of understanding" and *synderesis*

1. Based upon what he has said about the nature of virtue, what does St. Thomas reasonably conclude about intellectual virtue?

2. As subject to taking directions from the human will, what does he maintain about the speculative intellect in relation to the infused virtue of faith?

3. What does St. Thomas say about the way the four cardinal moral virtues exist in the intellectual and sensory faculties and appetites?

4. Regarding the species of intellectual virtue, what does he say these are and where does he say they exist?

5. Considered in general, what does he say about the three speculative intellectual virtues?

6. According to St. Thomas, how do the intellectual virtues enhance the quality of intellectual operation related to the human intellect's ability to consider truths and command well-done good deeds?

7. What does St. Thomas claim about the speculative intellectual virtue of science?

8. Absolutely and relatively considered, what does St. Thomas say about the speculative intellectual virtue of wisdom?

9. What does St. Thomas say about the chief concern of the practical intellectual virtue of art?

10. According to St. Thomas, do artists and scientists have any moral responsibilities essentially related to their arts and sciences? Explain.

11. Do liberal arts and speculative sciences involve work? If so, why does St. Thomas call them "liberal" and "speculative"?

12. What does St. Thomas understand to be the nature of the moral virtue of prudence?

13. What does St. Thomas understand to be the nature of the principle of *synderesis*?

14. According to St. Thomas, how does the principle of *synderesis* essentially relate to the moral virtue of prudence, and how is it analogous to the "habit of understanding"?

The moral virtues considered in general and identified specifically

1. According to St. Thomas, what is the etymology of the words "ethics" and "morals"?

2. Following Aristotle, how does St. Thomas define "moral virtue"?

3. What does St. Thomas always consider moral virtues to be?

4. Considering the way the human appetites are inclined to operate, in contrast to the way it rules the body, what does St. Thomas say about the way that reason rules the appetites the moral virtues are inclined to direct?

5. According to St. Thomas, how do the moral virtues relate to the human passions?

6. Identify the ten moral virtues that Aristotle lists as being related to the human passions. Why does Aristotle omit prudence and justice from this list?

The nature and causes of virtue, and especially of moral virtue

1. Specifically and individually, what does St. Thomas say about the moral and intellectual virtues?

2. In their early stages, how does St. Thomas say these moral virtues exist within our bodily and psychological constitution?

3. Chiefly what does St. Thomas consider moral virtues to be?

4. According to him, how does imperfect moral virtue differ from perfect moral virtue?

Properties of moral virtues

1. According to St. Thomas, what is the mean in relation to *the acquisition of* right moral habits by imperfectly-formed moral virtues?

2. According to him, what is the mean in relation to *the exercise of* moral virtue?

3. According to St. Thomas, what is the condition of human beings at birth in relation to the possession of moral virtue? Explain.

4. In genus and species, does St. Thomas think that one moral or

intellectual virtue can be qualitatively better than, superior to, another? If so, which ones are better, superior, to which, and how are they better, superior?

A brief consideration of the nature and division of theological virtues

1. According to St. Thomas, what are the three theological virtues and how does the way in which they are acquired differ from the way in which the natural intellectual and moral virtues are acquired and strengthened?

2. According to St. Thomas, where is each of these theological virtues respectively located within the human soul, and what is the formal object of each?

3. What does St. Thomas say regarding the relationship of the natural moral virtues and the infused theological virtues in relation to charity?

Exterior principles of moral activity: God, the Devil, and law (especially natural law)

1. Regarding the exterior principles of moral activity, where does St. Thomas first began to consider these within his *Summa theologiae*? Prior to his consideration of these exterior principles of moral activity, to how many other questions had he replied within his *Summa*?

2. In his prologue to question 90, what does St. Thomas say about God and the Devil?

3. How many questions comprise St. Thomas's "Treatise on Law" in the First Part of the Second Part of his *Summa theologiae*?

4. According to St. Thomas, what is the nature of law? How does he define "law"?

5. According to him, chiefly, what are the two good effects that every good law causes?

6. According to him, what are the five different species of law?

7. Explain the nature of each of these species of law and explain why each is necessary for the perfection of human life.

8. Within his *Summa theologiae*, how many questions does St. Thomas devote to the topic of law?

9. How many questions does he vote to the topic of natural law? How many articles does he devote to the topic of natural law? What are the topics of these articles?

10. Within Western culture, what is the origin of natural law teaching?

11. According to St. Thomas, what is the nature of natural law and why is it needed for human governance?

12. According to him, why is natural law called natural "law" and not natural "instinct"?

13. According to St. Thomas, from what single, generic principle known through the natural habit of *synderesis* are all the precepts of natural law derived? In what way are these other principles of natural law derived from the principle of *synderesis*?

14. According to him, what four needs does natural law command us to satisfy, and why is natural law insufficient as a moral principle to guide human life to moral perfection?

15. Does St. Thomas think that natural law is one and the same for all human beings?

16. Does he think that the first principle of natural law can ever be entirely eradicated from the human heart?

17. Strictly speaking, why is the mis-named "moral principle of double effect" not a moral principle for St. Thomas? What are the moral principles at work when two effects follow from an unavoidable moral choice and one of them is unintendedly evil? Why?

18. Beyond natural law, what laws does St. Thomas think human beings need in order to be brought to moral perfection? Why?

19. What does St. Thomas consider to be the relationship between civil law and natural law?

20. Does St. Thomas think that civil law should command all acts of virtue and forbid all acts of vice? Why or why not?

Chapter 7

St. Thomas's introduction to his *Commentary on the Nicomachean Ethics of Aristotle*: An essential responsibility of the wise man is to recognize and execute order

1. In his first "Lecture" in his *Commentary on the Nicomachean Ethics of Aristotle*, why does St. Thomas state that different habitual ways of considering unequally perfect modes of order cause differentiation in the sciences? Explain.

2. Why does St. Thomas maintain that, qualitatively considered and *qua* science, metaphysics is an intellectual quality that studies beings of utmost perfection in existence and difficulty for the human intellect to know in the qualitatively most perfect intellectual way of knowing?

3. What does St. Thomas say is the most powerful cause in the universe? What does he say about the way in which the most powerful cause in the universe operates?

4. What two things does St. Thomas say about the way in which order exists in the finite order?

5. What does he say about a twofold order existing within finite things? What does this order constitute?

6. Based upon the fact that different sciences study different species of order, what does St. Thomas conclude about what the different divisions of moral science study?

7. According to St. Thomas, what are the different divisions of moral science and what are the specific subjects of study?

8. Generically considered as a whole, what does St. Thomas claim are science's two widest divisions?

9. According to St. Thomas, how do theoretical (or speculative), practical, and productive sciences specifically differ one from another?

10. Why do Aristotle and St. Thomas maintain that the arts and sciences are architectonically ordered?

11. According to St. Thomas, what is the fourfold order that the human intellect, reason, considers?

The order, organizational whole, that moral philosophy/science studies and the way it studies it

1. According to St. Thomas, what does moral philosophy/science (subject of ethics) study? What is its formal object?

2. Why does St. Thomas say that moral science must study the three different divisions of monastics, domestics, and civics (or politics)?

3. What comments does St. Thomas make about Aristotle's statement in Book 1 of his *Nicomachean Ethics* that practical sciences like ethics are diversified by a diversity of ends and means?

4. According to St. Thomas, what is not the proper procedure to be used in moral education? According to him, what is the proper procedure for moral education to use?

5. Why does he say that political science naturally inclines to dictate to other practical and theoretical sciences specification of their exercise?

6. Regarding speculative and practical sciences, according to its nature, what does St. Thomas maintain political science can rightly dictate?

7. According to him, what can political science never rightly dictate to other sciences? Why?

8. According to St. Thomas, how do we derive the specification of the nature of any and every science?

9. According to him, properly considered, in relation to command and control of other sciences, what is the right way for political science to use the art of legislation? In relation to command and control of these other sciences, what does he say is the wrong way for political science to use the art of legislation? Why?

The essential connection between the moral science of politics and human happiness

1. After having discussed the nature, divisions, and general intrinsic principles of ethics (like reason, will, habit), how does St. Thomas start to specify the subject (chief good intended by) of moral science?

2. Why does St. Thomas say that the ends and means ethics studies must be finite?

3. Why does St. Thomas maintain that moral science has to belong to the supremely architectonic science of politics?

Essential qualities needed by students and teachers of moral science, and the method of study proper to the science

1. According to St. Thomas, what qualities must students and teachers of moral science have, and what is the method of study proper to this science?

2. According to him, what people tend to be morally unteachable? Why?

3. According to him, young people, the emotionally immature, and the habitually morally vicious are defective in what needed principle of moral education?

Peter A. Redpath

4. Today, by what term would such people be likely to refer to Aristotle's and St. Thomas's teaching about moral science?

5. For what people does St. Thomas think that the study of moral science is especially useful?

Start of part one of Aristotle's investigation of the supreme human good: happiness

1. According to St. Thomas, in what does Aristotle's three-part investigation into the nature of happiness precisely consist?

2. How does St. Thomas start his study about part one of Aristotle's investigation into the nature of happiness?

3. What does Aristotle claim that, around and before his time, *the Many* had said about happiness?

4. What does Aristotle claim some Platonists had said about happiness?

5. According to St. Thomas, what is Aristotle's method for studying the opinions of others to induce the first principles of right reason in practical matters?

6. As described by St. Thomas, what did Aristotle appear to consider to be one of the essential psychological foundations for the generation of moral universals?

7. Could the teaching of Plato in some way have influenced the method that Aristotle used when studying practical matters to consider the opinion of others to induce moral universals? If so, how?

A sketch of happiness: "Happiness" provisionally defined generically

1. Generically, how did Aristotle provisionally define "happiness"? What method did Aristotle use to induce this provisional definition?

2. In what sense does St. Thomas understand from Aristotle that happiness is man's proper operation? Precisely what does this claim mean?

603

3. In a human being, what does St. Thomas claim is man's highest perfection?

4. According to St. Thomas, what are the two essential parts, or divisions, of the human soul?

5. On the basis of Aristotle's identification of happiness as consisting in a human being's highest activity, what does St. Thomas maintain?

6. As the product of a highest virtue, habit, what does St. Thomas claim happiness requires?

7. Having finished giving *a sketch* (general, and good description) of happiness, according to St. Thomas how does Aristotle start to move beyond this good description to a good definition?

8. According to St. Thomas, what does Aristotle mean when he claims that the proper method of study in practical science is to examine the natures of things for their utility?

9. Whether our chief aim is to examine the nature of things to understand the causes of those natures in depth and considered as such, or for their utility, according to St. Thomas, where must all human reasoning, including philosophical/scientific reasoning, start?

10. Despite popular and widespread contemporary misunderstandings of the nature of induction, precisely understood, what is the nature of induction? Explain what the act of induction essentially involves.

11. Regarding the nature of induction, according to the author of this book, what did Aristotle and St. Thomas understand much better than did René Descartes, Sir Francis Bacon, or the overwhelming majority of contemporary self-professed "intellectuals"?

12. According to him, what crucial truth did Aristotle and St. Thomas recognize about principles and their relation to science?

How Aristotle and St. Thomas confirm the soundness of Aristotle's generic definition of happiness

1. If Aristotle's generic definition of happiness is sound, and if, to some extent, human beings have a natural ability to know the nature of happiness as the formal object of human nature considered as a whole, what should this fact indicate about the way Aristotle and St. Thomas *confirm* the soundness of this definition.

2. Why does St. Thomas maintain that thoroughly understanding principles, including definitions, at the start of the reasoning process is crucial for best hope of success in the end?

3. To ensure a more careful scientific study, what does St. Thomas tell us that, as part of our reasoning process, we have to examine? Why?

4. To carry out his stated goal to examine the opinions of others in relation to his provisional definition of happiness, what does St. Thomas say Aristotle does?

5. According to Aristotle, what two chief claims did some philosophers in ancient Greece make about the nature of happiness?

6. In addition to the opinions of these *Learned*, ancient philosophers, what other opinions does Aristotle also consider? Why?

7. After Aristotle completes his survey of the opinions of *the Many* and *the Learned*, what does Aristotle claim to be the likelihood regarding the truth or falsity of these opinions?

8. From the standpoint of reason and customary speech, how does Aristotle show why he considers his definition to be better than all these opinions cited?

9. Beyond these instances of confirmation already given, how does Aristotle prove his claim about the superiority of his definition of happiness?

10. What is crucial to note about what Aristotle says regarding the unhealthy pursuit of unnatural pleasures of imprudent individuals?

11. In contrast to the many external and unhealthy pleasures that incontinent and intemperate people pursue as instances of happy activity, what does Aristotle maintain that the virtuous life needs and does not need? Why?

12. Strictly speaking, why cannot people who do not delight in doing morally virtuous deeds be morally virtuous?

13. Since happiness consists in virtuous actions, what does Aristotle conclude about happiness as an action, and about happiness properly understood?

14. How does Aristotle prove his definition of happiness to be superior to definitions of happiness given by those who claim that happiness consists in possession of external goods?

The cause of happiness

1. Having started to consider the cause of happiness in general to consist in the exercise of perfect moral virtue, how does Aristotle start to specify our understanding of this cause?

2. How does St. Thomas answer the question whether happiness is divinely caused?

3. While St. Thomas claims that God is its chief cause, how does he maintain human beings contribute to happiness?

4. According to St. Thomas, what is evident from the preceding inquiry concerning the proper definition of happiness and its cause?

5. What does St. Thomas maintain about political science regarding framing laws and apportioning rewards and punishments of citizens?

6. According to St. Thomas, what follows from Aristotle's definition of happiness in this life regarding irrational animals and children?

How Aristotle answers Solon's problem regarding whether, because of changes in fortune, strictly speaking, anyone can be called "happy" in this life

1. According to St. Thomas, precisely what is Solon's problem regarding whether anyone can be called "happy" in this life?

2. According to him, how does Aristotle reject the claim that we can only judge a person happy after death?

3. According to St. Thomas, how does Aristotle answer Solon's problem regarding whether, because of changes in fortune, strictly speaking, anyone can be called "happy" in this life?

4. Unlike some Stoics, who considered external, bodily things not humanly good and the virtuous person to be someone who was not saddened by misfortune, what did Aristotle maintain about the way in which a morally virtuous person reacts to sorrow and misfortune?

What causes happiness and moral virtue to be goods deserving of honor and praise

1. According, to Aristotle, what two kinds of excellence exist? To which one should honor be given? To which one should praise be given?

2. According to him, based upon these two different kinds of excellence, considering happiness and moral virtue, which merits praise and which merits honor?

Aristotle returns to the discussion of the relation between happiness and virtue

1. According to Aristotle, why cannot we fully comprehend happiness without fully comprehending, and relating happiness to, virtue?

2. According to him, why does political science need to study his soul?

3. Why does Aristotle end Book 1 of the *Nicomachean Ethics* by considering the human soul and its subdivisions?

The sensory part of the soul and its subdivisions

1. According to Aristotle, what is the human soul?

2. According to him, considered strictly from the standpoint of it being a biological principle, what relation does the human soul have to moral science or ethics?

3. What does Aristotle think is the chief concern of moral science or ethics regarding the human soul?

4. In relation to the human passions, how does St. Thomas maintain that human reason works?

5. According to Aristotle, what are the two parts of the human soul that are the concern of ethics or moral science? Does he think that the political scientist needs to study both these parts of the soul?

Chapter 8

The habits that cause virtue: How and why habit, not human nature, proximately causes virtue

1. According to Aristotle and St. Thomas, in moral science, in contrast to a speculative science, how does moral virtue chiefly aim at habit formation and habit perfection? At what does it not chiefly aim, and why?

2. Why do they maintain that moral knowledge must be in accord, harmonize, with right reason and the virtue of prudence?

3. Since *investigation must be conducted in harmony with the subject investigated*, what do Aristotle and St. Thomas maintain about the method of investigation used within moral science?

4. Why should most people not be surprised that the provisional

method of investigation Aristotle recommends in moral science closely models that of a medical doctor?

5. What is evident about what Aristotle knows from what he says about the provisional method used by a moral scientist?

6. According to St. Thomas, unlike in speculative science, in moral science, when do we know we have achieved our goal?

7. According to Aristotle and St. Thomas, what does moral science chiefly study?

8. According to them, what destroys all virtues and actions that cause virtue? With what evidence do they support their claim?

9. For Aristotle and St. Thomas, in moral matters, ethics, how do we determine the golden mean, right measure, of choice and action within the individual situation?

10. When dealing with moral matters, what two major questions must we repeatedly ask ourselves when considering performance of an action or making a choice?

How pleasures and pains, joys and sorrows, act as signs indicating that moral virtue or vice is generating an action

1. While they do not claim that pleasure is the formal object of all virtues, what do Aristotle and St. Thomas claim about the relation of pleasure to all virtue, both theoretical and practical?

2. According to them, in what way do virtuous and vicious people experience pleasure in relation to making morally right and wrong choices? How does Aristotle use the teaching of Plato in support of this claim?

3. While Aristotle and St. Thomas admitted that pleasure exists in both the intellectual and sensitive powers, and that all animals are capable of experiencing it, for what two reasons do they say that only the human intellect recognizes the virtuous and the useful?

4. According to St. Thomas, what is "proper pleasure" and how is it essentially related to natural facultative inclination?

5. According to St. Thomas, how are pleasure and cogitative reason (or the estimative sense) essentially related to setting the mean of moral choice and action within the individual circumstance?

6. According to him, in naturally pursuing perfection of facultative health and operation, in what does a virtue naturally incline to take delight?

7. According to Aristotle and St. Thomas, more than pleasure and pain, what else accompanies all our acts of virtue?

8. According to them, why does the whole business of moral, and political, science concern the moral psychology of right and wrong use of pleasures and pains within individual circumstances?

9. According to them, why does moral education always essentially involve training the concupiscible appetite in acts of temperance?

10. According to St. Thomas, since, in the individual circumstance, moral education always essentially involves prudently and with pleasure doing the more difficult deed, choosing the higher good over the lower and the real good over the apparent, what species of morally virtuous activity does it also, necessarily, always essentially involve?

11. According to St. Thomas, what role does the *temperately-educated estimative sense faculty* (particular reason) always play in moral education within the individual circumstance?

Comparison of moral virtue and art

1. How does Aristotle answer the objection that what is true of art is true of moral activity; and, in art, the truth is that just as no person produces a work of art except a person who possesses the art, no one does a good moral deed without possessing moral virtue?

2. What does Aristotle say about the importance of speculative knowledge in a person becoming morally virtuous? What is his attitude toward those people who think they can become morally virtuous through speculative study?

Aristotle starts defining virtue generically

1. According to Aristotle and St. Thomas, what three principles of life activity exist within an animal soul?

2. How does Aristotle use the existence of these three principles to start defining virtue generically?

3. According to Aristotle, why cannot moral virtues be passions or faculties (powers) of the soul?

4. According to Aristotle, how do we judge and measure the power and virtue of a thing?

Aristotle defines virtue specifically

1. After Aristotle defines virtue generically, how does he start to find it specifically?

2. Under what three headings does Aristotle next investigate the specific difference of virtue in terms of a virtue's quality (strength of having, participating in, form)?

3. With what three things does St. Thomas claim virtue deals?

4. What does he maintain about *the equal* in relation to these three things?

5. According to St. Thomas, how do we derive the mean according to *absolute quantity*? And how do we derive the mean *relative to us*?

6. According to Aristotle, in what twofold way does every practical science work?

7. According to him, how does moral virtue incline us to work, and why is moral virtue better than art?

8. Relative to actions and passions, what does Aristotle claim the morally virtuous mean does and what it indicates?

St. Thomas concludes Aristotle's definition of moral virtue

1. According to St. Thomas, like health and beauty, how does moral goodness arise?

2. In attempting as completely as possible accurately to represent Aristotle's complete specification of moral virtue, what four points does St. Thomas make?

3. According to St. Thomas, how does moral virtue discover the mean, and how does it choose it?

4. According to him, in its genus is moral virtue a mean or an extreme? In its species, is it a mean or an extreme?

5. In their specific nature, why does St. Thomas maintain that some actions and passions, appetitive dispositions, can never be prudent/beautiful, while other actions moderated by prudence have a kind of intrinsic harmony and beauty?

By applying Aristotle's definition of moral virtue in a special way to individual virtues, St. Thomas makes this definition more precise

1. According to St. Thomas, how must a practical scientist consider definitions? Why?

2. Focusing attention on the way in which moral virtues act as principles of action in the individual situation, in what two ways does St. Thomas distinguish moral virtues? What does he tell us is the reason for this distinction?

3. In what two ways does St. Thomas maintain that the passions involve a kind of inclination that can be contrary to prudential reason?

4. On the basis of the two ways that emotional inclination can be contrary to prudential reason, how does St. Thomas distinguish the operations of the four cardinal moral virtues?

Aristotle's initial discussion of the moral virtues of courage and temperance, liberality and magnificence

1. According to St. Thomas, in his initial discussion of the moral virtues of courage and temperance, how does Aristotle talk about these virtues?

2. In his initial discussion of the external moral virtues of liberality and magnificence, how does St. Thomas say Aristotle talks about these virtues?

Aristotle's initial discussion of some other moral virtues related to external matters related to riches and honors

1. Before he begins his discussion of the cardinal moral virtue of justice and the virtue of friendship, why does Aristotle first discuss moral virtues related to riches and honors like liberality and magnificence, amiability and magnanimity, and their respective vices?

2. How does Aristotle define amiability and magnanimity? What are the extremes, vices, of these respective virtues, and explain the natures of these vices?

Opposition among virtues and vices

1. According to St. Thomas, what three things does Aristotle do when considering the way opposition exists between virtues and vices?

2. In saying that virtue opposes both extremes, according to St. Thomas, to some extent, what is Aristotle maintaining? According to Aristotle, to persons of both extremes of moral vice, how does the person of moral virtue appear?

3. For what two reasons does St. Thomas maintain Aristotle shows that vices are more greatly opposed to each other than to the mean?

4. For what two reasons does St. Thomas claim Aristotle says one extreme is more opposed to virtue than the other?

5. Regarding the opposition among virtues and vices, what does St. Thomas state is the chief aim of virtue?

6. What does he assert about those vices that are somewhat innate to us as opposed to those not innate to us?

7. What emotional inclination does St. Thomas say is in us most inordinately to pursue, not flee? As a result, what moral vice does he say tends to be stronger than any other?

Aristotle's teaching about how to become morally virtuous

1. Reviewing Aristotle's teaching about moral virtue, what three things does St. Thomas tell us about it?

2. To help alleviate the difficulty that moral vice poses for us to become morally virtuous, what two things does Aristotle do?

3. Regarding how to discover the mean in general, what four things does Aristotle tell us?

4. Finally, what three points and advice about determining the mean in the individual situation do Aristotle and St. Thomas give us?

Chapter 9

Voluntary and involuntary activity considered in general and in relation to praise, blame, reward, punishment, and moral virtue and vice

1. St. Thomas starts his examination of Aristotle's Book 3 of his *Nicomachean Ethics* by doing what three things?

2. Concerning Aristotle's prior discussion of moral virtue in his

Nicomachean Ethics, what four claims does Aristotle make regarding praise and blame related to the acts and passions that concern ethics?

3. According to St. Thomas, in what does the difference between pardon and pity consist? According to him, why does Aristotle say that, more than pardon, pity is due and total exoneration of blame for a wrong choice?

4. Why does he maintain that people who want to study moral virtue and vice need to study voluntary and involuntary acts? And, why does St. Thomas say they need to do so first, externally, from their effects: from the praise and blame, reward, and punishment that their actions and choices publicly receive? Regarding the nature of first principles of understanding as first principles of right reason, why are the answers to the immediately-preceding questions crucial to understand?

5. What does the readily-observable fact that, within all social communities, we human beings incline publicly to praise and blame, reward and punish, human beings for choices we make indicate to Aristotle and St. Thomas?

6. Of what sound moral induction and external sign does the effect of praise and blame, reward and punishment indicate that human beings universally incline to take for granted, consider as an evident inductive truth?

7. Why does Aristotle maintain that legislators should find study of voluntary and involuntary acts especially useful for determining honors and rewards for the law-abiding and punishment for law-breakers?

Involuntary and voluntary acts

1. According to St. Thomas, when considering involuntary and vol-

untary acts, why does Aristotle study involuntary activity first and voluntary activity second?

2. According to him, in what three stages does Aristotle achieve his explanation of the nature of involuntary activity?

3. Why does St. Thomas maintain that involuntariness can be caused by: 1) exclusion of the appetite violence; or 2) cognition due to ignorance?

4. Into what two species does St. Thomas divide the involuntariness that violence causes?

5. According to St. Thomas, what five claims does Aristotle make about the nature of violence?

6. What do Aristotle and St. Thomas maintain about involuntary acts done out of fear, about acts that St. Thomas refers to as acts of "mixed-voluntariness"?

7. In moral activity, what does Aristotle mean by what he calls "the ultimate particular"? In relation to moral activity, why is knowledge of the ultimate particular crucial to understand?

8. Why are we justified to call "scientific" the composite act (the corporate, practical, universal act) that generates moral activity?

9. According to St. Thomas, why does Aristotle include acts of mixed-voluntariness among the many voluntary acts that merit praise, blame, reward, punishment, and pardon?

10. In contrast to people who make an effort to avoid involuntarily choosing an evil, what does Aristotle observe about people who suffer evil to preserve no greater good?

11. What does Aristotle maintain about precisely what acts merit praise, blame, reward, punishment, and pardon?

12. According to Aristotle, what is even more difficult than judging

what should be chosen to avoid as evil and to be endured so as not to be deprived of a greater good?

13. According to him, why does remaining passionately steadfast in a decision involving mixed-voluntariness require courage, and why does it merit praise?

14. Chiefly what three things does St. Thomas claim Aristotle says about acts of mixed voluntariness?

15. According to Aristotle and St. Thomas, what sort of rule cannot we use when judging about the nature of an act as morally good or morally evil? According to them, what sort of rule must we use?

16. While Aristotle and St. Thomas do not say so precisely in this part of their work, why is the reason for using the sort of rule they indicate clear?

17. Why cannot people who deny the existence of natures in things make prudent choices within an individual situation?

18. How does St. Thomas summarize five reasons Aristotle rejects the claim made by some philosophers that, because reason is man's specific difference, only acts performed in agreement with the determination of reason are voluntary?

19. How does Aristotle distinguish three kinds of moral ignorance regarding involuntary acts resulting from ignorance?

20. According to Aristotle, emotionally how do involuntary acts done out of ignorance incline to affect a person? What does he say about acts *of* ignorance in general and how they differ, if at all, from acts done *out of* ignorance, *with* ignorance, and *in* ignorance?

21. Relative to states of ignorance, what do Aristotle and St. Thomas say about the way every vicious person acts?

22. At this part in the discussion, what do they say happens to the

intemperate/angry person who repeatedly acts in ignorance of the real good to be done? What do they omit saying happens to this person, but, nonetheless, results to such a person from such repeated acts of ignorance?

23. In addition to voluntary, involuntary, and non-voluntary ignorance, what other species of ignorance does Aristotle say exists relative to the performance of actions? Explain the nature of this ignorance.

24. In what two ways does Aristotle claim a person can be ignorant of what is suitable, proportionate, under the circumstances?

25. According to St. Thomas, what are the eight circumstances of an act?

26. According to St. Thomas, why does Aristotle define the cause he calls "voluntary" by *removal* of what two causes of an act of being involuntary?

27. For what five reasons does Aristotle reject the assertion that not everything an agent originates through knowledge of circumstances is voluntary because sometimes the passions, not the will, chiefly cause human act?

Choice, voluntary activity, the passions, wishing, and opinion

1. Among other reasons, what three reasons does Aristotle give for examining the nature of choice?

2. In what ways does Aristotle prove that choice is a species of the genus of voluntary activity?

3. On the basis of the fact that, to be identical, no difference or opposition can exist between two things, Aristotle claims that choice cannot be identical with what passions or activities?

4. How does Aristotle refute the claim that choice consists in any human passion?

5. How does Aristotle show that choice cannot be identical with opinion and wishing?

Counsel, its order and method, and how it compares and contrasts with choice

1. According to St. Thomas, how does Aristotle start his study of counsel?

2. According to Aristotle, about what matters do human beings not take counsel? Why?

3. According to Aristotle, what four species of cause can generate things?

4. What does Aristotle say about how counsel occurs related to human arts?

5. According to Aristotle, what are the only matters about which we take counsel and in what respect?

6. While, at this point in the discussion, Aristotle and St. Thomas make no explicit note of this fact, *of what human sense faculty does deliberation, counsel always involve work*? From this fact, what implications necessarily follows regarding people who are unaware of, or deny the reality of, human nature and an estimative sense faculty (particular, or cogitative, reason)?

7. According to Aristotle, about what doubtful matters do we deliberate more and less than about others? Give some examples of such doubtful matters.

8. According to him, essentially what three qualities relative to the subjects about which we deliberate do matters about which we take counsel involve?

9. What does Aristotle say is the method employed when using counsel? Today, what might we call this "method" of taking counsel?

10. How does St. Thomas define counsel? How does he contrast the way we reason in relation to principles in speculative science to the way reason in relation to them in practical science?

11. What four examples does Aristotle give about what people who take counsel do not do?

12. Taking for granted that a numerically-one, last act is a first prin-ciple of practical investigation, what three points does St. Thomas note about the order and method (steps) to be taken related to acts involving deliberation?

13. According to St. Thomas, if only one means (action and/or in-strument) exists to achieve the end, and if it is readily available, what does he say the prudent counselor concludes? If this means should not be readily at hand, what does he say this person concludes?

14. Just as in geometry, what does St. Thomas maintain about the reasoning method used in practical investigations? According to him, why is counsel a kind of deliberation that seeks to get to the first principles of operation?

15. As a prime example of analytical reasoning related to counsel, how does St. Thomas talk about *the moral psychology of prudent business leaders*, about *how business professionals* tend to think, and *how hope of success tends to guide their reasoning from start to finish*?

16. To put what St. Thomas says in more contemporary business language, what sort of questions and in what order does a good, pru-dent, counselor proceed about means to be taken to achieve an end?

17. According to St. Thomas, what are the three generic consider-ations that Aristotle determines to be the universal, intensive quan-tum, or qualitative, limits of all real counsel?

18. To make even more evident the precise nature of counsel, what

final comparison does Aristotle make between counsel and choice related to possible means of action, including when several means exist to achieve an end? What example does Aristotle give from ancient Greek politics to emphasize this comparison?

19. In concluding his comparison between choice and counsel, in a general way, how does Aristotle define choice?

The formal object of willing: Real, or apparent, good?

1. According to Aristotle, what has been the existing disagreement about whether the formal object of the will is real or apparent good?

2. How does Aristotle resolve this disagreement? In answering this disagreement, what crucial role does the estimative sense, or particular reason, of the prudent and imprudent man play?

Why behaving morally virtuously and viciously must be within our power

1. According to St. Thomas, how does Aristotle demonstrate that moral virtue must be within our power?

2. How does Aristotle refute the claim made by some that no person is voluntarily (willingly) evil or involuntarily (unwillingly) good because, by nature, the will tends toward the good? Why does Aristotle say the way private individuals behave in their everyday lives supports his argument?

3. Relative to the role that cogitative reason, or the estimative sense, plays in our ability to perform acts of moral virtue or vice, what special note should be taken regarding Aristotle's argument's reference to use of restraint and encouragement in dealing with moral behavior on an everyday basis?

4. According to Aristotle, what influence, if any, does ignorance, in some way, have on causing our acts not to be within our power?

5. How does St. Thomas refute the claim that: 1) not everyone is naturally able to be diligent about acquiring good habits of soul; 2) some people have a negligent disposition which prevents them from developing virtuous habits; 3) by nature, some people take pleasure in pursuing and doing evil?

6. How does he refute the claim that we have no knowing faculty that knows the good?

7. How does St. Thomas refute the claim that human beings have no power over the way things appear to us because our imagination can cause them to appear to us other than they are?

8. How does he refute the sophistic argument that: 1) some people are born with the ability to see the real good and take delight in what is really good for us, while others are not; 2) this ability is not teachable; 3) nor is the self-control over the imagination that supposedly can be taught?

Courage (fortitude) and vices that oppose it

1. According to St. Thomas, how does Aristotle define courage considered in general?

2. Strictly speaking, according to him, what does Aristotle maintain is the formal object of courage?

3. Does St. Thomas claim that some species of fear are naturally good and naturally bad not to experience? If so, why?

4. According to Aristotle, how does the unqualifiedly courageous person behave in the face of the most terrifying dangers while fighting for noble cause? What does the courageous person precisely do within such a situation that makes him or her unqualifiedly brave?

5. According to him, in what does courage consist, what is virtue as the maximum in the faculty of courage?

6. Generically considered, what does St. Thomas maintain is courage's formal object?

7. How does St. Thomas describe the moral psychology of the courageous man? According to him, what is the chief reason that this way of behaving is the moral psychology of someone who is courageous?

8. Why does St. Thomas say that the proximate, proper, end of every habit is to impress a likeness of that habit on its act? According to him, in acting in this way, what do habits and/or customs, act like?

9. While St. Thomas maintains that the remote end of every naturally-operating agent is a perfect good (the good of the created universe), what does he state is proximate end of such an agent? Consequently, what does he assert the brave men intends and does not intend to imprint on another?

10. In what five ways, does St. Thomas contrast real courage with counterfeit courage in relation to three ways an act of courage can fall short of real courage?

11. What does St. Thomas say about counterfeit courage motivated by anger?

12. In contrast to emotionally-generated, counterfeit courage of such individuals, how does St. Thomas maintain a really brave man inclines to react?

13. According to St. Thomas, what are the properties of courage related to pleasure and pain?

14. According to him, how does courage differently relate to fear and daring, and in what does he think praise of this virtue more consists? Why does he make this claim?

15. According to St. Thomas, in what psychological faculty does the

passion of daring start? In what act does the moral psychology of the daring person start?

16. What common generic object does St. Thomas say fear and pain share and how does this object differently relate to these two passions?

17. What special relationship does St. Thomas maintain exists between courage and pain?

18. How does he claim the brave man behaves in the face of future and present dangers?

19. According to St. Thomas, to what does praise of a courageous person essentially relate?

20. What observation does St. Thomas make about the way we praise virtue considered in general and the way we praise the virtue of courage?

21. Why does St. Thomas maintain that moral virtue of courage is more praiseworthy than the moral virtue of temperance?

22. What does St. Thomas say about the special relationship that Aristotle reports exists between courage and pleasure?

23. According to St. Thomas, what was Aristotle's attitude toward the Stoic understanding of the relationship between moral virtue and the passions of pleasure and pain?

24. How does Aristotle modify a claim that, previously, he had made about virtuous operations being pleasurable?

25. With what general definition does Aristotle finish his discussion of courage?

Temperance and intemperance

1. According to St. Thomas, in what ways does Aristotle claim temperance and courage agree?

2. According to him, what is a chief reason temperance exists in the sensitive appetite?

3. How does Aristotle start to define temperance generically?

4. Immediately to locate temperance's specific difference, what does Aristotle do?

5. What does Aristotle give as an example of psychological pleasure purely of the soul? What does he say about it?

6. In relation to knowledge that we possess love, what does Aristotle say about awareness of this on the sense level?

7. What does Aristotle maintain about the relation of temperance to bodily pleasures and external goods?

8. What does Aristotle claim about the relation of the passion of pleasure to the external sense faculties of sight, hearing, and smell in animals other than human?

9. Strictly speaking, what does Aristotle say is the formal object of temperance? How does he support his claim that other animals take delight in the sense of sight, hearing, and smell only indirectly, by reference to the external senses of taste and touch?

10. According to him, in what respect does the chief aim, by nature, for which brute animals have sense faculties and appetites differ from the chief aim, by nature, for which human beings possess them?

11. Before considering the relationship of touch and taste to temperance and intemperance, what five things that St. Thomas has already noted are most helpful to recall? And what five things that Aristotle tells us about the sense of taste and touch do we need to know?

12. According to Aristotle, why does intemperance naturally incline to appear to human beings to be *the most beastly*, and least-properly human, of all moral vices?

13. What is Aristotle's opinion about the vice of intemperance? What affect does he say the vice of intemperance has on human beings? Through its performance what does he say results?

14. What does Aristotle say in reply to the objection that, aside from beastly pleasure, some properly human delight, good, should pertain to touch?

15. To explain the nature of intemperance more precisely, what distinctions does Aristotle make among several modes of human choice (generic, specific, and individual) related to generic and specific nature? In making these distinctions, what does he say about the natural need of human beings to satisfy natural desire and the difference between natural need and individual preference?

16. In the case of generic and specific desires to eat and drink for the chief aim of staying healthy, what does Aristotle maintain about the propensity or lack of propensity of human beings to make mistakes? Related to eating and drinking, about what does he say most of us tend to make mistakes when we do make them?

17. According to Aristotle, precisely what does the natural animal desire related to the preservation and promotion of animal life and health seek?

18. Related to intemperance, what is the chief point Aristotle seeks to make about how it damages human life? According to him, what psychological disorder does the act of intemperance resemble?

19. Why does Aristotle say that "belly-mad" people, gluttons, are very brutish?

20. In short, like all vices, what mistake does the vice of intemperance make?

21. What do Aristotle and St. Thomas mean by *the prudent measure*?

22. As a result of their intemperance, what tends to be the moral psychology, the moral inclination, of intemperate people regarding pleasure?

23. On the basis of the moral psychology of intemperate people, what does Aristotle conclude about such people in general?

24. As they relate to temperance and intemperance, what six things does Aristotle say about temperance and intemperance?

25. Contrasting courage and temperance, what does Aristotle maintain about them?

26. What does St. Thomas say about Aristotle's apparently incongruous claim that pleasure is a cause of sadness for the intemperate man?

27. According to St. Thomas, relative to temperance, what does Aristotle say about the opposing vice of insensibility?

28. What six things does Aristotle say about how the temperate man *should behave* toward pleasures? Accordingly, what three things does Aristotle say about how the temperate man *actually* behaves?

29. In contrast to the way the temperate man is disposed toward pleasures considered in general, how does Aristotle say the intemperate man is disposed to them?

30. In relation to voluntariness, how do Aristotle and St. Thomas compare the moral vice of intemperance to the vices of cowards and children?

Chapter 10

1. How does St. Thomas start his analysis of Book 4 of Aristotle's *Nicomachean Ethics*?

Liberality as an external good for preserving and protecting individual and species human life

1. Why does Aristotle select liberality as the chief external good with which to begin his examination of external goods involving the reward of riches?

2. According to St. Thomas, how is the way temperance moderates the desires related to *having* tactile pleasures analogous to the way liberality moderates the desire related to *the desire to get*, have, wealth?

3. According to Aristotle, what other vices relate to liberality?

4. Loosely considered, what does Aristotle mean by the term "wealth"? To whom does he compare the spendthrift? What does he consider the term "spendthrift" signify?

5. What does Aristotle considered to be the chief act of the virtue of liberality, and what does he maintain having this virtue tends to enhance?

6. How does Aristotle distinguish liberality from saving?

7. According to Aristotle, does a person who is liberal with money tend more to distribute wealth to the right people than to take it from the right sources and refuse it from the wrong sources? According to him, what is more characteristic of the person who is liberal with money: to spend well or to avoid spending badly, to give well instead of receiving well?

8. According to Aristotle, of friendships chiefly based upon honor or utility, which is more characteristic of the liberal spender?

The act of liberality

1. According to Aristotle, what are the two chief qualities of liberal giving? What is a third quality that Aristotle stresses about liberal giving?

2. What are three other acts and four properties that Aristotle mentions related to liberal giving?

The illiberal vices of the spendthrift and the miser

1. Because opposites are mutually revealing, what does St. Thomas say Aristotle does to make the nature of the virtue of liberality more evident?

2. What does St. Thomas reply regarding the question whether being a miser or a spendthrift is worse?

3. What does he claim about the moral psychology of a person who is a mixture of a spendthrift and the miser? According to him, what tends to be the result of such behavior?

4. What do Aristotle and St. Thomas maintain inclines some people to become misers? How do they account for the existence of many species of stinginess?

5. Why do they maintain that the vices of being a spendthrift and a miser do not simultaneously tend to dominate within the same person?

6. What people does Aristotle identify as having the moral psychology of being cheap, deficient givers?

The moral psychology of misers and why miserliness is difficult to cure

1. How does Aristotle explain the moral psychology of misers, or tightfisted people?

2. For what two chief reasons does Aristotle maintain that being cheap is a greater vice than being a spendthrift?

The moral virtue of magnificence: Being a doer of great deeds, giver of great gifts

1. According to St. Thomas, how does the virtue of liberality con-

trast with the virtue of magnificence? What does he maintain is evident about the virtue of magnificence?

2. What two remarks does St. Thomas make regarding the terms "magnificent" and "great" when applied to the virtue of magnificence?

3. What does he say are the two vices opposed to the virtue of magnificence?

4. How does the author of this book support his claim that the virtue of magnificence can only be understood in relation to the notion of virtual quantity?

5. According to Aristotle and St. Thomas, what are five qualities that the magnificent giver and magnificent giving include?

The objects of magnificence

1. How does St. Thomas start his discussion about Aristotle's treatment of the objects of magnificence?

2. According to St. Thomas, in what three things does all virtue consist?

3. According to him, how does the prudent man behave?

4. Considered in what respect is virtuous, prudent, choice beautiful?

5. In executing a particular act, what does a beautiful choice include? Such being the case, how does moral virtue operate analogously to an internal modulator or gyroscope?

6. As a command and control universal, how does a moral universal work?

7. As a particular moral virtue, what two things does magnificence involve?

8. Chiefly and secondarily, what does Aristotle maintain are the objects of magnificent expenditures?

9. In giving, how does Aristotle say the magnificent person measures expenses?

10. Unlike the magnificent person, related to magnificent expenditures, how does Aristotle describe the vices of the classless and the tacky, or gaudy, person?

The moral virtue of magnanimity and the moral psychology of the magnanimous person

1. According to St. Thomas, what is the virtue of magnanimity?

2. According to him, considered in a wide sense, how does a magnanimous person compare and contrast to a temperate person?

3. What does he say is the vice by excess of magnanimity? What does he say is the vice by defect of magnanimity?

4. What does St. Thomas claim is the chief object of concern that is part of the moral psychology of the magnanimous person?

5. When it accompanies other virtues, what do Aristotle and St. Thomas maintain about the virtue of magnanimity?

6. Because prudence generates magnanimity, what three conclusions does Aristotle draw about magnanimity?

7. Following Aristotle, what five things does St. Thomas say about the magnanimously courageous person?

8. What five properties does St. Thomas identify as belonging to the moral psychology of the magnanimous person?

9. What other traits does he say the behavior of the magnanimous man include?

10. What four traits of magnanimity does St. Thomas identify as being especially related to the human intellect?

11. What thirteen traits related to the human appetites, the will, and

the passions, does St. Thomas identify as qualities of the moral psychology of a magnanimous person?

Vices opposed to magnanimity: Being conceited and small-souled

1. According to Aristotle, what are the vices by defect and excess of magnanimity? How does Aristotle describe the moral psychology of persons possessed of these vices?

2. Of the two vices, which does Aristotle claim is the more opposed to the virtue of magnanimity, and why?

The virtue concerned with desiring small, ordinary honors

1. According to Aristotle, what does the virtue concerned with desiring small, ordinary honors essentially involve?

2. What does he say about vices related to this virtue?

The moral virtue and vices related to inhibiting and provoking anger

1. What qualities does St. Thomas identify with the moral virtue related to inhibiting and provoking anger?

2. What does Aristotle say about the extremes by excess and defect (vices) of this virtue?

3. How does he describe the mean that exists between these two extremes? What names might we give to such a person today?

4. What three claims does Aristotle make in refuting the teaching of some Stoics that all anger is blameworthy?

5. What three species of hot-temperedness does St. Thomas identify? How does he describe the moral psychology of them?

6. In general, what does St. Thomas say about the vice of hot-temperedness? Why does St. Thomas say that no human being can endure the vice of hot temperedness for long?

7. What does Aristotle say about the excess of anger especially of the morose kind?

8. What five things does he say about how, when, and in what way a virtuous person should get angry?

The essential connection between possessing the friendship-like virtue of good personal-relations (amiability) and being able to exercise moral virtue toward others

1. In the last chapters of Book 4 of his *Nicomachean Ethics*, what external human actions that chiefly impact upon social life does Aristotle start to discuss?

2. According to St. Thomas, related to what matters does Aristotle discuss these actions and how does he first start his study of personal relations?

3. What two things does St. Thomas say about the social vice by defect of being socially disagreeable?

4. In contrast to these moral flaws in social, personal relations, what does Aristotle maintain about the moral virtue of being socially amiable? According to St. Thomas, how did Aristotle derive the name of this moral virtue? In a way, what sort of friendship does St. Thomas say the virtue of amiability resembles?

5. According to St. Thomas, how does the virtue of amiability differ from the virtue of friendship?

6. Considered as such, whom does St. Thomas say the amiable person resembles? According to him, to what acts does the virtue of amiability extend?

7. From his observation of the way in which amiable people incline to communicate with each other, what five properties of the moral psychology of amiability does Aristotle enumerate?

An Introduction to Ragamuffin Ethics

The amiable, social virtue of veracity

1. According to Aristotle, by examining individual virtues as he has done in studying moral science, what useful conclusion has he been able to derive about the relation of all virtues to particular habits?

2. According to him, how does consideration of veracity, truth-telling in words and deeds, further extend moral science? What contribution does Aristotle think truth-telling makes to human sociability? What does he say are the vices by excess and defect of truth-telling?

3. What does Aristotle say about the moral psychology of the boaster and the dissembler? According to him, can these habits relate to a means to an end or just to an end (taking pleasure in being what you are)?

4. According to Aristotle, why are liars vicious, evil?

5. Why does St. Thomas say that someone who speaks the truth constitutes the mean in human communication? What six things does he maintain regarding the truthful person about whom Aristotle speaks?

The moral psychology underlying boasting and dissembling, the objects about which people boast and dissemble, and why; and when, if ever, these acts are evil

1. Considering the boaster, what does Aristotle identify as three motives that underlie the moral psychology of the boaster? What does he maintain about the moral good or evil of boasting for these different aims?

2. What does Aristotle say regarding the objects about which people tend to boast and why they tend to boast?

3. What does he say underlies the moral psychology of dissemblers?

4. What does Aristotle say regarding which vice, that of the boaster or dissembler, is worse?

Amusement, laughter

1. What two things does St. Thomas say about behavior related to non-serious, relaxing activities?

2. What does Aristotle say we call people with the virtue of amusement? Today, what other names might we give such people ? How does he describe such people?

3. What names does Aristotle use to refer to the naming people possessed of the vices of excess and defect related to the virtue of amusement?

4. In what three ways does Aristotle describe the moral psychology of the amusing, or witty, person?

5. How does Aristotle conclude his discussion of amusement and laughter?

Shame

1. Why does St. Thomas claim that shame is a passion, not a virtue? In what passion does St. Thomas think shame consists? What does he tell us we tend to notice about the physiological condition of people when they are experiencing shame?

2. How does he contrast this with the physiological condition that terrified people tend to manifest? How does St. Thomas account for the difference between these two physiological conditions?

Chapter 11

1. After finishing his study of the definition of moral virtue, in Book 5 of the *Nicomachean Ethics*, how does Aristotle chiefly consider justice as a mean between excess and defect in social relations between people?

2. To start to do so, how does St. Thomas maintain that Aristotle talks about justice and the previously-examined virtues?

3. According to St. Thomas, how had Aristotle chiefly thought about the moral virtues, and, in contrast to that approach, how will he think about justice in Book 5 of the *Nicomachean Ethics*? How will he start discussion of the mean of commutative justice and how did he prepare to do this toward the end of Book 4?

Justice considered chiefly as a mean between excess and defect in social relations between people

1. According to Aristotle, between what two extremes of excess and defect (vices) are the moral virtues of temperance and courage means? According to him, between what two extremes of excess and defect is the virtue of justice a mean?

2. After explaining the difference in approach to what Aristotle has done and what he will do, how does St. Thomas say Aristotle distinguishes between particular, or individual, justice, and legal justice?

3. According to St. Thomas, how does Aristotle start to examine particular justice?

4. According to him, making the appropriate changes, how does Aristotle define injustice as a habit by which men are disposed to perform unjust deeds and by which they will and do unjust acts? By so doing, upon what does St. Thomas say Aristotle intentionally focuses attention?

5. According to St. Thomas, what is a chief aim of the will as a moral principle? To support his claim, to what observation of Aristotle about opposition and unfixed and firmly-fixed habits of the soul does St. Thomas make reference?

6. Toward the beginning of Book 5 of the *Nicomachean Ethics* and throughout this Book, about what should note be taken regarding the way Aristotle reasons? Keeping this note in mind, what is easily observable about the way in which Aristotle approaches preliminary definitions of justice and injustice?

7. According to Aristotle, in what three ways do we talk about the unjust person? From these ways of talking about injustice, what does Aristotle conclude about the way we speak about the just person?

8. Regarding an act of injustice by excess, what does St. Thomas say about the moral psychology of the greedy person? What does he say about the negative result of pursuing goods the way the greedy man does?

9. What observation does Aristotle make regarding two different reasons that cause people to refer to someone as "unjust"?

10. According to Aristotle, why is the lawbreaker called unjust? According to him, how is *what is illegal* a kind of inequality? According to him, is the lawbreaker within a political order always the unjust man? If not, in such a situation, who or what is the principle of injustice?

Legal justice

1. What does Aristotle mean when he says that legal justice concerns legal enactments as *relatively, somewhat, just acts*? According to him, why is it that what a political order commands as just might not conform to what is really just?

2. According to Aristotle, what is the difference between "civic justice" and "justice"? According to him, which species of justice do civic laws chiefly promote, and how do good civic laws do this?

3. Because justice commands the work of all the virtues, what does St. Thomas maintain about it?

4. According to St. Thomas, what makes legal justice perfect justice? According to him, why is legal justice the most perfect species of moral virtue?

5. According to St. Thomas, why are ruling and legislation essentially communications arts?

6. According to him, in what sense are illegal acts general vices and in what way are virtue and justice identical?

7. In what way does St. Thomas say that temperance approaches justice?

Particular, or individual, justice

1. In what three ways does Aristotle start his examination of individual justice? Explain.

2. Just as nothing is contained in a genus that is not contained in the species, what do Aristotle and St. Thomas maintain about whatever is legally unjust?

3. According to Aristotle, how do we determine the mean of legal and particular justice? Explain.

4. Why does Aristotle say that injustices that violate just civil law conform to the nature of complete vice?

5. According to Aristotle, considered in general, how does civil law command us to live? Why, then, does he maintain that some laws do not *directly* relate to any virtue?

6. Why does Aristotle claim that, in its relation to justice, positive law tends to educate the soul in virtue? Beyond this kind of legislative instruction in virtue, what other kind of moral instruction about how to become morally virtuous does Aristotle say exists, and where does he say he will discuss this form of instruction?

7. What observation does St. Thomas make about the nature of the best polity as a form of political rule?

Distributive and commutative justice as forms of particular justice

1. What does St. Thomas say about distributive justice as a form of particular justice?

2. In contrast to distributive justice, what does St. Thomas say about the nature of commutative justice?

3. Into what two species does St. Thomas divide commutative justice?

4. According to St. Thomas, what can cause species of commutative injustice to double, become twofold?

5. Since involuntary acts can be done out of violence and ignorance, into what two species does Aristotle divide involuntary acts of injustice?

6. Having made these initial observations about the natures of commutative and distributive justice, about what does Aristotle next start to talk?

7. According to Aristotle, how do we derive the just as a mean in activities related to distributive justice? Explain.

8. What does Aristotle mean by "proportionate equality" and how is the principle of virtual quantity related to proportionate equality?

9. According to Aristotle and St. Thomas, how is the principle of proportionate equality, or virtual quantity, applied in relation to acts of distributive justice?

10. According to them, what is the one vice that exists against distributive justice?

The mean of commutative justice and how to find it

1. According to Aristotle and St. Thomas, in exchanges involving

commutative justice, why is the mean that is used arithmetical and not proportional?

2. In matters of commutative justice, what do they say is the only thing the judge attempts to do? What does the judge not attempt to do?

3. According to Aristotle and St. Thomas, in commutative exchanges, how are the exchanges chiefly measured?

4. From what he has said thus far about commutative justice, what two conclusions does Aristotle draw about the uses of the terms "gain" and "loss" in relation to commutative transactions? Why does he say that use of these terms does not appear suitable? From where does he say these terms were first derived?

5. Because of the difficulty involved precisely in determining the mean in commutative and distributive relations, what does Aristotle conclude should be the nature of a judge? What example does Aristotle give to indicate how a judge determines a mean in commutative justice?

6. From what Aristotle has said thus far about commutative justice, what does St. Thomas think is evident?

The false opinion of some Pythagoreans about the mean: That it is reciprocation, an eye for an eye and a tooth for tooth

1. In what ways does Aristotle criticize the retributive teaching about the just mean attributed to some Pythagoreans?

2. According to Aristotle, why do commutative exchanges sometimes require use of proportional equality as a mean?

3. According to him, without just retribution, what tends to develop within a political order?

4. According to Aristotle and St. Thomas, what would happen with-

in a political order without the presence of equality of proportion and arithmetical equality as just means of measuring exchanges?

Money

1. While Aristotle's and St. Thomas's teachings about economics are often ridiculed today, according to the author of this book, in what way, if any, is what they say about the nature of money actually quite profound?

2. According to them, why is a type of proportionality in commutative exchanges an essential part of business activity that qualitatively makes intelligible the nature of money and economic exchange?

3. According to them, why was money, currency, invented?

4. What example do they give to make intelligible the nature of money as a measure of fair price and market demand?

5. According to them, if human beings do not recognize the hierarchical inequality of business and other professions for the unequal contribution they make toward the preservation and promotion of human life and safety, perfecting the quality of human life, what will happen?

6. According to Aristotle and St. Thomas, how does money serve as a just mean for commutative exchange of goods? According to St. Thomas, what is the only standard that truly measures all goods, including economic ones?

7. According to St. Thomas, why do we not measure economic good according to a metaphysical standard of greatness?

8. What does St. Thomas say as further proof that human need is a chief measure of economic price?

9. What does St. Thomas say about the etymology of the word "money"?

10. Why does St. Thomas maintain that money has to be backed up by the force of law?

11. According to him, what good does money serve in relationship to the existence and preservation of States? According to him, how is money a measure of the health of a State?

12. According to St. Thomas what is money's *virtue*? How does money serve as a kind of balance scale, and of what is it chiefly a sign or measure?

13. What does St. Thomas say is a great good that money provides to social human life?

14. According to him, what additional power, virtue, does money possess?

15. Why does St. Thomas state that, more so than other things, money needs legal protections to be put in place to enable it to retain its exchange utility?

16. Why does St. Thomas maintain that no measure of the hierarchy of human needs, arts, and sciences can exist according to reality and the natures of things? What does he say is the best we can do to compare the contributions made by the arts and sciences to human needs at this or that time, and in this or that circumstance?

Just action as a mean, or equal

1. From what he has said thus far about justice, what does Aristotle conclude about the nature of justice as an equal?

2. What does he conclude about justice as a mean in *having, possessing*?

3. In the most precise sense, why does Aristotle claim that justice is not a mean in the same way as other moral virtues are means?

4. Because virtue is a habit by which, through deliberate choice, a

642

man acts virtuously, in what two ways does Aristotle maintain that justice can be a virtue?

5. According to Aristotle, in relation to distributive goods like rules and honors, how do the just man and just judge do the just deed?

6. According to him, contrary to justice, what kind of habit is injustice? What twofold evil effect does he say injustice produces?

7. What three conclusions does Aristotle derive from his preceding remarks about the nature of justice as a mean related social interaction?

The unjust man and political justice

1. After finishing his treatment of justice and injustice in a general way, how does Aristotle start to talk about unjust deeds related to the unjust agent?

2. According to St. Thomas, after considering the nature of justice and injustice in a general way, why does he start to talk about unjust deeds related to the unjust agent?

3 According to Aristotle, in what does political justice consist? According to him, where *does* political justice exist, where *can it only* exist? Why?

4. Hence, in what does Aristotle maintain it cannot exist? According to Aristotle, in what sort of dominion does free exercise over human beings consist?

5. What does Aristotle say are the two species of political justice?

6. Why does Aristotle think that the extension of political justice to human beings capable of being unjust is evident?

7. What does Aristotle conclude from the fact that not every virtuous or vicious action is an act generated by virtue or vice (virtuous or vicious people)?

8. According to St. Thomas, why should the prudent man, and not someone else, rule in the political order?

9. To what kind of rule within the State does St. Thomas analogously relate the moral psychology of justice of a master over a slave or a child (over someone psychologically incapable of self-rule)?

10. Even though, previously, Aristotle, had conflated political and legal justice, at this point, for the sake of greater precision, into what two species does he divide political justice?

11. In political regimes, what sort of force and power does Aristotle claim political justice possesses? According to him, how does natural justice differ from justice by decree/legal enactments?

12. According to Aristotle, in what three ways are some ways of behaving called "legal justice"?

13. What does St. Thomas say about how legal/positive justice always originates? What two examples of positive justice arising from natural justice does he give?

14. At this point in his analysis, how does Aristotle start to prove the universal nature of natural justice?

15. According to Aristotle, why cannot civil law and State administration be universal and uniform?

Actions that make a person just or unjust

1. Having considered the nature of justice and what just and unjust actions are, what three questions related to justice and injustice does Aristotle next consider?

2. According to Aristotle, when and where does what is just considered in itself and considered as a just action exist?

3. According to Aristotle and St. Thomas, what three conditions must be fulfilled for a person to act voluntarily?

4. Since all the circumstances of an act influence the voluntariness of an act, and since only a voluntary act can be a moral, or ethical act (a freely-chosen act), what does St. Thomas maintain about the circumstances and the specification of an individual act as voluntary, non-voluntary, or involuntary and the determination of the nature of the individual choice and act as morally virtuous or vicious?

5. According to him, what do we have to know in order to be able accurately to judge a whole human act as morally virtuous or vicious? Why? Why does this knowledge necessarily depend upon our ability to comprehend the power of an agent's particular reason or estimative sense?

Whether a person can voluntarily suffer injustice and a just person easily execute unjust acts

1. In what three ways does Aristotle start to answer the question of whether a person can voluntarily suffer injustice? How does he attempt to answer the three questions he poses as to whether a person can voluntarily suffer injustice? What conclusion does he finally draw related to this question?

2. How does Aristotle answer the question about which person engaged in a distributive relation does injustice: the giver, the taker, or both?

3. In proposing his solution to this question, what twofold difficulty does Aristotle note about this situation?

4. For what three reasons does Aristotle maintain that a person who accepts too little or too much good from another does not always commit an injustice?

5. According to St. Thomas, how does Aristotle start to undermine the false notion that being habitually unjust is easy?

6. How does Aristotle refute the false claim that the just man can do injustice as easily as anyone else because he has a greater knowledge of how to do unjust acts?

Equity

1. Under what three topics does Aristotle consider equity and how does he start his inquiry into these topics?

2. How does he resolve the question about how the equitable person can be better than the just person?

3. According to Aristotle and St. Thomas, why does application of natural justice to positive law invariably generate defective precepts? According to them, what role does equity play in relation to this problem?

4. According to them, what mistake in positive law always arises? What do they maintain is the nature of the equitable?

5. According to them, why cannot positive law be absolutely rigid in individual cases? Why must it be applied proportionately to the situation?

6. Based upon this study of the nature of equity, what do Aristotle and St. Thomas conclude should be the qualities possessed by an equitable judge?

Whether a person can be unjust to himself

1. For what two reasons does Aristotle claim that, strictly speaking, according to legal justice, a person cannot be unjust to himself?

2. For what three reasons does Aristotle say that, in terms of particular, or individual, justice, no one can commit an injustice against himself?

3. According to him, how is the problem of whether or not a person can act unjustly toward himself completely solved?

4. What does Aristotle assert about the moral condition of doing injustice, doers of injustice, and those who suffer injustice?

5. How does Aristotle answer the question about whether doing or suffering injustice is more shameful and which is morally worse?

Chapter 12

1. According to St. Thomas, in Book 6 of the *Nicomachean Ethics*, how does Aristotle start his consideration of the definition of intellectual virtue?

2. Toward the start of the *Nicomachean Ethics*, does Aristotle consider the intellectual virtues of speculative science and practical science, or does he examine only one of these? If only one, which one? Why?

Right reason and practical science

1. Before discussing the species of practical right reason, what does St. Thomas note about right reason as a mean?

2. While Aristotle and St. Thomas do not precisely say so at this point, according to the author of this book, what would right reason as a mean be in speculative science?

3. To explain more precisely the nature of right reason in practical science, what does St. Thomas claim about all moral virtues considered thus far and all art?

4. To what does St. Thomas say virtue's formal object is analogous?

5. At this point in Book 6, why does St. Thomas add to, specify, Aristotle's claim that further inquiry about the nature of right reason is needed? How does St. Thomas start this further inquiry?

6. According to St. Thomas, why will the man who considers common measure of rule alone not know how rationally to use it in the individual situation? Give an example.

7. To make up for the deficiencies in a generic definition of a measure of right reason, how does St. Thomas start to specify this definition of measure? In so doing, why does he preface this study with an examination of the soul's nature?

8. According to St. Thomas, how does Aristotle resume study of the human soul?

9. How does St. Thomas justify Aristotle's twofold division of the human soul into rational absolutely considered and rational relationally considered?

10. According to St. Thomas, knowledge exists within the soul according to some sort of likeness to what?

11. According to him, each faculty of the soul is qualitatively proportioned in receptive capacity to what?

12. What does St. Thomas call that part of the rational soul whose formal object is contingent beings? Why does Aristotle say that deliberation is an inquiry not yet concluded?

13. Why does St. Thomas doubt Aristotle's division of the soul to be suitable? How does he solve the apparent contradiction between his teaching and that of Aristotle?

14. According to St. Thomas, what kind of consideration is used in speculative sciences like physics and the division of physics like astronomy? What kind of consideration is used in practical sciences like prudence and art?

15. According to him, what role does particular reason, the estimative sense, play in concrete consideration of the nature of contingent beings? For him, how can contingent beings and operational universals be formal objects of the speculative intellect?

Intellectual virtues as they relate to different parts of the soul

1 After dividing the parts of the soul, what does St. Thomas tell us Aristotle examines, and how does he do so?

2. After giving a generic definition of virtue, what does St. Thomas say Aristotle does?

3. To determine the proper operation of each part of the soul, what does St. Thomas say Aristotle does?

4. What does Aristotle say regarding the intellectual part of the soul?

5. Because they lack an intrinsic principle of voluntary activity (the power rationally, abstractly, to deliberate), while brute animals have senses, according to St. Thomas, what do these animals do not have within them?

6. According to St. Thomas, what kind of harmony, peace, is found in human beings that is found in no other species of animal?

7. According to him, what enables the appetitive faculty and the intellect within a human being to harmonize? According to him, what two chief actions in judging does the human intellect possess? Analogously, proportionately, to what two acts of the appetitive faculty does St. Thomas say these two intellectual acts correspond?

8. In well-ordered moral choice and activity, how does St. Thomas say the actions of the human intellect and appetite behave toward each other?

9. What does St. Thomas call *choice*? Why? Essentially, what does St. Thomas understand the nature of choice to be?

10. What does he say is required for choice to be completely good? In what respect does St. Thomas consider choice to be an efficient cause, proximate principle, of action?

11. According to St. Thomas, in speculative knowing, what is the absolutely-considered true and the absolutely-considered false? For him, what is practically-considered good?

12. For him, in what does truth of the practical intellect consist? For him, what is the measure of truth for practical reason?

13. According to St. Thomas, what is the proximate principle of moral choice? According to him, what is moral virtue?

14. From where does St. Thomas claim that practical intellect, including practical science, starts and terminates its reasoning?

15. According to St. Thomas, why does particular reason, the estimative sense, specify the action that universal reason generically considers?

16. As a voluntary activity, toward what does St. Thomas consider free choice to be directed? According to him, when is the appetitive faculty called "right"?

17. Considered as a principle of action, how does St. Thomas consider the speculative and practical divisions of the human intellect to differ? In the act of choice, how does St. Thomas consider deliberation to be related to consent?

18. Why does St. Thomas maintain that, prior to choice being effected, the human intellect and estimative sense (particular reason) must cooperate in comparing choice as a cause and the appetitive faculty commanded to cooperate in effecting a cause?

19. Why does St. Thomas maintain that, considered in and of itself, the speculative intellect moves nothing else? According to him what is the intellect as a principle of practical action? Give an example.

20. In the individual situation, what does St. Thomas consider to be the choices that prudence arranges?

Enumeration of the intellectual virtues and how every science can be taught

1. After finishing his study of the nature of human choice, how does Aristotle start to examine particular intellectual virtues?

2. How does he initially define science? Why does he maintain that certainty and necessity are proper to science?

3. Why does St. Thomas claim that even the science of the probable and perishable (like physics) can exist? How?

4. Explaining science by its cause, what does Aristotle say about the human ability to know noble things, and from what source does he maintain all teaching and science must arise?

5. By means of things known, according to Aristotle, what twofold teaching and way of learning exists? Explain.

6. According to him, does every syllogism generate scientific knowledge and cause speculative science? If not, why not?

7. According to Aristotle, before a person can have science, what must first exist and how must it be known? Explain.

8. What does Aristotle maintain we must use to perfect knowledge about different species of contingent things the intellect must use?

9. Why does Aristotle maintain that a habit which, through reason, causes action (prudence) is not specifically identical with a habit that, through reason, produces things (art)?

The nature of prudence

1. After considering in general the specific difference between the nature of prudence and art, how does Aristotle start to examine the nature of prudence?

2. In what two ways does he claim we commonly call a person "prudent"?

3. What does he maintain is a quality common to people who possess either or both forms of prudence? Why?

4. To start defining prudence through negative reasoning (from effect to cause), what observation does Aristotle make about how no human being deliberates? Why, from the outset of his attempt to define prudence negatively, does Aristotle take for granted that this method of definition must involve use of cogitative reason (particular reason), or the *estimative sense*?

5. From this intellectual first principle involving use of estimative reason, what does Aristotle conclude about principles of prudence?

6. Why does Aristotle maintain that prudence and art cannot be identical? How does he say that prudence and art differ regarding the genera they study and the chief aims?

7. Why do Aristotle and St. Thomas maintain that knowledge of contingent beings cannot possess and do in relationship to the intellect? What do they claim it can do regarding perfection of the intellect?

8. According to St. Thomas, what two parts does art's subject matter include? What threefold operation does he maintain exists in art? With what else does he maintain art is also concerned?

9. In productive arts, what two things does St. Thomas claim we need especially to consider about the work to be undertaken?

10. What does St. Thomas state that mathematics, metaphysics, and physics study in relation to their subjects? In contrast, what does he say art and prudence study? Give examples related to the way each of these intellectual virtues operates.

11. How does St. Thomas say the last act at which prudence aims differs from the last act at which art aims, and how does he explain this difference?

12. Other than prudence, do other species of performance excellence exist? If so, how do they specifically differ from the performance excellence of prudence? Historically, what people have been often identified as specialists in the profession of prudence? Why?

13. According to St. Thomas, what is the Greek etymology for the words "prudence" and "temperance"?

14. According to him, with what sort of judgments and reasoning is the moral virtue of temperance chiefly concerned?

15. Why does St. Thomas maintain that the passions of pleasure and pain have a greater impact on practical judgment and reasoning than they do on speculative judgment and reasoning? What problem does he maintain an intemperate man tends to have related to decision-making when experiencing intense pleasure and pain? What name would we incline to give to the behavior of such a person today?

16. Do you agree with St. Thomas's analysis that the moral psychology of the intemperate man is essentially unhealthy? If not, why not?

17. Precisely in what human faculty does St. Thomas consider the psychological weakness of the intemperate man to exist? Precisely in what way does he think the vice of intemperance distorts the health of this faculty?

18. From what he has said thus far about prudence, what does Aristotle conclude about its nature?

19. While not part of their chief aim according to their professional activity, nonetheless, what does St. Thomas claim that, to some extent, every productive and performance art depends upon prudence to be able to maintain a professional moral culture that sustains the health of the productive, or performance, activity generated by the art? Give an example.

20. Even if a moral virtue, like justice, might intervene and cause an imprudent artist to start to use his or her art out of a sense of duty (for example, to help a friend in need), after an art is acquired, why will an artist still need to exercise the moral virtue of prudence?

21. According to St. Thomas, what differing contributions to perfecting human activity within the individual circumstance does prudence make? Consequently, what sort of moral virtue does St. Thomas say is prudence?

22. Even though St. Thomas recognizes prudence to be chiefly an intellectual virtue, according to him, how is it an appetitive virtue existing within the estimative sense, or particular reason?

23. How does St. Thomas conclude his treatment of prudence?

The intellectual virtue of understanding

1. After examining the intellectual habits of right reason through which the intellect is perfected, what does St. Thomas say Aristotle next considers?

2. According to Aristotle, what kind of judgments does science involve?

3. According to him, why is the principle of demonstrable science necessarily not a prudence, an art, a science, not even the science of metaphysics?

4. According to Aristotle, why cannot art, science, and metaphysics provide principles of demonstrative science?

5. Why does Aristotle maintain that the intellectual virtue of understanding grasps the first principles of all other intellectual virtues? According to him, how do prudence, art, science, and wisdom relate to right reason?

6. By the habit, or virtue, of understanding, what does St. Thomas claim Aristotle does not mean? What does he say he does mean?

The intellectual virtue of wisdom

1. According to Aristotle, what is the difference between wisdom considered in a qualified sense and considered in an unqualified sense?

2. Of all the intellectual virtues, why does St. Thomas say Aristotle considers wisdom to be the highest? How does St. Thomas show that the chief intellectual virtue and science must be no ordinary science?

3. Following Aristotle, how does St. Thomas show that philosophers who maintain that political science or prudence is the highest science are wrong, that metaphysics is the highest science?

Prudence as the chief virtue in human relations

1. According to Aristotle and St. Thomas, what is the work of prudence and not the work of wisdom? What do they say that the prudent man is without qualification? What kind of principle to they say prudence is?

2. According to them, why must prudence consider both universals and singulars, and why must the prudent man possess knowledge of universals and singulars?

3. In what respect do they say prudence differs from wisdom?

4. In what respect do they maintain prudence is a command and control principle of practical reason?

5. According to Aristotle and St. Thomas, what is the difference between individual and civic prudence? How is the difference between individual and civic prudence analogous to the difference between individual justice and legal justice?

6. According to them, how is household prudence different from individual prudence and civic prudence?

7. What are the two parts into which Aristotle and St. Thomas maintain civic prudence is divided? To help make this division intelligible, to what does St. Thomas compare laws?

8. Why does St. Thomas call individual legal decree a "singular extreme"?

9. Why does Aristotle compare those who execute enacted laws to manual laborers?

10. What kind of prudence does St. Thomas refer to as being "especially" prudence, or prudence absolutely? According, to him how does Aristotle refer to the other types of prudence? Why do you think Aristotle and St. Thomas refer to these different kinds of prudence and these different ways of being prudent?

11. Considered in more detail, into what two parts does St. Thomas maintain that prudence is divided?

12. According to St. Thomas, does prudence exist only universally, or does it also exists in particular? Does it exist only in reason, or does it also exist in the appetites? According to him, where do all of the species of prudence to which he has so far referred exist?

13. If these aforementioned activities exist only in reason, what does St. Thomas say is their "proper" name? Why do you think he says this?

14. According to St. Thomas, why must civic prudence be of greater import than domestic prudence, domestic prudence be of greater import than personal prudence, and legislative prudence of greater import among the parts of civic prudence and absolutely of greatest import among acts a person must perform?

15. In reply to the objection that only a man who cultivates things having to do with himself appears prudent, while those who devote themselves to concerns of the multitude appear lacking in prudence, to what example does Aristotle refer? How does Aristotle's example show why legislative prudence is of greatest import?

16. Why does Aristotle claim that, without personal prudence, civic and domestic prudence are insufficient, and even with them in place, how to dispose personal affairs is not evident?

17. How does St. Thomas show that Aristotle's argument about prudence is concerned with universals?

18. Comparing prudence to understanding, why does St. Thomas say that both science and prudence are receptive of, in contact with, have some agreement with, understanding as a habit of principles?

19. What special role does the estimative sense, particular reason, of the prudent man, play in showing how the virtue of prudence is analogous to the virtue understanding?

20. According to St. Thomas, with what is prudence chiefly concerned, upon what does it chiefly focus its attention? According to him, why does no scientific knowledge exist for what the prudent man knows?

21. Why does St. Thomas claim that this singular extreme, the doable deed, is not apprehensible by any external sense faculty as a proper sensible? According to him, what sense faculty grasps this singular extreme, the doable deed?

22. According to St. Thomas, the possession of what sense faculty explains the reason why some people even call some animals "prudent"? According to him, why is the common sense faculty incapable of judging doable deeds?

23. According to him, as a property of the estimative sense, particular reason, how does prudence agree with understanding? How does prudence differ from understanding?

Virtues connected to, and closely resembling, prudence: *Eubulia* and *eustochia*

1. According to Aristotle, what is *eubulia*? What proverb does *eubulia* call to mind for St. Thomas?

2. According to Aristotle, what is *eustochia*?

3. According to Aristotle, how does the nature of prudence differ from the natures of the closely-resembling activities of *eubulia* and *eustochia*?

4, According to him, why can *eubulia* not be *eustochia*?

5. According to Aristotle, in what four senses do we predicate the term "rectitude"? According to him, in what does the rectitude of *eubulia* consist?

6. From Aristotle's analysis of *eubulia* and rectitude, what does St. Thomas conclude about the properties that *eubulia* possesses in relation to practical matters?

The virtue of *synēsis* as distinguished from common sense, opinion, and the virtues of science and *eustochia*

1. After showing how *eubulia* involves rightness of investigation, inquiry, how does Aristotle start to distinguish *synēsis* from common sense, science, opinion, and *eustochia*?

2. What does Aristotle do to make the idea of *synēsis* more precise?

3. According to St. Thomas, how does an act of practical reason resemble the acts of *eubulia* and *synēsis*? According to him, how does prudence differ from *synēsis*?

4. According to him, what is *gnome*, and how does *synēsis* resemble *gnome*?

5. According to St. Thomas, what does prudence combine, synthesize, from legal justice and equity?

6. According to Aristotle, what is the difference between *eubulia* and *synēsis*?

7. According to him, how is *eubulia* like and unlike speculative reason?

8. Referring to *eubulia*, *synēsis*, and prudence, how does St. Thomas describe the way practical reason investigates, judges, and commands?

9. According to St. Thomas, how is *synēsis* different from practical reasoning? According to him, what other kinds of judgments do judgments involving *synēsis* resemble?

10. According to St. Thomas, what does prudence combine, synthesize, with right judgment found in legal justice and equity, and what does it add to this combination?

11. According to him, how do *synēsis* and *gnome* resemble prudence in what they consider; and, like deliberation, what do they presuppose?

12. How does St. Thomas differentiate understanding from speculative and practical knowledge, and from reasoning?

13. According to St. Thomas, how many kinds of understanding exist, what are they, and what do they consider?

14. Because we take our understanding of universals from singulars, what does St. Thomas say is evident about singulars? For example, how does St. Thomas say we induce the universal medicinal power of the herb to cure?

15. What does he conclude from the fact that we know singular first principles through the senses?

16. To what sensory power of judging does St. Thomas maintain that prudence belongs?

17. Inasmuch as the object of particular reason is sensible and singular, what name does St. Thomas say we give to particular reason?

18. Because the habits of *eubulia*, *synēsis*, *gnome*, and prudence consider singulars, what does St. Thomas maintain must be their relationship to the sensitive faculties that operate by means of bodily organs? According to him, in what way do these principles appear to be "natural"?

19. Related to knowing principles, what does St. Thomas say about the natural aptitude of human beings to develop the speculative habits of geometry and metaphysics and the practical habits of *synēsis*, *gnome*, and sense understanding? What does St. Thomas give as an indication of the natural aptitude of human beings to develop a practical understanding of first principles?

20. From what he has said about first principles and the way the speculative and practical intellect acquire a knowledge of them, what does St. Thomas infer about particular reason (the estimative sense) in human beings?

21. What does St. Thomas remind us about the way demonstration proceeds in speculative matters? What difference does he note about the way demonstration proceeds in practical matters?

22. In practical argumentation, what does St. Thomas maintain about the nature of the major premise, the minor premise, and the conclusion?

23. Based upon what he has said about the nature of practical, and

particular, reason what does St. Thomas conclude about the perfection of particular reason?

24. Based upon what St. Thomas says about the relationship of prudence to perfecting particular reason, what conclusion follows regarding the chief aim of moral education? Such being the case, to what must we pay special attention in relationship to moral education? Why?

25. According to St. Thomas, in practical matters, why must we pay special attention to the opinions of experienced, prudent old men?

26. According to St. Thomas, just as, in speculative matters, absolute judgment about universal principles belongs to a speculative understanding (the habit, or virtue, of understanding), to what faculty does he maintain that absolute judgment about principles he calls "*singular extremes*" belong?

27. To which part of the soul does St. Thomas maintain that prudence, *synēsis*, *gnome*, and *eubulia*, chiefly belong? Why?

28. According to St. Thomas, do wisdom and prudence belong to the same, or different, parts of the soul? Why?

Answering some possible objections about the utility of wisdom and prudence for human life

1. How do Aristotle and St. Thomas counter a possible objection some people might make about the utility of wisdom and prudence for human life: that they appear useless to making human beings happy?

2. How do they answer the objection that, while prudence considers actions by which we might become happy, it appears unnecessary because, by an inner habit of inclination, not knowledge, a person

performs noble and honorable deeds toward himself and just deeds toward others?

3. How do they answer the objection that, while, in some cases from a knowledge of his art, an artist acts well as an artist, such intellectual influence is incidental to the art; the habit of the art, repetition of action, not knowledge, generates the good of the art; hence, virtuous habits, routines of action, not prudence, induce a man to do good?

4. How do they reject the claim that denies the superiority of wisdom over prudence?

5. How do they resolve general doubts about the usefulness of prudence and wisdom?

6. In what way do they further refute the claim that prudence contributes nothing to happiness?

7. In a morally virtuous operation, what kind of a relationship do Aristotle and St. Thomas claim exists between prudence and the other moral virtues?

8. According to them, for total moral virtue to exist, what two operative principles must exist?

9. According to them, what operative power resembling prudence exists in particular reason (the estimative sense)? Do they consider prudence to be a species of this operative power? Why, or why not?

10. According to Aristotle and St. Thomas, how does the supreme good, happiness, exist as a universal first principle of practical reason for the virtuous person?

11 According to them, how does the morally virtuous (prudent) man apprehend with precision universal and singular first principles of moral choice?

12. According to St. Thomas, how does moral vice pervert the judgment of reason and cause deception in the conception of practical principles, doable deeds, on the level of universal and particular reason? Why does he maintain that the imprudent, vicious, man cannot habitually reason well in practical matters?

13. Based upon what they have said about the nature of prudence and practical science, what does the author of this book think Aristotle and St. Thomas would conclude about the nature of modern science, mathematical physics, and its relation to the survival of Western civilization and global peace?

14. After considering in some detail that prudence cannot exist as a complete virtue without the other cardinal moral virtues, how do Aristotle and St. Thomas show that the cardinal moral virtues of temperance, courage, and justice cannot exist completely as virtues without prudence?

15. How do Aristotle and St. Thomas refute philosophers who claimed that one virtue can exist without another?

16. How does St. Thomas defend his claim that different species of prudence do not exist for different species of virtue?

17. From his previous discussions about prudence, what is evident to St. Thomas about the human need for prudence?

18. How do Aristotle and St. Thomas resolve the question whether prudence rules over wisdom or wisdom over prudence?

19. According to Aristotle, to claim that, because it gives directions about everything people do in a State, prudence rules over wisdom, is like claiming what?

Chapter 13

1. According to St. Thomas, why does Aristotle start Book 7 of his *Nicomachean Ethics* with a preliminary definition of incontinence?

2. What is this definition of incontinence?

The progression of moral vice from incontinence to intemperance through disease of particular reason, or the estimative sense, and the human will

1. According to St. Thomas, how does Aristotle's study determine a right definition of moral vice?

2. Why does St. Thomas maintain that the incontinent person is not vicious?

3. According to St. Thomas, precisely what happens to move a person from being incontinent to vicious?

4. According to him, what sort of personality change results from this movement from incontinence to viciousness? What role does St. Thomas maintain that particular reason (the estimative sense) and the human will play in this personality change?

5. As a result of the decline of a person from incontinence to viciousness, according to St. Thomas, what kind of moral condition results? How does St. Thomas compare this progressive decline to progressive debilitation of bodily health?

6. According to St. Thomas, how can psychological disharmony of this kind happen without totally destroying a person's ability to order choice like a psychologically healthy human being? If total psychological destruction does result, what kind of personality change does St. Thomas maintain happens to a human being?

7. What three ways does St. Thomas list in which human beings become brutish?

8. As healthy states contrary to the morally disordered states of brutishness, incontinence, and vice, what three states does St. Thomas identify?

9. After giving his general introduction to the devolution of human beings from moral virtue to moral vice, how does Aristotle start to talk about incontinence? How does he conclude his introduction to the study of continence and incontinence?

10. Despite the fact that Aristotle commends continence in relationship to pleasure and perseverance when concerned with pain as laudable, why do you think he maintains that neither is a virtue? Why does he conclude his general introduction to the devolution of human beings from moral virtue to moral vice by noting the limitations of the study?

11. What usual method does Aristotle say he will adopt for study, and why?

12. Using this method, what six probable statements does he make to start his investigations?

13. According to St. Thomas, what six steps does the proper way to consider, study, a subject involve?

14. According to him, how does this understanding this proper procedure for study help to explain why Aristotle does not address six doubts about six probable statements he has just made about continence and incontinence in the order in which he has presented them? How does it help to understand why Aristotle's first doubt addresses his probable statement three (the continent man knows particular acts are evil and avoids them because of reason; the incontinent man does the contrary opposite) instead of his first probable claim (continence and perseverance are good; incontinence and irresoluteness are bad)?

15. In addressing this third probable statement, St. Thomas realizes that Aristotle is directly criticizing what well-known claims of Socrates?

16. In what way does Aristotle reject the argument given by some (which claims the incontinent man acts under the influence of opinion, not knowledge) to salvage the teaching of Socrates?

17. For what two reasons does Aristotle reject the explanation given by some of Socrates' followers to defend Socrates' teaching related to why a prudent man cannot be incontinent?

18. What three doubts does Aristotle present against his probable claim that the temperate man appears continent and persevering and how does he resolve these doubts?

19. What argument does Aristotle present related to sophistic objections against his probable claim that the continent man appears prudent, while the incontinent man appears imprudent?

20. According to St. Thomas, how does Aristotle strengthen his claim that continence and perseverance are good and incontinence and irresoluteness are bad?

21. How does Aristotle resolve the fact that sometimes people who get angry and pursue honor and personal gain are called "incontinent"?

22. According to St. Thomas, how does Aristotle use distinctions among 1) continence in a qualified sense and continence and an unqualified sense; 2) two ways in which human beings habitually know and judge; and 3) two different ways in which a universal can be considered finally to resolve the teaching of Socrates (which appears to preclude the existence of continence and incontinence)?

23. What role does the realization of the existence of the faculty of particular reason (the estimative sense) play in the ability to resolve

the teaching of Socrates about whether or not continence and incontinence exist?

24. Beyond the distinctions that Aristotle makes, what further distinction about the intensity of habitual response to direction by universal reason on the part of particular reason can help to explain the reality of the existence of incontinent behavior in the face of knowledge?

25. How does Aristotle reply to someone who uses the following appeal as a means to refute Aristotle's claim that the incontinent man has an active appetitive habit restrained by reason: "The 'supposedly' incontinent man's use of scientific terminology indicates that he is too profoundly intelligent to be incontinent."

The moral psychology of the incontinent man

1. According to St. Thomas, if we want to understand how the incontinent man can, contrary to his knowledge, say one thing (know the right thing) and do another (the wrong thing), what two stages of judging involved in the natural process of practical reasoning do we have to comprehend?

2. According to him, since these two stages of judging unite to form one nature of a practical reasoning activity, practical science, what three conclusions necessarily follow?

3. According to St. Thomas, *analogously*, how does the incontinent man rightly reason abstractly in the same way about avoiding doing something shameful, *but*, nonetheless, choose to execute a shameful act?

4. While the moral psychology of the incontinent man is morally flawed, unhealthy, why does St. Thomas claim that it is not so morally flawed, unhealthy, as that of the intemperate man?

5. What causes St. Thomas to maintain that the process of practical reason happening in the way he has described in the case of the incontinent man is evident? According to St. Thomas, does concupiscence or reason chiefly cause the incontinent man to behave the way he does? Why?

6. According to St. Thomas, in contrast to human beings, why do brute animals make no distinction between apparent and real goods and evils? Why do they consider all goods and evils to be real?

7. What does St. Thomas propose as a prescription to cure the ignorance of the incontinent man? Do you agree or disagree with St. Thomas about this prescription? If not, why not?

8. Based upon what Aristotle has said about universal and particular reason, how does St. Thomas claim Aristotle is able to refute the argument of Socrates?

The generic matter (subject) of continence and temperance

1. Having shown that, in a way, human beings can knowingly perform evil acts, what two questions does Aristotle next consider? In short, what main question is Aristotle asking, and what is his reply to this question?

2. How does Aristotle explain why the formal object that externally stimulates action of the incontinent and intemperate man is precisely the formal object which it is?

3. How does Aristotle confirm that the formal object of continence and temperance is precisely the one he claims it to be?

4. While Aristotle locates the incontinent and intemperate man within the same genus, what does he claim is their specific difference?

5. Why does Aristotle say that the vice of the intemperate man is worse than that of the incontinent man?

Peter A. Redpath

6. In what way does Aristotle show that, in the case of unnecessary goods, no absolute incontinence can exist? Why?

7. According to Aristotle, what are the only kinds of goods to which absolute incontinence relates?

Natural and unnatural pleasure and the appetitive disposition and the moral psychology of incontinent and brutish men

1. Having considered the difference in calling a person "continent" and "incontinent" absolutely, totally, and partially, what other way of talking about continence and incontinence does Aristotle next examine?

2. How does Aristotle explain what he means when he says that we call, name, a person "continent" or "incontinent" in different senses?

3. What does Aristotle mean by "natural," or "proper," pleasures? How does he use the existence of such pleasures to identify "unnatural," "improper," and "brutish" pleasures? What does he give as examples of such pleasures?

4. According to him, why will no one accuse anyone who, from birth or bad education, has such a flawed nature with being incontinent absolutely and unqualifiedly?

5. What does St. Thomas say to concur with Aristotle's assessment that the behavior of such people is not an example of absolute and unqualified incontinence?

6. What other factors related to the nature of incontinent acts inclines Aristotle's to state that, strictly speaking, absolute incontinence does not apply to such people?

7. As far as brutish habits are concerned, relative to ordinary viciousness, what does Aristotle maintain about absolute brutishness? What sort of habit does Aristotle consider absolute brutishness to be?

669

8. According to him, what are different causes of absolute brutishness, and how do different species of brutish people behave relative
to acts of virtue? What people does Aristotle claim especially incline to be brutish?

**Comparison of different kinds of incontinence to different kinds
of pleasure and the moral psychology of the angry man**

1. Having shown how incontinence is related in different ways to
different pleasures, what subject does Aristotle next consider?

2. According to Aristotle, absolute, total, complete, incontinence
only concerns matters involving what activity? Why does he say
that a matter like anger concerns only partial incontinence?

3. Following Aristotle, what does St. Thomas add regarding incontinence related to anger? What four points does he make to support
his claim?

4. How does St. Thomas report Aristotle's analysis of the moral
psychology of the angry man? How does St. Thomas account for
this moral psychology of the angry man and how it differs from the
moral psychology of the incontinent man?

5. According to St. Thomas, what happens in human affairs when
the incontinent man does not listen to reason?

6. Why does St. Thomas maintain that the incontinent man absolutely considered is more shameful than the incontinent man acting
out of anger? What three arguments from Aristotle does St. Thomas
present to show that the incontinent man's behavior absolutely con-
sidreed is more shameful than that of the angry man?

7. How does St. Thomas summarize Aristotle's conclusion about
incontinence?

8. How does St. Thomas compare incontinence and intemperance

to brutishness? Why does he say that we sometimes call animals "temperate" and "prudent"? According to him, strictly speaking, can temperance and intemperance exist in animals other than human and brutish men, and what do insane people resemble?

9. Considering the animal condition of brutes and the brutish condition of brutish men, what does St. Thomas say about the evil and frightening nature of each?

A more detailed comparison of the moral psychology of continence and incontinence to that of temperance and intemperance

1. After discussing in detail the nature, and moral psychology, of continence and incontinence, to what does Aristotle next compare these in detail? How to does he start to do so?

2. According to Aristotle, in general, how does the moral psychology of the incontinent man contrast with that of the continent intemperate man?

3. Because the concupiscible appetite is not directly inclined to listen to reason, how does Aristotle say it inclines to behave toward its object and toward shame and guilt?

4. Relative to shame, embarrassment, sorrow, guilt, remorse, how does Aristotle describe the moral psychology of the intemperate man? Relative to these same psychological states, what does Aristotle say about the moral psychology of the frigidly intemperate man in contrast to the temperate man?

5. According to Aristotle, now and then how can the incontinent man restrain intense emotion? According to him, relative to intense emotion, how does the moral psychology of the incontinent man differ from that of the continent man? And how does the moral psychology of the continent man differ from that of the persevering man?

7. According to Aristotle, is the incontinent or the intemperate man more inclined to seek amusements as forms of pleasure? Why? Do you agree or disagree with Aristotle about this claim? If you disagree, why?

8. According to Aristotle, what are the two species of incontinence and in what sort of psychologically-disposed people do these species of incontinence tend to exist?

A special note about how the concupiscible and irascible passions relate to pleasurable and useful goods and the importance this has for understanding the nature of moral education

1. Why should special note be taken about how Aristotle considers the concupiscible and irascible passions to relate to pleasurable and useful goods?

2. What did recognizing the radical distinction that exists between these two sense appetites and their formal objects enable Aristotle to realize?

3. As St. Thomas came to realize even more than Aristotle, how are particular reason, or the estimative sense, the passion of pleasure, and the passions of the irascible appetite essentially involved in moral education and, especially, in moral education related to continence and temperance?

Some additional reasons why the intemperate man is morally worse than the incontinent man

1. Why do Aristotle and St. Thomas consider the intemperate man to be morally worse than the incontinent man and educationally incorrigible, unteachable, in the area of morals?

2. What does St. Thomas say that incontinence and intemperance resemble?

Peter A. Redpath

3. In relation to moral activity, why do Aristotle and St. Thomas maintain that continence and incontinence belong to different genera?

4. According to St. Thomas, precisely why is incontinence a quasi-vice and intemperance a full-fledged vice, and precisely why is the intemperate man morally worse than the incontinent man?

5. Why does St. Thomas maintain that the incontinent man (who sins out of soft bodily constitution and emotional dispositions) is more to be pitied, helped, than blamed? In contrast, why is the intemperate man not to be pitied, but to be blamed?

6. In the sphere of moral activity, what do Aristotle and St. Thomas claim that vice and virtue do regarding the end for the sake of which we engage in free acts? In practical knowledge, to what do they say the end is analogous in speculative knowledge?

7. According to St. Thomas, can first principles of practical knowledge be taught? If not, how does he say they are acquired?

8. According to St. Thomas, why cannot people, like the intemperate man, who make mistakes about first principles, easily be corrected by appeal to reason, or in any way be educated?

9. According to him, who is the right measure regarding the means and the end related to matters involving intense bodily pleasures and pains?

Continence: Its precise species, how the moral psychology of the continent man differs from that of the obstinate man, and more precisely from that of the incontinent, temperate, and intemperate man

1. According to St. Thomas, how does Aristotle start to settle the question about the precise species that is continence?

2. By considering what question does Aristotle start to narrow down

with precision the specific difference that makes a continent act continent? How does Aristotle answer this question?

The psychological difference between the prudent and incontinent man: why prudence cannot co-exist with incontinence

1. After comparing and contrasting in detail incontinence and intemperance, and the moral psychology of the incontinent man to that of the intemperate one, what two arguments does Aristotle employ to demonstrate that prudence cannot co-exist with incontinence?

2. According to Aristotle, why do incontinent people sometimes appear prudent?

3. According to Aristotle and St. Thomas, in what eight ways do the prudent and incontinent man differ?

Aristotle concludes his comparison and contrast of moral psychology of the continent man to that of incontinent, intemperate, and prudent man

1. Relative to the human will and intense pleasure, what does Aristotle conclude about the specific difference the intemperate, incontinent, and prudent man share relative to intense pleasures of taste and touch?

2. To what specifically different kinds of cities does Aristotle analogously compare the intemperate, incontinent, and prudent man?

3. According to St. Thomas, how does the mean of right reason that the continent man follows differ from the mean of right reason that the prudent man follows?

4. According to him, relative to moral activity, why do the majority of men lack the habit of right reason? How does he say that the measure of right reason that the incontinent man possesses measures up against the measure of right reason that the majority of human beings possess?

5. Of the two kinds of incontinence (of anger and concupiscence), which does St. Thomas say is easier to cure, and why?

Why moral science and the political philosopher need to study pleasure and pain

1. After explaining why prudence and incontinence cannot co-exist, what do Aristotle and St. Thomas start to examine?

2. According to St. Thomas, why do moral and political science need to study pleasure and pain?

3. In some way, do Aristotle and St. Thomas maintain that pleasure and human happiness are identical? If so, how? And what impact does this have on understanding the teaching about the nature of moral and political science?

4. According to Aristotle and St. Thomas, what connection, if any, does experience of pleasure have with the ability to perform acts of moral virtue and vice?

Aristotle's refutation of six arguments supporting four sophistic opinions held by some ancient Greek philosophers claiming to prove that pleasure is not good and the highest good

1. What four sophistic opinions does Aristotle present objecting to his claim that pleasure and human happiness are, in some way, identical?

2. What six arguments does Aristotle present in defense of these four sophistic opinions?

3. Having stated the six arguments favoring the four false opinions and the supporting arguments about the relation of pleasure and good, what distinctions do Aristotle and St. Thomas make to prepare to refute these arguments and the opinions these arguments defend?

4. Restate the six arguments that Aristotle and St. Thomas make to

refute the four sophistic opinions objecting to Aristotle's claim that pleasure and human happiness are in some way identical.

5. What distinction that Aristotle and St. Thomas make in preparation for the refutation of these six arguments is especially crucial for the success of their counter-arguments? Why?

That one pleasure (happiness) is the highest good, and why

1. As a first step in developing his complete proof that one pleasure, happiness, is the highest good, what two claims about truth does St. Thomas maintain Aristotle makes?

2. How does Aristotle refute the reported claim of Speucippus that pain is opposed to pleasure as a greater to the less evil, as one extreme evil to another (both pleasure and pain supposedly being evil)?

3. According to Aristotle, did the Platonists ever go as far as Speucippus in maintaining pleasure to be evil absolutely considered in itself? If not, what did they maintain about the relation of pleasure to good and evil?

4. Does the author of this book think that Aristotle's representation of the teaching of the Platonists regarding the relationship of pleasure to good and evil is accurate? If not, why not?

5. According to Aristotle, why does everyone, by nature, actually, understandably, essentially connect pleasure and happiness, actually think that the happy life is pleasurable and delightful?

6. According to him, why does happiness require all the enabling means for exercising unimpeded activity?

7. Why do Aristotle and St. Thomas maintain that, strictly speaking, people who, like some of the Stoics, claim that, even when tossed about and overcome by great misfortune, the virtuous man is happy, talk nonsense?

8. Because human beings so closely incline to identify happiness and pleasure, what does Aristotle say some philosophers considered to be the relationship between happiness and good fortune?

9. Does Aristotle agree with these philosophers that happiness and good fortune are identical? If not, why not?

10. Why do Aristotle and St. Thomas think that the opinion of *the Many* cannot be totally wrong in maintaining that happiness consists in pleasure?

11. How do Aristotle and St. Thomas defend the opinion of *the Many* that pleasure is the highest good against possible criticism of this opinion?

12. Even though Aristotle and St. Thomas identify this highest pleasure with a non-physical good, how do they count the fact that *the Many* tend to identify this with a physical good, with physical pleasure?

13. Strictly speaking, if pleasure and pleasurable activity are not good absolutely, if the life of the virtuous man and his activities are not essentially pleasurable, what conclusion might follow regarding the nature of the happy life and life of filled with pain?

Pleasure and pain as related to continence and incontinence

1. According to Aristotle, in what respect are bodily pleasures good?

2. According to Aristotle and St. Thomas, can too much good, pleasure, essentially exist within physical habit? If so, why? According to them, can too much good, pleasure, essentially exist within the habit of contemplation of the truth? If not, why not?

3. According to St. Thomas, can we blame some people for not experiencing bodily pleasures? If so, why?

4. According to Aristotle and St. Thomas, do we rightly avoid all

pain? According to St. Thomas, does even a man of virtue absolutely flee from all pain?

5. From the fact that all human beings naturally incline to flee from all pain, what does St. Thomas conclude about the nature of pain? Of what does he say pain cannot be the contrary opposite?

6. How do Aristotle and St. Thomas attempt more completely to explain the paradoxical phenomenon that, even though intellectual pleasure is qualitatively greater in nature than is physical pleasure, many people often desire physical pleasure more than they do intellectual pleasure?

7. What does St. Thomas say about the situation of some people who unwittingly attempt to satisfy the desire for pleasure as of a higher intellectual quality by substituting artificial stimulants or dangerous lifestyles of one sort or another?

8. According to him, why do young men especially seek pleasure and resemble alcoholics in bodily disturbances? And how does he account for the fact that emotionally-depressed people have a constant medicinal need for pleasure? As a result, what does he say often happens to depressed people?

9. Why does St. Thomas claim that intellectual pleasures provide a medicinal remedy for many young men, people in states of depression, and human beings considered in general?

10. Does St. Thomas think that the act of contemplation is always enjoyable, medicinal? If not, why not?

11. If human beings were only intellect, like God, what does St. Thomas claim would be our attitude toward the act of contemplation?

12. Since we are not only intellect, since we are physical and intellectual and constantly change, what does he say is the natural human attitude toward pleasure?

Chapter 14

Six reasons why moral philosophy/science must study friendship

1. With what six arguments does St. Thomas say Aristotle starts Book 8 of his *Nicomachean Ethics*?

2. What does Aristotle say in reply to the hypothetical objection that friends like people like them because likes like likes, but they do not like people who are competitors?

3. While, in ancient Greece, Aristotle says some intellectuals had attempted to give cosmological arguments to explain why friendship exists, in favor of what other kind of explanation does Aristotle reject considering such cosmological arguments?

4. What error made by some philosophers regarding the nature friendship does he also reject, and why?

Good as friendship's formal object, or external stimulus, and friendship as properly and improperly defined

1. Having finished his introduction regarding the need for moral philosophy to study friendship, what does St. Thomas say Aristotle next investigates? To simplify this investigation, what does Aristotle do in relation to the passion of love?

2. According to Aristotle, considered as such, is evil ever loved, ever lovable? If not, why not?

3. Absolutely and conceptually, what does Aristotle maintain about the identity of pleasure, or the pleasurable, and good?

4. To expose a falsehood so as to incline a student more readily to accept a truth, what problem does Aristotle pose regarding good as the formal object of love? How does Aristotle resolve this problem?

5. As another pedagogical tool to incline a student more readily to accept a truth, how does Aristotle argue against the conclusion

he just drew? In what twofold way does Aristotle reply to this criticism?

6. Considering friendship relative to human love's three possible objects of desire, what does Aristotle note about the nature of friendship in relationship to objects of love?

7. Following his consideration of the nature of friendship in relationship to objects of love, strictly speaking, how does Aristotle define friendship?

Aristotle's division, and discussion of, the three species of friendship: perfective, useful, and pleasurable *and how these relate to having the right moral psychology for a lasting friendship*

1. Having properly defined friendship and divided it into three species, on the basis of qualitatively unequal ways of having friendship, what does St. Thomas next report Aristotle notes about the nature of perfect and imperfect friendships, and especially about their ability to last?

2. To what human social groups does Aristotle maintain that imperfect friendship tends to belong? Why?

3. To what human social group does Aristotle claim perfect friendship tends to belong? Why?

4. Precisely why does Aristotle say that perfect friendship contains all the elements needed for friendship? What else does Aristotle note about perfect friendship?

5. Following his normal method of defining the subject considered as a whole before comparing and contrasting its parts, having defined friendship as a whole, what does Aristotle next do?

6. How does Aristotle start to compare imperfect friendships?

7. According to Aristotle, for what two chief reasons do friendships

tend to last, and what happens if one of these elements is missing from a friendship?

8. Why does Aristotle maintain that, based upon the moral psychology involved in them, friendships based upon pleasure and utility tend not to last? If what Aristotle says is true, what political implication follows from this claim in relation to the long-term existence of political orders chiefly based upon friendships of utility and pleasure?

9. For the sake of pleasure, what does St. Thomas note about all three species of friendship?

10. According to Aristotle, what are the only sorts of friendships that evil men are able to form? Why?

11. According to him, what kind of moral psychology is required for human beings to be able to form perfect friendships?

12. Why does Aristotle maintain that, in imperfect friendships, especially those based upon the moral psychology of pleasure, believing a friend acts unjustly, is morally evil, tends not to be a problem, or not to be a big problem?

13. Why, however, does Aristotle claim that discovery of professional dishonesty is a big problem in business friendships and perfect friendships?

Aristotle's consideration of the nature of perfect friendship in general and the moral psychology that it necessarily demands

1. After having compared and contrasted imperfect acts of friendship, what does St. Thomas say Aristotle next examines regarding friendship?

2. When examining the nature of perfect friendship considered in general, what distinctions does Aristotle first make between two ways in which we properly name natures? Give some examples.

3. Because maintaining regular, mutual activity tends to be necessary to cause friendships to last, what three classes of people does Aristotle claim have a hard time being lasting friends, and why?

4. According to Aristotle, what four acts *appear to be* essential acts of perfect friendship? What three acts does he say enduring friendship chiefly involves? Why?

Aristotle's consideration of the moral psychology of perfect friendship in relation to its chief subject: the friendworthy person

1. According to Aristotle, what qualities of sociability chiefly constitute a moral psychology capable of generating friendship and entering into friendships?

2. Chiefly what kind of activity does Aristotle consider friendship to be? Consequently, what kind of people does he maintain are able quickly to make friends, and what kind of people are not? Why?

3. According to Aristotle, why does this moral psychology of perfect friendship preclude one person from entering into perfect friendship with many people?

4. For what two reasons does Aristotle maintain that, in imperfect friendships, the moral psychology of imperfect friendship enables one person to have many friends?

5. Why does Aristotle claim that the moral psychology of young people inclines them to be able to form many friendships?

6. According to Aristotle, why do rich people tend to possess a moral psychology that inclines them to form friendships based upon pleasure instead of utility or perfect virtue?

7. In general, what does Aristotle maintain tends to be the psychological makeup of human beings related to the length of time they

are able to bear unpleasant behavior in others? What does he say about our ability to tolerate a good life that does not please?

8. Why does Aristotle claim that people in positions of power tend to form friendships based upon pleasure and utility, not upon virtue? For utility, what sort of people does Aristotle say such people especially tend to like?

9. How does Aristotle reply to a possible objection that, because virtuous people are also pleasant and useful, the powerful can be friends of the virtuous?

10. What does Aristotle note about proportionate equality and the ability to love and be loved in relation to a chief, and relative to all three, species of friendship? Of the three species of friendship he examines, which is the only one he considers to be properly named? How does he say the others are named?

The nature and moral psychology of friendships between un-equals, and the crucial role the estimative sense plays in being able to form them

1. After discussing three species of friendship based upon equal relations between friends, about what does Aristotle next talk regarding friendship?

2. In talking about unequal relation between friends, what problem and moral psychology does he say causes them to have difficulty in engaging in commutative exchanges and goods?

3. What does he give as examples of such friendships? What does he say tends to preserve them? What species of justice does he claim that justice between such friendships resembles?

4. How does Aristotle think that equality differently relates to justice and friendship regarding starting points and end points? Why does

Aristotle say knowing these differences is crucial in relation to establishing and maintaining friendships?

5. Such being the case, while neither Aristotle nor St. Thomas explicitly says so, from what Aristotle has said thus far about the nature of friendship, why must one starting point lie within the estimative sense, the particular, or cogitative, reason?

6. How does Aristotle reply to someone who might object that, from his prior discussion about friendship, what appears to follow is that human beings cannot wish the greatest of goods for friends because then they could no longer be friends?

The nature and moral psychology of loving and being loved as related to friendship

1. Having finished examining the moral psychology of friendship between unequals, what does Aristotle next consider regarding the relation that exists between loving and being loved and friendship, especially regarding the moral psychology of *the Many*? How does he start this examination?

2. In what ways does Aristotle show how the psychological excellence of friendship consists in loving and being loved?

3. Where does he say that likeness that preserves friendship is maximally and minimally found? Why?

4. What further observations does Aristotle make about the friendships of pleasure and utility as these exist among virtuous and non-virtuous people?

The nature and moral psychology of friendships that exist within civic associations

1. Having considered friendship between unequals, how does Aristotle start his consideration of friendships in relation to different human associations?

2. According to him, on what basis do we chiefly diversify friendships? What does he say would happen to friendship if no communication were to exist?

3. According to Aristotle, what happens to acts of injustice and justice as they involve closer associates, friends?

4. By nature, for what does Aristotle maintain all human associations are enabling means? How does this aim of natural inclination to associate influence the generation of private and civic associations?

Distinction of political societies and households based upon the number of people who rule and the moral psychology they employ to rule

1. After having shown that, by nature, all forms of friendship psychologically aim at generating civic friendship, what does St. Thomas report Aristotle next starts to discuss in relation to friendship?

2. On what basis is Aristotle well known to divide political societies? Restate this division. What does Aristotle say about the specific weaknesses of different forms of unjust political rule?

3. According to him, how does the moral psychology of different political orders resemble the moral psychology of different family/household relations?

4. Lest we incline to glory in our own contemporary moral superiority in considering Aristotle's claim that to use slaves for household profit is all right, what should we recall about Aristotle's understanding of the terms "slave" and "slavery"?

5. Given his more finely-nuanced understanding of the terms "slave" and "slavery," what should not surprise us to discover about his attitude toward the household relation between a husband and

wife? Essentially, what kind of rule did he maintain is that between a husband and wife?

6. According to him, what form of political rule does the rule of a household by brothers who are close in age resemble?

7. What does he say regarding democratic rule within a household or a political society?

The nature and moral psychology of friendships existing within political societies

1. After distinguishing the different kinds of political and household associations, how does Aristotle show that the moral psychology involved in organizations of political societies resembles that involved in friendships? According to him, in what way does the relation of the nature of a real political order to justice account for this resemblance?

2. To start showing how these two species of organizations of friendships and political societies analogously resemble each other in moral psychology, what does Aristotle say about the relation of friendship to kingly rule, aristocracy, democracy?

3. What does Aristotle say about the moral psychology underlying the kinds of friendships that exist within a tyranny?

4. In which forms of political rule does Aristotle say friendship exists least and most extensively? How does the moral psychology that generates these forms of rule account for the extent to which friendship exists in one and the other? According to him, what form of political rule manifests an extent of friendship in between that of a democracy a tyranny?

5. Why does Aristotle reason that no master *qua* master can have a real friendship with a slave *qua* slave, but can have a real friendship with a slave as a human being? Can you think of any relationship

that exists today between individuals of different social groups analogous to the one Aristotle has just described? Explain.

Division of friendships into species based upon their psychological awareness of sharing other kinds of things in common

1. Having distinguished personal, domestic, and civic friendship as forms of common participation toward an end, on what basis does Aristotle next divide friendship? Before making this division, what does Aristotle note about the nature of friendship existing between parents, a husband and a wife, and the influence that has on all subsequent friendships?

2. For what three reasons do Aristotle and St. Thomas maintain that, by nature, parents are psychologically inclined to love their children more than their children love them?

3. What do they maintain regarding the relationship of blood relatives one to another? According to them, what does this relationship resemble?

4. Why do they maintain that, by nature, mothers are inclined to love their children more than do their fathers?

5. As begotten by the same parents, how do they say brothers are inclined by nature to love each other?

6. How do they maintain that other blood relatives share a natural domestic proximity and close relation to each other?

7. On what basis do they maintain that children have a natural psychological inclination to experience friendship toward parents as to a superior good? Hence, in proportion as they live together in common, how do they maintain that children and parents tend to share pleasure and utility toward each other in contrast to the way they share pleasure and utility toward other friends?

8. Among family relations, what do they maintain is the friendship existing between and among brothers, and other blood relatives?

9. Regarding the special and unique familial friendship between a man and a wife, why do Aristotle and St. Thomas maintain that, while human beings are political animals, we are more conjugal than political? If this claim is true, what implication regarding the long-term existence of States that seek to redefine the nature of marriage appears necessarily to follow?

10. While union between a male and a female among other animals exists exclusively for species preservation (generation of offspring), what do they maintain that the conjugal friendship between a man and a woman proximately generates? Of what do they claim this conjugal friendship between a man and a woman is the proximate principle?

11. According to Aristotle, upon what species of friendship can this conjugal friendship between a man and woman be based? Based upon everything he has said previously within his *Nicomachean Ethics*, upon what form of conjugal friendship does he maintain the strongest of conjugal bonds result?

12. What does Aristotle say about the affect that children have on strengthening or weakening a conjugal union? To what does he refer as a sign of the truth of his claim?

The nature and moral psychology of quarrels and complaints that tend to arise within friendships between equals and advice about how to resolve them

1. After finishing his discussion of different kinds of friendship and their psychological foundations, what does Aristotle next discuss?

2. While Aristotle recognizes that quarrels can exist within any of the three species of friendship, in which species does he maintain they happen most? Why?

Peter A. Redpath

3. What advice does Aristotle give to people involved in utilitarian friendships about how to avoid quarrels? Why should this advice be especially useful to business professionals?

4. What advice does Aristotle give about how to measure repayments in utilitarian and virtuous friendships? How does he account for the different measures used in both cases?

Quarrels and complaints that tend to arise within friendships between unequals and advice about psychological, and other, means to resolve them

1. Generally considered, when does Aristotle maintain that quarrels in friendships tend to arise? What examples does he give from virtue-based, utility-based, and·pleasure-based friendships? What advice does Aristotle give about how to resolve such conflicts?

2. According to Aristotle, what creates proportionate equality among friends and preserves friendships within political societies?

3. What does he claim that, psychologically, friends tend to ask, expect, of friends?

Proportionate properties of friendship, and how a psychologically-healthy (prudently regulated) estimative sense can serve as a remedy for disturbances arising related to friendship

1. With a discussion of what topic does Aristotle start Book 9 of his *Nicomachean Ethics?* How does he initiate discussion of this topic; and, immediately after that, what does he do?

2. Before going into detail about the nature of such proportionate equality, what does Aristotle say about the nature of disagreements related to fair distribution in commutative exchanges?

3. According to him, what complicates the problem related to measuring fair distribution in matters regarding exchanges involving emotional affection and business services?

4. In what two stages does Aristotle maintain we human beings tend to judge repayment of friendship? Related to each of these stages, what do we tend to complain about people doing?

5. At times, what does Aristotle say psychologically causes such complaints to arise?

6. What does Aristotle recommend as a remedy against disturbances and friendships involving qualitatively unequal exchanges?

7. Why do Aristotle and St. Thomas maintain that a well-educated particular reason or estimative sense is crucial for being able to remedy against such disturbances in friendship? And upon what basis do they maintain measurement of payment should be made in different species of friendship?

Some doubts about duties related to friendship

1. Immediately after having given advice about how to preserve friendship through the proper moral psychology related to proportionate repayment, what doubts does Aristotle immediately raise about what he has said regarding repayment between unequals?

2. Why does Aristotle say that resolving these doubts is not always easy? How does Aristotle recommend they be resolved?

The crucial relation of self-love and good will to having the needed moral psychology to generate acts of friendship; and how the moral psychology of the good man differs from that of the evil man

1. After giving the above advice about how to preserve friendship through having the proper psychological attitude toward the nature

of proportionate repayment, what does Aristotle immediately consider related to the dissolution of friendship?

2. What sage observation does Aristotle make about fraudulent friends?

3. According to Aristotle and St. Thomas, what is the chief reason a person acts benevolently toward others? According to them, what is friendship's chief proximate cause within any and every human being?

4. Since benevolent acts are effects of benevolent wills, effects of friendship, into what three species does Aristotle divide such benevolent acts?

5. Because people tend to think that people having at least one of the qualities of benevolence have the essential quality of friendship, according to Aristotle, how do we tend to define friendship in relation to these qualities?

6. According to him, to what one human being do all these qualities essentially belong? How does he say, if in any way, do they belong to other people, including, the non-virtuous person?

7. In any order (genus) of reality, what does Aristotle claim is the measure? Why? Such being the case, in the moral order who does he say should be the measure?

8. According to Aristotle, who possesses what is suitably/proportionately proper to beneficence, good will, and peace/concord? Such being the case, how does Aristotle maintain such a person behaves? Explain in detail.

9. In contrast to the way the morally virtuous person tends to behave, how do Aristotle and St. Thomas say the morally vicious person tends to be behave?

10. According to St. Thomas, most fittingly, what psychological

qualities does the morally virtuous man possess? What two parts of the human soul does St. Thomas say operate harmoniously within such a person, and what effects does this harmony tend to generate within him?

11. According to Aristotle, how should friends be psychologically disposed to behave toward other people?

12. According to him, why can evil men never find self-satisfaction?

13. According to St. Thomas, how does the moral psychology of the evil man eventually incline to cause him to loathe himself and others?

14. According to Aristotle, why do wicked men not have the psychological qualities suitable for performing acts of friendship?

15. Because they lack good will, what does St. Thomas claim eventually happens to evil men psychologically and otherwise?

16. If living without self-love and real friends is among the greatest of human evils, what do Aristotle and St. Thomas recommend we do regarding moral virtue and vice?

How the moral psychology of good will relates to friendship

1. According to Aristotle, what is good will, what is it not, and how does it resemble friendship?

2. Why does Aristotle claim that good will cannot be identical with friendship? In contrast to perfect friendship, what does Aristotle say good will resembles?

3. Why does Aristotle consider good will to be a necessary condition of friendship?

4. According to him, why is not good will identical with love?

5. Where does Aristotle maintain good will appears to exist? According to him, where does good will not develop into friendship?

Peter A. Redpath

How the moral psychology of concord relates to friendship

1. What does Aristotle claim appears to be the relationship between concord and friendship?

2. Why does he reject the claims that no difference exists between concord and opinion, and that concord consists in common agreement about speculative topics, preferences, or likes; or unity of appetite about means and ends related things to be done?

3. To help more precisely to understand the nature of concord, what prime example of concord does Aristotle present, and what does Aristotle conclude about the nature of concord based upon the behavior of the individuals involved in his example?

4. Why does Aristotle maintain that concord only voluntarily exists between and among virtuous people? Why does he claim that it does not exist among vicious men?

5. According to Aristotle, what relationship does concord appear to have to political friendship?

How the moral psychology of beneficence relates to friendship

1. With what rationally paradoxical claim does Aristotle start his examination of beneficence? Precisely what is rationally paradoxical about the claim he examines?

2. Appearances to the contrary, why does Aristotle maintain that the situation he has described about the nature of beneficence in relation to benefactors and beneficiaries is actually not contrary to reason?

3. While Aristotle's resolution of this paradox tends to portray human nature in a bad light, why does he claim that, nonetheless, what he has said about the nature of beneficiaries and benefactors appears to be quite accurate?

4. What claim does Aristotle make to reinforce his argument?

Some doubts and answers about the moral psychology of self-love

1. After talking about the preservation and dissolution of friendship and its effects, what doubts does Aristotle articulate about self-love? How does he resolve these doubts?

2. What does St. Thomas claim about the benevolent relation that a human being has to himself individually, specifically, and generically and benevolent act towards others?

3. What does St. Thomas consider to be the connection between this benevolent relation of self-love and the development the moral virtue individually and socially?

4. What do Aristotle and St. Thomas agree about people who cannot rightly love themselves?

5. How does Aristotle contrast virtuous self-love to vicious self-love?

6. What do Aristotle and St. Thomas well understand regarding the relation of interior principles to the whole subject in which they exist? How does this understanding affect the way in which they understand the human soul to influence secondary principles of human operation like moral virtue?

7. What three arguments does Aristotle propose to prove that the person who wishes to be most perfect and do good works must love himself in a high degree?

8. After finishing his three arguments, why does Aristotle claim that the best of social situations results from virtuous self-love while the worst of situations arises from vicious self-love?

Resolving a doubt about a happy man needing friends

1. After solving the doubts about self-love, in two ways, how does Aristotle resolve another doubt about whether a happy man needs friends?

Some other reasons that a happy man needs friends

1. Having finished giving reasons related to moral virtue why a happy man needs friends, what further, more fundamental, reasons does Aristotle give for the happy man needing friends?

How many friends should a virtuous man have and why

1. According to Aristotle and St. Thomas, from the preceding analysis, why is the answer to this question evident? According to them, what is the evident answer?

2. Why do they claim that this is the evident answer?

3. From the preceding analysis, what else is evident to them about the need for friends? Consequently, how do they say people should behave toward friends in prosperity and adversity?

The nature of friends living together

1. According to Aristotle, upon what likeness is the desire for friends to live together based? What reasons does he give the truth of this claim?

2. From the preceding analysis in Book 9, what two things does Aristotle conclude?

Chapter 15

1. Having finished considering friendship in Book 9 of the *Nicomachean Ethics*, in Book 10, what does Aristotle next do, and how does he do it?

Three reasons St. Thomas gives for reconsidering the relationship between pleasure and happiness

1. For what three reasons does St. Thomas maintain Aristotle reconsiders the relationship between pleasure and happiness in Book 10 of his *Nicomachean Ethics*?

2. Why do Aristotle and St. Thomas disagree with people who think that misleading incontinent men to have aversion to all pleasure is a better teaching tool than telling them the truth?

Aristotle continues his discussion of pleasure by considering Eudoxus' teaching about it

1. Why does Aristotle continue his discussion of pleasure by considering Eudoxus' teaching about it?

2. Before immediately discussing the teaching of Eudoxus, what observation related to animal pursuit of pleasure does Aristotle make?

3. Considering Eudoxus' teaching first from the standpoint of pleasure, what two arguments does Aristotle present from Eudoxus to demonstrate that pleasure is the greatest animal good?

4. Why does Aristotle disagree with Eudoxus' conclusion that, because pleasure enhances goodness in all human actions, pleasure is the greatest of human goods? What arguments does Aristotle take from Plato against this conclusion of Eudoxus?

5. According to St. Thomas, what did Aristotle claim about the way in which Plato considered pleasure and good and good and perfection to be related?

6. According to St. Thomas, why was Aristotle especially critical of the way in which he understood Plato to relate goodness to perfection?

7. Why did Aristotle reject as "nonsense," evidently false, the claim of some Platonists which denied that what all animals/humans naturally desire is real good?

8. In defense of Aristotle's critique of these Platonists, what observation does St. Thomas note about the evident pursuit of real good by human beings and its relation to the faculty of particular reason, the estimative sense in human beings, and to brute animals?

9. What does St. Thomas maintain about the existence or non-existence of the pursuit of real good and of evil men?

10. According to Aristotle and St. Thomas, by nature, does pleasure divide or unite? According to them, in the moral psychology of evil men, what actually divides, fragments, them psychologically, and causes them to lose touch with reality?

Four arguments Aristotle gives against some people St. Thomas calls "the Platonists" related to pleasure not being a good

1. What four arguments does Aristotle present against some people St. Thomas calls "the Platonists" designed to show that they are wrong to claim pleasure is not a way of being good, a mode of goodness?

Aristotle starts properly to define pleasure

1. According to St. Thomas, after arguing against the opinions of "the Platonists," how does Aristotle start properly to define pleasure? What arguments does St. Thomas raise in defense of Aristotle's critique of "the Platonists"?

2. Having demonstrated that, strictly speaking, pleasure cannot be a motion or process, according to St. Thomas, how does Aristotle properly define pleasure's nature and properties?

3. According to St. Thomas, when is a pleasure experienced as maximally beautiful, passionate, for a human being?

4. According to him, in what way does pleasure maximize the activity of the sense or intellectual faculty?

5. According to St. Thomas, what is the twofold nature of formal perfection, and how does he apply this distinction to the nature of pleasure?

6. According to him, what does he say pleasure resembles?

7. According to Aristotle and St. Thomas, why cannot pleasure, even intellectual pleasure, last permanently in human beings.

8. What do Aristotle and St. Thomas say about the pleasure of intense cognitive activity?

9. According to them, why do all human beings naturally desire pleasure?

The difference of pleasures and pains according to species

1. Having explained pleasure's nature and properties, what does St. Thomas say Aristotle next considers, and how does Aristotle consider it?

2. According to St. Thomas, how do essential principles of species cause divisions within a genus?

3. On the animal and human levels, according to St. Thomas, how does this division of species within a genus relate to generation of differing specific pleasures, or proper pleasures?

4. According to him, what does a proper pleasure do in relation to facultative activity? Give an example.

5. In terms of intensive quantity, what are pleasure and pain in relationship to human nature and human faculties?

6. According to St. Thomas, how does every act of co-natural good and evil of a knowing faculty exist in the knowing faculty?

7. According to St. Thomas, what are proper and improper pleasures and what do they do wherever they exist?

The moral goodness and evil of pleasures and pains, joys and sorrows

1. After showing that pleasures and pains differ in species according to different activities, what do Aristotle and St. Thomas next show?

How does St. Thomas start to demonstrate their case, and how does he prove it?

2. According to Aristotle and St. Thomas, where is the chief pleasure found in the human species located? What do they maintain this chief pleasure synthesizes?

3. According to St. Thomas, what are the proximate facultative principles through which we human beings come to know with precision our proper pleasures?

4. According to Aristotle and St. Thomas, how are particular reason (or the estimative sense), loving, and knowing essentially connected to being able to apprehend proper pleasures?

5. Why does St. Thomas say that prudence is the measure by which we should judge all moral affairs, including whether or not a human being is morally good? Why does St. Thomas claim that no surprise exists why the delights of *the Many* and *the Prudent Man* (*the One*) tend to be contrary opposites?

Happiness: the one, chief pleasure of the prudent man

1. According to St. Thomas, after discussing the nature and species of pleasure and pain, joy and sorrow, what does Aristotle say he will next consider, and why does he say he especially needs to do so?

2. What does St. Thomas maintain Aristotle does to identify human happiness with utmost precision? Why does Aristotle maintain that defining happiness with such precision is necessary?

3. According to St. Thomas, strictly speaking, with what understanding of happiness do Aristotle, common human opinion, and he agree?

4. After having precisely located the genus of happiness as an activity, how does Aristotle proceed to identify its specific difference?

5. After doing this, by adding what three differences does he make this specific definition even more precise?

6. By saying that happiness is desirable *per se*, what precision about the nature of happiness does this enable them to make, to what mistaken understanding of happiness does it enable them to avoid?

7. Having shown that happiness is an activity in accord with virtue, according to St. Thomas, what six claims about happiness as an activity does Aristotle next make?

8. How does he prove these six claims?

Why Aristotle maintains that human happiness consists in the virtue of contemplation of the highest truth

1. According to St. Thomas, for what reasons does Aristotle claim that the highest, qualitatively greatest (or greatest in intensive, or virtual, quantity), most perfect and delightful human activity is contemplation of the highest truth?

2. Why does St. Thomas maintain the lasting enjoyment that constitutes happiness cannot be produced by the animal part of the soul, by an act like a dog eating a rabbit?

3. Why does St. Thomas claim that interruptions of intellectual delight rarely happen in philosophical, metaphysical, contemplation?

4. According to St. Thomas, in what respect is contemplation of truth twofold, which of the two does he consider to be better, and why?

5. According to him, how do people who already know the truth and have their reason perfected by its intellectual virtue through apprehension of forms of things spend their life?

6. Why does he claim the self-sufficiency that constitutes part of happiness exists most of all human activities in contemplation?

7. Why does St. Thomas maintain that the self-sufficiency of the contemplative man surpasses that of the prudent man?

8. Why does Aristotle say that, considered as contemplation of truth, happiness closely resembles amusement?

9. While, previously, Aristotle had said that rest is essentially ordered to subsequent activity, at this point in the *Nicomachean Ethics*, why does he no longer consider rest/leisure to be essentially ordered to subsequent activity?

10. According to Aristotle, is leisure in this sense found in the activities of the practical virtues? Do people of a practical bent, inclination, tend to understand leisure's nature in this sense?

11. Why does Aristotle claim that politicians and religious leaders have an especially difficult time understanding leisure in the sense of a contemplative activity?

12. Why do Aristotle and St. Thomas maintain that acts of war cannot be essentially ordered to more acts of killing?

13. According to them, in what ways is even political life ordered toward contemplative life?

14. Why does Aristotle consider political, especially military, life a preeminent act of moral virtue?

15. Why do Aristotle and St. Thomas maintain that the activity generated by the moral virtues, even that of prudence, cannot generate the contemplative virtue of happiness?

16. According to Aristotle, why does the proper pleasure of happiness proceeding from contemplative activity require a long life?

17. Why does Aristotle claim that a human being living a contemplative life is like something divine, unmixed with the bodily?

18. Rejecting the opinion of those who think otherwise, as far as

possible, what does Aristotle recommend human beings strive to do? Why does he claim that people like Simonides give foolish advice when they say a human being should not engage in contemplation of truth and metaphysical speculation?

The secondary kind of happiness that the activity of moral virtue causes

1. After showing how happiness consists chiefly in the intellectual virtue of contemplation, what two things do Aristotle and St. Thomas next show? How, in general, do they show it?

2. In what four ways does St. Thomas claim Aristotle proves that the contemplative life is happier than the practical life?

Human happiness and external goods

1. After having shown the twofold nature of perfect happiness in superior/contemplative, and inferior/practical, modes, what does St. Thomas say Aristotle next discusses about the happy man and how does he claim Aristotle discusses this?

2. According St. Thomas, since the happy man is most well disposed toward God and things God loves/honors, what two conclusions are we right to draw?

3. Hence, as St. Thomas says, what is evident about where Aristotle places happiness?

Why, according to Aristotle and St. Thomas, we need moral virtue plus prudent legislation to become happy: the moral psychology of the happy man as opposed to that of the incontinent and intemperate man

1. According to St. Thomas, after determining that, in both its contemplative and practical manifestations, happiness is pleasure, what does Aristotle next consider in relation to happiness? How does he consider it?

2. Regarding attainment of virtue during his period of time, what three chief philosophical teachings does Aristotle say existed? What does he state about these teachings?

3. What does St. Thomas add to what Aristotle states?

4. What do Aristotle and St. Thomas conclude about the relationship between good legislation and sound moral education?

5. How does Aristotle end his *Nicomachean Ethics*?

Conclusion

1. In his "Author's Introduction" to volume 2 of his *A Not-So Elementary Christian Metaphysics*, what had the author of this book claimed he had considered himself to be acting as? For whom, and for what chief aim, did he say he had written that work?

2. Analogous to that claim, in this work, what does he claim to have been doing? For whom, and for what chief aim, does he say he has written it? Do you think he has achieved what he claims to have set out to do in this book. If so, why? If not, why not?

Concluding Postscript

1. Close to 75 years ago, reflecting upon his career as a Ph. D. graduate in psychology from Columbia University, what had Mortimer J. Adler reported about his career as a student of modern psychology?

2. Having had experience with modern psychology, and having spent most of his professional academic career leading the fight in American higher education against, and exposing as intellectual frauds and sophists the many falsely-so-called "social scientists" that inhabited American colleges and universities while he was alive, were he still with us today, what does the author of this article suspect that Adler would be shocked and bewildered to find about the magazine *First Things*?

An Introduction to Ragamuffin Ethics

3. According to the author of this article, analogous to what is interviewing Jonathan Haidt to try to discover how to solve the problem of the contemporary coddling of the minds of contemporary American college and university students?

4. Were he alive today, what does the author of this book suspect Adler would have replied regarding such a positive portrayal of Haidt as someone who knows the chief causes and solutions to present problems facing American higher education?

5. Since Adler is not alive, why does the author of this article say he has written it?

General analysis of *The Righteous Mind*

1. What is the author of this article's general analysis of Jonathan Haidt's *The Righteous Mind*?

2. What does he maintain Haidt is claiming to show about Glaucon, Plato, and David Hume in *The Righteous Mind*?

3. From the start of his text, upon what does the author of this article maintain Haidt's argument essentially rests?

4. What does he say is Haidt's first unsupported, dogmatic assertion and false claim, and where does it appear in this text? Precisely why is that claim false?

5. Where and how does Haidt follow up this mistake by making what false disjunction and distinction? Why is this distinction false?

6. What false disjunction and what false distinction does Haidt immediately make about the nature of "empiricism" and "rationalism"? Why is this distinction false?

7. Just as Haidt grossly and anachronistically misunderstands Plato after the fashion of a modern rationalist, how does Haidt grossly misunderstand Hume as an "empiricist"?

Peter A. Redpath

8. Starting with his misinterpretations of Plato and Hume, and of himself as a "scientist" (apparently because he employs the "empirical method"), what conclusion does the author of this article maintain Haidt derives?

9. According to this article's author, while Haidt is right to challenge the rationalist delusions of Kohlberg and Kant, what is wrong about his use of Glaucon to challenge Plato?

Summary of Book 2 of Plato's *Republic*

Introduction

1. Summarize the actual request that Plato's brother Glaucon initially makes of Socrates at the start of Book 2 of Plato's *Republic*?

2. Explain what had happened in Book 1 of the *Republic* that had prompted Glaucon to make this request of Socrates.

3. If Socrates really wants to persuade Glaucon and Adeimantos that being just is always really better than seeming just, how does Glaucon evaluate the effectiveness Socrates has achieved thus far in their discussion? What does Glaucon initially do to assist Socrates to achieve what Socrates wants?

Initial discussion between Socrates and Glaucon (acting as Devil's Advocate for Thrasymachos' understanding of justice as praising injustice over justice)

1. According to Glaucon, why has Socrates not done justice to Thrasymachos' argument that appearing to be just is better, more profitable, than being just?

2. After saying that he disagrees with Thrasymachos and popular opinion about the nature of justice and the claim that the life of the unjust is better and more profitable than the life of the just, what does Glaucon say he has never heard adequately commended in an

705

argument? From whom does he claim he is most likely to hear such an argument?

3. To assist Socrates in the effort to commend the power of justice considered in itself (not related to anything else), what does Glaucon state he will do?

4. Since Socrates finds this proposal agreeable, how does Glaucon start his work?

5. According to Glaucon, in the popular view (the one Thrasymachos had commended), what is justice? According to this article's author, how does Jonathan Haidt's attitude to justice compare to that which Glaucon identifies as "the popular view" (that of Thrasymachos)?

6. According to Glaucon, what is justice in the popular view and how does justice originate?

7. According to the author of this article, why does Glaucon say he is telling "The Story of the Ring of Gyges"? Is Glaucon actually maintaining that he agrees with the moral of the story, or is he saying that he disagrees with it?

The Story of the Ring of Gyges

1. Summarize the "Story of the Ring of Gyges" as told by Glaucon?

2. According to Glaucon, who says the kinds of things that the message of the "Story of the Ring of Gyges" commends?

3. In telling the Story, is Glaucon, in any way, suggesting that the chief aim of the Story is to show that shame is important, in contrast to the attitude of Socrates that shame is not important?

4. What do Aristotle and St. Thomas maintain about the nature of shame in relation to the prudent, morally virtuous, man? Do they maintain that shame in any way motivates the behavior of the prudent, morally virtuous, man? Why, or why not?

5. According to Aristotle and St. Thomas, what person does shame motivate to do the right thing?

6. From what the author of this article has said about Jonathan Haidt's analysis of the "Story of the Ring of Gyges" and the relation of shame to moral education, moral psychology, and prudence, does Haidt show any awareness of the nature of moral virtue, prudence, or moral psychology as a science? If so, what is that awareness? If not, why not?

Discussion between Socrates and Adeimantos about the way popular opinion praises justice over injustice

1. At this point in Plato's *Republic*, why does Adeimantos say he needs to interrupt the conversation?

2. Summarize what Adeimantos claims "the many" (poets, priests, and others, like fathers to the sons) say when they talk about justice and injustice.

3. From how Adeimantos describes the way "the many" talk about justice and injustice, if the way the author of this article has summarized the teachings of Jonathan Haidt is right, do you think Adeimantos would include or exclude Haidt from belonging to the group he calls "the many"? Why?

4. Is Adeimantos maintaining that he and Glaucon are in disagreement with Socrates' teaching about justice? Or is he claiming that people who commend justice, virtue, chiefly for the sake of reputation make a mistake regarding the proper way morally to educate?

5. According to the author of this article, what does Jonathan Haidt incorrectly assume about Plato's understanding of the nature of reasoning and its relation to what Haidt calls "observation"?

6. According to this article's author, in contrast to what Haidt claims

An Introduction to Ragamuffin Ethics

Plato is doing (celebrating rationalist reason, abstract logic, and theoretical reason in the classical sense), what is Plato actually doing?

Summary of Book 1 of Plato's *Republic*

Introduction

1. Summarize the opening discussion of Book 1 of Plato's *Republic* by describing the encounter that Socrates and Plato's brother Glaucon had had with a friend of Socrates named Polemarchos and Plato's other brother, Adeimantos, before going to the home of Cephalos.

Discussion between Socrates and Cephalos

1. Summarize the discussion that Socrates has with Cephalos in Book 1 of the *Republic*.

2. How, if in any way, does this discussion indicate that Socrates' approach to moral investigation does not start with abstract logic and that Jonathan Haidt has close to no familiarity with the teaching of Plato and Socrates?

Discussion between Socrates and Thrasymachos

1. Summarize the discussion that Socrates has with Thrasymachos in Book 1 of the *Republic*.

2. How, if in any way, does this discussion indicate that Haidt has close to no familiarity with the teaching of Plato and Socrates and has grossly misrepresented the nature and moral of the "Story of the Ring of Gyges"?

Mortimer J. Adler's correct analysis of the Story of the Ring of Gyges

1. Does Mortimer J Adler agree or disagree with Haidt's claim that moral philosophy's first principle—its categorical imperative—is Haidt's moral psychology principle, "*Intuitions come first, strategic*

708

reasoning second"? If Adler disagrees with Haidt, what does Adler maintain is moral philosophy's first principle?

2. According to Adler, what is the age-old problem, the most difficult problem, in moral philosophy, that Plato's "Story of the Ring of Gyges" attempts to solve?

3. According to Adler, to solve this problem, what must we first recognize?

4. How does Adler proceed to solve this problem?

5. How does Adler's solution to this problem make evident that Jonathan Haidt totally misunderstands the teaching of Plato and the nature and moral of the "Story of the Ring of Gyges"?

A more detailed analysis of the sophistry of Jonathan Haidt's *The Righteous Mind*

1. While Jonathan Haidt cautions his readers (p. 316) to "Beware of anyone who insists," apparently like Mortimer Adler, "that there is one true morality for all people, times, and places—particularly if that morality is founded upon a single foundation," why does the author of this article maintain that the person to beware of is not the one like Adler, but the one like Jonathan Haidt and the person of supposed "moral excellence" Haidt celebrates: David Hume?

2. While Jonathan Haidt might want to claim that his moral psychology is radically different from that of Thrasymachos, according to this article's author, what statements that Haidt has made belie that claim?

3. According to the author of this article, what helps to explain the extensive number of absurdities that Haidt would have his readers accept?

4. What makes the claim that "anyone who tells you that all societ-

ies, in all eras, should be using one particular matrix, resting on one particular configuration of moral foundations, is a fundamentalist of one sort or another" false, absurd?

5. Why cannot the following claim being made by Jonathan Haidt possibly be right?: "Hume got it right. When he died in 1776, he and other sentimentalists had laid a superb foundation for moral science."

6. Identify some other similarly false and outrageous claims that the author of this article maintains Haidt makes? According to him, what makes these claims false and outrageous?

7. According to this article's author, to give their rationally incoherent thinking the aura of science, what do social science fundamentalists like Haidt and Hume maintain about the origin of words?

8. Why is Haidt wrong when he maintains that brain neurons think? Why does Haidt appear to think that he is a scientist? Why is his entire book an exercise in sophistry, not science?

9. How is the diagram of Jonathan Haidt's intuitionist model, with some incidental changes, largely a description of the Socratic method that Plato employs throughout his dialogues? What is the chief difference between Haidt's model and that of Plato and Socrates?

10. According to this article's author, how would Plato and St. Thomas agree and disagree with Haidt about the nature of intuitions? How does he think Mortimer Adler would evaluate the moral psychology of Jonathan Haidt?

11. According to the author of this article, why does Jonathan Haidt deserve praise and blame? Why does he conclude that "Jonathan Haidt's science of moral psychology is one more instance of the tradition of modern snake oil peddled by modern academic confidence men under the rubric of 'science'"?

12. What sage observation did Adler once make regarding the proper role of classroom instructors in relation to students? What did Adler well understand about the coddling and closing of the American mind that social scientists like Jonathan Haidt fail to comprehend?

13. What does the author of this article maintain about Haidt's claims that he is an expert in moral psychology and that his moral psychology is "moral science"?

14. If the author of this article has accurately reported the teaching of Jonathan Haidt as expressed in his book, *The Righteous Mind*, do you agree or disagree with the author's assessment of Haidt's teaching. If you disagree, explain why you disagree.

15. If this article's author has accurately reported the teaching of Jonathan Haidt as expressed in his book, *The Righteous Mind*, how would you evaluate Haidt's moral psychology and moral science in comparison and contrast to that of Aristotle and St. Thomas? Which do you think provides a better example of moral psychology and moral science? Why?

About the Author

PETER A. REDPATH is presently a Senior Fellow at the Center for the Study of The Great Ideas in Chicago, Rector of the Adler-Aquinas Institute (www.adler-aquinasinstitute.org); Chair of the St. John Paul II Thomistic Studies Graduate Philosophy Concentration in Christian Wisdom for Holy Apostles College and Seminary; CEO of the Aquinas School of Leadership (www.aquinasschoolofleadership.com); and a contributing scholar in the Thomistic Studies graduate program at the University Abat Oliba, Barcelona, Spain. Former Full Professor of Philosophy at St. John's University, New York, Redpath has taught philosophy on the college and university level for over forty-four years, plus courses at the Staten Island, Arthur Kill Correctional Facility and New York City's Rikers Island. He is author/editor of 12 philosophical books and dozens of articles and book reviews; has given over 200 invited guest lectures nationally and internationally; is president and co-founder of the International Étienne Gilson Society; co-founder of the Aquinas Leadership International group; co-founder and vice president of The Gilson Society, former vice-president of the American Maritain Association, Chairman of the Board of the Universities of Western Civilization and the Angelicum Academy home school program; a member of the Board of Directors of the Great Books Academy home school program; a member of Board of Trustees of the Institute for Advanced Philosophic Research; a member of Board of Directors and Executive Committee of the Catholic Education Foundation; Academician of The Catholic

Peter A. Redpath

Academy of Sciences in the United States of America; editor of the Brill/Rodopi Gilson Study Special Series; former executive editor of Value Inquiry Book Series (VIBS) for the Dutch publisher Editions Rodopi, B. V.; former editor of the Studies in the History of Western Philosophy special series for Editions Rodopi and former editor of the Editions Rodopi Gilson Studies Special Series; former associate editor, and current advisor of the journal *Contemporary Philosophy*; a recipient of St. John's University's Outstanding Achievement Award; a distinguished alumnus of Xaverian High School; a Fellow of the Priority Thinking Institute; and former Graduate Fellow at the SUNY at Buffalo. He currently resides with his wife, Lorraine, in Cave Creek, Arizona.

Index

Amsterdam, 17, 108, 559
amusement (see, also,
    playfulness), 186, 302–303,
    395, 493, 495, 635, 701
anachronistically, 516, 704
analogous(ly), 11–13, 30, 42,
    44, 61, 80, 89, 107, 138,
    141–142, 144, 160, 178, 193,
    224, 230–231, 241, 256, 265,
    290, 292, 296, 308–310, 312,
    323–324, 333–334, 339, 344,
    353, 356–357, 359, 376, 384,
    387, 398, 427, 430, 437–438,
    440, 459, 461, 465, 477, 485,
    487–488, 501, 509, 514, 538,
    592, 596, 628, 630, 644, 647,
    649, 655, 657, 667, 673–674,
    686–687, 703–704
analogy, 11, 105, 340, 358, 486,
    536, 540, 568
analysis, 13, 18–19, 58, 108, 145,
    238, 263, 279, 286, 309, 311,
    328, 363, 391, 455, 464, 466,
    514, 541, 544, 627, 644, 653,
    658, 670, 695, 704, 707–709
anarchic, 22, 326, 504, 506
anarchist(ic)(s), 327
anarchy, 22
ancestry, 420
ancient(s), 1, 5, 15, 23–25, 28,
    48–49, 63, 74, 93, 133–135,
    167, 193, 219, 233, 264, 280,
    328, 405, 419, 421, 436, 447,
    470, 490, 502, 515, 524, 526,
    547, 552, 554, 557, 562, 581,
    605, 621, 675, 679
anger, 8, 23, 104–106, 128–129,
    147, 151, 170–174, 188, 240,

243, 254, 256–258, 274,
    297–298, 312, 336, 371, 380,
    382, 386, 390–393, 403–404,
    460, 478, 506, 533, 551, 580,
    586–587, 593–594, 623,
    632–633, 670, 675
angry, 151, 171–173, 254, 258,
    274, 297–298, 377, 380,
    390–393, 396, 477–478, 526,
    594, 618, 633, 666, 670
Angelicum Academy, 712
Anglican, 2
animal(s), 7, 14, 55, 66–67,
    78, 80, 88–89, 92, 96–100,
    105–106, 109, 114–115,
    117–118, 121, 129–130, 135,
    141, 151–154, 156–158, 160,
    165, 193–195, 203, 219, 222,
    232, 235, 256–257, 270, 274,
    277–282, 298, 328, 344, 357,
    361, 372, 385, 389, 393, 406,
    411, 416–417, 420, 423, 440,
    458, 463, 470–471, 473–474,
    487, 490–491, 493–494, 501,
    551, 574, 588–591, 606, 609,
    611, 625–626, 649, 657, 668,
    671, 688, 698, 700
Apodaca, Christopher, 39
apologetic(al)(s), 18, 561, 714
apparent, 2, 12, 116, 119, 150,
    153, 156, 160, 208, 219–220,
    234, 240, 249, 253, 265–266,
    332–333, 342, 385–386, 394,
    398, 449–450, 470, 472, 474,
    480, 507, 512, 541, 587–588,
    610, 621, 648, 668
apparent good, 116, 156, 220,
    249, 265–266, 385, 398, 450,

doable, 115, 123, 131, 165–166,
204, 231, 260, 263–264, 329,
345, 349, 351–352, 358–359,
361–362, 364, 371, 465, 657,
663
doable deed, 115, 123, 131, 204,
329, 345, 349, 358–359, 361–
362, 364, 370–371, 657, 663
docilitas (see teachability), 34,
207, 505
doctor(s), 44, 183, 216, 226, 230,
261–262, 340, 349, 513, 609
doctrine(s), 18, 25, 31, 509–510,
553–554
dog, 156, 278, 291, 490, 494,
515, 553, 589, 700, 704
doing injustice, 332–334,
337–338, 647
domestic prudence (see, also,
household prudence), 358,
360, 656–657
doubt, 118, 227, 261, 267, 318,
342, 347, 364, 368, 374, 378,
380, 447–448, 458, 462–463,
619, 648, 662, 665–666, 690,
694
dream(ed)(s), 9, 17, 26, 108,
402–403, 559
drink, 153, 158, 211, 231, 242,
277, 279–281, 284, 386–388,
392, 416–417, 423, 466, 479,
537, 626
dualist(ic), 134, 193
Dumb Ox Books, 17
duplicitous, 243
Durkheim, Émile, 545
dut(ies)(y), 18, 41, 47, 193, 353,
358, 405, 443, 447, 454–455,

565, 654, 690
Dutch publisher, 713

Earth, 11, 62, 93, 139, 197, 329,
342, 509, 521
economic(s), 320–323, 421, 434,
641
Editions Rodopi, B.V., 17, 108,
559, 713
editor, 541, 559, 712–713
education(al)(ly), 8, 25, 30–35,
41, 96, 109, 160, 203,
232–234, 268, 308, 366, 368,
389, 396–397, 437, 447, 468,
500, 505, 507, 513, 514, 552,
559–560, 563, 601–602, 610,
661, 669, 672, 703–704, 707,
712
"Education of the Human Race"
(Lessing), 514
educationally incorrigible, 397,
672
effect(s), 30–31, 43, 47–48, 53,
61–62, 67, 69, 79, 81–82, 91,
94–95, 112, 136–138, 141–
142, 148–151, 158, 162–163,
166, 168–169, 171–172,
190–192, 198, 200, 209–210,
224, 230, 240, 248–249, 260,
262, 269, 276, 292, 294,
306–309, 325, 329, 337, 346,
348–349, 354, 359, 418, 420,
427, 448, 453–454, 456, 458,
502, 506–507, 516, 547, 554,
565–566, 569, 582–584, 586,
590–594, 598–599, 615, 631,
643, 650, 652, 691–692, 694,
705

113–114, 165, 181–182, 191,
194, 199, 203–204, 208–214,
217–219, 221–223, 225–226,
310, 368, 370, 398, 404–405,
409, 411–414, 468–469,
492–498, 500–503, 520, 523,
544, 554, 576, 602, 607, 662,
675–677, 695, 699, 702

harmonious(ly), 12–13, 42, 44,
51, 65–67, 69, 112–113, 147,
152, 200, 212–213, 215,
291–292, 376, 427, 451, 460,
464. 476–477, 482, 551, 564,
692

harmony, 54, 65–67, 69, 150,
152, 154, 163, 215, 230–231,
239, 266, 344, 376, 385, 421,
450, 474, 476–477, 569, 608,
649, 692

Harper's Magazine, 552

hate(ful), 32, 39, 68, 85, 104, 107,
128, 130, 141, 143, 146–147,
150, 152, 173, 208, 257, 299,
301, 303, 312, 333, 360, 400,
412, 434, 452, 468, 472, 478,
481, 504–505, 507, 528, 553,
586–587, 594, 638

hate-speech, 208, 481, 504

hatred, 8, 128, 133, 150, 170,
173, 240, 504–505, 526,
539–540, 586–587

have, 1, 7, 11–12, 15, 19–22, 27,
30–37, 44–45, 51, 53, 55, 60–
64, 68, 76–77, 80–82, 84–85,
87, 89, 93, 95, 98, 101–102,
107–108 112, 117, 120–122,
127–131, 133, 135, 138, 145,
147, 150, 153, 159, 164–166,

172–174, 178, 180, 187, 192–
193, 197, 199, 205–206, 208–
209, 211, 213–214, 216–217,
223, 227, 236, 240, 245, 252,
255–257, 259–260, 263–265,
267–271, 274, 278–279, 283,
285, 288, 292, 300–301, 311,
315, 321–323, 325, 328, 331,
334, 341–345, 348, 351, 353,
356, 361–363, 365, 368, 380,
382–383, 386, 389, 392–393,
397, 402–403, 408, 410–412,
414, 417, 420–421, 426–431,
434, 437–440, 442–444, 449,
451–545, 457, 462–465, 468,
469, 474–481, 490, 500–505,
508–510, 513–519, 521–526,
528–530, 536, 538–540, 542–
543, 545, 547–548, 551–554,
557, 561, 563, 566, 574,
579–580, 582–589, 592, 594,
596, 602–603, 605, 608–609,
612, 521, 622, 624–625, 627,
682–683, 686–688, 691–693,
695–696, 700–701, 703–704,
709

having(s), 23, 32, 45, 51, 54,
58–59, 63–64, 72–73, 75, 80,
82–83, 86, 88, 111, 113–114,
119–120, 141, 145–146, 152,
154–155, 164, 171–172, 177–
178, 185–186, 191, 196, 204,
208, 213, 219, 221, 225–226,
229, 235–237, 244, 259, 262,
264–265, 267–268, 271, 273,
275, 278–280, 282, 286–287,
289, 293–295, 297, 299, 303,
310–312, 314–315, 317–318,

484–486, 488, 502, 622
McInerny, Ralph M., 17
McVey, A. William, 16, 35, 39
mean, 8, 35, 81, 105, 135, 145,
185, 187, 231, 233, 237–240,
242, 244–247, 271, 277–278,
283, 291, 297–299, 301–303,
306–307, 309, 312, 314–319,
324–325, 339–340, 355, 358,
399–401, 403, 423, 520, 535,
537, 563, 565–566, 575, 582,
584–585, 588, 590, 597,
603–604, 609–612, 614, 616,
626, 628, 632, 634–643, 647,
655, 669, 674
means, 1, 13–15, 18–19, 21–22,
27, 41–42, 49, 55, 64, 78, 82,
86–87, 105, 111, 113, 116–
119, 121–123, 131, 138, 143–
144, 153, 155, 159, 187–189,
191, 194, 203–204, 206–207,
211, 216, 238, 242, 247, 252,
258–260, 262, 264–265,
267–277, 283, 286, 288, 292,
301–303, 310, 314, 322, 326,
328–331, 345–348, 352–353,
355, 363–366, 368–371, 373,
379, 383, 388–389, 391, 394,
399, 402, 405–406, 410–411,
413, 421–423, 425–427, 431,
435, 441, 444, 454, 462–463,
481, 493, 496, 499–500, 502,
514–517, 519, 524, 530, 532,
540–541, 543–544, 548–549,
557, 576–577, 601, 620–621,
634, 636, 641–642, 651, 660,
667, 669, 673, 676, 685, 689,
693

measure(d)(s), 9, 11, 16, 38, 41,
50, 53, 56, 58, 122, 147, 159,
173, 178, 190, 218, 231, 236,
239, 252, 257, 266, 281, 283,
287, 291–292, 295, 310, 315–
317, 319–324, 326, 329, 334,
340, 345, 388, 399, 401, 404,
413, 416, 424, 444, 446–447,
449, 464, 483, 487–488, 491,
502, 522, 525, 536, 546, 550,
568, 590, 609, 611, 626, 631,
640–642, 647, 650, 673–674,
689–691, 699
measuring, 118, 252, 489, 517,
537, 641, 690
mechan(ical)(istic), 49
medical(ly), 44, 113, 183,
215–216, 226, 230, 261–262,
340, 349, 386, 485, 532, 534,
537, 609
medical doctor, 44, 183, 216, 226,
230, 261–262, 340, 349, 609
Mediaeval, 37
medicinal, 156, 232, 300, 336,
365, 416–418, 659, 678
medicine, 43–44, 47, 112, 230,
340, 349, 364, 374, 407, 419,
519, 532, 534–536
*Medieval Tradition of Natural
Law, The* (Johnson, ed.), 198
Mein Kampf (Hitler), 553
melting, 149
memor(ies)(y), 7, 23, 84–85,
97, 99, 100, 162, 170, 386, 389,
450, 452, 457, 479, 481, 512
metaphysical, 3–4, 8–13, 15,
20–21, 25–26, 29–30, 322, 494,
498, 509, 562, 641, 700, 702

567, 570, 576–578, 581,
590–603, 606, 617, 620–621,
623–625, 627, 629–638, 642,
644–645, 647, 649–650, 653–
654, 661–665, 667, 669–675,
679–686, 690–695, 697–699,
701–703, 706–711
moral bankruptcy, 512
moral education, 8, 96, 109, 203,
232–234, 308, 396–397, 468,
500, 507, 601–602, 610, 661,
672, 703, 707
moral(ly) good, 121–123, 133,
135–136, 159, 164, 233, 238,
488, 577–578, 581, 590, 612,
617, 634, 698
moral(ly) evil, 136, 165, 192,
426, 592
morally-healthy, 183
moral principle, 19, 72–73, 192,
198, 207, 210, 307, 372, 459,
510, 542, 546, 561, 599, 636
moral psychology, i, ii, 1, 4–5,
7–15, 17–18, 21, 35, 65, 72–
73, 111, 115, 118, 164, 166,
169, 171, 182, 226, 233, 263,
272, 281, 289, 293–294, 297,
300, 302, 352, 370, 375, 381,
383, 388, 390–391, 393, 399,
401–403, 420, 424, 426–430,
432, 434–438, 441, 447–448,
453–455, 458–459, 503–505,
510, 514, 517, 522, 524, 534,
541, 545–546, 549, 555–557,
563, 570, 576–577, 592–594,
610, 620, 623–624, 627, 629,
631–635, 637, 644, 653, 667,
669–671, 674, 680–686, 688,

692–694, 697, 702, 707–711
*Moral Psychology of St. Thomas
Aquinas, The*: *An Introduction
to Ragamuffin Ethics* (Redpath), 5, 10, 12, 14, 17
moral science, 2, 12, 19–20, 28,
48, 50, 58, 111, 199, 201, 204,
206–208, 221, 227, 229–230,
233, 239, 300, 404, 468–469,
503, 509, 546, 557, 567, 576,
600–603, 608–609, 634, 675,
710, 711
moral virtue, 15, 19, 109, 113,
123–124, 135, 167, 180, 184–
188, 190, 192, 197, 203, 208,
214, 218, 221, 223, 225–227,
229, 231–232, 234, 236–242,
245, 247–248, 256, 267,
271–272, 275, 277, 286, 290,
292–293, 297–298, 306, 308,
324, 336, 339, 341, 345, 353,
361, 368–375, 377–379, 397,
401, 418, 430, 453, 468–469,
474, 479, 489, 496–507, 510,
542–543, 595–598, 606–615,
621, 624, 629–633, 635–637,
642, 647, 650, 653–654, 662–
663, 665, 675, 692, 694–695,
701–702, 707
moral worth, 135–136, 581
*Moral Wisdom of St. Thomas,
The*: *An Introduction* (Redpath), 4, 8
morose, 172, 298, 427–428, 633
morose anger, 298
mos (custom/habit), 185
motion(s), 8, 12, 15, 23–24, 32–
33, 49, 63, 65–66, 68–69, 74,

to the chase

pseudo-science, 513
psychic movement, 132, 147,
   154–155, 174, 588
psychology, 1–15, 17–18, 21–28,
   31, 35, 40, 65, 72–73, 77,
   111, 115, 118, 164, 166, 169,
   171–172, 182, 226, 233, 263,
   268, 272, 281, 289, 293–294,
   297, 300, 302, 352, 370, 375,
   381, 383–384, 388, 390–391,
   393–394, 399, 401–403, 420,
   424, 426–430, 432, 434–438,
   441, 447–448, 453–455,
   458–459, 503–505, 510,
   512–514, 517, 522, 524, 534,
   541, 545–546, 555–558,
   562–563, 570, 576–577,
   592–594, 610, 620, 623–624,
   627, 629, 631–635, 637, 644,
   653, 667, 669–671, 673–674,
   680–686, 688, 690, 692–694,
   697, 702–703, 707–711
psychological, 7, 14, 21–22,
   34–35, 43, 45, 66–68, 115–
   116, 149, 152, 160, 162–164,
   166–167, 169, 186, 210, 218,
   230, 251, 255, 268–270, 275,
   278, 281, 292, 295, 304, 306,
   314, 317–318, 327, 343, 368,
   375–376, 385, 391, 401, 411,
   417, 420, 426–427, 430–435,
   438–441, 443–446, 448, 450–
   452, 458, 481, 516, 525, 576,
   587, 589, 592–593, 597, 603,
   623, 625–626, 644, 653, 665,
   671–672, 674, 682, 684–685,
   687–692, 697
psychosomatic, 67, 70, 126, 154,

170, 499, 506
public, 30, 37, 39, 122, 125–126,
   175, 191, 198, 210, 228, 248,
   273, 288, 293–294, 296,
   298–299, 302–304, 311, 320,
   337–338, 443, 447, 467, 500–
   501, 510, 514, 518, 521–525,
   527, 533, 535, 538, 551, 615,
   705, 707–708
Pulydamas, 530
punishment, 124, 203, 222,
   244–249, 251, 268, 273, 298,
   319, 327, 336–337, 391, 503,
   505, 507, 522, 524–525, 529,
   578, 606, 614–616
pure, 26, 54, 60, 90, 278, 476,
   490, 494, 625
puritanical, 469
Pythagorean(s), 318–319, 640

qualitative(ly), 13, 42–45, 49–51,
   53–55, 58–61, 63–64, 66–67,
   76, 78, 80, 83–84, 87, 93–96,
   101–103, 114, 118, 120, 126,
   129–131, 137, 139, 149–150,
   153–155, 165, 168, 177–179,
   181–182, 188, 193, 199–200,
   206, 212–213, 229–231, 236,
   238, 252, 264, 266, 272, 274,
   276, 290–292, 301, 303, 314–
   316, 320–326, 328, 333–334,
   341, 348–349, 351, 374, 404,
   408–409, 415, 417–418, 425,
   430–432, 440, 445–446, 457,
   459, 460, 474, 478, 484–490,
   493–494, 496, 498, 500–502,
   564–565, 567, 571, 589, 598,
   600, 620, 641, 648, 678, 680,

690, 700

qualitative equality, 137, 314, 320

qualitative inequality, 320, 431

qualitatively unequal friendships, 446

qualit(ies)(y), 23, 34, 42, 45, 51, 60, 66, 77–78, 87–88, 93–100, 122–124, 140, 145, 148, 156, 172, 177–180, 183, 187, 200, 206, 208, 215–216, 236–239, 259–261, 266, 268, 283, 288, 291, 293, 301, 308, 312, 315–316, 320–324, 333, 335, 343, 348, 356, 368, 405, 408–409, 417, 426, 428, 430–431, 434, 449–452, 456, 458–459, 461, 475, 487, 490, 526, 540, 583, 595–596, 600, 602, 611, 619, 628, 630, 632, 641, 646, 652, 678, 682, 691–692

quantitative(ly), 85, 101, 141, 143, 394, 437

quantit(ies)(y), 9–10, 12, 28–30, 42, 50, 63, 78, 85, 97, 101–102, 114, 139–141, 143, 150, 154, 168, 177, 182, 186, 199, 220, 231, 236–237, 239, 245, 252, 272, 290–292, 314–316, 318, 323–333, 341, 343, 348, 356, 394–395, 408–409, 415, 418, 437, 459, 461, 480, 484, 486–487, 490, 494, 497–498, 568, 571, 582–583, 586, 593, 611, 630, 639, 698, 700

quarrel(s), 146, 300, 428, 441–444, 688, 619

quarrelsome, 300, 428

quick-tempered, 170, 243, 478

rabbit, 156, 278, 494, 589, 700

race(s), 25–26, 31, 67, 70, 112, 117, 151, 189–190, 219, 224, 250–251, 272–274, 276, 284, 290, 300, 304, 316–317, 390, 420, 448, 514

rare, 261, 282, 293, 295, 401, 407, 425, 442, 494, 700

Ragamuffin contemplative, 16

Ragamuffin Ethics, 4–5, 9–10, 12, 14, 17, 35, 509, 563

Ragamuffin Thomism 3–4, 35, 509, 563

Ragamuffin Thomist, 1, 3, 35

rash(ness), 161, 242, 244, 271

rational(ly)(ism)(ity), 2, 6, 13, 32, 45–46, 55, 60, 66, 69, 77, 88, 95, 105, 115, 121, 123, 132, 136, 139, 151, 156, 160, 167, 169–170, 188, 193–194, 203, 209, 213, 222, 226–227, 252, 256–257, 269, 325, 327–329, 340–344, 346, 353, 362, 366, 383, 389, 400, 414, 441, 455, 458, 474, 491, 504–506, 515–517, 527, 547–548, 553, 593, 606, 647–648, 649, 693, 704–705, 708, 710

rational animal, 55, 105, 115, 121, 156, 193–194, 203, 222, 256–257, 328, 606

read(ing)(s), 3–4, 8, 15, 18, 20–21, 33–37, 39, 81, 84, 91–92, 99, 105, 117, 149, 166, 174, 180, 187, 192, 202, 210, 214, 219, 236, 248, 263–264, 273, 291, 306, 312, 314, 319, 364, 368, 380, 393, 397, 410,

565–566, 571–572, 575–576,
578, 581, 583, 589, 591–592,
595, 597, 601–605, 608–610,
612–615, 617–621, 623, 625,
629, 636–637, 645–648, 650–
668, 670–674, 679–680, 682,
684, 686–687, 690–691, 693,
695–696, 699–700, 707–709
Reason/Will, 135
reasonable, 32, 171, 210, 221,
223, 243, 272, 368, 382, 450,
525, 528
Reasoned Judgment, 182
receptiv(e)(ity), 91–92, 101, 137,
141, 149, 151, 327, 341, 344,
361, 400, 478, 648, 657
reciprocal, 323, 426, 448, 453
reciprocat(e)(ion), 318, 426, 431,
640
recognition, 27, 142, 445, 542
recognize(d), 15, 21, 27–28,
33, 41, 45, 51, 61, 63, 142,
162, 167, 196, 199, 207, 214,
216, 232–233, 246, 252, 268,
320–321, 352, 396–397, 401,
405, 409–410, 414, 417, 424,
430, 442–443, 453, 474, 486,
506, 541, 543, 550, 564, 600,
604, 609, 641, 654, 688, 709
recognizing, 28, 214, 216–217,
245, 337, 394, 396, 672
recollection(s), 100, 516, 550
rectitiude, 159, 240, 345, 353,
363, 658
Redpath, Peter A., 3–5, 7–10,
12–13, 16–17, 37–38, 56, 108,
124, 198, 512, 559, 712
reduction(ism)(istic), 134, 319,

553
regime(s), 310, 315, 320, 327,
644
Reiss, Hans, 559
relat(able)(e)(ed)(es), 7–9, 18,
20, 24–25, 34–35, 37, 40, 43,
45–46, 48, 51–53, 61, 63, 68,
72, 76, 82, 85, 87–88, 93, 97,
99–100, 112, 116, 121, 123,
127–131, 133–136, 138–139,
142–145, 152, 156, 165–166,
170, 172, 178–179, 181,
185–186, 189–193, 196–197,
204, 210, 216–217, 219, 223,
226–227, 230, 233–234,
241–244, 247, 254–255, 258,
260, 262–264, 268–269, 271,
275–276, 278–281, 284,
286–287, 289–297, 299–300,
302–303, 307, 312, 315–316,
319, 321, 323, 325–326, 329,
337, 399, 403, 407, 409, 414,
417, 422, 431–432, 439, 445,
447, 454, 464, 469, 474, 479,
482, 491, 496, 517, 552–553,
568, 581–582, 584, 586, 593,
595–597, 610, 613, 615,
619–621, 623, 626, 628–629,
631–633, 635, 639, 643–645,
650, 652–653, 660, 666,
669–670, 672–673, 677, 682,
684, 689–691, 693, 695–697
relation(al)(ally)(ship)(s), 2,
4, 7, 9, 12–14, 17, 21, 28,
30–31, 40, 44, 46–49, 52, 54,
56–57, 60, 65–66, 73–74, 76,
79–82, 89, 100, 102, 105–106,
108–109, 111–113, 118–120,

146, 148, 150–158, 163–168,
170, 172–174, 178, 180–181,
184, 207–208, 210, 215–216,
220, 224, 227, 233–234, 237,
246, 249, 252, 261, 266–269,
273–275, 277–281, 290, 293,
295–296, 300, 304, 306, 324,
326, 331, 334, 336, 343–346,
349, 352–358, 361–363,
365–367, 369–373, 375–376,
381–387, 389–391, 393–394,
396, 398, 402, 405, 409–410,
413, 418, 424, 428, 430–432,
443, 445–446, 453, 455, 458,
462–463, 465–466, 473, 480,
484–487, 489–491, 495–497,
499, 503–504, 506, 516–517,
520, 527–528, 531–534, 540,
546–547, 549–553, 555,
573–576, 579, 581–582, 585,
587–589, 593–594, 603, 610,
619, 621, 625, 631, 638, 642,
645, 648–650, 652, 654–655,
657–658, 660, 662, 664, 666,
669, 672, 676, 683–684, 690,
696–697, 699, 707–708
sense impression(s), 516
sense reali(sm)(ty) 28, 33, 280
sensitive appetite, 103, 105–107,
127, 136, 236, 277, 333, 428,
625
sense wonder, 28
sensible(s), 7, 69, 75, 84, 93–94,
96–101, 128, 132–133, 144,
155, 157–158, 208–209, 361,
365, 386, 400, 476, 516, 574,
590, 657, 660
sense appetite, 8, 69, 103–104,

106–107, 117, 126–127, 132,
136, 138–139, 144, 150,
153–154, 157, 165, 174, 277,
344, 371, 396, 418, 575–576,
579, 581–582, 585, 587, 589,
672
sensitive part of the soul, 277,
451
sensual, 69, 103, 191, 196,
257–258, 282, 285, 391–393,
401, 403–404
Sentences (Peter the Lombard),
109
separation, 16, 21, 56, 126
Seraphim, 61–62
servile, 320, 436
sex, 105, 146, 194, 211, 242, 277,
279, 283–284, 316–317, 382,
387–389, 391, 406, 426, 440
shame(ful)(less), 164, 168, 239,
243, 269, 272–274, 280, 283,
289–290, 299, 301, 303–304,
306, 308–309, 311, 338, 384,
391–396, 399–400, 406, 458,
460, 480, 488, 500, 503–504,
507, 533, 538, 546, 591, 635,
647, 667, 670–671, 706–707
sheep, 99, 105–106, 151, 297–
298, 521, 533–534, 551
shepherd(ing), 521, 533–534
should, 7, 13, 17, 19–20, 35–36,
52, 65, 119–121, 136, 149,
165 –168, 172, 197–198, 206,
211, 213, 217, 223, 230, 249,
251–252, 254–256, 260, 262–
264, 266, 268, 273, 280–283,
285, 297–298, 309, 314, 318,
326–329, 335–336, 340–341,

271, 278, 280–285, 287–290,
295–297, 299, 301–302, 307,
310–312, 316, 325, 348–349,
352–353, 370, 375–378, 380,
386, 388, 390, 396–398, 405,
408, 441, 444–448, 457, 469,
474, 488, 498, 524, 535, 600,
609, 613–615, 621, 625–636,
638–639, 643, 653, 663–665,
668, 673, 675, 692, 712
vice-president, 712
vicious, 121, 164, 196, 197,
207, 220, 224, 232, 247–248,
253–254, 257, 266–267, 269,
271, 289, 293, 301, 303, 311,
317, 327, 331, 334, 370,
375–376, 378, 380, 389–390,
393, 397–398, 400, 405, 420,
450, 453–454, 458, 461, 464,
466, 474, 480, 488, 490, 503,
591–592, 602, 609, 617, 621,
634, 643, 663–664, 669, 691,
693–694
victim, 314, 332
vindictive, 170
violence, 115, 249–250, 253,
255–256, 314, 453, 504,
506–507, 616, 639
violent, 249–250, 252–253, 337,
507
virtual quantity, 9–10, 12–30, 50,
63, 78, 101, 139, 150, 168,
236, 245, 291, 343, 459, 490,
494, 568, 571, 582, 586, 593,
630, 639, 700
virtue(s)(*virtus*), 1–2, 7, 10,
12–13, 15, 19, 23, 49–50, 61,
73, 77, 107, 109, 113, 123–

124, 135, 161, 167, 177–192,
195–197, 199–200, 203, 206,
208, 211, 213–214, 218–227,
229–245, 247–248, 251,
256–257, 266–268, 271–273,
275–278, 282, 284, 286–288,
290–294, 296–300, 303–304,
306, 308–313, 323–327, 334,
336, 339–341, 343, 353–358,
361–363, 366–380, 390, 396–
401, 405–408, 410, 413–415,
418, 420–427, 430, 433, 436,
441–446, 449–450, 453, 461,
463–464, 468–469, 471, 474,
476, 479, 481, 487–489, 493–
507, 510, 523–525, 529, 535,
540, 542–544, 551, 557, 570,
595–600, 606–615, 621–624,
628–638, 642–643, 647, 649–
655, 657–658, 661–663, 665,
670, 673, 675, 678, 682–683,
689, 692, 694–695, 700–703
virtue ethics, 1–2
virtue of contemplation, 494, 498,
700, 702
virtuous, 12–14, 113, 121, 153,
164, 187, 197, 211, 213, 216,
219–221, 223–225, 232, 235,
237–238, 243–245, 247, 253,
257, 267–268, 271, 276–277,
291–292, 293, 295–296, 299,
301–303, 304, 309–313, 317,
325, 327, 331, 333, 368–370,
372, 379, 395, 401, 404,
405, 408, 410–411, 413–414,
425–427, 429–430, 433–434,
442, 444–445, 447, 449–451,
453–454, 457–458, 460–466,

469, 471, 476, 481, 486–490,
492, 494–495, 502–503, 505–
506, 524, 606–607, 609–612,
614, 621–622, 624, 630, 633,
638, 643, 645, 662, 671, 677,
683–684, 689, 691–695, 706
virtutis, 182
vision, 13, 25, 28–29, 55, 59, 61,
80, 92, 103–104, 114, 126,
138, 142–143, 155, 177, 189,
192, 201, 204, 206, 211–213,
218, 226–227, 230, 241, 249,
339, 341–342, 346, 359, 404,
424, 438, 487, 567, 573, 575,
578–579, 584, 598, 600–605,
608–609, 648, 650, 680, 685,
687, 698
volition, 103, 114, 116, 137, 202,
505, 576
voluntariness, 115, 117, 171,
247–251, 257, 269, 283, 292,
330, 337, 376, 393, 616–617,
627, 645
voluntary, 50, 115, 121, 171, 202,
247–260, 267–270, 283–284,
313–314, 318–319, 330–333,
337, 344–345, 402, 447, 460,
614–618, 639, 645, 649–650
voluntary act(ivty)(s), 50, 115,
202, 247–251, 253–258, 260,
267, 284, 314, 331, 337,
344–345, 402, 614–618, 639,
645, 649–650

Wauck, Mark A., 16
weak(en)(ness), 21, 29, 55, 67,
68, 115, 120, 139, 149, 166,
168–169, 177, 207, 215, 231,

245, 269, 274–276, 289, 304,
330, 362, 378, 380–381,
384–385, 387, 390, 394–395,
400–401, 403, 427, 432, 437,
441, 451, 460, 478, 480, 484,
488–489, 516, 520–521, 523,
526, 533, 538, 653, 685, 688
wealth, 113, 122, 154, 159, 165,
242, 286–290, 295, 304, 319,
322, 327, 417, 420, 436, 525,
528–529, 535, 556, 576, 628
Weismann, Max, 39, 510, 514,
559–560
West(ern), 15, 18–27, 30, 33, 40,
86–87, 124, 193, 198, 230,
371, 509–510, 514–515, 529,
543, 552–553, 556, 561–563,
570, 599, 663, 712–713
Western civilization, 22, 25, 27,
30, 33, 371, 563, 663, 712
Western culture(al)(e), 15, 18,
543, 556, 599
whole(s), 4–5, 7, 9, 12–15, 21,
23–27, 29–30, 40–42, 44,
46–55, 58, 60, 64, 66, 74–77,
79–80, 82–83, 106, 111–114,
116, 120–121, 145, 147, 151,
154, 156–157, 178, 181–182,
184–185, 191–193, 195,
199–202, 205–206, 212–218,
221, 230, 237–239, 250, 263,
266, 280, 282, 312, 319, 326,
328–331, 343, 348–349, 351,
355, 358, 360, 367–368, 370,
404, 407, 409–410, 422, 424–
425, 439, 450, 452, 458–460,
464, 466, 468, 474–479,
481–485, 489, 492, 497, 499,

599, 608, 610–612, 617, 619,
630, 637, 652, 655, 694, 703,
706
world(s), 15, 19, 21, 25, 41, 170,
187, 189, 329, 419, 472, 510,
516–517, 547, 552–553, 555,
561
worth(y), 2, 5, 33, 121, 135–136,
207, 275, 238, 243, 251–252,
269, 276, 280–281, 295, 297–
298, 301, 313, 323, 330, 335,
349, 378, 388, 393, 400, 414,
426, 428, 431, 444, 452–453,
456–458, 460, 488–489, 581,
624, 632, 682
wrong, 18, 22, 32, 37, 122, 124,
170, 209, 214, 219, 229–230,
232–233, 236, 248, 274, 281,
283, 287–288, 296, 298–299,
304, 313, 356, 376, 378, 381,
383–384, 388, 399–400, 403,
410, 412–413, 418, 473,
475, 477, 483, 487–489, 511,
514–515, 521, 524–525, 529,
539, 541, 543, 546, 558, 602,
609–610, 615, 628, 655, 667,
677, 697, 705, 710

young, 166, 194, 203, 207, 256,
274, 361, 417, 420, 425, 428,
507, 513, 524, 552, 557, 592,
602–603, 678, 682
youth, 18–19, 210, 232, 388, 429,
481, 507, 528, 552–553, 561

Zeno of Elea, 24
Zeus, 134–135

CPSIA information can be obtained
at www.ICGtesting.com
Printed in the USA
BVHW040209030720
582899BV00009B/180